John Henderson
821-6486

THE 8086/8088 FAMILY: DESIGN, PROGRAMMING, AND INTERFACING

JOHN UFFENBECK

PRENTICE-HALL, INC., Englewood Cliffs, New Jersey 07632

Library of Congress Cataloging-in-Publication Data
Uffenbeck, John E.
    The 8086/8088 family.

    Includes index.
    1. Intel 8086 (Microprocessor)
2. Intel 8088 (Microprocessor) I. Title.
QA76.8.I292U34 1986   004.165   86-22657
ISBN 0-13-246752-6

Editorial/production supervision and
    interior design: *Eileen M. O'Sullivan*
Cover design: *Edsal Enterprises*
Manufacturing buyer: *Carol Bystrom*

Printed in the United States of America

10 9 8 7 6 5 4 3 2

0-13-246752-6   025

PRENTICE-HALL INTERNATIONAL (UK) LIMITED, *London*
PRENTICE-HALL OF AUSTRALIA PTY. LIMITED, *Sydney*
PRENTICE-HALL CANADA INC., *Toronto*
PRENTICE-HALL HISPANOAMERICANA, S.A., *Mexico*
PRENTICE-HALL OF INDIA PRIVATE LIMITED, *New Delhi*
PRENTICE-HALL OF JAPAN, INC., *Tokyo*
PRENTICE-HALL OF SOUTHEAST ASIA PTE. LTD., *Singapore*
EDITORA PRENTICE-HALL DO BRASIL, LTDA., *Rio de Janeiro*

CONTENTS

PREFACE

This book is about the 8086 "family" of 16-bit microprocessors and microprocessor support components. It is a traditional book that concentrates on a particular processor, the 8086, but its intentions are much broader. First, I am assuming that this book represents your *introduction* to the world of microprocessors. Although you will need a background in digital logic (gates, flip-flops, counters, etc.), no other assumptions are made. In particular, I will not be assuming that you have previously studied one of the popular 8-bit microprocessors, such as the 8085 or 6800.

Second, the scope of this book goes beyond the 8086 to include all of the compatible processors and coprocessors in this 16-bit microprocessor family. This includes the 8-bit version of the 8086 called the 8088 (made popular in the IBM PC), and the 80186, a highly integrated version of the 8086 with the equivalent of 15 to 20 support components on-board.

Because these chips are compatible, software programs written for the 8086 can also be expected to run without changes on the 8088 or 80186. Thus you are really learning about an entire family of microprocessors, not just a single family member.

ORGANIZATION

You can think of this book as having four main parts. The first part (Chap. 1) describes the basic computer. This chapter introduces most of the topics and key words that are covered in detail in the later chapters. Its purpose is to present the "*big* picture."

The second part consists of Chaps. 2 through 5 and deals exclusively with software. Several tables in Chap. 2 summarize the complex instruction set of the 8086. Examples are included to illustrate the various instruction forms, depending on the addressing mode selected. A unique feature is the inclusion of hexadecimal object code for each example. You might think of Chap. 2 as your instruction set reference chapter.

Considerable time is spent in Chap. 3 developing the techniques of proper program design methodology. A "widget counter" is used for this first program example. It does a good job of illustrating the hardware-software integration process typical in microprocessor design problems. Chapter 4 includes several programming "tips" on topics such as bit manipulation, generating time delays, using procedures (subroutines), and modular programming.

You should be advised that the instruction set of the 8086 is quite extensive, with more than 3000 different forms of the various instructions! Hand assembly of 8086 programs, although quite tedious, is explained in Chap. 3. A better choice, however, is to use an assembler, such as Microsoft's macro assembler (MASM). An example using MASM, the line editor EDLIN, and the debugger DEBUG are also presented in this chapter. Note that all programs in this book are in list (XXXX.LST) form as output by MASM.

Chapter 5 concludes the software section by illustrating the problems that occur while trying to design a microprocessor-controlled VCR (video cassette recorder). The solution, a microcomputer *development system* with in-circuit emulation, finally emerges. Assembly language is also shown to be just one of several languages that can be chosen for a particular problem. Structured programming is also introduced in this chapter and shown to be an effective technique for tackling complex software problems. An additional example of structured programming, written in Pascal, is provided in Chap. 7.

Chapter 6 begins the hardware section of the book—that is, the third part. Its goal is the design of a CPU (central processing unit) module to which memory (Chap. 7) and I/O (Chap. 8) can be interfaced. Both minimum- and maximum-mode CPU modules are designed, and timing requirements imposed by the processor are listed in table form.

In addition to parallel and serial I/O ports, I/O control techniques are also discussed in Chap. 8. These include programmed I/O and interrupts. The general concept of DMA (direct memory access) is explained and its transfer rate and response time compared to polling and interrupt-driven techniques.

Several LSI peripheral controller chips that can be used to implement the I/O techniques presented in Chap. 8 are described in Chap. 9. Chips like the 8255 PPI, 8251A USART, and the 8259A PIC are explained in detail. Several examples, including control software, are given to aid in the understanding of these important support devices.

Chapter 10 continues the hardware part of our story but concentrates on topics that are not unique to the 8086 family. For example, data communications standards such as RS-232C and IEEE-488. These are standard data exchange techniques that can be used between any two computers.

Finally, Chap. 11, or part four of the text, covers the 80186 microprocessor in detail. Several design examples using the 80186's on-board peripherals are given, including a DMA-controlled disk transfer routine and a baud rate generator using the internal timers.

The 8087 and 8089 *coprocessors* are also described in Chap. 11. These chips expand the capabilities of the host CPU to allow scientific numeric processing (the 8087) and unattended I/O processing (the 8089). The 8089 is particularly important, as it is the only single-chip DMA controller currently available that is compatible with the 8086's request/grant protocol.

SPECIAL FEATURES

The ability to read and comprehend the data sheet for a complex component such as a microprocessor or peripheral controller chip is an increasingly important skill. For this reason you will find numerous data sheets distributed throughout the text. For example, a portion of the 8284A clock generator data sheet has been reproduced in Chap. 6 to aid in your understanding of the 8086 clock circuit.

Another important feature is the integration of software, that is, program listings, with hardware. In most cases, a control program accompanies each hardware interface. As mentioned, each program has been assembled with MASM. Thus the program listings provide additional examples of 8086 assembly language syntax.

At the end of each subsection you will find a set of Self-Review questions. The answers to these questions are provided at the end of the chapter. They are intended to highlight the key points in that section, and you are encouraged to try each of these before proceeding to the next section.

At the end of each chapter a set of 15 to 20 Self-Test questions tests your understanding of the main concepts developed in that chapter. These questions are normally of the fill-in-the-blank or multiple-choice variety. To test your ability to apply the material covered in the chapter, several Analysis and Design Questions are provided. These are more complex problems, often requiring you to write a program or design a hardware interface. In other cases you will be asked to analyze a program or circuit, perhaps to locate a program "bug" or hardware design error. Answers to selected questions are provided in the back of the book.

Finally, the IBM PC should again be mentioned. This computer (or a compatible system), when equipped with an 8086 assembler, editor, and debugger, makes a powerful and economical development system. In-circuit emulation capabilities are also available, further enhancing the PC's utility. If you are using a development kit like Intel's SDK-86, do not overlook the possibility of downloading programs from the PC to the SDK-86.

The IBM PC can also be used to explore the hardware interfaces presented in Chaps. 6 through 11. Appendix F provides a description of the PC's bus structure and gives a practical design example between the PC and an 8255A-5 PPI chip.

ASSUMPTIONS

To make effective use of this book, you will need to be familiar with the various digital logic elements and circuits. An understanding of the binary and hexadecimal number systems is also important. A brief review of the latter topic is provided in App. A.

Although most of the chips are regarded as "black boxes," a familiarity with voltage and current will help you understand the use of pull-up resistors, loading rules, and power-on-reset circuits.

ACKNOWLEDGMENTS

Writing a book of this magnitude required the help of several people. I would particularly like to thank Intel Corporation for their permission to reproduce the many data sheets scattered throughout this book. Tom Lehmann of Intel was especially helpful with the development systems chapter. David Hati reviewed the manuscript twice and provided many useful comments and suggestions which I have incorporated.

Finally, it is traditional for the author to thank his wife for typing the manuscript. Although she has done so in the past, I typed this one (with the help of WORDSTAR). Her encouragement and support, however, have been just as important. So this book is dedicated to you, Katie; thanks.

1

THE BASIC COMPUTER

Until recently, most digital design problems were solved using the same set of tools. Combinational circuits were derived from Boolean logic equations, truth tables, and Karnaugh maps. Sequential designs utilized flip-flop excitation tables and state diagrams. Designers then chose "off the shelf" logic components —typically 7400 family integrated circuits—to implement these equations in hardware. If the design specifications changed, the process was repeated and the hardware was modified or rebuilt.

In the early 1970s a new logic component changed all of this. That component is the *microprocessor*. Rather than implement a rigid set of logic equations, the microprocessor fetches, from a *memory unit*, "instructions" about the problem to be solved. These instructions are called the *control program*.

Figure 1.1 shows how this new approach to digital design works. A *microcomputer* system is built around the microprocessor. It includes the microprocessor, a memory unit, and a number of input and output devices. In this example the switch contacts function as an input device, perhaps representing a smoke detector or "temperature-too-high" sensor. When closed, the control program instructs the microprocessor to activate its output device—in this case a LED warning light.

Because the function of the design is controlled by *software*, that is, a program stored in memory, new features can easily be added (or old ones modified) without having to change the hardware. The result is a more flexible design that can be adapted to changes in the problem statement without requiring expensive hardware "fixes."

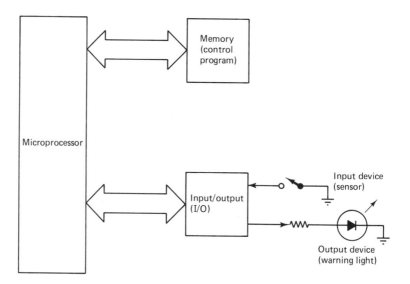

Figure 1.1 The microprocessor has revolutionized the digital design process. Combined with a memory unit and a set of I/O devices, a microcomputer is formed.

This book is about Intel's family of 16-bit microprocessors and the 8086 and 8088 microprocessors in particular (the bit specification of a microprocessor is explained later in this chapter). The word "family" is used because the design of a microcomputer system is not as simple as Fig. 1.1 might make it appear. Most microprocessors require several support circuits or "chips" to become a functioning microcomputer system. Typical examples are clock generators, bus controllers, and bus buffers.

In this chapter we present a core of digital computer principles on which the following chapters build. In it you will find a brief introduction to much of the terminology used in the later chapters. You will also learn that microprocessors can be used in many different ways, from simple single-board microcontrollers to "full-blown" systems with multiple microprocessors, floppy disks, keyboards, video displays, and printers. Keep in mind that this chapter is intended as an introduction; we will return to most of the topics several times between here and Chap. 11.

The major topics of this chapter include:

1.1 Intel Family of 16-Bit Microprocessors

1.2 Stored Program Computers

1.3 Computer Instructions and Bus Cycles

1.4 Computer Codes

1.5 Computer Programming

1.6 Digital Logic

1.7 Microcomputer Applications

1.1 INTEL FAMILY OF 16-BIT MICROPROCESSORS

The 8086 microprocessor is actually just one integrated-circuit (IC) chip in a family of 16-bit microprocessors designed by Intel. Table 1.1 lists the chip members for the various system configurations. All together, there are five microprocessors and five coprocessors. The note beneath the table provides a brief description of each chip.

A basic philosophy behind all the circuits in this family is one of providing a powerful but general-purpose microprocessor supported by optional special-purpose *co-processors*. For example, the iAPX86/21 is a three-chip microcomputer system based on the 8086 microprocessor, the 8087 *numeric data processor* (NDP), and the 8089 *I/O processor* (IOP).

The 8087 and 8089 expand the capabilities of the 8086. Using the 8087, the 8086 microprocessor can perform complex mathematical operations up to 100 times faster than it can alone. Using the 8089, much of the burden of controlling the peripheral devices (printers, disk drives, etc.) is lifted from the 8086, allowing it to concentrate on other tasks.

The 8088 microprocessor is identical to the 8086 but can read memory only 8 bits at a time (in Sec. 1.3 we explain the consequences of this in more detail). The 80186 and 80188 are upgrades of the 8086 and 8088 processors, expanded to include 15 to 20 of the most common iAPX86 and iAPX88 system components on a single chip. All the instructions for the 8086 are incorporated in the 80186 instruction set, including 10 new instruction types.

The 80286 is an even-higher-performance processor. It is designed with multiple users and multitasking (the execution of several programs at once) in mind. The 80286 is supported by the 80287 numeric data processor in the iAPX286/20 version.

The 80130 and 80150 are special *operating system processors* (OSPs). They contain system control programs in a special type of permanent memory called ROM (read-only memory). The 80130 supports the iRMX 86 operating system and the 80150 supports CP/M 86. More details on operating systems are given in Chap. 3.

1.2 STORED PROGRAM COMPUTERS

One of the first digital computers was a machine called ENIAC (Electronic Numerical Integrator and Computer). It was designed and built at the Moore School of Electrical Engineering at the University of Pennsylvania in 1946. ENIAC contained over 18,000 vacuum tubes, weighed more than 30 tons, and required 1500 square feet of floor space. It was programmed by setting up to 6000 switches and connecting cables between the various units of the computer.

While ENIAC was under construction, John von Neumann, also of the Moore School of Electrical Engineering, proposed a totally new computer architecture. Now called the *stored program concept*, von Neumann suggested that just like the data, the computer program be stored in memory. The computer would then be permanently wired to fetch its instructions from memory instead of being rewired for each new program.

TABLE 1.1 SYSTEM CONFIGURATION EXAMPLES FOR THE INTEL FAMILY OF 16-BIT MICROPROCESSORS[a]

System name	Microprocessor chips					Coprocessor chips				
	8086	8088	80186	80188	80286	8087	8089	80130	80150	80287
iAPX86/10	1									
iAPX86/11	1						1			
iAPX86/12	1						2			
iAPX86/20	1					1				
iAPX86/21	1					1	1			
iAPX86/22	1					1	2			
iAPX86/30	1							1		
iAPX86/40	1					1		1		
iAPX86/50	1								1	
iAPX88/10		1								
iAPX88/11		1					1			
iAPX88/12		1					2			
iAPX88/20		1				1				
iAPX88/21		1				1	1			
iAPX88/22		1				1	2			
iAPX88/30		1						1		
iAPX88/40		1				1		1		
iAPX88/50		1							1	
iAPX186/10			1							
iAPX186/11			1				1			
iAPX186/20			1			1				
iAPX186/21			1			1	1			
iAPX186/30			1					1		
iAPX186/40			1			1		1		
iAPX186/50			1						1	
iAPX188/10				1						
iAPX188/11				1			1			
iAPX188/20				1		1				
iAPX188/21				1		1	1			
iAPX188/30				1				1		
iAPX188/40				1		1		1		
iAPX188/50				1					1	
iAPX286/10					1					
iAPX286/20					1					1

[a]8086 16-bit microprocessor.

 8088 Identical to the 8086 except for 8-bit data bus width.

80186 High-integration 16-bit microprocessor. Includes clock generator, programmable interrupt controller, two DMA channels, three programmable 16-bit timers, and programmable chip select logic.

80188 Identical to the 80186 except for 8-bit data bus width.

80286 Higher-performance 8086 with 16M-byte address space. On-board memory management and support for virtual memory and operating systems.

 8087 Numeric data processor. Used with the 8086/88 and 80186/188 to decrease processing time for complex mathematical functions up to 100 times.

 8089 Input/output processor. Used with the 8086/88 and 80186/188 to provide high-speed DMA capabilities.

80130 iRMX 86 operating system processor containing many of the operating system primitive routines.

80150 Same as the 80130 but supports the CP/M 86 operating system.

80287 Same as the 8087 but supports the 80286 microprocessor.

Interestingly enough, virtually all computers today are still based on the von Neumann architecture and stored program concept.

Fetch and Execute

Figure 1.2 is a block diagram of a basic stored program computer. There are three major parts to this system: (1) the *central processing unit* (CPU), which acts as the "brain" coordinating all activities; (2) the *memory* unit, where the program instructions and data are temporarily stored; and (3) the *input/output* (I/O) *devices*, which allow the computer to input information for processing and then output the result.

The basic timing of the computer is controlled by a square-wave oscillator or *clock* generator circuit. This signal is used to synchronize all activities within the computer, and it determines how fast instructions can be fetched from memory and executed.

The basic processing cycle begins with a memory fetch or read cycle. The *instruction pointer* (IP) register (also called the *program counter*) holds the address of the memory cell to be selected. In *computerese*, it "points" at the instruction to be fetched. In the example shown, IP is storing the address 672,356, and the binary equivalent of this address is output onto the system address bus lines and routed to the memory unit.

The memory unit consists of a number of sequential storage locations, each with its own unique *address*. Each location in the memory unit is capable of storing one data element or computer instruction. In this example we assume that the memory is 8 bits wide, referred to as a *byte*. This memory organization is typical for Intel 16-bit microprocessors.

The address selector/decoder of the memory unit examines the address on the address lines and selects the proper memory location. Because the CPU must read from memory, it activates its MEMORY READ control signal. This causes the selected data byte in memory to be placed onto the data lines and routed to the *instruction register* within the CPU.

Once in the CPU, the instruction is decoded and executed. In this case the instruction has the decimal code 64, which is decoded to be INC AX, which means "increment the 16-bit accumulator." The *arithmetic-logic unit* (ALU) is instructed to add 1 to the contents of the accumulator, where the new result will be stored. In general, the ALU portion of the CPU performs all mathematical and Boolean logic functions, storing the result in the accumulator register.

With the instruction complete, the cycle repeats beginning with a new instruction fetch cycle. The control logic in the CPU is wired such that register IP is always incremented after an instruction fetch; thus the next sequential instruction in memory will be read. The entire process of reading memory, incrementing the instruction pointer, and decoding the instruction is known as the *fetch and execute* principle of the stored program computer.

The preceding discussion is not strictly true for the 8086 and 8088 microprocessors. This is because these processors utilize a separate *bus interface unit* (BIU) and a separate *execution unit* (EU). While the BIU is fetching instructions, the EU can be executing (previously fetched) instructions. Thus the fetch and execute phases are allowed to *overlap*. The BIU and EU of the 8086 are discussed in more detail in Chap. 2.

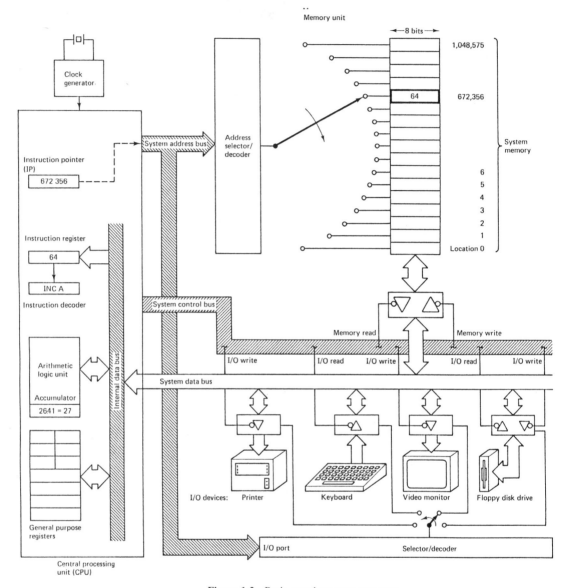

Figure 1.2 Basic stored program computer.

Three-Bus System Architecture

A collection of electronic signal lines all dedicated to a particular task is called a *bus*. In Fig. 1.2 there are three such buses, called the *address*, *data*, and *control* buses. This three-bus system architecture is common to nearly all microcomputer systems.

The width of the data bus in bits is usually used to classify the microprocessor.

Thus an 8-bit microprocessor has an 8-bit data bus, and a 16-bit processor has a 16-bit data bus. The width of the data bus determines how much data the processor can read or write in one memory or I/O cycle.

The 8088 microprocessor has an internal 16-bit data bus, but externally its data bus width is only 8 bits. This means that the 8088 requires two memory read operations to input the same information that the 8086 inputs in one memory read cycle. The result is that the 8088 operates less efficiently than the 8086.

You may be wondering how a 16-bit processor can access an 8-bit-wide memory. For the 8086 and 80186 this is done by designing the memory such that all even-addressed bytes are in one bank and all odd-addressed bytes are in another. In this way the processor can read (or write) an even-numbered byte and an odd-numbered byte simultaneously. For the 8-bit 8088 and 80188 processors, this division is not necessary. In Chap. 7 we discuss in detail memory interfaces for the 8086 and 8088.

The *address bus* is used to identify the memory location or I/O device (also called I/O *port*) with which the CPU wishes to communicate. For the 8086/88 and 80186/188 this bus is 20 bits wide and allows the microprocessor to output 2^{20}, or 1,048,576, unique addresses (all combinations of 20 bits from 00000000000000000000 to 11111111111111111111).

How can we tell if the address on the bus is a memory address or an I/O port address? This is where the *control bus* comes in. Each time the CPU outputs an address it also activates one of four control bus signals:

1. MEMORY READ
2. MEMORY WRITE
3. I/O READ
4. I/O WRITE

Thus if the address bus holds 10100100001001100100 ($672,356_{10}$) and the MEMORY READ signal is active, the data byte in memory location 672,356 will be selected to be read. The memory unit responds by outputting the contents of this location onto the data bus.

The control bus also identifies the *direction* of data flow on the data bus. When MEMORY READ or I/O READ is active, data is input to the CPU. When MEMORY WRITE or I/O WRITE is active, data is output by the CPU. That is, the control bus signals are defined from the CPU's point of view.

In summary, the CPU manages the flow of data between itself, memory and the I/O ports via the address, data, and control buses. The control and address buses are output lines (only), but the data bus is *bidirectional*.

CPU, Memory, and I/O Modules

In a practical microcomputer system the CPU, memory, and I/O blocks of Fig. 1.2 are built as separate electronic modules interconnected by the three system buses. These modules are then referred to as the computer *hardware*. The programs stored in the memory unit which control the operation of the computer are referred to as the *software*.

Regarding Fig. 1.2 as a microcomputer system block diagram, a microprocessor chip functions as the CPU, providing the ALU, accumulator, general-purpose storage registers, and overall system control. However, this chip must be supported by a clock generator, special bus drivers called buffers, and miscellaneous control logic to make it all work (sometimes called the "glue").

The memory module may contain read/write memory, called *RAM* (random-access memory), or special read-only memory, called *ROM*. Because the contents of ROM is not lost when the computer is turned off, this type of memory is useful when first starting the computer (called "booting"). In this way there will be a program in memory ready to begin executing as soon as the computer is started up. ROM is also referred to as *firmware*—software permanently stored in hardware.

Most computer systems actually have two types of memory. The first is *main memory*—RAM and ROM—from which the CPU fetches its instructions. The second type of memory is called *secondary storage*. A floppy-disk drive is a typical example. Secondary storage is required to save programs and data that are normally stored in RAM but will be lost when the computer is turned off.

The floppy-disk drive is one of a number of computer I/O devices called *peripherals*. Other examples are keyboards, video monitors, printers, Winchester or hard-disk drives (large-storage-capacity disks), and joysticks. The microprocessor connects or interfaces to all these devices via the three-bus system architecture as shown in Fig. 1.2.

Two general classes of I/O interface are possible. The most natural for the microprocessor is called the *parallel* interface port. All the data bus lines are connected in parallel to the I/O device. This results in very high speed data transfers but is limited to 10- to 20-ft cable lengths due to the cost of multiconductor cables and the limited drive capability of standard logic gates.

The second I/O interfacing technique is called the *serial* interface port. This technique transmits and receives the data one bit at a time. This is slower than the parallel technique, but with special line drivers and receivers can be used with cables several thousand feet long.

SELF-REVIEW 1.2 (answers on page 27)

1.2.1. The three major blocks of a stored program computer are the _____, _____, and the _____.

1.2.2. The instruction pointer: (a) holds the address of the next memory location to be fetched into the instruction register; (b) is located within the CPU; (c) is incremented by 1 as part of the basic fetch and execute cycle; (d) all of these.

1.2.3. Arithmetic operations are performed in the _____ _____ _____, with results stored in the _____.

1.2.4. A microcomputer system with a 16-bit address bus could potentially access _____ memory locations.

1.2.5. The memory unit for an 8086 microprocessor is organized as a set of _____ addressed bytes and _____ addressed bytes.

1.2.6. When the CPU is required to write data to the video monitor in Fig. 1.2, the _____ _____ control bus signal will be activated.

1.2.7. Of the three system buses, only the _____ bus is bidirectional.

1.2.8. In a microcomputer system _____ and _____ are considered main memory, and a floppy-disk drive is considered _____ storage.

1.3 COMPUTER INSTRUCTIONS AND BUS CYCLES

Depending on the current instruction, any of the four control bus signals—MEMORY READ, MEMORY WRITE, I/O READ, or I/O WRITE—may be active. For this reason, four basic types of bus cycles are possible. In this section we see how the different parts of an instruction determine the type of bus cycle that is to occur.

Operation Codes and Operands

Computer instructions are made up of two parts. The first part is called the *operation code* or *op-code* and specifies the action the CPU is to perform. The second part of the instruction indicates the source and/or destination of the data acted on by the op-code. This is called the *operand*.

As an example, the instruction INC AX is made up of the op-code INC (increment) and the operand AX (register AX; the 16-bit accumulator). In this case AX is the source and destination of the data.

The *instruction set* of a computer is a list of all the valid op-codes the CPU can execute. The valid operands depend on the internal organization of the processor and the different ways in which it can access these registers and memory. These are referred to as the *addressing modes*. The 8086 has nine different addressing modes.

Consider the instruction MOV [B040H],AX. This has the word interpretation "Move a copy of register AX to memory location B040H." The suffix H indicates that the address B040 is to be interpreted as a hexadecimal number.[1] The op-code for this instruction is MOV and the operand is [B040H],AX (in the form destination, source).

When an instruction is stored in memory it is the binary code representing that instruction that is actually stored. For the instruction INC AX the single byte 01000000 (40H or 64D) is stored. However, most 8086 instructions require more than one byte. For example, the (hex) codes for the instruction MOV [B040H],AX are A3 40 B0. Three bytes are required. Some instructions will require as many as seven bytes.[2]

This is where the difference between a 16-bit microprocessor and an 8-bit microprocessor become important. A 16-bit processor will require three memory read cycles to read a six-byte instruction, whereas an 8-bit processor will require six memory reads. These additional cycles slow down the 8-bit processor, making it less efficient than the 16-bit processor.

---

[1]Throughout this book, when not clear within context, the suffixes H, B, and D will be used to identify hexadecimal, binary, and decimal numbers.

[2]You may be puzzled as to why the address in the instruction MOV [B040H],AX is only 16 bits long when the address bus is 20 bits wide. This will be clarified in Chap. 2. For now, think of this 16-bit address as an *offset* from a 20-bit base address internally established by the CPU.

Memory Read and Write Bus Cycles

Once an instruction has been fetched from memory and decoded, it is executed. For some instructions, such as INC AX, this can be done internal to the CPU and require only two or three states of the clock. However, more complex instructions may require several additional clock cycles, particularly if the instruction requires additional memory or I/O references.

Let's consider the steps required of the CPU to fetch and execute the instruction MOV [B040H],AX.

1. Perform two memory read bus cycles fetching the op-code MOV and the operand [B040H],AX. Three bytes must be read.
2. The instruction decoder now determines that the contents of register AX must be written to memory location B040H.
3. The instruction is executed by outputting address B040H on the address lines, activating the MEMORY WRITE control bus line, and placing the contents of register AX on the data bus lines. This is called a memory write bus cycle.

Figure 1.3 summarizes the bus cycles required for an 8086 and 8088 microprocessor. Because the 8086 can read 16 bits at once, only three bus cycles are required. However, the 8088 requires five cycles, due to its 8-bit data bus width. Note that the convention of "high" and "low" refers to the most significant and least significant 8 bits of the address or accumulator.

I/O Read and Write Bus Cycles

Sometimes the execution of an instruction will require data to be read from or written to an I/O device or port. A typical instruction is IN AX,6DH, which has the word interpretation "Input the 16-bit data word from port 6DH to register AX." When the 8086 executes this instruction, the following steps take place:

1. Perform a memory read bus cycle, fetching the IN op-code E5H and the operand 6DH.
2. The instruction decoder determines that an I/O read bus cycle is required, outputs the port address on the address lines, and activates the I/O READ control bus signal. The I/O port responds by releasing its 16-bit data onto the data bus lines. The CPU copies this data into the 16-bit accumulator.

Figure 1.4 summarizes the bus cycles required for the instruction IN AX,6DH for the 8086 and 8088 microprocessors. Again, because the 8088 data bus is only 8 bits wide, additional memory and I/O read cycles are required.

In this section we have covered several important points about computer instructions and instruction cycle types. To summarize:

1. Computer instructions are made up of an operation code and an operand.
2. Every instruction cycle begins with an op-code fetch bus cycle, that is, a memory read of the instruction op-code.

Micro-processor	Bus cycles required				
8086					
Type:	Memory read (fetch)	Memory read	Memory write		
Data bus:	A3H (op-code)	B040H (address)	Contents of AX		
Control bus:	MEMORY READ	MEMORY READ	MEMORY WRITE		
	M1	M2	M3		
8088					
Type:	Memory read (fetch)	Memory read	Memory read	Memory write	Memory write
Data bus:	A3H (op-code)	40H (address low)	B0H (address high)	Contents of AX low	Contents of AX high
Control bus:	MEMORY READ	MEMORY READ	MEMORY READ	MEMORY WRITE	MEMORY WRITE
	M1	M2	M3	M4	M5

Figure 1.3 Bus cycles required of the 8086 and 8088 when fetching and executing the instruction MOV [B040H],AX. (*Note:* Because of the processor's pipelined architecture, the memory read cycles may not be necessary if these bytes are already in the pipeline. This is discussed in Chapter 2.)

Microprocessor	Bus cycles required			
8086				
Type:	Memory read (fetch)	I/O read		
Data bus:	E5H and 6DH (op-code and operand)	Contents of port 6DH		
Control bus:	MEMORY READ	I/O READ		
	M1	M2		
8088				
Type:	Memory read (fetch)	Memory read	I/O read	I/O read
Data bus:	E5H (op-code)	6DH (port address)	Contents of port 6DH (low)	Contents of port 6DH (high)
Control bus:	MEMORY READ	MEMORY READ	I/O READ	I/O READ
	M1	M2	M3	M4

Figure 1.4 Bus cycles required of the 8086 and 8088 when fetching and executing the instruction IN AX,6DH. (*Note:* Because of the processor's pipelined architecture, the memory read cycles may not be necessary if these bytes are already in the pipeline. This is discussed in Chapter 2.)

3. Additional memory reads may be required to fetch all bytes of the op-code and operand (especially for an 8-bit processor).

4. The execution phase of an instruction may be done internally by the CPU or require additional memory or I/O read or write bus cycles.

SELF-REVIEW 1.3 (answers on page 27)

1.3.1. The four bus cycle types are _____, _____, _____, and _____.

1.3.2. The op-code for the instruction IN AX,6DH is _____, and has the hex code _____.

1.3.3. The source of the data in question 1.3.2 is _____.

1.3.4. The first bus cycle of every instruction is always an _____ _____.

1.3.5. A 16-bit processor is more efficient than an 8-bit processor because: (a) it can address a larger number of memory locations; (b) fewer memory and I/O accesses are required for multibyte instructions; (c) a simplified control bus can be used; (d) all of these.

1.4 COMPUTER CODES

In Fig. 1.2 the instruction pointer register in the CPU is "pointing at" memory location 672356. In this location is the data word "64." Based on the preceding sections we now know that this data would actually be stored in memory in binary form as 01000000. But what does this number represent? Should we interpret it literally as decimal 64, or does it represent the op-code for some computer operation?

The answer to this question is that only the CPU knows for sure! If it is looking for an operation code, it will interpret this byte as an operation code (even if we meant it to be a data byte!). On the other hand, if it is looking for a data byte, it will be interpreted as data. It is up to the programmer to be sure that the data in memory is interpreted correctly. If this is not done, the CPU may end up trying to execute data instead of op-codes. The result is a (silent) *crash* as the programmer loses control of the machine.

The important point we need to make is that a byte may have many interpretations besides its decimal value. For example, the byte 01000000 is interpreted as decimal 64, hexadecimal 40, by an 8086 or 8088 microprocessor as the operation code INC AX (add 1 to the contents of the 16-bit accumulator), the operation code RTI (return from interrupt) by the 6502 microprocessor, and the operation code MOV B,B (copy register B to itself) by the 8085 microprocessor.

There is still another interpretation for this byte. In 1968 the American National Standards Institute (ANSI) established a 7-bit code for all the letters of the alphabet, the numerals 0 through 9, the common punctuation symbols found on most typewriters, and several special-purpose control codes. They called their code the American Standard Code for Information Interchange [ASCII (pronounced "ask-E")]. A copy of this code is given in Table 1.2.

Although ASCII is a 7-bit code, it is often written in byte (8-bit) form with bit 8 ignored (assumed 0) or used for error-detection purposes (see the discussion on parity in

TABLE 1.2 AMERICAN STANDARD CODE FOR INFORMATION INTERCHANGE (ASCII)[a]

Least significant bit	Most significant bit							
	0 0000	1 0001	2 0010	3 0011	4 0100	5 0101	6 0110	7 0111
0 0000	NUL	DLE	SP	0	@	P	`	p
1 0001	SOH	DC1	!	1	A	Q	a	q
2 0010	STX	DC2	"	2	B	R	b	r
3 0011	ETX	DC3	#	3	C	S	c	s
4 0100	EOT	DC4	$	4	D	T	d	t
5 0101	ENQ	NAK	%	5	E	U	e	u
6 0110	ACK	SYN	&	6	F	V	f	v
7 0111	BEL	ETB	'	7	G	W	g	w
8 1000	BS	CAN	(	8	H	X	h	x
9 1001	HT	EM	)	9	I	Y	i	y
A 1010	LF	SUB	*	:	J	Z	j	z
B 1011	VT	ESC	+	;	K	[	k	{
C 1100	FF	FS	,	<	L	\	l	|
D 1101	CR	GS	−	=	M	]	m	}
E 1110	SO	RS	.	>	N	^	n	~
F 1111	SI	US	/	?	O	—	o	DEL

[a]Bit 7 of the code is assumed to be 0.

Source: J. Uffenbeck, *Microcomputers and Microprocessors: The 8080, 8085, and Z-80.* Prentice-Hall, Englewood Cliffs, N.J., 1985.

Chap. 10). In Table 1.2 it is shown that the byte 01000000 (40 hex) is the code for the "@" symbol. Nearly all text information today is encoded in ASCII format, making it possible to transfer data between two different computer systems. Each time you type a key on a computer keyboard the ASCII code for that key is generated and sent to the computer for processing.

Actually, there are many binary codes. There is *BCD* (binary-coded decimal), useful for decimal arithmetic; the *Gray code*, in which only one bit changes between successive entries in the code (useful for testing digital circuits); the *2's-complement code* shown in Table A.2, in which the most significant bit of each word represents the sign (positive or negative) of the word; the *Extended Binary Coded Decimal Interchange Code* (EBCDIC), developed by IBM for its line of Selectric typewriters; and on and on.

So you can see that there is much more to a group of binary digits than their decimal value. It is up to the user to select and use the appropriate code for the application at hand.

SELF-REVIEW 1.4 *(answers on page 27)*

1.4.1. The data bytes stored in a computer's memory represent either instruction op-codes or program data. (True/False)

1.4.2. The byte 01101010 has the ASCII interpretation _____, but if interpreted as a 2's-complement signed binary number is _____decimal.

1.4.3. When a computer program "crashes" it is often caused by the CPU interpreting as an op-code what the programmer intended as a data byte.   (True/False)

1.5 COMPUTER PROGRAMMING

Computer programming requires learning a new language. But which one? There is *machine language*, *assembly language*, and a number of *high-level languages*. In this section we examine these different languages and discuss the merits of each.

Machine and Assembly Language Programming

Regardless of the programming language used, the CPU can only execute instructions encoded in binary. Needless to say, programming a computer in binary can be very awkward for a human being. Consider the following 8086 microprocessor program, which adds two numbers input from a keyboard.

```
11100101
00100111
10001011
11011000
11100101
00100111
00000011
11000011
11100111
00110000
11110100
```

Not too clear, is it? Of course, it is crystal clear to an 8086 microprocessor. This type of program is referred to as *object code* and is the only code a computer can execute; however, it is nearly impossible for a human being to work with.

Consider the same program encoded in hexadecimal:

```
E5
27
8B
D8
E5
27
03
C3
E7
30
F4
```

Certainly this is more readable, but the function of the program is still not clear. Let's add the *mnemonics* (abbreviations for the instruction operation codes) corresponding to these hex codes.

| Hex code | Mnemonic | | Comment |
	Op-code	Operand	
E5 27	IN	AX,27H	;Input first number from ;port 27H and store in AX
8B D8	MOV	BX,AX	;Save a copy of register AX ;in register BX
E5 27	IN	AX,27H	;Input second number to AX
03 C3	ADD	AX,BX	;Add contents of BX to AX ;and store the sum in AX
E7 30	OUT	30H,AX	;Output AX to port 30H
F4	HLT		;Halt the computer

The function of the program now becomes clear. The two numbers to be added are first input from port 27H (where the keyboard is assumed to be connected). The first number is temporarily saved in one of the 8086's general-purpose registers—register BX—so the second input operation will not overwrite it. The ADD AX,BX instruction adds the contents of registers AX and BX, leaving the result in register AX (the accumulator). This value is then output to port 30H (where the video display is assumed to be connected). Finally, the computer is instructed to halt.

Notice how the operation codes may be represented in binary, hexadecimal, or as a mnemonic. The comments on the far right help make the function of the program clear. Programming the computer by entering the instruction codes in hexadecimal or binary is referred to as *machine language programming*.

Machine language programming is very tedious because you must determine the hex code for each instruction you wish to use; this is called "hand assembly."[3] With over 100 mnemonics and 3800 different forms of the various 8086 instructions, this process is time consuming and error prone.

For this reason all microprocessors are supported by special *assembler programs*. These programs allow the programmer to directly enter the mnemonics for the program instructions. The assembler performs the tedious "bookwork" of encoding all the instructions. This technique is called *assembly language programming*.

The assembler program usually comes with some form of *editor* or word processor that allows for easy creation of the assembly language file (called the *source code*). When the source code version of the program is completed, the assembler is called on to determine the binary codes for the mnemonics and to create a new file called the *object code*. This file contains the binary code, which can be loaded into memory and executed. Using the standard 8086 assembler, the object code must be linked before it can be assembled. This is discussed in Chaps. 3 through 5.

---

[3]In Chap. 3 we provide details on how to calculate these hex codes for the 8086.

High-Level Languages

BASIC is a popular computer language and is supplied with most personal computer systems. The program to add two numbers when written in BASIC becomes

```
10    INPUT N1,N2
20    PRINT "SUM = ";N1 + N2
30    END
```

A comparison with the original binary program is striking. Of course that is the intent of a high-level language. Let the programmer communicate in a language as near his or her own as possible.

Programming in BASIC requires a BASIC *interpreter* or *compiler*. When using interpreted BASIC the application program may be entered to memory without an editor. The command *RUN* is then given, causing the interpreter to examine each BASIC statement and then execute a sequence of machine code instructions equivalent to that statement.

The use of an interpreter usually results in very slow program execution compared to that of the assembly language version. For example, if the computer is in a loop, the interpreter will needlessly reinterpret the instructions in that loop over and over. Because the computer is so fast, we do not usually notice (or care about) this delay.

The BASIC program given previously to add two numbers might require 10 ms to calculate the sum and print the result. The machine language version could do it in 7.4 μs (8086 microprocessor with a 5-MHz clock). You would certainly have to be pretty quick to notice the difference between 10 ms and 7.4 μs!

This time delay can become very noticeable, however, when the operation must be repeated a large number of times. For example, let's say that we had to perform the addition problem 1 million times. This would require $1,000,000 \times 10$ ms $= 10,000$ s or 2.8 hours with the BASIC program. The machine language version would require $1,000,000 \times 7.4$ μs $= 7.4$ s!

A *compiler* is used to convert a high-level-language program to object code form. Using a compiler is similar to using an assembler because an editor must be used for creating the application program file.

When the compiler is run it compiles the high-level-language program into a binary machine code file. This has several advantages over the interpreter. First, the code does not have to be reinterpreted over and over when loops are encountered. In addition, the resulting object code file will run all by itself without the need for the compiler to be resident in memory. This saves memory space and allows for larger programs to be written.

The main disadvantage of using a compiler is that errors will require reinvoking the editor, correcting the errors with the editor, and recompiling the program. This can be frustrating when simple syntax errors—missing commas, for example—appear.

Operating Systems

When you operate a computer—typing on its keyboard, observing its CRT display, directing files to the printer, saving other files to the disk drive—you do so under the control of a very special program. That program is known as the *operating system.*[4] This is a special program designed specifically to operate the computer. In effect, it is the software link that stands between you and the computer hardware.

For example, when instructed to print a text file, the operating system first checks that the printer is on-line and then begins sending one character at a time to the printer port. Because the printer is much slower than the computer, the operating system must always check that the last character has been received and printed before sending the next. Typically, this is done by *polling* a status signal output by the printer. Only when ready is the next character sent.

What makes the operating system so important is that all these operations are hidden from the computer operator. You give a command like

COPY MYFILE.TXT LST:

and the operating system does the rest (in this case sending a copy of the file MYFILE.TXT to the list device, that is, the printer).

Operating systems worry about the "nitty-gritty" details, such as printer port numbers, status bits, disk drive motor-turn-on delays, CRT cursor position, or keyboard decoding. They also provide a uniform entry point for the applications software to "hook into" the computer's hardware. In this way the applications program (and the program operator) need not be concerned with the exact details of how the keyboard is read or how the characters are sent to the CRT screen. This prevents software from becoming machine dependent.

Operating systems are normally customized by the computer manufacturer to the specific system hardware. The applications programs are then said to "run under" this particular operating system. That is, they become operating system dependent instead of machine dependent. The 8086 assembler MASM, for example, runs under MS-DOS (Microsoft Disk Operating System) and can be run on any computer equipped with this operating system. More details on MS-DOS and MASM are provided in Chap. 3.

SELF-REVIEW 1.5 (answers on page 27)

1.5.1. A mnemonic is: (a) an operation code written in binary form; (b) an operation code written in hex form; (c) a computer instruction in abbreviated form; (d) a special command written in BASIC.

1.5.2. To write a computer program in machine language requires: (a) an interpreter or compiler to generate the object code; (b) the hexadecimal codes for each instruction; (c) a text editor for creation of the source code; (d) a special assembler program.

1.5.3. Programs written in a high-level language are easier to write but execute more slowly than the corresponding machine language program. (True/False)

1.5.4. A computer program in binary or hexadecimal is also said to be in _____ code form.

[4] The operating system software is normally loaded from a disk when the computer is first started (this is called "booting up" the computer). As a result, the term DOS (disk operating system) is commonly applied.

1.5.5. Why is it advantageous for applications programs to be operating-system dependent instead of machine dependent?

1.6 DIGITAL LOGIC

Digital logic and control circuits are based on bistable electronic circuits called *logic gates*. These gates are so designed that they produce only two different output levels referred to by various names, such as high and low, 1 and 0, or true and false.

Several logic "families" have been developed to implement the common small-scale logic functions. These include basic logic gates—AND, OR, NOT, NAND, NOR—flip-flops, counters, and special buffer gates.

Logic Families

The TTL (transistor-transistor logic) family of logic devices is probably in most common use today. Also called the *7400 family*, all devices have part numbers prefaced by the number "74." A TTL gate produces a logic 1 output voltage of 2.4 V or greater and a logic 0 voltage of 0.4 V or less. Typical values are 3.4 V and 0.2 V. All TTL gates are powered by a single + 5-V power source. TTL gates are (usually) made with *npn* bipolar transistors and are best known for their high speed and moderate power consumption.

The best known competitor of TTL is the *CMOS* (complementary metal-oxide semiconductor) logic family, made up of alternate *n*-channel and *p*-channel field-effect transistors. A CMOS logic gate consumes only a fraction of the power of a TTL gate as long as the operating frequency is less than a few megahertz. The switching time for a CMOS gate is generally two to five times longer than for a corresponding TTL gate.

There are two popular CMOS logic families. The CD4000 series is the older of the two and features many of the devices available in the TTL family, plus a number of complex logic functions not available in TTL. The second CMOS logic family is the 74C00 family. As its part number suggests, 74C devices are pin compatible with the similarly numbered 74XX TTL parts.

Within either logic family there are several "subfamilies" offering special speed and power characteristics. For example, the 74HC family of CMOS devices are high-speed CMOS logic gates with typical gate delays of only 8 ns. Table 1.3 compares several variations of the TTL family of logic devices. Note that the 74ALS family probably offers the best choice of high speed and low power consumption.

Most microprocessors and semiconductor memories are built using MOS or CMOS technology. When interfacing to these devices special considerations regarding fanout, noise immunity, gate delays, and bus reflections must be made to ensure logic compatibility. This is discussed in detail in Chap. 6.

Testing and Troubleshooting

It is common to visualize a digital signal as a logic 1 or 0, that is, a high or low output voltage. A logic probe (see Fig. 1.5) is an inexpensive tool useful for monitoring the logic levels of circuits under test.

TABLE 1.3 SPEED AND POWER SPECIFICATIONS FOR THE TTL LOGIC FAMILY

Version	Description	Propagation delay (ns)	Power dissipation (mW)
74ASXX	Advanced Schottky	1.7	8
74SXX	Schottky	3	19
74ALSXX	Advanced low-power Schottky	4	1.2
74LSXX	Low-power Schottky	9	2
74XX	Standard	10	10
74LXX	Low power	33	1

Most digital signals are not static, however, and are continually changing in time. This is particularly true in a microcomputer system. An oscilloscope photograph of the A0 and A1 address lines of a microprocessor is shown in Fig. 1.6. Although a logic probe can also be used to detect this pulsing condition (the "pulse" indicator light will be lit), it is not possible to observe timing relationships between several signals.

An engineer was once asked what single tool he would take with him if he were to be stranded on a deserted island. His reply was: a dual-trace oscilloscope. That engineer might want to revise his answer following the advent of the microprocessor.

Consider the problem of trying to determine if a certain data word is being output on the data bus of a 16-bit microprocessor. There are two major problems: The data word is usually nonrepetitive (oscilloscopes rely on the repetitive nature of the signal being monitored), and 16 lines must be monitored simultaneously.

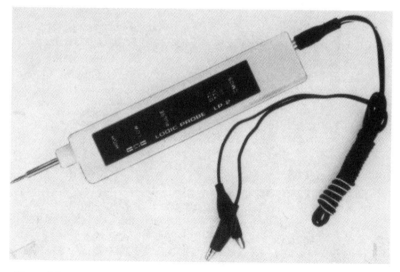

Figure 1.5 A logic probe is an inexpensive tool useful for monitoring logic 1s and 0s in digital circuits. (From J. Uffenbeck, *Hardware Interfacing with the Apple II Plus*, Prentice-Hall, Englewood Cliffs, N.J., 1983).

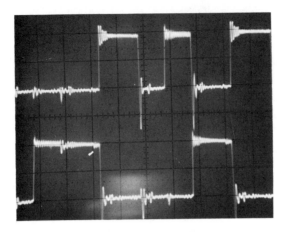

Figure 1.6 The address lines of a micro-processor are continually changing in time. The oscilloscope is set with vertical sensitivity = 2 V/div; horizontal sensitivity = 2 μs/div. From J. Uffenbeck, *Microcomputers and Microprocessors: The 8080, 8085, and Z-80.* Prentice-Hall, Englewood Cliffs, N.J., 1985.)

It soon becomes clear that a new type of test instrument is required. This instrument has become known as the *logic* or *data analyzer*. Figure 1.7 illustrates the Hewlett-Packard model 1630. Like an oscilloscope, the logic analyzer samples its inputs on a regular basis (the HP1630 allows up to 65 input channels) but stores the logic level in an internal memory. An internal or external clock signal is used to determine when to take the sample.

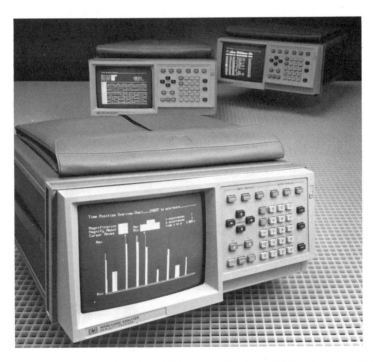

Figure 1.7 A logic analyzer is useful for troubleshooting and debugging the multiple signals on the address, data, and control buses of a microcomputer. (Courtesy of Hewlett-Packard.)

Logic analyzers generally offer two display modes. In the *timing mode* the data collected is shown as a multichannel waveform display similar to that of a conventional oscilloscope. The display can be expanded and horizontally scrolled for close scrutiny of a particular time period.

The same data can also be displayed in the *state mode*. In this case the data is shown in hex format or interpreted and displayed as a microprocessor op-code and operand. Usually, the state mode is selected when it is necessary to see if a particular sequence of data words is being placed on the bus.

SELF-REVIEW 1.6 *(answers on page 27)*

1.6.1. When measuring the output voltage of a 7400 quad NAND gate a typical logic 1 output voltage is _____ V.

1.6.2. The: (a) 74LSXX; (b) 74XX; (c) 74HCXX; (d) 74ASXX family offers the fastest switching speed among common logic families.

1.6.3. A logic analyzer may be operated in the _____ mode to obtain a multichannel waveform display or in the _____ mode to observe a hex or op-code display of data on the bus.

1.7 MICROCOMPUTER APPLICATIONS

Which is better, the 16-bit 8086 microprocessor or the 8-bit 8080 microprocessor? You probably answered the 8086. But what does ''better'' mean? When comparing microprocessors we usually think of higher clock rates, more capable instruction sets, and multiple addressing modes. Certainly, the 8086 excels in these categories. But does this mean that all 8-bit processors are now obsolete? If it does, perhaps this book should be about Intel's 80386 32-bit microprocessor.

I think a better perspective when comparing microprocessors is to consider the application at hand. In some cases the power afforded by a 16- or 32-bit microprocessor is a case of ''overkill.'' As an example, suppose that we wish to design a microprocessor-controlled food blender. Eight pushbuttons will select the speed required. The microprocessor will determine the speed by controlling the voltage applied to the motor's field winding. A photo sensor can be used to obtain pulses from the rotating armature proportional to the motor's speed. Monitoring these pulses, the microprocessor can adjust the field voltage to maintain a constant speed.

An 8086 microprocessor can certainly be used for this application, but much of its power will go unused. A simple 8-bit *microcontroller* with built-in RAM and ROM may actually provide a more economical solution.

Today, there are three broad categories of microprocessor applications:

1. Microcontrollers
2. Peripheral control processors
3. Microcomputer systems

In this section we consider a typical application for each of these.

Microcontrollers

A microcontroller is actually a single-chip computer. Contained in one integrated-circuit (IC) package are the CPU, ROM, RAM, and several input/output lines. It is only necessary to supply +5 V, ground, and the I/O devices to be interfaced.

Microcontrollers find applications in areas that have traditionally been designed with *hardwired* (i.e., permanently soldered in place) logic devices. Examples within the home include the control electronics in food blenders, microwave ovens, washing machines, and driers. The advantage of using a microcontroller is that many logic devices can be condensed into a single IC (improving reliability). Also, by changing the control program in ROM, new control functions can be added or modified without any rewiring.

Intel offers a family of microcontrollers, including the 8-bit 8048, 8049, and 8051. The 8051 contains 4K bytes of ROM, 128 bytes of RAM, and 32 I/O lines. In addition, two 16-bit timers are provided for accurate real-time recording of events. The 8051 also has a full-duplex (simultaneous transmission and reception) serial I/O port.

One of the fastest-growing applications of microcontrollers is in the automotive industry. Figure 1.8 shows the block diagram for a "trip computer" used by Chrysler Corporation in their Daytona and Laser sports cars. It will display instantaneous and average miles per gallon, average and current speed, elapsed time, distance to destination, and most other common automotive instrumentation functions. In this application the

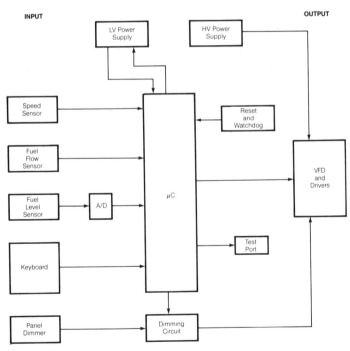

Figure 1.8 Block diagram of an automotive trip computer. (Courtesy of Intel Corporation.)

processor must run continuously, even when the car engine is off. Because of this, Chrysler selected the low-power 80C51 CMOS microcontroller.

It is interesting to note that even the microcontroller world has a 16-bit processor. One example is Intel's MCS-96 family. The 8096 has a 16-bit CPU, 8K bytes of ROM, 232 bytes of RAM, a 10-bit analog-to-digital converter, a full-duplex serial I/O port, and up to 40 I/O lines.

Peripheral Control Processors

Peripheral control processors are designed to interface to a general-purpose microprocessor on one side and to a complex peripheral on the other. A typical chip contains its own CPU, ROM, RAM, and I/O lines (like a microcontroller). However, unlike a microcontroller, it is designed to perform the I/O processing normally done by the host processor. In this way the host can do some other task, inputting or outputting data to the peripheral processor only when required.

Figure 1.9 illustrates an example using the UPI-42 (universal peripheral interface 8-bit 8042 microprocessor) as a dot-matrix-printer controller. On the left in this diagram the UPI-42 interfaces to a parallel output port of the host processor. On the right the print-mechanism-drive interface circuit to the UPI-42 is shown.

The 8243 is an I/O expander, providing eight output lines, labeled P40–P43 and P50–P53. These lines are used to control the stepper motors for paper feed and carriage head motion. Optical sensors detect the carriage home position (HR, home reset) and the print velocity (PTS, print timing sensor). The print head itself consists of nine wires and solenoids controlled by P10–P17 and P26, plus the print head trigger.

The UPI-42 makes BUSY = 0 when it is ready to receive a character from the host processor. This character is input on DB0–DB7 and then processed by the 8042 CPU. If a control character is received, such as the carriage return character, the proper control lines are activated and stepper motors pulsed to (in this case) advance the paper one line and return the print head to the left margin. Printable characters are converted to a nine-wire print code and output to the print head solenoid.

While all of this is going on, the host system need only monitor the BUSY and ACK outputs of the UPI-42. In this way the host system is relieved of the task of managing the "nitty gritty" details of controlling the printer.

Peripheral controllers such as the UPI-42 allow the processing functions of the microcomputer to be *distributed* throughout the system as needed. As a result, the main processor is able to concentrate on higher-level tasks, resulting in improved system performance. The concept of "distributed processing" is still evolving, and we can expect to see future microcomputer systems designed with separate processors for each I/O device in the system.

Microcomputer Systems

There are many applications in which the microprocessor serves as the host processor in a general-purpose microcomputer system. One example is the widespread use of the personal computer in education, business, and the home. At the other end of the spectrum

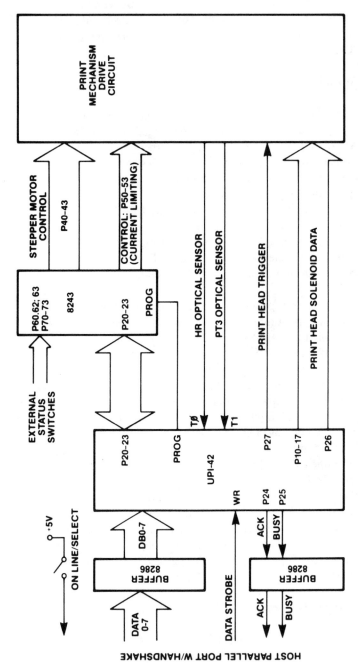

Figure 1.9 Using the 8042 UPI microcomputer to control a dot-matrix printer. (Courtesy of Intel Corporation.)

are *engineering workstations* used for computer-aided manufacturing (CAM), computer-aided design (CAD), and computer-aided engineering (CAE).

For example, consider the various steps required to bring a new concept to the marketplace:[5]

1. Product concept
2. Functional and design specifications
3. Register and gate-level design
4. Cell and mask layout
5. Manufacturing from pattern-generation tapes
6. Test
7. Distribution

The CAE workstation provides the engineer with all the tools needed to perform these tasks. In a *networked* system many engineers can have simultaneous access to a common data base as the product evolves.

With CAE tools such as circuit and logic simulators, automated printed-circuit-board layout systems, and statistical design programs, engineers can design and debug a product in software before committing that design to hardware, where mistakes can be very costly.

Figure 1.10 illustrates the Calcomp System 25 engineering workstation. This system features two Motorola MC68000 16-bit microprocessors operating at 10 MHz. It allows interactive design, storage, and retrieval of graphics images. Two viewing screens are provided: one color graphics screen with 832 × 624 picture elements, and a monochrome screen with 1024 × 768 pixel resolution.

The system also features 1MB of RAM, 1MB of floppy-disk storage, and 20MB of hard-disk storage. It can be interfaced to the DEC family of VAX mainframe computers for even greater storage capabilities. Prices for the basic configuration start at $65,000 and include software, installation, and a training program.

Summary

The point of this section should be clear. There is no such thing as a "typical" microprocessor application. In one instance it may be used as a microcontroller in a consumer appliance that sells for less than $20. In another case it may be combined with several other processors and peripherals capable of interfacing with large mainframe computers. The entire system may cost tens of thousands of dollars.

In the following chapters we discuss the common problems encountered when designing such systems. These include writing the control software, implementing the system hardware, and testing the final product.

[5]Stephen Evanczuk, "Integrating the Engineer's Environment," *Electronics*, Vol. 57, No. 10 (1984), p. 122.

Figure 1.10 CalComp System 25 engineering workstation. (Courtesy of CalComp.)

SELF-REVIEW 1.7 *(answers on page 27)*

1.7.1. The _____ is designed to function as a stand-alone single-chip microcomputer system.

1.7.2. The _____ is also a single-chip microcomputer but is designed to control the I/O functions of complex peripherals.

1.7.3. The microprocessor in a personal computer functions as the _____ in the CPU-memory-I/O devices stored program computer model.

CHAPTER 1 SELF-TEST

1. The 8086 outputs a _____-bit memory address allowing access to _____ memory locations.

2. Which control bus signal is active during an instruction fetch bus cycle?

3. The 8086 has a 16-bit internal data bus but an 8-bit external data bus.   (True/False)

4. A computer program must first be loaded into main computer storage before it can be executed. (True/False)

5. Main computer storage is made up of read/write memory called _____ and permanent memory called _____ .

6. Identify the op-code and operand for the 8086 instruction: AND BX,CX.

7. How does a memory read bus cycle differ from an I/O read bus cycle?

8. The first bus cycle of any instruction is always a(n) _____ _____ .

The Basic Computer   Chap. 1

9. A special multichannel test instrument used for troubleshooting microcomputer systems is called the _____ _____.

10. The byte 01101000 has the ASCII interpretation _____ but also represents _____ when interpreted as a signed binary number.

11. What is the main advantage of assembly language programming versus machine language programming?

12. What is meant by the term *distributed processing*?

ANALYSIS AND DESIGN QUESTIONS

1.1. The 8086 address bus carries the hex number A3E4C. What decimal memory address is indicated?

1.2. A 1K-byte memory actually has 1024 memory locations. What is the hex address of the last location in a 1K memory whose starting address is 10000H?

1.3. The accumulator of the 8086 contains the byte 10110110. How is this byte interpreted if it is encoded as a 2's-complement binary number?

1.4. With reference to Fig. 1.2, describe the contents of the address, data, and control buses when the CPU is writing the data byte 4CH to memory location 3F000H.

1.5. List the 8086 bus cycles required to fetch and execute the instruction IN AX,3CH.

1.6. Is it ever possible for two control bus signals to be active simultaneously? Explain your answer.

1.7. When you buy an expensive piece of software, the manufacturer will always supply the object code but seldom the source code. What is the reasoning behind this?

SELF REVIEW ANSWERS

1.2.1 cpu, memory, I/O

1.2.2 (d)

1.2.3 arithmetic logic unit, accumulator

1.2.4 65,536

1.2.5 even, odd

1.2.6 I/O write

1.2.7 data

1.2.8 RAM, ROM, secondary

1.3.1 memory read, memory write, I/O read, I/O write

1.3.2 IN, E56D

1.3.3 port 6Dh

1.3.4 instruction fetch

1.3.5 (b)

1.4.1 True

1.4.2 j, 106

1.4.3 True

1.5.1 (c)

1.5.2 (b)

1.5.3 True

1.5.4 object

1.5.5 The same operating system can be run on many different computers.

1.6.1 3.4V

1.6.2 (d)

1.6.3 timing, state

1.7.1 microcontroller

1.7.2 UPI

1.7.3 CPU

2

8086/88 CPU ARCHITECTURE AND INSTRUCTION SET

When studying microprocessors there are two major topics to consider:

1. The CPU architecture, including the internal registers and flags and the instruction set—that is, the dictionary of program instructions the microprocessor will recognize and execute
2. The electrical interface, including the data, address, and control buses and the clock generation circuitry

The first consideration is often referred to as the *programming model* and the latter as a *CPU module* to which the memory and I/O devices can be connected or interfaced.

In this chapter we introduce the CPU architecture of the 8086 and 8088 microprocessors and survey the instruction set in the form of several summary charts. In Chaps. 3 through 5 we continue to explore this programmer's viewpoint by developing the tools necessary to write 8086/88 assembly language programs. As you read these chapters and begin to write your own programs, you will want to return to this chapter to review the 8086's many different instructions and addressing modes.

In Chap. 6 we resume the hardware part of the story by developing practical CPU modules for the 8086 and 8088. For now, however, we concern ourselves with becoming software "experts."

The major topics in this chapter include:

2.1 8086/88 CPU ARCHITECTURE

As mentioned in Chap. 1, the microprocessor functions as the CPU in the stored program model of the digital computer. Its job is to generate all system timing signals and synchronize the transfer of data between memory, I/O, and itself. It accomplishes this task via the three-bus system architecture discussed in that chapter.

The microprocessor also has a software function. It must recognize, decode, and execute program instructions fetched from the memory unit. This requires an arithmetic-logic unit (ALU) within the CPU to perform arithmetic and logical (AND, OR, NOT, compare, etc.) functions.

Figure 2.1 is a model of the 8086 CPU. It is organized as two separate processors, called the *bus interface unit* (BIU) and the *execution unit* (EU). The BIU provides hardware functions, including generation of the memory and I/O addresses for the transfer of data between the outside world—outside the CPU, that is—and the EU.

The EU receives program instruction codes and data from the BIU, executes these instructions, and stores the results in the general registers. By passing the data back to the BIU, data can also be stored in a memory location or written to an output device. Note that the EU has no connection to the system buses. It receives and outputs all its data through the BIU.

The only difference between an 8088 microprocessor and an 8086 microprocessor is the BIU. In the 8088, the BIU data bus path is 8 bits wide versus the 8086's 16-bit data bus. Another difference is that the 8088 instruction queue (explained in the next section) is four bytes long instead of six.

The important point to note, however, is that because the EU is the same for each processor, the programming instructions are exactly the same for each. *Programs written for the 8086 can be run on the 8088 without any changes.*

Fetch and Execute

Although the 8086/88 still functions as a stored program computer (described in Chap. 1), organization of the CPU into a separate BIU and EU allows the fetch and execute cycles to *overlap*. To see this, consider what happens when the 8086 or 8088 is first started.

1. The BIU outputs the contents of the instruction pointer register (IP) onto the address bus, causing the selected byte or word to be read into the BIU.

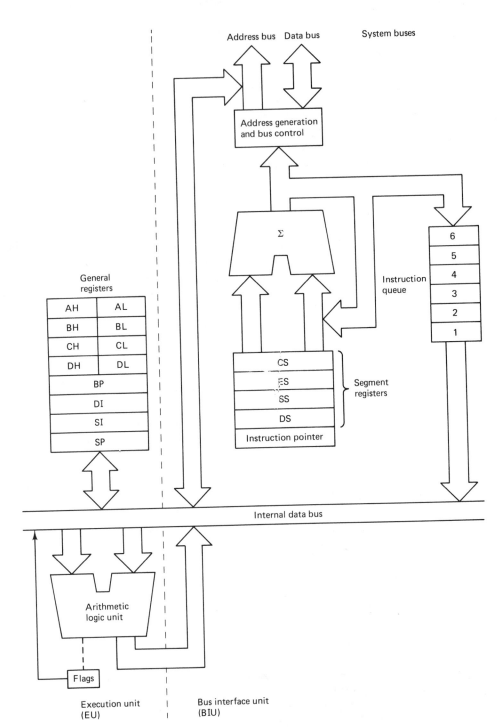

Figure 2.1 CPU model for the 8086 microprocessor. A separate execution unit (EU) and bus interface unit (BIU) are provided.

8086/88 CPU Architecture and Instruction Set   Chap. 2

2. Register IP is incremented by 1 to prepare for the next instruction fetch.

3. Once inside the BIU, the instruction is passed to the *queue*. This is a first-in, first-out storage register sometimes likened to a "pipeline."

4. Assuming that the queue is initially empty, the EU immediately draws this instruction from the queue and begins execution.

5. While the EU is executing this instruction, the BIU proceeds to fetch a new instruction. Depending on the execution time of the first instruction, the BIU may fill the queue with several new instructions before the EU is ready to draw its next instruction.

The BIU is programmed to fetch a new instruction whenever the queue has room for one (with the 8088) or two (with the 8086) additional bytes. The advantage of this pipelined architecture is that the EU can execute instructions almost continually instead of having to wait for the BIU to fetch a new instruction. This is shown schematically in Fig. 2.2.

There are three conditions that will cause the EU to enter a "wait" mode. The first occurs when an instruction requires access to a memory location not in the queue. The BIU must suspend fetching instructions and output the address of this memory location. After waiting for the memory access, the EU can resume executing instruction codes from the queue (and the BIU can resume filling the queue).

The second condition occurs when the instruction to be executed is a "jump" instruction. In this case control is to be transferred to a new (nonsequential) address. The queue, however, assumes that instructions will always be executed in sequence and thus will be holding the "wrong" instruction codes. The EU must wait while the instruction at the jump address is fetched. Note that any bytes presently in the queue must be discarded (they are overwritten).

One other condition can cause the BIU to suspend fetching instructions. This occurs during execution of instructions that are slow to execute. For example, the instruction AAM (ASCII adjust for multiplication) requires 83 clock cycles to complete. At four clock cycles per instruction fetch, the queue will be completely filled during the execution of this single instruction. The BIU will thus have to wait for the EU to pull one or two bytes from the queue before resuming the fetch cycle.

A subtle advantage to the pipelined architecture should be mentioned. Because the next several instructions are usually in the queue, the BIU can access memory at a somewhat "leisurely" pace. This means that slow-memory parts can be used without affecting overall system performance. In Chap. 7 we discuss memory access times in detail.

Programming Model

As a programmer of the 8086 or 8088 you must become familiar with the various registers in the EU and BIU. Figure 2.3 places these registers (originally presented in Fig. 2.1) into logical groups to form a *programming model*.

The *data* group consists of the accumulator and the BX, CX, and DX registers. Note that each can be accessed as a byte or a word. Thus BX refers to the 16-bit base

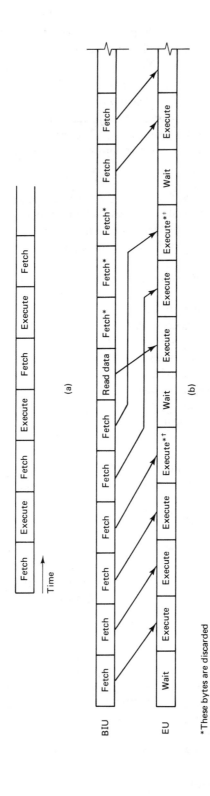

BIU

EU

Time

(a)

(b)

*These bytes are discarded
*† This instruction requires a request for data not in the queue
*‡ Jump instruction occurs

Figure 2.2 (a) The conventional (nonpipelined) microprocessor follows a sequential fetch and execute cycle. (b) The 8086/88's pipelined architecture allows the EU to execute instructions without the delays associated with instruction fetching.

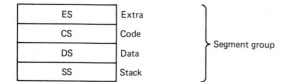

AX	AH	AL	Accumulator	⎫
BX	BH	BL	Base	⎬ Data group
CX	CH	CL	Count	
DX	DH	DL	Data	⎭

SP	Stack pointer	⎫
BP	Base pointer	⎬ Pointer and
SI	Source index	index group
DI	Destination index	
IP	Instruction pointer	⎭

| Flags_H | Flags_L | Status and control flags |

ES	Extra	⎫
CS	Code	⎬ Segment group
DS	Data	
SS	Stack	⎭

Figure 2.3 8086/88 programming model.

register but BH refers only to the high-order 8 bits of this register. The data registers are normally used for storing temporary results that will be acted on by subsequent instructions.

The *pointer and index* group are all 16-bit registers (you cannot access the low or high bytes alone). These registers are used as memory *pointers*. For example, the instruction MOV AH,[SI] has the word interpretation "Move the byte whose address is contained in register SI to register AH." SI thus "points" at the desired memory location. The brackets around SI are used to indicate *the contents of memory pointed to by SI*, not the value of SI itself.

Example 2.1

If SI= 1000H in Fig. 2.4, what is the contents of register AH after the instruction MOV AH,[SI] is executed?

Solution Study Fig. 2.4 and you will see SI pointing at the byte 26H. Thus AH will store 26H.

Sometimes a pointer register will be interpreted as pointing at a memory *byte* and at other times a memory *word*. In Fig. 2.4, [SI] = 26H but [SI+1:SI] = 3A26H. Note

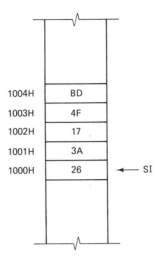

1004H	BD
1003H	4F
1002H	17
1001H	3A
1000H	26	← SI

Figure 2.4 Register SI is "pointing at" memory location 1000H.

the nomenclature for expressing the contents of a word versus a byte. As you will see, the 8086/88 always stores words with the high-order byte in the high-order word address.

Register IP is included in the pointer and index group, but this register has only one function—to point to the next instruction to be fetched to the BIU. Register IP is physically part of the BIU and not under direct control of the programmer as are the other pointer registers (see Fig. 2.1).

Figure 2.5 shows the bit definitions for the 16-bit flag register. Six of the flags are status indicators, reflecting properties of the result of the last arithmetic or logical instruction. For example, if register AL = 7FH and the instruction ADD AL,1 is given (add 1 to AL), the following results:

```
AL = 80H    ;7FH + 1 = 80H
CF = 0      ;There is no carry out of bit 7
PF = 0      ;80H has an odd number of logic 1's
AF = 1      ;There is a carry out of bit 3 into bit 4
ZF = 0      ;The result is not 0
SF = 1      ;Bit 7 is set
OF = 1      ;The result (+128) exceeds the capacity
             of (signed) register AL
```

The 8086/88 has several instructions that can be used to transfer program control to a new memory location based on the state of the flags. For example, the instruction sequence

```
ADD AL,1    ;Add 1 to register AL
JNZ 0100H   ;Jump to location 0100H if
             ;the result is not zero (ZF = 0)
```

Flags$_H$								Flags$_L$							
X	X	X	X	OF	DF	IF	TF	SF	ZF	X	AF	X	PF	X*	CF

*Bits marked X are undefined.

Bit position	Name	Function
0	CF	Carry flag: Set on high-order bit carry or borrow; cleared otherwise
2	PF	Parity flag: Set if low-order 8 bits of result contain an even number of 1-bits; cleared otherwise
4	AF	Set on carry from or borrow to the low-order 4 bits of AL; cleared otherwise
6	ZF	Zero flag: Set if result is zero; cleared otherwise
7	SF	Sign flag: Set equal to high-order bit of result (0 is positive, 1 if negative)
8	TF	Single step flag: Once set, a single-step interrupt occurs after the next instruction executes; TF is cleared by the single-step interrupt
9	IF	Interrupt-enable flag: When set, maskable interrupts will cause the CPU to transfer control to an interrupt vector specified location
10	DF	Direction flag: Causes string instructions to auto decrement the appropriate index register when set; clearing DF causes auto increment
11	OF	Overflow flag: Set if the signed result cannot be expressed within the number of bits in the destination operand; cleared otherwise

Figure 2.5 8086/88 flag word. DF, IF, and TF can be set or reset to control the operation of the processor. The remaining flags are status indicators.

will transfer control to location 0100H if the result of the ADD AL, 1 instruction is *not zero*. If it is desired to test for the zero condition, the JZ (jump if zero) instruction can be used. Section 2.8 covers these transfer-of-control instructions in more detail.

Three of the flags can be set or reset directly by the programmer and are used to control the operation of the processor. These are TF, IF, and DF.

When TF (the trap flag) is set, control is passed to a special address (previously defined by the programmer) after each instruction is executed. Normally, a program to display all the CPU registers and flags is stored there. Setting TF therefore causes the processor to operate in a software *single-stepping* mode, pausing after each instruction is executed. This is very useful for program debugging.

When IF (the interrupt flag) is set, external interrupt requests on the 8086/88 INTR input line will be enabled. When INTR is driven high (i.e., an interrupt occurs), control is transferred to an *interrupt service routine*. When this routine has finished, it normally executes an IRET (interrupt return) instruction and control is transferred back to the instruction in the main program that was executing when the interrupt occurred. Software interrupts are discussed in Sec. 2.8 and hardware interrupts in Chap. 8.

The last control flag is DF (the direction flag). This flag is used with the block move (also called "string") instructions. When DF is set the block memory pointer will automatically decrement; if reset, the pointer will increment. The block instructions are discussed in Sec. 2.5.

The final group of registers in Fig. 2.3 are called the *segment* group. These registers are used by the BIU to determine the memory address output by the CPU when it is reading or writing from the memory unit. To fully understand these registers, we must first study the way the 8086/88 divides its memory into *segments*. This is done in the next section.

SELF-REVIEW 2.1 *(answers on page 108)*

2.1.1. The CPU of the 8086 or 8088 microprocessor is divided into an _____ unit and a _____ _____ unit.

2.1.2. The pipelined architecture of the 8086/88 allows the fetch and execute cycles to _____.

2.1.3. What are the conditions that will cause the BIU to suspend fetching instructions?

2.1.4. What is the word interpretation of the 8086/88 instruction MOV CH,[DI]?

2.1.5. If register DI = 1002H, what is [DI + 1:DI] in Fig. 2.4?

2.1.6. The 8086/88 can be single-stepped if the _____ flag is set.

2.1.7. If register AL = FFH and the instruction ADD AL,1 is given, specify the contents of the six status flags.

2.2 SEGMENTED MEMORY

Even though the 8086 is considered a 16-bit microprocessor, (it has a 16-bit data bus width) its memory is still thought of in bytes. At first this might seem a disadvantage— why saddle a 16-bit microprocessor with an 8-bit memory? Actually, there are a couple of good reasons. First, it allows the processor to work on bytes as well as words. This is especially important with I/O devices such as printers, terminals, and modems, all of which are designed to transfer ASCII-encoded (7- or 8-bit) data.

Second, many of the 8086's (and 8088's) operation codes are single bytes. Other instructions may require anywhere from two to seven bytes. By being able to access individual bytes, these odd-lengthed instructions can be handled.

We have already seen that the 8086/88 has a 20-bit address bus, allowing it to output 2^{20}, or 1,048,576, different memory addresses. Figure 2.6 shows how this memory space is typically drawn on paper. As you can see, 524,287 words can also be visualized.

As mentioned in Chap. 1, the 8086 reads 16 bits from memory by simultaneously reading an odd-addressed byte and an even-addressed byte. For this reason the 8086 organizes its memory into an even-addressed bank and an odd-addressed bank, as shown in Fig. 2.7(a). If you are curious as to how this works, note that the 8086 provides control bus signals that can be decoded by the memory to determine if a byte or a word is to be accessed. We provide the details in Chaps. 6 and 7.

With regard to Fig. 2.7(a), you might wonder if all words must begin at an even address. For example, is it possible to read the word stored in bytes 5 and 6? The answer is yes, as you can see in Fig. 2.7(b). However, there is a penalty to be paid. The CPU must perform two memory read cycles: one to fetch the low-order byte and a second to fetch the high-order byte. This slows down the processor but is transparent to the programmer.

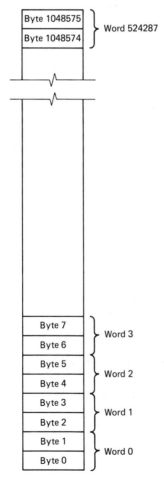

Figure 2.6 The memory space of the 8086/88 microprocessor consists of 1,048,576 bytes or 524,288 words.

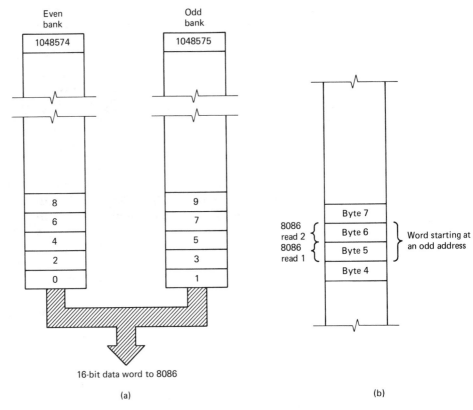

Even bank
1048574

Odd bank
1048575

8 | 9
6 | 7
4 | 5
2 | 3
0 | 1

16-bit data word to 8086

(a)

8086 read 2 { Byte 7
8086 read 1 { Byte 6
Byte 5
Byte 4

Word starting at an odd address

(b)

Figure 2.7 (a) By reading from an even-addressed bank and an odd-addressed bank the 8086 can read two bytes from memory simultaneously. (b) If a 16-bit word begins at an odd address, the 8086 (and 8088) will require two memory read or write cycles.

The last few paragraphs apply only to the 8086. The 8088 with its 8-bit data bus interfaces to the 1MB of memory as a single bank. When it is necessary to access a word (whether on an even- or an odd-addressed boundary) two memory read (or write) cycles are performed. In effect, the 8088 pays a performance penalty with every word access. Fortunately for the programmer, except for the slightly slower performance of the 8088, there is no difference between the two processors.

Memory Map

Still another view of the 8086/88 memory space is shown in Fig. 2.8. There are 16 64K-byte blocks beginning at hex address 00000 and ending at address FFFFFH. This division into 64K-byte blocks is an arbitrary but convenient choice. This is because the most significant hex digit increments by 1 with each additional block. That is, address 20000H is 65,536 bytes higher in memory than address 10000H. Be sure to note that five hex digits are required to represent a memory address.

The diagram in Fig. 2.8 is also called a *memory map*. This is because, like a road

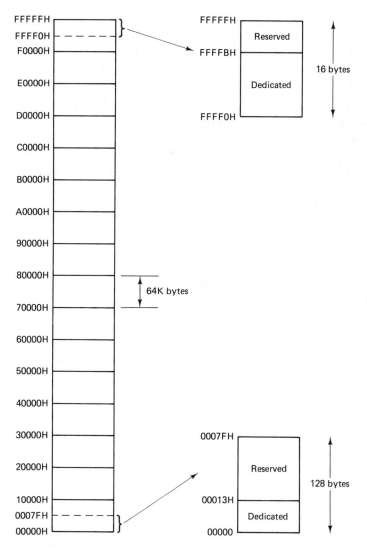

Figure 2.8 Memory map for the 8086/88 microprocessor. Some memory locations are *dedicated* or *reserved*.

map, it is a guide showing how the system memory is allocated. For example, it might show RAM (read/write memory) from 00000 to 3FFFFH, ROM (read-only memory) from FF000H to FFFFFH, and the remainder of the memory space unused. This type of information is vital to the programmer, who must know exactly where his or her programs can be safely loaded.

Note in Fig. 2.8 that some memory locations are marked *reserved* and others *dedicated*. The dedicated locations are used for processing specific system interrupts and the reset function. Intel has also reserved several locations for future hardware and software products. If you make use of these memory locations, you risk incompatibility with these future products.

Segment Registers

Within the 1MB of memory space the 8086/88 defines four 64K-byte memory blocks called the *code* segment, *stack* segment, *data* segment, and *extra* segment. Each of these blocks of memory is used differently by the processor.

The code segment holds the program instruction codes. The data segment stores data for the program. The extra segment is an extra data segment (often used for shared data). The stack segment is used to store interrupt and subroutine return addresses (explained more fully in Sec. 2.8).

You should realize that the concept of a segmented memory is a unique one. Older-generation microprocessors such as the 8-bit 8085 or Z-80 could access only one 64K-byte segment. This meant that the program instructions, data, and subroutine stack all had to share the same memory. This limited the amount of memory available for the program itself and led to disaster if the stack should happen to overwrite the data or program areas.

The four segment registers shown in Figs. 2.1 and 2.3 (CS, DS, ES, and SS) are used to "point" at location 0 (the base address) of each segment. This is a little "tricky" because the segment registers are only 16 bits wide, but the memory address is 20 bits wide. The BIU takes care of this problem by appending four 0's to the low-order bits of the segment register. In effect, this multiplies the segment register contents by 16. Fig. 2.9 shows an example.

The CS register contains B3FFH but is interpreted as pointing to address B3FF0H. The point to note is that the beginning segment address is not arbitrary—*it must begin at an address divisible by 16*. Another way of saying this is that the low-order hex digit must be 0.

Also note that the four segments need not be defined separately. In Fig. 2.9 the stack and extra segments are partially overlapped. Indeed, it is allowable for all four segments to completely overlap (CS = DS = ES = SS).

Example 2.2

Calculate the beginning and ending addresses for the data segment assuming that register DS = E000H.

Solution   The base address is found by appending four 0's. Base address: E0000H. The ending address is found by adding FFFFH (64K). Ending address: E0000H + FFFFH = EFFFFH.

Memory locations not defined to be within one of the current segments cannot be accessed by the 8086/88 without first redefining one of the segment registers to include that location. Thus at any given instant a maximum of 256K (64K × 4) bytes of memory can be utilized. As we will see, the contents of the segment registers can only be specified via software. As you might imagine, instructions to load these registers should be among the first given in any 8086/88 program.

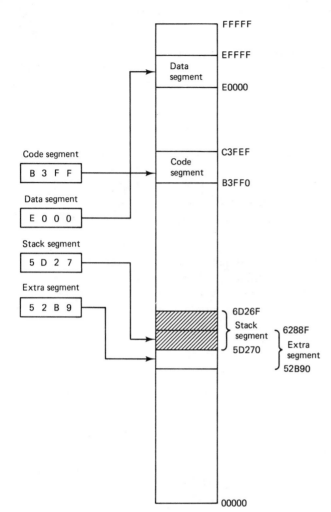

Figure 2.9 The 8086/88 divides its 1M bytes of memory address space into four segments, called the data, code, stack, and extra segments. The four segment registers DS, CS, SS, and ES point to location 0 of the current segment. In this example the stack and extra segments are partially overlapped. (From J. Uffenbeck, *Microcomputers and Microprocessors: The 8080, 8085, and Z-80*. Prentice-Hall, Englewood Cliffs, N.J., 1985.)

Logical and Physical Addresses

Addresses within a segment can range from address 0 to address FFFFH. This corresponds to the 64K-byte length of the segment. An address within a segment is called an *offset* or *logical address*. For example, logical address 0005H in the code segment shown in Fig. 2.9 actually corresponds to the real address B3FF0H + 5 = B3FF5H. This "real" address is called the *physical address*.

What is the difference between the physical and the logical address? The physical address is 20 bits long and corresponds to the actual binary code output by the BIU on the address bus lines. The logical address is an offset from location 0 of a given segment.

Example 2.3

Calculate the physical address corresponding to logical address D470H in the extra segment. Repeat for logical address 2D90H in the stack segment. Assume the segment definitions shown in Fig. 2.9.

Solution   For the extra segment

$$
\begin{array}{ll}
52\text{B}90\text{H} & \text{(base address)} \\
+ \ \underline{\text{D}470\text{H}} & \text{(offset)} \\
60000\text{H} &
\end{array}
$$

and for the stack segment

$$
\begin{array}{ll}
5\text{D}270\text{H} & \text{(base address)} \\
+ \ \underline{2\text{D}90\text{H}} & \text{(offset)} \\
60000\text{H} &
\end{array}
$$

The result of this example might be surprising. However, when two segments overlap it is certainly possible for two different logical addresses to map to the same physical address. This can have disastrous results when the data begins to overwrite the subroutine stack area, or vice versa. For this reason you must be very careful when segments are allowed to overlap. In Chaps. 3 and 4 we provide more detail on how these segments are defined in a program.

You should also be careful when writing addresses on paper to do so clearly. To specify the logical address 2D90H in the stack segment, use the convention SS:2D90H. Similarly, the logical address D470H in the extra segment is written ES:D470H. As we have just seen, both addresses map to physical address 60000H. There should be no ambiguity here, as five hex digits are required to specify a physical address.

Now that we have seen the differences between physical and logical addresses, we must dig a little deeper and see how the instruction set uses each of the four segments. For example, if register IP = 1000H, where exactly is the next instruction fetch going to come from? Or where will the instruction MOV [BP],AL—"move a copy of register AL to the memory location pointed to by register BP"—store register AL?

The answer is contained in Table 2.1. Every instruction that references memory has a *default* segment register, as shown. Instruction fetches occur only from the code segment, with IP supplying the offset or logical address. Similarly, register BP used as a pointer defaults to the stack segment.

Table 2.1 is programmed into the BIU. If IP = 1000H and CS = B3FFH, the BIU will form the physical address B3FF0H + 1000H = B4FF0H and fetch the byte stored at this physical address.

Example 2.4

What physical memory location is accessed by the instruction MOV [BP],AL if BP = 2C30H? Assume the segment definitions shown in Fig. 2.9.

Solution   Table 2.1 indicates that the stack segment will be used. The physical address is

$$
\begin{array}{l}
5\text{D}270\text{H} \\
+ \ \underline{2\text{C}30\text{H}} \\
5\text{FEA}0\text{H}
\end{array}
$$

TABLE 2.1 SEGMENT REGISTER ASSIGNMENTS

Type of memory reference	Default segment	Alternate segment	Offset (logical address)
Instruction fetch	CS	None	IP
Stack operation	SS	None	SP
General data	DS	CS, ES, SS	Effective address
String source	DS	CS, ES, SS	SI
String destination	ES	None	DI
BX used as pointer	DS	CS, ES, SS	Effective address
BP used as pointer	SS	CS, ES, DS	Effective address

Table 2.1 indicates that some memory references can have their segment definitions changed. For example, BP can also be used as a pointer into the code, data, or extra segments. On the other hand, instruction codes can only be stored in the code segment with IP used as the offset. Similarly, string destinations always use the extra segment. In Sec. 2.4 we show how the *segment override* is used to access these alternate segments.

Advantages of Segmented Memory

Segmented memory can seem confusing at first. What you must remember is that the program op-codes will be fetched from the code segment, while program data variables will be stored in the data and extra segments. Stack operations use registers BP or SP and the stack segment. As we begin writing programs the consequences of these definitions will become clearer.

An immediate advantage of having separate data and code segments is that one program can work on several different sets of data. This is done by reloading register DS to point to the new data.

Perhaps the greatest advantage of segmented memory is that programs that reference logical addresses only can be loaded and run anywhere in memory. This is because the logical addresses always range from 0000 to FFFFH, independent of the code segment base.

Consider a *multitasking* environment in which the 8086/88 is doing several different jobs at once. An inactive program can be temporarily saved on a magnetic disk and a new program brought in to take its place—without concern for the physical location of this new program. Such programs are said to be *relocatable*, meaning that they will run at any location in memory. The requirements for writing relocatable programs are that no references be made to physical addresses, and no changes to the segment registers are allowed.

Defining Memory Locations

As a programmer you will seldom need to know the physical address of a memory location. Usually, only the logical addresses are important. Indeed, as we have just seen, the physical address depends on the contents of the segment registers even though the logical address remains constant.

When writing assembly language programs it is convenient to assign logical addresses *labels* or *names*. For example, the sequence

```
DATA      SEGMENT
MEMBDS    DB        ?
DATA      ENDS
```

assigns the label MEMBDS to the byte at logical address 0 in the data segment. None of the three statements is a microprocessor instruction. However, they are *pseudo instructions* recognized by an assembler program.

The operator

```
DATA    SEGMENT
```

tells the assembler to store the following codes in the data segment. The second line uses the define byte operator (DB) to assign the label MEMBDS to a byte in the data segment. The "?" symbol indicates that the contents of this byte is undefined. Because MEMBDS is the first entry after the segment identifier, it maps to logical address 0. The statement

```
DATA    ENDS
```

ends the data segment (in this case only a single byte is defined).

If it is desired to define a word, the DW operator can be used: for example,

```
MEMWDS    DW    1234H
```

In this case the label MEMWDS will refer to a memory word location and the contents of that location will be initialized to 1234H (instead of being left undefined).

The DD operator can be used to define a 32-bit *double word*; DQ, a *quad word* (8 bytes); and DT defines 10 bytes (useful with the 8087 NDP). An *array* of uninitialized elements can be defined as

```
100    DUP  ?
```

which reserves 100 bytes of consecutive storage. If you wish to specify the values of the array, use

```
100    DUP(0)
```

which initializes each byte to 0. The statement

```
DB     'This is a message'
```

will cause the assembler to reserve 17 consecutive bytes, inserting the ASCII values for the string of characters enclosed within apostrophes.

The most important feature of the DB, DW, DD, DQ, or DT operators is that they allow the programmer to specify memory locations by a *name* rather than by their specific address. Even if you are not using an assembler and must hand assemble your 8086 or 8088 programs, you will find that using these operators will make your programs clearer and more understandable.

In the following sections we examine many of the 8086/88 instructions. In these examples descriptive labels are used to describe memory bytes, words or double words in the data, code, or stack segment. It will be presumed that these labels have been defined using the DB, DW, or DD operators in the appropriate segment. Thus you should interpret MEMBDS to be a memory byte defined in the data segment. Similarly, MEMWES is a memory word in the extra segment.

SELF-REVIEW 2.2 (answers on page 108)

2.2.1. The 8086 and 8088 can read or write a byte or word in a single memory access. (True/False)

2.2.2. To maximize 8086 processor performance, a data word should be stored beginning at a(n) _____ memory address.

2.2.3. Each memory segment is _____ bytes long and addresses within a segment are referred to as _____ or _____ addresses.

2.2.4. The four memory segments can be located anywhere within the 1MB of address space of the 8086/88. (True/False)

2.2.5. What is the physical address corresponding to DS:103FH if DS = 94D0H?

2.2.6. Which segment will be accessed for the instruction MOV [BX],AH?

2.2.7. What are the requirements to ensure that an 8086/88 program is relocatable?

2.2.8. Explain the meaning of the following assembly language pseudo instructions.

```
EXTRA       SEGMENT
COUNTER     DW          5678H
EXTRA       ENDS
```

2.3 ADDRESSING MODES

From Chap. 1 we learned that a computer instruction is made up of an operation code and zero, one, or two operands. The op-code identifies the operation to be performed while the operands identify the source and destination of the data operated on. The operands can specify a CPU register, a memory location in one of the memory segments, or an I/O port. The different ways in which the microprocessor generates these operand addresses are called the *addressing modes*. Table 2.2 lists the nine modes available with the 8086/88 microprocessor.

Immediate Addressing Mode

Instructions that use the immediate addressing mode get their data as part of the instruction. This mode represents a special case in which the data (located within the instruction) is stored in the code segment instead of the data segment. Note the *object code* column in Table 2.2. The data for the MOV AX,1000H instruction is supplied immediately after the instruction op-code B8.

TABLE 2.2 ADDRESSING MODES OF THE 8086/88 MICROPROCESSOR

Addressing mode	Object code	Mnemonic	Segment for memory access	Coding example — Symbolic operation	Description
Immediate	B8 00 10	MOV AX,1000H	Code	AH ← 10H; AL ← 00	Source of data is within instruction
Register	8B D1	MOV DX,CX	Within CPU	DX ← CX	Source and destination of data are CPU registers
Direct	8A 26 00 10	MOV AH,[MEMBDS][a]	Data	AH ← [1000H]	Memory address is supplied within the instruction
Register indirect	8B 04	MOV AX,[SI]	Data	AL ← [SI]; AH ← [SI+1]	Memory address is supplied in an index or pointer register
	FF 25	JMP [DI]	Data	IP ← [DI+1:DI]	
	FE 46 00	INC BYTE PTR[BP][b]	Stack	[BP] ← [BP]+1	
	FF 0F	DEC WORD PTR[BX][b]	Data	[BX+1:BX] ← [BX+1:BX] − 1	
Indexed	8B 44 06	MOV AX,[SI+6][c]	Data	AL ← [SI+6]; AH ← [SI+7]	Memory address is the sum of the index register plus a displacement within the instruction
	FF 65 06	JMP [DI+6][c]	Data	IP ← [DI+7:DI+6]	
Based	8B 46 02	MOV AX,[BP+2][c]	Stack	AL ← [BP+2]; AH ← [BP+3]	Memory address is the sum of the BX or BP base registers plus a displacement within instruction
	FF 67 02	JMP [BX+2][c]	Data	IP ← [BX+3:BX+2]	

Mode	Machine code	Assembly	Segment	Operation	Description
Based and indexed	8B 00	MOV AX,[BX+SI]	Data	$AL \leftarrow [BX+SI]$ $AH \leftarrow [BX+SI+1]$	Memory address is the sum of an index register and a base register
	FF 21	JMP [BX+DI]	Data	$IP \leftarrow [BX+DI+1:BX+DI]$	
	FE 02	INC BYTE PTR[BP+SI][b]	Stack	$[BP+SI] \leftarrow [BP+SI]+1$	
	FF 0B	DEC WORD PTR[BP+DI][b]	Stack	$[BP+DI+1:BP+DI] \leftarrow [BP+DI+1:BP+DI]-1$	
Based and indexed with displacement	8B 40 05	MOV AX,[BX+SI+5][c]	Data	$AL \leftarrow [BX+SI+5]$ $AH \leftarrow [BX+SI+6]$	Memory address is the sum of an index register, a base register, and a displacement within instruction
	FF 61 05	JMP [BX+DI+5][c]	Data	$IP \leftarrow [BX+DI+6:BX+DI+5]$	
	FE 42 05	INC BYTE PTR[BP+SI+5][b,c]	Stack	$[BP+SI+5] \leftarrow [BP+SI+5]+1$	
	FF 4B 05	DEC WORD PTR[BP+DI+5][b,c]	Stack	$[BP+DI+6:BP+DI+5] \leftarrow [BP+DI+6:BP+DI+5]-1$	

Strings	A4	MOVSB	Extra,Data	$[ES:DI] \leftarrow [DS:SI]$
				 If DF = 0, then
				 $SI \leftarrow SI+1; DI \leftarrow DI+1$
				 If DF = 1, then
				 $SI \leftarrow SI-1; DI \leftarrow DI-1$
					The memory source address is register SI in the data segment, and the memory destination address is register DI in the extra segment

[a] MEMBDS is assumed to point at location 1000H in the data segment. The brackets are optional.

[b] BYTE PTR and WORD PTR avoid the ambiguity of byte or word access.

[c] The displacement is added to the pointer or base register as a 2's-complement signed binary number.

You might also note in the object code column that the data is supplied *backward*, with the most significant byte first (this is very important if you are hand assembling your programs).

The immediate addressing mode is commonly used to load a register or memory location with some initial data. Following instructions then operate on this data. The one restriction is that the segment registers may not be specified. In the following section we show how to get around this problem.

Register Addressing Mode

Some instructions simply operate on or move data back and forth between CPU registers. MOV DX,CX puts a copy of register CX in register DX. Similarly, INC BH adds 1 to the contents of register BH. Note that the operand requires no memory reference.

The register addressing mode can be combined with the immediate addressing mode to load a segment register: for example,

```
MOV   AX,8010H      ;Load AX with 8010H
MOV   DS,AX         ;Copy AX into DS
```

The result is to move 8010H into register DS.

Direct Addressing Mode

All of the remaining addressing modes listed in Table 2.2 require an access to memory for at least one of the instruction operands. In the direct addressing mode the memory address is supplied directly as part of the instruction. However, as mentioned at the end of Sec. 2.2, labels are often given to these addresses so that the programmer need not be concerned with the numeric address. The instruction MOV AH,MEMBDS has the word interpretation "Store the contents of memory location MEMBDS in register AH."[1]

As note a in Table 2.2 indicates, MEMBDS is presumed to have been defined as a memory byte location in the data segment—in this specific case, address 1000H. You can see this address as the last two bytes in the object code column.

Indirect Memory Access Addressing Modes

The direct addressing mode is useful for infrequent memory accesses. However, when a memory location must be read from or written to several times within a program, the repeated fetching of the two-byte logical address makes this mode inefficient.

The indirect addressing modes solve this problem by storing the memory address in a pointer or index register (BX, BP, SI, or DI). In addition, a 2's-complement displacement can be added to the pointer or index to offset the location pointed at.[2] Table 2.3 shows the various combinations possible.

---

[1]Because MEMBDS is presumed to have been defined with the DB operator, the assembler knows that this label represents the contents of a memory location, not a constant.

[2]In App. A we review 2's-complement numbers.

TABLE 2.3 EFFECTIVE ADDRESS CALCULATIONS FOR THE INDIRECT MEMORY ACCESS ADDRESSING MODES

Addressing mode	Effective address				
	Displacement		Base register		Index register
Register indirect	None	+	BX or BP	+	None
	None	+	None	+	SI or DI
Indexed	+ 127 to − 128	+	None	+	SI or DI
Based	+ 127 to − 128	+	BX or BP	+	None
Based and indexed	None	+	BX or BP	+	SI or DI
Based and indexed with displacement	+ 127 to − 128	+	BX or BP	+	SI or DI

In general, a displacement can be added to a base register and the result added to an index register. This is the "deluxe" mode, called "based and indexed with displacement." In between are the "economy" modes, which use only a base or index register with or without a displacement. The resulting address is often referred to as the *effective address* (EA).

Note that the displacement is limited to a single byte, allowing the EA to be varied + 127 bytes (7FH) or − 128 bytes (80H) from the pointer base. Probably the most powerful feature of these indirect addressing modes is that the memory address can be changed based on program conditions. For example, we might set BX to point to the base of a table, perform a calculation in register SI to determine an index into this table, and finally test a flag to determine an offset value into this indexed table. This technique is explored in Chap. 4.

Sometimes you will see the indirect addressing mode operands written as in the instruction MOV AX, TABLE[SI], where TABLE is a label given to some memory location (presumably the base of a data table). This instruction can also be written MOV AX,[TABLE + SI]. However, the first form suggests that SI is used as an *index* into an array called TABLE. Thus if SI = 5, the fifth element in the TABLE array is accessed. Most assemblers will accept either form of the instruction.

Example 2.5

Identify the addressing mode for each of the following instructions:
(a) MOV AH,47H
(b) MOV AH,[BP + 2]
(c) MOV AH,[BP + SI]
(d) MOV AH,[XRAY]   ;XRAY defines a memory location
(e) MOV AH,TEMP[BX]   ;TEMP defines a memory location

Solution   (a) Immediate; (b) based; (c) based and indexed; (d) direct; (e) based.

When studying Table 2.2 you probably noticed two operators that we have not yet mentioned: BYTE PTR and WORD PTR. These are assembler pseudo operators needed to help the assembler determine if a byte or word memory access is required. For example, does the instruction INC [BP] mean "increment the memory *word*" or "increment the memory *byte* pointed to by register BP''? You cannot tell. By using the BYTE PTR or WORD PTR prefix, the proper instruction codes will be generated by the assembler.

When the instruction specifies two operands, the register operand will determine the byte or word access. For example, MOV AX,[BP]—move to register AX the contents of memory pointed to by register BP—indicates the word pointed at by BP because register AX (a word register) is indicated as the destination.

Finally, note that the default memory segments for all the indirect addressing modes are the stack segment when register BP is involved, and the data segment when register BX, SI, or DI is involved.

String Addressing Mode

In ''computerese'' a *string* is a sequence of bytes or words stored in memory. Word processors store their text as long strings of ASCII characters. A data table is another string example. Because of their importance, the 8086/88 has several instructions designed specifically for handling strings of characters.

These instructions have a special addressing mode of their own and use DS:SI to point to the string source and ES:DI to point to the string destination. MOVSB moves the source data byte to the destination location. Note that SI and DI are automatically incremented or decremented depending on the value of DF. In Sec. 2.5 we cover all the string instructions in detail.

SELF-REVIEW 2.3 (answers on page 108)

2.3.1. An instruction operand may reference a _____, a _____, or an _____.

2.3.2. The instruction MOV BH,23H uses the _____ addressing mode.

2.3.3. The instruction DEC BYTE PTR[BX + 2] uses the _____ addressing mode and decrements the _____ pointed to by register BX + 2.

2.3.4. When using the _____ addressing mode, the memory address is supplied as part of the instruction.

2.3.5. MEMBDS is an example of a _____ given to a memory location.

2.3.6. What is meant by NOTE[BP]?

2.3.7. Write the mnemonic for the instruction required to move the word pointed at by register SI offset by 27D to register CX.

2.3.8. Which memory segment will be accessed for the word described in question 2.3.7?

2.3.9. Which 8086/88 general-purpose registers cannot be used as base pointer or index registers in the indirect memory access addressing modes?

2.4 DATA TRANSFER INSTRUCTIONS

Now that we are familiar with the 8086/88 programming model and the various addressing modes, it is time to turn our attention to the instruction set itself. You should realize that this is quite a job. There are over 3000 different 8086/88 instructions to consider if each op-code is combined with each addressing mode!

What I would like you to do is consider the remaining sections of this chapter to be a first "tour" through this complex instruction set. We will look at the various instructions organized into logical groups and presented in table form. These tables will then serve as a reference for you as we begin to assemble increasingly more complex programs in Chaps. 3 and 4.

The data transfer group of instructions presented in this section allow the microprocessor to communicate with the outside world via the input and output instructions. They also provide the means for moving data into and out of memory and between the CPU registers.

MOV Instruction

Table 2.4 lists the various types of data transfers possible using the MOV instruction. Note that the operand is always written in the form *destination,source*. The data moved can be a byte or a word, although the pointer, index, and segment registers can only be accessed as words. The destination and source cannot both specify memory locations. Note that the flags are unaffected by this group of instructions.

Many more combinations of the MOV instruction are possible than are shown in Table 2.4: for example,

```
MOV   AX,[BX]
MOV   AX,[BX + 4]
MOV   AX,[SI]
MOV   AX,[SI − 6]
MOV   AX,[BP + SI]
MOV   AX,[BP + SI + 3EH]
```

These are all memory-to-register instructions but use the various forms of the memory indirect addressing modes.

Example 2.6

Assume that memory (byte) location COUNT holds the number of counts that a certain operation is to be repeated. Write an 8086/88 program to load CH with 00 and CL with the contents of COUNT.

Solution

```
MOV   CH,0        ;Move 0 to register CH
MOV   CL,COUNT    ;Copy the contents of COUNT
                  ;to register CL
```

Special Data Transfer Instructions

There are other data transfer instructions that do not use the MOV mnemonic. These are shown in Table 2.5. The XCHG instruction performs a register-to-register or register-to-memory swap that takes the place of three MOV instructions.

The 8 low-order flag bits can be stored in or loaded from register AH. These flags

TABLE 2.4 MOV INSTRUCTION[a]

Addressing mode MOV *dest,source*	Object code	Mnemonic	Coding example			
			Segment for memory access	Symbolic operation		Description
	8B C3	MOV AX,BX	Within CPU	AX ← BX		Register to register
	8A E3	MOV AH,BL	Within CPU	AH ← BL		Register to register
	A1 00 10	MOV AX,MEMWDS[b]	Data	AL ← [1000H] AH ← [1001H]		Memory to register
	A0 02 10	MOV AL,MEMBDS[c]	Data	AL ← [1002H]		Memory to register
	89 1E 00 10	MOV MEMWDS,BX[b]	Data	[1000H] ← BL [1001H] ← BH		Register to memory
	88 1E 02 10	MOV MEMBDS,BL[c]	Data	[1002H] ← BL		Register to memory
	C7 06 00 10 34 12	MOV MEMWDS,1234H[b]	Data	[1000H] ← 34H [1001H] ← 12H		Immediate data to memory

C6 06 02 10 34	MOV MEMBDS,34H[c]	Data	[1002H] ← 34H	Immediate data to memory
B0 10	MOV AL,10H	Code	AL ← 10H	Immediate data to register
B8 00 10	MOV AX, 1000H	Code	AL ← 00H; AH ← 10H	Immediate data to register
8E D8	MOV DS,AX	Within CPU	DS ← AX	General register to segment register
8C C2	MOV DX,ES	Within CPU	DX ← ES	Segment register to general register
8E 06 00 10	MOV ES,MEMWDS[b]	Data	ES ← [1001H:1000H]	Memory to segment register
8C 0E 00 10	MOV MEMWDS,CS[b]	Data	[1001H:1000H] ← CS	Segment register to memory

[a]The memory location can be specified using any of the addressing modes shown in Table 2.2. In this table the direct addressing mode is shown for all memory access examples.

[b]MEMWDS is assumed to point at the word beginning at location 1000H in the data segment.

[c]MEMBDS is assumed to point at the byte at location 1002H in the data segment.

TABLE 2.5 SPECIAL DATA TRANSFER INSTRUCTIONS[a]

General mnemonic Op-code Operand	Object code	Mnemonic	Segment for memory access	Coding example Symbolic operation	Description
XCHG *dest,source*	93 86 C7 87 14	XCHG AX,BX XCHG AL,BH XCHG [SI],DX	Within CPU Within CPU Data	AX⇆BX AL⇆BH [SI]⇆DL; [SI+1]⇆DH	Switch the contents of the word or byte source operand with the destination operand; none of the flags are affected.
LAHF	9F	LAHF	Within CPU	AH ← Flagsl	Copy the low-order flag byte into AH
SAHF	9E	SAHF	Within CPU	flagsl ← AH	Copy AH into the low-order flag byte
IN *accumulator,port*	E4 26 E5 26	IN AL,26H IN AX,26H	b b	AL ← port 26H AL ← port 26H; AH ← port 27H	Input a byte or word from direct I/O ports 0–255
	EC ED	IN AL,DX IN AX,DX	b b	AL ← port DX AL ← port DX; AH ← port DX+1	Input a byte or word from indirect I/O ports 0–65535; the port address is in DX; none of the flags are affected
OUT *port,accumulator*	E6 26 E7 26	OUT 26H,AL OUT 26H,AX	b b	port 26H ← AL port 26H ← AL; port 27H ← AH	Output a byte or word to direct I/O ports 0–255

	OUT DX,AL	EE	b	port DX ← AL	Output a byte or word to indirect I/O ports 0–65535; the port address is in DX; none of the flags are affected
	OUT DX,AX	EF	b	port DX ← AL; port DX+1 ← AH	
LEA dest,source[c]	LEA BX,MEMBDS[c]	8D 1E 00 10	Data	BL ← 00; BH ← 10H	The effective address of the source operand is transferred to the destination operand; none of the flags are affected
LDS dest,source[d]	LDS BX,DWORD PTR[SI]	C5 1C	Data	BL ← [SI]; BH ← [SI+1]; DS ← [SI+3:SI+2]	Transfer a 32-bit pointer variable from the source operand in memory to the destination register and register DS or ES; none of the flags are affected
LES dest,source[d]	LES BX,DWORD PTR[SI]	C4 1C	Data	BL ← [SI]; BH ← [SI+1]; ES ← [SI+3:SI+2]	
XLAT	XLAT	D7	Data	AL ← [BX+AL]	Replace the byte in AL with a byte from the 256-byte table beginning at [BX]; use AL as an offset into this table; none of the flags are affected

---

[a]Memory operands may be accessed using any of the addressing modes shown in Table 2.2. In this table the register indirect mode is used for example only.

[b]The IN and OUT instructions do not involve the segment registers.

[c]MEMBDS is assumed to point at the byte at location 1000H in the data segment.

[d]The destination must be a 16-bit CPU register.

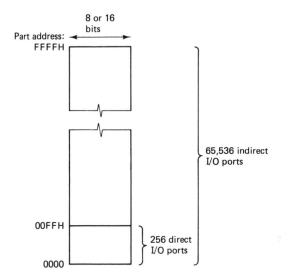

Part address:

8 or 16 bits

FFFFH

00FFH

0000

65,536 indirect I/O ports

256 direct I/O ports

Figure 2.10 The 8086/88 can access up to 65,536 different 8- or 16-bit I/O ports.

are in the same position as those in the 8-bit 8080 and 8085 microprocessors. Thus LAHF and SAHF are useful when translating programs from these processors to the 8086/88.

The IN and OUT instructions allow the 8086/88 to transfer data between itself and the outside world. A byte or word of data can be input or output but must pass through the accumulator. AL must be used as the source or destination for 8-bit I/O operations.

The I/O device address, also called the *port* address, can range from 0 to FFFFH. This allows up to 65,536 different I/O ports. The port address can be specified in two ways. In the *direct mode*, the instruction supplies the address but is limited to ports 0–255 (i.e., one byte). In the *indirect mode*, register DX holds the 16-bit port address, allowing access to all 65,536 ports. This is shown in Fig. 2.10.

Example 2.7

Write the 8086/88 program required to output the word in BX to I/O ports 8004H and 8005H.

Solution

```
MOV   DX,8004H      ;Point DX at the port address
MOV   AX,BX         ;Data must be in AX
OUT   DX,AX         ;Output the data
```

All the indirect memory access addressing modes require a pointer or index register to hold the memory address. This register can be loaded using the immediate addressing mode as

```
MOV   BX,1000H
```

but this requires the programmer to know the address of the target memory location—violating one of the goals of assembly language programming. A better technique is to use the LEA (load effective address) instruction. For example, assume that address 1000H has been given the label MEMBDS. Then the instruction

LEA   BX,MEMBDS

will load register BX with the EA of MEMBDS—in this case 1000H. The point is, we would not have to know this address; the assembler would look it up and insert it as part of the LEA object code.

In some cases an entirely new address, including the segment register, must be determined. The LDS (load pointer using DS) and LES (load pointer using ES) instructions are intended for this purpose. They load the 16-bit destination register and ES or DS segment register with the contents of the double-word memory operand.

Example 2.8

Assume that MEMWWDS defines a double word beginning at address 1000H in the data segment as shown in Fig. 2.11. What physical address will BX be pointing to after the following instruction sequence?

LEA   SI,MEMWWDS
LDS   BX,DWORD PTR[SI]

Solution The first instruction loads SI with the address of MEMWWDS—1000H. The second instruction loads BX and DS with the contents of the double word pointed at by SI. In this case BX = 8010H and DS = E000H. Now because BX defaults to the data segment, the physical address pointed to by BX becomes

E0000H + 8010H = E8010H

Note: The single instruction LDS BX,MEMWWDS could be used with the same effect.

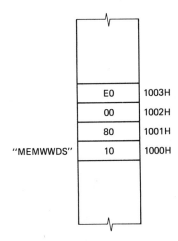

Figure 2.11 Memory organization for Ex. 2.8.

The last instruction in Table 2.5 is XLAT and is useful for extracting data from a table using register AL as the offset into the table. In Chap. 4 we provide an example of the use of this special instruction.

Segment Override

Every instruction that accesses memory has a particular segment register that it uses to determine the EA of the memory operand. Table 2.1 has shown the default segment register assignments.

The alternate segment column in this table indicates that the default assignment can be overridden for some types of memory references. Table 2.6 shows examples of the four segment override prefix instructions CS:, DS:, ES:, and SS:. Note in the object code column that the effect is to precede the normal object codes with the single byte 2E, 26, 3E, or 36. The segment override is in effect for the one instruction only and thus must be specified for each instruction to be overridden.

A typical application for the segment override is to allow data to be stored in the code segment. For example, consider the instruction sequence

```
CODE      SEGMENT
COUNT     DB    OFFH
MOV   AL,CS:COUNT
. . . (program continues)
```

The variable COUNT is defined within the code segment, requiring the MOV instruction to use the CS: override to access this memory location. Some assembler programs are smart enough to insert the segment override prefix on their own. If COUNT is known to the assembler to be in the code segment (due to the DB operator), the correct prefix will be generated automatically. Using CS: does not hurt, however, and serves as a check that COUNT is really in the code segment.

There is another way to store variables in the code segment—and that is to define CS = DS.

Example 2.9

Explain the operation of the following program:

```
MOV   CX,CS        ;Copy CS into CX
MOV   DS,CX        ;Copy CS into DS
MOV   AL,COUNT     ;Load AL with the contents of COUNT
```

Solution   The first two instructions make DS = CS. The last instruction loads AL with the contents of COUNT in the data segment. However, because DS = CS, COUNT is actually in the same physical memory space as the program. No segment override is needed.

Because a segment override is required to access data in the code segment, programs that use this technique must pay a penalty of one extra byte of code per data access instruction. For this reason, you are encouraged to store program data in the data segment. The resulting programs will require fewer bytes and execute faster.

TABLE 2.6 SEGMENT OVERRIDE PREFIX

General mnemonic			Coding example		
Op-code	Operand	Object code	Mnemonic	Segment for memory access	Symbolic operation	Description

General mnemonic Op-code	Operand	Object code	Mnemonic	Segment for memory access	Symbolic operation	Description
CS:		2E A1 00 10	MOV AX,CS:MEMWCS[a]	Code	AX ← CS:[1001H:1000H]	The default segment for the memory source or destination operand is overridden to become the code segment
		2E 89 4E 00	MOV CS:[BP],CX	Code	CS:[BP] ← CX	
ES:		26 A1 00 10	MOV AX,ES:MEMWES[a]	Extra	AX ← ES:[1001H:1000H]	The default segment for the memory source or destination operand is overridden to become the extra segment
		26 89 4E 00	MOV ES:[BP],CX	Extra	ES:[BP] ← CX	
DS:		3E 89 4E 00	MOV DS:[BP],CX	Data	DS:[BP] ← CX	The default segment for the memory source or destination operand is overridden to become the data segment
SS:		36 A1 00 10	MOV AX,SS:MEMWSS[a]	Stack	AX ← SS:[1001H:1000H]	The default segment for the memory source or destination operand is overridden to become the extra segment
		36 89 0F	MOV SS:[BP],CX	Stack	SS:[BP] ← CX	

[a]The assembler will automatically generate the segment override if these memory words have previously been defined to be in the appropriate segment. Each word is assumed to begin at address 1000H in the defined segment.

2.4.1. Using the MOV instruction, which of the following data transfers is illegal? (a) memory to memory; (b) memory to register; (c) register to memory; (d) segment register to memory.

2.4.2. Write the mnemonic for the instruction to load memory location MEMWDS with the contents of the DX register.

2.4.3. The 8086/88 can access _____ indirect I/O ports using register _____ to hold the port address.

2.4.4. Data can be input or output through any of the 8086/88 general-purpose registers.   (True/False)

2.4.5. Write the mnemonic for the instruction to load register DI with the base address of a data table starting at location TABLE.

2.4.6. Instruction op-codes are normally fetched from the code segment but can be overridden and fetched from the stack, data, or extra segments.   (True/False)

2.5 STRING INSTRUCTIONS

As mentioned in Sec. 2.3, the 8086/88 has several instructions for moving large blocks of data or *strings*. Table 2.7 lists the five string instructions. For all these instructions the memory source is DS:SI and the memory destination is ES:DI. Segment overrides can be applied only to the source address—the destination must be the extra segment.

The offset memory pointers, SI and DI, are automatically incremented or decremented depending on the state of DF—by 1 for bytes or by 2 for words. Because the instructions use dedicated registers defining the source and destination of data, the destination operand is not required (note that the object code is the same for both forms). Using the operand does make the assembly listing easier to read, however.

The STOS (store string byte or word) and LODS (load string byte or word) instructions transfer a byte or word from the accumulator to memory or from memory to the accumulator. The MOVS (move string byte or word) instruction combines these two operations, transferring the byte or word from the memory source to the memory destination.

The SCAS (scan string byte or word) and CMPS (compare string byte or word) instructions allow the destination byte or word to be compared with the accumulator (SCAS) or the memory source (CMPS). After execution the flags are set to reflect the relationship of the destination element to the source element. The conditional jump instructions can then be used to make decisions such as "Jump if AL is greater than the memory byte" or "Jump if the destination memory word equals the source memory word."

Repeat Prefix

You might be wondering how the string instructions are used to operate on large blocks of data. So far we have seen only the ability to handle single bytes or words. This is where the REP (repeat) prefix shown in Table 2.8 comes in.

Preceding the string instructions STOS or MOVS with the REP instruction causes

TABLE 2.7 STRING INSTRUCTIONS

General mnemonic Op-code	Operand	Object code	Mnemonic	Segment for memory access	Symbolic operation	Description
STOSB	None	AA	STOSB	Extra	ES:[DI] ← AL If DF = 0, DI ← DI + 1 If DF = 1, DI ← DI − 1	Transfer a byte or word from register AL or AX to the string element addressed by DI in the extra segment; if DF = 0, increment DI, else decrement DI; the flags are not affected
STOSW	None	AB	STOSW	Extra	ES:[DI] ← AL ES:[DI + 1] ← AH If DF = 0, DI ← DI + 2 If DF = 1, DI ← DI − 2	
STOS	dest[a]	AA	STOS MEMBES	Extra	Same as STOSB if DI = MEMBES	
		AB	STOS MEMWES	Extra	Same as STOSW if DI = MEMWES	
LODSB		AC	LODSB	Data	AL ← DS:[SI] If DF = 0, SI ← SI + 1 If DF = 1, SI ← SI − 1	Transfer a byte or word from the string element addressed by SI in the data segment to register AL or AX; if DF = 0, increment SI, else decrement SI; the flags are not affected
LODSW		AD	LODSW	Data	AL ← DS:[SI] AH ← DS:[SI + 1] If DF = 0, SI ← SI + 2 If DF = 1, SI ← SI − 2	
LODS	source[a]	AC	LODS MEMBDS	Data	Same as LODSB if SI = MEMBDS	
		AD	LODS MEMWDS	Data	Same as LODSW if SI = MEMWDS	

61

TABLE 2.7 (continued)

General mnemonic Op-code	Operand	Object code	Mnemonic	Segment for memory access	Coding example — Symbolic operation	Description
MOVSB	None	A4	MOVSB	Data, extra	ES:[DI] ← DS:[SI] If DF = 0, DI ← DI+1 SI ← SI+1 If DF = 1, DI ← DI−1 SI ← SI−1	Transfer a byte or word from the string element addressed by SI in the data segment to the string element addressed by DI in the extra segment; if DF = 0, increment SI and DI, else decrement SI and DI; the flags are not affected
MOVSW	None	A5	MOVSW	Data, extra	ES:[DI] ← DS:[SI] ES:[DI+1] ← DS:[SI+1] If DF = 0, DI ← DI+2 SI ← SI+2 If DF = 1, DI ← DI−2 SI ← SI−2	
MOVS	dest,source[a]	A4	MOVS MEMBES, MEMBDS	Extra, data	Same as MOVSB if SI = MEMBDS and DI = MEMBES	
		A5	MOVS MEMWES, MEMWDS	Extra, data	Same as MOVSW if SI = MEMWDS and DI = MEMWES	
SCASB		AE	SCASB	Extra	AL − ES:[DI]; update flags If DF = 0, DI ← DI+1 If DF = 1, DI ← DI−1	Subtract the byte or word of the string element addressed by DI in the extra segment from AL or AX; if DF = 0, increment DI, else decrement DI; the flags are updated to reflect the relationship of the destination operand to the source operand
SCASW		AF	SCASW	Extra	AX − ES:[DI+1:DI]; update flags If DF = 0, DI ← DI+2 If DF = 1, DI ← DI−2	
SCAS	dest[a]	AE	SCAS MEMBES	Extra	Same as SCASB if DI = MEMBES	

	AF	SCAS MEMWES	Extra	Same as SCASW if DI = MEMWES	Subtract the byte or word of the destination string element addressed by DI in the extra segment from the byte or word of the source string element addressed by SI in the data segment; if DF = 0, increment DI and SI, else decrement SI and DI; the flags are updated to reflect the relationship of the destination operand to the source operand
CMPSB	A6	CMPSB	Extra, data	DS:[SI] − ES:[DI]; update flags If DF = 0, DI ← DI+1 　　　　　SI ← SI+1 If DF = 1, DI ← DI−1 　　　　　SI ← SI−1	
CMPSW	A7	CMPSW	Extra, data	DS:[SI+1:SI] − ES:[DI+1:DI]; update flags If DF = 0, DI ← DI+2 　　　　　SI ← SI+2 If DF = 1, DI ← DI−2 　　　　　SI ← SI−2	
CMPS	A6	CMPS MEMBES, MEMBDS	Extra, data	Same as CMPSB if SI = MEMBDS and DI = MEMBES	
CMPS *dest,source*[a]	A7	CMPS MEMWES, MEMWDS	Extra, data	Same as CMPSW if SI = MEMWDS and DI = MEMWES	

[a]The destination or source operand must identify the string element as a byte of a word. Specifying the operand makes the instructions intent clear; however, the object code is the same as the nonoperand form.

TABLE 2.8 REP PREFIX

General mnemonic		Object code	Mnemonic	Coding example		
Op-code	Operand			Segment for memory access	Symbolic operation	Description
REP		F3 AA	REP STOSB	Extra	STOSB; CX ← CX − 1 Repeat until CX = 0	The string instruction following the REP prefix is repeated until CX is decremented to 0
		F3 AB	REP STOSW	Extra	STOSW; CX ← CX − 1 Repeat until CX = 0	
		F3 A4	REP MOVSB	Extra, data	MOVSB; CX ← CX − 1 Repeat until CX = 0	
		F3 A5	REP MOVSW	Extra, data	MOVSW; CX ← CX − 1 Repeat until CX = 0	
REPE/REPZ[a]		F3 AE	REPZ SCASB	Extra	SCASB; CX ← CX − 1 Repeat if ZF = 1 and CX ≠ 0	Repeat the string operation if the scan or compare is equal (i.e., ZF = 1) *and* CX ≠ 0; decrementing CX does not affect the flags
		F3 AF	REPZ SCASW	Extra	As above except SCASW	
		F3 A6	REPZ CMPSB	Extra, data	As above except CMPSB	
		F3 A7	REPZ CMPSW	Extra, data	As above except CMPSW	
REPNE/REPNZ[a]		F2 AE	REPNE SCASB	Extra	SCASB; CX ← CX − 1 Repeat if ZF = 0 and CX ≠ 0	Repeat the string operation if the scan or compare is not equal (i.e., ZF = 0) *and* CX ≠ 0; decrementing CX does not affect the flags
		F2 AF	REPNE SCASW	Extra	As above except SCASW	
		F2 A6	REPNE CMPSB	Extra, data	As above except CMPSB	
		F2 A7	REPNE CMPSW	Extra, data	As above except CMPSW	

[a]Either form of the memonic can be used.

these instructions to be repeated a number of times equal to the contents of the CX register. By loading CX with the number of words or bytes to be moved, a single string instruction (and REP prefix) can move up to 65,536 bytes.

Example 2.10

Write the 8086/88 program required to fill the 1000D-byte block of memory in the extra segment beginning at address BLOCK with the data byte 20H (ASCII space).

Solution

```
MOV   AL,20H        ;AL holds the data byte
LEA   DI,BLOCK      ;DI holds the address of BLOCK
MOV   CX,03E7H      ;Load CX with 1000D
REP   STOSB         ;Store AL at ES:DI, increment
                    ;DI, and repeat 1000 times
```

Note: DF is assumed to be 0.

The REPE/REPZ (repeat while equal or zero) and REPNE/REPNZ (repeat while not equal or not zero) forms of the REP prefix are intended for use with the SCAS and CMPS string instructions. They allow the string operation to be repeated while equal (REPE/REPZ) or while not equal (REPNE/REPNZ). These can be taken advantage of when performing a table-lookup operation or testing to ensure that two strings are equal.

SELF-REVIEW 2.5 (answers on page 108)

2.5.1. A block of sequential characters stored in memory is also called a _____.

2.5.2. When it is desired to move a block of data from one location in memory to another, the _____ instruction should be used with the REP prefix.

2.5.3. When DF = 1 the LODSW instruction will automatically _____ register _____ by _____.

2.5.4. Under what two conditions will the REPNE CMPSB instructions pass control to the following instructions?

2.6 LOGICAL INSTRUCTIONS

The logical instructions refer not to those instructions that seem logical (then the others are illogical?) but to the Boolean logic functions, such as AND, OR, NOT, exclusive-OR, and to the rotate and shift instructions. These instructions are all performed in the arithmetic-logic unit and usually affect all the flags.

Boolean Functions

Table 2.9 lists the five logic functions available with the 8086/88 microprocessor. Each function is performed bit by bit between the source and destination operands. An example will help illustrate this concept.

TABLE 2.9 LOGICAL INSTRUCTIONS

General mnemonic		Object code	Mnemonic[a]	Coding example			Description
Op-code	Operand			Segment for memory access	Symbolic operation		
NOT	*dest*	F7 D3	NOT BX	Within CPU	BX ← $\overline{\text{BX}}$		Complement all bits of the byte or word operand; none of the flags are affected
		F6 14	NOT BYTE PTR[SI]	Data	[SI] ← $\overline{\text{[SI]}}$		
AND	*dest,source*	23 CA	AND CX,DX	Within CPU	CX ← CX · DX		Perform a bit-by-bit AND of the source and destination byte or word operands storing the result in the destination operand; AF is undefined, all other flags are updated[b]
		22 3C	AND BH,BYTE PTR[SI]	Data	BH ← BH · [SI]		
		25 00 80	AND AX,8000H	Code	AX ← AX · 8000H		
OR	*dest, source*	0B CA	OR CX,DX	Within CPU	CX ← CX + DX		Perform a bit-by-bit OR of the source and destination byte or word operands storing the result in the destination operand; AF is undefined, all other flags are updated[b]
		0A 3C	OR BH,BYTE PTR[SI]	Data	BH ← BH + [SI]		
		0D 00 80	OR AX,8000H	Code	AX ← AX + 8000H		

XOR *dest,source*	33 CA	XOR CX,DX	Within CPU	CX ← CX ⊕ DX	Perform a bit-by-bit exclusive-OR of the source and destination byte or word operands storing the result in the destination operand; AF is undefined, all other flags are updated[b]
	32 3C	XOR BH,BYTE PTR[SI]	Data	BH ← BH ⊕ [SI]	
	35 00 80	XOR AX,8000H	Code	AX ← AX ⊕ 8000H	
TEST *dest,source*	85 D1	TEST CX,DX	Within CPU	CX · DX; update flags	Perform a bit-by-bit AND of the source and destination byte or word operands; the operands remain unchanged; AF is undefined, all other flags are updated[b]
	84 3C	TEST BH,BYTE PTR[SI]	Data	BH · [SI]; update flags	
	A9 00 80	TEST AX,8000H	Code	AX · 8000H; update flags	

[a] Any of the addressing modes can be used.
[b] CF and OF are reset.

Example 2.11

Determine the contents of register AL and the state of the flags after the following instructions are executed.

```
MOV   AL,6DH      ;Load AL with 6DH
MOV   BH,40H      ;Load BH with 40H
AND   AL,BH       ;AND AL with BH
```

Solution   Write the register contents in binary:

$$01101101 \quad (AL)$$
$$\cdot \underline{01000000} \quad (BH)$$
$$01000000 = 40H \quad (AL)$$

The flags are affected as follows:

```
CF = 0      ;CF is reset by the AND instruction
PF = 0      ;40H has an odd number of logic 1's
AF = X      ;AF is undefined
ZF = 0      ;The result is not zero
SF = 0      ;Bit 7 is reset
OF = 0      ;OF is reset by the AND instruction
```

The AND operation has several applications. As pointed out in Ex. 2.11, selected bits of the destination operand can be forced low by choosing those bits as 0 in the source operand. Another application is to consider the source operand a *mask* for testing selected bits of the destination operand. In Ex. 2.11 all bits are masked except bit 6. If this bit is 0, the result is 0; if it is a 1, the result is nonzero. The instruction sequence

```
AND   AL,BH
JZ    START
```

will transfer control to memory location START if bit 6 of register AL is a 0 (assuming that BH = 40H).

Using the AND instruction as a mask results in a "destructive" bit test because the contents of the destination operand is altered by the instruction. The TEST instruction, however, performs the same function but does not alter the source or destination operands. The conditional transfer to location START can be rewritten

```
TEST   AL,40H
JZ     START
```

This is a particularly handy instruction to use when several bits must be tested. If the first test fails, the second bit can be tested, and so on.

The OR instruction can be used to force selected bits high. For example, OR AL,80H will force bit 7 of AL high without changing any of the other bits in this register. Similarly, the exclusive-OR function can be used to *complement* selected bits. For example, XOR AL,80H will complement bit 7 of register AL without changing any of the other bits.

TABLE 2.10 SHIFT AND ROTATE INSTRUCTIONS

| General mnemonic | | Object code | Mnemonic | Coding example[a] | | Description |
Op-code	Operand			Segment for memory access	Symbolic operation	
SAL/SHL[b]	dest,count	D1 E0	SAL AX,1	Within CPU	See Fig. 2.12	Shift word or byte operand left or right once or CL times; AF is undefined; all other flags are updated; for single-bit shifts, OF is set if the sign of the operand changes
		D3 E0	SAL AX,CL	Within CPU	See Fig. 2.12	
SAR	dest,count	D0 F8	SAR AL,1	Within CPU	See Fig. 2.12	
SHR	dest,count	D2 F8	SAR AL,CL	Within CPU	See Fig. 2.12	
		D1 2C	SHR WORD PTR[SI],1	Data	See Fig. 2.12	
		D2 2C	SHR BYTE PTR[SI],CL	Data	See Fig. 2.12	
RCL	dest,count	D1 D3	RCL BX,1	Within CPU	See Fig. 2.12	Rotate word or byte operand left or right once or CL times; only CF and OF are affected; for single-bit rotates, OF is set if the sign of the operand changes
		D3 D3	RCL BX,CL	Within CPU	See Fig. 2.12	
RCR	dest,count	D0 DB	RCR BL,1	Within CPU	See Fig. 2.12	
		D2 DB	RCR BL,CL	Within CPU	See Fig. 2.12	
ROL	dest,count	D1 04	ROL WORD PTR[SI],1	Data	See Fig. 2.12	
		D2 04	ROL BYTE PTR[SI],CL	Data	See Fig. 2.12	
ROR	dest,count	D1 0E 00 10	ROR MEMWDS,1[c]	Data	See Fig. 2.12	
		D2 0E 04 10	ROR MEMBDS,CL[d]	Data	See Fig. 2.12	

[a]Any of the addressing modes can be used.
[b]Either form of the mnemonic can be used.
[c]MEMWDS is assumed to point at the word beginning at location 1000H in the data segment.
[d]MEMBDS is assumed to point at the byte at location 1004H in the data segment.

Shift and Rotate Instructions

There are several shift and rotate instructions; these are listed in Table 2.10 and diagrammed in Fig. 2.12. Be sure to notice that the rotated quantity can be an 8- or a 16-bit CPU register or memory location.

The main difference between a shift and a rotate is that the shifted bits "fall off" the end of the register, whereas the rotated bits "wrap around." Within the shift group of instructions there are both *arithmetic* (SAL and SAR) and *logical* (SHL and SHR) shift instructions.

The arithmetic shifts operate so that the sign bit (in bit 7 or 15) does not change

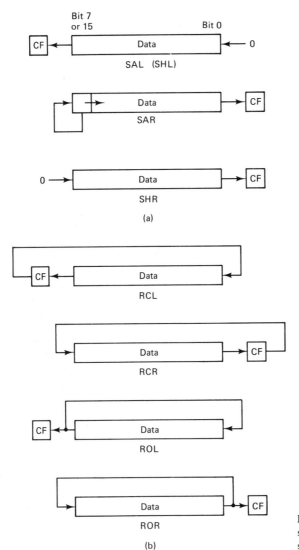

Figure 2.12 The 8086/88 has (a) three shift instructions and (b) four rotate instructions.

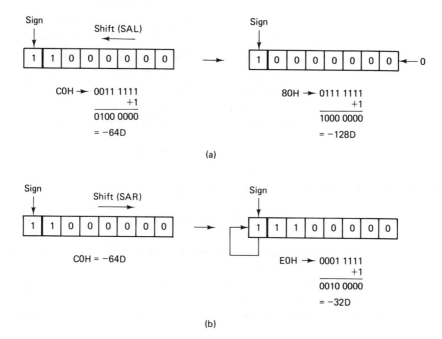

Figure 2.13 (a) The SAL instruction *multiplies* the signed binary number by a power of 2. (b) The SAR instruction *divides* the signed binary number by a power of 2.

when the shift occurs. Figure 2.13 shows the effect of the SAL and SAR instructions on the data byte C0H. As you can see, the SAL instruction in effect multiplies the data by 2 (maintaining the correct sign), and SAR divides the data by 2. The overflow flag (OF) will be set if the shifted quantity exceeds the limits for an 8- or 16-bit register ($+127$ to -128 for bytes and $+32767$ to -32768 for words).

The shift and rotate instructions can be repeated up to 255 times by loading register CL with the desired count. For example, to rotate the contents of register DX left five times through the carry, the following instructions should be given:

```
MOV   CL,5
RCL   DX,CL
```

Example 2.12

Determine the contents of registers AX, BX, and CX after the following program is run.

```
MOV   CL,3
MOV   AX,7FH
MOV   BX,0505H
ROL   AX,CL
AND   AH,BH
OR    BL,AL
```

Solution   The results are as follows.

		AX	BX	CX
MOV	CL,3	????	????	??03
MOV	AX,7FH	007F	????	??03
MOV	BX,0505H	007F	0505	??03
ROL	AX,CL	03F8	0505	??03
AND	AH,BH	01F8	0505	??03
OR	BL,AL	01F8	05FD	??03

SELF-REVIEW 2.6 (answers on page 108)

2.6.1. Which logical instruction should be used to force bits 0 and 1 of register DH low without changing any of the other bits?

2.6.2. Which logical instruction should be used to force bits 0 and 1 of register DH high without changing any of the other bits?

2.6.3. You need to determine if bit 3 of register AH is high without changing the contents of AH. Which instruction should be used?

2.6.4. What is the content of register BL after the following instructions are executed?

```
MOV    BL,0B2H
MOV    CL,2
SAR    BL,CL
```

2.6.5. Which two instructions will have the effect of dividing register BX by 8?

2.7 ARITHMETIC INSTRUCTIONS

The arithmetic instructions give the microprocessor its computational capabilities. But unlike earlier 8-bit processors, these instructions are not limited to addition and subtraction of 8-bit numbers in the accumulator. The 8086/88 can add and subtract 8- and 16-bit numbers in any of the general CPU registers, and using certain dedicated registers, perform multiplication and division of signed or unsigned numbers.

Addition and Subtraction Instructions

Examples of the various addition and subtraction instructions are given in Table 2.11. Note that the destination and source operands can be register and register, register and memory, memory and register, immediate data and register, or immediate data and memory.

There are two forms of addition and subtraction instructions. One includes the carry and the other does not. The ability to include the carry allows *multiple-precision* numbers to be handled. For example, suppose that we wish to add the 32-bit number in registers BX:AX to the 32-bit number in registers DX:CX storing the result in DX:CX. The addition would look as follows:

$$\begin{array}{cc} \text{BX} & \text{AX} \\ +\text{DX} & \text{CX} \\ \hline \text{DX} & \text{CX} \end{array}$$

Although there are no 32-bit addition instructions, the problem is easily solved using the ADC (add with carry) instruction.

```
ADD  CX,AX     ;CX ← CX + AX
ADC  DX,BX     ;DX ← DX + BX + CF
```

The first instruction does not include the carry, as there is no carry in at this point. If the addition of AX and CX sets CF, the second addition will add this to the sum of DX and BX.

The SUB (subtract) and SBB (subtract with borrow) instructions work similarly, with CF representing the borrow condition. When adding or subtracting one from a memory pointer or counter variable, the INC (increment) and DEC (decrement) instructions should be used. Note that the contents of a memory location can also be specified as the destination operand for these instructions.

The NEG (negate) instruction forms the 2's complement of the destination operand, effectively reversing its sign. This is done by subtracting the destination operand from 0.

Example 2.13

Determine the value of AL and the value of the flags following the instruction sequence

```
MOV  AL,5
NEG  AL
```

Solution AL → 00000000 − 00000101 = 11111011 = FBH = −5. The flags are affected as follows:

```
CF = 1    ;NEG sets CF except when the operand is 0
PF = 0    ;FBH has an odd number of logic 1's
AF = 1    ;There is a borrow out of bit 4
ZF = 0    ;The result is not 0
SF = 1    ;Bit 7 is set
OF = 0    ;There is no overflow condition
```

The CMP (compare) instruction is useful for determining the relative size of two operands. Normally, it is followed by a conditional jump instruction such as "jump if equal" or "jump if greater than or equal."

Multiplication and Division Instructions

Multiplication and division can be performed on signed or unsigned numbers as indicated in Table 2.12. The source operand can be a memory location or a CPU register, but the destination operand must be register AX (and DX for 32-bit results). The register usage

TABLE 2.11 ADDITION AND SUBTRACTION INSTRUCTIONS

| General mnemonic | | Object code | Mnemonic | Coding example | | Description |
Op-code	Operand			Segment for memory access	Symbolic operation	
ADD	dest,source	03 F2	ADD SI,DX	Within CPU	SI ← SI + DX	Replace the destination byte or word with the sum of the source and destination operands; update all flags
		00 2F	ADD BYTE PTR[BX],CH	Data	[BX] ← [BX] + CH	
		81 C7 00 80	ADD DI,8000H	Within CPU	DI ← DI + 8000H	
		81 06 00 10 00 80	ADD MEMWDS, 8000H[a]	Data	[1001H:1000H] ← [1001H:1000H] + 8000H	
ADC	dest,source	13 F2	ADC SI,DX	Within CPU	SI ← SI + DX + CF	Replace the destination byte or word with the sum of the source and destination operands plus the carry; update all flags
		10 2F	ADC BYTE PTR[BX],CH	Data	[BX] ← [BX] + CH + CF	
		81 D7 00 80	ADC DI,8000H	Within CPU	DI ← DI + 8000H + CF	
		81 16 00 10 00 80	ADC MEMWDS,8000H[a]	Data	[1001H:1000H] ← [1001H:1000H] + 8000H + CF	
SUB	dest,source	2B F2	SUB SI,DX	Within CPU	SI ← SI − DX	Replace the destination byte or word with the difference between the destination operand and source operand; update all flags
		28 2F	SUB BYTE PTR[BX],CH	Data	[BX] ← [BX] − CH	
		81 EF 00 80	SUB DI,8000H	Within CPU	DI ← DI − 8000H	
		81 2E 00 10 00 80	SUB MEMWDS,8000H[a]	Data	[1001H:1000H] ← [1001H:1000H] − 8000H	
SBB	dest,source	1B F2	SBB SI,DX	Within CPU	SI ← SI − DX − CF	Replace the destination byte or word with the difference between the destination operand and source operand plus carry; update all flags
		18 2F	SBB BYTE PTR[BX],CH	Data	[BX] ← [BX] − CH − CF	
		81 DF 00 80	SBB DI,8000H	Within CPU	DI ← DI − 8000H − CF	
		81 1E 00 10 00 80	SBB MEMWDS,8000H[a]	Data	[1001H:1000H] ← [1001H:1000H] − 8000H − CF	

INC *dest*[b]	FE C3	INC BL	Within CPU	BL ← BL + 1	Add one to the byte or word destination operand; store the result in the destination operand; all flags except CF are updated
	FF 05	INC WORD PTR[DI]	Data	[DI + 1:DI] ← [DI + 1:DI] + 1	
	FE 06 04 10	INC MEMBDS[c]	Data	[1004H] ← [1004H] + 1	
DEC *dest*[b]	FE CB	DEC BL	Within CPU	BL ← BL − 1	Subtract one from the byte or word destination operand, store the result in the destination operand; all flags except CF are updated
	FF 0D	DEC WORD PTR[DI]	Data	[DI + 1:DI] ← [DI + 1:DI] − 1	
	FE 0E 04 10	DEC MEMBDS[c]	Data	[1004H] ← [1004H] − 1	
NEG *dest*[b]	F6 DB	NEG BL	Within CPU	BL ← 0 − BL	Form the 2's complement of the byte or word destination operand; update all flags (CF = 1 except when the operand is zero)
	F7 1D	NEG WORD PTR[DI]	Data	[DI + 1:DI] ← 0 − [DI + 1:DI]	
	F6 1E 04 10	NEG MEMBDS[c]	Data	[1004H] ← 0 − [1004H]	
CMP *dest,source*	3A C4	CMP AL,AH	Within CPU	AL − AH; update flags	Subtract the byte or word source operand from the similar destination operand; the operands remain unchanged; the flags are updated to reflect the relationship of the destination operand to the source operand
	39 0D	CMP [DI],CX	Data	[DI + 1:DI] − CX; update flags	
	81 3E 00 10 00 80	CMP MEMWDS,8000H[a]	Data	[1001H:1000H] − 8000H; update flags	
	81 FF 00 80	CMP DI,8000H	Within CPU	DI − 8000H; update flags	

[a]MEMWDS is assumed to point at the word beginning at location 1000H in the data segment.

[b]Immediate operands are not allowed.

[c]MEMBDS is assumed to point at the byte at location 1004H in the data segment.

183

TABLE 2.12 MULTIPLICATION AND DIVISION INSTRUCTIONS

General mnemonic				Coding example		
Op-code	Operand[a]	Object code	Mnemonic	Segment for memory access	Symbolic operation	Description
MUL	*source*	F6 E3	MUL BL	Within CPU	AX ← AL*BL	Unsigned multiplication of the byte or word source operand and the accumulator; word results are stored in AX and double word results are stored in DX:AX (see Fig. 2.14); if the result cannot be stored in a single byte (for byte multiplication) or a single word (for word multiplication) CF and OF are set; cleared otherwise, all other flags are undefined
		F7 E1	MUL CX	Within CPU	DX:AX ← AX*CX	
		F6 27	MUL BYTE PTR[BX]	Data	AX ← AL*[BX]	
		F7 26 00 10	MUL MEMWDS[b]	Data	DX:AX ← AX*[1001H:1000H]	
IMUL	*source*	F6 EB	IMUL BL	Within CPU	AX ← AL*BL (signed)	Same as MUL except signed numbers are allowed; the source operand is limited to −128 to +127 for byte multiplication and −32768 to +32767 for word multiplication; CF and OF are set if the result cannot be represented in the low order register of the result; cleared otherwise, the sign is extended to the high order register; the other flags are not affected
		F7 E9	IMUL CX	Within CPU	DX:AX ← AX*CX (signed)	
		F6 2F	IMUL BYTE PTR[BX]	Data	AX ← AL*[BX] (signed)	
		F7 2E 00 10	IMUL MEMWDS[b]	Data	DX:AX ← AX*[1001H:1000H] (signed)	

Mnemonic	Operand	Opcode	Transfer	Operation	Description
DIV	source				Unsigned division of the accumulator (for byte divisors) or accumulator and DX (for word divisors); for byte divisors the result is returned in AL with the remainder in AH; for word divisors the result is returned in AX with remainder in DX (see Fig. 2.14); if the quotient exceeds the capacity of its destination register (AL or AX) a type 0 interrupt is generated; all flags are undefined
	DIV BL	F6 F3	Within CPU	AX ← AX/BL	
	DIV CX	F7 F1	Within CPU	DX:AX ← AX/CX	
	DIV BYTE PTR[BX]	F6 37	Data	AX ← AX/[BX]	
	DIV MEMWDS[b]	F7 36 00 10	Data	DX:AX ← AX/[1001H:1000H]	
IDIV	source				Same as DIV except signed division is performed; the source operand is limited to -128 to $+127$ for byte division and -32768 to $+32767$ for word division
	IDIV BL	F6 FB	Within CPU	AX ← AL/BL (signed)	
	IDIV CX	F7 F9	Within CPU	DX:AX ← AX/CX (signed)	
	IDIV BYTE PTR[BX]	F6 3F	Data	AX ← AL/[BX] (signed)	
	IDIV MEMWDS[b]	F7 3E 00 10	Data	DX:AX ← AX/[1001H:1000H] (signed)	

[a]Immediate operands are not allowed (except with the 80186).
[b]MEMWDS is assumed to point at the word beginning at location 1000H in the data segment.

is shown in Fig. 2.14 for both byte and word operations. Note that immediate operands are not allowed.

Example 2.14

Write a program to input two 8-bit unsigned numbers from input ports A0H and B0H and output the product to 16-bit output port 7080H.

Solution

```
IN    AL,0A0H      ;Get first number to AL
MOV   BL,AL        ;Save in BL
IN    AL,0B0H      ;Get second number to AL
MUL   BL           ;From product in AX
MOV   DX,7080H     ;Port address to DX
OUT   DX,AX        ;Output the product
```

Division can be performed on the word in AX or the double word in DX:AX. The divisor can be an 8- or a 16-bit memory location or CPU register. Note that a remainder is returned in register AH or DX when the result does not come out even.

Example 2.15

Write a program to divide the unsigned word input at indirect I/O port 8000H by 500D. Determine the result if the input data is 56,723.

Solution   The program is as follows:

```
MOV   DX,8000H     ;DX holds port address
MOV   BX,01F4H     ;BX holds divisor (500D)
IN    AX,DX        ;Input word
DIV   BX           ;Calculate quotient in AX and
                   ;remainder in DX
```

The result is AX = INT(56,723/500) = 113 = 71H and DX = MOD(56,723/500) = 223 = 00DFH.[3]

A special problem can occur when the divisor is so small as to cause the quotient to overflow the register dedicated to the result. For example, dividing 65,000 by 2 leaves a result too large to fit in register AL alone. When this occurs a special *divide by zero* software interrupt is automatically generated by the 8086/88. This causes control to be transferred to the address stored in locations 00000–00003H. Section 2.8 includes a description of software interrupts.

The integer multiplication and division instructions are similar to the unsigned forms except that the most significant bit represents the sign of the number. For integer byte division the quotient is limited to the range +127 to −128 and to the range +32767 to −32768 for word division. IDIV and IMUL are often used with the CBW and CWD (convert byte to word and word to double word) instructions described in the next section.

---

[3]The MOD operator represents the remainder after the indicated division.

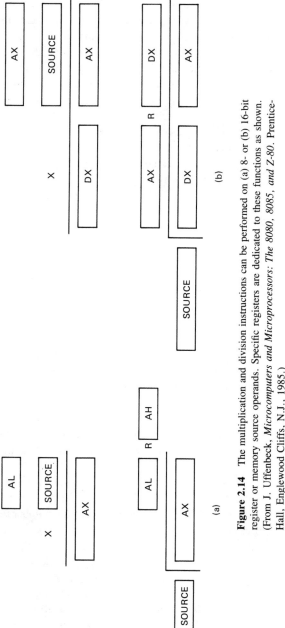

Figure 2.14 The multiplication and division instructions can be performed on (a) 8- or (b) 16-bit register or memory source operands. Specific registers are dedicated to these functions as shown. (From J. Uffenbeck, *Microcomputers and Microprocessors: The 8080, 8085, and Z-80.* Prentice-Hall, Englewood Cliffs, N.J., 1985.)

Arithmetic Adjust Instructions

In some cases the data to be operated on by the arithmetic instructions is encoded in BCD (decimal) or ASCII form. BCD encoding uses 4 bits to represent the decimal digits 0–9. The hex digits A–F are considered invalid. This means that one byte can hold two decimal digits—referred to as *packed decimal*. For example, the binary number 10011001 (99H) is the largest (one byte) packed decimal number allowed.

A decimal number can also be *unpacked* with one digit per byte. For example, 00001001 (09H) represents the unpacked decimal number nine.

An ASCII number is similar to an unpacked decimal number in that one byte can hold only one digit. In fact, it is very easy to convert an ASCII digit to decimal—simply subtract 30H. For example, the number 9 in ASCII is 39H (see Table 1.3). Subtracting 30H results in 09H − 9 in unpacked decimal form.

There are no special instructions for adding, subtracting, multiplying, or dividing these encoded numbers. This can lead to invalid results if care is not taken. For example, consider the following addition of two unpacked decimal numbers:

```
MOV   AL,7
MOV   BL,5
ADD   AL,BL
```

The result will be AL = 7 + 5 = 0CH (not 12!). The result is correct in binary form but invalid as a BCD number.

Fortunately, there are several arithmetic adjust instructions that can be used immediately before or after the arithmetic instructions to ensure valid decimal results. Table 2.13 lists these instructions.

In the preceding example, following the ADD AL,BL instruction with DAA—decimal adjust for addition—will correct the result so that AL = 12H. The DAS (decimal adjust for subtraction) instruction performs a similar function following the subtraction of two decimal operands.

When it is desired to convert the results of a decimal addition or subtraction to ASCII the AAA (ASCII adjust for addition) and AAS (ASCII adjust for subtraction) instructions should be used. However, they are to be used with unpacked decimal numbers only.

Note that the AAA and AAS instructions do not actually convert the result to ASCII form. However, the result in AL (and AH if a carry or borrow occurred) will be a valid unpacked decimal number. Adding 30H will convert this number to ASCII. For example, the decimal addition program becomes

```
MOV   AH,0          ;Be sure AH is 0
MOV   AL,7          ;First number
MOV   BL,5          ;Second number
ADD   AL,BL         ;AX = 000CH
AAA                 ;AX = 0102
ADD   AX,3030H      ;AX = 3132H
```

TABLE 2.13 ARITHMETIC ADJUST INSTRUCTIONS

General mnemonic		Object code	Mnemonic	Coding example		
Op-code	Operand			Segment for memory access	Symbolic operation	Description
DAA	none	27	DAA	Within CPU	If AL · 0F > 9 or AF = 1, then AL ← AL+6; AF ← 1 If AL > 9F or CF = 1, then AL ← AL+60H; CF ← 1	Adjust AL to a pair of valid packed decimal digits following the addition of two valid packed or unpacked decimal operands; all flags except OF (undefined) are affected
DAS	none	2F	DAS	Within CPU	If AL · 0F > 9 or AF = 1, then AL ← AL−6; AF ← 1 If AL > 9F or CF = 1, then AL ← AL−60H; CF ← 1	Adjust AL to a pair of valid packed decimal digits following the subtraction of two valid packed or unpacked decimal operands; all flags except OF (undefined) are affected
AAA	none	37	AAA	Within CPU	If AL · 0F > 9 or AF = 1, then AL ← AL+6; AH ← AH+1; AF ← 1; CF ← AF; AL ← AL · 0F	Adjust AL to a single unpacked decimal number following the addition of two valid unpacked decimal operands; the high-order half-byte of AL is zeroed and AH is incremented by 1; all flags except AF and CF are undefined

TABLE 2.13 (continued)

General mnemonic		Object code	Mnemonic	Segment for memory access	Coding example		Description
Op-code	Operand				Symbolic operation		
AAS	none	3F	AAS	Within CPU	If AL · 0F > 9 or AF = 1, then AL ← AL−6; AH ← AH − 1; AF ← 1; CF ← AF; AL ← AL · 0F		Adjust AL to a single unpacked decimal number following the subtraction of two valid unpacked decimal operands; the high-order half-byte of AL is zeroed and AH is decremented by 1; all flags except AF and CF are undefined
AAM	none	D4 0A	AAM	Within CPU	AH ← AL/0AH AL ← remainder		Following the multiplication of two valid unpacked decimal operands, AAM converts the result in AL to two valid unpacked decimal digits in AH and AL; all flags except PF, SF, and ZF are undefined

Mnemonic	Flags	Opcode		Operation	Description
AAD	none	D5 0A	Within CPU	AL ← (AH * 0AH) + AL AH ← 0	Before dividing AX by a single-digit unpacked decimal operand, AAD converts the two-digit unpacked decimal number in AX to a binary number in AL and 0 in AH; the quotient produced by the following division will then be a valid unpacked decimal number in AL and remainder in AH; all flags except PF, SF, and ZF are undefined
CBW	none	98	Within CPU	If AL < 80H, then AH ← 0 If AL > 7F, then AH ← FFH	Before dividing AX by a byte operand, CBW extends the sign of a byte dividend in AL into AH, thus converting AL into a valid signed word in AX; none of the flags are affected
CWD	none	99	Within CPU	If AX < 8000H, then DX ← 0 If AX > 7FFFH, then DX ← FFFFH	Same as CBW but extends the sign of a word dividend in AX into a double word in DX:AX; none of the flags are affected

The result in AX is now encoded in ASCII form and represents the correct decimal result: 12.

When multiplying two unpacked decimal numbers the result is almost always an invalid decimal number. For example, if AL = 06H and CL = 09H, the instruction MUL CL leaves 36H (54D) in AL. The correct binary result but incorrect decimal result. The AAM (ASCII adjust for multiplication) instruction converts this result to two valid unpacked decimal numbers in AH and AL. These digits can then be easily converted to ASCII if desired.

Example 2.16

Write a program to multiply the two ASCII digits in CH and CL and leave the ASCII result in AH and AL. Determine the contents of AX if CX = 3639H.

Solution The program is as follows:

```
AND   CX,OFOFH     ;Unpack CH and CL—CX = 0609H
MOV   AL,CH        ;Multiplier to AL
MUL   CL           ;Form product—AX = 0036H
AAM                ;Form two unpacked decimal digits
                   ;AX = 0504H
ADD   AX,3030H     ;Add the ASCII bias—AX = 3534H
```

It might also be worth noting that the AAM instruction can be considered a special form of the DIV instruction. This is because it divides AL by 10, leaving the quotient in AH and the remainder in AL.

When dividing a two-digit unpacked decimal number in AX by an unpacked decimal operand the AAD (ASCII adjust for division) instruction should be used *before* the division. This will convert AX to a binary number in AL and 0 in AH. (Remember: The largest decimal number in AX would be 99, which can be represented as the single binary byte 63H—thus AH is made 0.) The result of the division will then be two unpacked decimal numbers—the quotient in AL and the remainder in AH.

As an example, if AX = 0607H (67D) and CL = 09H, AX can be divided by CL using the following sequence.

```
AAD           ;Convert AX to 0043H (67D)
DIV   CL      ;AL = 07 and AH = 04 (7 remainder 4)
```

When signed division is performed, the CBW and CWD instructions may be required. For example, if it is desired to divide two signed bytes, a problem occurs. IDIV requires one of the digits to be in AX—a 16-bit register. CBW solves the problem by converting the byte in AL to a word in AX. It does this by extending the sign of the byte in AL to AH. Thus the number FBH (− 5) becomes FFFBH in AX following the CBW instruction.

CWD performs the same function when it is desired to divide two signed 16-bit words. Following the CWD instruction, the signed word in AX is converted to a signed *double word* in DX:AX.

2.7.1. Determine the contents of register AL after the following instructions are executed.

```
MOV   AL,3AH
MOV   CH,0A9H
ADD   CH,06H
ADD   AL,CH
NEG   AL
DEC   AL
```

2.7.2. Determine the contents of register AX after the following instructions are executed.

```
MOV   AX,6242H
MOV   BL,0FAH
DIV   BL
```

2.7.3. C3H is a valid packed number.   (True/False)

2.7.4. When decimal addition is to be performed, the DAA instruction should be used immediately _____ the addition instruction.

2.7.5. If, following an addition, register AX = 000EH, executing the AAA instruction will cause register AX to become _____.

2.7.6. Determine the final contents of register AX in Ex. 2.16 if CX = 3336H initially.

2.7.7. If AX = 0805H and CL = 09H, determine the final contents of register AX after the following two instructions are executed.

```
AAD
DIV   CL
```

2.7.8. You would use the CWD instruction before dividing two signed words, forcing the dividend to become a signed double word.   (True/False)

2.8 TRANSFER OF CONTROL INSTRUCTIONS

The stored program computer repeatedly follows the sequence: fetch the instruction whose address is in IP, increment IP, and execute the instruction. This implies that all programs will execute in a sequential manner. However, there are times when it is necessary to transfer program control to an address that is not the next instruction in sequence.

Examples are groups of instructions that must be executed repeatedly, groups of instructions that are shared throughout a program (subroutines), conditional transfers based on the state of the flags, and software interrupts. In this section we look at the 8086/88 instructions that allow program control to be transferred to new (nonsequential) addresses.

Unconditional Jump Instructions

Table 2.14 lists the five forms of the jump instruction. The first three are *unconditional*, meaning that control is transferred to the target address without regard for the state of

TABLE 2.14 JUMP INSTRUCTIONS

General mnemonic		Object code	Mnemonic	Segment for memory access	Coding example Symbolic operation	Description
Op-code	Operand					
JMP	*near target*	E9 — —[a]	JMP MEMN[b]	Code	IP ← MEMN	Transfer control to (near) target location within the segment; the addressing mode may be direct, memory indirect, or register indirect
		FF 26 00 10	JMP [MEMWDS][c]	Data	IP ← [MEMWDS + 1:MEMWDS]	
		FF 27	JMP [BX]	Data	IP ← [BX + 1:BX]	
		FF E0	JMP AX	Within CPU	IP ← AX	
JMP SHORT	*target*	EB —[d]	JMP SHORT MEMS[e]	Code	IP ← MEMS	Transfer control to the (short) target location; there are no indirect forms of this instruction
JMP	*far target*	EA 03 00 D3 9E	JMP FAR PTR MEMF[f]	Code	IP ← 0003H; CS ← 9ED3H	Transfer control to the far target location outside the segment
		FF 2E 05 10	JMP [MEMWWDS][g]	Data	IP ← [1006H:1005H]; CS ← [1008H:1007H]	
		FF 2F	JMP DWORD PTR[BX]	Data	IP ← [BX + 1:BX]; CS ← [BX + 3:BX + 2]	

	Code				
Jcond[h] *short target*	73 — [d]	JNC MEMS	Code	If CF = 0, then IP ← MEMS	Transfer control to the short target address if the condition is true; all conditional jumps require short targets
JCXZ *short target*	E3 — [d]	JCXZ MEMS	Code	If CX = 0, then IP ← MEMS	Transfer control to the short target address if CX = 0

[a]These two bytes are the 2's-complement offset between near memory location MEMN and the instruction immediately following the JMP instruction. For example, if the jump is to be 12 locations forward, the offset is 00 0C. Similarly, 12 locations backward requires an offset of FFF4. The offset is limited to 32767 locations forward (7FFFH) and −32768 locations backward (8000H).

[b]MEMN is assumed to point to a near-memory location (i.e., within the segment).

[c]MEMWDS is assumed to point at the word beginning at location 1000H in the data segment. The brackets are optional because MEMWDS defines a word, not a location to jump to.

[d]This byte is the 2's-complement offset between short memory location MEMS and the instruction immediately following the jump SHORT instruction. The offset is limited to 127 locations forward (7FH) and 128 locations backward (80H).

[e]MEMS is assumed to point to a short memory location (i.e., +127 or −128 locations from the address of the instruction immediately following the JMP SHORT instruction). The SHORT operator is optional if MEMS is already known by the assembler.

[f]MEMF is assumed to point to the far memory location 9ED3H:0003H.

[g]MEMWWDS is assumed to point to the double word beginning at location 1005H in the data segment. The brackets are optional because MEMWWDS defines a double word, not a location to jump to.

[h]See Table 2.15 for a list of testable conditions.

the processor flags. This form is used when it is required to repeat a group of instructions. For example, consider the program loop in Fig. 2.15.

This program repeatedly divides the data input at ports 6 and 7 by 4, outputting the result to port 9AH. The JMP REPEAT instruction transfers control back to the input instruction. REPEAT is a label given to the memory location storing the first byte of the IN AX,06H instruction. Note the column labeled *ADDR* in Fig. 2.15. This column keeps track of the logical address of each byte in the program. In this case you can see that REPEAT represents address 0002H and E5 is stored in this location (the operand 06H is stored in 0003H).

The direct form of the near jump (shown in Fig. 2.15) is also called a *relative jump*. This is because program control is transferred to a new address relative to the value in IP. The two bytes following the JMP op-code E9 are added to IP to form the target address.

Referring to Fig. 2.15, the assembler has generated the two bytes F7 FF for the target address REPEAT. Yet the IN AX,06H instruction is actually stored beginning at address 0002H. Does this make sense? The answer, of course, is yes if we do our arithmetic correctly. After fetching the jump instruction IP = 000BH. Now adding FFF7 (remember that the high-order byte is in the high-order address), we have

$$\begin{array}{r} 000\text{BH} \\ + \underline{\text{FFF7H}} \\ 1\ 0002\text{H} \end{array}$$

Ignoring the final carry, the correct address (0002) is found. FFF7 is actually -9, the number of bytes to jump *backward* in 2's-complement form.

When the target address is located within -128 or $+127$ bytes of IP, one byte of object code can be saved by using the *short jump*. This can be seen in Fig. 2.16. The distance to jump is now (minus) eight bytes, which can be represented in one 2's-complement byte as F8.

Which jump should you use—near or short? Because one less byte is required, the short form is best. In fact, when assembling your program, the assembler will automatically generate a short jump if it can determine that the target address is located within -128 to $+127$ bytes. The word SHORT is therefore optional. However, you are en-

ADDR	HEX CODES	LABELS	OP-CODE	OPERANDS	COMMENTS
0000	B3 04		MOV	BL,04H	;Load divisor to BL
0002	E5 06	REPEAT:	IN	AX,06H	;Get data word
0004	F6 F3		DIV	BL	;Divide by four
0006	E7 9A		OUT	9AH,AX	;Output result
0008	E9 F7 FF		JMP	REPEAT	;Repeat the cycle
000B					

Figure 2.15 Assembly language program demonstrating the near jump instruction.

ADDR	HEX CODES	LABELS	OP-CODE	OPERANDS	COMMENTS
0000	B3 04		MOV	BL,04H	;Load divisor to BL
0002	E5 06	REPEAT:	IN	AX,06H	;Get data word
0004	F6 F3		DIV	BL	;Divide by four
0006	E7 9A		OUT	9AH,AX	;Output result
0008	EB F8		JMP SHORT REPEAT		;Repeat the cycle
000A					

Figure 2.16   The program in Fig. 2.15 is rewritten using the JMP SHORT instruction. One byte of code is saved.

couraged to use it, as there may be some cases where the assembler will select a near jump when a short jump would be best. This can happen when the target's label has not yet been seen by the assembler and it must therefore assume the worst case.

The memory indirect and register indirect forms of the jump instruction specify the actual 16-bit target address. These two forms are thus not relative. As an example, we could replace the JMP SHORT REPEAT instruction in Fig. 2.16 with the two instructions

```
MOV  BX,0002H       ;BX points at REPEAT
JMP  BX             ;Jump to 0002H
```

The advantage in using the indirect jump instructions is that any address within the code segment can be specified. However, as we have just seen, an extra instruction is required to set up the target address. This is not always a disadvantage, as it allows the program the ability to compute the target address depending on program conditions.

The main advantage of using relative jumps is that the resulting program is *relocatable* anywhere within the code segment. Moving the program in Fig. 2.16 so that it begins at address E800H will not require the jump target address to be changed. It is still eight locations backward.

Finally, it is also possible to transfer control to a target address in a new code segment. This is called a *far jump*. Again direct and indirect forms are possible but neither form is relative. The direct form requires the assembler operator FAR PTR to identify the label as being in a new code segment. The indirect forms must specify a double word for the new CS and IP values.

Conditional Jump Instructions

The conditional jump instructions perform a short jump based on the condition of the status flags. The general form is shown in Table 2.14. Table 2.15 lists all the testable conditions. Usually, a conditional jump instruction is placed after an arithmetic or logical instruction, transferring control depending on the result of that instruction.

TABLE 2.15 CONDITIONAL JUMP INSTRUCTIONS

Mnemonic	Condition
Signed Operations	
JG/JNLE	Greater/not less nor equal $((SF \oplus OF) + ZF) = 0$
JGE/JNL	Greater or equal/not less $(SF \oplus OF) = 0$
JL/JNGE	Less/not greater nor equal $(SF \oplus OF) = 1$
JLE/JNG	Less or equal/not greater $((SF \oplus OF) + ZF) = 1$
JO	Overflow $(OF = 1)$
JS	Sign $(SF = 1)$
JNO	Not overflow $(OF = 0)$
JNS	Not sign $(SF = 0)$
Unsigned Operations	
JA/JNBE	Above/not below nor equal $(CF \oplus ZF) = 0$
JAE/JNB	Above or equal/not below $(CF = 0)$
JB/JNAE	Below/not above nor equal $(CF = 1)$
JBE/JNA	Below or equal/not above $(CF \oplus ZF) = 1$
Either	
JC	Carry $(CF = 1)$
JE/JZ	Equal/zero $(ZF = 1)$
JP/JPE	Parity/parity even $(PF = 1)$
JNC	Not carry $(CF = 0)$
JNE/JNZ	Not equal/not zero $(ZF = 0)$
JNP/JPO	Not parity/parity odd $(PF = 0)$

Source: J. Uffenbeck, *Microcomputers and Microprocessors: The 8080, 8085, and Z-80.* Prentice-Hall, Englewood Cliffs, N.J., 1985.

Example 2.17

Explain the operation of the following program.

```
MOV   BL,47H
IN    AL,36H
CMP   AL,BL
JE    MATCH
JA    BIG
JMP   SMALL
```

Solution   The program inputs a data byte from input port 36H and then compares it with 47H. If a match occurs, control is transferred to the program beginning at address MATCH. If the input byte is >47H, control is transferred to the program beginning at address BIG. If none of these conditions are met, control is passed to the program beginning at address SMALL.

Note: MATCH, BIG, and SMALL must be located within -128 to $+127$ bytes of the corresponding conditional jump instruction.

The JCXZ instruction is a special conditional jump that does not test the status flags. Instead, it tests the contents of CX and transfers control to the target address if CX = 0. This has application with the LOOP instructions explained in the next section.

In summary, the conditional jump instructions are among the most important in the processor's instruction set. This is because they allow the processor to make decisions based on program conditions. You will see numerous examples throughout this book.

Loop Instructions

One common programming problem is to set up a group of instructions that must be executed several times. One of the CPU registers is loaded with the loop count and this register is decremented by 1 at the end of each loop. A JNZ (jump if not zero) instruction transfers control back to the start of the loop if the counter register is not zero.

The 8086/88 loop instructions are designed exactly for this application. They combine the decrement counter and transfer of control instructions into one. Table 2.16 lists the three forms.

Example 2.18

Using the loop instructions, write a program segment to output 256 bytes from a data table beginning at address TABLE to output port A0H.

Solution

```
        LEA    SI,TABLE      ;Load SI with base address of TABLE
        MOV    CX,0100H      ;CX holds the number of bytes to output
AGAIN:  LODSB                ;Data byte to AL and INC SI
        OUT    0A0H,AL       ;Output the data byte
        LOOP   AGAIN         ;Repeat until CX = 0
```

Note: We have assumed that DF = 0. In Sec. 2.9 we show how to set or reset this flag.

This example shows how the string and loop instructions actually perform two operations each. LODSB (load string byte) is the equivalent of

```
MOV  AL,[SI]
INC  SI
```

and LOOP AGAIN replaces the equivalent instructions

```
DEC  CX
JNZ  AGAIN
```

The LOOPE or LOOPZ (loop if equal or zero) and LOOPNE or LOOPNZ (loop if not equal or not zero) instructions text CX and ZF. For example, LOOPE "loops while equal." This means that if CX ≠ 0 and ZF = 1, the loop will be repeated. Similarly, LOOPNE "loops while not equal." These two forms are useful when comparing two strings or looking for a match between a CPU register and a byte or word in a data table.

TABLE 2.16 LOOP INSTRUCTIONS

General mnemonic				Coding example		Description
Op-code	Operand	Object code	Mnemonic	Segment for memory access	Symbolic operation	
LOOP	short target	E2 —[a]	LOOP MEMS [b]	Code	CX ← CX − 1 If CX ≠ 0, then IP ← MEMS	Decrement CX and transfer control to the short target address if CX ≠ 0
LOOPE/[c] LOOPZ	short target	E1 —[a]	LOOPZ MEMS [b]	Code	CX ← CX − 1 If (CX ≠ 0)·(ZF = 1), then IP ← MEMS	Decrement CX and transfer control to the short target address if CX ≠ 0 AND the last instruction to affect the flags resulted in zero (ZF = 1)
LOOPNE/[c] LOOPNZ	short target	E0 —[a]	LOOPNZ MEMS[b]	Code	CX ← CX − 1; If (CX ≠ 0)·(ZF = 0), then IP ← MEMS	Decrement CX and transfer control to the short target address if CX ≠ 0 AND the last instruction to affect the flags resulted in a nonzero result (ZF = 0)

[a]This byte is the 2's-complement offset between short memory location MEMS and the instruction immediately following the LOOP instruction. The offset is limited to 127 locations forward (7FH) and 128 locations backward (80H).

[b]MEMS is assumed to point to a short memory location (i.e., +127 or −128 locations from the address of the instruction immediately following the LOOP instruction).

[c]Either form of the mnemonic may be used.

All forms of the loop instruction repeat until CX = 0. This means that the loop will be repeated 65,536 times if CX = 0 initially. Although the programmer normally controls the value in CX, the JCXZ instruction can be used before entering the loop "just to be sure" that CX has not somehow become zero.

Push and Pop Instructions

The PUSH and POP instructions are not really transfer-of-control instructions, but they do use the stack area of memory, which you will need to understand before studying the CALL, RET, and software interrupts in the next two sections.

Recall that the stack is a 64K-byte memory segment whose base address is determined by the SS segment register. Two CPU registers normally point into this area. These are SP and BP.

The stack is not another data segment but a special area in memory used by the processor for temporary data storage. What makes the stack unique is that it is a last-in, first-out type of memory. Just as plates are pushed into a spring-loaded dispenser in a cafeteria, data is pushed onto the stack by the PUSH *source* instruction. The POP *destination* instruction causes the data currently on top of the stack to be popped into the destination operand. Table 2.17 explains the four push and pop instructions in detail.

Figure 2.17 shows the stack segment with register SP pointing to location 1000H —currently the top of the stack. Now assume that the instruction PUSH CX occurs. SP is decremented by 2 and CL and CH are then pushed onto the stack. The new stack top is address 0FFEH (SP'). As you can see, the stack actually grows *downward* with each successive PUSH instruction. The stack top moves to 0FFCH (SP'') after the instruction PUSH BX is executed.

Now that BX and CX are safely stored in the stack segment, these registers can be used for some other purpose. When it is desired to recover the old values of BX and CX, the POP instruction is used. However, we must be careful. SP is currently pointing to location 0FFCH, where the BX register is stored. We can say that BX is "sitting atop the stack." The next POP instruction will thus cause BX to be popped into the destination operand.

Based on this observation we can state a general rule for using the stack. "Registers should be popped off the stack in the *reverse* order in which they were pushed on." In this case POP BX causes the contents of 0FFCH and 0FFDH to be popped into BL and BH and SP to be incremented by 2. CX now sits atop the stack and SP = 0FFEH (SP'). A POP CX instruction will recover CL and CH and restore SP to its original value (1000H).

Before using the stack it is important that register SP be initialized. This is accomplished with an immediate mode data move instruction such as MOV SP,1000H, which establishes the stack top at location 1000H in the stack segment. Because the stack grows downward, SP is usually initialized to a high memory location allowing room for the stack to grow.

The stack location is very important, especially if the data, code, and stack segments are all the same or allowed to overlap. If you are not careful, the stack can overwrite program data or even the program itself. This is a difficult problem to debug because there is no program left to check!

TABLE 2.17 PUSH AND POP INSTRUCTIONS

Addressing mode	Object code	Mnemonic op-code operand	Segment for memory access	Symbolic operation	Description
			Coding example		
PUSH source[a]	51	PUSH CX	Stack	SP ← SP − 2; [SP + 1] ← CH; [SP] ← CL	Decrement SP by 2 and transfer the word from the source operand to the top of the stack now pointed to by SP
	1E	PUSH DS	Stack	SP ← SP − 2; [SP + 1:SP] ← DS	
	FF 75 02	PUSH [DI + 2]	Stack, data	SP ← SP − 2; [SP + 1] ← [DI + 3]; [SP] ← [DI + 2]	
POP dest[a]	59	POP CX	Stack	CL ← [SP]; CH ← [SP + 1]; SP ← SP + 2	Transfer the word from the top of the stack pointed to by SP to the destination operand; increment SP by 2
	1F	POP DS	Stack	DS ← [SP + 1:SP]; SP ← SP + 2	
	8F 45 02	POP [DI + 2]	Data, stack	[DI + 3] ← [SP + 1]; [DI + 2] ← [SP]; SP ← SP + 2	
PUSHF none	9C	PUSHF	Stack	SP ← SP − 2; [SP + 1:SP] ← flags	Push the 16-bit flag word onto the stack
POPF none	9D	POPF	Stack	flags ← [SP + 1:SP]; SP ← SP + 2	Pop the top of the stack into the 16-bit flag word

[a]Immediate operands are not allowed (except with the 80186).

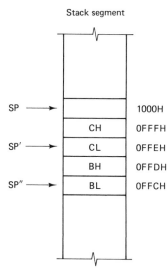

Stack segment

SP → 1000H
CH OFFFH
SP' → CL OFFEH
BH OFFDH
SP" → BL OFFCH

Figure 2.17 Contents of the stack and register SP after the PUSH CX and PUSH BX instructions have executed. SP" is the final value of register SP.

Finally, note that the PUSHF and POPF instructions allow the processor flags to be stored on the stack. This can be useful with interrupts and subroutines as the entire state of the machine (all CPU registers and flags) can be saved and then restored later. These concepts are explored in later chapters.

Call and Return Instructions

The CALL and RET instructions allow the programmer to use a group of instructions as a *subroutine* or *procedure* that can be executed several times from within the main program. As an example, the following instructions will generate a short time delay.

```
DELAY    PROC    NEAR      ;Define near procedure
         PUSH    AX        ;Save AX on stack
         MOV     AX,0000   ;Set counter for 65536 cycles
REPEAT:  DEC     AX        ;Bump counter
         JNZ     REPEAT    ;Do 65536 times
         POP     AX        ;Restore AX
         RET               ;Return to main program
DELAY    ENDP
```

The first line defines to the assembler the following group of instructions as a *near* procedure (i.e., a subroutine within the segment) and gives it the name DELAY. The subroutine itself kills time by repeating the DEC AX and JNZ REPEAT instructions 65536 times. This will require approximately 250 ms with a 5-MHz system clock. Once the time delay has ended, the value of AX before the procedure began is popped back into AX and control is transferred back to the main program via the RET instruction. The last line tidies things up, telling the assembler that this is the end of the procedure.

The DELAY subroutine can be called by any program in which a 250-ms time delay is required. This might be required when outputting data to a peripheral that cannot accept data as fast as the microprocessor can output it, for example. Another application would be waiting for a mechanical switch to stop bouncing before testing its value. The calling procedure would look as follows:

```
                         main program
                              .
                              .
                              .
                         CALL DELAY
                   (main program continues)
                              .
                              .
                              .
```

The CALL instruction is similar to an unconditional jump except that the value of IP (now pointing to the instruction immediately following the CALL) is pushed onto the stack. Control then transfers to address DELAY.

After the DELAY subroutine has executed, it must end with a RET (return) instruction. This causes the top of the stack to be popped into IP, neatly returning control to the instruction in the main program with which it left off.

Table 2.18 describes the various forms of the CALL and RET instructions. The CALL we have just been discussing is referred to as a *near* CALL because the subroutine is located within the same code segment. It is also possible to execute a *far* CALL to a procedure in a different code segment.

The far CALL differs from the near CALL in that the value of CS (in addition to IP) is saved on the stack. For this reason you must also use a far RET instruction to pop CS and IP from the stack when the far procedure has ended. The assembler will automatically generate the proper RET instruction if you have defined the procedure using the NEAR or FAR attribute.

Like the near jump instructions, the near CALL can be direct or indirect. The direct forms are relative, allowing the subroutine to be located within $+32767$ to -32768 bytes of the address in IP. There are no short forms. The indirect forms specify the absolute address in a memory location or CPU register.

A direct far CALL requires the operator FAR PTR to tell the assembler that the subroutine is located in another segment. The indirect forms require a double word to specify the new CS and IP values.

You will note in Table 2.18 that the RET instructions can specify an optional *pop value*. This allows data to be passed to a subroutine on the stack instead of in a CPU register: for example,

```
                         PUSH   CX
                         PUSH   BX
                         CALL   SUB
                SUB:        .
                            .
                            .
                         RET    4
```

TABLE 2.18 CALL AND RETURN INSTRUCTIONS

General mnemonic Op-code	General mnemonic Operand	Object code	Mnemonic	Segment for memory access	Coding example Symbolic operation	Coding example Description
Call	near target	E8 — —[a]	CALL MEMN[b]	Code	SP ← Sp−2; [SP+1:SP] ← IP; IP ← MEMN	IP is pushed onto the top of the stack and control is transferred within the segment to the near target address
		FF 16 00 10	CALL [MEMWDS][c]	Data	SP ← SP−2; [SP+1:SP] ← IP IP ← [1001H:1000H]	
		FF 15	CALL [DI]	Data	SP ← SP−2; [SP+1:SP] ← IP; IP ← [DI+1:DI]	
		FF D7	CALL DI	Within CPU	SP ← SP−2 [SP+1:SP] ← IP; IP ← DI	
CALL	far target	9A 00 10 D3 09	CALL FAR PTR MEMF[d]	Code	SP ← SP−2; [SP+1:SP] ← CS; CS ← 09D3H; SP ← SP−2; [SP+1:SP] ← IP; IP ← 1000H	CS and IP are pushed onto the top of the stack and control is transferred to the new segment and far target address
		FF 1E 00 10	CALL [MEMWWDS][e]	Data	Same as above except: CS ← [1003H:1002H]; IP ← [1001H:1000H]	
		FF 1D	CALL DWORD PTR[DI]	Data	Same as above except: CS ← [DI+3:DI+2]; IP ← [DI+1:DI]	

TABLE 2.18 (continued)

General mnemonic		Object code	Mnemonic	Coding example		Description
Op-code	Operand			Segment for memory access	Symbolic operation	
RET	n (near)[f]	C3	RET	Stack	IP ← [SP+1:SP]; SP ← SP+2	The word at the top of the stack is popped into IP transferring control to this new address; RET is normally used to return control to the instruction following a near subroutine call; if included, the optional pop value (n) is added to SP
		C2 08 00	RET 8	Stack	IP ← [SP+1:SP]; SP ← SP+2+8	
RET	n (far)[f]	CB	RET	Stack	IP ← [SP+1:SP]; SP ← SP+2; CS ← [SP+1:SP]; SP ← SP+2	As above except that the double word at the top of the stack is popped into IP and CS transferring control to this new far address
		CA 08 00	RET 8	Stack	IP ← [SP+1:SP]; SP ← SP+2; CS ← [SP+1:SP]; SP ← SP+2+8	

[a]These two bytes are the 2's-complement offset between near memory location MEMN and the instruction immediately following the CALL instruction. For example, if the CALL is to be 12 locations forward, the offset is 00 0C. Similarly, 12 locations backward requires an offset of FFF4.

[b]MEMN is assumed to point to a near memory location (i.e., within the segment).

[c]MEMWDS is assumed to point to the word beginning at location 1000H in the data segment. The brackets are optional because MEMWDS defines a word not a location to jump to.

[d]FAR PTR indicates that MEMF is located in a different code segment. In this case it is assumed that MEMF points at location 09D3H:1000H.

[e]MEMWWDS is assumed to point to the double word beginning at location 1000H in the data segment. The brackets are optional because MEMWWDS defines a double word, not a location to jump to.

[f]The same mnemonic is used for a near or far return. The assembler will generate the proper code based on the procedure definition statement (near or far).

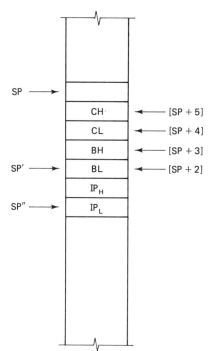

Figure 2.18 Passing parameters to a near subroutine on the stack. In this example four bytes are passed by the calling routine.

The main program pushes four bytes (registers CX and BX) onto the stack before calling the subroutine. This data can then be accessed by the subroutine using register BP to point to locations SP+2 through SP+5 (assuming a near call) as shown in Fig. 2.18. When the subroutine has ended and the data is no longer important, the RET 4 instruction pops IP off the stack, incrementing SP to SP′. The pop value of 4 then causes SP′ to be incremented to SP, its original value before the data was pushed onto the stack. This effectively deletes the data, as it will be overwritten with the next stack operation.

Software Interrupts

An interrupt is a request of the processor to suspend its current program and transfer control to a new program called the *interrupt service routine* (ISR). The interrupt request can be initiated in hardware or software. For the 8086/88, applying a logic 1 to the INTR or NMI input lines will initiate the interrupt request. In Chap. 8 we discuss in detail the processing of hardware interrupts.

Software interrupts are initiated by giving the instruction INT *type*. The processor responds by pushing the flags, CS, and IP onto the stack. This is shown in Fig. 2.19. It then loads new values for CS and IP from an interrupt jump table located in absolute memory from 00000 to 003FFH. These 1K bytes allow 256 different software interrupt requests. This is shown in Fig. 2.20.

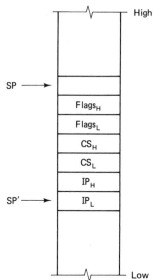

Figure 2.19 Stack area after executing an INT *type* instruction. SP' is the new value of register SP.

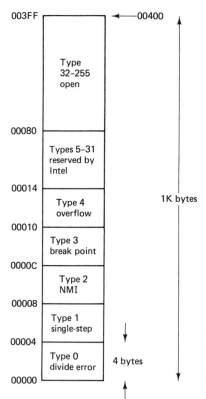

Figure 2.20 The 8086/88 software interrupt jump table will accommodate 256 interrupt types. (From J. Uffenbeck, *Microcomputers and Microprocessors: The 8080, 8085, and Z-80*. Prentice-Hall, Englewood Cliffs, N.J., 1985.)

Table 2.19 provides the specific details for the software interrupt instructions. If an INT 23H is executed, the processor will multiply 23H by 4 (rotate left twice), resulting in the jump table address 0008CH.

$$00100011 \times 4 = 10001100 = 0008CH$$

CS and IP will then be loaded with the double word stored in 0008CH through 0008FH (CS in the high-order word, IP in the low-order word). In effect, INT 23H performs a far call to the address stored in the double word at 0008CH through 0008FH.

When the interrupt service routine has finished, the IRET (interrupt return) instruction should be executed. This instruction is similar to the far return instruction but also pops the flag register from the stack (in addition to CS and IP). The main program then resumes with the instruction immediately following INT 23H.

Because a hardware interrupt can also generate an INT 23H, one of the uses for software interrupts is to debug interrupt service routines without having to build or use the hardware to request the interrupt.

Some of the interrupt jump table locations are reserved for special functions, as shown in Fig. 2.20. For example, whenever a divide-by-zero error occurs, the double word in 00000–00003H is used to determine the address of the error response routine. Similarly, if TF is set control transfers to the routine whose address is stored in locations 00004H–00007H after the execution of each main program instruction.

The INTO (interrupt on overflow) instruction is special in that no type number need be specified. After performing a signed arithmetic instruction, executing INTO will generate a type 4 interrupt if an overflow condition has occurred.

Note that executing an interrupt instruction (either software or hardware initiated) will clear IF and TF. This ensures that the interrupt service routine is not single-stepped and also blocks external (maskable) interrupts on INTR. Nonmaskable interrupt requests on NMI will still be accepted, as will other software interrupts. Executing the IRET instruction will restore the flags to their original values before the interrupt occurred. Thus you need not be concerned about setting IF or TF before returning from the interrupt service routine. The use of interrupts is explored more fully in later chapters.

SELF-REVIEW 2.8 (answers on page 108)

2.8.1. List the five instruction types that can be used to transfer control to a new (nonsequential) address.

2.8.2. What is the difference between a short, near, and far memory location?

2.8.3. All direct jumps or procedure calls are relative, but the indirect forms must specify the absolute address.   (True/False)

2.8.4. What is the advantage in using *relative* jump or procedure calls versus the absolute address forms?

2.8.5. The instruction JMP DWORD PTR CS:[BP] is an example of a(n) _____ jump.

2.8.6. In question 2.8.5 the target address is stored in the _____ segment.

2.8.7. The instruction codes below will transfer control to location ZERO if the data input is _____ .

Table 2.19 SOFTWARE INTERRUPT INSTRUCTIONS

General mnemonic		Object code	Mnemonic	Coding example		Description
Op-code	Operand			Segment for memory access	Symbolic operation	
INT	*type*	CD 23	INT 23H	Stack and interrupt jump table at 00000–003FFH	$SP \leftarrow SP - 2$; $[SP+1:SP] \leftarrow$ flags $IF \leftarrow 0$; $TF \leftarrow 0$; $SP \leftarrow SP - 2$; $[SP+1:SP] \leftarrow CS$; $CS \leftarrow [0008FH:0008EH]$;[a] $SP \leftarrow SP - 2$ $[SP+1:SP] \leftarrow IP$; $IP \leftarrow [0008DH:0008CH]$[b]	Save the flag, CS, and IP registers on the stack and transfer control to the far address stored in the double word beginning at absolute address *type* * 4
INTO	none	CE	INTO	Stack and interrupt jump table at 00000–003FFH	If $OF = 1$, then $SP \leftarrow SP - 2$ $[SP+1:SP] \leftarrow$ flags; $IF \leftarrow 0$; $TF \leftarrow 0$; $SP \leftarrow SP - 2$; $[SP+1:SP] \leftarrow CS$; $CS \leftarrow [00013H:00012H]$;[a] $SP \leftarrow SP - 2$; $[SP+1:SP] \leftarrow IP$; $IP \leftarrow [00011H:00010H]$[b]	If an overflow condition exists ($OF = 1$), a type 4 interrupt is executed
IRET	none	CF	IRET	Stack	$IP \leftarrow [SP+1:SP]$; $SP \leftarrow SP + 2$; $CS \leftarrow [SP+1:SP]$; $SP \leftarrow SP + 2$; flags $\leftarrow [SP+1:SP]$; $SP \leftarrow SP + 2$	Transfer control back to the point of interrupt by popping the IP, CS, and flag registers from the stack; IRET is normally used to exit any interrupt procedure whether activated by hardware or software

[a][(type * 4) + 3: (type * 4) + 2].
[b][(type * 4) + 1: (type * 4)].

```
INPUT:  IN   AL,80H
        DEC  AL
        JNZ  INPUT
        JMP  ZERO
```

2.8.8. The LOOP instruction is the equivalent of the two instruction types _____ and _____.

2.8.9. As data is pushed onto the stack, the stack grows _____ in memory.

2.8.10. How many bytes are pushed onto the stack by a far CALL instruction? What do they represent?

2.8.11. After executing the instruction INT 80H, from which memory location will the next instruction be fetched?

2.9 PROCESSOR CONTROL INSTRUCTIONS

The final group of instructions to be discussed are those used to control the operation of the processor and set or clear the status indicators. These are shown in Table 2.20.

The carry, direction, and interrupt flags can each be set or cleared, and the carry flag can also be *inverted*. The remaining status flags (PF, AF, ZF, and OF) cannot be accessed with specific control instructions. However, their values are determined by the results of particular arithmetic and logical instructions.

DF, IF, and TF are processor control bits rather than status indicators. DF is used with the string group of instructions to determine if the pointer registers are to be incremented or decremented. The STD (set direction flag) and CLD (clear direction flag) instructions are used to set or clear this flag.

STI (set interrupt enable flag) and CLI (clear interrupt enable flag) enable or disable maskable interrupts on the INTR input line. Clearing this bit blocks all interrupts on INTR effectively *masking* this input.

The third processor control bit is TF, the trap flag. When set, a type 1 interrupt is generated after completion of each processor instruction. There is no instruction for setting or resetting this flag (Intel design error?), but the following sequence of instructions can be used (in this example) to set TF. Refer to Fig. 2.21 for the flag bit positions.

```
PUSHF                          ;Copy flags onto stack
MOV  BP,SP                     ;Point BP at stack top
OR   BYTE PTR[BP+1],01H        ;Set bit 0—TF
POPF                           ;Restore flags
```

The HALT instruction will stop the processor and cause it to enter an idle loop. However, once halted it can be restarted only via a hardware interrupt or a system reset. For this reason, ending your programs with a HALT instruction may not be a good idea (restarting the computer may erase your program).

The NOP instruction may seem rather useless; after all, it is a "no operation" instruction. However, during debugging it may be useful to "NOP out" several instructions to avoid a long loop or other program condition. Later, the original instructions can be replaced. NOPs may also be used to "pad" time-delay routines.

TABLE 2.20 PROCESSOR CONTROL INSTRUCTIONS

| General mnemonic | | Object code | Mnemonic | Coding example | | |
Op-code	Operand			Segment for memory access	Symbolic operation	Description
STC	None	F9	STC	Within CPU	$CF \leftarrow 1$	Set carry flag
CLC	None	F8	CLC	Within CPU	$CF \leftarrow 0$	Clear carry flag
CMC	None	F5	CMC	Within CPU	$CF \leftarrow \overline{CF}$	Complement carry flag
STD	None	FD	STD	Within CPU	$DF \leftarrow 1$	Set direction flag (auto decrement for string instructions)
CLD	None	FC	CLD	Within CPU	$DF \leftarrow 0$	Clear direction flag (auto increment for string instructions)
STI	None	FB	STI	Within CPU	$IF \leftarrow 1$	Set interrupt flag (enabling interrupts on the INTR line)
CLI	None	FA	CLI	Within CPU	$IF \leftarrow 0$	Clear interrupt flag (disabling interrupts on the INTR line)
HLT	None	F4	HLT	Within CPU	None	Halt
WAIT	None	9B	WAIT	Within CPU	None	Enter wait state if $\overline{TEST}$ line = 1
LOCK	*instruction*	F0 A1 00 10	LOCK MOV AX,MEMWDS[a]	Data	None	Output line $\overline{LOCK}$ = 0 while the instruction following LOCK executes; used to prevent coprocessors from accessing the bus during a particular instruction
NOP	None	90	NOP	Within CPU	None	No operation
ESC	*number, source*	DE 0E 00 10	ESC 31H,MEMWDS[a]	Data	Data bus ← [MEMWDS]	Place the contents of the memory source operand on the data bus and execute a NOP; the first operand identifies a particular escape instruction to be executed by a coprocessor

[a]MEMWDS is assumed to point at the word beginning at location 1000H in the data segment.

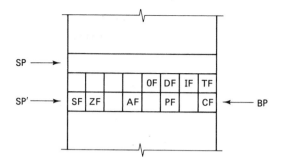

Figure 2.21 Contents of the stack after executing PUSHF. TF is bit 0 of [SP + 1].

Three processor control instructions are intended for use with special *coprocessors*. The WAIT instruction is used to synchronize the 8086/88 with the 8087 NDP via the $\overline{\text{TEST}}$ input. When the 8087 is busy executing an instruction and cannot accept new data or instructions from the 8086/88, it will drive this input high. By preceding each instruction that requires data from the 8087 with a WAIT instruction, the 8086/88 ensures that data will not be lost between these two processors.

The LOCK instruction is executed by the 8086/88 when it is important that no other processor attempt to control the system buses. LOCK is in effect for the single instruction only. It prevents a coprocessor from changing or accessing a memory location that the 8086/88 is about to access.

The ESC (escape) instruction is used as a prefix to the coprocessor instructions. The 8086/88 will place the source operand on the data bus but will take no further action. The coprocessor, constantly examining the data bus contents, is activated by the ESC prefix, causing it to read the two operands and begin execution. The 8087 and 8089 coprocessors are discussed in Chap. 11.

SELF-REVIEW 2.9 (answers on page 108)

2.9.1. To be sure that the carry flag is 0 before the execution of a particular set of instructions, the _____ instruction should be used.

2.9.2. Executing the instruction STD will affect only the string instructions. (True/False)

2.9.3. The 8086/88 has three instructions for controlling a coprocessor. These are _____

_____, and _____.

CHAPTER 2 SELF-TEST

1. Under what conditions will the contents of the queue hold the "wrong" op-codes?
2. Because of its pipelined architecture, the 8086 can execute several instructions at the same time. (True/False)
3. List all 8086/88 registers that can be accessed as bytes or as words.
4. Because of its segmented memory, the 8086/88 requires a minimum of 4 × 64K or 256K bytes of memory. (True/False)
5. Which of the following addresses are valid base addresses for one of the segment registers? (a) FFFFFH; (b) A0FF0H; (c) 90000H; (d) 10008H.

6. How would you tell the assembler to initialize a memory word TEMP with 0000H?

7. What is the logical code segment address corresponding to physical address 6A3F7H? Assume that CS = 5C00H.

8. Which addressing mode would you use to initialize a CPU register with data?

9. What is the advantage of the register indirect addressing modes versus the direct addressing mode?

10. Which CPU registers, when used as memory pointers, cannot have their default memory segment assignments overridden?

11. Each of the following instructions is invalid: (1) MOV DS,1234H; (2) IN AL,70FFH; (3) MOV CX,[AX]. Explain why.

12. Which string instruction should be used to ensure that two strings in memory are equal?

13. Which instruction should be given to ensure that the memory pointers in question 12 will automatically increment?

14. What is the difference between a rotate and a shift instruction?

15. To mask bits 4–7 of register CH and force these bits low, the instruction _____ should be used.

16. When performing _____ _____ arithmetic, the ADC and SBB instructions should be used.

17. If AL = 09H and BL = 08H, the instruction sequence

$$\text{MUL} \quad \text{BL}$$
$$\text{AAM}$$

will store _____ in register AX.

18. All conditional jump instructions perform _____ jumps.

19. To repeat a string instruction while a particular condition is zero, use the _____ instruction.

20. To transfer control to the address stored in the double word beginning at address 00084H, the software interrupt instruction _____ should be used.

ANALYSIS AND DESIGN QUESTIONS

2.1. The Intel manual for the 8086 indicates that ''a series of fast-executing instructions can drain the queue and increase instruction execution time.'' Explain this statement.

2.2. Determine the contents of register AL,BL and the six status flags after the following instructions are executed.

```
STC
MOV   AL,4CH
SBB   AL,3EH
XOR   BL,BL
MOV   [SI],BL
```

2.3. Determine the values of the 8086's six status flags after the program in Ex. 2.12 has executed.

2.4. Determine the value of register SP after the following instructions are executed.

```
MOV    SP,0FFFFH
PUSHF
PUSH   CX
CALL   DELAY
POP    CX
```

2.5. Using the segment register assignments shown in Fig. 2.9, what is the physical address of the memory operand for the following AND instruction?

```
MOV   BP,1080H
MOV   BX,007FH
AND   BYTE PTR[BP + BX + 30H],80H.
```

2.6. Write the programming sequence required to load the extra and data segment registers with 80A0H.

2.7. What is "wrong" with the instruction REP LODSB?

2.8. Write a program to input a data byte from I/O port 8800H and test bit 1. If this bit is low, transfer control to location START; if high, repeat the sequence.

2.9. Describe the output produced by the following program:

```
           MOV    AL,0
REPEAT:    OUT    0,AL
           INC    AL
           DAA
           JMP    REPEAT
```

2.10. What single 8086/88 instruction is the equivalent of the following four instructions?

```
PUSH  BX
PUSH  AX
POP   BX
POP   AX
```

2.11. The following program is written to compare two strings stored in memory. However, it contains at least two "bugs." What do you think is wrong with the program?

```
         LEA    SI, STRING1
         LEA    DI,STRING2
         CLD
         MOV    CX,NO_OF_BYTES
REPNE    SCASB
         JNZ    ERROR
         JMP    OK
```

SELF REVIEW ANSWERS

2.1.1 execution, bus interface

2.1.2 overlap

2.1.3 The current instruction requires access to a memory location or I/O port, a transfer of control (jump) instruction occurs, the queue is full.

2.1.4. Move the byte whose address is in register DI to register CH.

2.1.5 4F17

2.1.6 trap

2.1.7 CF = 1, PF = 1, AF = 1, ZF = 1, SF = 0, OF = 0 (−1 + 1 = 0)

2.2.1 False (true for 8086 only)

2.2.2 even

2.2.3 64K, offsets, logical

2.2.4 False−must begin at an address divisible by 16.

2.2.5 95D3FH

2.2.6 data

2.2.7 No references to physical addresses, no changes to segment registers.

2.2.8 The label COUNTER is assigned to the first word in the EXTRA segment and initialized to 5678H.

2.3.1 CPU register, memory location, I/O port

2.3.2 immediate

2.3.3 based, byte

2.3.4 direct

2.3.5 label

2.3.6 Memory location BP + NOTE, or the BPth element in the NOTE array.

2.3.7 MOV CX,[SI + 27]

2.3.8 data

2.3.9 AX, CX, DX

2.4.1 (a)

2.4.2 MOV MEMWDS,DX

2.4.3 65536, DX

2.4.4 False (AX or AL only)

2.4.5 LEA DI, TABLE

2.4.6 False

2.5.1 string

2.5.2 MOVS

2.5.3 decrement, SI, 2

2.5.4 source byte = destination byte and CX ≠ 0

2.6.1 AND DH,OFCH

2.6.2 OR DH,03H

2.6.3 TEST AH,8

2.6.4 ECH

2.6.5 MOV CL,3 and SAR BX,CL

2.7.1 16H

2.7.2 9A64H

2.7.3 False (C is invalid)

2.7.4 after

2.7.5 0104H

2.7.6 3138H

2.7.7 0409H

2.7.8 True

2.8.1 conditional and unconditional jumps, LOOP instructions, procedure calls, software interrupts

2.8.2 short: +127 bytes to −128 bytes; near: +32767 to −32768 bytes, far: address located in a different segment

2.8.3 True

2.8.4 Resulting program is relocatable anywhere within the code segment.

2.8.5 far

2.8.6 code segment (note CS: override)

2.8.7 01

2.8.8 DEC CX, JNZ

2.8.9 downward (towards lower addresses)

2.8.10 4 bytes−two for CS and two for IP

2.8.11 CS = [00203:00202H], IP = [00201:00200]

2.9.1 CLC

2.9.2 True

2.9.3 WAIT, LOCK, ESC

3

FROM SPECIFICATION TO PROGRAM DESIGN

The process of writing a computer program is not unlike that of developing a good composition. The microprocessor's instruction set is the programmer's "dictionary." Unfortunately, knowing all the words in the dictionary is not enough. Just as there are certain accepted rules for good grammar, there are accepted steps for developing a computer program.

In this chapter we follow the development of a "widget counter" control program. This begins with the receipt of the problem specification and preparation of the *global* solution. Next the hardware and software are partitioned and detailed solutions are proposed for each. The design is finished when the hardware and software have been debugged and the project has been documented.

Pay particular attention to the creative part of this process—the translation of ideas into computer instructions. Because this is an art in itself, Chap. 4 is devoted entirely to this topic. The major topics in this chapter include:

3.1 Modularizing the Problem
3.2 Coding the Program
3.3 Creating and Assembling the Source Code
3.4 Testing and Debugging
3.5 Documentation

3.1 MODULARIZING THE PROBLEM

Every problem begins with a specification. It identifies the problem to be solved and specifies the unique requirements that the solution must possess.

When the specification is received, you must resist the urge to immediately begin drawing hardware schematics or writing the program instructions. Instead, ask yourself: Is the problem clearly stated? Often the specification comes from a layman unfamiliar with the peculiarities of the hardware and software. Perhaps rewriting the specification will reveal a simpler solution.

In this section we look at the initial steps to be taken upon receiving a problem specification. Our goal is to prepare a general or *global* solution to the problem. This solution will then be refined as the hardware is designed and the software flowcharted.

The Specification

You have just been hired as chief design engineer for the Widget Manufacturing Corporation. Your first assignment is to design a *widget counter* that will allow the company president to see a running total of each day's widget production prominently displayed on his or her office wall.

As you walk back to your office your head is filled with visions of decade counters, seven-segment displays, and proximity switches. However, after several hours you discard the discrete logic solution as too inflexible. Instead, you propose the 8086-based microcomputer solution shown in Fig. 3.1.

In your solution, a *widget detector* will supply a pulse each time a new widget passes by. Software will be used to count these pulses and produce a decimal display of

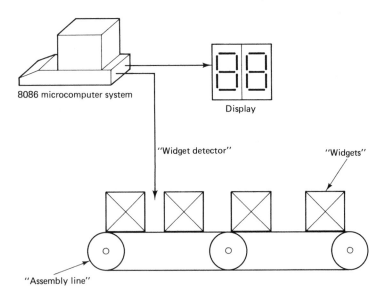

Figure 3.1 "Global" (general but all-inclusive) solution to the widget counter design problem.

the day's production on two LED (light-emitting diode) displays. You have determined that widget production will never exceed 99, so a third digit is not required.

It is important to note that your solution does not yet specify the particular integrated circuits to be used or the kind of signal the widget detector will produce. Nor have any program instructions been written. The goal at this point is to propose a general but complete problem solution. Now is also the time to be sure that the solution is correct —before any resources have been committed. Later, as you begin to formulate the specific hardware and software, changes will be much more costly and time consuming.

Refining the Hardware

Assuming that the global solution in Fig. 3.1 is satisfactory, we can begin breaking the design process into smaller modules. Beginning with the hardware, let's consider the widget display module first. A detailed schematic diagram is given in Fig. 3.2.

One 8-bit output port will be sufficient to drive the two displays. Bits 0–3 of this port will supply the least significant digit (LSD) and bits 4–7 the most significant digit (MSD). To minimize the number of components involved, TIL311 displays have been selected. These displays include a latch, decoder, and dot-matrix display all in one package. They will display all 16 combinations of the four input lines as a hex digit between 0 and F.

The 8086/88 instruction

OUT   port,AL

can be used to display the current number of widgets. Note that the software will have to be written in such a way that only decimal numbers are displayed.

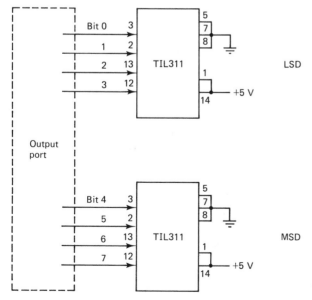

Figure 3.2 Widget display module. An 8-bit output port is used to drive two TIL311 hex decoder/displays.

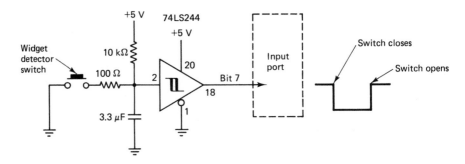

Figure 3.3 Widget detector module. The *RC* network and buffer gate are needed to *debounce* the mechanical switch.

Figure 3.3 is a schematic diagram for the widget detector module. As the widgets roll down the assembly line they will activate a normally open pushbutton switch. When the contacts of this switch momentarily close, a pulse will be produced that can be detected by the computer. However, because the switch is mechanical, the contacts will actually *bounce* open and closed for several milliseconds. If we are not careful, the computer will interpret these bounces as new widgets coming down the assembly line.

There are several ways to debounce this switch, and both hardware and software techniques can be used. In this example, a hardware approach is chosen consisting of an *RC* network and a logic gate buffer (74LS244). The output of this circuit is the "clean" pulse shown in the figure (see Analysis and Design Question 3.1 for the complete analysis). We return to the topics of buffers and switch debouncing in Chaps. 6 and 8.

Flowcharting the Control Program

A *top-down* approach to design is one in which the problem is first visualized at the abstract global level. Smaller modules are then defined and solved. This same approach can be taken with the software.

A good starting point is to prepare a diagram listing all the input signals and desired outputs. This is shown in Fig. 3.4. Note that we have given the input signal the name IN7 and similarly named the eight output lines OUT0–OUT7. The significance of the two IN7 logic levels is also clearly indicated.

It is a good idea to assign the particular I/O ports you plan to use at this time. These will depend on the specific system you are using, unless you are also designing the I/O port hardware. In the latter case you will have to consult the system I/O map to determine available port addresses. In Chap. 8 we cover I/O port design in detail, so we defer that topic until later.

Once the inputs and outputs have been defined, a system-level flowchart can be drawn. This is shown in Fig. 3.5. The basic flow of the program can now be seen, although specific instructions have not yet been written. Note that different symbols are used to identify different types of operations (*start/stop, I/O, decision, and process*).

Our next step is to refine the flowchart in Fig. 3.5 by expanding each of the blocks in this figure into a number of more detailed steps (approaching one computer instruction per step). This will require developing an *algorithm* for accomplishing each block's

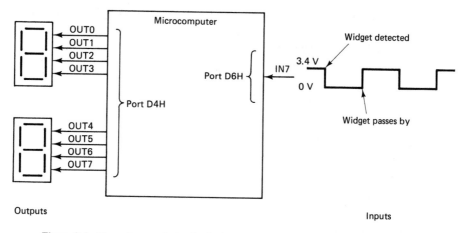

Figure 3.4 The software solution begins by specifying the program inputs and outputs.

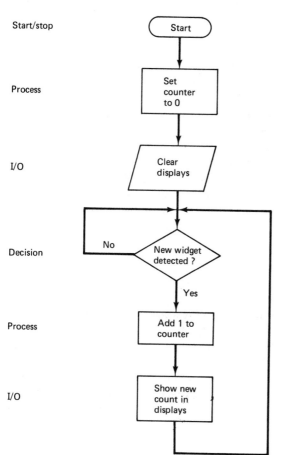

Figure 3.5 System-level flowchart for the widget counter control program. Four different flowchart symbols are commonly used: start/stop, process, I/O, and decision.

function. This is a precise step-by-step procedure or method for solving a particular problem. In Fig. 3.5, all the blocks are straightforward except for the decision block labeled "new widget detected?"

One possible algorithm for accomplishing this function is as follows:

1. Wait until IN7 = 0.
2. Wait until IN7 = 1.
3. Widget detected!
4. Go to step 1.

You might be wondering why we need step 2 since the widget is actually detected as soon as IN7 = 0. However, by including this step we ensure that the widget has passed by and is not counted twice. Remember, the entire program will require only a few microseconds to execute. Simply detecting IN7 = 0 would cause the same widget to be counted several thousand times.

Figure 3.6 is a detailed flowchart for the widget counter program. Note that three sections or *modules* are identified—output, input, and process. Even though this is a simple problem, it is still a good idea to break it into small manageable pieces (modules) which can then be solved separately. Modular programming is discussed in more detail in Chaps. 4 and 5.

Because the counter is a "mirror image" of the output display, we are able to combine the two I/O blocks in Fig. 3.5 into one. Thus the output module simply sends the contents of the counter to the display output port.

The input module follows the four-step algorithm presented above. The rising edge of the IN7 signal causes control to transfer to the process module. This module increments the counter each time a widget is detected. The "adjust for decimal" block is required because the computer will normally count in binary (causing hex characters to be displayed in the LED displays). Adjusting the count to decimal eliminates this problem.

Although no instructions have yet been written, we now have a detailed picture of the steps the widget counter program must follow. In the next section we begin to write the program.

SELF-REVIEW 3.1 (answers on page 138)

3.1.1. In general, using a microcomputer to solve a control problem will require a _____ solution and a _____ solution.

3.1.2. The system-level flowchart provides a detailed description of the control software. (True/False)

3.1.3. The _____-_____ approach to design is one in which the solution is first proposed at the global level and then broken into smaller easier to solve modules.

3.1.4. A step-by-step method to be followed for solving a particular part of a problem is called an _____.

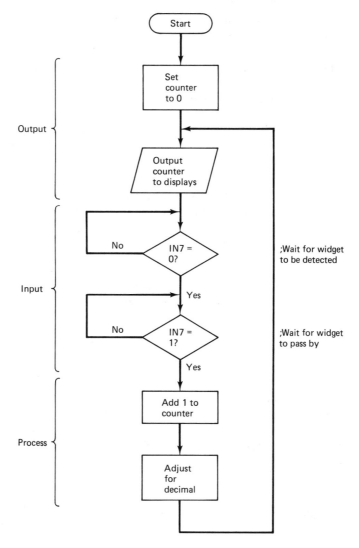

Figure 3.6 Detailed flowchart for the widget counter control program.

3.2 CODING THE PROGRAM

The process of writing the widget counter program is also called *coding*. This is because we must translate each block in the flowchart of Fig. 3.6 to a code (the program instructions) to accomplish that function.

We must also decide which computer language to use to write the program. High-level languages such as BASIC or Pascal are much easier to use than assembly language, but the resulting code will usually execute more slowly. The high-level language program will also require more memory space than the assembly language version.

Because we are trying to learn 8086/88 programming, we will use this language. But remember, in many cases a high-level language will do the job just as well as assembly language and require much less of your time. In Chap. 5 we provide additional guidelines for determining when to select a high-level language for a microprocessor application.

The Six Programming Fields

The result of coding the widget counter program is shown in Fig. 3.7. For the moment concentrate on the *form* on which the program has been written. The heading includes space for the program name, author, and date. Space is also provided to describe the purpose or function of the program as well as the expected inputs and desired outputs. The program itself is written over six fields, called the *address, hex codes, label, op-code, operand,* and *comment* fields.

Program Name __WIDGET__ Date __8-23-84__

Author __A. Programmer__ page __1__ of __1__

Function: _Count and display widgets proceeding down an assembly line_

Inputs: _Switch status on bit 7 of port ØD6H_

Outputs: _Two seven-segment displays at port ØD4H_

Calls: ___none___ Destroys: __AL, BL, flags__

Address	Hex Codes					Label	Op-code	Operand	Comments
0000	B0	00					MOV	AL,Ø	; Counter = 0
0002	8A	D8				CYCLE:	MOV	BL,AL	; Save in BL
0004	E6	D4					OUT	ØD4H,AL	; Display counter
0006	E4	D6				READ1:	IN	AL,ØD6H	; Read switch
0008	A8	80					TEST	AL,80H	; Test bit 7
000A	75	FA					JNZ	READ1	; Wait until low
000C	EA	D6				READ2:	IN	AL,ØD6H	; Read switch
000E	A8	80					TEST	AL,80H	; Test bit 7
0010	74	FA					JZ	READ2	; Wait until high
0012	8A	C3					MOV	AL,BL	; Counter to AL
0014	FE	C0					INC	AL	; Add 1 widget
0016	27						DAA		; Decimal counter
0017	EB	E9					JMP	CYCLE	; Repeat loop

Figure 3.7 Source and hex codes for the widget counter control program. The hex codes are determined by hand assembly in Sec. 3.3.

The programming form in Fig. 3.7 will not write the program for you, and using it will not guarantee that your programs will work. However, it will force you to write your programs in a standard, easy-to-read format. It will also remind you of the information you need to supply when writing an assembly language program. Because of this, you are encouraged to adopt this format for all your assembly language programs.

Ignoring the address and hex code fields (these are discussed in Sec. 3.3), the label field is used to give a memory location a name (see Sec. 2.2 for a discussion of labels in assembly language programs). Note that some instructions do not have labels because they are not referenced anywhere else in the program.

The program instructions are entered under the *op-code* and *operand* fields. This division is done to make the program easier to read. Note that the operands for the jump instructions are the labels CYCLE, READ1, and READ2.

The comment field is included to explain what the programmer intended for that instruction. Be careful that you do not fall into the trap of commenting an instruction by explaining its mnemonic. For example, a poor comment would be

```
MOV  AL,0      ;Put 0 in AL
```

On the other hand, if register AL is being used as a counter, say so in your comment.

```
MOV  AL,0      ;Counter = 0
```

Widget Counter Program Logic

Let's compare the widget counter program with its flowchart in Fig. 3.6. The "set counter to 0" and "output counter to displays" blocks are accomplished with the first three instructions. It would seem convenient to use register AL as the widget counter. Then the instruction OUT 0D4H,AL would output the counter to the displays.[1] Although this will work, the IN instruction (needed to check the widget detector) also uses AL and will overwrite the counter. For this reason the count is saved in BL while the two decision blocks are executed.

The first decision block, "IN7 = 0?", is accomplished with the three instructions IN AL,0D6H, TEST AL,80H, and JNZ READ1. These three instructions will be repeated over and over until IN7 goes low. When IN7 finally does go low, control is transferred to the second decision block. The same instructions are repeated except that the jump instruction is changed to JZ READ2.

Remembering that BL holds the widget counter, the "add 1 to counter" block is accomplished with the MOV AL,BL and INC AL instructions. The "adjust for decimal" block is accomplished with the DAA instruction. This instruction works only on AL and should occur immediately after the INC AL instruction. It adjusts the accumulator so that AL contains two valid packed BCD numbers.

The arrow transferring control back to the output block is accomplished with the

---

[1]Constants that begin with one of the hex digits A–F must be preceded by a 0 when using an assembler. If this is not done, the assembler will assume that the constant is a label.

JMP CYCLE instruction. After saving the new count in BL, the new widget count is displayed and the program then begins waiting for the next widget.

In summary, we can say that the coding process is one in which the detailed flowchart is translated into program instructions. When assembly language is used, the instruction set of the microprocessor may impose restrictions on which registers to use (the I/O and DAA instructions are examples).

SELF-REVIEW 3.2 (answers on page 138)

3.2.1. List the six fields to be included when writing an assembly language program.

3.2.2. If the widget detector were connected to input port bit 5, which program instruction(s) would have to be changed? Specify the new instruction(s).

3.2.3. What is the binary value of the byte output to the displays as the thirty-sixth widget passes down the assembly line?

3.3 CREATING AND ASSEMBLING THE SOURCE CODE

Although the widget counter program is written, we still face two problems. The 8086/88 cannot execute the mnemonics (source code) shown in Fig. 3.7. We must determine the binary codes for each instruction and then find some means of loading those codes into memory so that the program can be run and tested.

There is an easy and a hard way to do this. The easy way is to use an *assembler* and a *linker*. The assembler will generate an *object code* file consisting of the binary codes for the widget counter program. The linker then takes this file and creates an executable run file that can be loaded into memory and tested.

The hard way is to do these tasks by hand. First look up or calculate the binary instruction codes for each instruction, then enter each code into memory manually. This is the so-called "hand assembly" process. In this section we examine both alternatives.

Hand Assembly

One of the big differences between 8- and 16-bit microprocessors is the number of instructions in each processor's instruction set. Because of their 8-bit word size, processors such as the 8085 and 6800 are limited to recognizing 256 (2^8) unique op-codes. This means that it is possible to list the hexadecimal op-code for every 8085 instruction on a single sheet of paper. To hand assemble an 8085 program, you need only look up each instruction in this chart and jot down its corresponding hex code.

But now consider the 8086. The 16-bit word size means that as many as 65,536 (2^{16}) op-codes are possible. Although all these combinations are not utilized (and some are only a single byte), there are close to 4000 unique instructions. Just as an example, Table 3.1 lists the various forms of the MOV instruction that involve register AX. Now consider that a similar table could be written for registers BX, CX, DX, BP, SP, SI, and DI. When you recall that registers AX, BX, CX, and DX can also be accessed as a high-

TABLE 3.1 FORMS OF THE MOV INSTRUCTION INVOLVING REGISTER AX

Register to Register			*Indexed*	
MOV AX,BX	BX,AX	MOV	AX,[DI + disp]	[DI + disp],AX
AX,CX	CX,AX		AX,[SI + disp]	[SI + disp],AX
AX,DX	DX,AX			
AX,BP	BP,AX		*Based*	
AX,SP	SP,AX	MOV	AX,[BP + disp]	[BP + disp],AX
AX,SI	SI,AX		AX,[BX + disp]	[BX + disp],AX
AX,DI	DI,AX			
AX,CS	CS,AX		*Based and Indexed*	
AX,DS	DS,AX			
AX,ES	ES,AX	MOV	AX,[BP + SI]	[BP + SI],AX
AX,SS	SS,AX		AX,[BP + DI]	[BP + DI],AX
			AX,[BX + SI;]	[BX + SI],AX
Immediate			AX,[BX + DI]	[BX + DI],AX
MOV AX,data16				
			Based and Indexed with Displacement	
Direct		MOV	AX,[BP + SI + disp]	[BP + SI + disp],AX
MOV AX,MEMW			AX,[BP + DI + disp]	[BP + DI + disp],AX
MOV MEMW,AX			AX,[BX + SI + disp]	[BX + SI + disp],AX
			AX,[BX + DI + disp]	[BX + DI + disp],AX
Register Indirect				
MOV AX,[BP]	[BP],AX			
AX,[BX]	[BX],AX			
AX,[SI]	[SI],AX			
AX,[DI]	[DI],AX			

order or low-order byte, you begin to appreciate the magnitude of the 8086's instruction set.

For this reason, hand assembly of an 8086 program will require you to *calculate* —versus look up in a chart—the hex codes for each instruction. To see how this is done, let's dig a little deeper into the 8086 instruction set.

Figure 3.8 shows how each byte of an instruction is interpreted, depending on the number and type of operands. The first byte is optional and specifies a segment override if required. For example, to specify the extra segment (ES:), the first byte would be 001 00 110, or 26H.

The second byte specifies the instruction op-code and the destination (D) and word/ byte (W) identifier. The third byte is the MOD-REG-R/M byte, which is used to indicate the addressing mode and CPU registers involved. The coding of these bits is shown in Table 3.2. The remaining bytes, shown in Fig. 3.8, are optional depending on the instruction and are used to specify an 8- or 16-bit displacement or date value.

How do you actually use all this information to encode a particular instruction? Begin by turning to App. D, which is an instruction set summary for the 8086/88. The general form of each instruction is shown here, but Intel has left the details for you to work out depending on the addressing mode and registers involved.

TWO OPERAND FORMAT, SECOND OPERAND IS REGISTER

| 001 | SEG | 110 |
(optional)

| OPCODE | D | W |

| MOD | REG | R/M |

| DISP-LO |
(optional)

| DISP-HI |
(optional)

TWO OPERAND FORMAT, SECOND OPERAND IS CONSTANT

| 001 | SEG | 110 |
(optional)

| OPCODE | S | W |

| MOD | OPCODE | R/M |

| DISP-LO |
(optional)

| DISP-HI |
(optional)

| DATA-LO |

| DATA-HI |
(optional)

ONE OPERAND FORMAT

| 001 | SEG | 110 |
(optional)

| OPCODE | W |

| MOD | OPCODE | R/M |

| DISP-LO |
(optional)

| DISP-HI |
(optional)

FOR DEFINITION OF MOD AND R/M FIELDS, SEE FIGURE 2-5.

OTHER BIT FIELDS:

W = 0: 8-BIT OPERAND(S)
    1: 16-BIT OPERAND(S)

D = 0: DESTINATION IS FIRST OPERAND
    1: DESTINATION IS SECOND OPERAND

S = 0: DATA = DATA HI, DATA LO   } APPLIES IF
    1: DATA = DATA-LO SIGN EXTENDED   }   W = 1

SEG:	SEGMENT REG
00	ES
01	CS
10	SS
11	DS

| | REGISTER | |
REG:	8-BIT (W = 0)	16-BIT (W = 1)
000	AL	AX
001	CL	CX
010	DL	DX
011	BL	BX
100	AH	SP
101	CH	BP
110	DH	SI
111	BH	DI

Figure 3.8 Instruction format for one- and two-operand instructions. (Courtesy of Intel Corporation.)

TABLE 3.2   CALCULATING THE MOD-REG-R/M BYTE

MOD = 11[a]	MOD = 00	MOD = 01	MOD = 10	R/M	REG	W = 0	W = 1
R/M specifies	[BX + SI]	[BX + SI + disp8]	[BX + SI + disp16]	000	000	AL	AX
a register	[BX + DI]	[BX + DI + disp8]	[BX + DI + disp16]	001	001	CL	CX
operand	[BP + SI]	[BP + SI + disp8]	[BP + SI + disp16]	010	011	DL	DX
	[BP + DI]	[BP + DI + disp8]	[BP + DI + disp16]	011	011	BL	BX
	[SI]	[SI + disp8]	[SI + disp16]	100	100	AH	SP
	[DI]	[DI + disp8]	[DI + disp16]	101	101	CH	BP
	Direct address[b]	[BP + disp8]	[BP + disp16]	110	110	DH	SI
	[BX]	[BX + disp8]	[BX + disp16]	111	111	BH	DI

[a] See Table 3.3, lines 1 and 3.

[b] See Table 3.3, lines 5 and 6.

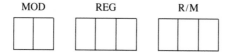

Table 3.3 should help with these details. There are six different combinations of operands that will affect the MOD-REG-R/M byte as shown in this table. The two MOD bits select the different forms of the register indirect addressing mode. Note that there is an exception when MOD = 11, as this selects the register or immediate addressing modes (lines 1 and 3). The REG field specifies a CPU register or an op-code when a constant is involved (lines 3 and 4). The R/M field identifies the memory location or additional CPU register to be used.

Let's try an example. Assume that we wish to encode the instruction MOV DX,CX. Because there is no segment override or displacement, we need only determine the op-code and MOD-REG-R/M bytes. In App. D under the MOV mnemonic we see the heading

Register/memory to/from register

(which we will interpret as register to register). The coding is

100010 d w   mod   reg   r/m

We consult Table 3.3; the operands are in the form shown in line 1. Thus MOD = 11 and REG and R/M are used to specify the two registers. Arbitrarily selecting REG = CX = 001 and R/M = DX = 010 (from Table 3.2) results in the MOD-REG-R/M byte 11001010 or CAH.

The destination and byte/word identifiers (bits d and w in the first byte of the instruction) must now be determined. Consulting Fig. 3.8, w = 1 because we are selecting the 16-bit forms of registers C and D. Bit d must be 0 because the first operand (identified by the R/M field) is register DX—the destination of the data. The op-code byte thus has

TABLE 3.3 OPERAND COMBINATIONS FOR THE MOD-REG-R/M BYTE

Operands	Mod.	Reg.	R/M	Example:	Op-code	_D_W	Mod	Reg	R/M
1. Register, register	11	Register[a]	Register[b]	MOV DX,CX	100010 0 1 (89H)	11 001 010 (CAH)			
2. Register, memory	00 01 10	Register[a]	Memory location[b]	MOV BX,[SI]	100010 1 1 (8BH)	00 011 100 (1CH)			
3. Register, constant	11	Op-code	Register	ADD BX,1000H	100000 0 1 (81H)	11 000 011 (C3H)	00H	10H	
4. Memory, constant	00 01 10	Op-code	Memory location	MOV [BX + 8000H],1234H	1100011 1 (C7H)	10 000 111 (87H)	00H	80H	34H 12H
5. Register, memory (direct addressing)	00	Register	110	MOV AH,[1000H]	100010 1 0 (8AH)	00 100 110 (26H)	00H	10H	
6. Memory, constant (direct addressing)	00	Op-code	110	MOV [1000H],34H	1100011 0 (C6H)	00 000 110 (06H)	00H	10H	34H

[a]Second operand.

[b]First operand.

the coding 1000010 0 1, or 89H. The final coding for the instruction MOV DX,CX is 89H CAH.

It is interesting to note that had we chosen the REG field to represent register DX and R/M to represent register CX, the destination bit would have to be a 1. The same instruction would now have the coding 8BH D1H. The same instruction can have two different sets of hex codes! This happens only with the MOV group of instructions, in which the choice of first and second operands is arbitrary.

Example 3.1

Determine the hex codes for the instruction ADD BX,[SI].

Solution   The general form is shown in App. D. The coding is

000000 d w   mod reg r/m

Because the operands specify a memory location and a CPU register, the form is similar to line 2 of Table 3.3. When we refer to Table 3.2, we see that MOD = 00, R/M = 100, and REG = 011. In the first byte d = 1 because the register (the second operand) is the destination and W = 1 because of the 16-bit destination register size. The result is ADD BX,[SI] → 03H 1CH.

There is one peculiarity that you should note when determining the MOD-REG-R/M byte. When register BP is used without a displacement you would expect the encoding to be MOD = 00 and R/M = 110. However, as shown in Table 3.2, this combination of bits has been chosen to identify the *direct addressing mode*. To use register BP with 0 displacement, you will have to select MOD = 01 and supply a displacement byte with value 00. (*Note:* If you are using an assembler, this is done automatically.)

Example 3.2

Hand assemble the widget counter program in Fig. 3.7 beginning at effective address 0000.

Solution   The result is shown under the address and hex codes fields in Fig. 3.7. Pay particular attention to the second bytes of the three jump instructions. All use *short jumps* in which the second byte of the instruction specifies a 2's-complement displacement. For example, JNZ READ1 requires a jump backward of six bytes. The proper code is

00000000 − 00000110 = 11111010 = FAH

The JZ READ2 instruction also requires a jump backward of six bytes and thus has the same displacement. The JMP CYCLE instruction requires a jump backward of 23 bytes or E9H.

Note: When the displacement distance is not too far, a simple "trick" can be used to calculate the displacement byte. Beginning with the displacement byte position, count backward from FF until the target location is reached. The result will be the displacement byte value. It really works!

Machine Assembly

It may have occurred to you that the job (drudgery?) of calculating hex codes for assembly language instructions is well suited for a computer. Indeed, hand assembly is suitable only for short programs and/or people with a great deal of patience.

Unfortunately, the "price of the game" goes up considerably when you elect to

```
A:EDLIN WIDGET.ASM

EDLIN  version 1.02
End of input file
*I
     1:*PROG      SEGMENT
     2:*          ASSUME   CS:PROG
     3:*WIDGET:   MOV      AL,0      ;COUNTER=0
     4:*CYCLE:    MOV      BL,AL     ;SAVE IN BL
     5:*          OUT      0D4H,AL   ;DISPLAY COUNTER
     6:*READ1:    IN       AL,0D6H   ;READ SWITCH
     7:*          TEST     AL,80H    ;TEST BIT 7
     8:*          JNZ      READ1     ;WAIT UNTIL LOW
     9:*READ2:    IN       AL,0D6H   ;READ SWITCH
    10:*          TEST     AL,80H    ;TEST BIT 7
    11:*          JZ       READ2     ;WAIT UNTIL HIGH
    12:*          MOV      AL,BL     ;COUNTER TO AL
    13:*          INC      AL        ;ADD 1 WIDGET
    14:*          DAA                ;DECIMAL COUNTER
    15:*          JMP      CYCLE     ;REPEAT LOOP
    16:*PROG      ENDS
    17:*          END      WIDGET
    18:*^Z
*E

A:DIR WIDGET.*
WIDGET   ASM      434    8-23-84   9:36a
       1 File(s)
A:
```

Figure 3.9 Using EDLIN (the MS-DOS line editor) to create the source code for the widget counter program.

go the machine assembly route. First you will need an 8086- or 8088-based microcomputer system (sometimes called a *development system*) with typewriter-like keyboard, a video monitor for displaying the text, and one or two floppy disk drives.

You will also need an *editor* program that will allow you to type in the source code, an *assembler* for creating the object codes (i.e., the instruction hex codes), and a *linker* for creating the run file. These programs are normally stored on a disk and called up through the development system's *disk operating system* (DOS) when the system is first turned on. Normally, 64K of RAM or more will be required to run these programs.

One popular operating system for 8086- and 8088-based microcomputers is called MS-DOS (Microsoft Disk Operating System). In this section we use several programs available under MS-DOS to create the widget counter source, object, and run files. In Sec. 3.4 we use MS-DOS's DEBUG program to test the widget counter program and verify that it has met our design goals.

Let's begin by creating the source code file for the widget counter. In Fig. 3.9, the prompt **A:** indicates that MS-DOS is logged onto drive A and ready for a command.[2] We respond **EDLIN WIDGET.ASM**. This causes the line editor (EDLIN) to be loaded into memory and a file created with the primary name WIDGET and extension ASM. You will see how the extension works as we proceed.

The editor prompt is a *, to which we have responded **I** to enter the insert mode. Line numbers now appear as we type each successive line of the widget counter program into the computer. Note that EDLIN does not care what we type for the source file. It

---

[2]In some systems the prompt is **A>**.

can be 8086 assembly instructions, Pascal statements, or a letter to a friend. It simply assists us in creating the file that we have named.[3]

After all statements are entered, pressing control Z (^Z) leaves the edit mode. We can now list the file, add additional lines, or correct or insert new lines. When the file is complete we enter **E** to end the edit and return to the operating system. To see the files we have created, the **DIR WIDGET.*** command is given. This causes a directory of all widget files to be displayed. The * character is a "wildcard," causing any file with primary name WIDGET to be listed. In this case there is only one—the file WIDGET.ASM.

You have probably noticed that the widget program in Fig. 3.9 looks similar to, but not exactly like, the program in Fig. 3.7. We have had to add two statements to the beginning and end of the program. These are not 8086 assembly language instructions but "helpers" for the assembler and linker.

The **PROG SEGMENT** and **PROG ENDS** statements tell the assembler that all the instructions between these two statements are to be considered part of a segment with name PROG. This allows you to have several different program segments, each with its own unique name. The linker can then be used to link all these different segments together into one large program.

The ASSUME statement is critical because it tells the assembler which of the many segments you may have defined should be assigned to the four 8086/88 segments as the following instructions are assembled. The assembler needs this information so that it can determine if a segment override or near or far attribute should be assigned to a variable or symbolic address.

In this case the **ASSUME CS:PROG** statement indicates that CS should correspond to those codes in the segment named PROG. Be careful about the ASSUME statement. It *does not* load the CS, DS, SS, or ES registers. It simply tells the assembler which segment to currently assume from the many you may have defined. In this example, the stack, extra, and data segments are not required and thus they need not be mentioned in the ASSUME statement.

The last end statement, **END WIDGET**, identifies the end of the entire program. The assembler will ignore all instructions following this statement. The optional operand WIDGET is used by the linker to identify the instruction to pass control to when the file is loaded into memory and run.

The WIDGET.ASM file is now ready to be assembled. Figure 3.10 shows the steps. The command **MASM WIDGET.ASM** causes the assembler (called MACRO-86 or MASM) to be loaded with the file WIDGET.ASM as the source. The normal output of the assembler is an object code file that can be read by the linker. In this example MASM is suggesting that it will name this file WIDGET.OBJ. If we wish, we can override this name selection.

MASM can also produce two optional files. The source listing contains the relative addresses and hex codes together with the original source code in a file that can be read or output to a printer. The cross-reference is a file containing an alphabetical listing of

---

[3]Any word-processing program can be used to create the source file. Indeed, because a word processor offers full-screen editing, such programs will be more convenient to use than EDLIN.

```
A:MASM WIDGET.ASM
The Microsoft MACRO Assembler
Version 1.07, Copyright (C) Microsoft Inc. 1981,82

Object filename [WIDGET.OBJ]:
Source listing  [NUL.LST]: WIDGET.LST
Cross reference [NUL.CRF]:

Warning Severe
Errors  Errors
0       0

A:DIR WIDGET.*
WIDGET    ASM    434   8-23-84   9:36a
WIDGET    OBJ     68   8-23-84   9:38a
WIDGET    LST   1304   8-23-84   9:38a
        3 File(s)
A:
```

Figure 3.10 The assembler is loaded and told to assemble the file WIDGET.ASM. The results are two new files, WIDGET.OBJ and WIDGET.LST.

all labels and symbols. In this example we have requested that the list file be created but not the cross-reference file.

The assembly then begins and after a short time we are pleased to see that no errors were detected. This does not mean that the program will count widgets as we desire, only that we have used the proper mnemonics for the instructions and not forgotten any labels.

The **DIR WIDGET.*** command now reveals three widget files: the ASM file with the original source code, the OBJ file ready to be linked, and the LST file.

Let's take a look at the LST file and compare it to the hand-assembled version in Fig. 3.7. The command **TYPE WIDGET.LST** will display the list file on the video monitor as shown in Fig. 3.11.

Comparing the hex codes and address fields, you can see that they match with those given in Fig. 3.7 exactly. The list file also provides a list of segment names and symbols used.

Loading the Program into Memory

Now that the hex codes for the widget counter program have been determined—either by hand or machine assembly—we can turn our attention to the problem of getting those codes into memory. Again our approach depends on the type of system with which we are working.

The manual approach will require the use of a program that will allow hex data to be entered into memory and displayed or examined to verify proper loading. A *GO* command will also be necessary to transfer control to the loaded program. Such a program is often called a *monitor*.

The MS-DOS operating system contains such a monitor program, called *DEBUG*. Figure 3.12 illustrates its use with the widget counter program. From the operating system prompt **A:** the command **DEBUG** is typed. DEBUG loads and issues its prompt, >.[4] In this example we have arbitrarily elected to load the widget counter hex codes into memory beginning at address A0000H (A000:0000).

---

[4]In some systems the prompt is a dash (–).

```
The Microsoft MACRO Assembler                     08-23-84       PAGE     1-1


0000                               PROG     SEGMENT
                                            ASSUME   CS:PROG
0000   B0 00                       WIDGET:  MOV      AL,0      ;COUNTER=0
0002   8A D8                       CYCLE:   MOV      BL,AL     ;SAVE IN BL
0004   E6 D4                                OUT      0D4H,AL   ;DISPLAY COUNTER
0006   E4 D6                       READ1:   IN       AL,0D6H   ;READ SWITCH
0008   A8 80                                TEST     AL,80H    ;TEST BIT 7
000A   75 FA                                JNZ      READ1     ;WAIT UNTIL LOW
000C   E4 D6                       READ2:   IN       AL,0D6H   ;READ SWITCH
000E   A8 80                                TEST     AL,80H    ;TEST BIT 7
0010   74 FA                                JZ       READ2     ;WAIT UNTIL HIGH
0012   8A C3                                MOV      AL,BL     ;COUNTER TO AL
0014   FE C0                                INC      AL        ;ADD 1
0016   27                                   DAA                ;DECIMAL COUNTER
0017   EB E9                                JMP      CYCLE     ;REPEAT LOOP
0019                               PROG     ENDS
                                            END      WIDGET




Segments and groups:

                 N a m e                    Size     align     combine class

PROG . . . . . . . . . . . . . .            0019     PARA      NONE

Symbols:

                 N a m e                    Type     Value     Attr

CYCLE. . . . . . . . . . . . . .            L NEAR   0002      PROG
READ1. . . . . . . . . . . . . .            L NEAR   0006      PROG
READ2. . . . . . . . . . . . . .            L NEAR   000C      PROG
WIDGET . . . . . . . . . . . . .            L NEAR   0000      PROG

Warning Severe
Errors  Errors
0       0

A:
```

Figure 3.11 Widget list file created by the assembler.

The **E** command is used to begin entering data at this address. DEBUG responds by displaying the contents of that address and a period. Typing the new hex code and pushing the space bar advances the memory pointer to the next address. When you proceed in this manner, all the widget counter codes (determined in Fig. 3.7) can be loaded into memory.

The **D** (display) command can be used to verify that the codes have been entered correctly. This is done with **DA000:0 18**—display 18H bytes of memory beginning at address A000:0000. Note that the ASCII interpretation of these bytes is also given.

DEBUG also has an *unassemble* command that will display the 8086 mnemonics of a block of memory. This is very useful to verify that we have assembled the correct codes when performing a hand assembly. In this case the command is **UA000:0 18**—

```
A:DEBUG

DEBUG   version 1.08
>EA000:0
A000:0000   DC.B0    04.00    00.8A    FF.D8    79.E6    24.D4    00.E4    3F.D6
A000:0008   80.A8    DF.80    00.75    FF.FA    DE.E4    21.D6    D2.A8    CE.80
A000:0010   00.74    FF.FA    00.8A    BF.C3    00.FE    FF.C0    00.27    5F.EB
A000:0018   00.E9
>DA000:0 18
A000:0000   B0 00 8A D8 E6 D4 E4 D6-A8 80 75 FA E4 D6 A8 80    0..XfTdV(.uzdV(.
A000:0010   74 FA 8A C3 FE C0 27 EB-E9                         tz.C~ɔ'ki
>UA000:0 18
A000:0000   B000        MOV      AL,00
A000:0002   8ADB        MOV      BL,AL
A000:0004   E6D4        OUTB     D4
A000:0006   E4D6        INB      D6
A000:0008   A880        TEST     AL,80
A000:000A   75FA        JNZ      0006
A000:000C   E4D6        INB      D6
A000:000E   A880        TEST     AL,80
A000:0010   74FA        JZ       000C
A000:0012   8AC3        MOV      AL,BL
A000:0014   FEC0        INC      AL
A000:0016   27          DAA
A000:0017   EBE9        JMPS     0002
>
```

Figure 3.12 Using the monitor's E (enter) command, the hex codes are loaded into memory beginning at address A000:0000. The D (display) and U (unassemble) commands verify that the program has been loaded correctly.

unassemble the 18H bytes of memory beginning at address A000:0000. The unassembled mnemonics do not always agree exactly with the source code. For example, the IN AL,0D6H instruction unassembles as INB D6—input a byte from port D6.[5]

If an assembler has been used to create an object code file of the widget counter program, the *linker* can be used to prepare the executable run file. This process is shown in Fig. 3.13. The command **LINK WIDGET.OBJ** loads the linker, and like the assembler, offers the creation of three new files. The EXE file is the executable run file which must be selected. The (optional) list file or link map lists the segment names used in the program and their starting and ending addresses. The (optional) library file contains program modules that can be searched for by LINK and added to your run file.

After LINK has been run it reports any errors it has found. In this case, because WIDGET.OBJ did not define a stack segment, a warning is issued. This will not be a problem for this program because none of the widget counter instructions reference the stack. In more complex programs a stack segment should be defined. This is illustrated in Chap. 4.

The command **TYPE WIDGET.MAP** displays the contents of the map file which shows that the program utilizes one segment of length 19H bytes. Unlike the manual process shown in Fig. 3.12, you cannot tell LINK where to load your program. The physical location is determined by the operating system when the program is loaded to be run. Therefore, interpret the addresses in the map as *relative addresses*—relative to the first load address.

---

[5]Beginning with MS-DOS version 2, DEBUG includes an assemble (A) command. Using this command mnemonics can be entered directly to memory.

```
A:LINK WIDGET.OBJ

   Microsoft Object Linker V1.10
(C) Copyright 1981 by Microsoft Inc.

Run File [WIDGET.EXE]:
List File [NUL.MAP]: WIDGET.MAP
Libraries [.LIB]:
 Warning: No STACK segment

There was 1 error detected.

A:TYPE WIDGET.MAP

Warning: No STACK segment

 Start  Stop    Length  Name                      Class
 00000H 00018H  0019H   PROG

Program entry point at 0000:0000

A:DIR WIDGET.*
WIDGET   ASM     434    8-23-84    9:36a
WIDGET   OBJ      68    8-23-84    9:38a
WIDGET   LST    1304    8-23-84    9:38a
WIDGET   MAP     256    8-23-84    9:56a
WIDGET   EXE     640    8-23-84    9:56a
      5 File(s)
A:
```

Figure 3.13 LINK is used to create the run file WIDGET.EXE. WIDGET.MAP shows that the program is 19H bytes long.

The directory of widget files has now grown to five files, including the executable file WIDGET.EXE. In Sec. 3.4 we (finally) test the widget counter and see if it works.

SELF-REVIEW 3.3 (answers on page 138)

3.3.1. Hand assemble the hex codes for the instruction CMP BYTE PTR[BX],24H.

3.3.2. With reference to the MOD-REG-R/M byte, if MOD = 00, the _____ _____ addressing modes are indicated unless R/M = 110. In this case the _____ addressing mode is selected.

3.3.3. When MS-DOS is ready to accept a command it displays the prompt _____.

3.3.4. A(n) _____ is used to create the source code for an assembly language program.

3.3.5. The output of the assembler is called the _____ code file.

3.3.6. The _____ converts the object code file into a run file.

3.3.7. List the three steps required to create an executable run file with a typical development system.

3.3.8. Which of the following files contains the original source code, instruction hex codes, and program relative addresses in a form that can be displayed on a video monitor? (a) PRINTER.ASM; (b) PRINTER.OBJ; (c) PRINTER.LST; (d) PRINTER.MAP.

3.4 TESTING AND DEBUGGING

Once a program has been written, two types of problems can keep it from working. These are errors in the program *syntax* and *logical* errors. Again the computer can come to our aid to help track down and eliminate these problems.

Errors in Syntax

Refer to the widget counter program in Fig. 3.7. Suppose that we had forgotten the label READ1 or misspelled the test instruction TSET AL,80H. How would these errors be detected?

With hand assembly they would not really matter as long as we still determined the proper hex codes. You would probably see the misspelling or forgotten label and correct it on your paper.

A more serious problem occurs if you assemble an instruction incorrectly. For example, if you are assembling the instruction MOV DX,CX but incorrectly make the destination bit (d) a 1 instead of a 0, the result is the instruction MOV CX,DX. The syntax on your paper appears correct but the coding is wrong. This can be a difficult problem to detect. A monitor with an unassemble command is invaluable in this instance.

If machine assembly is used, the assembler will "flag" syntax errors (missing labels, spelling errors) and issue an error message such as "Symbol not defined." The assembler has all the syntax rules "built in." When an error is noted, you must return to the editor, make the correction, and reassemble. Eventually, you will get a "clean" assembly—no warnings or severe errors.

Logical Errors

The widget counter program we have written has passed the syntax error test imposed by the assembler. But does that mean that the program works? No. We have yet to test the program logic and verify that it does indeed count widgets.

There are two ways of doing this. The optimistic approach is to load the program and run it—hoping that it will work. The pessimistic approach is to load the debugger and single step through the program, verifying that each instruction is doing what was expected.

Let's be optimistic and try the first approach. We start up the program as the widgets begin moving down the assembly line. Our eyes are glued on the widget counter displays. Unfortunately, nothing happens. The displays seem stuck at 00. What could be wrong? Our "window" into the operation of the program is limited to the view provided by the two displays. Because they are not changing, we can only guess what the problem might be.

Unfortunately, this is a common occurrence when testing hardware controlled by a microprocessor. The first thing to do is to *isolate* the problem to the hardware or software. Remember, the program may be working perfectly but the displays could be miswired or the widget detector switch may not be working.

In this example we can test the hardware with a logic probe and a simple test program. As the widgets move down the assembly line, pulses should be observed at IN7. If the logic probe does not show these pulses, the widget detector circuit should be carefully tested.

The output displays can be tested with a simple test program such as

```
START:  MOV  AL,55H
```

```
OUT   0D4H,AL
JMP   START
```

This program repeatedly writes the data pattern 01010101 to the displays on output lines OUT0–OUT7. The correct operation of the displays can now be quickly verified.

But what if these hardware tests all check out as being okay? Then it is time to test the software. Most monitor programs include two features for this purpose. They are the insertion of *breakpoints* and *single stepping*.

The breakpoint technique involves replacing one of the program instructions with a special breakpoint instruction. Recall that the 8086 has a single-byte software interrupt intended exactly for this purpose. This is INT 3. When this instruction is executed, control is transferred to the program whose address is stored in memory locations 0000CH–0000FH.

The breakpoint program normally displays the contents of the CPU registers so that the programmer can "see" the state of the machine up to the breakpoint. If everything appears correct, the breakpoint can be moved further into the program until the problem is located.

The second approach to software troubleshooting is to single-step through the program instruction by instruction. Again the contents of all CPU registers are normally displayed after each single step. Figure 3.14 illustrates this approach using the **T** (trace) command in DEBUG.

DEBUG is first loaded together with the executable widget file via the command **DEBUG WIDGET.EXE**. The **R** command causes DEBUG to display all CPU registers at this point. Note that the operating system has decided to load the program at address 09E3:0000 and IP is set to 0000, the first instruction in the program.

The contents of the various registers can now be seen. The condition of the eight flags is also given. Table 3.4 explains the symbology used when a flag is cleared or set. Giving the command **T** causes the first instruction to be traced (MOV AL,00). IP advances to 0002, AL is set to 0, and the next instruction to be executed is displayed (MOV BL,AL).

Repeatedly giving the **T** command causes the first loop of the program to be single-stepped. Because IN7 is high, the program repeats the READ1 loop. Manually closing the widget counter switch causes IN7 to be low on the next pass, and program control transfers to the READ2 test loop (ZF changes from NZ to ZR).

Once in this loop, releasing the switch causes IN7 to be high (ZF = NZ) and program control passes to the MOV AL,BL instruction followed by INC AL. However, before AL is incremented, the **RAX** command—examine register AX—is given. This gives us the opportunity to change this register. In this case we enter 09 in order to test the DAA instruction. The INC AL instruction causes AL to become OA as expected and the DAA corrects this to 10. Control then transfers back to the beginning of the program.

As you can see, the single-stepping feature of DEBUG is very useful and allows you quickly to verify the proper operation of a program. In this case we have seen that the widget counter program is working correctly so we can proceed to the final step in the design process—the documentation.

```
A:DEBUG WIDGET.EXE

DEBUG  version 1.08
>R
AX=0000  BX=0000  CX=0019  DX=0000  SP=0000  BP=0000  SI=0000  DI=0000
DS=09D3  ES=09D3  SS=09E3  CS=09E3  IP=0000   NV UP DI PL NZ NA PO NC
09E3:0000 B000        MOV     AL,00
>T

AX=0000  BX=0000  CX=0019  DX=0000  SP=0000  BP=0000  SI=0000  DI=0000
DS=09D3  ES=09D3  SS=09E3  CS=09E3  IP=0002   NV UP DI PL NZ NA PO NC
09E3:0002 8AD8        MOV     BL,AL
>T

AX=0000  BX=0000  CX=0019  DX=0000  SP=0000  BP=0000  SI=0000  DI=0000
DS=09D3  ES=09D3  SS=09E3  CS=09E3  IP=0004   NV UP DI PL NZ NA PO NC
09E3:0004 E6D4        OUTB    D4
>T

AX=0000  BX=0000  CX=0019  DX=0000  SP=0000  BP=0000  SI=0000  DI=0000
DS=09D3  ES=09D3  SS=09E3  CS=09E3  IP=0006   NV UP DI PL NZ NA PO NC
09E3:0006 E4D6        INB     D6
>T

AX=0080  BX=0000  CX=0019  DX=0000  SP=0000  BP=0000  SI=0000  DI=0000
DS=09D3  ES=09D3  SS=09E3  CS=09E3  IP=0008   NV UP DI PL NZ NA PO NC
09E3:0008 A880        TEST    AL,80
>T

AX=0080  BX=0000  CX=0019  DX=0000  SP=0000  BP=0000  SI=0000  DI=0000
DS=09D3  ES=09D3  SS=09E3  CS=09E3  IP=000A   NV UP DI NG NZ NA PO NC
09E3:000A 75FA        JNZ     0006
>T

AX=0080  BX=0000  CX=0019  DX=0000  SP=0000  BP=0000  SI=0000  DI=0000
DS=09D3  ES=09D3  SS=09E3  CS=09E3  IP=0006   NV UP DI NG NZ NA PO NC
09E3:0006 E4D6        INB     D6
>T

AX=0000  BX=0000  CX=0019  DX=0000  SP=0000  BP=0000  SI=0000  DI=0000
DS=09D3  ES=09D3  SS=09E3  CS=09E3  IP=0008   NV UP DI NG NZ NA PO NC
09E3:0008 A880        TEST    AL,80
>T

AX=0000  BX=0000  CX=0019  DX=0000  SP=0000  BP=0000  SI=0000  DI=0000
DS=09D3  ES=09D3  SS=09E3  CS=09E3  IP=000A   NV UP DI PL ZR NA PE NC
09E3:000A 75FA        JNZ     0006
>T

AX=0000  BX=0000  CX=0019  DX=0000  SP=0000  BP=0000  SI=0000  DI=0000
DS=09D3  ES=09D3  SS=09E3  CS=09E3  IP=000C   NV UP DI PL ZR NA PE NC
09E3:000C E4D6        INB     D6
>T

AX=0080  BX=0000  CX=0019  DX=0000  SP=0000  BP=0000  SI=0000  DI=0000
DS=09D3  ES=09D3  SS=09E3  CS=09E3  IP=000E   NV UP DI PL ZR NA PE NC
09E3:000E A880        TEST    AL,80
```

Figure 3.14 Using DEBUG to single-step through the widget counter program.

```
>T

AX=0080   BX=0000   CX=0019   DX=0000   SP=0000   BP=0000   SI=0000   DI=0000
DS=09D3   ES=09D3   SS=09E3   CS=09E3   IP=0010     NV UP DI NG NZ NA PO NC
09E3:0010 74FA            JZ        000C
>T

AX=0080   BX=0000   CX=0019   DX=0000   SP=0000   BP=0000   SI=0000   DI=0000
DS=09D3   ES=09D3   SS=09E3   CS=09E3   IP=0012     NV UP DI NG NZ NA PO NC
09E3:0012 8AC3            MOV       AL,BL
>T

AX=0000   BX=0000   CX=0019   DX=0000   SP=0000   BP=0000   SI=0000   DI=0000
DS=09D3   ES=09D3   SS=09E3   CS=09E3   IP=0014     NV UP DI NG NZ NA PO NC
09E3:0014 FEC0            INC       AL
>RAX
AX 0000
:09
>T

AX=000A   BX=0000   CX=0019   DX=0000   SP=0000   BP=0000   SI=0000   DI=0000
DS=09D3   ES=09D3   SS=09E3   CS=09E3   IP=0016     NV UP DI PL NZ NA PE NC
09E3:0016 27              DAA
>T

AX=0010   BX=0000   CX=0019   DX=0000   SP=0000   BP=0000   SI=0000   DI=0000
DS=09D3   ES=09D3   SS=09E3   CS=09E3   IP=0017     NV UP DI PL NZ AC PO NC
09E3:0017 EBE9            JMPS      0002
>T

AX=0010   BX=0000   CX=0019   DX=0000   SP=0000   BP=0000   SI=0000   DI=0000
DS=09D3   ES=09D3   SS=09E3   CS=09E3   IP=0002     NV UP DI PL NZ AC PO NC
09E3:0002 8AD8            MOV       BL,AL
>
```

Figure 3.14 (continued)

TABLE 3.4 FLAG SYMBOLS

Flag name	Set		Clear	
Overflow	OV		NV	
Direction	DN	Decrementing	UP	Incrementing
Interrupt	EI	Enabled	DI	Disabled
Sign	NG	Negative	PL	Plus
Zero	ZR		NZ	
Auxiliary carry	AC		NA	
Parity	PE	Even	PO	Odd
Carry	CY		NC	

SELF-REVIEW 3.4 (answers on page 138)

3.4.1. If we had forgotten to include the DAA instruction in the widget counter program shown in Fig. 3.11, this would be considered a _____ error.

3.4.2. Errors in program syntax will normally be detected by an assembler program.   (True/False)

3.4.3. When debugging a microcomputer design problem like the widget counter, the first step should be determining if the problem is due to _____ or _____.

3.4.4. Assume that a breakpoint is inserted in location 0012 of the program in Fig. 3.11. Under what conditions will the breakpoint be executed?

3.5 DOCUMENTATION

By their very nature, assembly language programs are difficult to read and understand. For example, refer to the unassembled widget counter mnemonics shown at the bottom of Fig. 3.12. With only these mnemonics to read, can you tell that this is a program intended for counting the flow of widgets down an assembly line?

The problem is that the instructions themselves convey very little about what is in a programmer's mind as he or she is writing the program. When we see the instruction MOV AL,0 we really do not know *why* the programmer wants to put 0 in register AL. This, of course, is the reason for adding a comment field to each instruction. It gives the programmer the opportunity to explain the intention of each instruction.

Why should we be so concerned about comments? One answer is that software costs now represent the major time (and money) investment for companies designing microprocessor-based products. The cost to develop a program that will fill 64K bytes of ROM may easily exceed $100,000. Yet the cost of the ROM chips themselves is less than $100!

Maintaining and modifying a program over its useful life span will undoubtedly involve several different programmers. A well-commented and documented program can save many hours of labor.

What constitutes "good" documentation? First we might define two separate classes of documentation. There is the *user's manual*, intended for the end user of the product. This document explains in lay terms how to use the product as its designers intended.

The second type of documentation, the one we are more concerned about, is intended to help other programmers, designers, and technicians understand and maintain your work. Here are some suggestions on the kinds of documents to include.

1. Abstract global-level block diagrams of the system (see Figs. 3.1 and 3.4)
2. General and detailed flowcharts of the system software (see Figs. 3.5 and 3.6)
3. Detailed schematic diagrams of the system hardware (pin numbers and part numbers of all integrated circuits must be shown; see Figs. 3.2 and 3.3)
4. A well-commented copy of the system software in source code form

It is no accident that all the documentation for the first three items has already been completed. Good documentation is done in parallel with the design phase, not after the job has been completed (somehow it never seems to get done when put off until the design is working).

Figure 3.15 shows the final version of the widget counter program rewritten to provide a clear description of its function. You are encouraged to adopt the following rules as you develop your own programs.

1. Always include a title block with the current date or program version number. This should provide a brief description of the function of the program.

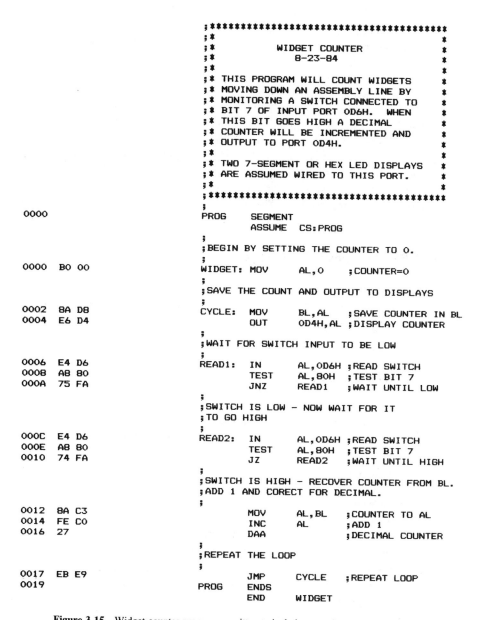

```
                                ;***************************************
                                ;*                                     *
                                ;*             WIDGET COUNTER          *
                                ;*               8-23-84               *
                                ;*                                     *
                                ;* THIS PROGRAM WILL COUNT WIDGETS     *
                                ;* MOVING DOWN AN ASSEMBLY LINE BY     *
                                ;* MONITORING A SWITCH CONNECTED TO    *
                                ;* BIT 7 OF INPUT PORT 0D6H.  WHEN     *
                                ;* THIS BIT GOES HIGH A DECIMAL        *
                                ;* COUNTER WILL BE INCREMENTED AND     *
                                ;* OUTPUT TO PORT 0D4H.                *
                                ;*                                     *
                                ;* TWO 7-SEGMENT OR HEX LED DISPLAYS   *
                                ;* ARE ASSUMED WIRED TO THIS PORT.     *
                                ;*                                     *
                                ;***************************************
                                ;
0000                            PROG    SEGMENT
                                        ASSUME  CS:PROG
                                ;
                                ;BEGIN BY SETTING THE COUNTER TO 0.
                                ;
0000  B0 00                     WIDGET: MOV     AL,0      ;COUNTER=0
                                ;
                                ;SAVE THE COUNT AND OUTPUT TO DISPLAYS
                                ;
0002  8A D8                     CYCLE:  MOV     BL,AL    ;SAVE COUNTER IN BL
0004  E6 D4                             OUT     0D4H,AL  ;DISPLAY COUNTER
                                ;
                                ;WAIT FOR SWITCH INPUT TO BE LOW
                                ;
0006  E4 D6                     READ1:  IN      AL,0D6H  ;READ SWITCH
0008  A8 80                             TEST    AL,80H   ;TEST BIT 7
000A  75 FA                             JNZ     READ1    ;WAIT UNTIL LOW
                                ;
                                ;SWITCH IS LOW - NOW WAIT FOR IT
                                ;TO GO HIGH
                                ;
000C  E4 D6                     READ2:  IN      AL,0D6H  ;READ SWITCH
000E  A8 80                             TEST    AL,80H   ;TEST BIT 7
0010  74 FA                             JZ      READ2    ;WAIT UNTIL HIGH
                                ;
                                ;SWITCH IS HIGH - RECOVER COUNTER FROM BL.
                                ;ADD 1 AND CORECT FOR DECIMAL.
                                ;
0012  8A C3                             MOV     AL,BL    ;COUNTER TO AL
0014  FE C0                             INC     AL       ;ADD 1
0016  27                                DAA              ;DECIMAL COUNTER
                                ;
                                ;REPEAT THE LOOP
                                ;
0017  EB E9                             JMP     CYCLE    ;REPEAT LOOP
0019                            PROG    ENDS
                                        END     WIDGET
```

Figure 3.15 Widget counter program rewritten to include more descriptive comments.

2. Think of the program as a number of small modules each with a specific function. Provide comments before each group of instructions which describe the intent of the module.

3. Provide comments for each line of code explaining why this instruction is included.

Sec. 3.5 Documentation   **135**

Summary

The top-down approach to hardware and software design is one in which the problem and its solution are first visualized from an abstract global viewpoint. After defining the hardware and software requirements, each of these areas are further refined into smaller, easier-to-handle modules.

Developing the software consists of the creative coding process in which the program is actually written, and the mechanical assembly process in which the binary or hex codes are determined and loaded into the machine. The hardware and software are then tested together and any problems are isolated and debugged. Finally, the product is documented in such a way that others may understand and maintain your work.

Most microprocessor-based products are designed and tested with the aid of special *development systems*. These systems often include special hardware and software debugging "tools" that can be used to minimize the amount of time required to bring the product to the marketplace. These topics are covered in more detail in Chap. 5.

SELF-REVIEW 3.5 (answers on page 138)

3.5.1. Explain the three ways that an assembly language program should be documented.

3.5.2. List at least four items that should be included in the documentation package of a hardware/software design problem.

CHAPTER 3 SELF-TEST

1. Sketch and define the four common flowcharting symbols.
2. If the widget counter switch is manually operated, the displays will increment each time the switch is _____.
3. List the steps to follow when using a top-down approach to hardware and software design.
4. Symbolic addresses are recorded in the: (a) address field; (b) label field; (c) op-code field; (d) comment field.
5. Because some microprocessor instructions require dedicated CPU registers, the choice of which registers to use when developing a program is not arbitrary. (True/False)
6. Which instruction in Fig. 3.7 causes the widget counter display always to be decimal?
7. Using hand assembly, determine the hex codes for the instruction MOV BH,CS:[BP].
8. Give an example of an 8086 instruction that has no operands. What is its hex code?
9. Using hand assembly, determine the hex codes for the instruction ADD [8010H],65H.
10. When developing an assembly language program the file created by the editor is called the _____ code and has the file extension _____.
11. A(n) _____ is used to create the object code file.
12. The file created by the linker is called the _____ file and has the file extension _____.

13. When the assembler begins the assembly process, how does it know which program segment to use for the code, data, extra, and stack segments?

14. What is the DEBUG command to display the hex codes from 24000H to 240FFH?

15. Two techniques used for troubleshooting software are _____ and _____

ANALYSIS AND DESIGN QUESTIONS

3.1. Explain how the circuit in Fig. 3.3 debounces the switch contacts by comparing the charge and discharge time constants with the switch bounce time of 5 to 20 ms.

3.2. Figure 3.16 shows a common-anode seven-segment display being driven directly from a microcomputer output port. Write a program that will cause the number "5" to appear in this display.

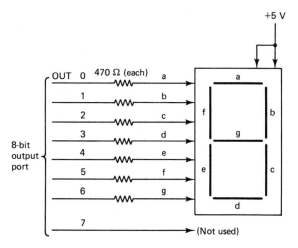

Figure 3.16 Driving a seven-segment display from an 8-bit microcomputer output port.

3.3. Modify the list of inputs and outputs in Fig. 3.4 to include a second input, IN6. When this input is high, the widget counter program should operate normally. When this input is low, the program should reset the count and displays to 00. Provide a diagram of the new hardware required, system-level and detailed flowcharts, and a commented assembly language program listing.

3.4. Figure 3.17 is a list of inputs and outputs for a computer monitoring system for an industrial process. You are to design and write the system software that monitors the temperature and pressure sensors for both processes. The alarm is to be sounded whenever the temperature and pressure for process A or B are both high or both low. Develop system-level and detailed flowcharts and a commented assembly language program listing.

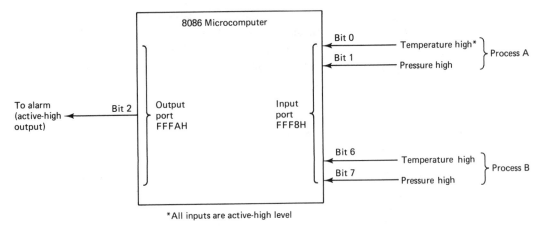

Figure 3.17 Program inputs and outputs for Analysis and Design Question 3.4.

3.5. In this problem you are to design a simple frequency counter with 10-Hz resolution. Use the same hardware as in the widget counter but replace IN7 with a 5-HZ 50% duty cycle square wave. Apply the unknown frequency input signal to IN0 (bit 0 of the same input port). By counting pulses during the time that IN7 is high, the frequency of the IN0 signal can be determined. Provide a standard documentation package with your solution.

SELF REVIEW ANSWERS

3.1.1 hardware, software

3.1.2 False

3.1.3 top-down

3.1.4 algorithm

3.2.1 address, hex codes, label, op-code, operand, comments

3.2.2 TEST AL,20H

3.2.3 00110110

3.3.1 82H (or 80H) 3FH 24H (the s bit is a "don't care")

3.3.2 register indirect, direct

3.3.3 A: or A> (assuming drive A)

3.3.4 editor

3.3.5 object

3.3.6 linker

3.3.7 edit, assemble, link

3.3.8 (c)

3.4.1 logical

3.4.2 True

3.4.3 hardware, software

3.4.4 After IN7 pulses low and then high

3.5.1 title block, module descriptions, instruction comments

3.5.2 global-level system block diagrams, flowcharts, schematic diagrams, commented source code

4

MICROPROCESSOR PROGRAMMING TECHNIQUES

Writing a computer program is as much an art as it is a skill. Indeed, a dictionary definition of an artist is that he or she is a person who does anything well, with a feeling for form or effect. Certainly this applies to the computer programmer as well as to the sculptor. Developing an ''elegant'' solution to a programming problem can be as satisfying to the author as is the creation of a fine piece of art to the sculptor.

In Chap. 3 we learned how to partition a microprocessor problem into its hardware and software components. Normally, the hardware defines a number of inputs and outputs that are to be monitored and controlled via the software.

The development of the software solution to the problem proceeds in several well-defined steps:

1. Design the program logic.
2. Code the instructions.
3. Assemble and link the program.
4. Test and debug.
5. Document.

The first two steps are usually the most difficult (although the fourth may cause the most frustration). These steps also represent the creative part of the problem. Because the experienced programmer ''has been there before,'' he or she can often translate the solution into program instructions with apparent ease. This is not so for the inexperienced programmer.

It is the intention of this chapter to begin developing that experience by illustrating several well-known programming techniques. One example is the use of subroutines (or *procedures*) to eliminate duplicating the same code several times within a program. By studying the examples presented in this chapter, you can avoid "reinventing the wheel" each time you are faced with a new programming problem.

In parallel with these examples, you will also have the opportunity to learn more about the 8086, its segmented memory, and its assembly language (using MACRO-86, LINK, and DEBUG—all available under the MS-DOS operating system). The chapter concludes with an introduction to modular programming and the use of macros—techniques appropriate for very large programming projects. This includes the use of a library facility (LIB) for storing often-used program modules.

The major topics in this chapter include:

4.1 Logical Processing
4.2 Arithmetic Processing
4.3 Time-Delay Loops
4.4 Procedures
4.5 Data Tables
4.6 Modular Programming
4.7 Macros

4.1 LOGICAL PROCESSING

The basic processing cycle performed by all computers is one of inputting information, processing that information, and outputting the result. Often the input data is *coded* and may represent characters typed on a keyboard (ASCII), decimal data (BCD), or the magnitude of some quantity expressed in binary. Processing of this type of data consists of performing arithmetic operations such as multiplying the input data by 10, dividing the product by 256, and outputting the result to port AOH.

In other cases the data input to the processor may represent outside world *status*

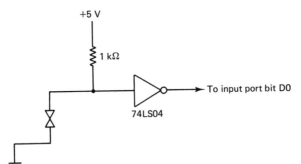

Figure 4.1 The open or closed status of a switch can be monitored using one bit of an input port.

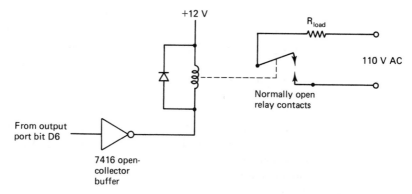

Figure 4.2 One bit of an output port can be used to control an external device, in this example a 12-V relay.

information. This is shown in Fig. 4.1. If bit 0 of the input port is a 0, it may be interpreted that the switch contacts are open. If this bit is a 1, the switch contacts are closed.

Processing of status information will require the microprocessor to perform logical tests such as "Make output bit 5 high if input bits 2 or 3 are low." Figure 4.2 shows an example where output bit 6 is used to turn a mechanical relay on or off, thereby controlling a 110-V ac device.

Logical processing of input status information is an important concept that we will use throughout this book. In this section the control of an industrial process requiring logical processing is covered as an example. In Sec. 4.2 we cover the case where the input data must be manipulated arithmetically.

Bit Testing and Masking

There are several ways of testing a bit to determine if it is a 1 or a 0. For example, consider the following program sequence:

```
AGAIN:  IN   AL,PORT    ;Status information to AL
        AND  AL,01H     ;Test bit 0
        JNZ  AGAIN      ;Repeat if not zero
```

Notice what happens when the AND instruction is executed. If the input data is 37H, the result is

$$
\begin{array}{l}
0011\ 0111 \\
\underline{0000\ 0001} \\
0000\ 0001 \qquad \text{ZF} \leftarrow 0
\end{array}
$$

Because the result is not zero, the jump is taken and the group of instructions repeated. Only when bit 0 becomes a 0 will control pass to the instructions following the JNZ.

The immediate data in the AND instruction (01H) is called a *mask*. As you can see, choosing a particular mask bit to be 0 effectively removes that bit from consideration when the AND instruction is performed.

In some cases data that is to be processed arithmetically is first passed through a mask to force certain bits to be zero. A common example is ASCII-encoded data. Because the digits 0–9 are coded as 30H–39H, the instruction AND AL,OFH will result in a BCD number between 0 and 9 in register AL (assuming that the input data was a valid ASCII number). This process of masking the high-order ASCII nibble is sometimes called "removing the ASCII bias."

One disadvantage to using the AND instruction for masking is that the contents of the ANDed register are altered. If the data input in the IN AL,PORT instruction above contains status information about another device, say on bit 3, it will be masked (lost). A second IN instruction will be required.

Here is a solution to this problem using the TEST instruction:

```
AGAIN:  IN    AL,PORT    ;Status information to AL
        TEST  AL,01H     ;Test bit 0
        JZ    BIT0       ;If zero, go to BIT0 routine
        TEST  AL,08H     ;If not zero, test bit 3
        JNZ   BIT3       ;If bit 3 = 1, go to BIT3 routine
        JMP   AGAIN      ;If bit 0 = 1 AND bit 3 = 0, then
                         ;repeat the process
```

Because the TEST instruction does not destroy the contents of AL, the second test can be done without the need to perform a second input.

Example 4.1

Write the sequence of instructions required to input a byte of data from symbolic port address PORT, test if bits 4 and 7 are low, and transfer control to symbolic address READY. If both bits are not low, repeat the loop.

Solution   Both bits can be tested simultaneously.

```
AGAIN:  IN    AL,PORT
        TEST  AL,90H
        JZ    READY
        JMP   AGAIN
```

The rotate instructions can also be used to test status bits; for example,

```
AGAIN:  IN    AL,PORT    ;Status information to AL
        ROR   AL,1       ;Move bit 0 to the carry
        JC    AGAIN      ;Repeat if carry set
```

The main advantage to this technique is that the single-bit rotate instruction requires only two clock cycles to execute versus four for the AND and TEST instructions. Thus this technique will be slightly faster. However, if the bit to be tested is not in the "end" position, multiple rotates will be required, canceling the speed advantage.

Outputting a Bit Pattern

Once the input data has been processed, the selected output device must be activated. This involves outputting a logic 1 or 0 to the appropriate output port bit. There are two cases to consider. In the first, a bit pattern is determined, loaded into register AL or AX, and output to the desired port. For example, suppose that we wish to turn on devices connected to bits 6 and 7 and turn all other devices off (if any). Assuming an active high level, the following instructions could be used:

```
MOV  AL,0C0H      ;Bits 6 and 7 high
OUT  PORT,AL      ;Output the data
```

This technique works fine when the desired condition of all the output devices is known. But what if we do not know if the device connected to bit 0 should be off (as it will be after executing this program)? In this case we must save the old bit pattern after outputting it. When a new pattern is to be output, the old pattern is retrieved and selected bits updated. Consider the following sequence, in which device 7 is to be turned on but device 6 off. TEMP is a memory location used to store the previous bit pattern.

```
MOV  AL,TEMP      ;Recover old pattern from memory
OR   AL,80H       ;Set bit 7 but change no others
AND  AL,0BFH      ;Clear bit 6 but change no others
MOV  TEMP,AL      ;Save pattern for next time
OUT  PORT,AL      ;Output the data
```

Note how the AND and OR instructions are used to set or clear individual bits of the data pattern without affecting the other bits.

Design Example

Figure 4.3 illustrates one step in an industrial process that is to be computerized. In this example a chemical solution is to be heated before being passed on to the next processing station. You will notice that several input sensors and output controls have been added to allow the computer complete control over this processing step.

The following specifications have been received from the engineer in charge of the process (with the control and sensor information added by the programmer).

1. Fill the tank to its capacity.
   a. Open the inlet valve: $\overline{\text{INFLOW}} = 0$
   b. Close the outflow valve: $\overline{\text{OUTFLOW}} = 1$
   c. Turn off the heater: HTRON = 0
   d. Wait until the tank is full: TANKFUL = 1
2. Heat the solution in the tank until its temperature is 90° C.
   a. Close the inlet valve: $\overline{\text{INFLOW}} = 1$
   b. Turn on the heater: HTRON = 1
   c. Wait for the solution to heat: $\overline{\text{TEMPOK}} = 0$

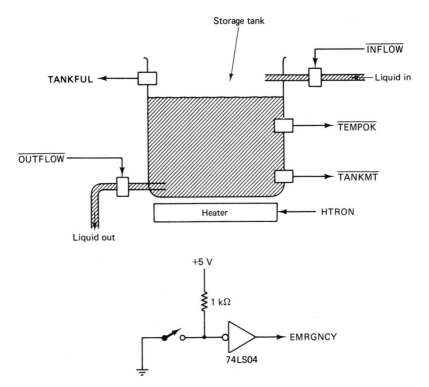

Figure 4.3 Industrial process designed

3. Empty the tank.
   a. Turn off the heater: HTRON = 0
   b. Open the outlet valve: $\overline{\text{OUTFLOW}}$ = 0
   c. Wait for the tank to empty: $\overline{\text{TANKMT}}$ = 0
4. Go to step 1.

The process also has an emergency shutdown switch. Whenever this switch is pushed the entire process should be shut down, allowing a manual override of the entire process. When the emergency condition is removed, the process should be restarted from the beginning.

Figure 4.4 shows the computer interface, the I/0 ports selected, and the bit assignments. Three output bits are required. Bit 0 ($\overline{\text{INFLOW}}$) is active low and will open the inlet valve, allowing the tank to be filled. Bit 1 ($\overline{\text{OUTFLOW}}$) is also active low and opens the outlet valve to empty the tank. Bit 7 (HTRON) will cause the solution in the tank to be heated when this output bit is high.

Four input status bits are provided. Bit 4 (TANKFUL) will go high when the level in the tank reaches the height of this sensor. Similarly, bit 5 ($\overline{\text{TANKMT}}$) will go low when the level in the tank falls below this sensor. Bit 6 ($\overline{\text{TEMPOK}}$) will go low when the temperature of the solution in the tank reaches (or exceeds) a predefined limit. Finally, bit 7 (EMRGNCY) will be high whenever the emergency override switch is closed.

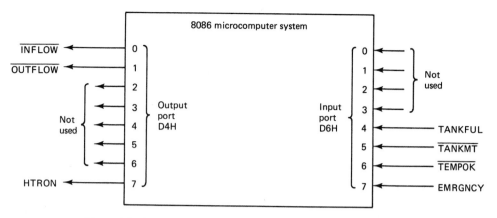

Figure 4.4 Input and output port bit assignments for the process controller.

Figure 4.5 is a flowchart of the control program required. The bits to be monitored and patterns to be output are also indicated. In this example we are assuming that the unused bits are "don't cares." This means that previous output bit patterns need not be stored.

As an example, consider the code required to fill the tank. The heater should be turned off (bit 7 = 0), the inlet valve opened (bit 0 = 0), and the outlet valve closed (bit 1 = 1). The instructions

```
            MOV    AL,02
            OUT    0D4H,AL
```

will accomplish this (the don't cares are made 0).

The assembly language listing of the program is provided in Fig. 4.6. It follows the flowchart very closely. To make the program more readable, the EQU operator has been used. This allows a name to be *equated* with a constant. Thus OFF equates to 03H (00000011B), and when output, closes all valves and turns off the heater ($\overline{\text{INFLOW}}$ = 1, $\overline{\text{OUTFLOW}}$ = 1, HTRON = 0). Note that equates are also used for each bit pattern being tested. For example, the emergency condition occurs when bit 7 = 1. Thus the instruction sequence

```
            TEST   AL,EMRGNCY      ;EMRGNCY = 80H
            JNZ    SHTDWN
```

will branch to the shutdown routine if bit 7 is high.

Following the equate statements, the program instructions are defined to exist in a segment called CODE. The assembler is then told to assume that CS = CODE for the following instructions (until the **CODE ENDS** statement).

The program ends with the statement **END START**. This tells the linker program which instruction is the first to be executed. In this simple program, the label START could be omitted, as there is only one code segment. However, later in this chapter we will see cases where this is not so. For this reason it is a good habit always to identify the starting point of the program for the linker.

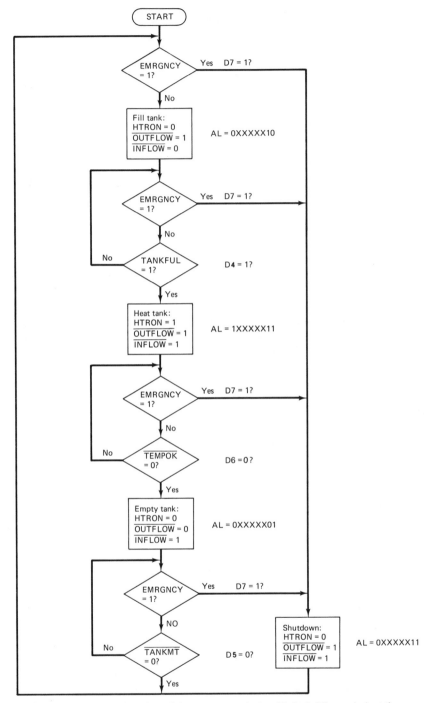

Figure 4.5 Detailed flowchart of the process required to fill the holding tank, heat the liquid, and then empty the tank.

```
                         ;**************************************************
                         ;*              Process Controller               *
                         ;*                 version 1.0                    *
                         ;*                                                *
                         ;* This program controls the industrial pro-      *
                         ;* cess shown in Fig. 4.3 and follows the         *
                         ;* flow chart in Fig. 4.5                         *
                         ;*                                                *
                         ;**************************************************

                         ; The following "equate" statements assign
                         ; constants to the labels shown.  This
                         ; makes the program more readable and will
                         ; allow changes to be made more easily.

= 00D6                   SPORT     EQU  0D6H    ;Status port
= 00D4                   DPORT     EQU  0D4H    ;Data port
= 0080                   EMRGNCY   EQU  80H     ;Emergency mask
= 0010                   TANKFUL   EQU  10H     ;Tankful mask
= 0040                   TEMPOK    EQU  40H     ;Temp OK mask
= 0020                   TANKMT    EQU  20H     ;Tank empty mask
= 0002                   FILLTANK  EQU  02H     ;Fill tank code
= 0083                   HEATTANK  EQU  83H     ;Heat tank code
= 0001                   EMPTYTANK EQU  01H     ;Empty tank code
= 0003                   OFF       EQU  03H     ;All off code

                         ;Program begins here.  Give the name "CODE"
                         ;to the segment where the program is stored.

0000                     CODE      SEGMENT
                                   ASSUME  CS:CODE

                         ;Test for an emergency and then fill the tank.

0000  E4 D6              START:    IN    AL,SPORT      ;Read sensors
0002  A8 80                        TEST  AL,EMRGNCY    ;Emergency?
0004  75 2C                        JNZ   SHTDWN        ;Go to shutdown
0006  B0 02                        MOV   AL,FILLTANK   ;Else fill tank
0008  E6 D4                        OUT   DPORT,AL      ;
000A  E4 D6              FILL:     IN    AL,SPORT      ;Read sensors
000C  A8 80                        TEST  AL,EMRGNCY    ;Emergency?
000E  75 22                        JNZ   SHTDWN        ;Go to shutdown
0010  A8 10                        TEST  AL,TANKFUL    ;Tank full?
0012  74 F6                        JZ    FILL          ;No - continue

                         ;The tank is full.  Now close the inlet valve
                         ;and turn on the heater.

0014  B0 83                        MOV   AL,HEATTANK   ;Heater on
0016  E6 D4                        OUT   DPORT,AL      ;
0018  E4 D6              HEAT:     IN    AL,SPORT      ;Read sensors
001A  A8 80                        TEST  AL,EMRGNCY    ;Emergency?
001C  75 14                        JNZ   SHTDWN        ;Go to shutdown
001E  A8 40                        TEST  AL,TEMPOK     ;Temp OK?
0020  75 F6                        JNZ   HEAT          ;No - continue

                         ;The tank is heated.  Now open the outlet valve
                         ;and empty the tank.
```

Figure 4.6   Assembly language listing for the process controller.

```
0022   BO 01                        MOV      AL,EMPTYTANK   ;Open the valve
0024   E6 D4                        OUT      DPORT,AL       ;
0026   E4 D6               EMPTY:   IN       AL,SPORT       ;READ SENSORS
0028   A8 80                        TEST     AL,EMRGNCY     ;Emergency?
002A   75 06                        JNZ      SHTDWN         ;Go to shutdown
002C   A8 20                        TEST     AL,TANKMT      ;Tank empty?
002E   75 F6                        JNZ      EMPTY          ;No - continue

                           ;The tank is empty.  Repeat the cycle.
                           ;
0030   EB CE                        JMP      START          ;
                           ;
                           ;This is the shutdown routine.  Everything
                           ;is turned off.

0032   BO 03               SHTDWN:  MOV      AL,OFF         ;
0034   E6 D4                        OUT      DPORT,AL       ;
0036   EB C8                        JMP      START          ;

0038                       CODE     ENDS           ;End of CODE segment
                                    END      START ;End of program
```

Figure 4.6 (Continued)

SELF-REVIEW 4.1 (answers on page 191)

4.1.1. Explain the difference between bit testing and bit masking.

4.1.2. What instruction should be used to test bit 3 of register AX without changing the contents of AX?

4.1.3. The instruction sequence

```
              IN    AL,32H
              AND   AL,81H
              JNZ   ERROR
```

will branch to the error routine if bit _____ or bit _____ is _____.

4.1.4. Which of the following instructions will set bit 2 of register AL without changing any of the other bits? (a) AND AL,OFBH; (b) AND AL,40H; (c) OR AL,04H; (d) OR AL,20H.

4.1.5. Write the assembly statement required to assign 42H to the label COUNT.

4.2 ARITHMETIC PROCESSING

Arithmetic processing requires that the entire data word or byte be processed instead of individual bits. For example, a program may be required to look for a special character from the keyboard. When this character arrives, control should be transferred to another routine. The *control-C* character (ASCII 03H) is often used in this way. Typing this character will cause the currently executing program to be suspended.

In other cases the input data must be *translated* to some new value based on a mathematical formula. As an alternative, the translated value can be stored in a table and the input data used as an *index* into this table. This technique is covered in more detail

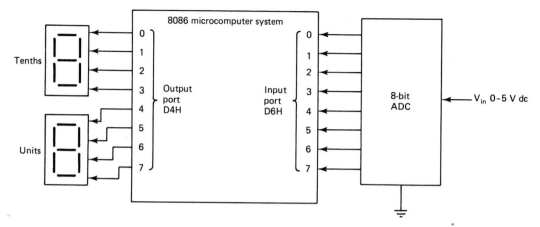

Figure 4.7 Analog-to-digital converter interface. Typical hardware would be TIL311 hexadecimal displays (see Fig. 3.2 for pin numbers) and a National Semiconductor ADC0800 8-bit analog-to-digital converter.

in Sec. 4.5. In this section we see how the 8086's extensive arithmetic instructions can be used to process data and also see how to set up a jump table.

Analog-to-Digital Conversion Program

Figure 4.7 shows an 8086 microcomputer system designed to collect analog data samples and display the result on a two-digit LED display. The analog input voltage is restricted to voltages less than 5.0 V, the full-scale range of the analog-to-digital converter (ADC). The output of the ADC is an 8-bit byte in the range 00–FFH.

Example 4.2

If the input voltage to the ADC in Fig. 4.7 is 1.25 V, determine the digital input seen by the 8086.

Solution This can be calculated by determining the portion of full scale represented by 1.25 V.

$$\frac{1.25 \text{ V}}{5.0 \text{ V}} \times 256 = 64 = 40\text{H}$$

Thus the input data will be 40H.

In this particular application the 8086 is to be converted into a two-digit voltmeter. An input of 1.25 V should appear as 13 in the two LED displays.[1] Working Ex. 4.2 in reverse, the conversion program must calculate the fraction of 256 that the input data represents, and then scale this to a number between 0 and 5 V. That is,

$$40\text{H} \rightarrow \frac{64}{256} \times 5.0 = 1.25$$
$$= 1.3 \quad \text{(rounded to the nearest tenth)}$$

[1]Certainly, the 8086 is capable of finer resolution than this. However, the point of this example is to illustrate the 8086's arithmetic processing capabilities, not to build a digital voltmeter.

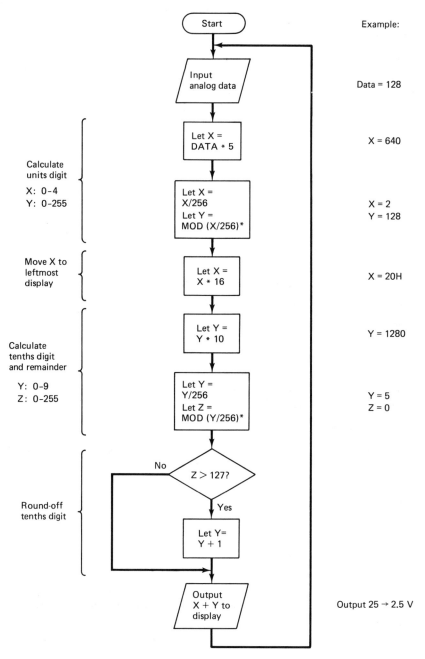

*MOD represents the remainder of the indicated division

Figure 4.8 Flowchart of the steps required to convert the input analog data byte into a two-digit-decimal output byte.

Microprocessor Programming Techniques   Chap. 4

```
                              ; *********************************************
                              ; *                                           *
                              ; *              ADC 0-5V Scaler               *
                              ; *               version 1.0                  *
                              ; *                                           *
                              ; * This program accepts the 8-bit output     *
                              ; * from an analog-to-digital converter and    *
                              ; * scales it to a value between 0V and 5V.    *
                              ; * The ouput is displayed on two seven       *
                              ; * segment displays as a units digit and a   *
                              ; * 'tenths' digit.  For example 27 => 2.7V.   *
                              ; *                                           *
                              ; *********************************************

= 00D6                        DPORT    EQU      0D6H           ;Data in port
= 00D4                        DSPY     EQU      0D4H           ;Display port
= 0005                        MPLR     EQU      5              ;Full scale
                                                              ; = 5V

                              ;One byte of (uninitialized) storage is
                              ;required.  TEMP is defined in a segment
                              ;called DATA.

0000                          DATA     SEGMENT
0000   ??                     TEMP     DB       ?         ;Undefined
0001                          DATA     ENDS

                              ;The program codes are stored in a segment
                              ;called CODE.  The ASSUME statement tells the
                              ;assembler to use CODE for CS and DATA for DS.
                              ;The SS and ES segment registers are
                              ;not defined.

0000                          CODE     SEGMENT
                                       ASSUME   CS:CODE,DS:DATA

                              ;The op system loads CS at run time but not DS.
                              ;The next two instructions load DS with the
                              ;DATA segment base address.

0000   B8   ---- R            START:   MOV      AX,DATA ;Segment base
0003   8E D8                           MOV      DS,AX    ;to DS.

                              ;Get data from ADC and form value
                              ;between 0V and 5V.

0005   E4 D6                  AGAIN:   IN       AL,DPORT       ;GET data
0007   B3 05                           MOV      BL,MPLR        ;Multiply times
0009   F6 E3                           MUL      BL             ;full scale.
000B   BA 0000                         MOV      DX,0           ;Divide 32 bit
                                                              ;dividend in
                                                              ;DX:AX
000E   BB 0100                         MOV      BX,256         ;by 256 for an
0011   F7 F3                           DIV      BX             ;8 bit ADC.
```

Figure 4.9 Assembly language listing for the ADC problem flowcharted in Fig. 4.8.

```
                              ; Shift quotient four bits left so it will
                              ; appear in the leftmost display.

0013  B1 04                           MOV     CL,4         ;4 shifts left
0015  D2 E0                           SAL     AL,CL        ;
0017  A2 0000 R                       MOV     TEMP,AL      ;Save units
                                                           ;digit.

                              ;Fetch remainder and calculate 'tenths' digit.

001A  8A C2                           MOV     AL,DL        ;Remndr to AL
001C  B3 0A                           MOV     BL,10        ;Multiplier
001E  F6 E3                           MUL     BL           ;
0020  BA 0000                         MOV     DX,0         ;Do division
0023  BB 0100                         MOV     BX,256       ;for the
0026  F7 F3                           DIV     BX           ;tenths digit.

                              ;Check remainder, round tenths digit up and
                              ;output result to the displays.

0028  80 FA 80                        CMP     DL,128       ;Less than
002B  72 03                           JB      SKIP         ;half?
002D  FE C0                           INC     AL           ;No
002F  27                              DAA                  ;Keep decimal
0030  02 06 0000 R            SKIP:   ADD     AL,TEMP      ;Form result
0034  E6 D4                           OUT     DSPY,AL      ;and show it.
0036  EB CD                           JMP     AGAIN        ;Repeat cycle

0038                          CODE    ENDS
                                      END     START
```

Figure 4.9 Continued

Figure 4.8 is a flowchart of the program. In this chart the units digit is called X and the tenths digit is called Y. After inputting the digital word, the units digit is calculated using the formula above. Note that to divide the data by 256 will require a 16-bit divisor (and thus a 32-bit dividend in registers DX:AX—see Fig. 2.14). After the division X will be a number between 0 and 4. At this point Y represents the remainder of the division and could be any number between 0 and 255.

Because the units digit must appear in the leftmost display, it is shifted left four places (or multiplied by 16). The remainder is then multiplied by 10 and divided by 256 to calculate the tenths digit. If the remainder from this division is greater than 127, one is added to Y to round up one-tenth.

Finally, adding X and Y assembles the two-digit result and it can be output to the displays. The process then repeats.

Figure 4.9 is the assembly language listing for the program. Again EQU statements are used to give names to constants and port addresses. After calculating a value for X, the result is temporarily stored until the tenths digit has been calculated. One byte in a (data) segment called DATA is used for this purpose. Notice how this segment is bracketed between the **DATA SEGMENT** and **DATA ENDS** statements. All segments must have an opening and closing statement like this or the assembler will issue an error message (*'open segments'*).

The program itself is stored in a segment called CODE. The **ASSUME CS:CODE,DS:DATA** statement tells the assembler what to assume for the segment registers as it assembles the following instructions. *Note that this statement does not load these registers.* Rather, ASSUME is required so that the assembler will know if it needs to generate far or near calls and jumps. It is also required to determine if a segment override is required.

How are the segment registers loaded? The operating system will pick a value for CS based on available memory. Thus you need not worry about loading this register.[2] However, the remaining segment registers must be loaded by your program.

Notice the two instructions beginning at the label START. The MOV AX,DATA instruction will cause the assembler to reserve two bytes of the MOV op-code for the segment address.[3] This can be seen in the leftmost column: B8 ---- R. The R means that this address is *relative* and cannot be determined at this time. When the program is linked and loaded, the actual segment address will be placed in these two bytes.

When the program is run, the data segment address will be loaded into AX and the next instruction will transfer this value to DS. The remainder of the program follows the flowchart.

Creating a Jump Table

Figure 4.10 is a flowchart for a program that processes the input data by using that data as an *index* into a jump table. This is a common programming technique for branching control to several different routines, depending on a selection key. In this example four input keys are allowed, corresponding to the number keys 1 through 4 on an ASCII keyboard.

If the key value is within range, the high-order ASCII bits are masked, the appropriate routine's address extracted from the table, and control transferred to that address. For example, pushing key 2 (32H) will cause routine 2 to be executed.

Figure 4.11 shows how the jump table is arranged in memory. TABLE represents a memory location corresponding to the base of the table. In the actual program this will be address 0000 in the data segment. To calculate the proper table address, the following formula must be used:

$$address = TABLE + (data \times 2) - 2$$

The data value must be multiplied by 2 because there are two bytes for each entry in the table. Also note that the table is offset by two locations relative to the key values; that is, the address for routine 1 is stored at address 0—thus the need to subtract 2.

Figure 4.12 is the program listing. A segment called TABLE is created and one word is reserved for the address of each routine. If you look at the end of the program, you will see the four routines at addresses 001BH, 001DH, 001FH, and 0021H. These routines are just "dummies" to illustrate the concept. The important point for you to note is that the assembler, upon encountering the DW ROUTINE1 statement, automatically inserted the address of routine 1 in this location. This can be seen in the hex op-codes listing along the left margin. Similarly, the addresses of routines 2–4 are also inserted.

---

[2]Using a special *locator* utility program, it is possible to force the operating system to locate a program at a specific address.

[3]Normally, this move instruction would load the *contents* of memory location DATA to AX. In this case, however, because DATA identifies a segment statement, the segment address is used.

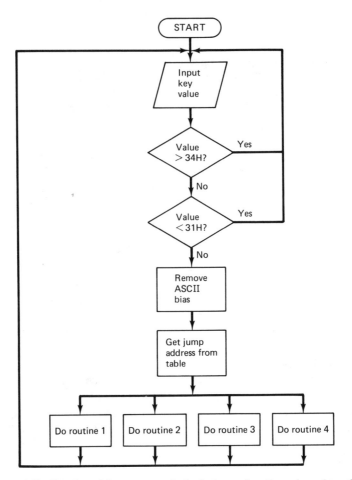

Figure 4.10 Flowchart of the process required to look up an input key value and transfer control to the appropriate routine.

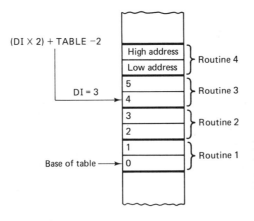

Figure 4.11 The jump table consists of eight consecutive memory bytes. The base address is stored in the variable TABLE. DI holds the offset into the table, depending on the key value (1–4).

Microprocessor Programming Techniques   Chap. 4

```
                    ;**************************************************
                    ;*                                                *
                    ;*             Creating a Jump Table              *
                    ;*                 version 1.0                    *
                    ;*                                                *
                    ;* This program reads an ASCII key value from *
                    ;* the input data port.  If the key value is  *
                    ;* between 1 and 4 control is transferred to   *
                    ;* the routine whose address is stored in      *
                    ;* the jump table.                             *
                    ;*                                                *
                    ;**************************************************

= 00D4              DPORT    EQU     0D4H        ;Data-in port
= 0007              MSK      EQU     07H         ;ASCII mask

                    ;Define a Data segment called TABLE to store
                    ;the address of the first instruction of
                    ;each routine.

0000                TABLE    SEGMENT
0000  001B R                 DW      ROUTINE1
0002  001D R                 DW      ROUTINE2
0004  001F R                 DW      ROUTINE3
0006  0021 R                 DW      ROUTINE4
0008                TABLE    ENDS

0000                CODE     SEGMENT
                             ASSUME  CS:CODE,DS:TABLE

0000  B8   ---- R   START:   MOV     AX,TABLE    ;Data segment
0003  8E D8                  MOV     DS,AX       ;value to DS.

0005  E4 D4        NEWKEY:   IN      AL,DPORT    ;Read key value
0007  3C 34                  CMP     AL,34H      ;Too big?
0009  77 FA                  JA      NEWKEY      ;Try again
000B  3C 31                  CMP     AL,31H      ;Too small?
000D  72 F6                  JB      NEWKEY      ;Try again

                    ;Got a valid key.  Now look up address
                    ;in the table.

000F  24 07                  AND     AL,MSK      ;AL holds 1-4
0011  B4 00                  MOV     AH,0        ;Offset in AX
0013  8B F8                  MOV     DI,AX       ;Offset in DI
0015  D1 E7                  SHL     DI,1        ;Times 2
0017  FF A5  ---- R          JMP     [TABLE+DI-2];Transfer control
                                                 ;to the routine.
```

Figure 4.12 Assembly language listing for the jump table program.

Sec. 4.2   Arithmetic Processing   **155**

```
                                    ;The four routines should be placed here.
                                    ;Each ends by jumping to NEWKEY.

                                    ROUTINE1:       ;The code for the first
           001B                                     ;routine is placed here.

                                         JMP        NEWKEY          ;End of routine
           001B   EB E8
                                    ROUTINE2:       ;Second routine here.
           001D                          JMP        NEWKEY
           001D   EB E6
                                    ROUTINE3:       ;Third routine here.
           001F                          JMP        NEWKEY
           001F   EB E4
                                    ROUTINE4:       ;Fourth routine here
           0021                          JMP        NEWKEY
           0021   EB E2
                                    CODE      ENDS
           0023                          END        START
```

Figure 4.12 Continued

The R after each address in the table again indicates *relative* and means that these addresses are relative to the base address of the CODE segment, which is unknown at this time.

The program begins by loading DS with the segment address of TABLE and then follows the flowchart. Control is transferred to the proper routine with the indirect jump instruction: JMP [TABLE + DI − 2]. This instruction has the word interpretation "Transfer control to the address stored in the data segment word pointed to by the offset of TABLE + DI − 2." Notice that the MOV AX,TABLE instruction uses the *segment* address of TABLE, but the jump instruction uses the *offset* address of TABLE.

Segment Alignment

After the jump table program has been assembled it must be linked as discussed in Chap. 3. This is done with the command (assuming that the program name is JUMP) **LINK JUMP.OBJ**. The result of this operation is the creation of the actual run file (JUMP.EXE) and the (optional) *link map*. This map indicates the relative addresses of the various segments in the program. For example, the map for the jump program appears as follows:

START	STOP	LENGTH	NAME
00000H	00022H	0023H	CODE
00030H	00037H	0008H	TABLE

Refer to Fig. 4.12, where you will see that the lengths correspond to the lengths of the TABLE and CODE segments. Although LINK is indicating physical addresses, the actual addresses used are still relative and will not be determined until the program is actually loaded into memory.

Studying the link map further you may notice a "gap" at the end of the CODE segment from 00023H to 0002FH. Why didn't the linker begin the TABLE segment immediately after the CODE segment ended, instead of wasting these 13 bytes? The

```
09E3:0000 B8E609    MOV     AX,09E6
09E3:0003 8ED8      MOV     DS,AX
09E3:0005 E4D4      INB     D4
09E3:0007 3C34      CMP     AL,34
09E3:0009 77FA      JA      0005
09E3:000B 3C31      CMP     AL,31
09E3:000D 72F6      JC      0005
09E3:000F 2407      AND     AL,07
09E3:0011 B400      MOV     AH,00
09E3:0013 8BF8      MOV     DI,AX
09E3:0015 D1E7      SHL     DI
09E3:0017 FFA5FEFF  JMP     [DI+FFFE]
09E3:001B EBE8      JMPS    0005
09E3:001D EBE6      JMPS    0005
09E3:001F EBE4      JMPS    0005
09E3:0021 EBE2      JMPS    0005
09E3:0023 0000      ADD     [BX+SI],AL
09E3:0025 0000      ADD     [BX+SI],AL
09E3:0027 0000      ADD     [BX+SI],AL
09E3:0029 0000      ADD     [BX+SI],AL
09E3:002B 0000      ADD     [BX+SI],AL
09E3:002D 0000      ADD     [BX+SI],AL
09E3:002F 001B      ADD     [BP+DI],BL
09E3:0031 001D      ADD     [DI],BL
09E3:0033 001F      ADD     [BX],BL
09E3:0035 0021      ADD     [BX+DI],AH
09E3:0037 0008      ADD     [BX+SI],CL
>
```

```
09E3:0000 B8E509    MOV     AX,09E5
09E3:0003 8ED8      MOV     DS,AX
09E3:0005 E4D4      INB     D4
09E3:0007 3C34      CMP     AL,34
09E3:0009 77FA      JA      0005
09E3:000B 3C31      CMP     AL,31
09E3:000D 72F6      JC      0005
09E3:000F 2407      AND     AL,07
09E3:0011 B400      MOV     AH,00
09E3:0013 8BF8      MOV     DI,AX
09E3:0015 D1E7      SHL     DI
09E3:0017 FFA50200  JMP     [DI+0002]
09E3:001B EBE8      JMPS    0005
09E3:001D EBE6      JMPS    0005
09E3:001F EBE4      JMPS    0005
09E3:0021 EBE2      JMPS    0005
09E3:0023 001B      ADD     [BP+DI],BL
09E3:0025 001D      ADD     [DI],BL
09E3:0027 001F      ADD     [BX],BL
09E3:0029 0021      ADD     [BX+DI],AH
09E3:002B 001C      ADD     [SI],BL
>
```

Figure 4.13 Unassembled program listing with (a) paragraph alignment of the jump table, and (b) word alignment of the jump table.

reason is found in the SEGMENT statement—**TABLE SEGMENT**. Unless we include a *segment alignment type*, the linker assumes that the named segment is to be aligned on the next *paragraph* boundary. For the jump table program, the CODE segment ended at address 00022H and thus the linker began the TABLE segment at the next paragraph address, 00030H.

Figure 4.13(a) shows the result of using DEBUG to unassemble the jump program after it has been loaded into memory (forcing the physical addresses to be resolved). Along the left margin you will see that the program is loaded beginning at address

09E3:0000. That is, CS was loaded with 09E3. The 13-byte gap was filled in with 0's (which unassembled to ADD [BX + SI],AL). The jump table itself begins at address 09E3:0030H.

The physical address corresponding to the last instruction in the CODE segment is 09E30H + 0022H = 09E52H. Because the TABLE segment must be loaded at the next available *paragraph* address, it begins at physical address 09E30 + 0030H = 09E60H, which is indeed the next paragraph address following 09E52H.

Now turn your attention to the first instruction in the program listing shown in Fig. 4.13(a). This is the instruction MOV AX,TABLE. Notice that the segment address of TABLE has been resolved to 09E6 (which checks with the physical address of the TABLE segment calculated). The next instruction copies this value into the data segment register.

The other unresolved address in Fig. 4.12 was that of the indirect jump. In this case we are concerned with the *offset* address of the table, which is 0000 because the segment is loaded at a paragraph boundary. The indirect jump address is thus 0000 + DI − 2 = DI + FFFEH. This is confirmed in the unassembled program listing in Fig. 4.13(a).

The segment alignment is defined in the SEGMENT statement. The complete form of this statement is

name   SEGMENT   *align-type*   *combine-type*   *class name*

The align type can be specified as byte, word, or paragraph. The default is paragraph. Figure 4.13(b) shows the result of changing the jump table segment definition to

TABLE   SEGMENT   WORD

The linker now chooses the first even address (word boundary) following the last CODE segment instruction and begins the jump table there. In this case it is at offset address 0024H. Notice that only the single byte at 0023H is now wasted.

The physical address of the table thus begins at address 09E30 + 0024H = 09E54H. But is this correct? Doesn't the DS register have to be loaded with an address whose last hex digit is 0 (i.e., an address divisible by 16)? The answer to this question can be seen in the first line of Fig. 4.13(b). The *segment* address for TABLE is now 09E5. However, the *offset* address is 0004 (09E50 + 0004 = 09E54H).

This may seem strange at first, but there is no reason that the table must begin at offset address 0 in its segment. When the program is linked and loaded, the addresses will be resolved as before—in this case by inserting an offset of 0004H and a segment address of 09E3 for the label TABLE.

This all seems very complicated, but it is instructive to learn how the linker aligns the segments of a multiple-segment program. It is also important when memory usage must be kept to a minimum. For that matter it might seem best to align all segments on byte boundaries; then there will be no wasted bytes. For the 8088 this would be acceptable; however, for the 8086 an extra bus cycle (four clock states) is required to access a word beginning at an odd address. For this reason, word-oriented data segments (including the stack segment) should be word aligned.

4.2.1. If DX:AX = 00C0H and BX = 0100H, determine the contents of DX:AX after the instruction DIV BX is executed.

4.2.2. What change is required to the program in Fig. 4.9 if V_{FS} = 10.0 V?

4.2.3. The ASSUME statement loads the CS and DS registers when the program is loaded and run. (True/False)

4.2.4. In Fig. 4.9 the instruction MOV AX,DATA moves the _____ address of DATA to AX.

4.2.5. In Fig. 4.12 ROUTINE3 is located at address 001FH in the TABLE segment. (True/False)

4.2.6. What is the (relative) base address of the jump table in Fig. 4.12 if the table segment is defined with the following statement?

TABLE   SEGMENT   WORD

4.2.7. What is the advantage of using word alignment versus paragraph alignment for a word-oriented data table?

4.3 TIME DELAY LOOPS

Nearly all computer programs involve *loops*. These are groups of instructions that are to be executed repeatedly. Figure 4.14 flowcharts a typical loop-controlled program. The instructions in the "task box" are repeated until the loop counter has been reduced to 0.

The 8086 has three instructions specifically designed for implementing loops. These are LOOP, LOOPNE, and LOOPE and were discussed in Table 2.16. In all cases the

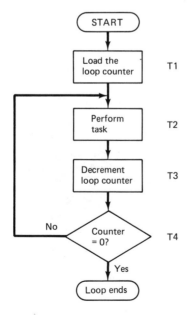

Figure 4.14 Flowchart of a typical program loop. T1–T4 refer to the number of processor T states required to accomplish the function in that box.

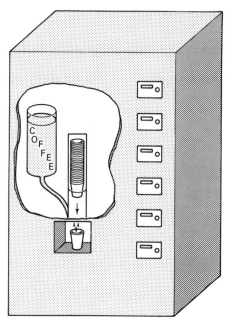

Figure 4.15 Microprocessor-controlled coffee vending machine.

CX register must be dedicated to holding the loop count. Note that the LOOPNE and LOOPE instructions allow the loop counter and ZF to both be tested.

As an alternative to using the loop instructions, any of the CPU general registers can be used as a loop counter. The sequence

```
AGAIN:    .

          .

          .

          DEC  r
          JNZ  AGAIN
```

will repeat the loop until register r has been counted down to zero.

Sometimes a group of instructions are to be repeated until a certain condition occurs. This was the case in Fig. 4.6, in which the status bits were tested until the tank was full (or the temperature OK, or the tank empty). This type of looping is given the special name *polling* and is one way of synchronizing the microprocessor to a slow peripheral. Polling is covered in detail in Chap. 8.

Another loop application is simply to "waste time." Consider the microprocessor-controlled vending machine shown in Fig. 4.15. This particular machine dispenses coffee by releasing a cup from a dispenser, allowing it to fall down a chute to a window opening. The cup is then filled from the coffee reservoir located above.

The control program for this coffee machine must release a cup, wait for it to fall down the chute, turn on the coffee, wait for the cup to fill, and then turn off the coffee. Because the microprocessor can perform each activity so quickly, it must be told to *idle* for short periods, giving the other tasks time to complete.

MOV Operands	Clocks	Transfers	Bytes	MOV Coding Example
memory, accumulator	10(9)	1	3	MOV ARRAY AL
accumulator, memory	10(8)	1	3	MOV AX,TEMP_RESULT
register, register	2(2)	-	2	MOV AX, CX
register, memory	8(12)+EA	1	2-4	MOV BP, STACK_TOP
memory, register	9(9)+EA	1	2-4	MOV COUNT [DI],CX
register, immediate	4(3-4)	-	2-3	MOV CL,2
memory, immediate	10(12-13)+EA	1	3-6	MOV MASK[BX][SI],2CH
seg-reg, reg16	2(2)	-	2	MOV ES, CX
seg-reg, mem16	8(9)+EA	1	2-4	MOV DS,SEGMENT_BASE
reg16, seg-reg	2(2)	-	2	MOV BP, SS
memory, seg-reg	9(11)+EA	1	2-4	MOV[BX],SEG_SAVE,CS

Figure 4.16 T states for the various forms of the MOV instruction. (Courtesy of Intel Corporation.)

Time delays can be generated in hardware (via one-shots and programmable timers) or with software. Referring to Fig. 4.14, if the loop counter is loaded with a very large number, say 50,000, the time required to execute all the instructions in the loop can become significant. In effect we are instructing the processor to count backward from 50,000 to 0! Not a very efficient use of the microprocessor but a simple way of generating a time delay.

In this section we see how the execution time of a loop can be predicted and use this information to synthesize a 1-kHz square wave on one bit of an output port.

Calculating the Execution Time of a Loop

Every instruction requires a specific number of clock cycles or T states. This number varies with the complexity of the instruction (a NOP requires only 3 T states, but the AAM instruction requires 83 T states). It also depends on the addressing mode. Figure 4.16 lists the number of clock cycles required for the various forms of the MOV instruction. The numbers enclosed within parentheses represent 80186 T states and are usually (much) less than those for the 8086.[4]

> **Example 4.3**
>
> Calculate the time required to execute the instruction MOV AX,BX if the system clock frequency is 5 MHz.
>
> **Solution** According to Fig. 4.16, 2 T states are required or $2 \times \dfrac{1}{5 \text{ MHz}} = 2 \times 200$ ns = 400 ns.

Instructions that must calculate an effective address require an additional amount of time to execute. This is shown in Table 4.1 for the various addressing modes. The instruction MOV CX,[BX+SI+3], for example, will require $8 + 11 = 19$ T states to execute (8 for the instruction, 11 for the EA calculation).

[4]For example, AAM requires only 19 T states with the 80186.

TABLE 4.1 EFFECTIVE ADDRESS CALCULATION TIME (8086,88 ONLY)

	EA components	Clocks[a]
Displacement only		6
Base or index only	(BX,BP,SI,DI)	5
Displacement + base or index	(BX,BP,SI,DI)	9
Base + index	BP + DI, BX + SI	7
	BP + SI, BX + DI	8
Displacement + base + index	BP + DI + DISP	11
	BX + SI + DISP	
	BP + SI + DISP	12
	BX + DI + DISP	

[a]Add 2 clocks for segment override.

All the T states listed in Fig. 4.16 assume that the instruction to be executed is already in the queue. If this is not true, an additional four T states will have to be added to account for the instruction fetch time (this points out another advantage of the prefetch queue—faster instruction execution times). It is also possible that the BIU will have just begun an instruction fetch when the EU requires a memory operand. An additional four T states will have to be added to account for the instruction fetch time.

The 8088 microprocessor requires two bus cycles to access memory words. This means that four additional T states will have to be added to the 8086 execution times for each 8088 16-bit transfer. The instruction MOV CX,[BX + SI + 3] will thus require 23 T states with an 8088 processor.

Finally, there is a bus cycle penalty when accessing words beginning at an odd address, and 4 T states must be added to such instructions. The 8088 pays this penalty with each memory word access.

As you can see, predicting the *exact* execution time of an 8086/88 program can become quite involved. In fact, the program may have different execution times depending on where it (and its data) are loaded in memory. Intel states that using the numbers

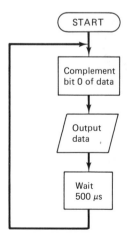

Figure 4.17 Flowchart of a program to generate a 1-kHz square-wave signal.

supplied with each instruction (like those in Fig. 4.16) and adding the EA calculation time normally yields a number within 5 to 10% of the actual execution time. However, in a worst case, the actual time could be much longer than calculated.

If the precise time period is required, a logic analyzer can be used to time out the instructions exactly. However, for many applications, like the coffee machine, a delay of 0.45 s or 1.45 s will not matter (now if someone would only add a sensor that detects that all the cups are gone!).

Example 4.4

Determine the DELAY parameter to be used in the delay loop that follows to produce a 500-μs time delay. Assume a 5-MHz system clock. T states for each instruction are shown along the right margin.

```
              MOV   CX,DELAY    [4]
       COUNT: LOOP  COUNT       [17/5]

            ;Program continues
```

Solution The LOOP instruction requires 17 T states if the jump is taken but only 5 T states if it is not. Thus the total time delay can be calculated as

$$t = [4 + (17 \times DELAY) - 12] \times 200 \text{ ns}$$
$$= -1.6 \text{ μs} + 3.4 \text{ μs} \times DELAY$$

Solving for $t = 500$ μs yields DELAY = 147.

Generating a 1-kHz Square Wave

Figure 4.17 flowcharts the process required to implement a square-wave generator in software using one bit of an 8086 output port. If this bit is held in each state for 500 μs, the period becomes 1 ms and a 1-kHz square wave is realized.

Figure 4.18 shows the program listing. It uses the delay loop calculated in Ex. 4.4. Accounting for the extra instructions, the delay parameter is 146 instead of 147.

Because a frequency of 1 kHz is in the audio range, the output bit can be used to drive a loudspeaker as shown in Fig. 4.19. By using different delay parameters, different tones can be generated. In fact, this is the basis for many of the simpler computer music programs.

Self-Review 4.3 (answers on page 191)

4.3.1. The 8086/88 has two types of instructions useful when testing for the end of a program loop. They are the _____ jump instructions and the _____ instructions.

4.3.2. The process of monitoring an external status bit and repeating the loop if not ready is called _____.

4.3.3. How many T states are required to execute the instruction MOV BYTE PTR[BX],12H? Assume that the instruction is in the queue of an 8086 microprocessor.

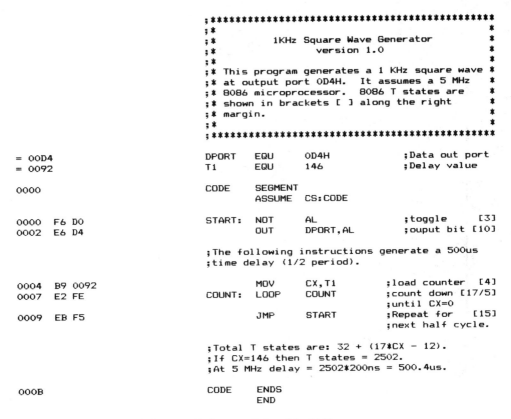

```
                    ;************************************************
                    ;*                                             *
                    ;*            1KHz Square Wave Generator        *
                    ;*                  version 1.0                 *
                    ;*                                             *
                    ;* This program generates a 1 KHz square wave *
                    ;* at output port 0D4H.  It assumes a 5 MHz    *
                    ;* 8086 microprocessor.  8086 T states are     *
                    ;* shown in brackets [ ] along the right       *
                    ;* margin.                                     *
                    ;*                                             *
                    ;************************************************

= 00D4              DPORT     EQU     0D4H            ;Data out port
= 0092              T1        EQU     146             ;Delay value

0000                CODE      SEGMENT
                              ASSUME  CS:CODE

0000  F6 D0         START:    NOT     AL              ;toggle        [3]
0002  E6 D4                   OUT     DPORT,AL        ;ouput bit [10]

                    ;The following instructions generate a 500us
                    ;time delay (1/2 period).

0004  B9 0092                 MOV     CX,T1           ;load counter  [4]
0007  E2 FE         COUNT:    LOOP    COUNT           ;count down [17/5]
                                                      ;until CX=0
0009  EB F5                   JMP     START           ;Repeat for    [15]
                                                      ;next half cycle.

                    ;Total T states are: 32 + (17*CX - 12).
                    ;If CX=146 then T states = 2502.
                    ;At 5 MHz delay = 2502*200ns = 500.4us.

000B                CODE      ENDS
                              END
```

Figure 4.18 Assembly language listing of the 1-kHz square-wave program.

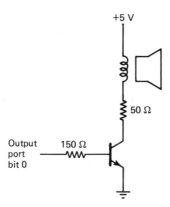

+5 V

50 Ω

Output
port
bit 0

150 Ω

Figure 4.19 Driving a loudspeaker
with one bit of an output port.

4.3.4. The execution time for the instruction MOV AX,[TEMP] is increased by 4 T states when run on an 8088 microprocessor versus an 8086 processor. (True/False)

4.3.5. The 8086/88 T state specifications do not include the fetch cycle time. Why is this?

4.3.6. What changes are needed to the program in Fig. 4.17 to generate a 5-kHz square wave?

4.4 PROCEDURES

As the programs you write become more complex you will probably find that certain instruction sequences are required several times in the same program. For example, if we were writing the coffee machine control program, we would need code to wait for the cups to drop, and also code to wait for the cup to be filled. Rather than write this time-delay routine twice, we can place it in a *procedure* (or subroutine) and use a CALL instruction to transfer control temporarily to this routine. When the procedure executes a RETurn instruction, control will be transferred back to the main program.

The CALL instruction acts like a jump but pushes IP (and CS for a far call) onto the stack. This allows the RET instruction to recover the address in the main program where it left off. The cardinal rule when using procedures is that *every call must have a return* (far calls require far returns, near calls require near returns).

Procedures also facilitate the practice of *modular programming*. This is a programming technique in which a large problem is broken into several small modules (or procedures). The main program then consists of several procedure calls. For example, the process controller program shown in Fig. 4.6 could be written in modular form as

```
START:  CALL  FILL_TANK
        CALL  HEAT_TANK
        CALL  EMPTY_TANK
        JMP   START
```

Modular programming allows many people to work on one large project by assigning separate modules to each person.

In this section we see how to write a procedure, pass data to it, and finally document it. In Sec. 4.6 we show how several modules or procedures can be linked into one large program or added to a library.

Passing Parameters to a Procedure

In many cases the calling program will supply the procedure with one or more *parameters*. In the coffee machine example we might want to supply a delay parameter. In this way the time delay for the cups to drop can be different from the delay required to fill the cups.

There are several ways of passing parameters to a procedure. One way is to use one of the CPU registers: for example,

```
MOV   CX,T1
CALL  DELAY
```

where T1 is the delay parameter. Another technique is to use a memory location.

```
MOV   TEMP,T1
CALL  DELAY
```

A variation of this technique is to pass the *address* of the memory variable: for example,

```
MOV   SI,POINTER
CALL  DELAY
```

The procedure extracts the delay parameter with an instruction such as MOV CX,[SI]. This technique has the additional advantage of allowing an entire *table* of values to be passed to the procedure.

All these techniques have a built-in disadvantage in that a register or memory location must be dedicated to holding the parameter when the procedure is called. When one procedure calls another (*nested* procedures), this can become confusing. It also puts a burden on you to remember in which register this particular procedure expects its data to be.

An alternative is to pass the parameter on the *stack*: for example,

```
MOV   DX,T1
PUSH  DX
CALL  DELAY
```

The procedure can pop its parameters off the stack without requiring any dedicated CPU registers or memory locations.

Figure 4.20 shows the flowchart for a program called "BEEP." It produces a short (~0.25 s) beep in a loudspeaker connected to one bit of an output port. This might be used to alert an operator that an error has occurred.

BEEP is basically the 1-kHz square-wave generator program but restricted to 500 one-half cycles. The delay loop is written as a procedure with the delay parameter passed on the stack. The program is shown in Fig. 4.21.

Notice that the program consists of two segments. One is STACK, which is word aligned and consists of 64 undefined words (a larger stack area than is actually required for this program). The word STACK on the end of the SEGMENT statement identifies this segment as stack-combinable (the combine-type option of the SEGMENT statement is explained in Sec. 4.6). The other segment is called CODE and holds the main program and the delay procedure.

The program begins with the label START and loads SS with the segment address of STACK. The statement

TOP   LABEL   WORD

assigns the label TOP to the topmost (highest addressed) word in the stack segment. This allows the instruction LEA SP,TOP to load the stack pointer register with the (effective) address of the stack top. You might notice the segment override automatically generated by the assembler for this instruction (LEA normally references the data segment, but TOP has previously been defined in the stack segment).

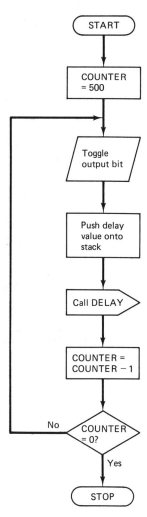

Figure 4.20 Flowchart for the "beep" program. A near procedure called DELAY is used and the delay parameter is passed on the stack.

The main program follows the flowchart, toggling the output port bit and then pushing the delay parameter (T1) onto the stack. A near call is then made to DELAY (DELAY is in the same segment as the main program).

The DELAY procedure includes several comment lines documenting its function. This includes information on input and output parameters, additional calls it might make, and the registers it changes. In this case DELAY expects a 16-bit delay value to be passed on the stack and does not call any other procedures; and because the contents of the CPU registers are not altered, it is considered *transparent*. The time-delay parameter required is slightly different from the program in Fig. 4.18 because of the additional PUSH and POP instructions.

Figure 4.22 shows how the delay parameter (T1) is passed on the stack. Initially, register SP is pointing at memory location 0080H in the stack segment. The main program pushes DX (T1) onto the stack and then performs a near call to DELAY. This decrements SP to 007CH. DELAY saves all registers that it will be using (in order to make itself

```
                                     TITLE    Beep      V1.0
                              ;**********************************************
                              ;* This program produces a 0.25s beep in a    *
                              ;* loudspeaker connected to bit 0 of output    *
                              ;* port 0D4H.                                  *
                              ;**********************************************
= 00D4                        DPORT    EQU      0D4H      ;Output port
= 008E                        T1       EQU      142       ;500us delay value
= 01F4                        CYCLES   EQU      500       ;Number of cycles

                              ;**********************************************
                              ;*          Set up a stack segment            *
                              ;**********************************************
0000                          STACK    SEGMENT WORD STACK
0000     40 [                          DW       64 DUP (?)
              ????
                    ]

0080                          TOP      LABEL    WORD
0080                          STACK    ENDS

                              ;**********************************************
                              ;*   Define a code segment called CODE        *
                              ;**********************************************
0000                          CODE     SEGMENT
                                       ASSUME   CS:CODE,SS:STACK

0000     B8   ---- R          START:   MOV      AX,STACK  ;Get stack segment
0003     8E D0                         MOV      SS,AX     ;to SS.
0005     36: 8D 26 0080 R              LEA      SP,TOP    ;Point to stack top

000A     B9 01F4                       MOV      CX,CYCLES ;Cycle counter
000D     F6 D0                AGAIN:   NOT      AL        ;Toggle
000F     E6 D4                         OUT      DPORT,AL  ;output bit.
0011     BA 008E                       MOV      DX,T1     ;Put delay value
0014     52                            PUSH     DX        ;on stack.
0015     E8 001B R                     CALL     DELAY     ;Wait 1/2 cycle
0018     E2 F3                         LOOP     AGAIN     ;Do CX times
001A     F4                            HLT

                              ;**********************************************
                              ;*  The main program ends here.  The delay    *
                              ;*  procedure follows.                         *
                              ;**********************************************
```

Figure 4.21   Assembly language listing of the BEEP program.

```
                              ;Function:   Time delay
                              ;Inputs:     16 bit delay value passed on
                              ;            stack.
                              ;            T = [3.4us * T1] + 17us
                              ;Outputs:    None
                              ;Calls:      Nothing
                              ;Destroys:   Nothing

001B                          DELAY    PROC    NEAR
001B   51                              PUSH    CX          ;Save all registers
001C   9C                              PUSHF               ;and the flags.
001D   55                              PUSH    BP
001E   8B EC                           MOV     BP,SP       ;Recover delay value
0020   8B 4E 08                        MOV     CX,[BP+8]   ;from stack.
0023   E2 FE               COUNT:      LOOP    COUNT       ;Delay loop
0025   5D                              POP     BP          ;Restore all
0026   9D                              POPF                ;registers.
0027   59                              POP     CX
0028   C2 0002                         RET     2           ;Discard delay param
002B                          DELAY    ENDP

                              ;**************************************************
                              ;*  The delay procedure ends here                *
                              ;**************************************************

002B                          CODE     ENDS                ;CODE segment ends
                                       END     START       ;End of program
```

Figure 4.21 Continued

transparent) by pushing CX, the flags, and BP onto the stack. The stack pointer decrements to 0076H.

The DELAY procedure now prepares to retrieve the delay parameter by copying SP into BP. The instruction MOV CX,[BP + 8] uses SS for its segment register and thus copies T1 into CX. The delay loop is then executed, after which the BP, flags, and CX

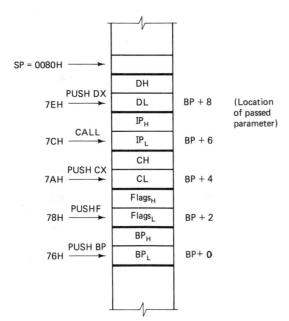

Figure 4.22 Once DELAY is called and the CX, BP, and flag registers saved, the delay parameter is located on the stack at SP + 8.

registers are restored. At this point register SP is pointing at location 007CH, the location of the return address. An RET 2 instruction pops this word into IP (SP = 007EH) and adds 2 to SP. The result is to remove T1 from the stack and restore SP to its original value (0080H) before the parameter was passed.

Using the stack to pass parameters is convenient, as no CPU registers or memory locations are required. However, it does require extra instructions to push the data onto the stack and pop it back off. This will slow the response time of the procedure. When several parameters must be passed, passing a memory pointer is usually more efficient.

Avoiding Forward Reference Errors

When the assembler is called on to assemble a program, it does so in two passes. On the first pass any instructions that reference symbols that have not yet been defined generate errors ('undefined symbol') that it assumes will be resolved on the second pass, when these symbols are known. This is known as a *forward reference error*—there is a reference to an address or symbol forward of the present location counter.

Forward reference errors are normally of no concern—provided that they are resolved on the second pass! However, when multiple segments are used within the same program, a problem can occur. If the assembler encounters an undefined symbolic address on the first pass, it *assumes* that that address can be reached within the same segment. That is, it assumes a *near* location. However, if during the second pass, the symbol is subsequently defined in a new segment (i.e., a *far* location), an error message will be issued.

A similar problem can occur with data references. The assembler assumes that forward-referenced data can be found in the data segment, which may not always be true. The following code will produce a *phase error*:

```
CODE    SEGMENT
        ASSUME CS:CODE
        MOV    AX,COUNT
COUNT   DW     00
         .
         .
         .
CODE    ENDS
```

On the first pass two bytes are reserved for the address of *count*, which is assumed to be in the data segment. However, on the second pass, when COUNT is known to be in the CODE segment, a segment override must be generated requiring an additional byte.

Phase errors occur when the number of bytes allocated on the first pass do not agree with those required on the second pass. When the CALL DELAY instruction in Fig. 4.21 is assembled on the first pass, two bytes are allocated for the address of the DELAY procedure. In this case, because DELAY is located in the same segment as the CALL, there is no problem (i.e., the assembler "guessed" correctly). However, if the DELAY procedure had been located in a different segment, a far call would have been needed

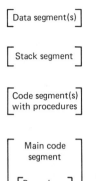

Figure 4.23 Recommended assembly language program structure for the 8086 and 8088 microprocessors. This organization will prevent forward reference errors.

and four bytes would have to have been allocated for the address. The result would have been an error message following the CALL instruction.

How can you guard against forward reference errors? The best way is to define all symbols *before* they are referenced by an instruction. In the DELAY example, place the DELAY procedure at the top of the listing so that its address will be known before the CALL instruction is assembled. The alternative is to help the assembler by using the FAR operator (CALL FAR DELAY). However, this shifts the burden to you to make sure that all symbols are properly identified.

Figure 4.23 shows the recommended form for an 8086/88 assembly language program. After the data and stack segments are defined, any procedures in different code segments are listed. Finally, the main code segment is given with all procedures preceding the main program itself. In this way all symbols will be known before the main program is assembled.

Self-Review 4.4 (answers on page 191)

4.4.1 Why is it advantageous to pass parameters to a procedure?

4.4.2. State four different ways of passing parameters to a procedure.

4.4.3. When is a procedure *transparent*?

4.4.4. When the assembler encounters a CALL instruction it normally generates the code for a _____ CALL.

4.4.5. The instructions

```
CODE    SEGMENT
        ASSUME  CS:CODE
        MOV   AX,CS:COUNT
COUNT   DW    0
CODE    ENDS
```

will assemble without forward reference errors.   (True/False)

4.5 DATA TABLES

In this chapter we have seen examples of both logical and arithmetic processing of input data. One other technique is also common. This is to use the input data as an *index* into a table. For example, the analog-to-digital conversion program in Fig. 4.9 could be replaced by a program that stores all 256 possible voltage values in a table. The binary input from the ADC can then be used to point to the appropriate value in the table to be output to the display.

The main advantage of this technique is much faster processing speed. The instruction MUL BL used in the ADC program requires 77 T states and the DIV BX instruction requires 162 T states. However, the instructions XLAT and LODSB (which can be used to extract data from a table) require only 11 and 12 T states, respectively.

In this section we see how to set up and use a data table of sequential and non-sequential items.

Looking Up Sequential Data Items

When performing a lookup of sequential data items a pointer can be established at the base of the table. Incrementing this pointer will step through the table item by item. This will be the case in this first example, in which a seven-segment display is to be driven without benefit of an external hardware decoder.

Figure 4.24 shows the hardware interface. Each segment is driven by one bit of an output port. The problem is to output codes to the display such that it appears to count slowly from 0 through 9 and A through F.

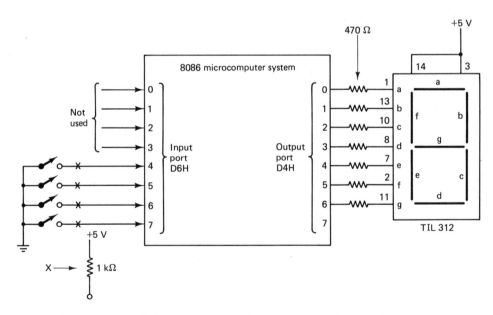

Figure 4.24 Interfacing a (common-anode) seven-segment display to an 8-bit microcomputer output port. The input port is not used in this example.

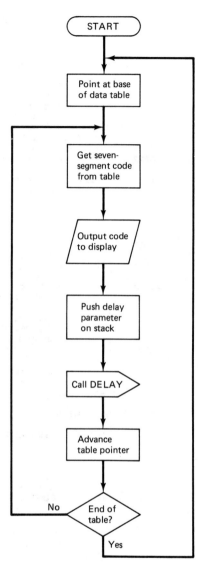

Figure 4.25 Seven-segment counter program flowchart.

A flowchart of the control program is provided in Fig. 4.25. The codes for the 16 digits are assumed to be stored in a data table and a pointer register (SI) is used to step through this table, fetching each byte to be output. The LODSB instruction is effective in this problem because it automatically increments SI (if DF = 0) and puts the data in AL ready for output.

The assembly language program is provided in Fig. 4.26. Four segments are used, labeled STACK, SEVEN, PROCED, and CODE. STACK consists of 10 uninitialized words used for storing the delay procedure return address and miscellaneous registers.

The segment named SEVEN holds the seven-segment codes for the 16 digits. For example, 40H (01000000B) will cause all but segment g to light up, thus displaying a 0.

                                        TITLE   Seven Segment Counter

                              ;***
                              ;*   This program will cause the hexadecimal *
                              ;*   digits 0 through F to appear in sequence *
                              ;*   in a seven-segment display connected to   *
                              ;*   output port 0D4H.   It illustrates   *
                              ;*   the use of a data table to store the   *
                              ;*   segment codes.   *
                              ;***

0000   STACK   SEGMENT WORD STACK
0000   0A [DW   10 DUP (?)
               ????
                        ]

0014   TOP   LABEL   WORD
0014   STACK   ENDS

0000   SEVEN   SEGMENT WORD

                              ;This (data) segment is used to store the
                              ;codes for each of the 16 digits.

0000 40 79 24 30 19   CODES   DB   40H,79H,24H,30H,19H
0005 12 02 78 00 18 08   DB   12H,02H,78H,0,18H,08H
000B 03 46 21 06 0E   DB   03H,46H,21H,06H,0EH
0010   SEVEN   ENDS

                              ;This is a delay procedure called by the
                              ;main program below. Note that it is in
                              ;its own segment.

0000   PROCED   SEGMENT BYTE   ;Same code as
0000   DELAY   PROC   FAR   ;Fig. 4.21 except
                                       ASSUME CS:PROCED   ;DELAY must be a
0000 51   PUSH   CX   ;FAR procedure.
0001 9C   PUSHF
0002 55   PUSH   BP
0003 8B EC   MOV   BP,SP
0005 8B 4E 0A   MOV   CX,[BP+10]
0008 E2 FE   COUNT: LOOP   COUNT
000A 5D   POP   BP
000B 9D   POPF
000C 59   POP   CX
000D CA 0002   RET   2   ;FAR return
0010   DELAY   ENDP
0010   PROCED   ENDS

Figure 4.26 Assembly language listing for the seven-segment counter program.

```
0000                                    CODE      SEGMENT BYTE
                                        ASSUME    CS:CODE,DS:SEVEN,SS:STACK

                                        ;The main program begins here.
= 00D4                                  DPORT     EQU       0D4H        ;Data output port
= 0000                                  T1        EQU       0           ;0.2s delay parameter

0000    B8    ---- R                    START:    MOV       AX,STACK    ;Begin by loading the
0003    8E  D0                                    MOV       SS,AX       ;SS and DS registers
0005    B8    ---- R                              MOV       AX,SEVEN    ;and point SP at the
0008    8E  D8                                    MOV       DS,AX       ;top of the stack.
000A    36: 8D 26 0014 R                          LEA       SP,TOP

000F    8D 36 0000 R                    FOREVR:   LEA       SI,CODES    ;Get offset of table
0013    FC                                        CLD                   ;Auto increment of SI
0014    BB 0000                                   MOV       BX,T1       ;Get delay parameter
0017    B9 0010                                   MOV       CX,16       ;16 digits to output

001A    AC                              NUDIGT:   LODSB                 ;Fetch byte to AL
001B    E6 D4                                     OUT       DPORT,AL    ;Display digit
001D    53                                        PUSH      BX          ;Pass delay parameter
001E    9A 0000 ---- R                            CALL      DELAY       ;Wait .2s
0023    53                                        PUSH      BX
0024    9A 0000 ---- R                            CALL      DELAY       ;Another .2s
0029    E2 EF                                     LOOP      NUDIGT      ;Next digit

002B    EB E2                                     JMP       FOREVR      ;Repeat indefinately
002D                                    CODE      ENDS
                                        END       START
```

Figure 4.26 Continued

The segment named PROCED is used to hold the delay procedure, which by now we are quite familiar with. Note that because this procedure is in a different segment from the main program, it must be declared a *far procedure*. This means that the delay parameter (passed by the main program) is located 10 bytes relative to the base of the stack (instead of eight). To produce the maximum delay, T1 is equated to 0 (65,536 loops) in the main program.

Finally, the CODE segment contains the main program. It begins by loading SS and DS with the proper segment addresses and then points SP to the top of the stack. Next, LEA SI,CODES is used to get the *offset* address of the base of the table. A loop is then entered in which the codes are fetched from the table with the LODSB instruction and output to the display. The delay procedure is called twice to produce a 0.4-s delay. The LOOP NUDIGT instruction tests to see if all 16 digits have been output, and if not, the loop is repeated.

Because there are so many segments, the link map for this program is rather interesting and is shown in Fig. 4.27. Note that the PROCED segment follows immediately after the CODE segment because it is defined to be *byte combinable*. The SEVEN segment and STACK segment are *word combinable* and thus begin on word boundaries.

Looking Up Nonsequential Data Items

In most cases looking up data in a table involves a random selection of a particular data item dependent on some input index. For example, the input data may request that item 67 be extracted from the table. The XLAT instruction—replace AL with the contents of memory pointed to by BX + AL—is very useful in this case. For example, by pointing

Sec. 4.5   Data Tables

```
Start   Stop    Length  Name            Class
00000H  0002CH  002DH   CODE
0002DH  0003CH  0010H   PROCED
0003EH  0004DH  0010H   SEVEN
00050H  00063H  0014H   STACK

Program entry point at 0000:0000

B:
```

Figure 4.27 Link map for the seven-segment counter program.

BX to the base of the table and moving 67 (the table index) to AL, XLAT will retrieve the desired item.

Figure 4.28 flowcharts a table-lookup problem based on this technique. In this case the program is to input a 4-bit binary number, look up the seven-segment code corresponding to this number, and output the result to a nondecoded display. The hardware is the circuit shown in Fig. 4.24 but now includes the input port.

Figure 4.29 is the assembly language listing of the program. Again a data segment called SEVEN is used to store the seven-segment codes. The program itself is stored in a segment called CODE. It begins by loading DS with the segment address of SEVEN and then points BX at the base of the table.

The index into the table is formed by inputting the value set on the four switches wired to the input port. To ensure that bits 0–3 are zero, the instruction AND AL,0F0H masks these bits. The number in AL now ranges from 00 to F0. Unfortunately, the 4

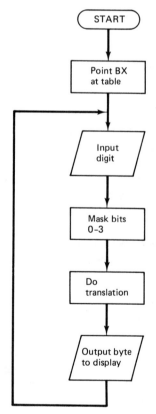

Figure 4.28 Flowchart for a table-lookup program.

```
                                TITLE   Table Lookup
          ;***********************************************
          ;  This program reads the four bit binary    *
          ;* number input from port 0D6H bits 4-7.  It  *
          ;* looks up the seven segment code for this   *
          ;* number and outputs the pattern to a non    *
          ;* decoded seven segment display wired to     *
          ;* output port 0D4H.                          *
          ;***********************************************

          ;These are the codes for the digits 0-F

0000                          SEVEN     SEGMENT WORD
0000  40 79 24 30 19 12       CODES     DB      40H,79H,24H,30H,19H,12H
0006  02 78 00 18 08 03                 DB      02H,78H,0,18H,08H,03H
000C  46 21 06 0E                       DB      46H,21H,06H,0EH
0010                          SEVEN     ENDS

0000                          CODE      SEGMENT

= 00D6                        IPORT     EQU     0D6H
= 00D4                        DPORT     EQU     0D4H

                                        ASSUME  CS:CODE,DS:SEVEN

0000  B8    ---- R            START:    MOV     AX,SEVEN     ;Load DS with
0003  8E D8                             MOV     DS,AX        ;segment address.
0005  8D 1E 0000 R                      LEA     BX,CODES     ;Point BX at table
0009  B1 04                             MOV     CL,4         ;Need four rotates

000B  E4 D6                   AGAIN:    IN      AL,IPORT     ;Get digit
000D  24 F0                             AND     AL,0F0H      ;Mask other bits
000F  D2 C0                             ROL     AL,CL        ;Prepare for XLAT
0011  D7                                XLAT                 ;Lookup code
0012  E6 D4                             OUT     DPORT,AL     ;Display digit
0014  EB F5                             JMP     AGAIN        ;Repeat
0016                          CODE      ENDS
                                        END     START
```

Figure 4.29   Table-lookup program listing.

bits are being input in the "wrong" position for the XLAT instruction. This is fixed by performing four rotate lefts. Now the translate instruction can be executed and the data output to the display. The program then repeats indefinitely.

The XLAT instruction has one limitation—the table length cannot exceed 256 bytes. However, the instruction MOV AX,[BX + SI] will retrieve the item indexed by SI in a table with base address in BX. Because SI is a 16-bit number, the table length can be up to 65,536 bytes in length.

SELF-REVIEW 4.5 *(answers on page 191)*

4.5.1. What are the advantages to using a data lookup table? Are there any disadvantages?

4.5.2. When using the LODSB instruction to extract data from a table the instruction _____ must first be given to initialize register SI.

4.5.3. To look up a particular item in a 256-byte table, use register _____ as the index, register _____ to point to the base of the table, and give the instruction _____.

4.6 MODULAR PROGRAMMING

As we have seen in this chapter, 8086 assembly language programs, even with only a few segments and procedures, can easily become long and complex. For this reason, the *top-down* approach to program design, in which the problem is broken into several smaller and easier-to-conceptualize modules, is often chosen.

With this technique, each program module is written, tested, and debugged and then linked together to form the main program. Because short, single-function modules are easier to understand, they are also easier to write, test, and debug. Routines that are frequently used can be stored in a "library" to avoid "reinventing the wheel" each time that program is needed.

The principal problem with the modular programming technique is the reference that one module must make to symbols and addresses in another module. For example, the instruction CALL DELAY will yield the error message "undefined symbol" if the symbol DELAY cannot be located in the present module.

In this section we study an example of modular programming based on the "BEEP" program in Sec. 4.4. It illustrates how symbols can be declared *public*, *private*, or *external* and shows how a program module can be added to a library.

Linking Multiple Program Modules

Let's rewrite the program in Fig. 4.21 titled BEEP to have three separate program modules:

Module 1. Main program; set up stack and call BEEP.
Module 2. BEEP procedure; produce the beep.
Module 3. DELAY procedure; provide a time delay.

Figure 4.30 is the assembly language listing of the main program. Note that a word-aligned stack segment is set up with only two words of storage. The reason for this small stack will become clearer as we proceed.

Before the main program begins, the symbol BEEP is declared to be an *external* far symbol. This avoids the *undefined symbol* error message mentioned previously. The type attribute—far or near— is necessary so that the assembler will know how many bytes to reserve for this address. In this case, because BEEP is located in a far segment, four bytes are reserved.

The EXTRN directive can also be used to identify data located in other modules. In this case the type can be any of the valid sizes, such as BYTE, WORD, or DWORD. For example, to reference the data byte COUNT in another module, use the statement

                    EXTRN   COUNT:BYTE

```
                                        TITLE    Main Program

                                ;**************************************************
                                ;*   This program produces a beep in a           *
                                ;*   loudspeaker connected to bit 0 of            *
                                ;*   output port 0D4H.                            *
                                ;**************************************************

0000                            STACK    SEGMENT WORD STACK
0000      02 [                           DW       2 DUP (?) ;Two words for
                 ????
               ]

0004                            TOP      LABEL    WORD        ;the far call.
0004                            STACK    ENDS

                                         EXTRN    BEEP:FAR    ;BEEP is a symbol
                                                              ;located in a far
                                                              ;external segment

0000                            CODE     SEGMENT
                                         ASSUME   CS:CODE,SS:STACK

0000  B8   ---- R               START:   MOV      AX,STACK    ;Stack segment
0003  8E D0                               MOV      SS,AX       ;to SS.
0005  36: 8D 26 0004 R                    LEA      SP,TOP      ;Point SP at TOP

000A  9A 0000 ---- E                      CALL     BEEP        ;This is a far CALL
000F  F4                                  HLT

0010                            CODE     ENDS
                                         END      START
```

Figure 4.30 MAIN program assembly language listing.

The main program in Fig. 4.30 is located in a segment called CODE. It begins by loading SS and SP and then performs a CALL to BEEP, after which the program halts. In practice, HLT would be replaced with a return to the operating system.

Notice the object code generated by the assembler for the CALL BEEP instruction. Because the address of BEEP is unknown at this point, two 00 bytes are allocated for the offset and two undefined bytes for the segment. The "E" indicates that this address is located in an external module and will be resolved by the linker when all the program modules are linked.

The BEEP procedure is shown in Fig. 4.31. A title and description block introduce the procedure. The statement

STACK   SEGMENT   WORD   STACK

defines a segment called STACK that is word aligned and *stack combinable*. The word STACK at the end of this statement means that this segment can be combined with the stack segment defined in the main program. In this particular case, because it defines two words of storage, it will have the effect of adding two words to the stack length. These are added before the label TOP in Fig. 4.30 so that this symbol continues to identify the stack top.

Sec. 4.6   Modular Programming   **179**

The procedure itself is located in a segment called SUBRT (for subroutine). Notice that this segment is defined to be byte aligned and *public* combinable. The public declaration means that this procedure can be referenced by other program modules. In general, the combine type can be *public*, *stack*, or *private*. The default is private, which means that the code in this segment cannot be combined (or accessed) by another program module.

The next statement, **PUBLIC BEEP**, allows the symbol BEEP to be referenced in other modules—as it was in the main program with the statement **EXTRN   BEEP:FAR**. Every symbol identified in an external statement must also be declared public in some other program module.

The BEEP procedure calls a routine called DELAY located in still another program module. Thus DELAY must be declared external. In this case DELAY will be located in the same segment (SUBRT) as BEEP and therefore has the attribute NEAR.

EXTRN   DELAY:NEAR

Note that the object code for the CALL DELAY instruction reserves two bytes for the offset of DELAY.

Figure 4.32 is the program listing for the DELAY procedure. It adds three more words to the stack length. As you can now see, the advantage of using the stack combine-type is that the stack can grow with each additional program module. In this way the main program need not guess at how large a stack it will need.

Because DELAY was declared to be NEAR in the BEEP procedure, it must be located in the SUBRT segment, declared public combinable, and written as a near procedure. The symbol DELAY must also be declared public.

Once all three modules have been written and assembled, they may be linked with the command

LINK MAIN.OBJ + BEEP.OBJ + DELAY.OBJ

The result is the executable file MAIN.EXE. The name for this file is chosen by the linker from the file name of the first module in the link list. The name selection can be overridden if desired.

Figure 4.33 shows the result of giving the command

TYPE MAIN.MAP

This is the link map created for the three program modules. It should be compared with the three program modules in Figs. 4.30 through 4.32. The main program occupies addresses 00000–0000FH. The stack segment is next beginning at 00010H. It is 14 bytes long, consisting of two words for the main program, two words for the BEEP procedure, and three words for the DELAY procedure.

The SUBRT segment follows immediately. This is because it was defined to be byte aligned. You cannot see the two separate procedures in this segment, but the length, 21H bytes, is consistent with the length of BEEP (11H bytes) plus DELAY (10H bytes).

```
                                TITLE    Beep   (far procedure)

                        ;Function:   Produce short beep (0.25s)
                        ;Inputs:     none
                        ;Outputs:    none
                        ;Calls:      DELAY (near procedure)
                        ;Destroys:   CX,DX,AL,flags

0000                    STACK    SEGMENT WORD STACK
0000    02 [                     DW      2 DUP (?)    ;Add two words
          ????
             ]

0004                    STACK    ENDS                 ;to stack length.
0000                    SUBRT    SEGMENT BYTE PUBLIC  ;The code in this
                                                      ;segment is public
                                                      ;and byte
                                                      ;combinable.

                        ;The next two lines declare BEEP to be a public
                        ;symbol (accessible to other external modules)
                        ;and DELAY to be a near symbol (in the same
                        ;segment but in an external module).

                                PUBLIC   BEEP
                                EXTRN    DELAY:NEAR
                                ASSUME   CS:SUBRT

= 008E                  T1       EQU     142          ;500us delay value
= 00D4                  DPORT    EQU     0D4H         ;Output port
= 01F4                  CYCLES   EQU     500          ;Number of cycles

0000                    BEEP     PROC    FAR

0000  B9 01F4                    MOV     CX,CYCLES ;Cycle counter
0003  F6 D0            AGAIN:    NOT     AL        ;Toggle
0005  E6 D4                      OUT     DPORT,AL  ;output bit.
0007  BA 008E                    MOV     DX,T1     ;Put delay value
000A  52                         PUSH    DX        ;on stack.
000B  E8 0000 E                  CALL    DELAY     ;This is a near CALL
000E  E2 F3                      LOOP    AGAIN     ;Do CX times
0010  CB                         RET               ;This is a far RET
0011                    BEEP     ENDP
0011                    SUBRT    ENDS
                                 END
```

Figure 4.31 BEEP procedure assembly language listing.

To get a better feeling for exactly how this program is located in memory, DEBUG has been used to load MAIN.EXE and the UCS command given to disassemble the object code. The result is shown in Fig. 4.34. The operating system loaded the CODE segment at address 09E3:0000. The STACK segment begins at 09E4:0000 (09E3:0010) and runs through 09E4:000D (09E30:001D).

The SUBRT segment, because it is byte aligned, begins immediately after the stack segment at address 09E3:001E. This is also address 09E4:000E (the address seen in the CALL BEEP instruction). The BEEP procedure ends with the instruction RET L (a far return) in location 09E3:002E. The DELAY procedure, also byte aligned, follows immediately.

Sec. 4.6   Modular Programming   **181**

```
                                    TITLE    Delay    (near procedure)

                              ;Function:      Time delay
                              ;Inputs:        16 bit delay value (T1)
                              ;               passed on stack.
                              ;               T = [3.4us * T1] + 17us
                              ;Outputs:       none
                              ;Calls:         nothing
                              ;Destroys:      nothing

0000                          STACK    SEGMENT WORD STACK
0000      03 [                         DW      3 DUP (?)  ;Add 3 words to
               ????
                     ]
0006                          STACK    ENDS                ;stack length.

0000                          SUBRT    SEGMENT BYTE PUBLIC
                                       PUBLIC  DELAY
                                       ASSUME  CS:SUBRT

0000                          DELAY    PROC    NEAR
0000   51                              PUSH    CX          ;Save all registers
0001   9C                              PUSHF               ;and the flags.
0002   55                              PUSH    BP
0003   8B EC                           MOV     BP,SP       ;Recover delay value
0005   8B 4E 08                        MOV     CX,[BP+8 ]  ;from stack.
0008   E2 FE                  COUNT:   LOOP    COUNT       ;Delay loop
000A   5D                              POP     BP          ;Restore all
000B   9D                              POPF                ;registers.
000C   59                              POP     CX
000D   C2 0002                         RET     2           ;Discard delay param
0010                          DELAY    ENDP
0010                          SUBRT    ENDS
                                       END
```

Figure 4.32   DELAY procedure assembly language listing.

Managing Program Modules with LIB

LIB is another utility program, like MASM and LINK used for program development. It allows you to create a library of master object code files (.OBJ). Assembled program modules can be added to the library with the sequence of commands

>**LIB LARGE.LIB**
>Operations: **+BEEP.OBJ+DELAY.OBJ**

```
Start   Stop    Length  Name              Class
00000H 0000FH  0010H   CODE
00010H 0001DH  000EH   STACK
0001EH 0003EH  0021H   SUBRT

Program entry point at 0000:0000

B:
```

Figure 4.33   Link map for the combined program modules in Figs. 4.30 through 4.32.

```
09E3:0000 B8E409      MOV    AX,09E4
09E3:0003 8ED0        MOV    SS,AX
09E3:0005 36          SEG    SS
09E3:0006 8D260E00    LEA    SP,[000E]
09E3:000A 9A0E00E409  CALL   09E4:000E
09E3:000F F4          HLT
09E3:0010 0000        ADD    [BX+SI],AL
09E3:0012 0000        ADD    [BX+SI],AL
09E3:0014 0000        ADD    [BX+SI],AL
09E3:0016 0000        ADD    [BX+SI],AL
09E3:0018 0000        ADD    [BX+SI],AL
09E3:001A 0000        ADD    [BX+SI],AL
09E3:001C 0000        ADD    [BX+SI],AL
09E3:001E B9F401      MOV    CX,01F4
09E3:0021 F6D0        NOT    AL
09E3:0023 E6D4        OUTB   D4
09E3:0025 BA8E00      MOV    DX,008E
09E3:0028 52          PUSH   DX
09E3:0029 E80300      CALL   002F
09E3:002C E2F3        LOOP   0021
09E3:002E CB          RET    L
09E3:002F 51          PUSH   CX
09E3:0030 9C          PUSHF
09E3:0031 55          PUSH   BP
09E3:0032 8BEC        MOV    BP,SP
09E3:0034 8B4E08      MOV    CX,[BP+08]
09E3:0037 E2FE        LOOP   0037
09E3:0039 5D          POP    BP
09E3:003A 9D          POPF
09E3:003B 59          POP    CX
09E3:003C C20200      RET    0002
>
```

Figure 4.34 The executable program loaded by DEBUG showing the placement of the main program, the stack area, and the two subroutines.

which adds the BEEP and DELAY object code modules to the library file LARGE.LIB.

The advantage of using the library utility is that individual modules do not need to be mentioned when linking and creating the main program run file. For example, after BEEP and DELAY have been added to the library, the command

LINK MAIN.OBJ,MAIN.EXE/M,MAIN.MAP,LARGE.LIB

links the file MAIN.OBJ, creates the run file MAIN.EXE and the map file MAIN.MAP (the /M switch), and searches the library file LARGE.LIB for external symbols.

Using LIB, often-used program modules can easily be added to new programs without your having to enter (or remember) all the individual program module names.

Self-Review 4.6 *(answers on page 191)*

4.6.1. Write the assembly language statement that declares XRAY to be a word variable in an external module.

4.6.2. What is the corresponding statement that allows XRAY to be accessed by other program modules?

4.6.3. The combine-type in the SEGMENT statement can specify _____, _____, or _____.

4.6.4. The STACK combine-type allows each program module to add only as many bytes to the stack as that module requires. (True/False)

4.6.5. Explain how the LIB utility can speed up the modular programming development process.

4.7 MACROS

Although the instruction set of the 8086 is quite extensive, using macros you can create new instructions that will be recognized by the assembler. For example, we might write a (macro) instruction DELAY T1 to generate a time delay equal to the value of T1 in seconds. Using this macro, whenever a time delay is needed in a program—say, 5 s— we simply specify the instruction DELAY 5.

The advantages to using macros in your programs are that the resulting code is easier to read and easier to write. In fact, libraries of macros can be written (or purchased) and then INCLUDED in your source code. This can greatly expand the (apparent) instruction set of your assembler.

In this section we see how to write and invoke a macro in an assembly language program. We also compare macros and procedures and determine the advantages of each.

Writing a Macro

The general form of a macro is

        name   **MACRO**   *arg1*   *arg2*   *arg3*   . . .
                  statements . . .
                  . . .
                  ENDM

where *name* is the name given to the macro and *arg* represents the arguments of the macro. The (optional) arguments allow the same macro to be used in different places within a program with different sets of data. Each argument must represent a constant; that is, you cannot specify a CPU register.

Example 4.5

Suppose that a program requires register AX to be inverted and then rotated right a given number of times. Write a macro called FIXAX to accomplish this function.

Solution

        FIXAX MACRO   TIMES
               NOT   AX
               MOV   CL,TIMES
               ROR   AX,CL
               ENDM

After adding this macro to your program the assembler knows a "new" instruction: **FIXAX** *n*. Figure 4.35 shows how the instruction might be used in a typical program. The macro definition is given at the head of the program so that it will be known when invoked in the main program.

In this program, note that the assembler "expands" the macro into the assembly language instructions it represents. The "+" symbol indicates that these statements are part of the macro definition. You can also see that the argument of the macro can be defined literally (2) or through an equate statement (N1).

```
                                TITLE      Macro Illustration Program

                         ;Create a macro called FIXAX

                                FIXAX    MACRO    TIMES     ;;This comment is in
                                         NOT      AX        ;;the macro
                                         MOV      CL,TIMES  ;;definition only.
                                         ROR      AX,CL     ;This one in both
                                         ENDM

                         ;The assembler now knows a new instruction
                         ;called "FIXAX".

= 0006                          N1       EQU      6

0000                            CODE     SEGMENT
                                         ASSUME   CS:CODE

                                         FIXAX    2
0000  F7 D0                +               NOT      AX
0002  B1 02                +               MOV      CL,2
0004  D3 C8                +               ROR      AX,CL     ;This one in both

                                         FIXAX    N1
0006  F7 D0                +               NOT      AX
0008  B1 06                +               MOV      CL,N1
000A  D3 C8                +               ROR      AX,CL     ;This one in both

000C                                     CODE     ENDS
                                         END
```

Figure 4.35   Program to illustrate the macro FIXAX. The assembler marks the expanded instructions with a " + "

INCLUDE Files

It is not necessary to write each macro's definition at the head of the main program. Instead, you can create a special file—call it MACRO.LIB—which contains the definitions of all your macros. At the beginning of the main program you must then enter the statement

INCLUDE   MACRO.LIB

This will cause the assembler to include automatically all the statements (presumably macro definitions) in the file MACRO.LIB.

In fact, the INCLUDE statement can be used to include program statements from other (non macro) files as well. In this way program modules can be read into a main program at any point. You are discouraged from abusing this privilege, however. Long program modules should be written and assembled separately and then linked to the main program using the linker utility, as discussed in Sec. 4.6.

When the INCLUDE statement is used, the assembler will expand the required macros during the first pass of the assembly. During the second pass, *all* the macros in the INCLUDE file will be listed, just as if you had entered them at this point in the

Sec. 4.7   Macros   **185** program. This may be undesirable, especially when the INCLUDE file is very long and you are not using many of the macros in the file.

The following statements can be used to include the macro library file but suppress the listing of each macro.

```
IF1
INCLUDE MACRO.LIB
ENDIF
```

The **IF** and **ENDIF** are *conditional* assembly directives. In this case the assembler is instructed to INCLUDE the file MACRO.LIB during the first pass—when the macros are expanded—but not during the second pass—when the macros are listed. Of course, the body of each *expanded* macro is included in the list file (and identified with the "+" symbol). So you will still be able to see the code generated for each (invoked) macro.

Local Names

There is a problem when a symbolic address is used within a macro. Consider the macro shown in Fig. 4.36 to generate a time delay (you will recognize it as the delay procedure introduced in Fig. 4.21). When the assembler first expands this macro, there is no problem. However, if DELAY is used a second time in the same program, the assembler will issue an error message (*'Redefinition of symbol'* or *'Symbol is multidefined'*).

The problem is the label COUNT. On the first expansion it identifies one memory location, but on the second, it identifies a *different* location. Fortunately, there is a way around this problem. At the beginning of the macro all labels within that macro must be declared LOCAL. For example,

```
DELAY    MACRO    DELTA
         LOCAL    COUNT
```

defines COUNT to be a *local* address. When assembled, the assembler will replace the label COUNT with the name ??0000 the first time the DELAY macro is invoked. If DELAY is invoked a second time, the name ??0001 will be chosen, and then ??0002, and so on.

Figure 4.37 shows how the DELAY macro is used in the seven-segment counter program (Fig. 4.26). In this example the macro is defined at the beginning of the program instead of being included from a macro library file.

```
DELAY    MACRO    DELTA
         PUSH     CX
         PUSHF
         MOV      CX,DELTA
COUNT:   LOOP     COUNT
         POPF
         POP      CX
         ENDM
```

Figure 4.36 Time-delay procedure written as a macro.

```
                                    TITLE    Seven Segment Counter

                              ;************************************************
                              ;*  This program will cause the hexadecimal   *
                              ;*  digits 0 through F to appear in sequence   *
                              ;*  in a seven-segment display connected to    *
                              ;*  output port 0D4H.   It illustrates         *
                              ;*  the use of a data table to store the       *
                              ;*  segment codes.                             *
                              ;************************************************

                              DELAY    MACRO    DELTA
                                       LOCAL    COUNT
                                       PUSH     CX
                                       PUSHF
                                       MOV      CX,DELTA
                              COUNT:   LOOP     COUNT
                                       POPF
                                       POP      CX
                                       ENDM

0000                          STACK    SEGMENT WORD STACK
0000     0A [                 DW       10 DUP (?)
              ????
                    ]

0014                          TOP      LABEL    WORD
0014                          STACK    ENDS

0000                          SEVEN    SEGMENT WORD

                              ;This (data) segment is used to store the
                              ;codes for each of the 16 digits.

0000  40 79 24 30 19          CODES    DB       40H,79H,24H,30H,19H
0005  12 02 78 00 18 08                DB       12H,02H,78H,0,18H,08H
000B  03 46 21 06 0E                   DB       03H,46H,21H,06H,0EH
0010                          SEVEN    ENDS


0000                          CODE     SEGMENT BYTE
                                       ASSUME  CS:CODE,DS:SEVEN,SS:STACK

                              ;The main program begins here.

= 00D4                        DPORT    EQU      0D4H        ;Data output port
= 0000                        T1       EQU      0           ;0.2s delay parameter

0000  B8   ---- R             START:   MOV      AX,STACK    ;Begin by loading the
0003  8E D0                            MOV      SS,AX       ;SS and DS registers
0005  B8   ---- R                      MOV      AX,SEVEN    ;and point SP at the
0008  8E D8                            MOV      DS,AX       ;top of the stack.
000A  36: 8D 26 0014 R                 LEA      SP,TOP

000F  8D 36 0000 R            FOREVR:  LEA      SI,CODES    ;Get offset of table
0013  FC                               CLD                  ;Auto increment of SI
0014  BB 0000                          MOV      BX,T1       ;Get delay parameter
0017  B9 0010                          MOV      CX,16       ;16 digits to output

001A  AC                      NUDIGT:  LODSB                ;Fetch byte to AL
001B  E6 D4                            OUT      DPORT,AL    ;Display digit
                                       DELAY    T1
001D  51                  +            PUSH     CX
001E  9C                  +            PUSHF
001F  B9 0000             +            MOV      CX,T1
0022  E2 FE               + ??0000:    LOOP     ??0000
0024  9D                  +            POPF
0025  59                  +            POP      CX
                                       DELAY    T1
0026  51                  +            PUSH     CX
0027  9C                  +            PUSHF
0028  B9 0000             +            MOV      CX,T1
002B  E2 FE               + ??0001:    LOOP     ??0001
002D  9D                  +            POPF
002E  59                  +            POP      CX
002F  E2 E9                            LOOP     NUDIGT      ;Next digit

0031  EB DC                            JMP      FOREVR      ;Repeat indefinately
0033                          CODE     ENDS
                                       END      START
```

Figure 4.37 Seven-segment counter program rewritten using the DELAY macro. Note the names assigned to the symbolic address COUNT when the macro is expanded.

Comparing Macros and Procedures

As you have seen, a macro and a procedure are very similar. Indeed, in the last example we replaced the DELAY procedure with a macro. What are the differences between a macro and a procedure, and what are the advantages of each?

A procedure is easily identified because it is invoked with a CALL instruction and terminated with a RET instruction. In addition, the code for that procedure appears only once in the program—no matter how many times the procedure is called.

A macro, on the other hand, is invoked during program assembly, not when the program is run. You can think of it as a *text substitution* process. Each time the macro is required, the assembler substitutes the defined sequence of instructions. As a result, macros almost always require more memory than the equivalent procedure.

The advantage to using a macro is that there is no overhead associated with the procedure's CALL and RET instructions. This means that the macro will execute faster. It also means that in some cases the macro may require less code than is required by the equivalent procedure.

Example 4.6

The 8086 assembler, MACRO-86, will not recognize the instructions for the 8087 numeric data processor. Use a macro to create a "new" 8086 instruction FDECSTP—decrement the 8087 stack pointer—which has the hex coding D9 F6.

Solution The macro is very simple:

```
FDECSTP  MACRO
         DB      0D9H, 0F6H
         ENDM
```

In this case the macro substitutes the two bytes D9 F6 for the 8087 instruction whenever the FDECSTP macro is encountered. Although this could also be done with a procedure, it would be awkward and not nearly as readable as the macro form. Also note that the procedure would require several more bytes (the CALL instruction alone requires at least three bytes).

SELF-REVIEW 4.7 (answers on page 191)

4.7.1. A macro is expanded into the machine code it represents when it is: (a) assembled; (b) linked; (c) loaded; (d) executed.

4.7.2. Write the code for a macro that adds register BL to the contents of memory location MEMLOC. If bit 7 of register AL is set MEMLOC should also be incremented by 1.

4.7.3. Macro INCLUDE files are expanded by the assembler during pass _____ of the assembly.

4.7.4. Why must symbolic addresses within macros be defined with a LOCAL statement?

4.7.5. List two ways in which a macro differs from a procedure.

CHAPTER 4 SELF-TEST

1. Determine the contents of register BL after the following instructions have been executed.

```
MOV   AL,0ABH
AND   AL,07H
MOV   BL,0C0H
OR    BL,AL
TEST  BL,84H
JNZ   ERROR
```

2. In question 1, control is transferred to the ERROR routine only if bit 7 and bit 2 of register BL are high.   (True/False)

3. Given the segment definition

```
DATA1   SEGMENT
FIRST   DB  ?
DATA1   ENDS
```

Write an instruction sequence that will load the data segment register with the segment address of DATA1 and the BX register with the offset address of FIRST.

4. The data segment defined in question 3 is _____ aligned.

5. The data segment defined in question 3 is _____ combinable.

6. What is wrong with the 8086/88 instruction: MUL AL,80H?

7. The data table shown in Fig. 4.13(b) has its base (starting address) at physical address 09E5: _____.

8. The 8088 microprocessor will require _____ T states to execute the instruction MOV CH,[BX].

9. In Fig. 4.18, changing the T1 equate to

```
T1   EQU   0
```

changes the oscillation frequency to _____.

10. FIX_UP is a far procedure expecting a 16-bit data parameter to be passed on the stack. After the instructions

```
PUSH  AX
CALL  FIX_UP
```

at which memory location relative to register SP can the data be found?

11. A forward reference error will occur when a call to a _____ procedure precedes the definition of that procedure.

12. What changes are needed to the program in Fig. 4.26 to make the display count *backward*?

13. To call the far procedure DEC_BIN located in the file LARGE.LIB, what assembly language directive must be included?

14. In Fig. 4.31 the assembler reserves two bytes for the address of DELAY in the instruction CALL DELAY. What do these two bytes become when all three program modules are linked and loaded as shown in Fig. 4.34?

15. Identify any errors in the following macro.

```
ADDM    MACRO  DATA
AGAIN:  ROR    AX,1
        JNC    AGAIN
        INC    DATA
        ENDM
```

16. A routine written as a macro will execute faster than when written as a procedure. (True/False)

ANALYSIS AND DESIGN QUESTIONS

4.1. Assume the two displays in Fig. 4.7 are to be decoded in software similar to the interface in Fig. 4.24. Using port addresses FFFA (low order digit) and FFFB (high order digit), write a DISPLAY procedure to accept a display byte in register AL and display its hex equivalent on the two displays.

4.2. Calculate the total time delay created by the nested loop below assuming a 5-MHz 8086 microprocessor.

```
        MOV   CX,OFFFFH
OUTER:  MOV   DX,CX
        MOV   CX,OFFFFH
INNER:  LOOP  INNER
        MOV   CX,DX
        LOOP  OUTER
```

4.3. The instruction sequence

```
        MOV  CS:TEMP,AX
TEMP    DB  ?
```

may or may not generate an assembly error. Explain the problem.

4.4. Redesign the coffee machine in Fig. 4.15 so that time delays in software are not necessary. Provide a complete documentation package including a list of hardware inputs and outputs, flowcharts, and the 8086/88 assembly language program.

4.5. Write a procedure that converts a two-digit decimal number (*packed* decimal) to a single-byte binary number. Assume that the decimal number is passed on the stack (low order byte). Write the routine so that it can be added to LARGE.LIB.

4.6. Sketch the link map for the program given in Fig. 4.21.

4.7. Refer to the link map in Fig. 4.27 for the seven-segment counter program. If the operating system loads the program beginning at address 09E30, what value will the program load into DS? Will the code for digit 0 be stored at DS:0000? Explain.

4.8. What changes would be needed to the program in Fig. 4.12 if each of the routines was located in a different segment from the main program?

4.9. Assume 8086 input port FFF8 has three active high sensors wired to bits 0, 1, and 2. Write a procedure that monitors this port and returns only when the three sensors are turned on in sequence (ie., bit 0 only is on, then bits 0 and 1 only are on, and finally all three bits are on). An incorrect sequence should cause the procedure to start over.

4.10. Write a procedure that accepts an ASCII letter between "a" and "z" passed on the stack. The procedure should determine if the letter is contained within a string of characters, and return with the character *position* in AL (00 if not found). *Example:* If letter = "a" and the string = "This is a string," then return with AL = 09H. (*Hint:* Use the loop instructions.)

4.11. Rewrite the ADC 0-5V scaler program given in Fig. 4.9 assuming all 256 possible voltage values have been stored in a data table. (*Hint:* Use the XLAT instruction with the input binary number used as an index.)

4.12. The 8086 trap flag cannot be set with a single instruction. Write a macro SET_TF to accomplish this.

SELF REVIEW ANSWERS

4.1.1 Bit testing is nondestructive

4.1.2 TEST AX,0008H

4.1.3 7, 0, high

4.1.4 (c)

4.1.5 COUNT   EQU 42H

4.2.1 DX:AX = 00C0:0000

4.2.2 MPLR EQU 10

4.2.3 False

4.2.4 segment

4.2.5 False (001FH in the CODE segment)

4.2.6 0004H

4.2.7 fewer wasted bytes

4.3.1 conditional, loop

4.3.2 polling

4.3.3 15

4.3.4 True (assuming TEMP begins at an even address)

4.3.5 Instructions are assumed to be in the queue

4.3.6 T1 EQU 28

4.4.1 same procedure can be used with different sets of data

4.4.2 CPU register, memory location, memory pointer, stack

4.4.3 when all CPU registers are unchanged

4.4.4 near

4.4.5 True (due to the CS: segment override)

4.5.1 faster than arithmetic processing, data table requires memory space

4.5.2 LEA SI,BASE_OF_TABLE

4.5.3 AL, BX, XLAT

4.6.1 EXTRN XRAY:WORD

4.6.2 PUBLIC XRAY

4.6.3 public, stack, private

4.6.4 True

4.6.5 programs in library need not be reinvented

4.7.1 (a)

4.7.2 INCMEM MACRO
             LOCAL EXIT
             TEST AL,128
             JZ   EXIT
             INC MEMLOC
EXIT: ADD
             MEMLOC,BL
             ENDM

4.7.3 1

4.7.4 prevent one symbol from identifying more than one address

4.7.5 no CALL or RET required, code for the macro is expanded each time it is invoked

5

MICROPROCESSOR PRODUCT DEVELOPMENT

Unlike conventional electronic designs whose functions are rigidly fixed in hardware, a microprocessor-based product is *programmable*. This single feature of the microprocessor is responsible for revolutionizing the electronics industry. Designers need no longer scrap entire circuit boards when redesigns are necessary. Instead, the microprocessor control program, stored in ROM, can be rewritten and a new ROM programmed. No changes to the hardware are necessary.

Viewed in this way, hardware is simply computing potential. It is the software that will determine if this potential is realized in the form of a useful product. Not surprisingly, writing, debugging, and documenting the system software for a microprocessor product often accounts for more than 50% of the total development cost.

In this chapter we consider the steps and choices to be made when designing a microprocessor-based product. This process is known as the *development cycle* and is diagrammed in Fig. 5.1. We will be paying particular attention to the software development phase of this cycle (Chaps. 6 through 9 deal with microprocessor hardware in detail). Among our considerations will be the need for a *development system*—that is, a system on which the software can be written and tested prior to its incorporation in the prototype hardware.

Although all of our programs thus far have been written in 8086 assembler, higher-level languages such as Pascal or FORTRAN should also be considered. Such languages allow the programmer to develop control structures in a clear and concise manner. The

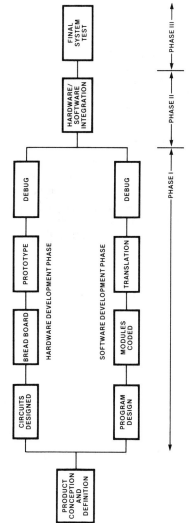

Figure 5.1 Design of a microprocessor-based product requires a hardware and software development phase. (Courtesy of Intel Corporation.)

result is a program that is often easier to debug and maintain than the corresponding assembler version.

The chapter concludes with a description of *in-circuit emulation*. This is a technique that allows the development system to emulate the microprocessor in the prototype—even though all the features of the prototype may not yet be completed. In this way software development can proceed in parallel with hardware development, shortening the time through the development cycle.

The main topics in this chapter are:

5.1 The Development Cycle
5.2 Defining the Product's Software
5.3 Debugging the Software
5.4 Integrating the Hardware and Software

5.1 THE DEVELOPMENT CYCLE

The programs we wrote and studied in Chap. 4 assumed that some sort of "system" existed on which these programs could be tested. This might have been a system design kit such as Intel's SDK-86 or an MS-DOS personal computer running MACRO-86. When interfaced to additional hardware these systems can become useful microprocessor-controlled products. For example, using several solid-state relays, an IBM PC could be used to control the heating and cooling systems in a large building. Appropriate software would allow an energy management control system to be designed.

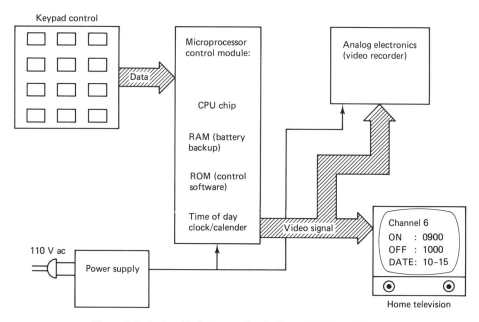

Figure 5.2 System block diagram for the "smart" VCR machine.

But what if we are interested in a stand-alone microprocessor application: for example, a computer-controlled video cassette recorder (VCR) or microwave oven? The keyboard and video display of the personal computer are not required in these products. But without these devices, how are we to write and test the system software and mate it to the hardware?

In this section we look more closely at the development cycle and show the need for a *development system*.

A Microprocessor-Controlled Video Cassette Recorder

You have been charged with designing and bringing to market a new brand of "smart" VCR. Your machine is to have the following capabilities:

1. Accept input from a calculator-like keypad.
2. Prompt the user via a "menu" of options that display on the user's home television set.
3. Allow program selection to be specified up to 30 days from the current time and date.

As a first step in the design of this machine you have prepared the system block diagram shown in Fig. 5.2. The analog electronics, that part of the system that records and plays back the video signal, is available from a previous design and will simply be incorporated into this new smart machine. The real job is designing the microprocessor control module, interfacing it to the analog electronics and keypad, and then writing the system software that is to reside in the control module's ROM.

With regard to the development cycle in Fig. 5.1, you decide to organize separate hardware and software design teams. The software group can then begin work writing modules to scan the keypad, read the clock/calendar, perform table lookups for the various command functions, display the screen menus, and perform the command functions. The hardware group can begin designing the control module and the interfaces to the keypad, clock/calendar, and analog electronics.

Shortly after the design teams have been organized, the two group leaders request a meeting. At this meeting several questions are raised. "How many bytes of RAM and ROM will you need in this system?" "Should we write the program in a high-level language, or should we use assembler?" "How many keys do you want on the keypad?" "How are my programmers supposed to write the software? Your *smart* machine has no keyboard or video display for program development."

Quickly you glance at your development cycle chart (Fig. 5.1), but it offers no help. The hardware and software people are supposed to go off and perform their respective tasks independently. But now it appears that the hardware cannot be designed until the software is written, and the software cannot be written because the product provides no means to write and test the program!

The end result? The project never gets off the ground and the company goes out of business. Obviously, there has to be a better way.

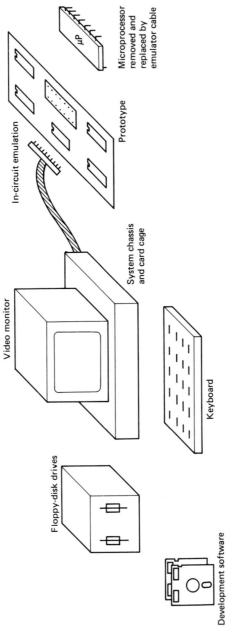

Figure 5.3 Components of a typical microcomputer development system.

Microprocessor removed and replaced by emulator cable

μP

Prototype

In-circuit emulation

System chassis and card cage

Video monitor

Keyboard

Floppy-disk drives

Development software

The Need for a Development System

There is another scenario for the development of the smart VCR machine. Before the two design groups are formed, a microprocessor *development system* is purchased. A diagram of such a system is shown in Fig. 5.3. Because it uses the same microprocessor as is intended in the smart machine, the software group can use the development system to begin writing some of the program modules—even though the hardware is not yet ready. They are supported in their endeavor by a set of *software development tools*. These include text editors, assemblers, linkers, debuggers, and high-level-language compilers.

With the software group now at work, details of the system (like the number of keys on the keypad) can be clarified, allowing the hardware group to begin building portions of the prototype. When it comes time to test these first modules, the *emulation* capabilities of the development system can be put to work.

An in-circuit emulator is a circuit in the development system that can be programmed to "look like" or *emulate* the microprocessor in the prototype. However, there is one important difference. The emulated microprocessor is under control of the development system. The software can thus be traced, single-stepped, and generally debugged using all the facilities of the development system.

In-circuit emulation allows portions of the prototype hardware and software to be tested—before the entire machine has been designed. Design errors can then be spotted early in the development cycle when it will be less costly to "design them out."

As time proceeds, the debugged program modules can be transferred to ROM in the prototype. Eventually, the entire program will have been tested (on the development system) and verified to work in the ROM of the prototype. Finally, the emulator is unplugged and the prototype's microprocessor inserted in its place. A *logic analyzer* can now be used to track down any remaining hardware bugs. The product can then proceed to the final test phase of the project.

What Is a Development System?

A development system is a computer used to write and debug software for another computer. As shown in Fig. 5.3, its basic components include a system unit containing the host microprocessor, a keyboard, a video display monitor, and disk drives. The system unit must also include sufficient memory to run the various text editors, assemblers, debuggers, and high-level languages required to develop the product's software.

The purpose of a development system is to provide an *environment* within which the microprocessor product can be designed. This is particularly important when the product does not include these facilities itself (like the VCR example). Some systems include support for hardware debugging via in-circuit emulators and integrated logic analyzers.

A personal computer such as the IBM PC can be used as an inexpensive development system for 8086- and 8088-based microprocessor products. This computer provides a programming environment called MS-DOS (or PC-DOS) that includes the EDLIN text editor, the MACRO-86 assembler, and DEBUG for tracing and single-stepping the software. In Chap. 3 we discussed the use of these software "tools" in some detail. Numerous high-level languages, full-screen editors, and symbolic debuggers are available for the

intel®

iMDX 430/431/440/441
INTELLEC® SERIES IV
MICROCOMPUTER DEVELOPMENT SYSTEM

- **Complete Microcomputer Development System for the iAPX 86/87/88/186/188/286, the MCS® -80/85 and the MCS® -48/51 family microprocessors.**

- **Advanced, friendly human interface with menu-driven function keys, HELP, and syntax builder/checker capabilities for increased user productivity.**

- **Foreground/Background multiprocessing for simultaneous execution of two jobs, increasing system throughput.**

- **Hierarchical file system provides file sharing and protection for large software projects.**

- **Software compatible with both Series IIE and Series IIIE development systems.**

- **Supports PL/M, Pascal, C, and FORTRAN, and Basic high-level languages as well as assemblers.**

- **Provides Program Management Tools (PMTs), advanced AEDIT™ text editor and supports powerful PSCOPE symbolic, source level debugger.**

- **Can be fully integrated into the NDS-II Network Development System.**

The Intellec® Series IV is a new generation development system specifically designed for supporting the iAPX family of advanced microprocessors. It also supports the MCS-80/85 and the MCS-48/51 families.

Figure 1. Intellec® Series IV Microcomputer Development System

Figure 5.4 The Intellec Series IV development system. This system is based on the 8086 microprocessor but can also be run in an 8085 mode. (Courtesy of Intel Corporation.)

PC. In-circuit emulation and logic analysis hardware can also be added via separate plug-in cards.

Intel supports its family of 8- and 16-bit microprocessors with the *Intellec Microcomputer Development System* series. A description of the Intellec Series IV is given in Fig. 5.4. This system has both an 8085 and an 8086 CPU, allowing it to support the 8-bit 8080 and 8085, as well as the 16-bit 8086, 8088, 80188, 80186, and 80286 microprocessors.

Software can be run from one or two built-in 640K byte floppy disks, or from an optional 10M- or 35M-byte Winchester disk drive. Running under Intel's iNDX multitasking operating system, it is possible to assign one job to the *foreground* and another to the *background*. For example, a program that is known to require 10 to 20 minutes to assemble can be assigned to the background while another file is being edited in the foreground.

When very large projects are involved, the Series IV can become a *workstation* in a network of development systems. In this way software development can be broken into modules and assigned to several different people, all of whom share a common database.

SELF-REVIEW 5.1 *(answers on page 219)*

5.1.1. Most microprocessor-based products include conventional keyboards, floppy-disk drives, and video monitors. (True/False)

5.1.2. A _____ _____ is a computer system designed for writing, testing, and debugging microcomputer software.

5.1.3. What is meant by the term *programming environment*?

5.1.4. What is wrong with the development cycle chart shown in Fig. 5.1?

5.2 DEFINING THE PRODUCT'S SOFTWARE

The unique feature of a microprocessor product is the ability to control that product via software. Changes need not require expensive hardware modifications. Instead, new sections of code can be written that change or add to the product's function.

Because of the software's importance, the *organization* of that software is critical. Programs written in a monolithic style with numerous branch statements can be as difficult to maintain and modify as a product based on a fixed-in-hardware design. The BASIC programming language, for example, is well known for its GOTO statement. When abused, the resulting programs can be very difficult to trace and debug. The term "spaghetti code" has aptly been applied.

In Chap. 3 we introduced the topic of *modular* programming. Applying the "divide and conquer" principle, modular programs break the problem into several manageable pieces or *modules*. When written correctly, the details of one module need not affect another. In this way changes to the program can be effected by simply rewriting those modules involved.

Another advantage of modular programming is that each module can be written in a programming *language* best suited for the job. Assembler, for example, can be chosen

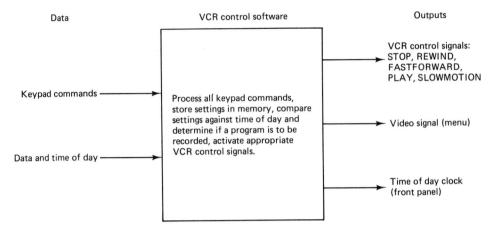

Data   VCR control software   Outputs

VCR control signals:
STOP, REWIND,
FASTFORWARD,
PLAY, SLOWMOTION

Keypad commands

Process all keypad commands,
store settings in memory, compare
settings against time of day and
determine if a program is to be
recorded, activate appropriate
VCR control signals.

Video signal (menu)

Data and time of day

Time of day clock
(front panel)

Figure 5.5 Block diagram of the "smart" VCR control system.

when fast execution or direct bit manipulation is required. Modules requiring complex mathematical calculations can be coded in FORTRAN. Pascal is best known for its rigid type checking of variables and its control structure, which eliminates the need for the GOTO statement. By matching the module to the language and then using a linker to join these modules, you can effectively "have your cake and eat it, too!"

In this section we reemphasize the advantages of modular programming, particularly in a development system environment. The need for a set of software development tools will also be explained. Finally, an example of a structured program using Pascal to code one of the VCR control modules will be given.

Modularizing the Problem

When faced with any complex task the first question that usually comes to mind is: "Where should I begin?" Certainly, this is true when writing a computer program. You must be careful at this point not to let your knowledge of a particular programming language dominate your thought process. That is, do not let yourself begin thinking in terms of computer instructions before the *purpose* of the software has been clearly defined.

Rule 1: Define the overall purpose of the software. A diagram such as the one shown in Fig. 5.5 may be helpful at this point. It specifies the program's inputs and outputs in general terms. The purpose of the software can then be thought of as processing the inputs to produce the desired outputs.

Rule 2: Define the structure of the software. The structure of a program defines the logical sequence in which tasks must be performed. This is best identified by using a pseudo-high-level language (such as English!) and avoiding GOTO constructs. Instead, think of the problem as a set of tasks that should be done WHILE a particular condition is true, or UNTIL something occurs. Decisions can be handled with a IF-THEN-ELSE structure. When multiple choices exist, a CASE statement can be used.

Figure 5.6 shows how the VCR control software can be structured. A variable ERROR is set to FALSE when the system is first started. As each module in the program

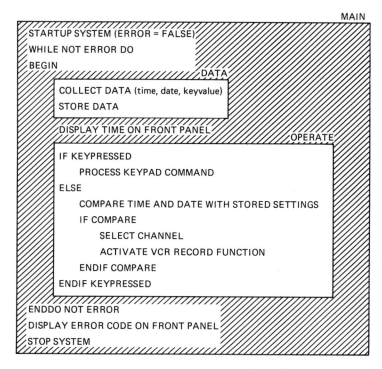

```
                                                              MAIN
STARTUP SYSTEM (ERROR = FALSE)
WHILE NOT ERROR DO
BEGIN
                                            DATA
      COLLECT DATA (time, date, keyvalue)

      STORE DATA

      DISPLAY TIME ON FRONT PANEL
                                                    OPERATE
         IF KEYPRESSED

               PROCESS KEYPAD COMMAND

         ELSE

               COMPARE TIME AND DATE WITH STORED SETTINGS

               IF COMPARE

                     SELECT CHANNEL

                     ACTIVATE VCR RECORD FUNCTION

               ENDIF COMPARE

         ENDIF KEYPRESSED

ENDDO NOT ERROR
DISPLAY ERROR CODE ON FRONT PANEL
STOP SYSTEM
```

Figure 5.6 The VCR control program is broken into three independent modules. Further refinement will result in smaller submodules that can then be coded.

executes, it has the option of setting this variable to TRUE. As long as there is no error, the program will run, collecting data, and processing that data.

Rule 3: Modularize the problem. Once the structure of the program has been defined, it can be broken into several general-purpose modules. When defining these modules it is important to "hide" the nitty-gritty details. That is, do not let the definition of one module depend on the exact details of another.

In the VCR example, the OPERATE module need not know exactly how the DATA module will be collecting data. In this way the port assignments can be changed, the keypad interface redesigned, all without affecting the OPERATE or MAIN modules. The result is a program that is more easily understood and maintained.

Once these key modules have been identified, they can be assigned to separate programmers. Submodules can then be defined as the program is broken into ever-smaller (and manageable) pieces.

Software Development Tools

Just as a carpenter requires special tools to build a house, a programmer requires special tools to develop a program. For example, a Pascal compiler may be required to write one module, an 8086 assembler to write another. Both modules will require a text editor to produce the source code. A LINKER can then be used to combine the two modules. The testing phase will require a special debugging utility so that the contents of variables,

8086 SOFTWARE TOOLBOX

- **Collection of Tools That Speed Software Development**
- **MPL, a Standalone Macro Processor, is Ideal for Debugging Macros**
- **SCRIBL and SPELL Assist Text Preparation**

- **OMC 286 and 287 EMULATOR Aid 80286 and 80287 Software Development**
- **Many Other Valuable 16-Bit Software Tools Are Included**
- **Runs on Series III and Series IV Microcomputer Development Systems**

The 8086 Software Toolbox is a collection of 16-bit software tools that can significantly improve programmer productivity. These tools are valuable for text formatting and preparation, software testing and performance analysis, 286/287 software development, and a multitude of other applications.

Text processing tools ease document formatting and preparation. SCRIBL is a text formatting program that uses commands embedded in text to do paging, centering, left and right margins, subscripts, etc. SPELL finds misspelled words in a text file and comes with a user expandable dictionary. COMP compares two text or source files and displays their differences.

Test and performance analysis tools aid software testing and performance evaluation. PERF, a performance analysis tool for 8086 software, is ideal for isolating code "hot spots." PASSIF is a general-purpose assertion checking and reporting tool perfect for running test suites.

Software development for 286/287 components is assisted by two software tools: OMC 286, an 8086 to 80286 object module convertor, and 287 EMULATOR, an 80287 emulator that runs on the 80286.

Additional tools are included that aid 16-bit software development efforts. All tools run on Series III and Series IV Microcomputer Development Systems.

TEXT PROCESSING
SCRIBL
SPELL
MPL
WSORT
COMP

PERFORMANCE MEASUREMENT & TESTING
PERF
GRAPHIT
PASSIF

286/287 DEVELOPMENT
OMC 286
287 EMULATOR

MISCELLANEOUS TOOLS
FUNC
XREF
DC
HSORT

8086 SOFTWARE TOOLBOX TOOLS

Figure 5.7 Intel offers an 8086 programmer's toolbox consisting of utility programs for the 8086 microprocessor. (Courtesy of Intel Corp.)

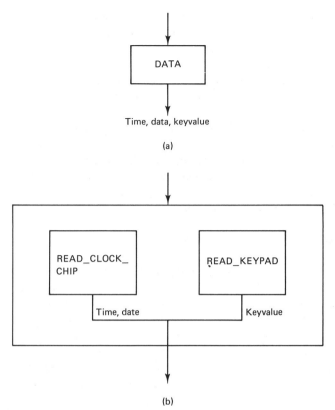

(a)

Time, data, keyvalue

(a)

READ_CLOCK_
CHIP

READ_KEYPAD

Time, date

Keyvalue

(b)

Figure 5.8 (a) The DATA module has a single entry point and a single exit point. (b) Refining the DATA module into two submodules, READ_CLOCK_CHIP and READ_KEYPAD.

CPU registers, and memory locations can be examined. Often modules written for one project can be shared with another. A library manager utility can facilitate this process.

Based on the above we might define a programmer's basic set of "tools" to include:

1. High-level-language compilers and machine code assemblers
2. Text editors for file creation and modification
3. Library managers to allow storage and retrieval of "canned" routines
4. Linkers to combine modules into the final program
5. Debuggers for program test and checkout

Other tools can also come in handy. Intel supplies an "8086 Software Tool Box," shown in Fig. 5.7. Included are text formatting and printing utilities, spelling checkers, performance measurement utilities used to isolate code "hot spots," a floating-point desk calculator, and utilities for use with the 80286 and 80287.

Compiled or Interpreted?

Computer languages can be *interpreted* or *compiled*. Interpreted languages execute more slowly than compiled languages. This is because a special interpreter program is required.

Its job is to interpret each high-level command and convert it to corresponding machine instructions. This process must be done each time the program is run.

The advantage of this scheme is that the operator can interact directly with his or her program. For example, the program can be told to stop or start at any given point. Once halted, the state of any of the program variables can be examined and altered. In addition, new program statements can easily be added. These features provide an ideal debugging environment.

Despite these advantages, most microprocessor control programs are compiled rather than interpreted. That is, the source code is written and then compiled into corresponding machine instructions. The resulting code can then be run just like any other machine code file. The result is a more compact program—the compiler need not be resident in memory to run the program—that executes much faster than the corresponding interpreted version. These features are particularly important when the object code is to be stored in a ROM.

VCR Example: A Pascal Data Collection Module

How can you determine which sections of a program should be assigned to a particular module? One way is to adopt the *single-entry, single-exit* rule. This rule states that a program module must have only one entry point and one exit point.

Following this rule, the VCR DATA module identified in Fig. 5.6 could be diagrammed as shown in Fig. 5.8(a). We enter the module via a single path, and exit—with the time, date, and keypad value (if any)—also via a single path.

Once a module has been identified, it can be broken into several smaller modules. In the case of the DATA module, the next step in this refinement is the definition of the READ_CLOCK_CHIP and READ_KEYPAD modules shown in Fig. 5.8(b). In this example we are assuming that the hardware design group has selected a particular clock chip (the OKI Semiconductor MSM5832 for example) that will be used to keep track of the time and date for the smart VCR machine. Table 5.1 lists the 13 register addresses within this chip that must be read to determine the time and date.[1]

Before attempting to write the code for the READ_CLOCK_CHIP module, we should again define the purpose and structure of this module in a pseudo-high-level language. The result might be

```
BEGIN
     READ SECONDS, MINUTES, HOURS
     STORE AS THE VARIABLE TIME
     READ MONTHS, DAYS
     STORE AS THE VARIABLE DATE
END
```

The purpose of the READ_CLOCK_CHIP module can thus be defined as: *Read the appropriate clock chip registers and I/O ports, process this data, and return with the current time and date stored in the variables TIME and DATE.*

---

[1]Analysis and Design Question 9.7 explores a technique for interfacing this chip to the 8086 microprocessor. Pinouts and timing diagrams for the MSM5832 are given in Figs. 9.38 and 9.39.

TABLE 5.1 CLOCK/CALENDAR CHIP REGISTERS

Register address	Register accessed
0	Seconds (units)
1	Seconds (tens)
2	Minutes (units)
3	Minutes (tens)
4	Hours (units)
5	Hours (tens)
6	Weekday (0–6)
7	Monthday (units)
8	Monthday (tens)
9	Month (units)
10	Month (tens)
11	Year (units)
12	Year (tens)

```
(*   ############################################################   *)

Procedure Read_Clock_CHIP   (VAR TIME,DATE :integer);

(*   ############################################################   *)

(*  This procedure returns the time - in 24 hour format - and the    *)
(*  date - in MMDD format as the two integer variables time and date. *)


const
    base_port=$FFF8;      (* base port of clock chip *)
    control_port=$FFFA;   (* used to output clock chip register addresses *)

var
    register: integer;
    clock_chip: array[0..12] of integer;

begin
    for register:=0 to 12 do

        begin
            port[control_port]:=register;   (* output register address *)

            clock_chip[register]:=port[base_port];   (* read register *)
        end;

    TIME:=1000*clock_chip[5] + 100*clock_chip[4] + 10*clock_chip[3]
            + clock_chip[2];

    DATE:=1000*clock_chip[10] + 100*clock_chip[9] + 10*clock_chip[8]
            + clock_chip[7];

end;
```

Figure 5.9 Pascal source code for the READ_CLOCK_CHIP VCR program module.

Figure 5.9 lists a Pascal procedure to accomplish this module. Pascal has been chosen for its ability to *hide* details within a module, passing only the data required. In this example, whenever the time and data are required, the single statement

```
READ_CLOCK_CHIP (t,d);
```

will load variables t and d with the current time and date. Notice that the calling program need not be concerned about how the READ_CLOCK_CHIP procedure accomplishes this function. In fact, because the variable names (t and d) are assigned by the calling routine, we need not even be concerned with the variable names used in the READ_CLOCK_CHIP procedure itself.

Referring to the program listing, the variable names base_port and control_port are assigned to the ports to be used to control the clock chip. The integer variable *register* is defined and used as an index for the array *clock_chip*.

The program consists of a loop of instructions to be repeated 13 times. The register address is first output to the clock chip control port. The data at that address is then read and stored in the array. Although all 13 registers are read and stored, only registers 2 through 5 (for the time) and 7 through 10 (for the date) are actually used. The last two lines of the program process and assemble the TIME and DATE variables.

The listing in Fig. 5.9 represents the *source code* for the READ_CLOCK_CHIP module. It must be compiled and debugged before it is ready for use (discussed in the next two sections). Once converted to object code form, it can be linked with other modules in the VCR control software to form the final version of the program. The entire program can then be tested and ultimately stored in a ROM in the microprocessor control module.

SELF-REVIEW 5.2 (answers on page 219)

5.2.1. Before a program module is written, the _____ and _____ of that module must be clearly defined.

5.2.2. The details of one module should purposely be _____ from other modules in the program.

5.2.3. List a minimum set of "tools" with which every programmer should be equipped.

5.2.4. Why do interpreted programs run more slowly than the corresponding compiled versions?

5.2.5. Assume that registers 2 through 5 of the MSM5832 clock chip store the data "4", "3", "2", "1". What is the output produced by the following Pascal statements?

```
BEGIN
    READ_CLOCK_CHIP (x,y);
    Writeln('The time is ',x);
END
```

5.3 DEBUGGING THE SOFTWARE

The source code for each program module must be compiled or assembled to object code form before it can be tested. This compilation process will reveal any errors in the program's *syntax*. Typical examples are misspelled words, missing delimiters (each line in Pascal must end with a semicolon, for example), and type mismatches (trying to assign an integer to a Boolean variable, for example).

Correcting syntax errors is relatively simple, as the compiler or assembler will normally locate the line in the source code that is in error. More difficult to detect are errors in the program logic. These can be found only by exercising all the various paths through the program. As complex programs may have thousands of different paths, some program errors can go undetected for years.

Such errors are referred to as ''bugs'' and the process of correcting these bugs as *debugging*. Note that debugging is different from *testing*. Once a program module has been written, it should be tested. This involves inputting a subset of data to the program and verifying the output. A good test will check the extreme limits of valid input data. For example, the READ_CLOCK_CHIP module should return a time between 0 and 2359. But will the program calling this module accept numbers outside this range? What if the operator types in 2360? Will the VCR hang up, waiting for this nonexistent time?

Few people actually enjoy debugging a computer program. This is especially true when the program has been written by someone else. Yet for most projects, more time is devoted to this activity than any other. Therefore, this section is devoted to software debugging. We begin by outlining steps that can be followed while the program is still being written. These in turn can simplify the debugging process to follow.

A set of debugging procedures will also be presented. These are just ''common-sense'' rules that define the best way to attack a software problem. The section concludes with a description of DEBUG-86, a symbolic debugger that can be used to locate errors in assembly-language or high-level-language programs.

Anticipating the Debugging Cycle

It is nearly impossible to write a bug-free program on the first attempt. Recognizing this, a good program will be written such that it *anticipates* the debugging cycle to follow. How is this done? As a first step, you should be sure to follow the three rules presented in Sec. 5.2. By structuring your programs in a logical way, and breaking the problem into manageable tasks, the program will be much easier to understand, and therefore debug. When errors are detected, the module at fault can quickly be identified and corrections made.

It may also be a good idea to build a debugger into your code as it is being written. For example, consider the Pascal module shown in Fig. 5.10. This module has a ''built-in'' debugger which can be turned on or off via the variable *debug*. If an error is detected, debug can be set true, causing the first 10 values of the *Data_Array* to be output to the system printer. This information can then be studied to determine whether the module is operating correctly.

```
const
      debug=True;

var
      j: integer;

begin                           (* module begins *)

 .

 .

 .

if debug then          (* Is the debugger on? *)
begin

      writeln(Lst,"Data_Array values 1 through 10")

      for j:=1 to 10 do

      begin

          writeln(Lst,Data_Array[j]);

      end          (* for j:=1 to 10 *)

end     (* if debug *)

 .                       (* module continues *)

 .

 .
```

Figure 5.10 Building a debugger into the program code. Setting the Boolean variable *debug* to true causes the contents of the DATA_ARRAY to be output to the printer each time this module is executed.

Debugging Procedures

Debugging a computer program involves software troubleshooting. And like hardware troubleshooting, you begin with a hypothesis based on all the facts available at the time. Next you test your theory. This can be done by inputting a specific set of data, forcing a variable to take on a certain value, or simply printing out the value of one or more variables to confirm your suspicions.

As an example, suppose that you are testing our smart VCR machine and the following problem occurs. When programmed to record, the machine fails to activate itself—but only for certain times. While studying the problem, you also note that the minutes digits on the front-panel display never exceed 14. In fact, the time changes from 10:09 to 10:01 (and 11:09 to 11:01, etc.).

At first you decide that this must be a hardware problem (it is always easier to blame another group!). However, the hardware people test the displays and verify that they are working correctly. So it must be software. But where?

What about the READ_CLOCK_CHIP module? If the time is read wrong here, it will propagate throughout all the other control modules. This could explain the recording problem—perhaps even the strange problem with the minutes.

Now to test the hypothesis. We add a new statement just before the end of the READ_CLOCK_CHIP module:

Writeln(Lst,time);

This will cause the time—as read directly from the clock chip—to be output to the printer each time this module is called. Let's assume that your hunch is correct—the time is being read incorrectly. But what could be wrong? The logical place to look is the line in which the variable TIME is calculated.

TIME: = 1000*clock_chip[5] + 100*clock_chip[4] + clock_chip[3] + clock_chip[2];

And there is the problem! We forgot the multiplier of 10 for clock_chip[3]. This caused clock_chip[3] and clock_chip[2] to be added directly. This also explains why the minutes never exceeded 14. A quick edit and recompile fixes the problem.

Of course, troubleshooting is not always that easy. But even if your hypothesis is wrong, you have at least ruled out one possibility. Armed with this new information, you can propose your next theory. If you are diligent, you will eventually determine the module in error.

While proceeding in this manner you are well advised to heed the following two troubleshooting rules:

1. *Make changes one at a time. Consider that the corrections themselves may introduce errors, masking the original problem.*
2. *Always keep a backup copy of the module you are changing. If the "fix" does not work, you can quickly "unfix" the module and explore another possibility.*

Another common debugging problem is "missing the forest for the trees," that is, looking for a program bug by searching through the program on a line-by-line basis. Often the program flowcharts or pseudo diagrams will reveal logic errors not readily seen when studying the code line for line.

Finally, do not rule out rewriting a "problem" module entirely. This may require less time than trying to patch up a section of code that was poorly written in the first place.

Debugging Tools

As outlined in the preceding section, debugging involves testing your theories about why a program is not working. The best way to do this is with a debugging program. One example is DEBUG, which operates under the MS-DOS (or PC-DOS) operating system.[2]

Most debuggers are designed to allow you to set *breakpoints* and to *single-step* the program one instruction at a time. For example, the DEBUG command

>GCS:7550

---

[2]DEBUG was covered in detail in Chap. 3.

will cause the program to execute starting at the current CS:IP value and halt when IP = 7550H. DEBUG will then display all the 8086 CPU registers and flags. A typical display was shown in Fig. 3.14.

Breakpoints are used in the early stages of debugging when you are not sure where the problem is. A typical question in your mind at this point would be: "Am I getting through the data input routine correctly?" By inserting a breakpoint at the end of this routine, you can confirm that this part of the program is working as expected. The breakpoint can then be advanced further into the program. Eventually, the breakpoint will either not be "hit," or the contents of the CPU registers will indicate that a problem exists. Now is the time to turn to the single-step mode.

With DEBUG, giving the command

>**T**

(for trace) will cause the current instruction to be executed and all CPU registers and flags displayed (again refer to Fig. 3.14). Stepping through the problem section in this way, you should be able to find the exact spot where the program goes astray.

DEBUG also allows you to "force" a CPU register or flag to take on any value you wish. For example, to load register AX with 1234H, the command is

```
>RAX         ;display contents of AX
AX 0000      ;AX = 0000 (in this example)
:1234        ;New value: AH = 12H, AL = 34H
```

This can be convenient when you need to escape from a long loop (just set the counter to 1). You can also use this technique to test a debugging theory. Load the registers with the desired worst-case data and then single-step through the problem lines.

The debugger available on the Intellec Series IV development system is called DEBUG 86. It is a *symbolic debugger*, meaning that you can refer to memory locations and program variables by their symbolic names (established when the program was edited).

To illustrate the capabilities of DEBUG 86, consider the following 8086 program:

```
START:   MOV   AX,09D3H
         MOV   DS,AX
         MOV   CX, 1000H
COUNT:   LOOP  COUNT
```

This program loads the data segment register with a particular value and then enters a time-delay loop. In DEBUG 86 this program can be single-stepped from the beginning with the command

*STEP FROM .START

where * is the DEBUG 86 prompt. Typing R will cause all the CPU registers to be displayed so that the program's progress can be checked.

Breakpoints can also be set symbolically: for example, to set a breakpoint at the LOOP instruction, use

*GO FROM .START TILL .COUNT

DEBUG 86 commands can also be made part of a compound structure, such as

*REPEAT
.*STEP
.*R
.*END

which will cause the program to single-step and display all CPU registers continually until a control-D is used to abort the process.

DEBUG 86 can also be used with high-level languages. Consider the Pascal READ_CLOCK_CHIP procedure we have been working with. After loading the object code for this module into memory, the command

*DEFINE .START = CS: IP

assigns the label START to the current value of CS:IP (the start of the program). Now assume that we need to check the value of the variable TIME (as we did in the preceding section). The command

*GO TILL .TIME WRITTEN

will begin execution at the current value of CS:IP and halt when a value is written into the variable TIME. Thus this command is a sort of *symbolic breakpoint* based on a memory write condition to a particular variable.

In some debugging cases you are looking for a specific data value. The command

*GO TILL WRITE AT .:READ_CLOCK_CHIP.TIME IS 1209T

will halt when 1209 decimal is written to the variable TIME, located in the module READ_CLOCK_CHIP.

The advantages of using a symbolic debugger are the same as those a high-level language enjoys over an assembly language program. You can reference program variables by their names. This allows you to concentrate on the program's logic, not memory addresses.

SELF-REVIEW 5.3 (answers on page 219)

5.3.1. Explain the purpose of a built-in debugger.

5.3.2. How does software testing differ from software debugging?

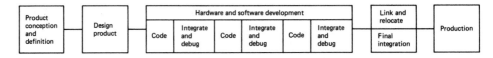

Product conception and definition		Design product		Hardware and software development							Link and relocate		Production
				Code	Integrate and debug	Code	Integrate and debug	Code	Integrate and debug		Final integration		

Figure 5.11   Revised development cycle chart. The hardware and software are developed together and debugged together.

5.3.3. The first step in debugging a computer program is to propose a _____ that if true will explain the problem.

5.3.4. If a breakpoint is set in a program but not "hit," what is indicated?

5.4 INTEGRATING THE HARDWARE AND SOFTWARE

Based on the preceding sections, you should now be able to see that the development cycle chart originally proposed in Fig. 5.1 is not realistic. It suggests that the hardware and software proceed in parallel, but separately. But as we have seen, many of the software modules cannot be tested until the hardware they support is available. Similarly, many of the hardware modules require software control programs to verify their operation.

Figure 5.11 offers a more realistic picture of the development cycle. The hardware and software are developed together (integrated) and then debugged together. What makes this possible is the development system. Because it can *emulate* the processor in the prototype, the software and hardware can be tested and debugged even though the prototype may not yet be capable of running a program on its own. In this way software development can track hardware development.

In this section, using the VCR clock module as an example, we focus on the *integrate and debug* phase of the development cycle. The SDK-86 system design kit will be used to breadboard the hardware, which will then be tested using the in-circuit emulation capabilities of the Intellec Series IV development system.

Designing and Building the Prototype Hardware

One of the important hardware circuits in the VCR machine is the time-of-day clock module. As mentioned in Sec. 5.2, our mythical hardware team has chosen the OKI Semiconductor MSM5832 clock/calendar chip. This device is designed specifically to be controlled by a microprocessor. In fact, it cannot be tested unless a microprocessor interface is provided. For this reason the hardware design team has selected an SDK-86 as a "test bed" for this chip.

The SDK-86 is an 8086 microprocessor system programmed via a keypad and set of six hexadecimal displays. A photograph is shown in Fig. 5.12. Included on the circuit board are 4K of RAM, 8K of ROM, one serial port, and six 8-bit input/output ports. A wire-wrapping area is also provided with access to all the system control signals. A block diagram is given in Fig. 5.13.

As chief engineer of the VCR project, your "game plan" is to interface the MSM5832 to two of the I/O ports available in the SDK-86. The 8086 processor in the kit will then be removed and replaced with a connector and cable to the Series IV development system.

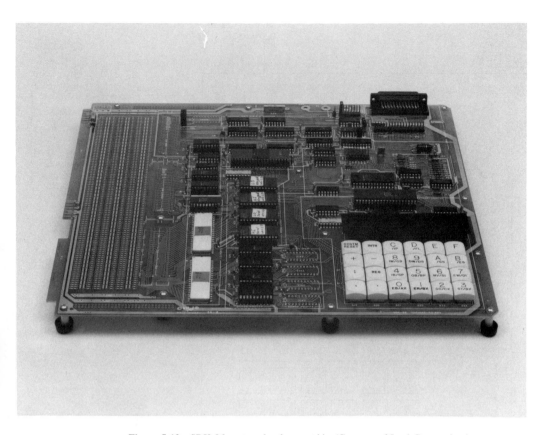

Figure 5.12 SDK-86 system development kit. (Courtesy of Intel Corporation.)

The hardware and software can then be debugged together, using all the facilities of the Series IV.

Using the SDK-86 as a development system.   The SDK-86 can be used as an inexpensive hardware/software development system. It can be controlled via the keypad shown in the block diagram in Fig. 5.13, or via an external video terminal connected to its serial port. Note that separate monitor (control) program ROMs are provided for each option.

Programs written for the SDK-86 must be entered in object code form. One way of doing this is to "hand assemble" the program and then enter the hex codes via the keypad or terminal's keyboard. A better choice is to develop the software using an assembler on another system. The object code can then be entered from the assembled listing. A better choice still is to use the serial monitor's **L** command to download the object code directly into the SDK-86's RAM. This requires a cable between the SDK-86 and the development system.

Once the program is in memory, it can be single-stepped and traced. The contents of any of the CPU registers can be requested and displayed on the terminal's screen or the system displays. Once a program has been debugged, a PROM can be programmed

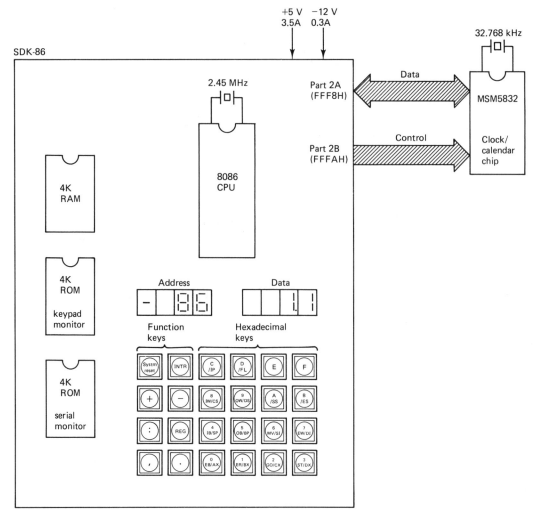

Figure 5.13 SDK-86 block diagram. Two of the six 8-bit I/O ports are used to control the MSM5832 clock/calendar chip.

and interfaced to the processor in the SDK-86. In this way the hardware and software of the prototype can be integrated, debugged, and built on the SDK-86 hardware "skeleton."

In-Circuit Emulation

Let's assume that the MSM5832 has been interfaced to the SDK-86 and appears to be working. That is, pulses are detected from the crystal oscillator and on the chip's data lines. Of course, we cannot really test the circuit until the software is run. This will require the *in-circuit emulator*.

Using Intel's Series IV development system, the emulator is started by typing the command.

– RUN I2ICE

This transfers control to the I^{2}ICE (integrated instrumentation and in-circuit emulation) hardware in the development system (see Fig. 5.14 for an overview of this system). Using the emulator, the clock chip hardware and software can now be integrated and debugged in stages. Before the prototype hardware is available the software can be written and *simulated* using the memory and I/O of the development system. In this initial development stage, the emulation cable is left open-circuited, as no prototype hardware yet exists.

Before emulation is begun, the memory and I/O must be *mapped* to the development system. For example, the command.

*MAP 0K LENGTH 32K HS

defines the first 32K bytes of memory to be high-speed memory in the I^{2}ICE instrumentation chassis. The MAP command determines where the memory physically resides. Other choices are:

1. *User*. The prototype system itself contains the memory.
2. *MB*. The host development system contains the memory.
3. *Guarded*. The memory does not reside anywhere. Access to guarded memory will result in a halt in emulation, and an error message will appear on the system video display.

When the prototype is not yet available, the I/O can also be mapped to the development system. In this case input data will be received from the keyboard and output data displayed on the system console. The command

*MAPIO FFC0H LENGTH 64T ICE

will map the last 64 8086 I/O ports to the I^{2}ICE system.

The next step is to load the object code for the READ_CLOCK_CHIP procedure (Fig. 5.9) into memory:

*LOAD :F1:clock.86

where F1 indicates that drive 1 is to be read. The extension (86) indicates the object code form of the file. Emulation is then begun with the command

*GO

In this example, the console responds

?UNIT 0 PORT FFFAH OUTPUT BYTE 0000H

I^{2}ICE has intercepted the first output statement in the READ_CLOCK_CHIP procedure. This is the statement

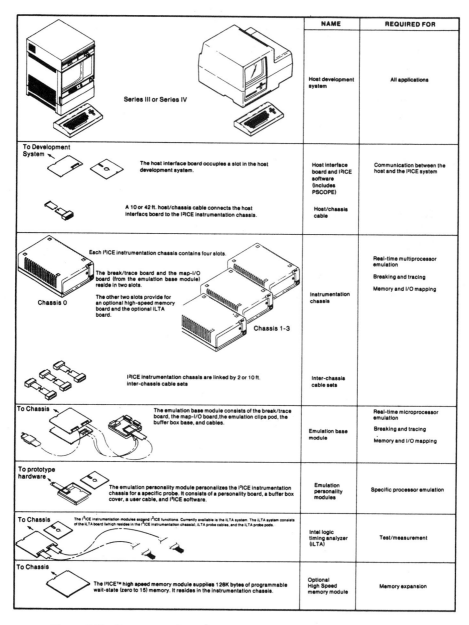

	NAME	REQUIRED FOR
Series III or Series IV	Host development system	All applications
To Development System — The host interface board occupies a slot in the host development system.	Host interface board and I²ICE software (includes PSCOPE)	Communication between the host and the I²ICE system
A 10 or 42 ft. host/chassis cable connects the host interface board to the I²ICE instrumentation chassis.	Host/chassis cable	
Each I²ICE instrumentation chassis contains four slots. The break/trace board and the map-I/O board (from the emulation base module) reside in two slots. Chassis 0. The other two slots provide for an optional high-speed memory board and the optional ILTA board. Chassis 1-3	Instrumentation chassis	Real-time multiprocessor emulation Breaking and tracing Memory and I/O mapping
I²ICE instrumentation chassis are linked by 2 or 10 ft. inter-chassis cable sets	Inter-chassis cable sets	
To Chassis — The emulation base module consists of the break/trace board, the map-I/O board, the emulation clips pod, the buffer box base, and cables.	Emulation base module	Real-time microprocessor emulation Breaking and tracing Memory and I/O mapping
To prototype hardware — The emulation personality module personalizes the I²ICE instrumentation chassis for a specific probe. It consists of a personality board, a buffer box cover, a user cable, and I²ICE software.	Emulation personality modules	Specific processor emulation
To Chassis — The I²ICE instrumentation modules expand I²ICE functions. Currently available is the ILTA system. The ILTA system consists of the ILTA board (which resides in the I²ICE instrumentation chassis), ILTA probe cables, and the ILTA probe pods.	Intel logic timing analyzer (ILTA)	Test/measurement
To Chassis — The I²ICE™ high speed memory module supplies 128K bytes of programmable wait-state (zero to 15) memory. It resides in the instrumentation chassis.	Optional High Speed memory module	Memory expansion

Figure 5.14 Components of the I²ICE emulation and logic timing analysis system. (Courtesy of Intel Corporation.)

```
port[control_port]: = register;
```

Because this port has been mapped to the development system console, the data is sent to the video display, not to the prototype. The program then continues and the console responds

?UNIT 0 PORT FFF8H REQUESTS BYTE INPUT (ENTER VALUE)*

I^2ICE has intercepted the next line in the program, which corresponds to the input statement

```
clock_chip[register]: = port[base_port];
```

Because this port is also mapped to the development system, you must enter the data to be input using the keyboard.

As the program continues to loop, each data byte output is displayed on the system console, and each data input request must be answered from the keyboard. When the program ends, we can check the values of the variables TIME and DATE by requesting I^2ICE to display their values.

*TIME
+1247

*DATE
+850813

These numbers are interpreted as 12:47 and August 13, 1985. They should agree with those input from the keyboard.

As you can see, the emulator allows you to simulate the prototype hardware and in this way test the control software. All the commands in DEBUG-86 are valid in the I^2ICE system. This includes the use of breakpoints and single-stepping. Using these facilities to debug our software, we can feel fairly confident that the control program is correct, even though the hardware itself has not yet been built.

The next phase in the development cycle calls for a test with the prototype hardware. In our example, this means the SDK-86 with MSM5832 clock chip interface. After removing the 8086 from its socket and replacing it with the emulation cable, we must remap the I/O space to the prototype.

*MAPIO FFC0H LENGTH 40H USER

Now when the emulation is run, the data will be read from the prototype and output to the prototype. If the hardware is working, the time and data will be read and stored in the variables TIME and DATE.[3]

The final step in the program development cycle is to move the (tested and debugged) control software to the prototype itself. Now running from its own RAM and ROM, the prototype is ready for final testing. If any new problems occur, the emulator can be plugged back in, and the hardware/software debugged.

Of course, in practice, a microprocessor-controlled product has many hardware and

---

[3]A SET_CLOCK_CHIP procedure is obviously required for any practical application of this chip. This submodule would be part of the OPERATE module defined in Fig. 5.6.

software modules. Each must be tested and debugged by following the program development cycle just described. In the end, all these modules will be linked together to form the final version of the control software.

SELF-REVIEW 5.4 (answers on page 219)

5.4.1. List the three stages of hardware/software development when using an in-circuit emulator.

5.4.2. What is meant by the term SDK-86 "skeleton"?

5.4.3. An in-circuit emulator can be used to test a prototype even though that prototype does not yet contain RAM or ROM. This is done by _____ the prototype's memory to the emulator or development system.

5.4.4. The I²ICE command to specify that the first 128 8086 I/O ports are to be accessed from the development system console is _____.

CHAPTER 5 SELF-TEST

1. System integration refers to the creation and testing of _____ and _____ in a prototype microprocessor product.

2. Because its functions are controlled by _____, a microprocessor-based product is more flexible than a fixed-in-hardware product.

3. The development cycle for a microprocessor product consists of a(n) _____ and _____ cycle repeated for each hardware and software module.

4. A development system can be used to: (a) debug system software; (b) debug prototype hardware; (c) develop applications programs; (d) all of the above.

5. Is a structured program also a modular program? Explain.

6. A program module should have only a _____ _____ _____ and a _____ _____ _____.

7. Which of the following is *not* an advantage of using a high-level language versus assembly language? (a) more efficient code; (b) reduced development time; (c) more reliable code; (d) easier maintenance.

8. What is the "hidden" information concept as applied to modular programming?

9. For program debugging, a(n) _____ language is most convenient.

10. Syntax errors are normally caught when the program is _____.

11. Specify the DEBUG command to execute the program beginning at the current CS:IP with a breakpoint at CS:0010H.

12. If CS:0010H has the label ERROR, give the DEBUG-86 command to execute the program beginning at address START with a breakpoint at address ERROR.

13. A(n) _____ _____ _____ allows portions of the prototype hardware to be tested before the entire system has been built.

14. Using Intel's I²ICE, development software may reside in _____ memory, _____ memory, or _____ memory.

15. Specify the I²ICE command(s) that will map the first 64K bytes of memory to high-speed memory in the I²ICE instrumentation chassis, and map all remaining memory as guarded.

ANALYSIS AND DESIGN QUESTIONS

Note: The following questions assume that you have been put in charge of developing a micro-processor-controlled washing machine. The following hardware capabilities are required:

1. Variable-speed control of the motor/agitator.
2. Water temperature selection: cold, warm, hot.
3. Water flow control to fill and empty the washer.
4. Timed control of the various wash cycles (normal, prewash, knit-delicate, permanent press).

5.1. Sketch a block diagram of the entire system (washer and microprocessor controller). Be sure to include the following: motor, inlet valves for hot and cold water, drain valve for emptying the tank, and control electronics.

5.2. Sketch a diagram similar to Fig. 5.5 that defines the purpose of the washing machine control software in terms of the system inputs and outputs.

5.3. Create a chart similar to Fig. 5.6 that illustrates the *structure* of the control software described in question 5.2. Break your chart into several manageable modules, keeping in mind the *information-hiding* concept.

5.4. As group leader for this project, describe in detail the steps you would follow to develop this product. Be sure to indicate the sequence in which each step is to be performed and the hardware and software ''tools'' required.

SELF REVIEW ANSWERS

5.1.1 False

5.1.2 development system

5.1.3 the set of tools (editors, assemblers, compilers, debuggers) available to the programmer

5.1.4 it assumes the hardware and software development can proceed independently

5.2.1 purpose, structure

5.2.2 hidden

5.2.3 editor, assembler, high level language compiler, debugger, library manager, linker

5.2.4 each high level instruction must be translated to the equivalent machine instructions as the program is run

5.2.5 The time is 1234

5.3.1 a debugger built into the program that can be ''turned on'' when needed to view program variables

5.3.2 sample data is tested to verify correct operation of the program

5.3.3 hypothesis

5.3.4 the instruction in that location is never executed

5.4.1 test the software emulating the hardware, test the prototype hardware and software, final testing without the emulator

5.4.2 the basic 8086 microcomputer hardware which can be expanded to form the prototype's hardware

5.4.3 mapping

5.4.4 MAPIO 0 LENGTH 80 H ICE

6

DESIGNING THE 8086 CPU MODULE

Beginning with this chapter, we shift the focus of our attention from microcomputer software to microcomputer hardware. In particular, this and the following two chapters introduce the topic of *microcomputer systems design*. We begin by taking a detailed look at the pin functions of the 8086 microprocessor chip. This is followed by an introduction to the support circuits required to construct an 8086-based microcomputer. Our goal is the design of a hardware module to which the memory and I/O can be interfaced (connected). In Chaps. 7 and 8 we discuss memory and I/O interfacing in detail.

The 8086 microprocessor is a complex integrated circuit housed in a 600-mil-wide 40-pin package. Many of these pins are *time multiplexed*, providing two separate processor functions. Other pins are devoted to supporting the 8087 coprocessor or 8089 I/O processor. In this chapter we examine all these pins and their functions, but the primary emphasis will be on developing the three-bus system architecture introduced in Chap. 1.

Because the concept of an electrical bus is so important, we will take a brief "side trip" to study different types of microcomputer buses and their electrical characteristics. These concepts are applied throughout the remaining chapters of this book.

Although this chapter is devoted to the 8086 microprocessor, nearly all the comments apply to the 8-bit 8088 as well. In Sec. 6.7 the hardware differences between the two processors are specifically pointed out.

The main topics in this chapter are:

6.1 Reviewing the Three-Bus System Architecture
6.2 Basic 8086 CPU Hardware Design

6.1 REVIEWING THE THREE-BUS SYSTEM ARCHITECTURE

In one regard a microprocessor is a very simple machine. It endlessly follows the sequence:

1. Fetch the next instruction in sequence from memory.

2. Execute the instruction.

3. Go to step 1.

The fetch cycle is actually a *memory read* operation in which the byte or word "pointed to" by the program counter (or instruction pointer) is transferred from memory to the instruction register in the CPU. Execution of this instruction may require additional memory reads as in the 8086 instruction MOV BX,[MEMWDS]. Other possibilities for the execution phase include a *memory write* (MOV [MEMWDS],BX), an *I/O read* (IN AL,DPORT), an *I/O write* (OUT DPORT,AL), or an *internal* CPU activity (INC AX).

In all, there are five unique operations or *bus cycles* possible:

1. Memory read

2. Memory write

3. I/O read

4. I/O write

5. Bus idle (internal operation not requiring access to memory or I/O)

As we saw in Fig. 1.1, three sets of wires (or buses) are dedicated to this transferring of data between the CPU and the memory and I/O units. In this section we look at the timing between the address, data, and control buses for each of the (active) bus cycle types.

Bus Cycle Timing

Figure 6.1 illustrates bus cycle timing for the four active bus cycle types. Each cycle begins with the output of the memory or I/O port address during the T1 clock cycle. For the 8086 this can be a 20-bit memory address, a 16-bit indirect I/O address (using register DX), or an 8-bit direct I/O address.

Note that in Fig. 6.1 I have not attempted to draw all 20 address lines. Instead, the contents of the address bus is shown to change to a new address sometime during the T1 state. The parallel lines indicate that some of the lines are assumed to be high and others low. The specific address is unimportant for this discussion.

Examining the address lines only, it is not possible to determine if this is a memory or an I/O address. Neither can you tell the *direction* of the data flow. That is, is the CPU performing a read or a write cycle? For this reason a *control* bus is required. As shown in Fig. 6.1, this bus consists of the four active-low signals

1. $\overline{\text{MEMR}}$
2. $\overline{\text{MEMW}}$
3. $\overline{\text{IOR}}$
4. $\overline{\text{IOW}}$

To see how the three buses shown in Fig. 6.1 work together, consider the sequence of events that occur during a memory read bus cycle.

T1. The processor outputs the 20-bit memory address. The data lines are open circuited and all control lines disabled.

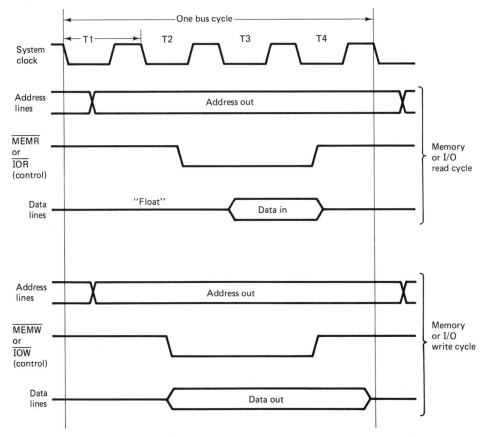

Figure 6.1 During an active bus cycle the microprocessor may perform a memory read, memory write, I/O read, or I/O write operation. The control and address buses are used to specify the memory or I/O address and the direction of data flow on the data bus lines.

T2. The $\overline{\text{MEMR}}$ control line is driven low. The memory unit recognizes this bus cycle as a memory read and prepares to place the addressed byte or word onto the data lines.

T3. The microprocessor configures its data bus lines for input but takes no further action. This state is provided primarily to give the memory time to "look up" the data byte or word.

T4. The microprocessor now expects the data to be on the data bus lines. Therefore, it latches the contents of these lines and releases the memory read control signal. This marks the end of the bus cycle.

The most important point to note is that the microprocessor controls all the bus timing. The memory must be able to supply the selected data byte or word by the time $\overline{\text{MEMR}}$ goes high during the T4 state. If it cannot do so, the CPU will read random information on the data bus lines. This will lead to unpredictable results.[1]

Example 6.1

Describe the contents of the address, data, and control bus lines when the instruction MOV [1000H],BX is executed. Assume that register DS = 09D3H and register BX = 1234H.

Solution   The instruction requires a memory write to location 1000H of the data segment. In this case the physical address is 09D30H + 1000H = 0AD30H. This 20-bit address will be placed on the address lines. The control bus signal $\overline{\text{MEMW}}$ will go low during T2 and the data bus will contain 1234H, the contents of register BX. The memory is assumed to latch this data word by the time $\overline{\text{MEMW}}$ returns high in the T4 state.

There is one final point to make about the control bus timing—but it should be obvious. *Only one control signal can be active at a given time.* The processor cannot read from its memory at the same time it is outputting to an I/O device, for example. This is a very important point and the key to the memory and I/O interface circuits covered in Chaps. 7 and 8.

SELF-REVIEW 6.1 *(answers on page 269)*

6.1.1. During an instruction fetch a _____ _____ bus cycle is performed.

6.1.2. Execution of the instruction OUT DPORT,AX requires a(n) _____ _____ bus cycle.

6.1.3. Under what conditions will the 8086 buses be idle?

6.1.4. Using a logic analyzer the three buses of an 8086 microprocessor are recorded at a particular instant.

> *Address bus:* 47000H
> *Control bus:* $\overline{\text{MEMR}} = 0$, $\overline{\text{MEMW}} = 1$, $\overline{\text{IOR}} = 1$, $\overline{\text{IOW}} = 1$
> *Data bus:* F3C0H

Explain the type of bus cycle occurring.

---

[1]In Chap. 7 we see how the memory unit can request "wait" states, effectively extending the T3 state by an integral number of clock cycles. In this way slow-memory devices can be interfaced.

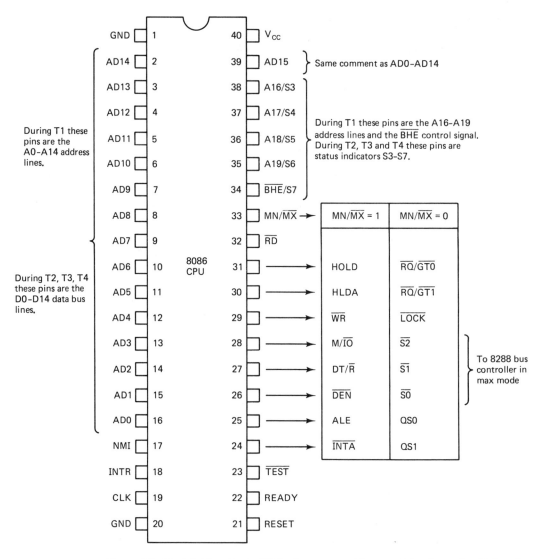

Figure 6.2 Pin definitions for the 8086 microprocessor. The control signals on pins 24 through 31 change depending on the mode of operation. (From J. Uffenbeck, *Microcomputers and Microprocessors: The 8080, 8085, and Z-80.* Prentice-Hall, Englewood Cliffs, N.J., 1985.)

6.2 BASIC 8086 CPU HARDWARE DESIGN

In this section we look at the pin descriptions for the 8086 microprocessor. This information will allow us to draw timing diagrams for the four active bus cycles similar to those in Fig. 6.1. A thorough understanding of 8086 timing will be essential when we cover memory and I/O interfacing in Chaps. 7 and 8.

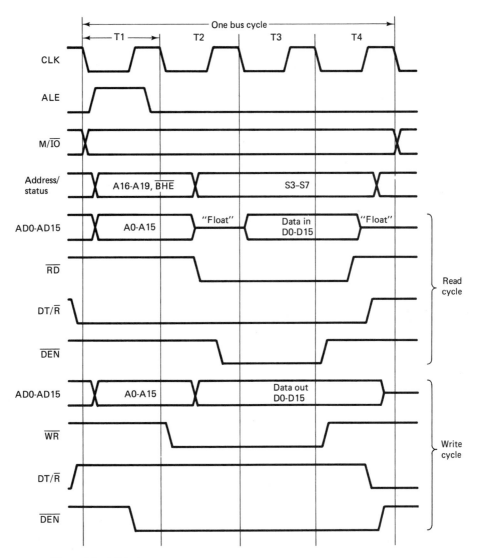

Figure 6.3 8086 microprocessor read and write bus cycles. The address lines are valid during the T1 state but become the data lines and status indicators during T2–T4.

8086 CPU Pin Descriptions

One of the challenges faced by the 8086 design engineers was providing access to all the functions of the processor with a standard 40-pin dual-in-line package (DIP). In fact, the 8086 has a 20-bit address bus, 16-bit data bus, three power pins, and 17 pins devoted to miscellaneous control and timing functions. Clearly, this does not add up.

The "trick" employed by Intel to make this work is called *time multiplexing*. This is a design technique in which one circuit pin has more than one function. For example, the 8086's 16 data pins (labeled AD0–AD15) are address lines during the T1 clock state, but become data lines during the T2–T4 states. A special "demultiplexing" circuit is required to extract the separate data and address lines. Using time multiplexing the pin breakdown becomes

16 data and address pins

4 address (and status) pins

3 power pins

17 control and timing pins

Figure 6.2 shows the specific pin assignments.

Another interesting feature of the 8086 is its ability to operate in a *minimum mode* or a *maximum mode*. The minimum mode is intended for simple single-processor systems on one printed circuit board (PCB). The maximum mode is intended for more complex systems with separate I/O and memory boards. This mode also supports coprocessors such as the 8087 NDP and 8089 IOP. In the discussion to follow, we assume that the minimum mode applies as each group of pins are explained. Maximum-mode operation is discussed in Sec. 6.6.

Data bus (AD0–AD15).   These 16 pins form the CPU's bidirectional data bus. These lines are valid only during the T2 through T4 clock states. During T1 they hold the low 16 bits of the memory or I/O address.

Address bus (AD0–AD15 and A16/S3–A19/S6).   These 20 pins correspond to the CPU's 20-bit address bus and allow the processor to access 1,048,576 unique memory locations. These output lines are valid only during the T1 state, switching to become the data and status lines during the T2–T4 clock states.

Address latch enable (ALE).   The signal output on this pin can be used to demultiplex the address, data, and status lines on AD0–AD15, A16/S3–A19/S6, and $\overline{\text{BHE}}$/S7. Figure 6.3 illustrates the (minimum mode) timing for read and write bus cycles. Every cycle begins with an ALE pulse during the T1 clock state. The 20-bit address is guaranteed to be valid when ALE switches from high to low near the end of T1. Therefore, this signal can be used to strobe the address into a latch. This technique is explored more fully in Sec. 6.5.

TABLE 6.1 SPEED AND POWER SPECIFICATIONS FOR THE 8086 AND 8088 MICROPROCESSORS

Processor	f_{max} (MHz)	I_{CC}(max) (mA)	Power dissipation (W)
8086	5	340	1.7
8086-2	8	350	1.75
8086-1	10	360	1.8
8088	5	340	1.7
8088-2	8	350	1.75
P8088	5	250	1.25

TABLE 6.2 S3–S7 STATUS BIT DEFINITIONS[a]

S4	S3	Bus cycle access is to:
0	0	Extra segment
0	1	Stack segment
1	0	Code segment (or none)
1	1	Data segment

[a]S5, IF (interrupts enabled flag); S6, 0; (indicates 8086 is on the bus); S7, spare status bit (not used).

Memory/IO (M/$\overline{\text{IO}}$).   The 8086 does not output separate memory and I/O read and write signals. Instead, the M/$\overline{\text{IO}}$ signal is output early in the T1 state and identifies the current bus cycle as a memory (M/$\overline{\text{IO}}$ = 1) or I/O (M/$\overline{\text{IO}}$ = 0) operation.

Read ($\overline{\text{RD}}$).   This active-low output signal indicates that the direction of data flow on the bus is from memory or I/O into the processor. It can be combined with M/$\overline{\text{IO}}$ to form $\overline{\text{MEMR}}$ and $\overline{\text{IOR}}$ control signals. It is output during the T2 state and removed during the T4 state. The memory or I/O device is assumed to have placed the addressed byte or word onto the data lines by the time $\overline{\text{RD}}$ returns high.

Write ($\overline{\text{WR}}$).   This signal is the counterpart of $\overline{\text{RD}}$ and indicates that data is to flow from the CPU to memory or to an I/O device. In either case, the data is output during the T2 state. This gives the memory or I/O plenty of time to latch the data byte or word before $\overline{\text{WR}}$ is removed during T4. Figure 6.4 shows how $\overline{\text{RD}}$, $\overline{\text{WR}}$, and M/$\overline{\text{IO}}$ can be combined to generate a conventional four-line control bus.

Clock (CLK).   All events in the microprocessor are synchronized to the system clock applied to the CLK pin. Table 6.1 indicates that the maximum clock frequency is

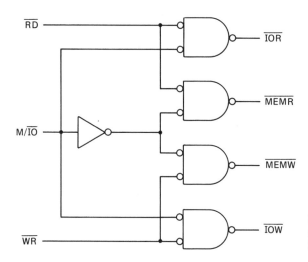

Figure 6.4   Generating the four memory and I/O control bus signals from the 8086'a $\overline{\text{RD}}$, $\overline{\text{WR}}$, and M/$\overline{\text{IO}}$ outputs.

10 MHz for the 8086-1 part. Section 6.3 provides more detail on the clock signal and the 8284A clock generator.

Status (A16/S3–A19/S6 and $\overline{\text{BHE}}$/S7).   These five status signals are output during states T2–T4. They are intended primarily for diagnostic testing purposes, as their definitions in Table 6.2 indicate. It is possible to decode S3 and S4 to provide four separate 1MB address spaces for the extra, data, code, and stack memory segments. This is shown in Fig. 6.5. All memory read or write operations are intercepted by this circuit, causing the appropriate physical memory block to be accessed. In practice, this is seldom done.

Bus high enable ($\overline{\text{BHE}}$/S7).   This signal is multiplexed with the S7 status indicator. It is output only during the T1 state. When $\overline{\text{BHE}}$ is low, it indicates that AD8–AD15 are involved in the data transfer. This can occur for memory or I/O word accesses or when accessing a data byte from an odd address. $\overline{\text{BHE}}$ and A0 are typically used to select even or odd memory banks or I/O ports. Table 6.3 shows the encoding.

Data transmit/receive (DT/$\overline{\text{R}}$).   This signal is intended to control the direction of data flow through the buffers (if any) connected to the system data bus. When low it indicates a read operation, and when high, a write operation. Bidirectional buffers suitable for this task are discussed in Sec. 6.4.

Data enable ($\overline{\text{DEN}}$).   This signal is intended to be used with DT/$\overline{\text{R}}$ to enable a set of bidirectional buffers connected to the system data bus. It prevents bus contention (two circuits attempting to drive the same bus line) by disabling the data bus buffers until the T2 state, when the address/data lines no longer hold the memory or I/O address.

Minimum/maximum mode (MN/$\overline{\text{MX}}$)..   As mentioned at the beginning of this section, the 8086 can be operated in one of two modes called the minimum and maximum modes. The function of pins 24 through 32 change depending on the logic level applied to this pin. In this section we are considering only the minimum mode (MN/$\overline{\text{MX}}$ = 1). The maximum mode is covered in Sec. 6.6.

RESET.   When pulsed high this input causes the 8086 to terminate its present activity and perform a reset sequence. The status of the "old" job is lost. RESET is

TABLE 6.3 8086 MEMORY ACCESS ENCODING

$\overline{\text{BHE}}$	A0	Action
0	0	Access 16-bit word
0	1	Access odd byte to D8–D15
1	0	Access even byte to D0–D7
1	1	No action

Source: J. Uffenbeck, *Microcomputers and Microprocessors: The 8080, 8085, and Z-80.* Prentice-Hall, Englewood Cliffs, N.J., 1985.

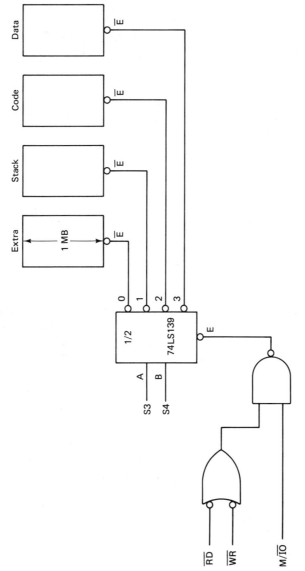

Figure 6.5 Decoding status signals S3 and S4 allows the extra, stack, code, and data segments to be located in physically separate 1M-byte address spaces.

normally used when first starting the system or after a system crash. In Sec. 6.3 we describe the reset sequence in detail.

$\overline{\text{TEST}}$. This input is used together with the WAIT instruction. If the $\overline{\text{TEST}}$ input is high when the WAIT instruction is encountered, execution of the program is suspended and the CPU enters an idle mode. Only when $\overline{\text{TEST}}$ returns low will execution resume (with the instruction following WAIT). Normally, this input is driven by the 8087. WAIT is then used as a prefix to those 8086 instructions that reference data operated on by the 8087. This prevents the CPU from accessing a memory result before the NDP has finished its calculation.

READY. The READY input is sampled on the rising edge of the T2 clock pulse. If this line is found low (''not ready''), an extra T3 state is inserted by the processor. The cycle repeats until the READY input is found high. The READY input is usually driven by a slow-memory device that cannot supply data as fast as required with normal CPU timing.

Interrupts (INTR, NMI, and $\overline{\text{INTA}}$). INTR and NMI are hardware-initiated interrupt requests that function exactly as software interrupts. NMI is rising-edge triggered and INTR is an active high-level trigger. The INTR input can be *masked* by resetting the IF processor status bit (CLI). NMI is a nonmaskable interrupt that will always be serviced. As such it should be reserved for ''catastrophic'' events such as power failure or memory errors.

When NMI is active, control automatically transfers to the address stored in locations 00008–0000BH. When INTR is active an *interrupt-acknowledge* cycle is performed. This is similar to a memory read cycle except that $\overline{\text{INTA}}$ is active instead of $\overline{\text{RD}}$. The interrupting device is expected to place an 8-bit *type* number onto the low-order data bus. Control then transfers to the address stored in locations *type* $\times$ 4 through *type* $\times$ 4 + 3.

Hold and hold acknowledge (HOLD and HLDA). HOLD is an active-high CPU input that causes the processor to open circuit all of its bus lines. This effectively disconnects the CPU from its memory and I/O, allowing a second processor to access these devices. This is referred to as *direct memory access* (DMA). HLDA acknowledges the DMA request to the DMA controller. This topic is covered in more detail in Chap. 8.

Power and ground (V_{cc} and GND). The 8086 requires a single +5-V power source and has two ground pins. Power consumption is indicated in Table 6.1 for the various speed versions of the chip.

SELF-REVIEW 6.2 *(answers on page 269)*

6.2.1. Explain the term *time multiplexed*.

6.2.2. The 8086 20-bit address is output during the _____ state and guaranteed to be valid on the falling edge of _____.

6.2.3. During which T state does the 8086 CPU read data from memory or an I/O device?

6.2.4. Assume that the 8086 is performing a memory-word read bus cycle. Complete the following chart for the T1 and T4 clock states, indicating the values of the signals indicated.

	T1	T4
AD0–AD15	————	————
A16/S3–A19/S6	————	————
$\overline{BHE}$/S7	————	————
$\overline{RD}$	————	————
$\overline{WR}$	————	————
M/$\overline{IO}$	————	————

6.2.5. The highest-performance 8086 is the ——————— version with a maximum clock frequency of ————— MHz.

6.2.6. When used with coprocessors such as the 8087 NDP, the 8086 should be operated in the ——————— mode.

6.3 GENERATING THE 8086 SYSTEM CLOCK AND RESET SIGNALS

The 8086 requires a clock signal with fast rise and fall times ($<$10 ns), logic 0 and 1 levels of -0.5 to 0.6 V and 3.9 to 5.0 V, respectively, and a duty cycle of 33%. The processor's RESET signal must be synchronized to the system clock and persist for at least 4 T states.

Because of these stringent requirements, Intel has made available the 8284A clock generator. This IC meets all the requirements mentioned for the clock and RESET signals and can also be used to synchronize wait requests from slow-memory parts.

In this section we show how to use the 8284A to generate the system clock signal in an 8086 microcomputer system and how to implement the reset function.

The 8086 Clock Signal

As we have seen, all the activities of the 8086 are sequential and synchronized to a system clock signal. During the T1 state of this clock the memory or I/O address is output, during T2 the control signals are activated, during T3 the memory and I/O are given time to respond, and finally, during the T4 state the data is input or output.

Without the clock signal to synchronize these events, we would have chaos. The memory and I/O devices need the *setup* and *hold* times provided by the basic four-clock-state bus cycle.

The clock is important for still another reason. Internally, the microprocessor is designed with *dynamic* logic gates that require periodic "refreshing" or they will lose their data. The clock signal provides this refresh. For this reason the clock must never be stopped. In fact, the 8086 has a *minimum* operating frequency specification (2 MHz) as well as a maximum.

8284A/8284A-1
CLOCK GENERATOR AND DRIVER FOR
iAPX 86, 88 PROCESSORS

- **Generates the System Clock for the iAPX 86, 88 Processors:**
  5 MHz, 8 MHz with 8284A
  10 MHz with 8284A-1
- **Uses a Crystal or a TTL Signal for Frequency Source**
- **Provides Local READY and Multibus™ READY Synchronization**
- **18-Pin Package**

- **Single +5V Power Supply**
- **Generates System Reset Output from Schmitt Trigger Input**
- **Capable of Clock Synchronization with Other 8284As**
- **Available in EXPRESS**
  - **Standard Temperature Range**
  - **Extended Temperature Range**

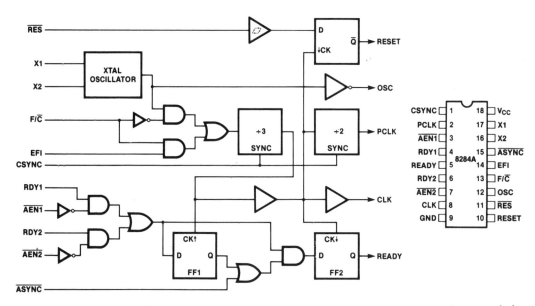

Figure 6.6 The 8284A is used in all 8086/88 microcomputer systems to generate the system clock signal. (Courtesy of Intel Corporation.)

Figure 6.6 is a portion of the 8284A data sheet with the clock generator portion of the chip highlighted. The clock source can be an internal crystal oscillator ($F/\overline{C} = 0$) or an external frequency input ($F/\overline{C} = 1$) applied to the EFI pin. In either case a divide-by-3 counter provides the necessary 33% duty cycle.

The 8284A has three frequency outputs. OSC is a TTL-level signal with a frequency equal to that of the internal crystal oscillator. PCLK is a TTL-level peripheral clock with frequency one-half that of the 8086 clock and a 50% duty cycle. CLK is the processor clock. Its frequency is one-third that of the crystal oscillator or EFI input and has a 33% duty cycle.

The CSYNC input allows the system clock to be synchronized to an external event. It can also be used to synchronize multiple 8284As to provide clock signals that are in phase. When high, the counters are reset but resume counting when this input is brought low.

Example 6.2

Describe the 8284A pin connections necessary to operate the 8086-2 at 8 MHz. Assume a crystal time base.

Solution   The circuit is shown in Fig. 6.7. The crystal connects between X1 and X2 with 510Ω resistors to ground at each pin (as recommended by Intel for oscillator stability). The EFI, $F/\overline{C}$, and CSYNC inputs are all grounded for this application.

"Cold Starting" the 8086

When power is first applied to the 8086, all its internal registers contain random data. This also applies to its read/write memory (RAM). Because of this, the processor will fetch its first instruction from a random memory location (containing a random instruction), leading to an unpredictable result. It is quite likely that the CPU will "tie itself up" in a loop endlessly executing some random group of instructions.

Obviously, some means must be provided for gaining control of the machine when it is first started. This is the purpose of the RESET input. When this pin is driven high, most of the 8086 CPU registers are reset, as shown in Table 6.4. Pay particular attention

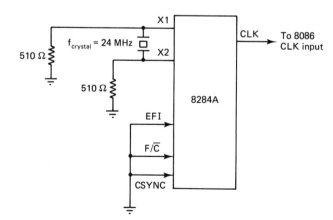

Figure 6.7   Generating the 8086 clock signal with the 8284A. The output duty cycle is 33% with a frequency one-third that of the crystal. If the $F/\overline{C}$ input is wired to +5 V, an external oscillator can be connected to EFI bypassing the crystal oscillator source.

TABLE 6.4 CPU STATE FOLLOWING RESET

CPU	Content
Flags	Clear
Instruction pointer	0000H
CS register	FFFFH
DS register	0000H
SS register	0000H
ES register	0000H
Queue	Empty

to the CS register, however. Because it contains FFFFH, the CPU will fetch its first instruction from physical address FFFF0H + 0000 = FFFF0H.

RESET thus solves the random-start-address problem associated with "cold starting" the processor. However, another problem remains. We must ensure that a useful program resides in memory beginning at the reset start address FFFF0H. Note that RAM cannot be used at this address, as this memory will be storing random data when power is first applied.

The solution is to map a read-only memory (ROM) into this address space. Because the contents of ROM are not lost when power is removed, we can be sure that the 8086 will have a useful program to execute when it is first started.

There are only 16 bytes between addresses FFFF0H and FFFFFH (the end of memory), so the instruction at FFFF0H is normally a "jump" to some other location where a longer program resides (again in ROM). For example, a 2K-byte 2716 ROM could be mapped to cover the address range FF800H–FFFFFH. A jump to location FFF80H will then allow most of the 2K-byte ROM to be used for a "bootstrap" loader program. This is a program that initializes the computer and then loads a more complex program from a disk drive (usually the operating system) into RAM.

Generating the RESET Signal

Figure 6.8 illustrates how the 8284A is used to generate a RESET signal that will meet the requirements of the 8086. The $\overline{\text{RES}}$ input is synchronized to the falling edge of the system clock signal, as shown in the 8284A block diagram in Fig. 6.6.

The circuit in Fig. 6.8 allows the processor to be reset in two ways. The most obvious is to depress the switch. The RESET output will be held high for an integral number of clock pulses until the switch is released. The 8086 will then begin execution at address FFFF0H.

The circuit also provides a *power-on reset* function. As the waveforms in Fig. 6.8 illustrate, when power is first applied to the system, the capacitor will charge toward +5 V. With a sufficient time constant, the $\overline{\text{RES}}$ input will be held low long enough to reset the processor.

The 8284A employs a Schmitt trigger on the $\overline{\text{RES}}$ input to protect the system from oscillations due to the slowly rising voltage across the capacitor. This circuit has 0.25 V of hysteresis, meaning that the logic 1 and 0 switching points will differ by at least this

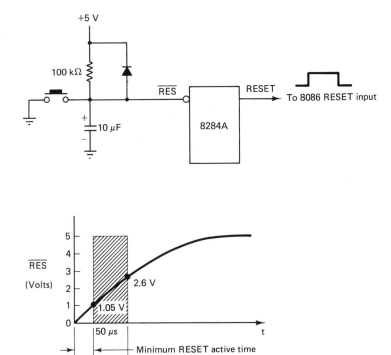

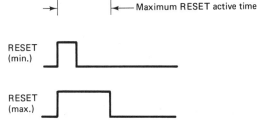

Figure 6.8 Resetting the 8086 with the 8284A. The *RC* network provides a power-on reset function by holding the $\overline{RES}$ input low for at least 50 μs when power is first applied to the system.

amount.[2] The output pulse shown in Fig. 6.8 will not terminate before the input voltage reaches 1.05 V but is guaranteed to terminate before the input reaches 2.6 V.

The *RC* time constant should be chosen to meet the minimum power-on reset active time of 50 μs. The diode provides a discharge path for the capacitor through the power supply (instead of the 8284A) when power is removed.

SELF-REVIEW 6.3 (answers on page 269)

6.3.1. All activities in the 8086 microprocessor are synchronized to the system _____ signal.

[2]In Sec. 6.4 we provide more detail on buffers with hysteresis.

6.3.2. The 8086-2 has a maximum clock frequency of _____ MHz and a minimum clock frequency of _____ MHz.

6.3.3. Assuming a 15-MHz crystal, determine the frequency and duty cycle of the three 8284A outputs: OSC, PCLK, and CLK.

6.3.4. Explain the purpose of a ''boot'' ROM in an 8086 microcomputer system. To what address range should it be mapped?

6.3.5. The circuit in Fig. 6.8 allows the 8086 to be reset in two different ways. Explain.

6.4 MICROCOMPUTER BUS TYPES AND BUFFERING TECHNIQUES

In Chap. 1 a *bus* was defined to be a set of electronic signal lines (wires) all dedicated to a particular task. The bus lines in a microcomputer system are critical, as all data, address, and control information must be reliably transmitted and received over these lines.

There are three types of buses to be found in a microcomputer system (not to be confused with the address, data, and control buses). If we refer to these arbitrarily as types 1 through 3, they are defined as:

> *Type 1*: one transmitter, several receivers
>
> *Type 2*: one receiver, several transmitters
>
> *Type 3*: several transmitters and receivers

Each of these bus types requires special buffering techniques to ensure reliable data transmission. For example, each receiver requires a dc load current from the transmitter. The effect of this load is to reduce the high-level output voltage (V_{OH}) and increase the low-level output voltage (V_{OL}). This in turn reduces the *noise immunity* of the system. This can be seen from the defining equations:

$$\text{high-level noise immunity} = V_{OH}\text{min} - V_{IH}\text{min}$$
$$\text{low-level noise immunity} = V_{IL}\text{max} - V_{OL}\text{max}$$

where V_{IH} is the logic 1 input voltage and V_{IL} the logic 0 input voltage. The noise immunity for standard TTL is 0.4 V and over 1.0 V for CMOS.

In addition to a dc load, each receiver also presents an ac load. This is the receiver's input capacitance that must be charged and discharged each time the transmitter's output changes state. The effect is to increase the propagation delay time for the transmitted signal. This decreases the time available to the memory or I/O device for reading or writing data.

In this section we discuss buffering techniques for all three types of microcomputer buses. Our goal will be to minimize the ac and dc loading effects associated with multiple receivers (and transmitters) on a single bus line.

Type 1 Bus

The type 1 bus is characterized by a single transmitter and several receivers. The address bus is an example of a type 1 bus. The need for buffering can best be seen with an example.

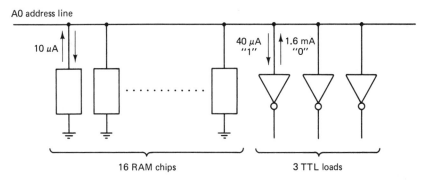

A0 address line

10 µA

40 µA "1" 1.6 mA "0"

16 RAM chips

3 TTL loads

Figure 6.9 Loading considerations for the A0 address line in Ex. 6.3.

Example 6.3

Assume that an 8086 microprocessor is interfaced to a 64K-word memory consisting of two banks of eight 2164A 64K × 1 RAM chips each. In addition to driving the RAM chips, assume that each address line must drive three standard TTL loads used for address decoding. Will the processor address lines require a buffer?

Solution   Figure 6.9 illustrates the interface for the A0 address line (in general, this is duplicated for all 20 address lines). Because the 2164A's are MOS (metal-oxide semiconductor) devices, they require only a small drive current—10 µA in this case. The three TTL loads will require 1.6 mA each in the low state and 40 µA each in the high state. The total loading on the 8086 A0 address line is thus

$$
\begin{array}{r}
16 \times 10 \ \mu\text{A} = 160 \ \mu\text{A} \\
+3 \times 40 \ \mu\text{A} = 120 \ \mu\text{A} \\
\hline
280 \ \mu\text{A in the logic 1 state}
\end{array}
$$

and

$$
\begin{array}{r}
16 \times 10 \ \mu\text{A} = 160 \ \mu\text{A} \\
+3 \times 1.6 \ \text{mA} = 4.8 \ \text{mA} \\
\hline
4.96 \ \text{mA in the logic 0 state}
\end{array}
$$

The dc characteristics data sheet for the 8086 in App. B indicates an I_{OH} (output high-level drive current) of 400 µA and an I_{OL} (low-level output sink current) of 2.5 mA. The 64K memory circuit will exceed the low-level specification and therefore a buffer will be required to drive this memory interface.

The result of Ex. 6.3 should come as no surprise. Microprocessors are MOS devices and as such have very limited drive capabilities. As a general rule, a bus buffer should be used whenever the bus loading exceeds the drive capabilities of the microprocessor, or when it is necessary to drive receivers off the main CPU card. The latter requirement is due to the capacitive loading associated with the edge connectors and backplane wiring in a multicard system.

Special buffers are available for this application, and Fig. 6.10 shows several

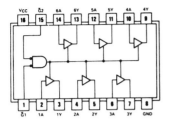

74LS365,

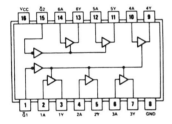

SN74LS366

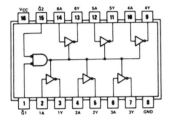

74LS367,

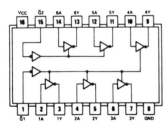

74LS368

74LS240 '

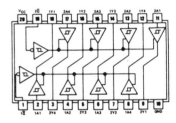

74LS241

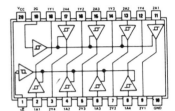

74LS244

Figure 6.10 Common bus buffers for use with microprocessors. (Courtesy of Texas Instruments.)

Designing the 8086 CPU Module   Chap. 6

recommended operating conditions

PARAMETER		SN54LS'			SN74LS'			UNIT
		MIN	NOM	MAX	MIN	NOM	MAX	
V_{CC}	Supply voltage (see Note 1)	4.5	5	5.5	4.75	5	5.25	V
V_{IH}	High-level input voltage	2			2			V
V_{IL}	Low-level input voltage			0.7			0.8	V
I_{OH}	High-level output current			−12			−15	mA
I_{OL}	Low-level output current			12			24	mA
T_A	Operating free-air temperature	−55		125	0		70	°C

NOTE 1: Voltage values are with respect to network ground terminal.

electrical characteristics over recommended operating free-air temperature range (unless otherwise noted)

PARAMETER		TEST CONDITIONS[†]			SN54LS'			SN74LS'			UNIT
					MIN	TYP[‡]	MAX	MIN	TYP[‡]	MAX	
V_{IK}		V_{CC} = MIN,	I_I = −18 mA				−1.5			−1.5	V
Hysteresis $(V_{T+} - V_{T-})$		V_{CC} = MIN			0.2	0.4		0.2	0.4		V
V_{OH}		V_{CC} = MIN, I_{OH} = −3 mA	V_{IH} = 2 V,	V_{IL} = MAX,	2.4	3.4		2.4	3.4		V
		V_{CC} = MIN, I_{OH} = MAX	V_{IH} = 2 V,	V_{IL} = 0.5 V,	2			2			
V_{OL}		V_{CC} = MIN, V_{IL} = MAX	V_{IH} = 2 V,	I_{OL} = 12 mA			0.4			0.4	V
				I_{OL} = 24 mA						0.5	
I_{OZH}		V_{CC} = MAX,	V_{IH} = 2 V,	V_O = 2.7 V			20			20	μA
I_{OZL}		V_{IL} = MAX		V_O = 0.4 V			−20			−20	
I_I		V_{CC} = MAX,	V_I = 7 V				0.1			0.1	mA
I_{IH}		V_{CC} = MAX,	V_I = 2.7 V				20			20	μA
I_{IL}		V_{CC} = MAX,	V_{IL} = 0.4 V				−0.2			−0.2	mA
I_{OS}[§]		V_{CC} = MAX			−40		−225	−40		−225	mA
I_{CC}	Outputs high	V_{CC} = MAX, Output open		All		17	27		17	27	mA
	Outputs low			'LS240		26	44		26	44	
				'LS241, 'LS244		27	46		27	46	
	All outputs disabled			'LS240		29	50		29	50	
				'LS241, 'LS244		32	54		32	54	

[†] For conditions shown as MIN or MAX, use the appropriate value specified under recommended operating conditions.
[‡] All typical values are at V_{CC} = 5 V, T_A = 25°C.
[§] Not more than one output should be shorted at a time, and duration of the short-circuit should not exceed one second.

switching characteristics, V_{CC} = 5 V, T_A = 25°C

PARAMETER	TEST CONDITIONS		'LS240			'LS241, 'LS244			UNIT
			MIN	TYP	MAX	MIN	TYP	MAX	
t_{PLH}	R_L = 667 Ω, See Note 2	C_L = 45 pF,		9	14		12	18	ns
t_{PHL}				12	18		12	18	ns
t_{PZL}				20	30		20	30	ns
t_{PZH}				15	23		15	23	ns
t_{PLZ}	R_L = 667 Ω, See Note 2	C_L = 5 pF,		10	20		10	20	ns
t_{PHZ}				15	25		15	25	ns

NOTE 2: See General Information Section for load circuits and voltage waveforms.

Figure 6.11 Electrical specifications for the 74LS240, 74LS241, and 74LS244. (Courtesy of Texas Instruments.)

Sec. 6.4   Microcomputer Bus Types and Buffering Techniques

239

common types. The 74LS240/241/244 are particularly attractive because they contain eight buffers in one package. A data sheet for the 74LS244 is included as Fig. 6.11.

Example 6.4

Assume that a type 1 bus line similar to Fig. 6.9 is to be buffered with a 74LS244 transmitter. Calculate the number of standard TTL loads (40-μA high-level input current, −1.6-mA low-level input current) that can be driven by this transmitter. How many loads can be driven if each input is also buffered by a 74LS244?

Solution   From the 74LS244 data sheet in Fig. 6.11, the high-level output-drive capability is 3 mA at V_{OH} = 2.4 V. This means that 3 mA/40 μA = 75 standard TTL loads can be driven in the high state.

In the low state the 74LS244 can sink 12 mA with V_{OL} = 0.4 V, and thus 12 mA/ 1.6 mA = 7.5 standard TTL loads can be driven. When the loads are also buffered with 74LS244's, the high-level drive current required drops to 20 μA per input (that of the 74LS244 itself), and 3 mA/20 μA = 150 loads can be driven. In the low state the buffered load requires only 0.2 mA and the calculation is 12 mA/0.2 mA = 60 loads.

In summary, for a type 1 bus with 74LS244 transmitters, seven standard TTL loads can be driven or 60 74LS244 buffered loads (not considering the ac loading effects).

The lesson from this example should be clear. Not only is it advantageous to use a buffer for the transmitter, but by also buffering each receiver input, the number of receivers that can be safely driven is increased considerably.

Tri-state Buffers with Hysteresis

Another advantage of the 74LS240 series of buffers is that each gate has a built-in *Schmitt trigger*. As mentioned previously, this is a circuit with a dual switching threshold—a property also called *hysteresis*. Figure 6.12 shows the effect that a Schmitt trigger can have on a waveform with excessive ringing. Once the input signal has crossed the upper switching threshold (1.7 V), the circuit will not switch back to the low state until the input falls below the lower switching threshold (0.9 V). The opposite occurs when

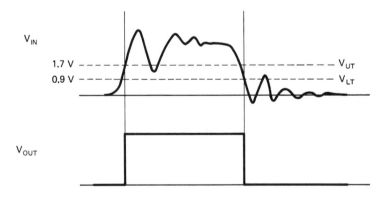

Figure 6.12   Effect of hysteresis on a waveform with excessive ringing. All 74LS240 series buffers have hysteresis. (From J. Uffenbeck, *Microcomputers and Microprocessors: The 8080, 8085, and Z-80*. Prentice-Hall, Englewood Cliffs, N.J., 1985.)

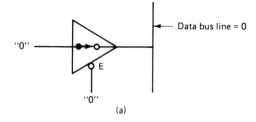

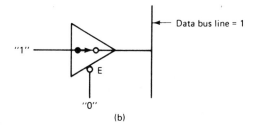

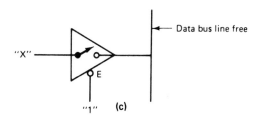

Figure 6.13 Tri-state gates are commonly used to gate data onto a data bus. In parts (a) and (b) the tri-state gate is enabled and the bus line is connected to the input logic level. In part (c) the tri-state gate is disabled and its output appears as an open circuit. The data bus line is now free to be controlled by another transmitter on the line. (From J. Uffenbeck, *Hardware Interfacing with the Apple II Plus*, Prentice-Hall, Englewood Cliffs, N.J., 1983.)

switching from high to low. This circuit is said to have 0.8 V of hysteresis. The 74LS240 series of buffers are guaranteed to have at least 0.2 V of hysteresis.

All the buffers in Fig. 6.10 also have *tri-state* capability. This means that in addition to the two logic states, a third output state, called the tri-state, can be realized. This state is actually a high-impedance or open circuit. A model of a tri-state gate is shown in Fig. 6.13.

Tri-state buffers will allow several transmitters to control the same bus line. By placing all but one transmitter in the tri-state mode (OFF), no interference occurs. This property will be taken advantage of in the type 3 bus.

Type 2 Bus

The type 2 bus has many transmitters but only one receiver. This type of bus cannot be realized with standard TTL gates. Figure 6.14 shows why. Everything is fine as long as both transmitters want the same voltage level on the bus line. But as shown in Fig. 6.14, when one output is high and the other low, the logic level on the bus line can become indeterminate. What is worse, an excessive current may flow from the logic 1 output to the logic 0 output, possibly damaging both devices. This is called *bus contention*.

One solution to this problem is to use tri-state gates for the transmitters. By enabling only one transmitter at a time, bus contention is eliminated. The problem with this technique is that extra logic will be required to ensure that only a single transmitter is enabled at a particular time.

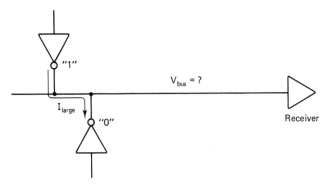

Figure 6.14 A type 2 bus has several transmitters and one receiver. If standard TTL gates are used, problems occur when one transmitter tries to drive the bus line high and another tries to drive it low. (From J. Uffenbeck, *Microcomputers and Microprocessors: The 8080, 8085, and Z-80.* Prentice-Hall, Englewood Cliffs, N.J., 1985.)

Another solution is to use an *open-collector* (or open-drain) bus, as shown in Fig. 6.15. In this scheme the transmitters have open-collector output stages. This means that they can pull the bus line down to a logic 0—by saturating their output transistor—but they require an external pull-up resistor to force a logic 1 onto the bus.

We can write the following logic equation for the READY signal in Fig. 6.15:

$$\overline{READY} = \overline{T1} + \overline{T2}$$

This connection is referred to as a "wired OR." An open-collector bus normally sits in the high state and is activated by any one transmitter pulling the bus line low. For this reason the receiver is normally a control function activated by a low logic level—that

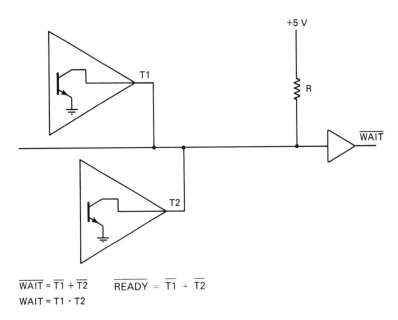

$\overline{WAIT} = \overline{T1} + \overline{T2}$ $\overline{READY} = \overline{T1} + \overline{T2}$

$WAIT = T1 \cdot T2$

Figure 6.15 Type 2 bus realized with open-collector gates. This connection is called a "wired-OR." (From J. Uffenbeck, *Microcomputers and Microprocessors: The 8080, 8085, and Z-80.* Prentice-Hall, Englewood Cliffs, N.J., 1985.)

is, an active-low input. In this example a wait condition (i.e., *not* READY) occurs whenever T1 or T2 is low.

A disadvantage associated with the open-collector bus is that it is not possible to tell which transmitter pulled the bus line low. This may require the processor to read a status port—a technique called *polling*—to determine the activating device.

In many cases the particular device pulling the bus line low is unimportant. For example, when the 8086's READY line is low, the microprocessor enters a wait or idling state. This is usually requested by a slow-memory circuit that cannot respond quickly enough with data for the processor. In this case the CPU waits until the memory is ready (when the READY line is released high) and then continues. The specific memory device requesting the wait does not matter.

For the 8086, wait requests must be synchronized to the system clock signal. For this reason the 8284A $\overline{\text{RDY1}}$ and $\overline{\text{RDY2}}$ inputs are normally used to request wait states. Chapter 7 provides more details on interfacing slow memory.

The value of the pull-up resistor used with an open-collector bus is not arbitrary. This is because loading of the transmitters must be considered.

Example 6.5

Assume that the open-collector bus in Fig. 6.15 has five transmitters, each using a 7401 open-collector NAND gate. Assume that the receiver is the READY input of the 8086 microprocessor. Calculate the value of the pull-up resistor.

Solution   When all transmitters are off, the pull-up resistor must supply a leakage current to each collector and the 8086's READY input. According to the 8086 dc characteristics data sheet in App. B, this is 10 μA for the READY input. The 7401 data sheet indicates 250 μA leakage maximum per collector. The total current is thus $5 \times 250\ \mu\text{A} + 10\ \mu\text{A} = 1.26$ mA.

The high level presented to the READY input must not be less than 2.4 V (to maintain 0.4 V of noise immunity). Therefore, the pull-up resistor must be less than

$$R \leq \frac{2.6\ \text{V}}{1.26\ \text{mA}} = 2\ \text{k}\Omega$$

The general result is

$$R \leq \frac{5\ \text{V} - 2.4\ \text{V}}{n \times I_{1\text{kg}} + I_{\text{IH}}}$$

where n is equal to the number of transmitters on the line.

In the low state the worst case occurs when only one output is low, as it must then sink all the current from the pull-up resistor. In this case the bus line must not exceed 0.4 V. The maximum sink current for the 7401 is 16 mA and the drop across R is 4.6 V. The value of R must thus be greater than

$$R \geq \frac{4.6\ \text{V}}{16\ \text{mA}} = 288\ \Omega$$

The general result is

$$R \geq \frac{5\ \text{V} - 0.4\ \text{V}}{I_{\text{OL}}}$$

For this particular bus, R must be greater than 288 Ω but less than 2 kΩ.

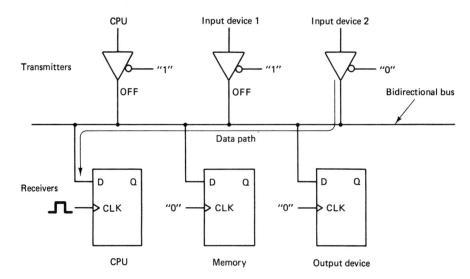

Figure 6.16 Data flow on a bidirectional bus line. (From J. Uffenbeck, *Microcomputers and Microprocessors: The 8080, 8085, and Z-80.* Prentice-Hall, Englewood Cliffs, N.J., 1985.)

Type 3 Bus

The type 3 bus is a bidirectional bus in which there are many receivers and many transmitters. The most common example is the data bus of a microprocessor. Figure 6.16 illustrates data flow from an input device to the CPU over a type 3 bus. Note that all transmitters are shown as tri-state gates and all receivers are shown as latches (D-type flip-flops).

The necessity for tri-state transmitters should be clear—only one transmitter can control the bus at a particular time. The need for receiving latches may not be so clear. What you must remember is that data is placed on the bus for a very brief time. For example, when performing an output instruction the data bus holds the output data only during the T2 through T4 clock states. Thus each receiver must quickly latch the data bus contents when "its turn comes up."

That is the main problem with the type 3 bus. How does a receiver (or transmitter) know when its turn is here? The answer to this question involves address and control bus *decoding* techniques, both covered in Chaps. 7 and 8. But the concept is simple enough. If the control bus I/O read line is active, and if the address bus holds "our" port address, it is time for the I/O device to put the data on the bus (enable the tri-state transmitter).

On the other hand, if the I/O write line is active and the address bus holds "our" address, it is time for the output device to clock the flip-flop and store the present contents of the data bus. For these reasons all three buses (control, address, and data) are involved in the transfer of data between a receiver and a transmitter on the data bus.

The CPU drive capabilities of its data bus lines are no better than the address lines. In addition, the routing of the data bus lines to other cards and peripherals will cause capacitive loading problems. Buffers will again be required.

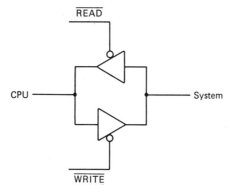

Figure 6.17 Bidirectional bus buffer. Only one gate is enabled at a particular time.

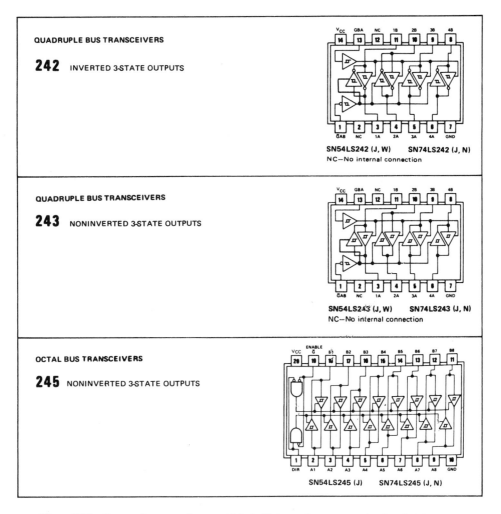

Figure 6.18 Common bus transceivers useful for buffering a microprocessor data bus. [(a) Courtesy of Texas Instruments; (b) courtesy of Intel Corporation.]

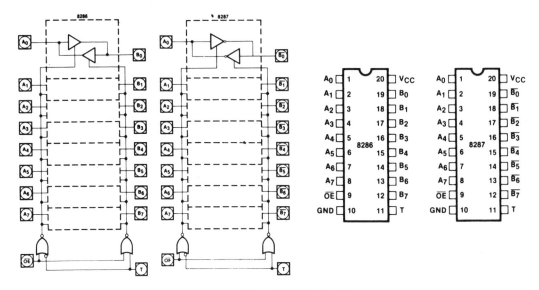

Figure 6.18 Continued

The technique for buffering a data bus line is slightly more complex, due to the bidirectional nature of the bus. Figure 6.17 shows the method. Two tri-state gates are required for each bus line with separate $\overline{\text{READ}}$ and $\overline{\text{WRITE}}$ enables. These enable signals must be derived from the control bus of the microprocessor.

Special bus *transceivers* (transmitter and receiver combinations) are available for this application. Examples from Texas Instruments [Fig. 6.18(a)] and Intel [Fig. 6.18(b)] are shown. The 74LS245 and 8286/8287 are preferred for microprocessor applications, as they contain eight transceivers in one package. Table 6.5 compares the dc drive characteristics of these two parts.

TABLE 6.5 COMPARING THE ELECTRICAL SPECIFICATIONS OF THE 8286 AND 74LS245 OCTAL TRANSCEIVERS

	8286	74LS245
I_{OL}	32 mA at 0.45 V	12 mA at 0.4 V
I_{OH}	5 mA at 2.4 V	3 mA at 2.4 V
I_{IL}	0.2 mA	0.2 mA
I_{IH}	50 μA	20 μA

Source: J. Uffenbeck, *Microcomputers and Micropro-cessors: The 8080, 8085, and Z-80.* Prentice-Hall, Englewood Cliffs, N.J., 1985.

6.4.1. The minimum logic 1 input level for the CMOS 74C00 is 3.5 V. The maximum logic 0 input level is 1.5 V. If $V_{OH} = 4.5$ V minimum and $V_{OL} = 0.5$ V maximum, calculate the high- and low-level noise immunities for this gate.

6.4.2. When driving a load the _____ and _____ loading effects must be considered.

6.4.3. Noisy signals with undershoot and overshoot can be cleaned up using special buffers with _____.

6.4.4. Under what conditions can *bus contention* occur? How does a tri-state buffer help avoid this problem?

6.4.5. If three open-collector buffers are driving a common bus line, the line will be high only if the output of each buffer is also high. (True/False)

6.4.6. Why are latches normally used as receivers on bidirectional data bus lines?

6.5 THE 8086 MINIMUM-MODE CPU MODULE

When the 8086 MN/$\overline{MX}$ pin is wired to +5 V, the processor operates in the *minimum mode*. In this mode the CPU provides all the control signals for the system. It is intended for small- to medium-sized designs with a single processor.

In this section we see how to implement an 8086 *minimum-mode CPU module*. This is a hardware module providing all the signals required to interface memory and I/O in a practical 8086-based microcomputer system.

Demultiplexing the Address/Data Bus

Very few memory or I/O devices are compatible with the 8086's multiplexed data and address lines. Instead, they require separate data lines and separate address lines. The process of forming these separate buses from the multiplexed address/data lines is called *demultiplexing*.

Figure 6.19 shows how the AD0 address/data line can be demultiplexed into a separate A0 address line and D0 data line. During the time that ALE is high, the latch is "transparent" and the Q output follows AD0 (an address line at this time). The falling edge of ALE causes the latch to store the address bit so that A0 continues to hold this address during the T2 through T4 clock states.

Note that D0 is not really demultiplexed—it continues to carry the A0 address during the T1 state. However, the memory and I/O devices do not access the data bus until the T2 state. Thus the contents of D0 can be considered a "don't care" until this second clock cycle.

Because all twenty 8086 address lines are multiplexed, it will be to our advantage to select a chip with several latches in one package for the demultiplexing job. Such a chip is available from Intel, called the 8282/8283 octal latch. It is described in Fig. 6.20. Eight transparent latches are provided with a common (ALE-compatible) strobe input. The 8282 provides noninverting outputs while the 8283 version inverts the input data.

In addition to their demultiplexing function, these chips also buffer the address

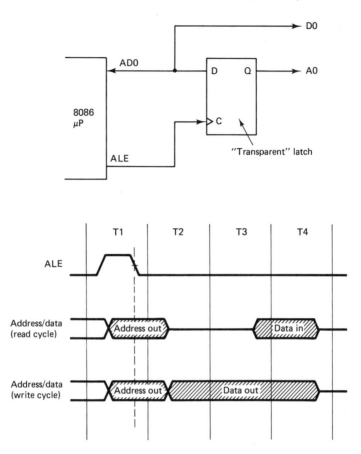

Figure 6.19 Demultiplexing the 8086 address/data bus. Q "follows" the D input latching the address bit on the falling edge of the ALE clock signal.

lines, providing increased output drive capability. For example, the output low level is specified as 0.45 V maximum with a sink current of 32 mA maximum. The high level is specified as 2.4 V minimum while supplying a 5-mA maximum high-level load current.

Example 6.6

Calculate the maximum number of standard TTL loads (I_{IH} = 40 μA and I_{IL} = − 1.6 mA) that can be driven by the 8282/8283. Calculate the noise immunity for this case.

Solution In the high state the drive current is 5000 μA, and therefore 5000 μA/40 μA = 125 loads can safely be driven in this state. In the low state the calculation is 32 mA/1.6 mA = 20 loads. The low level establishing the limit, a total of 20 standard TTL loads can safely be driven by the 8282/8283.

The high-level noise immunity is found as

$$V_{OH}\text{min } (8282/8283) - V_{IH}\text{max (TTL load)} = 2.4 \text{ V} - 2.0 \text{ V} = 0.4 \text{ V}$$

Similarly, for the low level,

$$V_{IL}\text{min (TTL load)} - V_{OL}\text{max } (8282/8283) = 0.8 \text{ V} - 0.45 \text{ V} = 0.35 \text{ V}$$

8282/8283
OCTAL LATCH

- **Address Latch for iAPX 86, 88, 186, 188, MCS-80®, MCS-85®, MCS-48® Famlies**

- **High Output Drive Capability for Driving System Data Bus**

- **Fully Parallel 8-Bit Data Register and Buffer**

- **Transparent during Active Strobe**

- **3-State Outputs**

- **20-Pin Package with 0.3" Center**

- **No Output Low Noise when Entering or Leaving High Impedance State**

- **Available in EXPRESS**
  – Standard Temperature Range
  – Extended Temperature Range

The 8282 and 8283 are 8-bit bipolar latches with 3-state output buffers. They can be used to implement latches, buffers, or multiplexers. The 8283 inverts the input data at its outputs while the 8282 does not. Thus, all of the principal peripheral and input/output functions of a microcomputer system can be implemented with these devices.

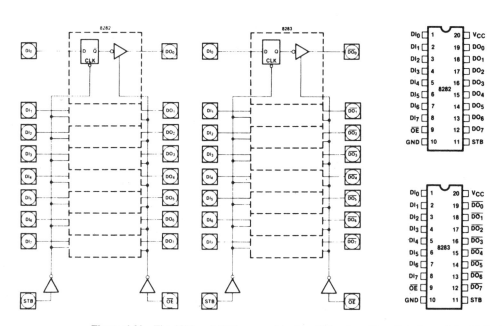

Figure 6.20 The 8282 and 8283 are used to demultiplex the address/data lines of the 8086 microprocessor. (Courtesy of Intel Corporation.)

249

There is one negative aspect associated with the 8282/8283 demultiplexing buffers. They introduce a *time delay* that reduces the time available to the memory or I/O device to read or write data. As mentioned in Sec. 6.4, this delay is strongly dependent on the latches capacitive loading. For example, when driving 20 TTL loads the capacitive load is approximately 100 pF and the propagation delay through the latch is 32 ns maximum. Increasing the load to 125 TTL inputs (the maximum allowable high-state load) increases the capacitive load to over 600 pF and increases the maximum propagation delay to nearly 40 ns.

The 8283 inverting buffer has one less internal inverting stage than the 8282. This means that it will switch faster. For the loading conditions specified in the paragraph above, the delay is about 22 ns and 30 ns maximum. In a double-buffered system (buffers onto and off the bus) the inversion introduced by the 8283 will be canceled by the (inverting) receiving buffer. This will allow up to 20 ns of propagation delay to be saved. We discuss double buffering, and its consequences on memory access time, in more detail in Chap. 7.

Minimum Mode CPU Module Design

Figure 6.21 shows the complete 8086 minimum mode CPU module. It incorporates the 8284A clock generator and reset circuit, three 8282 octal latches for demultiplexing the address/data lines, and a simple gating array to develop the standard memory and I/O control signals. The address lines are labeled AB0–AB19, where the "B" is used to indicate that these lines are buffered.

The four status lines S3–S6 are not used, being intended primarily for diagnostic testing, as mentioned previously. The control bus includes the signals $\overline{\text{BHE}}$ (demultiplexed), $\overline{\text{INTA}}$, and $\overline{\text{RESET}}$, as these signals may also be required in the memory and I/O interfaces.

The control and address bus signals are buffered through tri-state gates enabled via HLDA. During a DMA cycle this signal will be high, disabling these buffers, effectively disconnecting the CPU from the system. The pull-up resistors on the control signals are necessary to ensure that these lines remain inactive during the switchover between normal processing and the DMA cycle (and vice versa).

Troubleshooting the CPU Module

Clearly, the CPU module is the "heart" of any microcomputer system. Testing this module is thus a logical first troubleshooting step. This can be a frustrating experience unless a well-defined "game plan" is established.

Begin by measuring the power supply voltages. Nothing will work unless these are within 5 to 10 percent of their nominal values. Be wary of noise riding on these lines induced by the rapid switching of states of the logic gates (particularly TTL gates). Each TTL package should have a 0.01-μF capacitor to ground at the package site to supply the transient current needed as the output switches.

Assuming that the power supply voltages are within specification and free of noise, turn your attention to the system clock. An oscilloscope connected to the CPU CLK pin should reveal a 30% duty cycle square wave switching between 0 V and 3.9 V minimum.

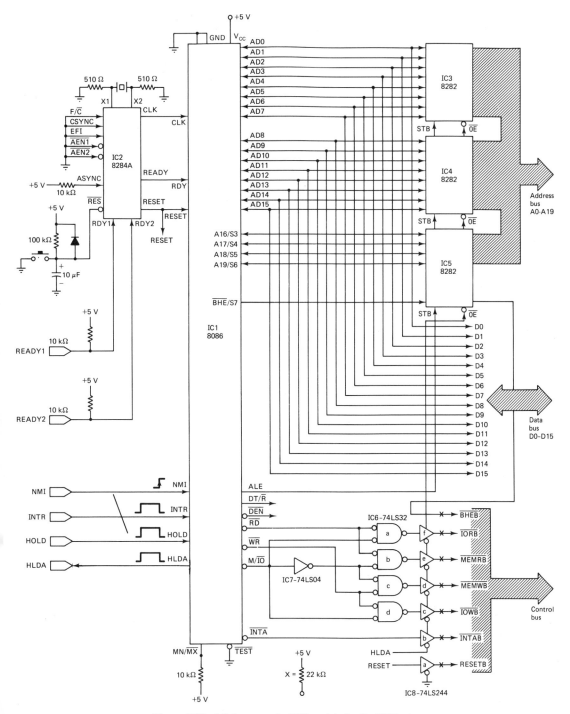

Figure 6.21 Minimum-mode CPU module for the 8086 microprocessor.

Sec. 6.5   The 8086 Minimum-Mode CPU Module

The frequency should be one-third that of the crystal connected to X1 and X2 of the 8284A.

Having passed these tests, we can make some general observations about the operation of the processor. Using a logic probe, examine each of the address/data and control bus signals. A *pulsing* condition should be observed, indicating that the line is switching. Lines "stuck" high or low should be checked carefully. Depending on the loop of instructions being executed, it is possible for a given line always to be high or low. Sometimes, resetting the processor will reveal that these lines are free to switch.

More detailed testing can best be accomplished with the use of a special test program. Assuming that a ROM is mapped to cover the reset address of FFFF0H, the following simple test program could be used.

```
START:  MOV  AX,5555H    ;Data test pattern
        OUT  0,AX        ;IOW pulse
        JMP  START       ;Set up cyclic pattern
```

Using a logic probe or oscilloscope, the $\overline{\text{IOW}}$ and $\overline{\text{MEMR}}$ control bus lines should pulse low once for each program cycle. $\overline{\text{MEMW}}$ and $\overline{\text{IOR}}$ should always be high, as these lines are not used. Knowing that the CPU is executing this simple program goes a long way in testing the system. It indicates that the microprocessor is functioning and that instructions are being fetched from memory correctly. This in turn means that the address, data, and control buses are (probably) wired correctly.[3]

The next step up in the testing hierarchy will require the use of a *logic analyzer*. Using this device, the actual instructions fetched from memory can be observed—either as their hex equivalents or, if disassembly is supported, as their 8086 mnemonic. This is done by selecting the *state* mode and monitoring D0–D15. $\overline{\text{MEMR}}$ should be used as a trigger to sample these lines each time a memory read or instruction fetch occurs. Using $\overline{\text{IOW}}$ as a trigger should show an alternating 1–0 data pattern (55H) on D0–D15.

The timing mode can be used to capture the actual waveforms on the buses. For example, setting the time base for a 50-ns sampling rate, four samples will be taken for each system clock pulse (assuming 5 MHz). This can reveal timing "glitches" caused by unequal time delays through buffers and decoders.

SELF-REVIEW 6.5 (answers on page 269)

6.5.1. What is the difference between an edge-triggered latch and a transparent latch?

6.5.2. Connecting the 8086's MN/$\overline{\text{MX}}$ input to +5 V configures the CPU for a multiprocessor environment. (True/False)

6.5.3. In addition to demultiplexing the 8086 address/data lines, the 8282 also provides a _____ function.

6.5.4. What is the purpose of the control bus signal $\overline{\text{BHEB}}$?

[3]In Chap. 7 we discuss a circuit modification that allows instructions to be *single-stepped* one bus cycle at a time. This circuit stops the CPU with valid data, addresses, and control signals intact.

6.5.5. In a demultiplexed minimum-mode CPU module the D0–D15 data lines function as the data bus only during the _____ clock state(s).

6.5.6. What is an advantage of using the 8283 to demultiplex the 8086 address/data lines versus the 8282?

6.5.7. The following test program is written to put a characteristic test pattern on the control bus of the CPU module shown in Fig. 6.21. Using a logic probe, what pattern would you look for?

```
START:   MOV    BL,5
         MOV    CX,0
AGAIN:   LOOP   AGAIN
         DEC    BL
         JNZ    AGAIN
         OUT    80H,AL
         JMP    START
```

6.6 THE 8086 MAXIMUM-MODE CPU MODULE

When operated in the maximum mode the 8086 requires the 8288 *bus controller* chip to generate most of the system control signals. Those pins previously dedicated to the control function are now redefined as coprocessor support signals. They provide two levels of processor preemption (similar to HOLD and HLDA), queue status for instruction execution tracking, and a bus lock mechanism to avoid conflicts when accessing resources (memory and I/O) shared between the CPU and another processor.

In this section we explain 8086 maximum-mode operation. This includes the 8288 bus controller, the coprocessor control bus, and the design of a maximum-mode CPU module. A brief discussion of the use of the 8086 in a multiprocessor environment is also given.

The Coprocessor Bus

When the 8086's MN/$\overline{\text{MX}}$ pin is wired to ground, pins 24–31 of the CPU change function as shown in Fig. 6.2. All of the control bus signals except $\overline{\text{RD}}$ are "lost"; that is, they are no longer generated by the CPU. The following discussion explains the new co-processor support signals.

Request/grant ($\overline{\text{RQ0}}/\overline{\text{GT0}}$, $\overline{\text{RQ1}}/\overline{\text{GT1}}$). These two pins are bidirectional, allowing a coprocessor to request control of the system buses (similar to the minimum mode's HOLD request). The 8086 responds by disconnecting itself from the system buses and pulsing the $\overline{\text{RQ}}/\overline{\text{GT}}$ line in acknowledgment. A direct memory access now occurs by the coprocessor. When finished, the coprocessor again pulses the $\overline{\text{RQ}}/\overline{\text{GT}}$ communications line and the CPU reclaims the system buses. If requests are received simultaneously on these pins, $\overline{\text{RQ0}}/\overline{\text{GT0}}$ is given higher priority.

$\overline{\text{LOCK}}$. $\overline{\text{LOCK}}$ is an output signal intended for use in a bus arbitration scheme with another processor. Arbitration refers to the process of determining which processor should have control of the system buses at any given time. The $\overline{\text{LOCK}}$ signal is output low during the execution of any instruction with the $\overline{\text{LOCK}}$ prefix. For example, the instruction

LOCK   XCHG   AL,STAT

exchanges the contents of memory location STAT with AL. While this instruction is executing the $\overline{\text{LOCK}}$ signal is used to prevent another processor from accessing the system buses.

Used in this way, STAT is referred to as a *semaphore*. This is a flag that indicates if a coprocessor (or other system resource, a shared printer, for example) is busy. Before entering a program section that requires the coprocessor, the CPU tests STAT. If available, the resource is "claimed" (STAT set to BUSY) to prevent another processor from preempting the CPU. LOCKing the instruction that makes this test prevents another processor from claiming the coprocessor simultaneously.

Queue status (QS0, QS1).   These two pins are intended for coprocessors that receive their instructions via the ESC prefix. They allow the coprocessor to track the progress of an instruction through the queue and help it determine when to access the bus for the escape op-code and operand. Table 6.6 provides the specific details.

Status outputs ($\overline{\text{S0}}$, $\overline{\text{S1}}$, $\overline{\text{S2}}$).   These three output pins are intended for the 8288 bus controller. They encode the control bus signals lost when the maximum mode of operation was selected. Table 6.7 shows the encoding. These pins are valid during the entire four-state bus cycle (including any wait states).

The 8288 Bus Controller

Figure 6.22 describes the 8288 bus controller used when the 8086 is operated in the maximum mode. It receives four inputs from the 8086: the $\overline{\text{S0}}$–$\overline{\text{S2}}$ status signals and CLK. There are two sets of output command (or control) signals.

One group are the MULTIBUS command signals. These are the conventional $\overline{\text{MEMR}}$, $\overline{\text{MEMW}}$, $\overline{\text{IOR}}$, and $\overline{\text{IOW}}$ control signals, renamed $\overline{\text{MRDC}}$, $\overline{\text{MWTC}}$, $\overline{\text{IORC}}$, and $\overline{\text{IOWC}}$. The suffix "C" stands for command. Also included in this group is the interrupt acknowledge signal, $\overline{\text{INTA}}$.

$\overline{\text{AMWC}}$ and $\overline{\text{AIOWC}}$ are *advanced* memory and I/O write commands, respectively. These outputs are enabled one clock cycle earlier than the normal write commands. Some

TABLE 6.6   QUEUE STATUS

QS1	QS0	Current instruction
0	0	No operation
0	1	First byte of op-code from queue
1	0	Empty the queue (transfer of control)
1	1	Subsequent byte from queue

8288
BUS CONTROLLER
FOR iAPX 86, 88 PROCESSORS

- Bipolar Drive Capability
- Provides Advanced Commands
- Provides Wide Flexibility in System Configurations
- 3-State Command Output Drivers

- Configurable for Use with an I/O Bus
- Facilitates Interface to One or Two Multi-Master Busses
- Available in EXPRESS
  - Standard Temperature Range
  - Extended Temperature Range

The Intel® 8288 Bus Controller is a 20-pin bipolar component for use with medium-to-large iAPX 86, 88 processing systems. The bus controller provides command and control timing generation as well as bipolar bus drive capability while optimizing system performance.

A strapping option on the bus controller configures it for use with a multi-master system bus and separate I/O bus.

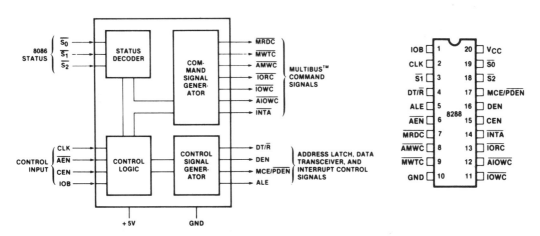

Figure 6.22 (Courtesy of Intel Corporation.)

Sec. 6.6   The 8086 Maximum-Mode CPU Module

TABLE 6.7 8288 STATUS WORDS BASED ON THE $\overline{S0}$, $\overline{S1}$, AND $\overline{S2}$ MAXIMUM MODE STATUS SIGNALS

$\overline{S2}$	$\overline{S1}$	$\overline{S0}$	Processor state	8288 active output
0	0	0	Interrupt acknowlege	$\overline{INTA}$
0	0	1	Read I/O port	$\overline{IORC}$
0	1	0	Write I/O port	$\overline{IOWC}$ (also advanced $\overline{IOWC}$)
0	1	1	Halt	None
1	0	0	Code access	$\overline{MRDC}$
1	0	1	Read memory	$\overline{MRDC}$
1	1	0	Write memory	$\overline{MWTC}$ (also advanced $\overline{MWTC}$)
1	1	1	Passive	None

Source: J. Uffenbeck, Microcomputers and Microprocessors: The 8080, 8085, and Z-80. Prentice-Hall, Englewood Cliffs, N.J., 1985.

memory and I/O devices require this wider write pulse width. In App. E we provide details on the specific timing for all 8288 control signals.

The second group of signals output by the 8288 are the bus control signals DT/$\overline{R}$, DEN, ALE, and MCE/$\overline{PDEN}$. We are already familiar with the first three, as they are output by the 8086 when operated in the minimum mode (note that DEN is now active high). MCE/$\overline{PDEN}$ is an output with two functions depending on the 8288's mode of operation—I/O bus control or system bus control.

The three 8288 control inputs CEN, IOB, and $\overline{AEN}$ determine the operating mode as shown in Table 6.8. When CEN (command enable) and IOB are wired high, the 8288 operates in the I/O bus mode. The MC/$\overline{PDEN}$ output acts as a *peripheral data enable*. Its function is identical to DEN except that it is active only during I/O instructions. In effect it allows the 8288 to control two sets of buses: the normal system buses (possibly shared with other processors) and a special I/O bus dedicated to the processor controlling this particular 8288.

In the system bus mode the control signals are active only if the $\overline{AEN}$ (address enable) and IOB inputs are low. This mechanism allows several 8288's (and 8086's) to be interfaced to the same set of bus lines. The bus arbiter selects the active processor by enabling only one 8288 (via the $\overline{AEN}$ input). In this mode MCE/$\overline{PDEN}$ becomes MCE —*master cascade enable*. This signal is used during an interrupt sequence to read the address from a master priority interrupt controller (PIC). In Chaps. 8 and 9 we provide more details on interrupts (and the PIC).

Maximum-Mode CPU Module Design

Figure 6.23 shows a maximum-mode CPU module design for the 8086. Like the minimum mode, it uses the 8284A to generate the clock signal and synchronize the RESET and READY requests. Unlike the minimum mode, a fourth bus is included called the *co-processor bus*. This bus includes those signals intended for the 8087 NDP and 8089 I/O processor.

TABLE 6.8 8288 I/O AND SYSTEM BUS MODES

CEN	IOB	$\overline{AEN}$	Description
1	1	X	I/O bus mode; all control lines enabled; $MC/\overline{PDEN} = \overline{PDEN}$
1	0	1	System bus mode but all control signals disabled; the bus is busy, that is, controlled by another bus master
1	0	0	System bus mode, all control signals active; the bus is free for use; $MCE/\overline{PDEN} = MCE$
0	X	X	All command outputs and the DEN and PDEN outputs are disabled (open-circuited)

The address/data lines are demultiplexed using 8282 (or 8283) latches as in the minimum-mode design. Note, however, that the STB signal is derived from ALE, now output by the 8288. In this single-processor system the 8288 is operated in the system bus mode with its control signals permanently enabled (IOB = 0 and $\overline{AEN}$ = 0).

The data bus lines are buffered with 8286 (or 8287) octal transceivers. Note that these buffers are enabled only when the DEN output is active. Figure 6.3 shows that this occurs only during the T2–T4 clock states. The direction of the transceivers is controlled by DT/$\overline{R}$.

The circuit in Fig. 6.23 is said to be *fully buffered*, as all of the address, control, and data bus signals are passed through buffers. To so indicate, the suffix ''B'' is appended to each signal name.

8086 Multiprocessor System Design

By designing a computer system to include more than one CPU, the computing capabilities of that system are greatly increased. This is because each processor can operate in parallel or *concurrently* with the others. This can have the effect of breaking the von Neumann ''bottleneck'' associated with the sequential processing of a single processor.

For this reason, it has become common to partition a microcomputer system into *subsystems*, each controlled by its own processor. One CPU detects and reads switch closures from the keyboard. Another handles floppy disk read and write operations. A special arithmetic processor may be assigned to handle time-consuming trigonometric and scientific calculations. A general-purpose CPU is then used to coordinate the activities of each subsystem.

When high reliability and fault tolerance are critical considerations, several CPUs may be assigned to the same task. A comparator checks the output of each system. If a particular system's output disagrees with the others, it is declared ''ill'' and a backup system is switched into its place.

The economics of VLSI (very large scale integration) makes all of this possible. It is cheaper to construct a microcomputer system with five separate CPUs than to design a similar system around a single high-performance processor.

The two main problems to be addressed in a multiple-CPU design are cycle arbitration and multicycle usage. The first problem relates to the fact that two CPUs cannot

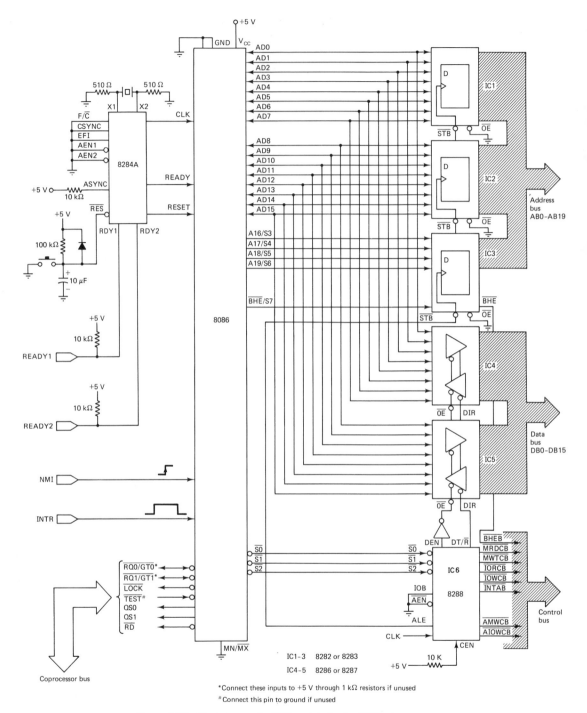

Figure 6.23 Maximum-mode CPU module for the 8086 microprocessor.

IC1-3   8282 or 8283

IC4-5   8286 or 8287

*Connect these inputs to +5 V through 1 kΩ resistors if unused

#Connect this pin to ground if unused

access the same memory location or I/O device simultaneously. Some means of arbitrating these requests must be employed.

Once a CPU has gained control of a system resource, it may require several cycles to read or write its data. During this time another processor must not inspect or modify this information. Again some means must be found to indicate to the other processors that this system resource is "BUSY" and not available for access.

The 8086 (and 8088) have been designed to facilitate the design of a multiprocessor microcomputer system. Three methods or modes of operation can be used: *shared single-bus, I/O bus*, or *resident bus*.

Shared single-bus mode.   In this mode two or more CPUs share all system resources, including the bus buffers, latches, and bus controller. The best example is an 8086 (or 8088) supported by the 8087 numeric data processor (NDP). This chip is discussed in detail in Sec. 11.2, and Fig. 11.22 shows a typical 8086–8087 interface.

The two processors are wired in parallel and together fetch instructions from memory. The NDP looks for special instructions, those with the "ESC" prefix. When such an instruction occurs, the 8086 computes an effective address but does not store the selected data. Instead, it performs a NOP (no operation). The 8087, however, captures the data and begins execution. The 8086 is free to continue fetching and executing instructions from its queue. Thus the NDP and host CPU operate *concurrently* while the NDP instruction is being executed.

When the result is to be stored in memory, the 8087 pulses the $\overline{\text{RQ}/\text{GT}}$ line of the CPU requesting use of the buses. A return pulse on this bidirectional line releases control of the buses to the NDP. One or more write cycles now occur as the 8087 stores the numeric result in memory. A third pulse on $\overline{\text{RQ}/\text{GT}}$ relinquishes control of the buses to the CPU. The $\overline{\text{RQ}/\text{GT}}$ line thus establishes a physical protocol that prevents bus contention between the CPU and NDP.

When the 8087 begins executing an instruction, its BUSY output is set. Connected to the 8086's $\overline{\text{TEST}}$ input, the CPU is alerted that results in memory are not yet valid. Instructions that reference these results should be prefaced with the "WAIT" prefix. This will cause the CPU to enter a wait state until its $\overline{\text{TEST}}$ input is low.

The 8087 effectively expands the instruction set of the 8086 to include numerous "number-crunching" instructions. In effect, the circuit in Fig. 11.22 can be considered a two-chip CPU. Intel calls this CPU configuration an iAPX 86/21. One of its main advantages is its simplicity. No extra hardware beyond the NDP chip itself is required. For this reason, many manufacturers include an *empty socket* for the NDP. This allows the user to expand to the iAPX 86/21 configuration as desired.

Sharing system resources does have disadvantages. When an NDP result is required, the 8086 must stop and wait for the result. The CPU must also suspend operations while the NDP is reading or writing memory. Thus some of the advantages of parallel processing are lost.

I/O bus mode.   In this mode a special processor is provided to handle I/O functions for the host CPU. Figure 6.24 shows an example using the 8089 I/O processor (IOP). Two sets of buses are used. The *local* I/O bus is accessible to the 8089 only. The

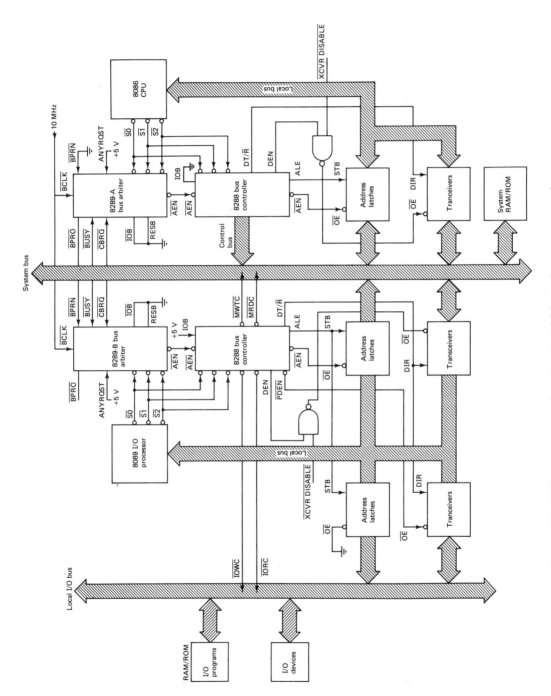

Figure 6.24 Multiprocessor system featuring a local I/O bus and a common system bus.

system bus is used by the host 8086 and provides access to system RAM and ROM. This bus also provides a common communications path between the two processors.

In this circuit the IOP is programmed for the remote mode and fetches instructions for its task program from local memory. The I/O devices are also (memory) mapped into this space. In typical operation, the CPU stores "messages" in system memory regarding the task to be performed. The IOP accesses system memory for these messages, but then carries out the task independent of the host. This maximizes system throughput, as both processors can operate in parallel (except when exchanging messages in system memory).

Notice that each processor is supported by an 8288 bus controller. On the 8089 side of the interface, this chip is operated in the IO bus mode. In this mode, any I/O instruction will activate $\overline{\text{PDEN}}$ (peripheral data enable). This signal, in turn, is used to enable the transceivers between the IOP and the local bus.

When an 8089 memory read or write cycle is detected (via $\overline{\text{S0}}$–$\overline{\text{S2}}$), the 8289 bus arbiter (8289-B) is alerted. It responds by driving $\overline{\text{CBRQ}}$ (common bus request) low. A delay then occurs until $\overline{\text{BPRN}}$ (bus priority in) is driven low (via 8289-A). Once enabled, the arbiter activates $\overline{\text{AEN}}$, enabling the 8288. The memory address and control signals are then driven onto the system bus by the IOP via the (now enabled) address latches and bus transceiver.

When several CPUs are involved, a priority must be established for simultaneous requests. In Fig. 6.24 a serial or "daisy chain" technique is used. $\overline{\text{BPRN}}$ of 8289-A is strapped permanently low, giving this arbiter highest priority. When accessing the bus its $\overline{\text{BPRO}}$ output will be high. Connecting this to the $\overline{\text{BPRN}}$ input of the next arbiter in the chain (8289-B) prevents lower-priority CPUs from acquiring the system bus.

Note that the bus can always be claimed by a lower-priority CPU when $\overline{\text{CBRQ}}$ is asserted. However, a time delay will ensue until the higher-priority CPU enters a state not requiring the bus (a higher-priority request would be granted the bus immediately without having to wait for another arbiter to release the bus through $\overline{\text{CBRQ}}$).

The advantage of an I/O bus is that the host can work on another task while the IOP controls (and waits for) the I/O devices. Because the IOP can fetch its instructions from local memory, both processors can operate concurrently. The principal disadvantage is the extra hardware required, including a bus arbiter for each CPU and two sets of transceivers and address latches.

Resident bus mode. In this mode multiple general-purpose CPUs can be accommodated, each with its own private (resident) bus. Figure 6.25 shows an example. Eight 8086 CPUs are interfaced to a common multiprocessor system bus. Each can access either a *resident* bus or the *system* bus. In this way expensive system resources such as high-capacity magnetic disks can be shared by all processors.

Notice that each 8086 is supported by two 8288 bus controllers. One drives the resident bus and the other drives the system bus. An address decoder is used to define a range of memory addresses as *system* addresses. When accessing such an address, the decoder output will be high causing the resident 8288 to become disabled but the system 8288 to become enabled (both via the CEN inputs). This disables all command outputs onto the resident bus.

The address decoder also activates the SYSB/$\overline{\text{RESB}}$ input of the 8289 bus arbiter, requesting use of the system bus. The arbiter responds by pulling $\overline{\text{BREQ}}$ low. This signal

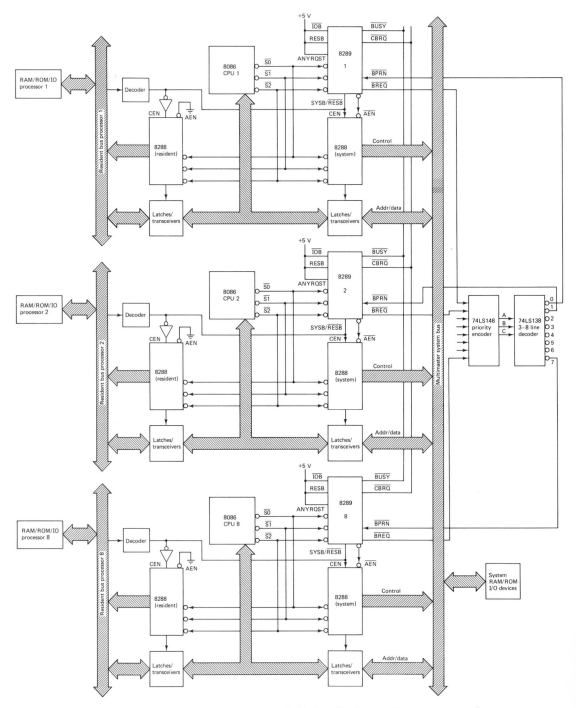

Figure 6.25 Multiprocessor system featuring individual resident buses and a common system bus.

is fed to a parallel priority resolving circuit. The 74LS148 encodes its highest active input and applies the result as a 3-bit code to the 74LS138. The eight outputs of this chip enable one of the eight bus arbiter $\overline{\text{BPRN}}$ inputs.

The selected arbiter enables its corresponding 8288 via $\overline{\text{AEN}}$, which in turn drives the memory read and write commands onto the system bus. The system resources are now accessible to the requesting CPU. If desired, the system bus can be *locked* during the data transfer by prefacing each instruction with the "LOCK" prefix. If this is not done, another CPU (even one of lower priority) can gain control of the system bus. This was explained previously for the serial priority resolving circuit. Again the requesting CPU will have to wait until the higher-priority CPU releases the bus through $\overline{\text{CBRQ}}$.

Multiple CPUs each interfaced to its own resident buses offers the maximum flexibility in a multiprocessor microcomputer system. Each CPU runs independent of the others except to access common system resources. This type of design could be taken advantage of to allow several users access to a common database, for example. In such a system, caution must be exercised so that data blocks operated on by one processor are not contaminated by another user. One way of preventing this is to LOCK all such data operations.

SELF-REVIEW 6.6 (answers on page 269)

6.6.1. When designing a maximum mode single-processor 8086 CPU module, several support ICs are required in addition to the 8086 microprocessor. List these chips and their function.

6.6.2. When accessing a memory location shared with a coprocessor, which of the following signals prevents the coprocessor from also accessing that location? (a) $\overline{\text{TEST}}$; (b) $\overline{\text{LOCK}}$; (c) $\overline{\text{BHE}}$; (d) DT/$\overline{\text{R}}$.

6.6.3. When the 8086 is wired for the maximum mode, the 8288 bus controller decodes _____ to generate the system control bus.

6.6.4. Memory chips that require a longer data setup time prior to the rising edge of the memory write control signal should be interfaced to the 8288's _____ signal.

6.6.5. When operated in the _____ mode, the 8288 controls the system bus and a separate I/O bus.

6.6.6. Refer to Fig. 6.23. What logic levels would you expect on DEN and DT/$\overline{\text{R}}$ during an I/O write bus cycle?

6.6.7. When interfaced to the 8087 NDP, the host CPU and 8087 _____ the system resources.

6.6.8. Which 8288 signal enables the data transceivers connected to the local bus in Fig. 6.24?

6.6.9. A low-priority processor cannot gain control of the system bus from a higher-priority processor unless the $\overline{\text{LOCK}}$ signal is asserted. (True/False)

6.6.10. What is the purpose of the address decoder shown with each CPU in Fig. 6.25?

6.7 THE 8088 MICROPROCESSOR

The only difference between the 8086 and the 8088 microprocessors is the latter's 8-bit (instead of 16-bit) bus interface unit. When fetching 16-bit memory or I/O operands, two bus cycles are required: one for the high byte and one for the low byte. To the programmer,

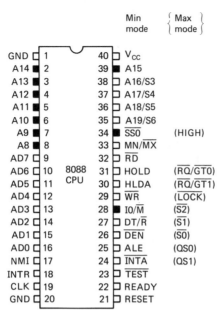

Figure 6.26 Pin assignments for the 8088 microprocessor. The shaded pins have different functions from those on the 8086.

these additional memory and I/O accesses are transparent except for the increased instruction execution time.

In this section we compare the pin configurations of the 8086 and 8088. We also look into the differences in CPU module design when using the 8088. Finally, a four-chip 8088-based microcomputer system is shown that features 2K bytes of ROM, 1K bytes of RAM, and 16 I/O pins.

Pin Comparison with the 8086

The 8088 is *not* pin compatible with the 8086. Figure 6.26 highlights the pin differences. Because the 8088 has an 8-bit external data bus, there is no need to multiplex the A8–A15 address lines. Thus these pins carry address information throughout the bus cycle and need not be latched. Note that A16/S3–A19/S6 are still multiplexed.

The 8086 M/$\overline{\text{IO}}$ signal becomes IO/$\overline{\text{M}}$ on the 8088. This seemingly odd redefinition is done to make this signal compatible with 8-bit 8085-microprocessor-compatible peripherals.

The only "new" signal on the 8088 is $\overline{\text{SS0}}$, which takes the place of $\overline{\text{BHE}}$/S7. $\overline{\text{BHE}}$ is no longer needed, as data is transferred only on the AD0–AD7 address/data lines. S7 was a spare status signal. Table 6.9 indicates that $\overline{\text{SS0}}$ can be combined with DT/$\overline{\text{R}}$ and IO/$\overline{\text{M}}$ to encode the current bus cycle. This information can then be used for diagnostic testing purposes.[4]

---

[4]In Chap. 7 a single-step circuit is discussed that allows individual bus cycles to be monitored by decoding these three signals.

TABLE 6.9 8088 STATUS DECODING

IO/$\overline{\text{M}}$	DT/$\overline{\text{R}}$	$\overline{\text{SS0}}$	
1	0	0	Interrupt acknowledge
1	0	1	Read I/O port
1	1	0	Write I/O port
1	1	1	Halt
0	0	0	Code access
0	0	1	Read memory
0	1	0	Write memory
0	1	1	Passive

8088 CPU Modules

Because the 8088 provides nearly the same set of data, address, and control signals as the 8086, the CPU module designs are very similar. The main difference is that only AD0–AD7 and A16/S3–A19/S6 need be demultiplexed. This saves one 8282/8283 latch. The clock generation, reset timing, and ready timing are identical, as are the control bus signals, with the exception of IO/$\overline{\text{M}}$.

MN/$\overline{\text{MX}}$ again selects the minimum or maximum mode of processor operation, with the latter supported by the 8288 bus controller. The coprocessor bus signals are the same as those shown in Fig. 6.23 for maximum-mode operation. Circuit diagrams for these minimum- and maximum-mode CPU modules are left as Analysis and Design Questions.

Four-Chip 8088-Based Microcomputer System

Because of its 8-bit data bus, the 8088 is compatible with a number of peripheral chips originally designed for the 8085 microprocessor. These are listed in Table 6.10. All of these devices have the address/data demultiplexing latches "built in." They also have a control bus directly compatible with that of the 8088 (when operated in the minimum mode). Using these chips, the 8088 CPU module can be reduced to two chips: the 8088 and the 8284A clock generator.

Figure 6.27 gives an example of such a design. This circuit is a complete micro-

TABLE 6.10 8088-COMPATIBLE MULTIPLEXED BUS COMPONENTS

Device	Description
8155/8156	256-Byte static RAM, I/O, and timer
8185	1024-Byte static RAM
8355	2048-Byte ROM and I/O
8755A	2048-Byte EPROM and I/O
8256	Multifunction UART
21821	4096-Byte pseudostatic RAM

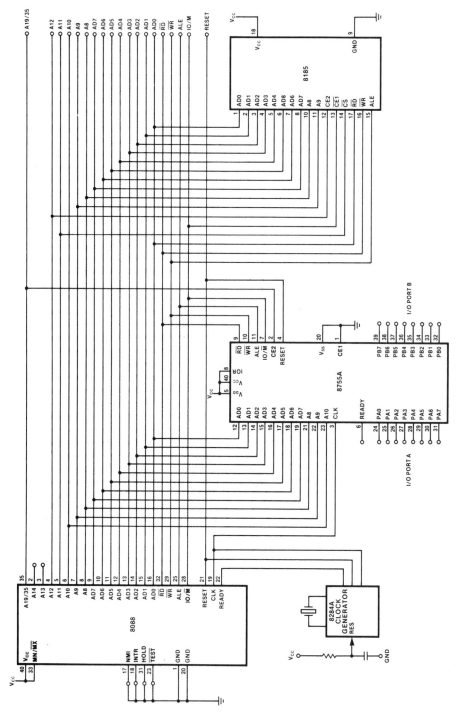

Figure 6.27 Four-chip 8088-based microcomputer system. (Courtesy of Intel Corporation.)

266

computer system featuring CPU, RAM, ROM, and I/O. The 8755A contains 2K bytes of ROM and 16 I/O pins. The ROM is mapped to cover the reset start address FFFF0H so that upon power-on a monitor program can take control of the system. The 8185 contains 1K bytes of read/write memory and can be used to store system variables or user programs.

Is this a practical microcomputer system? Yes and no. The 16 I/O pins could be used for some control function (the microwave oven application, for example) with the control program stored in ROM. However, as we have seen in Chap. 1, there are special *microcontroller* chips designed specifically for this purpose. For example, the 8051 8-bit microcontroller has (in one chip) 4K bytes of ROM, 128 bytes of RAM, 32 I/O pins, two 16-bit counter/timers, and a full-duplex serial transmission channel. The 16-bit 8096 has similar capabilities and includes a 10-bit analog-to-digital converter.

Because of the availability of these microcontrollers, the computer in Fig. 6.27 is probably better suited as a "learning" computer or microprocessor trainer. For high-volume industrial applications the single-chip microcontrollers offer superior performance with fewer total chips.

SELF-REVIEW 6.7 (answers on page 296)

6.7.1. It is possible to switch from an 8086 microprocessor to an 8088 microprocessor by simply plugging the 8088 into the 8086 socket. (True/False)

6.7.2. Why is the 8086 signal $\overline{BHE}$ not provided on the 8088?

6.7.3. The 8088 is directly compatible with 8085 peripheral chips when operated in the _____ mode.

6.7.4. Can the 8088 be operated in the maximum mode and be interfaced to the 8087 coprocessor?

CHAPTER 6 SELF-TEST

1. When the instruction OUT 0A0H,AX is executed (assume that AX = 1234H) the address bus will hold _____ and the data bus will hold _____.

2. For the instruction in question 1, indicate the values of the control signals: M/$\overline{IO}$ _____; $\overline{RD}$ _____; $\overline{WR}$ _____; $\overline{INTA}$ _____.

3. During idle bus cycles the 8086 is in a "wait" state. (True/False)

4. Which processor output signal is used to demultiplex the address/data lines?

5. A minimum-mode CPU module becomes a maximum-mode CPU module when the processor's MN/$\overline{MX}$ pin is connected to ground. (True/False)

6. When interfacing memory to the 8086, valid data must be placed on the data lines during the _____ and _____ clock states.

7. During a memory read bus cycle, how does the memory know whether a word or a byte is to be transferred?

8. Why is it necessary to have a reset input on a microprocessor?

9. Using a 24-MHz crystal, the system clock signal produced by the 8284A will have a frequency of _____.

10. What is the maximum sink current for the 74LS244 buffer? In which logic state does it occur?

11. What is the role of a test program in troubleshooting the CPU module?

12. Bus contention is most likely to occur: (a) with open-collector gates; (b) on a type 1 bus; (c) on a type 2 bus; (d) when the pull-up resistor is too small.

13. Explain how the 8087 coprocessor determines if the system data bus is carrying an operand intended for itself.

14. Explain the term *full buffering*.

15. The coprocessor bus is available only when the 8086 is operated in the maximum mode. (True/ False)

16. A _____ _____ is required in multiprocessor microcomputer systems to determine which processor can control the bus at a particular time.

17. Which signal and instruction is used by the 8086 to prevent it from accessing an 8087 result before the entire message has been transferred?

18. Either a _____ or a _____ priority resolving technique can be used in a multiprocessor microcomputer system.

19. The 8088 microprocessor is identical to the 8086 except for the _____ _____ _____.

20. In which operating mode or modes is the 8088 compatible with the 8085 family of multiplexed bus components?

ANALYSIS AND DESIGN QUESTIONS

6.1. Refer to Fig. 6.3. Why is $\overline{\text{DEN}}$ not enabled during the T1 clock state of a read bus cycle?

6.2. Refer to Fig. 6.28. This circuit is a type 2 bus implemented with tri-state buffers. Write the logic equation for the READY output. Show that this circuit also implements the "wired-OR" function.

6.3. Assuming that all gates in Fig. 6.28 are 74LS244's, calculate the maximum and minimum value for pull-up resistor "R."

6.4. Calculate the high- and low-level noise immunity of an address bus line buffered with 74LS244 receivers and transmitters.

6.5. In Fig. 6.25 the resident 8288 is permanently enabled ($\overline{\text{AEN}}$ = 0 V), but the system 8288 is controlled by the bus arbiter. Explain these connections.

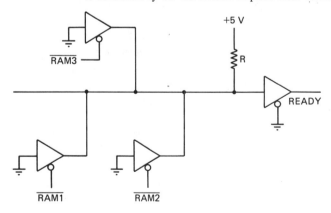

Figure 6.28 Circuit for Analysis and Design Questions 6.2 and 6.3.

6.6. Sketch a minimum-mode CPU module for the 8088 microprocessor similar to the 8086 diagram in Fig. 6.21.

6.7. Sketch a maximum-mode CPU module for the 8088 microprocessor similar to the 8086 diagram in Fig. 6.23.

SELF REVIEW ANSWERS

6.1.1 memory read

6.1.2 I/O write

6.1.2 internal operation not requiring access to the buses (INC AX for example)

6.1.4 data word F3COH is being read from memory location 47000H

6.2.1 a single pin sharing two different signals

6.2.2 T1, ALE

6.2.3 T4

6.2.4 ADO-AD15: memory offset address, memory word contents

A16/S3-A19/S6: memory segment address, status

$\overline{BHE}$/S7:   0, not used

$\overline{RD}$:   1, 0

$\overline{WR}$:   1, 1

M/$\overline{IO}$:   1, 1

6.2.5 8086-1, 10

6.2.6 maximum

6.3.1 clock

6.3.2 8, 2

6.3.3 OSC: 15 MHz, PCLK: 2.5 MHz 50%, CLK: 5 MHz 33%

6.3.4 The boot ROM initializes the computer and then loads the operating system from disk. It must cover (at least) the range FFFF0-FFFFFH.

6.3.5 depress the switch or power-on reset

6.4.1 1V, 1V

6.4.2 dc, ac

6.4.3 hysteresis

6.4.4 two outputs attempting to control the same line, the output stage of a tri-state buffer can be turned off

6.4.5 True

6.4.6 the data is present only briefly

6.5.1 in a transparent latch data passes through the latch while the clock is high (enabled)

6.5.2 False

6.5.3 buffer (or amplification)

6.5.4 when low it indicates that AD7-AD15 will be used in the data transfer

6.5.5 T2-T4

6.5.6 it is faster

6.5.7 one pulse per loop on the $\overline{IOW}$ line (as the OUT 80H,AL instruction is executed)

6.6.1 8284A clock generator, 8288 bus controller, 8282/83 bus buffers, 8286/87 address latches

6.6.2 (b)

6.6.3 $\overline{S0}$-$\overline{S2}$

6.6.4 $\overline{AMWC}$

6.6.5 I/O bus

6.6.6 DEN = 1, DT/$\overline{R}$ = 1

6.6.7 share

6.6.8 $\overline{PDEN}$

6.6.9 False ($\overline{LOCK}$ prevents another processor from accessing memory for the LOCKED instruction only)

6.6.10 enables the system or resident bus controller depending on the memory address

6.7.1 False

6.7.2 all data transferred on AD0-AD7 only

6.7.3 minimum

6.7.4 yes

7

MAIN MEMORY SYSTEM DESIGN

When the 8086 is reset, the next instruction executed will be fetched from memory location FFFF0H. This means that the 20-bit address 11111111111111110000 will be output on address lines A19–A0. As the instruction is fetched and executed, the op-code and data are transported to or from the memory via the 16 data bus lines. The direction of data flow—that is, a CPU read or write operation—is determined by the control bus signals.

Memory that interfaces directly to the microprocessor in this way is referred to as *main memory*. It has the following characteristics:

1. Any location can be accessed at random.
2. Each byte has its own unique address.
3. Data is read or written in one CPU bus cycle.

The best known examples of main memory are RAM and ROM. The basic RAM cell is a flip-flop that can be set or reset. It is this feature of RAM that allows it to be written as well as read. Because the transistors that comprise a RAM flip-flop require a dc voltage to operate, RAM cells will loose their data ("forget") when power is removed. Accordingly, RAMs are said to be a *volatile* memory type.

ROM is a *nonvolatile* main memory type that can only be read. A special programmer is required to write data into the device. Because of their nonvolatility, ROMs are often mapped to cover the CPU's reset address. In this way they can be used to "boot" the computer up from a "cold" start.

Any information stored in RAM must ultimately be lost. For this reason a more permanent type of memory is required to save important data and program files. The floppy disk is a common example. The 1's and 0's that comprise the data are stored as semipermanent magnetic impulses on the disk's surface.

Unlike main memory, the data from a floppy disk is read byte by byte from the same (I/O port) address. This means that to the CPU, each byte of data on the disk appears to be stored at the same address. To execute such programs the CPU must first transfer this data to main memory. This is accomplished by reading the data in sequence byte by byte as the disk rotates.

Devices like the floppy-disk drive, Winchester disk drive, and digital cassette recorder are referred to as *secondary storage* devices. They are not the CPU's main memory. However, they do allow data stored in RAM to be saved. Floppy disks also provide a convenient means of exchanging software between two computers.

In this chapter we examine briefly the various types of RAM and ROM commonly used in microcomputers today. This is followed by a study of the timing restrictions imposed by the 8086 when operated in the minimum and maximum modes. This timing will define the interface requirements for the various types of main memory and lead to *address decoding*—the technique of mapping a block of memory to a specific CPU address. Because the 8086 can access over 1 million bytes of memory, we will take a detailed look at dynamic RAM technology and the design of large memory arrays. The chapter concludes with a discussion of memory module test programs.

The major topics of this chapter are:

7.1 Types of Main Memory

7.2 8086 CPU Read/Write Timing

7.3 SRAM and ROM Interface Requirements

7.4 Address Decoding Techniques

7.5 Accounting for Buffer Delays in a Memory Design

7.6 Interfacing Dynamic RAM

7.7 Troubleshooting the Memory Module

7.1 TYPES OF MAIN MEMORY

To describe main memory as RAM and ROM is like describing a car as a sedan or a station wagon—there are many different models. In this section we look at those RAM and ROM types most commonly found in microcomputer systems. The discussion will center on the technology behind the part, not the CPU interface. Memory interfacing is covered in Sec. 7.3.

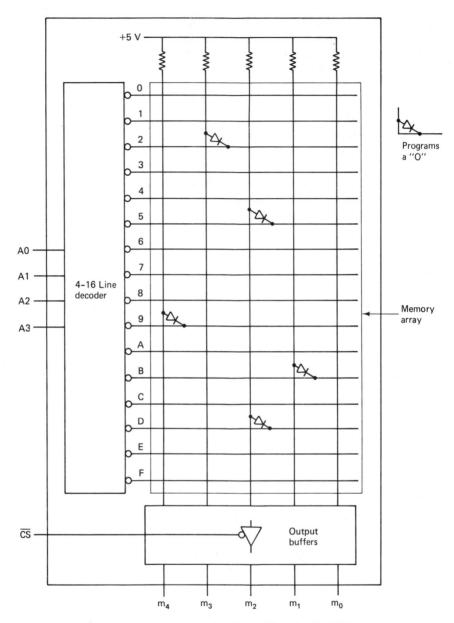

Figure 7.1 A diode ROM illustrating the *n*-input address decoder, $2^n \times m$ memory array, and *m* output buffers. (From J. Uffenbeck, *Microcomputers and Microprocessors: The 8080, 8085, and Z-80*. Prentice-Hall, Englewood Cliffs, N.J., 1985.)

Mask-Programmable ROMs

It is possible to view a ROM as a device with n inputs and m outputs. For each of the 2^n input combinations there is one output word of m bits. This is shown in Fig. 7.1.

A ROM is made up of an address decoder, a programmable memory array, and a set of output buffers. In Fig. 7.1, $n = 4$ and $m = 5$. When a 4-bit address is applied to the ROM, one of the 16 row lines will go low. A diode connected between a row line and a column line will program that output bit low. The absence of a diode will program a logic 1.

In essence, a ROM is nothing more than a *truth table* generator. It provides one m-bit output word for each possible input combination. Because of this, ROMs can be used to replace combinational logic networks (in Sec. 7.4 we provide an example in which a ROM is used as an address decoder).

A *mask-programmable* ROM is one in which the diode connections are programmed at the factory according to a truth table supplied by the user. In this way the manufacturer can sell the same ROM chip to many different customers, altering only the mask that defines the diode connections.

The economics of integrated-circuit manufacture are such that it would be impractical to make only one ROM chip. The integrated-circuit dies are grouped together on a wafer containing several hundred potential ROMs. Because there is no guarantee that a particular wafer will test as being good, several wafers must be manufactured. For this reason, mask-programmable ROMs are limited to production runs of several thousand parts. Needless to say, it is imperative that the truth table supplied to the manufacturer be accurate!

Field-Programmable ROMs

There are several types of ROMs that can be programmed by the user in the field. These devices are referred to as PROMs or *programmable read-only memories*.

Fusible-link PROMs. One type of PROM uses a low-current fusible link in series with the output. By applying a current pulse to the desired output, the fuse can be melted and a logic 1 or 0 permanently programmed. Figure 7.2 is a data sheet for the National Semiconductor DM77/87S180 series of high-speed bipolar PROMs. These devices have a typical access time (i.e., time from receipt of address to data out) of 35 ns. A typical application would be a "boot" PROM in a microcomputer system.

UV-light-erasable PROMs (EPROMs). Probably the most popular type of PROM used in microcomputer systems is the erasable programmable read-only memory (EPROM). This device can be programmed, erased, and reprogrammed many times over by the user. A block diagram and mode selection truth table for the Intel 2764 8K-byte EPROM is given in Fig. 7.3.

EPROMs use a *floating-gate avalanche-injection* MOS (FAMOS) transistor cell to store charge. This is shown in Fig. 7.4(a). Applying a special programming voltage (V_{pp}) causes a high electric field to be developed in the channel region of the transistor. This

 **National Semiconductor**

DM77/87S180/DM77/87S181; DM77/87S181A; DM77/87S280/DM77/87S281; DM77/87S281A (1024 × 8) 8192-Bit TTL PROMs

General Description

These Schottky memories are organized in the popular 1024 words by 8 bits configuration. Memory enable inputs are provided to control the output states. When the device is enabled, the outputs represent the contents of the selected word. When disabled, the 8 outputs go to the "OFF" or high impedance state. The memories are available in both open-collector and TRI-STATE® versions.

PROMs are shipped from the factory with lows in all locations. A high may be programmed into any selected location by following the programming instructions.

Features

■ Advanced titanium-tungsten (Ti-W) fuses
■ Schottky-clamped for high speed
    Address access—35ns typ
    Enable access—15ns typ
    Enable recovery—15ns typ
■ PNP inputs for reduced input loading
■ All DC and AC parameters guaranteed over temperature
■ Low voltage TRI-SAFE™ programming

	Military	Commercial	Open-Collector	TRI-STATE	Package	24-Pin Standard	24-Pin Narrow-Dip
DM87S180		X	X		N,J	X	
DM87S181		X		X	N,J	X	
DM77S180	X		X		J	X	
DM77S181	X			X	J	X	
DM87S280		X	X		N,J		X
DM87S281		X		X	N,J		X
DM77S280	X		X		J		X
DM77S281	X			X	J		X

Block and Connection Diagram

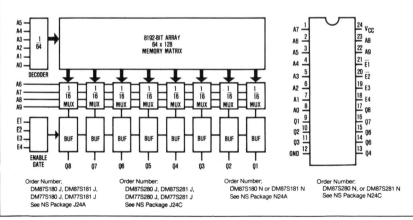

Order Number:
DM87S180 J, DM87S181 J,
DM77S180 J, DM77S181 J
See NS Package J24A

Order Number:
DM87S280 J, DM87S281 J,
DM77S280 J, DM77S281 J
See NS Package J24C

Order Number:
DM87S180 N or DM87S181 N
See NS Package N24A

Order Number:
DM87S280 N, or DM87S281 N
See NS Package N24C

Figure 7.2 Specifications for the DM77/87S180 family of fusible-link PROMs. (Courtesy of National Semiconductor.)

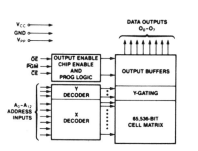

Figure 1. Block Diagram

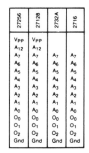

2764

NOTE: INTEL "UNIVERSAL SITE"-COMPATIBLE EPROM PIN CONFIGURATIONS ARE SHOWN IN THE BLOCKS ADJACENT TO THE 2764 PINS

Figure 2. Pin Configurations

MODE SELECTION

MODE	PINS $\overline{CE}$ (20)	$\overline{OE}$ (22)	$\overline{PGM}$ (27)	A_9 (24)	V_{PP} (1)	V_{CC} (28)	Outputs (11–13, 15–19)
Read	V_{IL}	V_{IL}	V_{IH}	X	V_{CC}	V_{CC}	D_{OUT}
Output Disable	V_{IL}	V_{IH}	V_{IH}	X	V_{CC}	V_{CC}	High Z
Standby	V_{IH}	X	X	X	V_{CC}	V_{CC}	High Z
Program	V_{IL}	V_{IH}	V_{IL}	X	V_{PP}	V_{CC}	D_{IN}
Verify	V_{IL}	V_{IL}	V_{IH}	X	V_{PP}	V_{CC}	D_{OUT}
Program Inhibit	V_{IH}	X	X	X	V_{PP}	V_{CC}	High Z
Intelligent Identifier	V_{IL}	V_{IL}	V_{IH}	V_H	V_{CC}	V_{CC}	Code
Intelligent Programming	V_{IL}	V_{IH}	V_{IL}	X	V_{PP}	V_{CC}	D_{IN}

1. X can be V_{IH} or V_{IL}
2. $V_H = 12.0V \pm 0.5V$

*HMOS is a patented process of Intel Corporation

PIN NAMES

A_0–A_{12}	ADDRESSES
$\overline{CE}$	CHIP ENABLE
$\overline{OE}$	OUTPUT ENABLE
O_0–O_7	OUTPUTS
$\overline{PGM}$	PROGRAM
N.C.	NO CONNECT

Figure 7.3 Specifications for the Intel 2764 8K-byte UV EPROM. (Courtesy of Intel Corporation.)

in turn causes electrons to jump the silicon dioxide barrier between the channel region and the floating gate.

During programming the select gate is given a positive bias which helps attract these electrons to the floating-gate electrode. Because the floating gate is surrounded by silicon dioxide (an excellent insulator), the injected charge is effectively trapped. The storage period is projected by Intel to exceed 20 years.

Cells with trapped charge cause the transistor to be biased ON, whereas those cells without trapped charge are biased OFF. Blank EPROMs have no trapped charge and each cell stores a logic 1. The EPROM can be erased by subjecting each gate to ultraviolet (UV) light, which has a wavelength of 2537 angstroms. The electrons on the floating gate absorb photons from the UV-light source and acquire enough energy to reverse the programming process and return to the substrate.

EPROMs are packaged in special ceramic packages with quartz windows to allow erasure. Commercial erasers are available that will erase several EPROMs at once in 15 to 20 minutes.

In operation the EPROM window should be covered with an opaque label because normal room fluorescent lighting could erase the device (Intel reports that approximately three years of exposure to fluorescent lighting or one week of direct sunlight would be required).

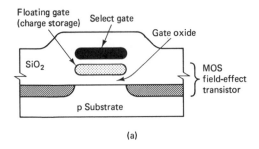

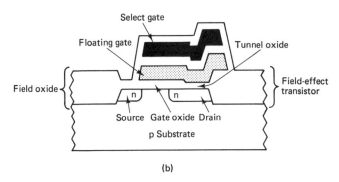

Figure 7.4 (a) Basic UV EPROM cell structure. A logic 0 is stored by trapping charge on the floating-gate electrode. (b) The E²PROM has a thin tunnel oxide covering the drain diffusion of the MOS transistor. Electrons are able to "tunnel" through this thin oxide to or from the floating gate. In this way, programming and erasure are both done electrically. (Courtesy of Intel Corporation.)

As indicated in the mode selection chart in Fig. 7.3, the 2764 can be programmed in two ways. The first method is consistent with the programming technique used for the lower-density devices, such as the 2716 (2K byte) and 2732 (4K byte) EPROMs. In this technique, pin 1, V_{pp}, is raised to 21 V, the chip enabled, data applied to outputs 0–7, and the desired address applied to A0–A12. Programming is accomplished by applying a 45- to 55-ms active-low TTL-level pulse to pin 27, the $\overline{PGM}$ pin.

Usually, the data is written, verified, and the next address selected. The 2764 (and 27128 16K-byte EPROM) can also be programmed using what Intel refers to as an *intelligent programming algorithm*. The advantage in using this algorithm is to reduce the programming time for a 2764 from nearly 7 minutes to less than 1½ minutes. V_{cc} equals 6.0 V for this mode.

PROM programmers are commercially available that allow programming of individual devices with a hex keypad, an external terminal, or an external computer. Universal "personality" modules allow most of the common EPROMs (and fusible-link PROMs) to be programmed with one machine. Figure 7.5 is a photo of the Pro-Log M980 PROM programmer.

The 2764 (and the 2732 and 27128) also support an *intelligent identifier* mode. In this mode, address line A9 is raised to +12 V. Two identifier bytes may then be read

Figure 7.5 Pro-Log M980 PROM programmer. (Courtesy of Pro-Log Corporation, Monterey, Calif.)

from the PROM by forcing A0 low and then high. The first byte represents a manufacturer code and the second byte a device code. This is intended to allow PROM programmers to "read" the device and automatically select the proper pinning and programming algorithm.

Electrically erasable PROMs (E^2 PROMs).   There are several disadvantages to the UV EPROM. These are:

1. The device must be removed from the circuit board to be erased.
2. Byte erasure is not possible; all cells are erased when exposed to UV light.
3. The quartz window package is expensive.

Because of these problems much research has been devoted to developing an electrically erasable nonvolatile memory device. The result is the E^2PROM. This device can be programmed and erased without removing the chip from its socket. In addition, both byte and bulk erasure modes are possible.

An example of an E^2PROM is the Intel 2817A, whose data sheet is given in Fig. 7.6. Figure 7.4(b) shows the difference between the FAMOS cell and the E^2PROM cell. Like the FAMOS cell, a floating gate and a select gate are used. However, a very thin tunnel oxide is provided over the drain diffusion of the MOS transistor in the E^2PROM cell. With a positive voltage applied to the select gate, electrons are attracted to the floating gate. Applying a positive voltage to the drain terminal with the select gate grounded discharges (erases) the cell.

Because the gate oxide over the drain is so thin, the process is controlled by a *tunneling* phenomenon instead of avalanche injection. Tunneling has the advantage that a large amount of charge can be injected during the write cycle but only a small amount

2817A
16K (2K x 8) ELECTRICALLY ERASABLE PROM

- **5 Volt Only Operation**

- **On-Chip Latches for Direct Microprocessor Interface**

- **Automatic Byte-Erase-before-Write**

- **Self Timed Byte Write**

- **Fast Read Access Time:**
  - —2817A-1   200ns max
  - —2817A-2   200ns max
  - —2817A   250ns max
  - —2817A-3   350ns max
  - —2817A-4   450ns max

- **Write Protect Circuit to Preserve Data on Power Up and Power Down**

- **10,000 Erase/Write Cycles per Byte**

- **Reliable Intel HMOS*-E FLOTOX Cell Design Technology**

- **READY/$\overline{\text{BUSY}}$ Line for End-of-Write Signal**

- **10 Year Data Retention For Each Write**

The Intel 2817A is a 16,384 bit Electrically Erasable Programmable Read Only Memory. Like the Intel 2816A it has completely Non-Volatile Data Storage. In addition, it offers a high degree of integrated functionality which enables in-circuit byte writes to be performed with minimal hardware and software overhead. The Intel 2817A is a product of Intel's advanced E^{2}PROM technology and uses the powerful HMOS*-E process for reliable, non-volatile data storage.

*HMOS is a patented process of Intel Corporation.

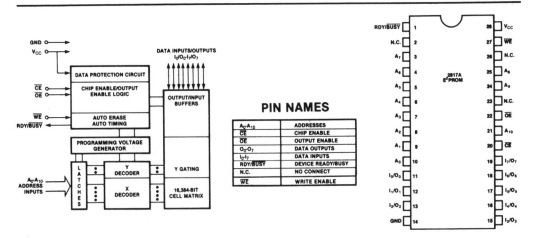

Figure 7.6   Specifications for the Intel 2817A electrically erasable E^{2}PROM. (Courtesy of Intel Corporation.)

of charge is lost during a read cycle. Intel projects data retention to be greater than 10 years.

Unfortunately, each read and write cycle causes a small amount of charge to be trapped in the gate oxide. Eventually, the E²PROM cannot be reprogrammed. This lifetime is between 10,000 and 1 million read/write cycles.

Read access times are comparable with present EPROM and RAM chips, but write times are slow (25 ms typical) compared with conventional RAM devices. For this reason, WAIT states will be required for all write cycles.

What are some applications for the E²PROM? Although it will not replace conventional RAM, it can be used to hold programs and data that are subject to frequent changes: for example, inventory records, set points for NC (numerically controlled) machine tools, and motion paths for industrial robots.

A particularly interesting application of the E²PROM is programming via a remote data link. Using a telephone interface called a *modem*, the central factory can "call up" the E²PROM field system and transfer new data or modify the system software. The cost savings can be substantial compared with conventional service calls and EPROM reprogramming techniques.

Static and Dynamic RAMs

Static RAMs.   Two types of semiconductor RAM are popular. In the first, called *static* RAM (SRAM), four to six transistors are connected to form a simple RS flip-flop. The standard six-transistor static memory cell is shown in Fig. 7.7. Q1 and Q2 are the

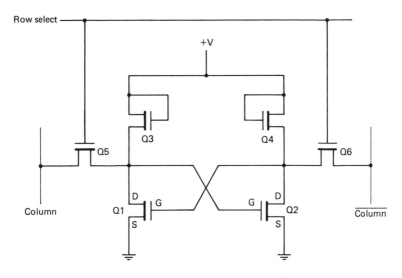

Figure 7.7   Basic six-transistor static memory cell. (From J. Uffenbeck, *Microcomputers and Microprocessors: The 8080, 8085, and Z-80.* Prentice-Hall, Englewood Cliffs, N.J., 1985.)

TABLE 7.1 COMMON STATIC RAM SPECIFICATIONS

Part	Total bits	Organization	Voltage supplied (V)	Access time[a] (ns)	P_D (mW)	Pins
2114AL-1	4K	1K × 4	+5	100	200	18
2147H-1	4K	4K × 1	+5	35	900	18
2167-2	16K	16K × 1	+5	70	900	20
2016	16K	2K × 8	+5	100	325	24

[a]Address to valid data out.

active devices, while Q3 and Q4 are biased as resistive loads. Transistors Q5 and Q6 are used to gate data onto the internal data bus.

As with all flip-flops, the latching mechanism is due to the *cross-coupling* of the active devices, Q1 and Q2. If the Q1 drain is at 0 V, this level will hold Q2 OFF and its drain terminal will be high. This high level, in turn, holds Q1 ON and its drain low.

Data is written to the cell by applying the desired data (and its complement) to the column and column lines with Q5 and Q6 ON. Data is read out by enabling Q5 and Q6 and reading the column line. This static cell is volatile because it will lose its data if power is lost. Each cell will also power-on in an unpredictable state.

Static memories are best known for their ease of interfacing and fast access times. No special timing circuits are required. We will see that the same is not true for the dynamic RAM. Table 7.1 lists several common specifications for popular static RAM chips.

Dynamic RAMs.   If we assume that one of the goals of main memory technology is to produce a high-bit-density component, a part that requires six transistors per cell may not be the best choice. It is this basic flaw of the static RAM that has led designers to the *dynamic RAM* technology.

Dynamic RAMs or DRAMs are based on the well-known capacitive input nature of an MOS transistor. In this scheme the basic storage cell is shrunk to a single bit-select transistor and storage capacitor. A portion of a dynamic RAM memory array is shown in Fig. 7.8.

For a given integrated-circuit die size, a DRAM will be four to six times as dense as the corresponding static die. For example, when the first 16K-bit static RAMs were being announced, 64K-bit dynamic RAMs were becoming available.

In addition to this density improvement, DRAMs generally require much less power than do their static counterparts. This is because current need flow only when charging the bit capacitors. Unfortunately, this can lead to rather large current *transients*. The 2164A 64K-bit DRAM requires only 5 mA when operated in standby but 55 mA during a read or write cycle. Momentary current peaks as high as 120 mA are not uncommon. For this reason, careful attention must be given to DRAM printed-circuit-board (PCB) layout. High-frequency 0.1-μF capacitors should be connected across V_{cc} and ground at each chip site to decouple the noise transients.

The latest trend is to fabricate DRAMs using CMOS technology versus the older NMOS technology. CMOS is easier to design with, consumes much less power, and

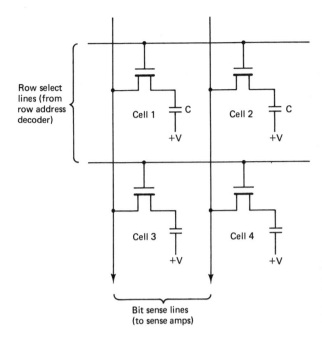

Row select
lines (from
row address
decoder)

Cell 1   C
+V

Cell 2   C
+V

Cell 3
+V

Cell 4
+V

Bit sense lines
(to sense amps)

Figure 7.8 Dynamic RAMs use an MOS capacitor as the basic storage cell. (From J. Uffenbeck, *Microcomputers and Microprocessors: The 8080, 8085, and Z-80.* Prentice-Hall, Englewood Cliffs, N.J., 1985.)

provides faster access times. Table 7.2 provides specifications for several popular DRAMs. Note that the 51C64 is a CMOS version of the 2164A. It is 30% faster than the 2164A and consumes 30% less power.

You may already be familiar with the DRAM's greatest shortcoming—the storage node is not perfect: it leaks. This necessitates a *refresh* operation—that is, sense the charge, amplify it, and then rewrite it. This must be performed once every 2 ms to each cell in the memory.

Refresh may not be as difficult to implement as it may at first seem. Referring to Fig. 7.8, each column in a DRAM has its own sense amplifier which can be used to

TABLE 7.2 COMMON DYNAMIC RAM SPECIFICATIONS

Part	Total bits	Organization	Voltage Supplied (V)	Access time[a] (ns)	P_D (mW)	Pins
2141-2	4K	4K × 1	+5	120	350	18
4116-5	16K	16K × 1	+12 + 5V	120	460	16
2118-10	16K	16K × 1	+5	100	135	16
2164A-15	64K	64K × 1	+5	150	275	16
4416-12	64K	16K × 4	+5	120	270	18
51C64HL-10	64K	64K × 1	+5	100	185	16
41256	256K	256K × 1	+5	120	300	16

[a]RAS low to valid data out.

recharge the bit cell in a given row. By sequencing through all *row* addresses—apply row address 0, then row address 1, and so on—the entire memory array can be refreshed. The data itself does not have to be read or written.

DRAMs are purposely designed to facilitate the refresh process. For example, the 2164A is organized as four 128×128 bit-cell quadrants. In this design the row address is common to all four quadrants. This means that a 7-bit refresh address is sufficient to access all rows in the chip. This in turn simplifies refreshing, requiring just 128 row addresses to be applied every 2 ms. Some 64K DRAMs (the 51C64/65) require sequencing through 256 rows every 4 ms.

To keep the PCB packing density high, DRAMs are packaged in an industry standard 16-pin 300-mil-wide DIP (dual-in-line package). In this standard there is one data-in and one data-out pin. The address lines are *multiplexed* and given to the chip as a *row* address followed by a *column* address. This increases the memory access time, explained in Sec. 7.6.

Because of the refresh and address multiplexing requirements, interfacing a DRAM to a microprocessor is more complex than an SRAM interface. However, DRAM controller chips are available to simplify this task. The Intel 8203 DRAM controller is discussed in Sec. 7.6.

Memory Organization

From the manufacturer's standpoint (and for better marketing appeal), the most important number describing a memory component is the total bit capacity. But from a user's standpoint, it is just as important to know how this memory is *organized*.

The organization of a memory refers to the number of bits in the output word. Referring to Tables 7.1 and 7.2, we see that this can range from *byte-wide* devices such as the 2016 to single-bit devices such as the 2164A or 2147. Most DRAMs are just 1 bit wide, to accommodate a maximum number of address lines. EPROMs are always 8 bits wide to simplify programming and allow one chip to store an entire program segment.[1]

The advantage of the byte-wide devices is that a single chip (two chips in a 16-bit computer) can be used to provide a practical memory in a small system. This, in turn, helps keep the package count low and allows miniaturization of the overall hardware.

The memory chips organized by 1 bit will require eight (or 16) devices to realize a useful memory but offer the advantage of higher board density in large memory systems. This is because there are only eight (or 16) pins devoted to the data, compared to eight data pins per chip with byte-wide devices.

The Universal Memory Site

The Joint Electron Devices Engineering Committee (JEDEC) has approved a standard pinning configuration for byte-wide memories. This is called the *byte-wide universal memory site*.

The universal memory site can accommodate EPROMs, E^2PROMs, static RAMs,

---

[1]Sixteen-bit processors such as the 8086 require a minimum of two byte-wide devices: one for the high byte and one for the low byte.

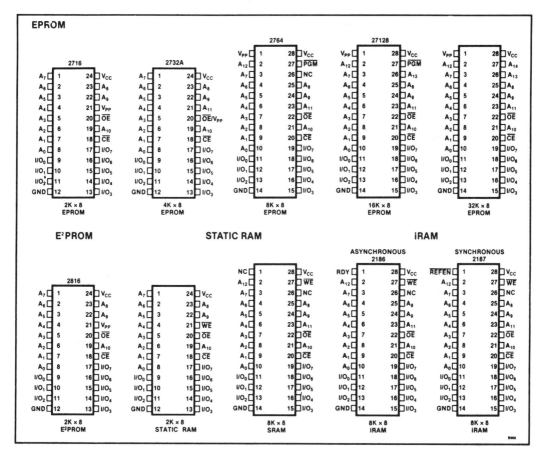

Figure 7.9 Intel family of universal memory site products. (Courtesy of Intel Corporation.)

and pseudostatic integrated RAMs (dynamic RAMs with the refresh controller included on-board). Figure 7.9 illustrates several different memory circuits that are all pin compatible. Note that although the standard is based on a 28-pin package, 24-pin devices can be accommodated by plugging the device into the bottom 24 pins.

Example 7.1

Show how the universal memory site can be designed to accommodate the 2K 2716 EPROM or the 16K 27128 EPROM.

Solution Figure 7.10 shows the circuit. Jumper wires are used to select the appropriate chip. In this case the jumpers are shown in the 27128 position. Notice that the 2716 plugs into the low 24 pins of the socket. The decoder is necessary to determine the value of the high-order address bits that will enable the EPROM. This topic is covered in more detail in Secs. 7.3 and 7.4.

One of the advantages of the universal memory site is that development software can be debugged in RAM, where changes are easily made. Once tested, an EPROM can

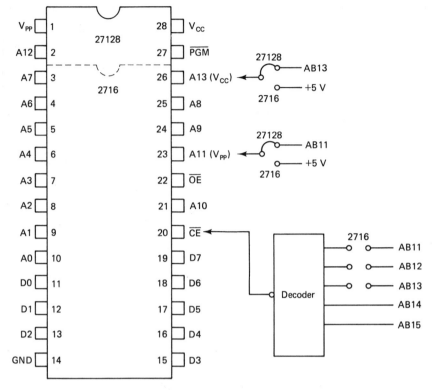

Figure 7.10 Memory design for a 2716/27128 EPROM interface. By using the universal memory site, 2716 designs can be upgraded to the larger 27128 without redesigning the circuit board. (From J. Uffenbeck, *Microcomputers and Microprocessors: The 8080, 8085, and Z-80.* Prentice-Hall, Englewood Cliffs, N.J., 1985.)

be programmed and plugged into the same socket with full confidence that the software has been debugged. As illustrated in Ex. 7.1, systems can be designed for expansion later, when the price of the higher-bit-density component will be less.

SELF-REVIEW 7.1 *(answers on pages 345-346)*

7.1.1. Each byte of _____ memory has its own unique address.

7.1.2. Explain the term *memory access time*.

7.1.3. ROM is a type of (volatile/nonvolatile) memory.

7.1.4. The diode ROM in Fig. 7.1 can store _____ words, where each word is _____ bits wide.

7.1.5. _____ is a type of ROM that can be programmed and erased in the field.

7.1.6. List two advantages and two disadvantages of the E²PROM.

7.1.7. Which memory type is selected when high-density memory arrays are required?

7.1.8. 64K refresh cycles are required every 2 ms to refresh the 2164A DRAM.   (True/False)

7.1.9. What is the difference between two 16K RAM chips, one organized as 16K × 1 and the other as 2K × 8?

To a "hardware type" a microprocessor is a complex timing unit. Turn the machine on and a carefully orchestrated set of signals can be observed on the data, address, and control buses. Looking for a way to force the M/$\overline{\text{IO}}$ and $\overline{\text{RD}}$ lines low while the address bus holds 00000H? Then execute an IN AL,0 instruction. To this person each instruction is known for the unique set of "footprints" it leaves on the system buses.

For now we must all become "hardware types" and look more closely at the sequence of events that occur during CPU read and write cycles. Armed with this information we will be able to design the hardware to connect or interface main memory (and system I/O devices) to the microprocessor.

In this section we look specifically at the timing restrictions imposed by the 8086 when operated in the minimum and maximum modes. I say "restrictions" because there is little we can do to change the CPU timing other than add WAIT states. Our goal will be to come up with a set of timing "windows" for transferring data between the CPU and main memory.

Minimum-Mode Read/Write Timing Specifications

Memory read timing. In App. C we provide a complete set of timing diagrams and ac specifications for the 8086. Figure 7.11 simplifies this by showing only those signals involved in a minimum-mode read cycle. Note the following sequence as the CPU reads a byte or word from memory.

1. The direction of the data bus transceivers is set to receive (DT/$\overline{\text{R}}$ = 0) and M/$\overline{\text{IO}}$ is driven high to indicate a memory cycle.
2. The 20-bit memory address is output on AD0–AD15 and A16–A19.
3. The $\overline{\text{RD}}$ line goes low to indicate to the memory and I/O that this will be a read bus cycle.
4. The data bus transceivers are enabled as $\overline{\text{DEN}}$ goes low.
5. The CPU waits for the memory to place the selected byte or word on D0–D15, the system data bus.
6. The cycle ends as $\overline{\text{RD}}$, $\overline{\text{DEN}}$, and DT/$\overline{\text{R}}$ all return high, disconnecting the CPU from the system bus. The (disabled) data bus buffers are left pointing in the transmit direction.

There are two important timing windows provided by the 8086. The first is the *address access time*: the time from output of the memory address on AD0–AD15 and A16–A19 until valid data is expected by the CPU. This is called TAVDV in Intel's literature. As shown in Fig. 7.11, this is calculated to be 460 ns minimum.[2]

The second parameter important to the RAM is the *read access time*: the time from $\overline{\text{RD}}$ active (low) until valid data is expected by the CPU. This is called TRLDV in Fig. 7.11 and is 205 ns minimum for a 5-MHz 8086 minimum-mode CPU.

[2]All calculations are based on the waveforms in App. C and use the worst-case specifications given in these data sheets.

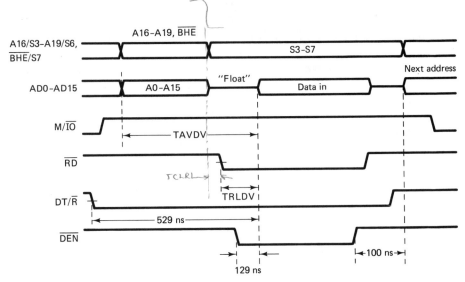

$$TAVDV = 3TCLCL - TCLAVmax - TDVCLmin = 3 \times 200 \text{ ns} - 110 \text{ ns} - 30 \text{ ns} = 460 \text{ ns (8086)}$$
$$TRLDV = 2TCLCL - TCLRLmax - TDVCLmin = 2 \times 200 \text{ ns} - 165 \text{ ns} - 30 \text{ ns} = 205 \text{ ns (8086)}$$

Figure 7.11 Read timing for the 5-MHz 8086 CPU when operated in the minimum mode.

The address access time is often referred to simply as the "access time" in RAM chip advertisements. Thus an ad for a 200-ns 2164A is interpreted as a 64K $\times$ 1 DRAM with an address access time of 200 ns maximum.

Example 7.2

Calculate the maximum allowable address access time (minimum CPU time) for a memory part interfaced to the 10-MHz 8086-1 CPU operated in the minimum mode.

Solution   Using the formula in Fig. 7.11 and referring to the specifications in App. C, we have

$$TAVDV = 3 \text{ TCLCL} - \text{TCLAVmax} - \text{TDVCLmin}$$
$$= 3 \times 100 \text{ ns} - 50 \text{ ns} - 5 \text{ ns} = 245 \text{ ns}$$

One word of caution is in order. The formulas in Fig. 7.11 assume a "naked" CPU. That is, they do not take into consideration any buffer delays. For example, the 8282/8283 address demultiplexer, data bus transceivers, and any buffers at the memory site will all "steal" time away from the memory and shorten the access timing windows. We consider this topic in more detail in Sec. 7.5.

Memory write timing.   Figure 7.12 shows the timing for a minimum-mode write cycle. The following sequence occurs:

1. The M/$\overline{\text{IO}}$ line is driven high to indicate a memory bus cycle.
2. The 20-bit memory address is output on AD0–AD15 and A16–A19.

3. The data bus transceivers are enabled. Note that DT/$\overline{\text{R}}$ is driven high at the end of every bus cycle and thus the buffers are already pointed in the transmit direction.

4. Shortly before the data is output $\overline{\text{WR}}$ becomes active (low). This alerts the memory (and I/O) to the direction of the data transfer.

5. Data is placed on the data lines and held by the CPU.

6. The cycle ends as $\overline{\text{WR}}$ and $\overline{\text{DEN}}$ are driven high, disabling the data bus transceivers. Data is held on the bus briefly after $\overline{\text{WR}}$ returns high.

One of the important points to note about the write timing is that data may not be valid as $\overline{\text{WR}}$ goes low. Thus the rising (or trailing) edge of $\overline{\text{WR}}$ should be used by the memory to latch the data—not the leading edge.

The memory *setup* time is the time from valid data out until $\overline{\text{WR}}$ goes high. It is labeled TDVWH by Intel and is 300 ns minimum for a 5-MHz minimum-mode 8086 CPU.

The data *hold* time is the time data is held on the bus after $\overline{\text{WR}}$ becomes inactive. This is called TWHDX and is a minimum of 88 ns for the 8086.

Finally, most memories have a minimum *write pulse width* or write-time specification. This is called TWLWH. The minimum mode 8086 provides a minimum write pulse width of 340 ns.

Again, the various bus buffers must be taken into account when analyzing a particular memory interface.

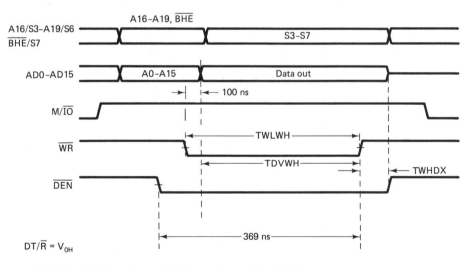

TWLWH = 2TCLCL − 60 ns = 2 × 200 ns − 60 ns = 340 ns (8086)
TDVWH = 2TCLCL − TCLDVmax + TCVCTXmin = 2 × 200 ns − 110 ns + 10 ns = 300 ns (8086)
TWHDX = TCLCH − 30 ns = 118 ns − 30 ns = 88 ns (8086)

Figure 7.12 Write timing for the 5-MHz 8086 CPU when operated in the minimum mode.

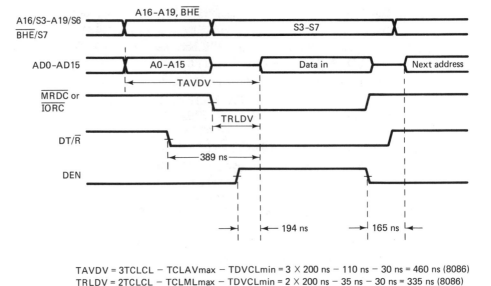

$$TAVDV = 3TCLCL - TCLAVmax - TDVCLmin = 3 \times 200 \text{ ns} - 110 \text{ ns} - 30 \text{ ns} = 460 \text{ ns (8086)}$$
$$TRLDV = 2TCLCL - TCLMLmax - TDVCLmin = 2 \times 200 \text{ ns} - 35 \text{ ns} - 30 \text{ ns} = 335 \text{ ns (8086)}$$

Figure 7.13 Read timing for the 5-MHz 8086 CPU when operated in the maximum mode.

Maximum-Mode Read/Write Timing Specifications

Memory read timing.   When operated in the maximum mode, the control bus signals originate at the 8288 bus controller. In this mode, specific memory and I/O read and write control signals are output by the 8288. The M/$\overline{\text{IO}}$ output is no longer needed and is not generated. Although the $\overline{\text{RD}}$ line is still available (from the CPU), it is intended for devices connected to the processor's local multiplexed bus only.

Maximum-mode memory timing is nearly identical to minimum-mode timing except for DEN, which has become an active-high signal. Because the relationship between address output and data input has not changed, the address access time (TAVDV) is the same as in the minimum mode. The read access time (TRLDV) is actually improved because $\overline{\text{MRDC}}$ is output earlier in the bus cycle in this mode. The read-cycle timing diagram is shown in Fig. 7.13.

Note that $\overline{\text{MRDC}}$ and $\overline{\text{IORC}}$ have the same timing, and thus the specifications in Fig. 7.13 also apply to I/O read cycles. In Chap. 8 we discuss 8086 I/O interfacing in detail.

Memory write timing.   There are two write signals available in the maximum mode. The *advanced* write command has the same timing as the maximum-mode read commands and nearly the same timing as the minimum-mode configuration. Data is output 100 ns (worst case) after the falling edge of $\overline{\text{AMWC}}$. The memory setup time to the rising edge of $\overline{\text{AMWC}}$ (TDVWH) is 300 ns minimum. The data hold time (TWHDX) is a minimum of 93 ns.

The normal write commands ($\overline{\text{MWTC}}$ and $\overline{\text{IOWC}}$) are delayed one T state with

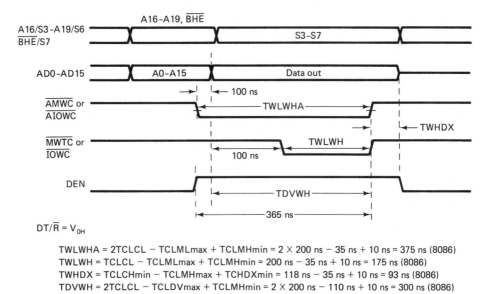

$$TWLWHA = 2TCLCL - TCLMLmax + TCLMHmin = 2 \times 200 \text{ ns} - 35 \text{ ns} + 10 \text{ ns} = 375 \text{ ns (8086)}$$
$$TWLWH = TCLCL - TCLMLmax + TCLMHmin = 200 \text{ ns} - 35 \text{ ns} + 10 \text{ ns} = 175 \text{ ns (8086)}$$
$$TWHDX = TCLCHmin - TCLMHmax + TCHDXmin = 118 \text{ ns} - 35 \text{ ns} + 10 \text{ ns} = 93 \text{ ns (8086)}$$
$$TDVWH = 2TCLCL - TCLDVmax + TCLMHmin = 2 \times 200 \text{ ns} - 110 \text{ ns} + 10 \text{ ns} = 300 \text{ ns (8086)}$$

Figure 7.14 Write timing for the 5-MHz 8086 CPU when operated in the maximum mode.

respect to the advanced commands. The data setup time (TDVWH) and data hold time (TWHDX) are the same as for the advanced write command. The minimum write pulse width for the advanced write commands is 375 ns and 185 ns for a normal write.

General 8086 CPU Timing Specifications

If you study the timing diagrams and specifications in App. C you will see many more parameters than those shown in Figs. 7.11 through 7.14. Each CPU memory or I/O interface must be handled separately. There is not one timing parameter that if met will guarantee that the design will work.

The numbers presented in this section are those most commonly used, but depending on the design, others may have to be taken into consideration; and, of course, we already noted the need to consider the delays introduced by the bus buffers. In Sec. 7.5 we present a design example in which all the timing specifications of the memory are verified against those of the CPU, including bus buffers.

In Table 7.3 we provide a brief word description of several of the most common memory and I/O timing specifications. The symbols in parentheses are used by Intel to describe the timing specifications for its family of peripheral interface chips (discussed in Chap. 9). Thus the timing requirements for each of these chips can be checked for compatibility with the 8086.

Table 7.4 provides formulas for most of the parameters listed in Table 7.3 for the minimum and maximum modes. These formulas are written in terms of the system clock period (TCLCL) and thus can be used for any CPU clock frequency. The remaining parameters appear in the 8086 ac timing specifications given in App. C.

TABLE 7.3 TIMING DEFINITIONS FOR PERIPHERAL COMPATABILITY[a]

TAVRL	Address stable before RD leading edge	(TAR)
TRHAX	Address hold after RD trailing edge	(TRA)
TRLRH	Read pulse width	(TRR)
TRLDV	Read to data valid delay	(TRD)
TRHDZ	Read trailing edge to data floating	(TDF)
TAVDV	Address to valid data delay	(TAD)
TRLRL	Read cycle time	(TRCYC)
TAVWL	Address valid before write leading edge	(TAW)
TAVWLA	Address valid before advanced write	(TAW)
TWHAX	Address hold after write trailing edge	(TWA)
TWLWH	Write pulse width	(TWW)
TWLWHA	Advanced write pulse width	(TWW)
TDVWH	Data set up to write trailing edge	(TDW)
TWHDX	Data hold from write trailing edge	(TWD)
TWLCL	Write recovery time	(TRV)
TWLCLA	Advanced write recovery time	(TRV)
TSVRL	Chip select stable before RD leading edge	(TAR)
TRHSX	Chip select hold after RD trailing edge	(TRA)
TSLDV	Chip select to data valid delay	(TRD)
TSVWL	Chip select stable before WR leading edge	(TAW)
TWHSX	Chip select hold after WR trailing edge	(TWA)
TSVWLA	Chip select stable before advanced write	(TAW)

[a]Symbols in parentheses are equivalent parameters specified for Intel peripherals.
Source: Intel Corp.

Example 7.3

The 2147H 4K × 1 SRAM has a read cycle specification (time from application of address to new address) of 70 ns. Is this memory part compatible with the 5-MHz 8086 CPU?

Solution From Table 7.3 the read cycle time provided by the 8086 is TRLRL. In Table 7.4 this is listed as 4 TCLCL (for either mode). At 5 MHz, the read cycle time is thus 4 × 200 ns, or 800 ns. The specification is easily met.

Finally, the 8088 microprocessor uses the same BIU as does the 8086, and thus all the timing specifications presented in this section apply to this processor as well.

SELF-REVIEW 7.2 (answers on page 346)

7.2.1. The time from memory address output by the CPU until valid data is received by the CPU is called the _____ _____ time.

7.2.2. The DT/R̄ and DEN control signals are only used when the 8086 is operated in the maximum mode. (True/False)

TABLE 7.4 8086 TIMING REQUIREMENTS

Minimum Mode[a,b]

TAVRL = TCLCL + TCLRLmin − TCLAVmax = TCLCL − 100

TRHAX = TCLCL − TCLRHmax + TCLLHmin = TCLCL − 150

TRLRH = 2TCLCL − 75 = 2TCLCL − 75

TRLDV = 2TCLCL − TCLRLmax − TDVCLmin = 2TCLCL − 195

TRHDZ = TRHAVmin = 155 ns

TAVDV = 3TCLCL − TDVCLmin − TCLAVmax = 3TCLCL − 140

TRLRL = 4TCLCL

TAVWL = TCLCL + TCVCTVmin − TCLAVmax = TCLCL − 100

TWHAX = TCLCL + TCLLHmin − TCVCTXmax = TCLCL − 110

TWLWH = 2TCLCL − 60

TDVWH = 2TCLCL + TCVCTXmin − TCLDVmax = 2TCLCL − 100

TWHDX = TCLCH − 30

TWLCL = 4TCLCL

Maximum Mode[b]

TAVRL = TCLCL + TCLMLmin − TCLAVmax = TCLCL − 100

TRHAX = TCLCL − TCLMHmax + TCLLHmin = TCLCL − 35

TRLRH = 2TCLCL − TCLMLmax + TCLMHmin = 2TCLCL − 25

TRLDV = 2TCLCL − TCLMLmax − TDVCLmin = 2TCLCL − 65

TRHDZ = TRHAVmin = 155

TAVDV = 3TCLCL − TDVCLmin − TCLAVmax = 3TCLCL − 140

TRLRL = 4TCLCL

TAVWLA = TAVRL = TCLCL − 100

TAVWL = TAVRL + TCLCL = 2TCLCL − 100

TWHAX = TRHAX = TCLCL − 35

TWLWHA = TRLRH = 2TCLCL − 25

TWLWH = TRLRH − TCLCL = TCLCL − 25

TDVWH = 2TCLCL + TCLMHmin − TCLDVmax = 2TCLCL − 100

TWHDX = TCLCHmin − TCLMHmax + TCHDXmin = TCLCLmin − 25

TWLCL = 3TCLCL = 3TCLCL

TWLCLA = 4TCLCL

---

[a]Delays relative to chip select are a function of the chip select decode technique used and are equal to: equivalent delay from address − chip select decode delay.

[b]Formulas with constants are for the 5MHz 8086 CPU.

Source: Intel Corp.

7.2.3. During a write bus cycle, data out is guaranteed to be valid on the _____ edge of $\overline{WR}$.

7.2.4. Under what conditions is data valid on the falling edge of the write control signal(s)?

7.2.5. At the end of every bus cycle the data bus transceivers are always left in the _____ direction.

7.2.6. Calculate the minimum advanced write pulse width for the 8086-1 CPU.

7.3 SRAM AND ROM INTERFACE REQUIREMENTS

The one basic characteristic of all 8086 memory designs is the requirement to partition the memory into two *banks*. One bank stores the even-addressed bytes and the other the odd-addressed bytes. The A0 address line and $\overline{BHE}$ control signal must be used in the memory interface to select the appropriate bank as required by the current CPU instruction.

In this section we provide examples of SRAM and ROM interfaces to the 8086 CPU. Also included is an 8088 memory design. Both processor interfaces will provide examples of *address decoding*. In Sec. 7.4 we explore this topic in more detail.

For the moment we concentrate on the electrical connections required to mate RAM and ROM to the microprocessor. Then in Sec. 7.5 we resume our memory timing analyses by considering the effects of bus buffers.

Interfacing Static RAM to the 8086 CPU

Figure 7.15 is a portion of the data sheet for the TMM2016 2K × 8 SRAM. This byte-wide RAM has three active-low control inputs, labeled $\overline{CS}$ (chip select), $\overline{OE}$ (output enable), and $\overline{WE}$ (write enable). The RAM idles in a low-power standby mode with all eight data pins open-circuited until the $\overline{CS}$ input is taken low.

When $\overline{CS}$ is low, a read cycle will occur provided that $\overline{WE}$ is high (i.e., disabled). The $\overline{OE}$ input is then used to enable the output buffers and place the selected data byte onto the data bus lines. Eleven address lines are required to select all 2K bytes.

If a memory write cycle is to occur, $\overline{CS}$ and $\overline{WE}$ are driven low. Normally, the $\overline{OE}$ input is left high throughout this cycle to avoid a momentary read cycle while $\overline{CS}$ and $\overline{OE}$ are low but $\overline{WE}$ has not yet been enabled.

Because the data lines of the TMM2016 can be tri-stated, they can be connected directly to the data lines of the (demultiplexed) 8086 data bus. To avoid bus contention, care must be taken to chip select the memory and enable its outputs only during a CPU memory read cycle (from this chip).

Figure 7.16 shows a memory interface that meets these requirements. Two chips are required—one stores the even bytes and connects to DB0–DB7, the other stores the odd bytes and connects to DB8–DB15. Thus the interface provides a total of 4K bytes (2K words) of memory.

It may seem odd to see AB1–AB11 connected to memory chip address lines A0–A10. However, you must remember that AB0 (and $\overline{BHE}$) is required to select the appropriate (even or odd) bank. Table 7.5 should help explain.

When AB11–AB1 = 000H, the bottom-most location in each chip is selected. If the 8086 is accessing a word location (the word at physical address 00000H and 00001H), AB0 and $\overline{BHEB}$ ($\overline{BHE}$ buffered) will both be low. Assuming that MEMORY SELECT is low, both RAMs will be chip selected. For even-byte transfers only AB0 will be low and SRAM-A selected. Similarly, SRAM-B will be selected for odd-byte transfers and $\overline{BHEB}$ only will be low.

Note that the $\overline{WE}$ input is driven by $\overline{MEMW}$ for a minimum-mode CPU (see Fig. 6.21) or $\overline{MWTC}$ (see Fig. 6.23) for a maximum-mode CPU module design. The output enable ($\overline{OE}$) is controlled by $\overline{MEMR}$ or $\overline{MRDC}$. In this way, the output pins are enabled

TOSHIBA MOS MEMORY PRODUCTS

2,048 WORD × 8 BIT STATIC RAM

TMM2016AP-90, TMM2016AP-12
TMM2016AP-10, TMM2016AP-15

DESCRIPTION

The TMM2016AP is a 16,384 bits high speed and low power static random access memory organized as 2,048 words by 8 bits and operates from a single 5V supply. Toshiba's high performance device technology provides both high speed and low power features with a maximum access time of 90ns/100ns/120ns/150ns and maximum operating current of 80mA/65mA/65mA/65mA. When $\overline{CS}$ is a logical high, the device is placed in a low power standby mode in which maximum standby current is 7mA. Thus the TMM2016AP is most suitable for use in microcomputer peripheral memory where the low power applications are required. The TMM2016AP is fabricated with ion implanted N channel silicon gate MOS technology for high performance and high reliability.

FEATURES

- Access Time and Current

Parameter / Part Number	Access Time (Max.)	Operating Current (Max.)	Standby Current (Max.)
TMM2016AP-90	90ns	80mA	7mA
TMM2016AP-10	100ns	65mA	7mA
TMM2016AP-12	120ns	65mA	7mA
TMM2016AP-15	150ns	65mA	7mA

- Single 5V Power Supply
- Fully Static Operation
- Power Down Feature: $\overline{CS}$
- Output Buffer Control: $\overline{OE}$
- Three Stage Outputs
- All Inputs and Outputs: Directly TTL Compatible
- Inputs Protected: All inputs have prtoection against static charge.

PIN CONNECTION

PIN NAMES

SYMBOL	NAME
$A_0 \sim A_3$	Column Address Inputs
$A_4 \sim A_{10}$	Row Address Inputs
$\overline{CS}$	Chip Select Input
$\overline{WE}$	Write Enable Input
$I/O_1 \sim I/O_8$	Data Input/Output
$\overline{OE}$	Output Enable Input
V_{CC}	Power (5V)
GND	Ground

BLOCK DIAGRAM

Figure 7.15 Specifications for the TM2016 2K × 8 static RAM. (Courtesy of Toshiba Corp.)

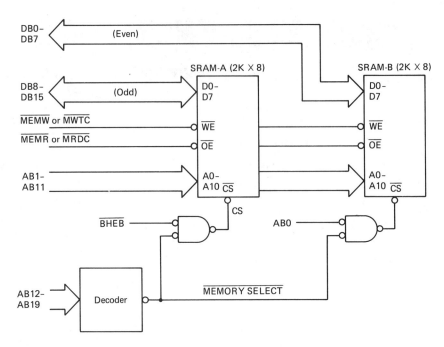

Figure 7.16 The TMM2016 is interfaced to the 8086 CPU in pairs. One chip stores the even bytes, the other the odd bytes.

only for memory read cycles (and $\overline{CS}$ = 0). This avoids bus contention with other bus cycles not involving this RAM.

You have probably noticed that the address lines to each chip are wired in parallel. This means that each chip starts to look up the same address as the bus cycle begins. However, the $\overline{\text{MEMORY SELECT}}$, $\overline{\text{BHEB}}$ and AB0 signals will determine which chip (if either) is actually selected. This leads us to inquire about the contents of the box labeled "decoder."

The decoder is required because the two RAM chips together require only 12 of the 20 address lines. AB12–AB19 are not required. Or are they? If these eight lines are always low, the memory will be mapped to cover the address range 00000H–00FFFH (i.e., all combinations of AB0–AB11 with AB12–AB19 low). But what if AB12–AB19

TABLE 7.5 8086 MEMORY ACCESS ENCODING

$\overline{\text{BHE}}$	A0	Action
0	0	Access 16-bit word
0	1	Access odd byte to D8–D15
1	0	Access even byte to D0–D7
1	1	No action

Source: J. Uffenbeck, *Microcomputers and Microprocessors: The 8080, 8085, and Z-80*. Prentice-Hall, Englewood Cliffs, N.J., 1985.

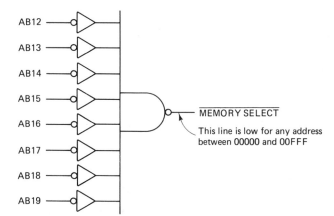

Figure 7.17 Address decoder for the memory interface in Fig. 7.16. MEMORY SE-LECT is low only when the high-order address lines AB12–AB19 = 00H.

= F0H? Now the memory is mapped to the range F0000H–F0FFFH—an entirely different address range.

Perhaps you can now see the need for the decoder. This is a circuit that activates MEMORY SELECT for a single combination of AB12–AB19. Figure 7.17 shows one possible circuit. Nothing very exotic—just a NAND gate driven by eight inverters. However, its output will be low only when AB12–AB19 = 00H. This maps the 4K-byte memory to the bottom 4K memory locations in the 8086's 1,048,576-byte memory address space.

In Sec. 7.4 we will study other types of address decoders. But the idea is always the same. Decode the unused address lines to map the memory interface to a particular memory range in the microprocessor's address space.

Interfacing ROM to the 8086 CPU

By definition, a ROM cannot be written to via a normal memory write cycle. Thus the processor's MWTC or MEMW control lines are not required in a ROM interface. As you will see, address line AB0 and the BHE control signal are also not required.

Figure 7.18 shows a 16K-byte EPROM interface between the 8086 and two 2764A 8K-byte EPROMs. As in the RAM interface, two chips are required, one for the even addresses and one for the odd addresses. Note, however, that both chips share the MEMORY SELECT signal. As a result, whenever MEMORY SELECT is low, no matter if it is an even, odd, or word address, both EPROM chips will be enabled.

How can this work? During an EPROM memory read cycle 16 bits of data will be presented to the CPU, even if the instruction calls for the odd- or even-addressed byte only. This is because AB0 and BHE are not being used. What allows this to work is the 8086's BIU, which will accept only the byte required—ignoring the extra byte.

If an EPROM memory write cycle is attempted, the BIU will output the data on the appropriate data lines—DB0–DB7 for an even-addressed byte and DB8–DB15 for an odd-addressed byte. Because *both* EPROM chips in Fig. 7.18 are enabled, one chip is going to receive indeterminate data, that is, the data on the "unused" set of data lines. For a RAM chip this would be a disaster, as this unknown data would be written to the

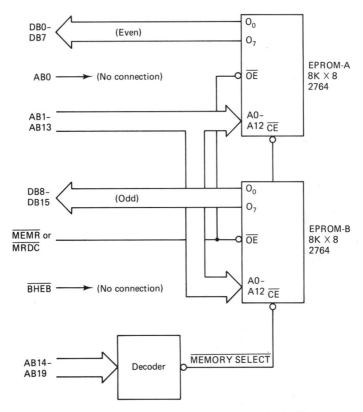

Figure 7.18 Interfacing the 2764 8K-byte EPROM to the 8086 CPU.

selected address. However, for a ROM there is no problem. This is because each chip's $\overline{OE}$ pin is driven by $\overline{MEMR}$ or $\overline{MRDC}$. During the memory write cycle, $\overline{OE}$ will therefore be high and each EPROM data pin in a high-impedance state. No data is written and no bus contention occurs. In other words, "You can't write data into a ROM—even though you can try!"

With this explanation out of the way, the rest of the EPROM interface in Fig. 7.18 is straightforward. Thirteen address lines are required, AB1–AB13, to select one of 8K bytes. The address decoder must decode the unused address lines AB14–AB19. Figure 7.19 shows one possibility. This circuit forces the unused address lines to be 111111B and maps the circuit to the range FC000–FFFFFH. You should verify to yourself that this corresponds to 16K bytes.

Finally, note that because each EPROM stores every other byte, care must be taken to program the chips accordingly.

Interfacing Memory to the 8088 Microprocessor

There is no need to divide the 8088's memory space into a set of even- and odd-addressed bytes as does the 8086. This is because the 8088 can access its memory only one byte

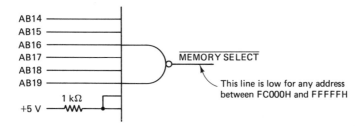

AB14 ——————
AB15 ——————
AB16 ——————
AB17 —————— ⊃o— MEMORY SELECT
AB18 ——————
AB19 ——————

1 kΩ
+5 V ——\/\/\—

This line is low for any address
between FC000H and FFFFFH

Figure 7.19 This address decoder causes the EPROM interface in Fig. 7.18 to reside in the 16K-byte range FC000H–FFFFFH.

at a time. This eliminates the need for the $\overline{\text{BHE}}$ control signal, which has been redefined as status signal $\overline{\text{SS0}}$. It also means that the 8088 can be interfaced to single memory chips.

Figure 7.20 shows how the TMM2016 2K × 8 SRAM is connected to a minimum- or maximum-mode 8088 CPU module. Because of its output tri-state capability, the eight data lines can be connected directly to the data bus. $\overline{\text{OE}}$ and $\overline{\text{WE}}$ are driven by the memory read and write control signals, respectively. The 11 address inputs are controlled by the processor's low-order address lines AB0–AB10.

The decoder must examine the 9 unused address lines AB11–AB19. The 74LS260 is a dual five-input NOR gate and is put to good use in this application, as its active-low representation provides five inverters per gate. The MEMORY SELECT output of this circuit requires all 9 of these address lines to be low. This maps the interface to the range 00000H–007FFH, where address 007FFH corresponds to the topmost location (2047D) in the TMM2016.

SELF-REVIEW 7.3 *(answers on page 346)*

7.3.1. When interfacing RAM or ROM to the 8086 microprocessor, separate _____ and _____ memory banks must be provided.

7.3.2. Assume that the 8086 is reading a memory byte from physical address 00003H. Indicate the logic levels expected on the following bus lines:

(1) AB15–AB0 _____;   (3) $\overline{\text{MEMR}}$ _____;
(2) $\overline{\text{BHE}}$ _____;   (4) MEMW _____.

7.3.3. Data to be read from or written to an even memory location is transferred over the 8086's _____ data bus lines.

7.3.4. The _____ address line is not used when interfacing _____ to the 8086 microprocessor.

7.3.5. It is important to enable the even and odd banks of RAM separately when the 8086 is performing a memory _____ cycle.

7.3.6. What range of addresses would be decoded by the circuit in Fig. 7.17 if the AB19 address line was *not* inverted?

7.3.7. Why is it simpler to interface memory to the 8088 microprocessor than to the 8086 microprocessor?

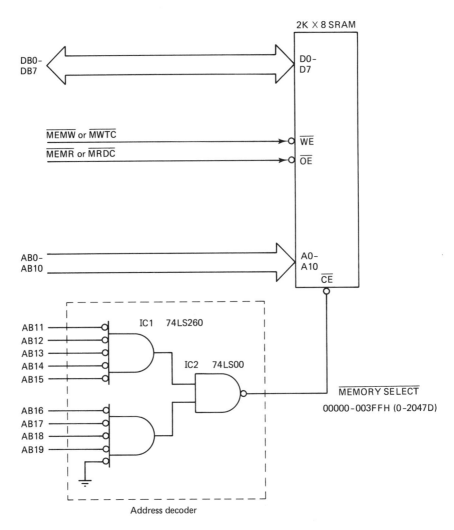

Figure 7.20 Interfacing the TMM2016 2K $\times$ 8 SRAM to the 8088 microprocessor.

7.4 ADDRESS DECODING TECHNIQUES

The 8086 microprocessor provides a 20-bit memory address that allows up to 1MB of main memory. Most memory interfaces, however, do not fill this entire range. This means that for a given memory design, several of the address lines are going to be "unused." However, these unused lines are very important because they determine the *range* of addresses the memory interface will occupy.

An *address decoder* is a circuit that examines these extra address lines and enables the memory for a specified range of addresses. This is an important part of any memory design, as one block of memory must not be allowed to overlap another. In this section

we consider several address decoder circuit designs. These range from simple NAND gates to programmable array logic (PAL) devices.

Full Decoding

A digital decoder is a circuit that recognizes a particular binary pattern on its input lines and produces an active output indication. For example, a two-input NAND gate recognizes the input pattern "11" and produces an active-low output only when this input combination is applied. A two-input AND provides a similar function but produces an active-high output indication.

OR and NOR gates can also be used as decoders when their alternate (active-low input) logic symbols are used. The four decoder combinations are shown in Fig. 7.21.

Example 7.4

Design an address decoder for the 16K-byte EPROM interface in Fig. 7.18 such that the memory begins at address 80000H.

Solution First we must determine the ending address of the 16K block. We can do this by noting that the fourth significant digit in a hex number has the value 16^3, or 4096D. Thus this digit counts *4K blocks*. In a 16K memory there are four such blocks, starting at 0000 and ending with 3FFFH (the last address in the fourth 4K block).

In this example the memory must thus extend from 80000H to 80000H + 3FFFH = 83FFFH. When this is written in binary, the decoding requirements can easily be seen.

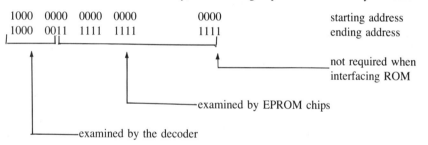

The memory should be enabled only when AB19–AB14 = 100000B. Figure 7.22(a) and (b) shows two ways of building this decoder. Both require two IC packages, but the version in part (b) has fewer connections.

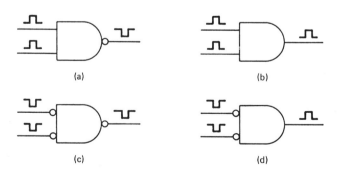

(a)

(b)

(c)

(d)

Figure 7.21 (a) NAND, (b) AND, (c) OR, and (d) NOR gates can all be used as address decoders, depending on the logic levels to be detected and the active output level required.

Figure 7.22(c) shows an alternative decoding scheme. It uses a 74ALS677 address comparator. This 24-pin chip is essentially a 16-input *programmable NAND gate*. When enabled ($\overline{G}$ = 0 V), the four P inputs define the number of NAND gate inputs that will be inverted. In this example "P" = 5, causing inputs A1–A5 to be inverted. Inputs A6–A16 are not inverted. Thus the circuit is equivalent to the decoders in Fig. 7.22(a) and (b) but requires only one package.

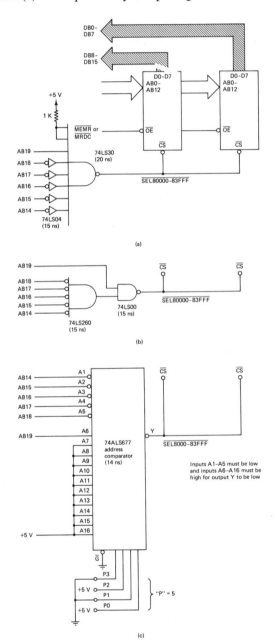

Figure 7.22   (a) and (b) Full address decoding using NAND and NOR gates; (c) Using the 74ALS677 programmable NAND gate.

Main Memory System Design   Chap. 7

The 74ALS677 is particularly useful when a large number of address lines must be decoded. Simply count the number of inputs that must be inverted and program "P" to this value. The inverted lines are then connected to the chip inputs in sequence beginning with A1. Programming "P" to be 0 implies that none of the inputs are to be inverted and results in a 16-input NAND gate.

Partial Decoding

The smaller the memory block, the more address lines there will be to decode. The 8088 2K-byte memory interface in Fig. 7.20 had to decode nine address lines. All of this decoding circuitry can become a nuisance, particularly in small systems where much of the memory space is unimplemented. In these systems *partial decoding* is often used. This is a technique in which some of the (normally decoded) address lines are simply ignored. Figure 7.23(a) gives an example for the 16K-byte EPROM interface just discussed.

In this circuit the decoder has been shrunk to a single inverter, with address lines AB18–AB14 left untested. In effect these lines become "don't cares." Certainly, this is a much simpler decoder circuit—but will the interface still work?

The $\overline{\text{MEMORY SELECT}}$ line in Fig. 7.23(a) will be active and the EPROM array enabled whenever AB19 is high. This corresponds to any address from 80000H to FFFFFH. In particular, it covers the range 80000H–83FFFH of the original design. But note that address 84000H will also enable the memory. It differs from address 80000H only in bit AB14, one of the bits not tested by the decoder. Thus a memory read from 84000H will return the same data—in fact, it reads the same EPROM location—as address 80000H.

In a similar manner, address 88000H will enable the memory and access the same EPROM location as address 80000H. All told, there are 32 different addresses (corresponding to the 32 different combinations of AB14–AB18) that access location 80000H. Since there are 32 combinations of each EPROM address, the entire 16K block appears to wrap around on itself 32 times from 80000H to FFFFFH. This is shown in *memory-map* form in Fig. 7.23(b).

This wraparound effect is characteristic of all partially decoded memories. At first glance it seems very wasteful to use 512K (32 × 16K) bytes of memory for a single 16K memory block. However, if this space is not required for other memory blocks, the simplification in the decoder circuitry may justify it. You must be careful, however, not to map any other memory into this space.

Partial decoding is often used in microcontroller applications where the microprocessor is *embedded* into the final product. In these applications the memory configuration is fixed and the ability to expand the memory not required.

Block Decoding

In a practical microcomputer the memory array often consists of several blocks of memory chips. This will require a separate decoder for each memory block unless a special *block decoder* is built.

A 256K-byte memory array is shown in Fig. 7.24. It consists of four 64K-byte blocks of memory and a 74LS138 (Intel part number 8205) 3-to-8-line decoder. The low-

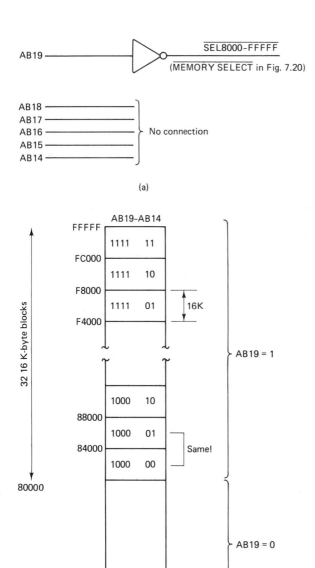

(a)

Figure 7.23 (a) Partial address decoder for the 16K EPROM interface in Fig. 7.18; (b) The memory wraps around on itself, reappearing 32 times between addresses 80000H and FFFFFH.

(b)

order address lines AB0–AB15 select one of 64K bytes in each memory bank. However, the decoder allows only one bank to be enabled at a time. For example, output 0 will be active when AB19 = 0 (enabling the decoder) and AB18–AB16 = 000 (selecting the 0 output). This corresponds to the address range 00000–0FFFFH.

The decoder in Fig. 7.24 provides eight block select outputs and thus can be used to decode up to 512K bytes of memory. This is shown in the memory map in Fig. 7.25. Using a 74154 4-to-16-line decoder, all 16 64K blocks could be decoded.

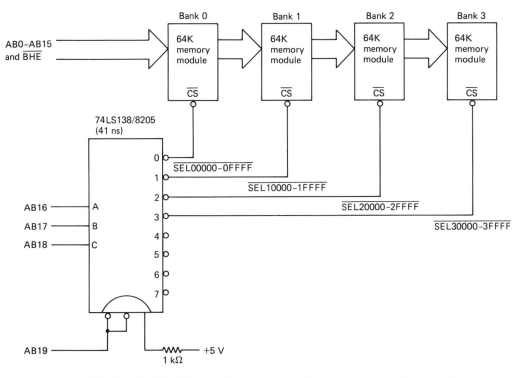

Figure 7.24 The 74LS138/8205 3-to-8-line decoder can be used to provide eight consecutive memory-block select signals.

It is often desirable to be able to move a block of memory about in the processor's memory space. For example, two 64K-byte memory boards might be constructed. If one could be mapped to begin at address 00000H and the other to address 10000H, both boards could be accommodated in the same system.

Figure 7.26 shows a decoder for a 64K-byte memory that allows the memory block to be positioned in one of 16 ranges as set by the four switches. When all four switches are open (in the "0" position), AB16–AB19 must equal 0000 to cause all four exclusive-OR gate open-collector outputs to be high. If any one of these address lines goes high, its exclusive-OR output will be low and the memory disabled. Thus to set this block of memory to begin at address C0000H, set the switches to 1100 (S4–S1).

PROM Decoders

It is somewhat incongruous to have the 50,000-transistor 8086 microprocessor sitting beside several SSI and MSI TTL devices providing address decoding and other miscellaneous gating functions. These chips, with 15 to 100 transistors per package, may collectively require as much board space as the more complex processor they support. There ought to be a better way.

And, of course, there is. One solution is to replace all of this combinational TTL logic with a high-speed PROM. After all, a PROM is nothing more than an elaborate

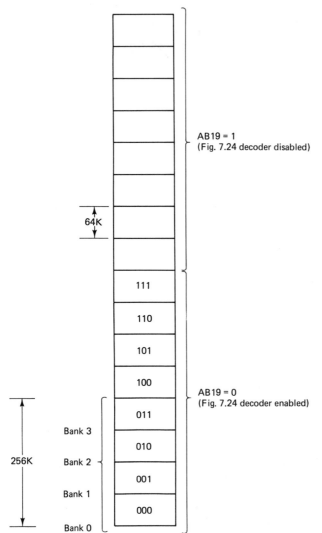

AB19 = 1
(Fig. 7.24 decoder disabled)

64K

111

110

101

100

AB19 = 0
(Fig. 7.24 decoder enabled)

011

Bank 3

010

256K   Bank 2

001

Bank 1

000

Bank 0

AB18–AB17–AB16

Figure 7.25 Memory map for the circuit in Fig. 7.24. There are 16 64K blocks in the 8086's 1M-byte address space.

truth-table generator. As discussed in Sec. 7.1, it stores one m-bit output word for each of its 2^n input combinations.

As an example, consider the design of an address decoder to implement the 8086 system whose memory is mapped in Fig. 7.27. What makes the design of this decoder difficult is the three different block sizes—1K, 16K, and 64K. A block decoder is impractical because the smallest block size—1K bytes—would require a decoder with 10 inputs and therefore 2^{10}, or 1024 outputs! It appears that we are stuck having to build three separate decoder circuits.

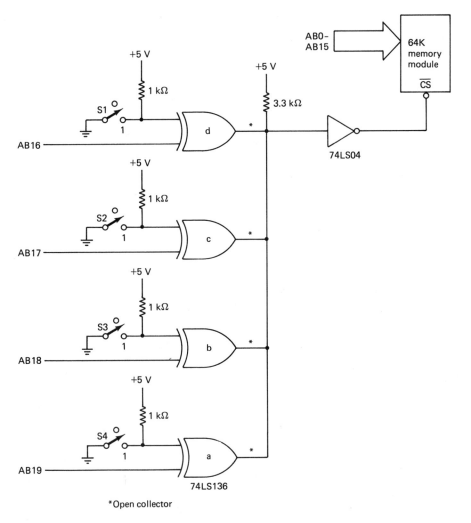

Figure 7.26 By setting the four switches, this decoder allows the 64K memory module to be mapped to any of 16 possible 64K address slots.

But now consider using a PROM with 10 inputs. Assuming an 8-bit word size, a 1K-byte PROM would be required, not a particularly exotic or expensive component. In fact, the 77/87S180 series of fusible-link PROMs studied in Sec. 7.1 (see Fig. 7.2) are all 1K-byte PROMs and could be used for this purpose.

Selecting the 87S181A with tri-state outputs, the memory interface in Fig. 7.28 can be drawn. The low-order address lines are connected to the memory chips, with the PROM used to decode the 1024 1K-byte block boundaries. Q1–Q4 have arbitrarily been selected to provide the four memory select signals.

These outputs should be programmed so that each is low when its address range is applied to the PROM. For example, Q4, the $\overline{RAM0}$ select signal, should be low for addresses in the range 00000H–0FFFFH. Over this range, AB19–AB10 vary from

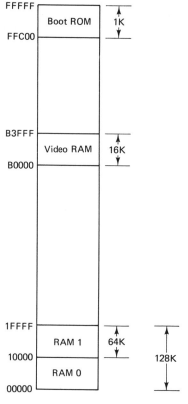

Figure 7.27 Memory map for an 8086 microcomputer system featuring three different block sizes.

0000000000B to 0000111111B, that is, location 0 to location 63D in the PROM. This corresponds to the first 64 1K blocks. Addresses outside this range should cause Q4 to be high (inactive).

Similar calculations can be made for the other three blocks. The result is the PROM truth table shown in Table 7.6. This data can be rewritten in the easier-to-program form shown in Table 7.7. In this table Q5–Q8 are left unprogrammed and store logic 0's.

The PROM decoder offers several advantages over its discrete logic TTL counterpart. Most important, it replaces several TTL packages with one 24-pin package. It also offers the versatility of allowing the system's memory map to be *programmable*. A new memory configuration can be obtained by simply inserting a new PROM. Finally, the circuit is fast. Typical access time (decoder delay) is 25 ns—probably faster than the TTL gates it replaces.

PLAs and PALs

The PROM decoder in Fig. 7.28 uses 64 + 64 + 16 + 1 = 145 of the 1024 possible memory locations. The remaining 879 locations store a memory disable code. This seems rather wasteful, as each of these 879 bytes stores exactly the same binary code (OFH).

TABLE 7.6 82S181A TRUTH TABLE

PROM address	PROM input AB19–AB16	PROM input AB15–AB12	PROM input AB11–AB10	PROM output Q4 $\overline{\text{RAM0 SEL}}$	PROM output Q3 $\overline{\text{RAM1 SEL}}$	PROM output Q2 $\overline{\text{VSRAM SEL}}$	PROM output Q1 $\overline{\text{BROM SEL}}$
				RAM0			
0	0000	0000	00	0	1	1	1
↓		↓	↓				
63D	0000	1111	11	0	1	1	1
				$\overline{\text{RAM1}}$			
64D	0001	0000	00	1	0	1	1
↓		↓	↓				
127D	0001	1111	11	1	0	1	1
				Unused			
128D	0010	0000	00	1	1	1	1
↓		↓	↓				
703D	0010	1111	11	1	1	1	1
				$\overline{\text{VRAM}}$			
704D	1011	0000	00	1	1	0	1
↓		↓	↓				
719D	1011	0011	11	1	1	0	1
				Unused			
720D	1011	0100	00	1	1	1	1
↓		↓	↓				
1022D	1111	1111	10	1	1	1	1
				$\overline{\text{BROM}}$			
1023D	1111	1111	11	1	1	1	0

TABLE 7.7 PROGRAMMING CODES FOR THE PROM DECODER IN FIG. 7.28

Prom address A9–A0	Data Q8–Q1	Memory block selected
0–63	07H	RAM0
64–127	0BH	RAM1
128–703	0FH	None
704–719	0DH	VRAM
720–1022	0FH	None
1023	0EH	BROM

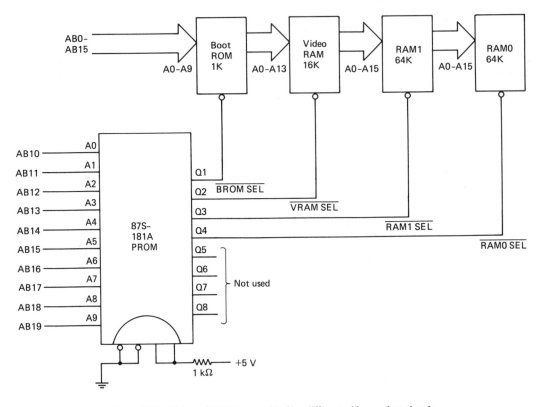

Figure 7.28 Using a PROM to provide four different address select signals.

Could we devise a component that has the decoding capability of the PROM but not the wasted storage space?

Before answering this question, let's develop an equivalent circuit for a PROM (or ROM) when it is used to replace combinational logic. Because the ROM develops all 2^n possible combinations of its inputs, we think of it as a *truth-table* generator. We also know that using the rules of Boolean algebra, any truth-table function can be expressed as a combinational logic circuit in standard *sum-of-products* form. Thus we might visualize a ROM as an array of AND gates (developing all possible product terms) driving one OR gate. ROMs with multiple outputs (i.e., word sizes greater than one bit) have several OR gates. This is shown in Fig. 7.29.

A ROM has certain restrictions. Each AND gate must develop one of the 2^n product terms, no simplifications are possible. For example, if the function to be implemented is

$$X = ABCD + ABC\overline{D} = ABC (D + \overline{D}) = ABC$$

it will still be implemented as $ABCD + ABC\overline{D}$ by the ROM. This is where the "wasted" space comes from. This restriction also has another negative effect. If the D input in

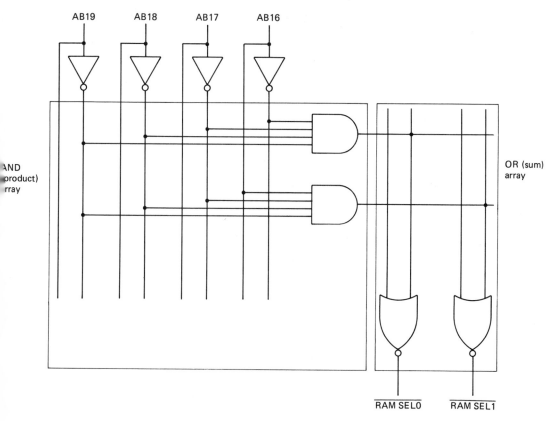

Figure 7.29 PROMs, PLAs, and PALs can be used to implement logic functions expressed in standard sum-of-products form. Each device consists of an AND array whose outputs can be used to drive an OR array.

the example above switches from a 1 to a 0, a different AND gate (the one developing the product ABC$\overline{\text{D}}$) will be enabled. This may cause a "glitch" (momentary pulse) in the ROM's output as one AND gate switches OFF and the other switches ON.

There are two alternatives to the ROM. They are called the PLA and PAL (for "programmable logic array" and "programmable array logic"). The PLA is the most versatile. It allows the entire *AND* array (see Fig. 7.29) to be programmed. Thus the term ABC required in the example above could be programmed. The PLA also allows the *OR* array to be programmed. This means that each OR gate has as many inputs as there are product terms.

A PAL is similar to a PLA but its *OR* array is limited so that each OR gate has a fixed number of inputs. For example, the Monolithic Memories PAL10L8 shown in Fig. 7.30 has 10 inputs and eight NOR gate outputs. However, each of these NOR gates is limited to two product terms.

The "wasted" storage space of the ROM is reduced in the PLA and PAL by limiting

Sec. 7.4   Address Decoding Techniques

309

10L8

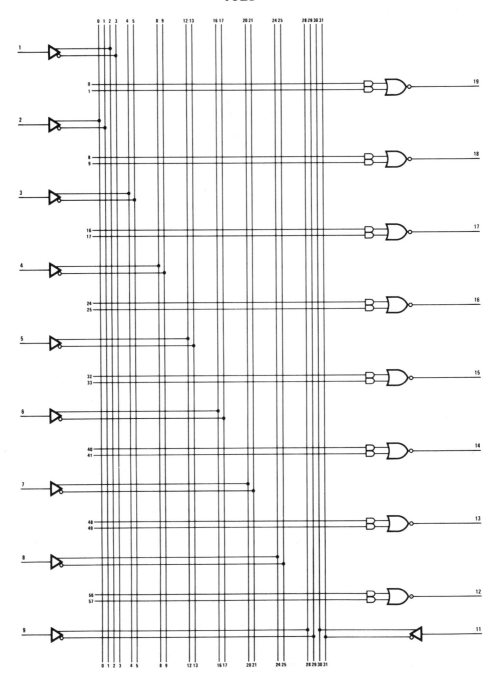

Figure 7.30 The PAL10L8 has 10 inputs and 8 outputs. The AND array is programmable, but the OR array is limited to two product terms per gate. (Courtesy of Monolithic Memories Inc. PAL is a registered trademark of Monolithic Memories, Inc. PLE is a trademark of Monolithic Memories, Inc.)

each to fewer than 2^n product terms. In Fig. 7.30, the intersection of a vertical line with a (NOR input) horizontal line represents a possible *AND* term. With eight OR gates and two inputs per OR gate, a total of $8 \times 2 = 16$ product terms can be generated. For example, output 19 could be programmed for

$$O_{19} = I_1 \, I_2 \, I_7 \, \overline{I_8} \, I_9 \, I_{11} + \overline{I_1} \, \overline{I_2} \, \overline{I_3} \, \overline{I_4} \, I_9$$

Note that with 10 inputs, there are 1024 possible product terms. The PAL (and PLA) are restricted to a subset of these terms.

Electrically, PALs and PLAs are available with TTL-compatible inputs and outputs. The PAL10L8 has a maximum propagation delay of 35 ns. A FAST series is available with typical delays of only 15 ns.

PALs are programmed using a fusible-link technique similar to that of a bipolar PROM. This makes the parts extremely versatile. A designer can quickly design and fabricate his or her own "custom" integrated circuit in a matter of hours. And there need not be a high volume to justify the part, as would be the case in the conventional four- to eight-month custom IC development cycle.

If a part is required in high volume, it can be mask-programmed at the factory. Such parts are called HALs (for *hard array logic*). Monolithic Memories has several such parts available off the shelf. An example is the 74LS380 shown in Fig. 7.31. This circuit combines the features found in the 74LS273 and 74LS374 8-bit registers.

PLAs and PALs are now the choice of most designers for replacement of combinational (and sequential) logic. PLAs are the most versatile but also the most expensive. They require special programmers, whereas PALs can be programmed with a conventional (fusible-link) PROM programmer. PROMs are chosen when all 2^n product terms are required—microprocessor memory applications, primarily.

SELF-REVIEW 7.4 (answers on page 346)

7.4.1. For full decoding of a 16K-byte memory module, which 8086 address lines must be examined by the decoder?

7.4.2. If a decoder requires AB19–AB16 = 0000, the memory block decoded will be mapped to cover the address range _____ through _____.

7.4.3. Output 7 of the block decoder in Fig. 7.24 will be active for addresses in the range _____ through _____.

7.4.4. A PROM decoder is particularly useful when memory blocks of _____ sizes are to be decoded.

7.4.5. PROMs, PLAs, and PALs can be visualized as an array of _____ gates driving an array of _____ gates.

7.4.6. Unlike PROMs, PLAs and PALs cannot develop all 2^n products of the input variables. (True/False)

7.4.7. Only the _____ allows a completely programmable output OR array.

7.4.8. The mask-programmable version of the PAL is called the _____.

HMSI Product Description

Selected members of the HMSI family will now be described.

Octal Register (SN54/74LS380)

The 8-bit register combines all of the three features found in the LS273 (CLEAR), LS374 (THREE-STATE), and LS273 (CLOCK ENABLE) into one 24-pin skinny DIP package. In addition to the above, this device has extra features: LOAD COMPLEMENT and PRESET, allowing inverting data operations. A Bus-structured pinout is also provided.

This convenient microprocessor interface lowers inventory requirements.

SN54/74LS380
Octal Register

Function Table

$\overline{OC}$	CLK	$\overline{LD}$	POL	$\overline{CLR}$	$\overline{PR}$	D7–D0	Q7–Q0	OPERATION
H	X	X	X	X	X	X	Z	HI-Z
L	↑	X	X	L	X	X	L	CLEAR
L	↑	X	X	H	L	X	H	PRESET
L	↑	H	X	H	H	X	Q	HOLD
L	↑	L	H	H	H	D	D	LOAD true
L	↑	L	L	H	H	D	$\overline{D}$	LOAD comp

Figure 7.31 HAL (hard array logic) 74LS380 octal register/latch. (Courtesy of Monolithic Memories, Inc. PAL is a registered trademark of Monolithic Memories, Inc. PLE is a trademark of Monolithic Memories, Inc.)

7.5 ACCOUNTING FOR BUFFER DELAYS IN A MEMORY DESIGN

In Sec. 7.2 we considered the timing windows provided by the 8086 for memory read and write bus cycles. But as we have seen, these windows are shortened due to the support circuits. These include:

> Address demultiplexers/buffers
> Data bus transceivers
> Memory address decoders

In this section we adjust the timing specifications given in Sec. 7.2 to account for the delays introduced by these support devices. An example will be presented using the 2167 16K × 1 SRAM.

8086 and 8088 CPU Configurations

The simplest CPU configuration occurs when the 8088 microprocessor is operated in the minimum mode. In this case all the 8085 bus-multiplexed components are directly compatible. One example was presented in Fig. 6.27. There are no buffers or address latches with which to be concerned. The equations presented in Table 7.4 can be used directly to calculate the memory timing requirements.

In most cases, however, the 8086 (and 8088) are used in considerably more complex configurations. Figure 7.32 provides four examples. In Fig. 7.32(a) the CPU is wired for the minimum mode and no buffers are used (other than those of the address demultiplexer). This design would be suitable for a single-board computer with a limited number of memory chips and I/O ports. If this system is to be expandable, a better design is the buffered version shown in Fig. 7.32(b). This circuit includes data and control bus buffers.

For more complex applications, possibly supporting the 8087 and 8089 coprocessors, the maximum mode must be selected. This configuration is shown in fig. 7.32(c). Note that the control signals are now generated by the 8288 bus controller.

Figure 7.32(d) shows a *double-buffered* maximum mode CPU configuration in which the memory and I/O are located on separate logic cards. All signals are buffered onto the system bus and off the bus at the memory or I/O site. The advantages of double buffering were explained in Ex. 6.4.

Unfortunately, the buffers also increase the amount of time required to exchange data with memory (or the I/O devices). Figure 7.33 shows the effects of the buffers on the address access time in a double-buffered 8086 system. Using noninverting buffers (8282, 8286), 120 ns is added to the round-trip time from address output until data is received by the CPU. With inverting buffers this is reduced to 88 ns. As the footnote indicates, high-speed (74AS family) buffers can be used to reduce these propagation delays even further.

Because the memory's chip select (CS) input must be active before the memory can release its data, the delay through the address decoder must also be accounted for.

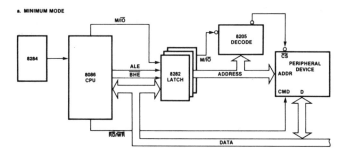

a. MINIMUM MODE

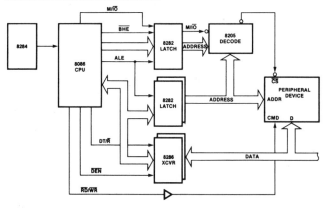

b. MINIMUM MODE BUFFERED DATA AND COMMAND BUSSES

Figure 4D1. 8086 System Configurations

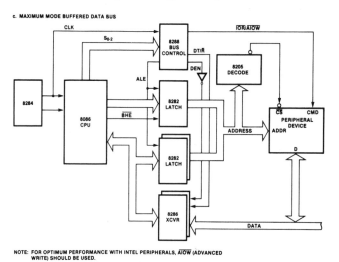

c. MAXIMUM MODE BUFFERED DATA BUS

NOTE: FOR OPTIMUM PERFORMANCE WITH INTEL PERIPHERALS, $\overline{\text{AIOW}}$ (ADVANCED WRITE) SHOULD BE USED.

Figure 7.32 8086 CPU configurations: (a) minimum mode; (b) minimum-mode buffered; (c) maximum-mode buffered data bus; (d) maximum-mode double buffered. (Courtesy of Intel Corporation.)

Figure 7.32 Continued

Example 7.5

Assume that a maximum mode double-buffered 8086 CPU is operating at 5 MHz. Calculate the maximum address access time allowed by the processor. Assume inverting buffers and an address decoder with 35-ns delay.

Solution The circuit configuration is as shown in Figs. 7.32(d) and 7.33. Referring to Table 7.4, the address access time is called TAVDV and is calculated as 3 TCLCL − 140 ns. Accounting for the 88 ns of buffer delay and 35 ns of decoder delay, the result is

$$\text{TAVDV} = 3 \times 200 \text{ ns} - 140 \text{ ns} - 88 \text{ ns} - 35 \text{ ns} = 337 \text{ ns}$$

The memory must have an address access time of 337 ns or less.

Not all of the timing specifications are affected by the buffers. For example, the leading and trailing edges of the memory write pulse are *skewed* (shifted) in time, but the pulse width itself remains approximately the same.

A Design Example

The 2167 is a 16K × 1S RAM. This chip stores the same number of bits as the TMM 2016 but has only one output bit. It is packaged in a standard 300-mil-wide 20-pin package, in contrast to the TMM2016's 600-mil-wide 24-pin package.

In this example a 32K-byte memory is to be interfaced to the 8086 maximum-mode CPU module. The 2167 SRAM is used because it will require less PCB area than the TMM2016. As pointed out in the next section, this is about the largest amount of RAM

Sec. 7.5   Accounting for Buffer Delays in a Memory   **315**

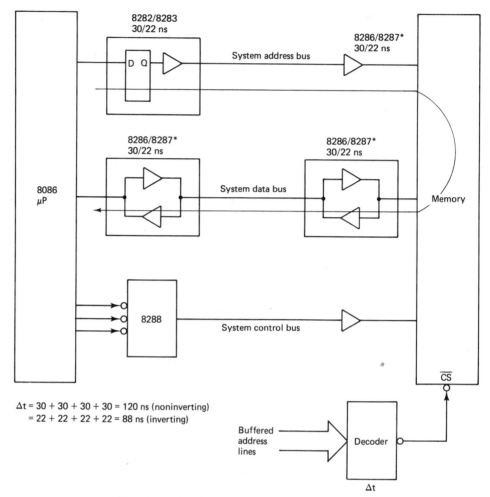

Δt = 30 + 30 + 30 + 30 = 120 ns (noninverting)
  = 22 + 22 + 22 + 22 = 88 ns (inverting)

*The 74LS240/244 may also be used (18/18 ns).
The 74AS versions of these parts have delays of less than 9 ns.

Figure 7.33 The propagation delays of the address and data bus buffers decrease the access time allowed the memory by the microprocessor.

that you would want to implement using SRAM parts. Larger memory arrays can be implemented more efficiently using denser DRAM memory chips.

The circuit diagram of the memory design is shown in Fig. 7.34. Two banks of memory chips are required: one for the even bytes and another for the odd bytes. Each bank requires eight chips to construct an 8-bit byte. The address decoder maps the interface to cover the range 00000–07FFF, that is, the low 32K bytes of the 8086's memory space. AB0 and $\overline{\text{BHEB}}$ ($\overline{\text{BHE}}$ buffered) select the even or odd byte.

Because the 2167 has a separate data-in and data-out pin, a special data bus buffer is required. If the current bus cycle is a memory read to an odd byte or a 16-bit word within the address range of the memory, $\overline{\text{MRDC}}$ and $\overline{\text{SEL ODD BYTE}}$ will both be low.

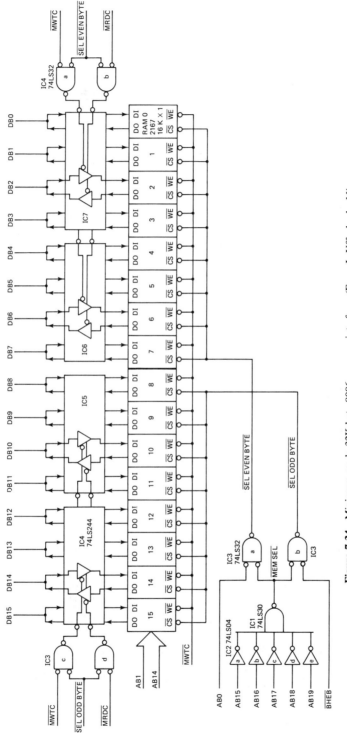

Figure 7.34 Minimum-mode 32K-byte 8086 memory interface. (From J. Uffenbeck, *Microcomputers and Microprocessors: The 8080, 8085, and Z-80.* Prentice-Hall, Englewood Cliffs, N.J., 1985.)

317

TABLE 7.8 TIMING VERIFICATION FOR THE 2167 SRAM INTERFACE IN FIG. 7.34

Parameter	2167-2		8086: Symbol/equation/value[a]
	Symbol	Value	
Read cycle time	t_{RC}	70 ns min.	TRLRL = 4 TCLCL = 800 ns min.
Address access time (assume chip selected)	t_{AA}	70 ns max.	TAVDV = 3 TCLCL − 140 − 108 ns (buffers) = 352 ns max.
Chip select access time	t_{ACS}	70 ns max.	TSLDV = TAVDV − address decoder delay = 352 ns − 57 ns = 315 ns max.
Write cycle time	t_{WC}	70 ns min.	TWLWL = TRLRL = 4 TCLCL = 800 ns min.
Chip select to end of write	t_{CW}	55 ns min.	TCW[b] = 3 TCLCL − TCLAVmax + TCLMHmin − address decoder delay = 600 ns − 110 ns + 10 ns − 57 ns = 443 ns min.
Address valid to end of write	t_{AW}	55 ns min.	TAW[b] = 3 TCLCL − TCLAVmax + TCLMHmin = 600 ns − 110 ns + 10 ns = 500 ns min.
Write pulse	t_{WP}	40 ns min.	TWLWH[c] = TCLCL − 25 ns = 200 ns − 25 ns = 175 ns min.
Write recovery time (address hold from end of write)	t_{WR}	15 ns min.	TWR = TCLCL + TCLLHmin − TCLMHmax = 200 ns + 0 ns − 35 ns = 165 ns min.
Data valid to end of write	t_{DW}	30 ns min.	TDVWH[d] = 2 TCLCL + TCLMHmin − TCLDVmax = 400 ns + 10 ns − 110 ns = 300 ns min.
Data hold time	t_{DH}	10 ns min.	TWDHX[d] = TCLCHmin − 25 ns = 118 ns − 25 ns = 93 ns min.

[a]Equations taken from Table 7.4 are derived from the 8086 ac characteristics data sheet in App. C. Clock frequency assumed to be 5 MHz.
[b]Buffer delays on MWTC and the memory address lines are assumed to cancel.
[c]Assuming normal write (not advanced).
[d]Address and data buffer delays are assumed to cancel.

This will enable the bus transmitters within IC5 and IC6 and gate the output data from the DO pins of RAMs 8–15 onto the DB8–DB15 data bus lines. Similarly, IC7 and IC8 control the gating of the even-order byte onto DB0–DB7. When a memory write occurs, the opposite buffer in IC5 and IC6 and/or IC7 and IC8 is enabled. The data bus contents are thus applied to the DI inputs of the RAM chips.

Analysis and Design Question 7.4 explores the possibility of shorting the DO and DI pins. Each bank of memory could then be buffered with one 74LS245 or 8286/8287 octal transceiver, eliminating two of the buffer packages.

Table 7.8 takes each of the 2167 timing parameters and compares them with the corresponding 8086 timing specifications in Table 7.4. A double-buffered noninverting system like that in Fig. 7.33 is assumed. Note, however, that the memory side of the data bus is buffered with a 74LS244, not an 8286/8287.

As can be seen, at 5 MHz the 8086's timing windows are quite relaxed and this static RAM easily meets all specifications. However, the lesson to be learned is that each memory interface must be analyzed separately, taking into account the unique support circuitry required. This will be especially true when we consider the DRAM in Sec. 7.6.

Adding Wait States

If the memory (or I/O) cannot respond quickly enough to supply the CPU with data, or store the data output by the CPU, a WAIT state must be requested. This is an additional T3 state in which the 8086 holds the data, address, and control signals in a static condition. At 5 MHz one WAIT state will add 200 ns to each timing parameter. For example, the address access time (without buffers) increases from 460 ns to 660 ns.

WAIT requests are asserted by pulling the 8086's READY input low just before the falling edge of the clock in the T3 state (i.e., just before state T3). This timing is shown in Fig. 7.35. READY must be then be held low until at least 30 ns after the clock returns high. To avoid an additional WAIT state, READY must have returned high 119 ns before the rising edge of the clock in the TW state.

Fortunately, the 8284A clock generator will guarantee these specifications if its RDY and $\overline{\text{AEN}}$ inputs are used. This can be done in two ways, as shown in Fig. 7.36. In part (a) the RDY line must be pulled low to request the WAIT state, whereas the circuit in part (b) requires that $\overline{\text{AEN}}$ be driven high to request a WAIT state.

The 8284A requires that the WAIT request occur 35 ns before the falling edge of the clock in the T3 state. If the requesting circuit cannot guarantee this, the $\overline{\text{ASYNC}}$

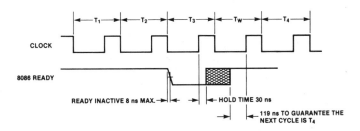

Figure 7.35 The 8086 samples its READY input at the beginning of each T3 clock cycle. (Courtesy of Intel Corporation.)

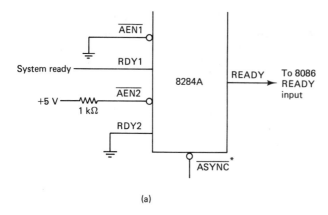

(a)

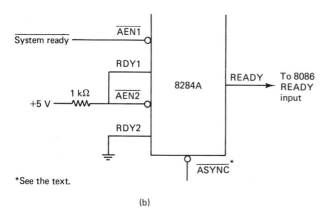

*See the text.

(b)

Figure 7.36 Using the 8284A, the system READY signal can be active high (a) or low (b).

input of the 8284A must be grounded. This provides an additional flip-flop synchronized to the rising edge of the T2 clock. Circuits meeting the 8284A setup requirement can leave the ASYNC input open (an internal pull-up resistor is provided).

How does the memory go about requesting a WAIT state? First, you as the designer must determine that a WAIT state is required—by performing a timing analysis similar to that done in the preceding section. If this analysis reveals that one WAIT state is required, the circuit in Fig. 7.37 can be used.

This circuit would normally be incorporated into the CPU module with the $\overline{\text{WAIT}}$ input driven by an open-collector gate. In this way any number of circuits can request a WAIT state by simply pulling the $\overline{\text{WAIT}}$ line low.

Circuit operation is as follows. With no WAIT requests occurring, each ALE pulse will reset the flip-flop and the RDY line will be high. The JK flip-flop operates in the "no-change" mode. The $\overline{\text{WAIT}}$ input is assumed to be driven by a $\overline{\text{MEMORY SELECT}}$ signal (e.g., $\overline{\text{SEL ODD BYTE}}$ + $\overline{\text{SEL EVEN BYTE}}$ in Fig. 7.34). This signal will become active during the T1 state when the memory address is first output.

During this time ALE is high, holding the 8284A RDY1 input high. Now when ALE returns low, the next rising edge of the clock will set the flip-flop and cause RDY

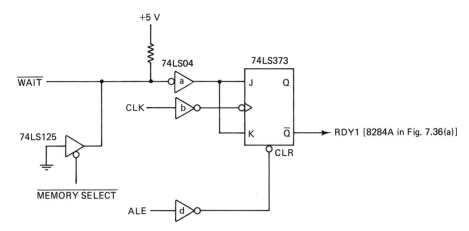

Figure 7.37 This circuit can be used by a memory array to request one wait state per bus cycle. It is guaranteed to meet the setup and hold requirements of the 8284A RDY input. Thus that chip's $\overline{ASYNC}$ input can be connected to +5 V.

to go low. According to the 8086 timing in App. C, this will occur on the rising edge of the clock in state T2. This in turn guarantees the RDY setup time of the 8284A. The next rising edge of the clock (in state T3) will toggle the flip-flop and release the WAIT request so that only one WAIT state is inserted.

The following clock pulses will continue to toggle the flip-flop, but the WAIT request timing window will have passed, and this will not matter. The ALE pulse at the beginning of the next bus cycle will ensure that RDY is high when a new bus cycle begins.

WAIT states are most often used with EPROMs that have long access times (greater than 350 ns). DRAMs also have a need to request WAIT states to avoid conflicts with their refresh operations.

There is one other application for the WAIT-state generator. Because all the data, address, and control bus signals are held in a valid condition, forcing the processor into a WAIT state can be an effective *troubleshooting tool*. A special single-stepping circuit can be constructed that allows the processor to execute one bus cycle at a time. A logic probe can then be used to trace the signal flow on the buses. Analysis and Design Question 7.9 explores this idea in more detail.

SELF-REVIEW 7.5 *(answers on page 346)*

7.5.1. Why must the address decoder's propagation delay be included in the address access time of the memory?

7.5.2. Which 8086 CPU configuration requires the fastest memory parts?

7.5.3. What is the logic condition of the 74LS244 outputs in Fig. 7.34 when an I/O read bus cycle is being performed?

7.5.4. A certain memory generates an active-low WAIT request signal. The _____ input of the 8284A should be used to request a WAIT state from the CPU.

7.5.5. The 8086 checks for a WAIT-state request once per bus cycle only. (True/False)

7.6 INTERFACING DYNAMIC RAM

The 32K-byte static memory interface in the preceding section required 24 chips, yet filled only about 3% of the 8086's 1MB of memory space. Because of the low bit density of SRAM chips, these parts are normally used only in systems requiring a small amount of RAM (<32K bytes) or very fast access times. These requirements would be met by a microcontroller-based system or a computer designed for high-speed data acquisition and analysis, for example.

It is not uncommon to find the 8086 supported by 128K to 512K bytes of dynamic RAM memory. The remaining memory space may be filled with a bootstrap ROM and additional RAM chips serving as the video screen memory.

In this section we study the specifications and timing requirements of the 2164A 64K × 1 DRAM. This is followed by a discussion of dynamic RAM refresh and the several techniques possible. Finally, a 256K-byte 8086 memory interface example will be covered. This circuit will introduce the Intel 8203 DRAM controller, which simplifies the task of designing a dynamic RAM memory module.

Dynamic RAM Timing

Packaging. To be consistent with the dynamic RAM's high bit density, most DRAM chips are packaged in standard 300-mil-wide 16-pin DIPs. This allows a very dense memory to be constructed in a minimum amount of PCB area. However, a 16-pin package does not have enough pins for all the address lines of a 256K (or 64K or 16K) memory part. For this reason, DRAMs are organized 1 bit wide with *multiplexed* address pins.

The industry standard pinning for 16-pin DIP 16K, 64K, and 256K DRAMs is shown in Fig. 7.38. It is interesting to note that the 16K and 64K chips actually have *unused* pins. By adopting this standard pinning arrangement, designers are able to design

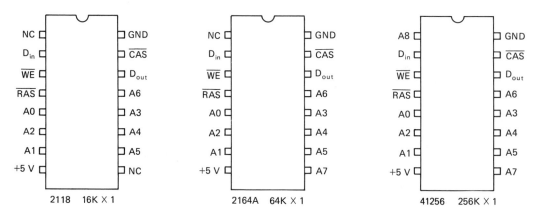

Figure 7.38 Pinouts for the JEDEC standardized 16K, 64K, and 256K dynamic RAM chips. All provide separate data-in and data-out pins and a multiplexed row and column address.

memory interfaces that can easily be upgraded. For example, the A7 and A8 address lines could be run to the 2118 socket. Jumper wires at the DRAM controller would then allow an upgrade from 16K parts to 256K parts by simply plugging in the higher-density chips.

Although the address pins are labeled A0 to A6 (or A7 or A8), the high-order address lines, A7 to A14 (or A15 or A16), are also applied to these pins via a multiplexing scheme. Thus each new package pin provides two additional address lines and *quadruples* the memory density. The next step in the evolution is the 1MB DRAM. Unfortunately, this chip will not fit in a 16-pin package, and at the moment there is no universally accepted package or memory organization.

$\overline{\text{RAS}}$ and $\overline{\text{CAS}}$ timing. Figure 7.39 illustrates basic timing for DRAM memory read and write cycles. Two clock signals are required: $\overline{\text{RAS}}$, row address strobe, and $\overline{\text{CAS}}$, column address strobe.

A read or write cycle begins with the falling edge of the $\overline{\text{RAS}}$ clock signal. This will latch the address currently applied to the chip, which should correspond to the low-order or row address. During the timing window t_{RCD}, the row address must be held stable to meet the t_{RAH} row address hold specification and then changed to the high-order or column address. The falling edge of $\overline{\text{CAS}}$ latches this address and also gates the data onto the data-out pin of the RAM.

There are two access times: the *row access time* (t_{RAC}), measured from the falling edge of $\overline{\text{RAS}}$ to valid data out, and the *column access time*, measured from the falling edge of $\overline{\text{CAS}}$ to valid data. Normally, DRAMs are characterized by their row access time. Thus a 200-ns 2164A is interpreted as having $t_{\text{RAC}} = 200$ ns.

The memory read cycle must include the cycle *precharge* time t_{RP}. This is the time required to charge the bit sense line (see Fig. 7.8) in preparation for the next memory cycle. The memory read cycle time (t_{RC}) is thus the sum of t_{RAC} and t_{RP}. The 2164A-15 has a 150-ns row access time but a 260-ns read cycle time.

From the microprocessor's standpoint, the row and column access times are the important parameters. The effect of the precharge is to cause the cycle time to be greater than the access time. Fortunately, this does not affect the microprocessor. Why? A minimum of four clock periods are required for any one microprocessor bus cycle. This prevents the processor from requesting consecutive memory cycles with periods shorter than 4 T states, or 800 ns, at 5 MHz. This is much longer than the memory cycle time.[3]

A DRAM memory write cycle occurs when the $\overline{\text{WE}}$ input is active. In this case data will be latched by the falling edge of $\overline{\text{CAS}}$ or $\overline{\text{WE}}$, whichever occurs last. The DRAM controller described in this section performs an *early-write* write cycle; that is, $\overline{\text{WE}}$ occurs before the falling edge of $\overline{\text{CAS}}$. This technique is preferred because it ensures that the data-out pin will be disabled when the new data is written. This, in turn, means that the data-out and data-in pins can be tied together without contention problems with the incoming write data.

---

[3]Some direct memory access (DMA) controllers may perform memory cycles with fewer than 4 T states. For example, the 8237A-5 DMA controller, when programmed for compressed timing, performs consecutive memory cycles in 2 T states, or 400 ns, at 5 MHz.

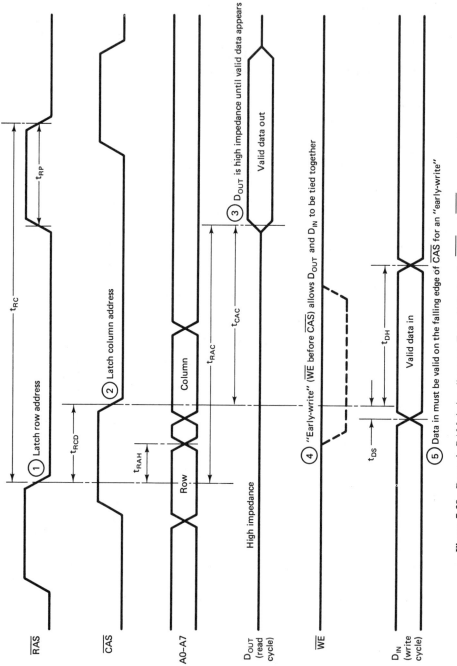

Figure 7.39 Dynamic RAM timing diagrams. Two clock signals ($\overline{\text{RAS}}$ and $\overline{\text{CAS}}$) are required to latch the multiplexed row and column addresses. (From J. Uffenbeck, *Microcomputers and Microprocessors: The 8080, 8085, and Z-80.* Prentice-Hall, Englewood Cliffs, N.J., 1985.)

Page mode. In certain applications the DRAM can be operated in a *page mode* (also called "*ripple*" *mode* by Intel). When the $\overline{\text{RAS}}$ clock falls low, all the memory cells in the selected row pass their data on to the sense amplifiers. In the 2164A the row address is 8 bits wide and 256 bits (one page) of data is selected. The $\overline{\text{CAS}}$ clock now gates in the high-order or column address and selects one cell on this page.

Page-mode operation takes advantage of the fact that all the data for one page is stored in the sense amplifiers after the trailing edge of the $\overline{\text{RAS}}$ clock. $\overline{\text{CAS}}$ can now be used to cycle through all addresses on that page and the access time becomes t_{CAC}. This is only 85 ns for the 2164A-15. The cycle time is equal to the width of the $\overline{\text{CAS}}$ pulse and the $\overline{\text{CAS}}$ precharge time. This is 125 ns for the 2164A-15.

CMOS DRAMs. Many manufacturers are turning to CMOS for the next generation of dynamic RAMs. Intel's 51C64 and 51C65 are 64K $\times$ 1 DRAMs featuring 100-ns row access times and 160-ns read cycle times. The 51C65 has a *static column decode* mode similar to the page mode except that $\overline{\text{RAS}}$ and $\overline{\text{CAS}}$ are both held low. New column addresses can be repeatedly applied without the need for the $\overline{\text{CAS}}$ clock. The access time drops to 50 ns in this mode.

Regardless of the technology behind the DRAM, you should be careful to note one important point. The timing requirements in Fig. 7.39 are those imposed by the DRAM chip itself, not the microprocessor. It will be the job of the DRAM controller to interface with the processor's three-bus architecture and provide those signals required by the DRAM.

Refresh

As mentioned in Sec. 7.1, the storage cell for a dynamic RAM is a capacitor. Because this capacitor is not perfect, the charge in each cell must be rewritten at least once every 2 ms or data will be lost. For the 64K $\times$ 1 2164A, the memory array consists of four quadrants arranged as 128 rows by 128 columns. Because the row lines of all four quadrants are common, the refresh operation can be accomplished by sequencing through all 128 row addresses. This means that the refresh address is 7 bits wide.

Although a refresh operation will occur whenever a memory read or write cycle occurs, we cannot usually guarantee that every row of the DRAM will be accessed at least once every 2 ms (an exception might be "screen" memory used in a memory-mapped video display interface).

The technique most commonly used in DRAM controllers is called *RAS-only* refresh and is illustrated in Fig. 7.40. In this scheme only a row address is output to the DRAM and no data is read or written during the cycle. All the bits in the selected row are refreshed. To maintain data in the memory, all 128 row addresses must be refreshed in this manner at least once every 2 ms. During a refresh cycle the CPU cannot access the memory.

A third method of refreshing a DRAM is called *hidden refresh*. The timing is illustrated in Fig. 7.41. After completing a normal memory read or write cycle, the $\overline{\text{CAS}}$ clock is left low. This will maintain data on the data-out pin. Now any number of $\overline{\text{RAS}}$ clocks can be applied, as the row address is incremented.

Hidden refresh is essentially a $\overline{\text{RAS}}$-only refresh but with the $\overline{\text{CAS}}$ clock held low.

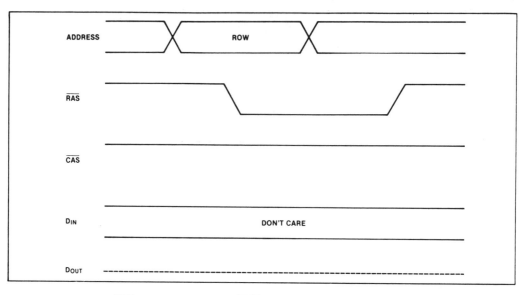

Figure 7.40 $\overline{RAS}$-only refresh cycle. The $\overline{CAS}$ clock is left high (disabling the data pins) as the $\overline{RAS}$ clock refreshes a row. 128 such cycles are required every 2 ms to refresh the 2164A. (Courtesy of Intel Corporation.)

The technique can be used to "hide" refresh cycles among processor cycles which require that data be held on the bus but do not require a new memory or I/O access.

There are three methods of distributing the necessary refresh cycles over the 2-ms refresh period.

1. *Burst refresh*. In this technique the processor is forced into a WAIT state and all 128 rows are refreshed in one "burst." Normal processing is then resumed until the next refresh period is required. Because one refresh cycle can take 260 ns (2164A-15), the time to refresh all 128 rows can exceed 30 μs. This implies 150 consecutive WAIT states. During this time the memory cannot be accessed.

2. *Distributed refresh*. Rather than refreshing the entire memory at once, the refresh cycles can be distributed over the entire 2-ms period. This will require a refresh cycle every 2 ms/128 cycles = 15.6 μs. Most DRAM controllers use this technique.

3. *Transparent refresh*. Ideally, we would like to "sneak" the refresh cycles into the microprocessor timing at points when access to the memory is not required. In this way the refresh operations would be "transparent" and never slow the processor down (i.e., zero WAIT states are required).

Transparent refresh is appropriate for *nonpipelined* processors such as the 8085 or Z-80. After these processors fetch an instruction, one or two CPU clock cycles are normally required to execute the instruction or prepare for the next bus cycle. During this time the DRAM controller can "sneak" in one or two hidden refresh cycles.

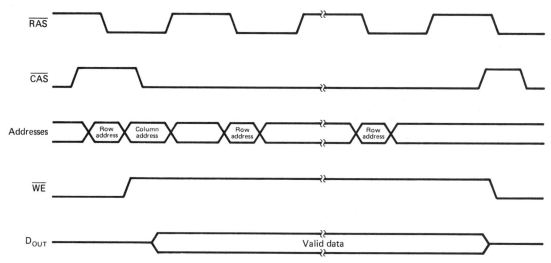

Figure 7.41 "Hidden refresh" cycle. Data-out is maintained valid throughout the cycle. (From J. Uffenbeck, *Microcomputers and Microprocessors: The 8080, 8085, and Z-80.* Prentice-Hall, Englewood Cliffs, N.J., 1985.)

Unfortunately, this technique will not work with a *pipelined* processor such as the 8086. This is because the 8086's queue maximizes use of the buses, resulting in very little "dead" time within which to "sneak" in a refresh cycle.

The 8203 DRAM Controller

There are several problems associated with interfacing dynamic RAM memory. Among these are:

1. *Address multiplexing.* The memory address must be "split in two" and time multiplexed with a $\overline{RAS}$ and $\overline{CAS}$ clock signal. In addition, during refresh cycles the memory address must be switched to a refresh address.
2. *Refresh.* Each row in the DRAM must be refreshed at least once every 2 ms. Several refresh techniques are possible.
3. *Arbitration.* Logic must be designed to decide if a refresh cycle or a normal memory read or write cycle is to be performed when simultaneous requests occur. This circuit is called an *arbiter*.
4. *WAIT states.* When refresh interferes with normal processor activity, WAIT states must be requested.

There are three approaches the designer can take to solving these problems. One is to design an interface using discrete logic components and/or one or more PAL devices. This will require several months for design, timing analysis, and protyping before the job is completed.

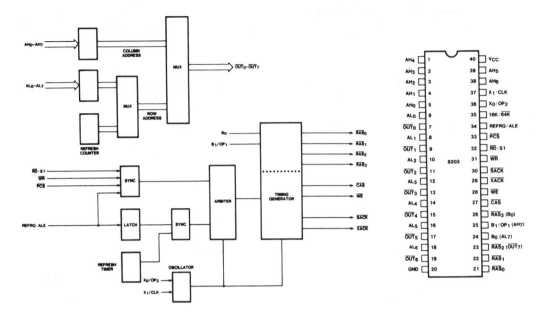

Figure 7.42 Intel 8203 dynamic RAM controller. (Courtesy of Intel Corporation.)

In some cases the designer may find it advantageous to design a custom interface that takes advantage of other LSI circuits already a part of the system design. The IBM PC, for example, uses a distributed refresh technique in which a timer automatically requests a refresh cycle every 72 clock cycles (approximately once every 15 μs). One channel of a DMA controller chip is then used to perform a "dummy" read cycle, refreshing all cells in that particular row. This is an example of software replacing hardware. Hardware is still required, however, to generate the $\overline{RAS}$ and $\overline{CAS}$ clocks and perform the address multiplexing.

The third approach is to select an LSI DRAM controller chip. This choice offers the advantage of a single IC replacing the 20 or more IC packages required in the discrete component version. It also means that the design can be made operational in a matter of weeks rather than months.

An example of such a chip is the Intel 8203 64K DRAM controller shown in Fig. 7.42. This chip supports both 16K and 64K DRAMs. Pin 35 must be grounded for the latter case. Referring to the block diagram, the low 16 (64K mode) or 14 (16K mode) address lines from the CPU are applied to AH0–AH7 (or AH6) and AL0–AL7 (or AL6). An internal multiplexer then routes these lines to the DRAM address pins as $\overline{OUT0}$–$\overline{OUT7}$ (or $\overline{OUT6}$).[4] During refresh cycles the row address is replaced by the refresh counter address.

The 8203 refresh counter is 8 bits wide and is thus compatible with both 128-row

---

[4]The outputs are inverted to reduce the propagation delay through the 8203. Address FFFFH thus becomes 0000H, and vice versa. Note, however, that these lines do not need to be reinverted before being applied to the RAM chips.

and 256-row DRAM chips. Although memory cycles are given the priority, a refresh cycle in progress will not be interrupted for a memory access. The $\overline{\text{SACK}}$ (system acknowledge) signal (explained in detail in the next section) can be used to request a WAIT state when this occurs. The 8203 normally performs a *RAS-only* refresh cycle every 10 to 16 μs.

A timing generator normally driven by a crystal oscillator generates the $\overline{\text{RAS}}$ and $\overline{\text{CAS}}$ clock signals. If desired, the X0/OP2 pin can be wired directly to +5 V (no pull-up resistor) and an external clock signal then applied to the X1/CLK pin. In either case, the clock signal must have a frequency between 18.5 and 25 MHz.

Pins 23 through 26 change function depending on the mode of operation. This is shown in Table 7.9. In the 16K mode, there are four $\overline{\text{RAS}}$ outputs, allowing four 16K banks. Pins 24 and 25 should be driven by high-order memory address lines, thereby selecting one of the four 16K banks. In the 64K mode only two banks are allowed. The former bank select inputs now input the extra address lines required. Pin 26 becomes the single bank select input.

Figure 7.43 shows a memory interface between the 8086 maximum mode CPU module and the 8203 operated in the 64K mode. Notice that there are two banks of 64K *words* with $\overline{\text{BHE}}$ and AB0 used to select the even or odd byte in each word. $\overline{\text{RAS0}}$ and $\overline{\text{RAS1}}$ select the high- or low-order 64K word bank. This is controlled by memory address line AB17 connected to the 8203 B0 input. Note that memory read cycles allow both the even and odd bytes to be read (the 8086 accepts only the byte or word it wants). Only for write cycles are the even and odd bytes enabled separately.

Because $\overline{\text{RAS}}$ and $\overline{\text{CAS}}$ must both be low to read or write data, the $\overline{\text{CAS}}$ clock can be a common connection to all memory chips in the array. The deselected RAMs perform $\overline{\text{CAS}}$-only cycles, which keeps them in a standby mode. This also allows the DO (data-out) and DI (data-in) pins of each row to be connected together without contention problems.

The 8203 must be chip selected in order to perform a memory read or write cycle. In this interface $\overline{\text{PCS}}$ (protected chip select) will be low whenever AB18 and AB19 are both low. This maps the interface to the address range 00000–3FFFFH. This corresponds to the bottom 256K bytes of the 8086's memory space.

$\overline{\text{RAS}}$-only refresh cycles are performed regardless of the state of the $\overline{\text{PCS}}$ input. During these cycles $\overline{\text{OUT0}}$–$\overline{\text{OUT7}}$ contain a refresh address, $\overline{\text{CAS}}$ is high, and $\overline{\text{RAS0}}$ and $\overline{\text{RAS1}}$ are both low. Thus both word banks are refreshed simultaneously. As mentioned, the 8203 uses the distributed refresh technique.

By driving the REFRQ input high, an external circuit can request a refresh cycle. This can be used to implement a ''transparent'' refresh design. In Fig. 7.43 REFRQ is grounded and all refresh cycles are initiated by the 8203 itself.

TABLE 7.9 16K/64K MODE SELECTION

Pin	16K Function	64K Function
23	$\overline{\text{RAS2}}$	Address output ($\overline{\text{OUT7}}$)
24	Bank select (BO)	Address input (AL7)
25	Bank select (B1)	Address input (AH7)
26	$\overline{\text{RAS3}}$	Bank select (BO)

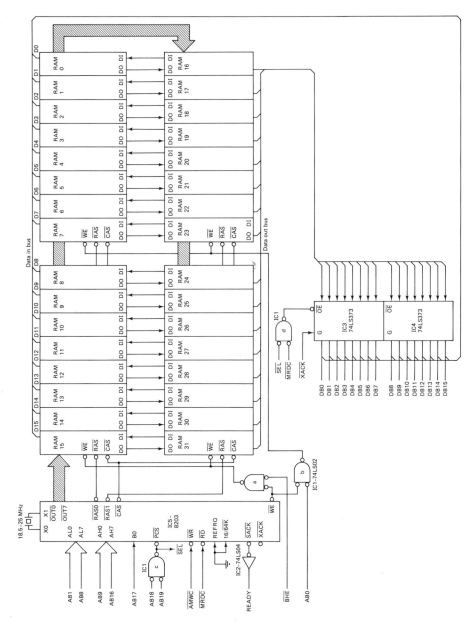

Figure 7.43 8086 256K-byte DRAM interface. The 8203 controls two banks of 64K words each.

8203 Memory Timing

The key point to remember about the DRAM is that unlike SRAM, data can be read or written only by following a precise sequence:

1. Pulse the $\overline{\text{RAS}}$ clock input low.
2. Wait t_{RCD} and then pulse the $\overline{\text{CAS}}$ clock input low.
3. Return $\overline{\text{RAS}}$ and $\overline{\text{CAS}}$ high within the maximum pulse width specifications (10 µs for the 2164A).

Be sure to note that this sequence implies that there is a "window" in which the data must be read or written by the CPU. This is quite different from the SRAM. With this device, as long as it is enabled, data is available to be read or written. The CPU can enter a WAIT state for 5 minutes and the memory will continue to hold the selected cells data on its output pins.

Figure 7.44 shows the DRAM timing as output by the 8203. The cycle begins when the 8086 outputs a memory address that is assumed to chip select the 8203 ($\overline{\text{PCS}}$ = 0). TAVRL nanoseconds later, $\overline{\text{MRDC}}$ or $\overline{\text{AMWC}}$ is output by the CPU, indicating the type of memory cycle. These outputs are connected to the 8203's $\overline{\text{RD}}$ and $\overline{\text{WR}}$ inputs, respectively. The falling edge of one of these control inputs begins the $\overline{\text{RAS}} - \overline{\text{CAS}}$ cycle. After t_{CR} nanoseconds, $\overline{\text{RAS}}$ goes low, and after t_{CC} nanoseconds $\overline{\text{CAS}}$ goes low. Data is available from the memory t_{CAC} after the falling edge of $\overline{\text{CAS}}$.

And now the "tricky" part. The data *disappears* t_{OFF} nanoseconds after $\overline{\text{CAS}}$ returns high. In effect, the data "spurts" out and must be read during the short time it is available. This is the reason for the two latches (IC3 and IC4) in Fig. 7.43. They store the data so that it will meet the setup and hold times required by the CPU. This latch is not required in an SRAM interface because the CPU keeps the SRAM enabled until it has read the data.

The 8203 $\overline{\text{XACK}}$ signal can be used to control the latch. It is output just before the rising edge of $\overline{\text{CAS}}$, when the data from the memory is known to be valid. Referring to Fig. 7.43, the output of each latch follows its input until $\overline{\text{XACK}}$ goes low, storing this data. IC1d enables the outputs onto the system data bus if the current bus cycle is a memory read from the selected address range. $\overline{\text{XACK}}$ remains low until the CPU removes its control signal—effectively holding the data on the bus (via the latch) just like an SRAM interface.

During a write cycle the latch's outputs are disabled and the write data is routed to the RAM DI pins via the data-in bus.

Example 7.6

Verify the memory read and write cycle timing for the DRAM interface in Fig. 7.43. Assume a 5-MHz maximum-mode 8086 CPU. Use the 8203 numbers provided in Fig. 7.44.

Solution From Table 7.4, the address access time provided by the 8086 is 460 ns. Using the numbers in Fig. 7.44, the interface will require

$$\text{TAVRL} + t_{\text{cc}} + t_{\text{CAC}} = 100 \text{ ns} + 245 \text{ ns} + 85 \text{ ns} = 430 \text{ ns}$$

Now if we assume full buffering, an additional 88 ns (with inverting buffers) will be required (see Fig. 7.33). Thus the interface will require a total of 430 ns + 88 ns = 518 ns. One WAIT state will be required.

The need for a WAIT state is also apparent by noting the position of $\overline{\text{MRDC}}$ relative to data out from the memory in Fig. 7.44. The data is not available until $\overline{\text{MRDC}}$ *has gone high*, resulting in 0 *setup* time. The dashed line shows the effect of adding one WAIT state. $\overline{\text{MRDC}}$ is extended 200 ns. Now, however, the data disappears before $\overline{\text{MRDC}}$ returns high; that is, there is no hold time! Again the need for a latch is demonstrated, as it will hold the data stable until $\overline{\text{MRDC}}$ is removed. In this way the data setup and hold times required by the CPU are met.

During a memory write cycle the DRAM requires that data be set up prior to the leading edge of $\overline{\text{CAS}}$ (t_{DS}) and then held after this edge (t_{DH}). For the 2164A-15 $t_{\text{DS}} = 0$ ns and $t_{\text{DH}} = 30$ ns. Using the advanced write command to start the $\overline{\text{RAS}}$–$\overline{\text{CAS}}$ cycle, these specifications are easily met. Note that the 8203 automatically performs "early-write" write cycles.

The (row) access time by which most DRAMs are characterized can be misleading. The 2164A-15 has a 150-ns "access time" but is not fast enough for the 5-MHz 8086 when interfaced with the 8203. The problem is twofold. The multiplexed address lines required a $\overline{\text{RAS}}$–$\overline{\text{CAS}}$ sequence in order to receive the memory address. Second, the 8203 cannot start this sequence until it receives the appropriate control signal. Thus even though the memory address is output during the T1 clock state, the 8203 does not begin the read or write cycle until T2, when its $\overline{\text{RD}}$ or $\overline{\text{WR}}$ inputs become active.

One option open to the designer is to decode the $\overline{\text{S0}}$, $\overline{\text{S1}}$, and $\overline{\text{S2}}$ status signals together with ALE to provide an *advanced read* signal during the T1 clock state. In fact, if the 8203 is used in the 16K mode, an advanced read can be generated by pulsing the REFRQ/ALE input while the $\overline{\text{RD}}$/S1 input is active (high). This option is not available in the 64K mode because pin 25 (which must select OP1) operates as the AH7 address input.

Intel's application note AP-133 describes 5-MHz and 10-MHz 8086 CPU dynamic RAM interfaces that operate without any WAIT states. However, a considerable amount of external logic is required.

When WAIT states are required, $\overline{\text{XACK}}$ (transfer acknowledge) or $\overline{\text{SACK}}$ (system acknowledge) can be used. Referring to the memory design Fig. 7.43, $\overline{\text{SACK}}$ is inverted and used to drive the 8284A's RDY input. The memory then operates in a "*normally not ready*" mode ($\overline{\text{SACK}} = 1$ and READY = 0). In order that a WAIT state *not* be requested, $\overline{\text{SACK}}$ must be high 135 ns before the rising edge of the clock in state T2 (see Fig. 7.35). This point in time is shown with arrows in Fig. 7.44.

$\overline{\text{SACK}}$ occurs early in the memory cycle and acknowledges to the CPU that a memory read or write cycle is occurring. If a refresh cycle is in progress, $\overline{\text{SACK}}$ will be delayed as shown and the CPU forced to enter a WAIT state. $\overline{\text{XACK}}$ can also be used to request the WAIT state, but this signal occurs much later in the cycle (when the data from the RAM is output) and may cause extra WAIT states to be requested. Using the timing in Fig. 7.44, $\overline{\text{XACK}}$ would cause two WAIT states per memory cycle (recall that only one was actually needed).

In this example, using $\overline{\text{SACK}}$ will cause one WAIT state as required. Care must be taken when using $\overline{\text{SACK}}$, however. If its leading edge occurs too soon, the WAIT

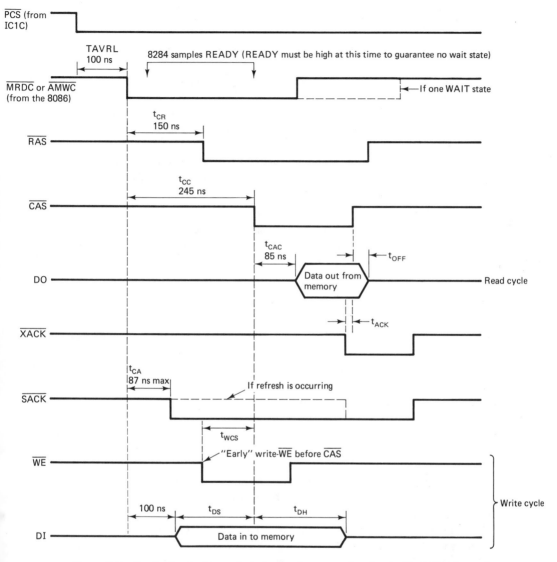

Figure 7.44 Read and write bus cycle timing for the memory interface in Fig. 7.43. The read cycle requires one WAIT state. All time delays are shown to scale. The 8203 clock is assumed to be 25 MHz.

request will be missed. Also note that $\overline{\text{SACK}}$ (or $\overline{\text{XACK}}$) will cause WAIT states for both memory read and write cycles.

In summary, each memory interface must be carefully analyzed and all memory timing parameters verified. DRAM controllers like the 8203 make the hardware interface easier, but often require one or more WAIT states per bus cycle. Future controllers will be designed to handle 256K DRAMs and include the circuitry needed to avoid WAIT states.

Sec. 7.6   Interfacing Dynamic RAM

333

7.6.1. The 2164A-15 has a 150-ns access time. This is the time from _____ to _____.

7.6.2. DRAMs with multiplexed address lines latch the low-order address on the falling edge of the _____ clock.

7.6.3. Why are the 8086 and 8088 microprocessors not suitable for transparent refresh?

7.6.4. A 256K DRAM operated in the page mode would allow access to _____ bits without latching a new row address.

7.6.5. Which RAM chip in the Fig. 7.43 stores bit 0 of the byte at address 30000H?

7.6.6. Under what conditions will $\overline{RAS0}$ and $\overline{RAS1}$ both be low in the memory interface in Fig. 7.43?

7.6.7. How long is data available at the DO pins of a DRAM? of an SRAM?

7.6.8. When the 8203 is chip selected, the falling edge of the _____ or _____ input signal causes the $\overline{RAS}$–$\overline{CAS}$ cycle to begin.

7.7 TROUBLESHOOTING THE MEMORY MODULE

In the preceding sections we have seen how to design and interface main memory to the 8086 and 8088 microprocessors. Before we end this chapter it is important to address one final point. Namely, how can we be sure that our memory module is indeed working? As an optimist you might plug the module in and load one of your favorite software programs. If the program seems to run correctly, you can declare the module to be operational. However, I think that you will agree that this is not a very exhaustive memory test.

But, then, what is a good memory test? In particular, what types of problems should this test look for? Memory errors are usually classified as "hard" or "soft." Hard errors can be attributed to defective memory cells, causing a bit to become "stuck" permanently high or low. This type of error can also be caused by component failures in the data bus buffers or the address decoding circuitry.

Soft errors are random in nature and nondestructive. These errors can be cleared by rewriting the data. Typical sources of soft errors are power supply noise, temperature effects, and ionizing radiation of alpha particles, changing the memory cell's charge (in dynamic RAMs).

The most effective way to test memory is via a software test program or *diagnostic*. This is a program that writes a particular data pattern to the memory and then attempts to read it back. Some programs provide diagnostic information that can pinpoint the chip in error. Because memory errors can go undetected for long periods of time, it is a good practice to perform a memory test as part of the routine maintenance performed on any computer system.

In this section we examine several memory test algorithms. A rigorous memory test program written in Pascal is also provided. This program also serves as an additional example of structured programming, discussed in Chap. 5.

A Simpleminded Approach

Figure 7.45 provides one example of a memory test program. Written as an 8086 procedure, it assumes that the starting address of the memory block to be tested is passed in register ES with the number of bytes to be tested in register CX. The program takes advantage of the 8086's string instructions, particularly STOSB to write the test byte and SCASB to read it back. When all bytes in the block have been tested, or when an error is detected, control returns to the calling program. In the latter case, CF is set to designate the error condition and ES:DI holds the address of the byte in error.

This is a simpleminded program because it performs many more read/write cycles than are necessary. For example, when testing bit 7's ability to store a 1, 128 read/write cycles are performed as bits 0–6 are cycled through all possible combinations. To test 64K bytes of memory, more than 16 million read/write operations must be performed. Assuming a 5-MHz system clock, nearly 3 minutes is required.

Two Faster Tests

By selecting a less rigorous memory test pattern, the time required to test a block of memory can be reduced substantially. One such test uses the "checkerboard" algorithm. The steps are as follows:

1. Write AAH to the even bytes.
2. Write 55H to the odd bytes.
3. Read and verify all bytes.
4. Repeat steps 1–3, reversing the even and odd bytes.

Because of the alternate 1's and 0's in the ("checkerboard") test pattern, the test is effective at locating adjacent shorted data or address lines. Note that only two read/write cycles are required per byte.

An even-speedier test is based on the complement algorithm. The steps are as follows:

1. Read a byte to AL and complement.
2. Write the byte to memory.
3. Compare the memory with the contents of AL.
4. Invert the memory byte.

This test has the advantage that the contents of memory are left undisturbed. For this reason the technique is often used to *size* memory. This is a process in which one complement cycle is performed at each memory block boundary—every 64K bytes if 64K RAM chips are used. When an error is detected because of no memory at that address, the size of memory can be computed. Because the test requires only one read cycle and two write cycles, it is very fast. However, there is no control over the memory test pattern, and some types of errors can go undetected.

```
                        ;Function:      Write all possible byte combinations
                        ;               to each byte in the test block and
                        ;               verify their contents.
                        ;
                        ;Inputs:        Starting address of block assumed in ES
                        ;               with offset 0.  Number of bytes in the
                        ;               block assumed passed in CX.
                        ;
                        ;Outputs:       If error, the proceedure ends with ES:DI
                        ;               pointing to the first byte in error and
                        ;               CF set.  If no errors are detected, the
                        ;               procedure returns with CF clear.
                        ;
                        ;Calls:         nothing.
                        ;
                        ;Destroys:      AL, CX, flags, memory test block.


0000                    CODE            SEGMENT
                                        ASSUME CS:CODE

0000                    MEM_TEST        PROC FAR
0000    51                              PUSH    CX          ;Save no. of bytes
0001    FC                              CLD                 ;Auto increment
0002    B0 00                           MOV     AL,0        ;Starting test pattern
0004    BF 0000                         MOV     DI,0        ;Offset = 0

0007    AA              WR_RD:          STOSB               ;Write byte
0008    4F                              DEC     DI          ;Point at byte
0009    AE                              SCASB               ;Read it back
000A    E1 FB                           LOOPE   WR_RD       ;Repeat for all bytes
                                                            ;in the block or until
                                                            ;the bytes don't match.
000C    75 0C                           JNZ     ERROR       ;Is there an error?
000E    59                              POP     CX          ;No - recover bytes
000F    51                              PUSH    CX          ;Save
0010    BF 0000                         MOV     DI,0        ;Reset offset to 0
0013    FE C0                           INC     AL          ;Next test pattern
0015    75 F0                           JNZ     WR_RD       ;All 256 patterns?
0017    EB 03 90                        JMP     DONE        ;Yes - we're done

001A    F9              ERROR:          STC                 ;Error so set carry
001B    4F                              DEC     DI          ;Point DI at bad byte
001C    CB              DONE:           RET     2           ;Return and discard CX

001D                    MEM_TEST        ENDP
001D                                    CODE    ENDS
```

Figure 7.45 Simpleminded memory test program for the 8086.

The Walking-Bit Test

This test goes by several names, including the "walking 1's" or "walking 0's" test, and the "barber pole" memory test. Each describes the pattern that is written to memory when the test is run. Table 7.10 shows the test pattern for bit-wide memory devices (such as the 2164A). The walking 1 or 0 can clearly be seen. The pattern has also been likened to that seen on a rotating barber pole.

TABLE 7.10 WALKING-BIT TEST PATTERN

Binary	Hex
00000000	00
00000001	01
00000010	02
00000100	04
00001000	08
00010000	10
00100000	20
01000000	40
10000000	80
11111110	FE
11111101	FD
11111011	FB
11110111	F7
11101111	EF
11011111	DF
10111111	BF
01111111	7F

One of the advantages of this test is that the memory chip in error can easily be identified by examining the data read when an error occurs. Figure 7.46 provides an example. The program begins by requesting a starting segment address and number of bytes to be tested (limited to 64K). Note that these numbers can be input in hex by preceding the response with a ''$'' symbol.

As the test is being run, error reports (if any) are printed on the screen. By examining the binary representation of the data read, it is clear (in this example) that bit 0 of memory

```
            Walking Bit Memory Test
            ========================

Enter the starting segment address: $4000

Enter the number of bytes to be tested: $1000


Error at    4000:07FFH    wrote:  00000000    read:  00000001
Error at    4000:07FFH    wrote:  00000010    read:  00000011
Error at    4000:07FFH    wrote:  00000100    read:  00000101
Error at    4000:07FFH    wrote:  00001000    read:  00001001
Error at    4000:07FFH    wrote:  00010000    read:  00010001
Error at    4000:07FFH    wrote:  00100000    read:  00100001
Error at    4000:07FFH    wrote:  01000000    read:  01000001
Error at    4000:07FFH    wrote:  10000000    read:  10000001
Error at    4000:07FFH    wrote:  11111110    read:  11111111
Memory test fails
```

Figure 7.46 Example of the screen produced by the walking-bit memory test program. Bit 0 is stuck high.

location 407FFH is stuck high. Furthermore, knowing which bank of RAM chips represents the base segment, the actual chip at fault can be identified (in this example, the chip storing the LSB).

The walking-bit test program is considerably more complex than the other programs mentioned in this section. The basic algorithm is as follows:

1. Write the test pattern (Table 7.10) to all bytes in the test block. Note that the pattern will repeat every 17 bytes.
2. Read the test block and compare with the test pattern. Note any errors.
3. Shift the test pattern by one position and repeat steps 1 and 2. For example, on the second pass, the first byte in the block receives the pattern 00000001.
4. Repeat step 3 until all 17 test patterns have been shifted through all bytes in the test block.

Figure 7.47 is a Pascal listing for the walking-bit test program. Normally, this program would be coded in assembler to minimize execution time. I have used Pascal to make the logic of the program clearer and to provide an additional example of structured programming.

The program begins by defining several procedures which are called by the main program at the very end of the listing. Referring to the main program, several modules can be identified.

1. *Initialize _ for _ memory _ test*. This module clears the screen and initializes the program variables.
2. *Data _ input*. This module gets the base segment address and number of bytes to be tested.
3. *Initialize _ for _ one _ pass*. This module initializes variables to make one pass over all bytes in the test block. Note that the variable *Index* determines the starting position in the test pattern array.
4. *Test _ for _ pass _ done*. This module advances the memory pointer and byte counter. It then tests to see if all bytes for this pass have been written (in which case Pass _ done is made true).
5. *Do _ error _ message*. This module reports the hex address of the byte in error, and the binary values of the bytes written and read. Note that the functions Bin (convert to binary) and Hex (convert to hexadecimal) are not shown (see Analysis and Design Question 7.13).
6. *Test _ for _ test _ done*. This module advances the position of the starting Index in the test pattern array. When each byte has been cycled through all 17 patterns, Test _ done is made true.
7. *Print _ end _ of _ test _ message*. This module prints a message identifying the end of the memory test and the test result—success or failure.

```
(*  Walking Bit Memory Test Program  *)

Program Mem_Test;


var
 No_of_bytes, Offset_address, Byte_counter: Integer;

 Pointer, No_of_cycles, Index, Data_read, Segment_address: Integer;

 Test_done, Error, Pass_done: Boolean;


const

 Test_pattern: array[1..34] of integer = (0,1,2,4,8,16,32,64,128,254,
                                          253,251,247,239,223,191,127,
                                          0,1,2,4,8,16,32,64,128,254,
                                          253,251,247,239,223,191,127);


(*  #################################  *)

Procedure Initialize_for_memory_test;

(*  #################################  *)

(*  This procedure initializes the program variables.  *)

Begin
   ClrScr;
   gotoxy(24,1);
   writeln('Walking Bit Memory Test Program');
   gotoxy(24,2);
   writeln('==============================');
   Index:=1;
   Test_done:=False;
   Error:=False;
End;
```

Figure 7.47 PASCAL source code for the walking-bit memory test program. The main program begins at the end of the listing.

```
(*  ###############################################  *)

Procedure Data_input;

(*  ###############################################  *)

(* This procedure gets the starting address and number of bytes  *)
(* for the test.                                                  *)

var
   valid_input: Boolean;

Begin
   valid_input:=False;
   While NOT(valid_input) do
      Begin
         gotoxy(1,5);
         writeln('Enter the memory test base segment address: ');
         gotoxy(45,5);
         readln(Segment_address);
         gotoxy(1,7);
         writeln('Enter the number of bytes to test: ');
         gotoxy(36,7);
         readln(No_of_bytes);
         If No_of_bytes <> 0 then valid_input:=True;
      End;
      writeln;
      writeln;
End;


(*  ###############################################  *)

Procedure Initialize_for_one_pass;

(*  ###############################################  *)

(* This procedure initializes all variables to make one read or  *)
(* write pass of all memory locations.                           *)

Begin
   Pass_done:=False;
   Pointer:=Index;              (* define starting test pattern *)
   No_of_cycles:=17;
   Offset_address:=0;
   Byte_counter:=No_of_bytes;
End;
```

Figure 7.47 (continued)

```
(*    ############################################    *)

Procedure Test_for_pass_done;

(*    ############################################    *)

(* This procedure updates all pointers and counters and determines *)
(* if all bytes for this pass have been tested (Pass_Done=True).    *)

Begin
    Byte_counter:=Byte_counter-1;
    If Byte_counter <> 0 then
       Begin
          Offset_address:=Offset_address+1;
          Pointer:=Pointer+1;
          No_of_cycles:=No_of_cycles-1;
          If No_of_cycles = 0 then
             Begin
                Pointer:=Index;
                No_of_cycles:=17;
             End;
       End
    Else Pass_done:=True;
End;




(*    ############################################    *)

Procedure Do_error_message;

(*    ############################################    *)

(* This procedure is called whenever the byte read does not match *)
(* the byte written.  It displays both byte values and the byte   *)
(* read in binary.                                                *)


Begin
    Error:=True;
    write('error at ',hex(segment_address):5,':',hex(offset_address):5);
    writeln('    wrote: ',Bin(test_pattern[pointer]):10,'    read: ',
      Bin(data_read):10 );
    writeln;
End;




(*    ############################################    *)

Procedure Test_for_test_done;

(*    ############################################    *)

(* This procedure checks to see if all bytes have been tested with *)
(* all 17 test patterns.                                           *)

Begin
    Index:=Index+1;          (* Define starting test pattern element *)
    If Index = 18 then Test_done:=True;
End;
```

Figure 7.47 (continued)

```
(*   ######################################################   *)

Procedure Print_end_of_test_message;

(*   ######################################################   *)

(* This procedure is called at the end of the program to indicate *)
(* if the test has succeeded or failed.                           *)

Begin
    If NOT(Error) then writeln('Memory test OK')
    Else writeln('Memory test fails');
End;




Begin                 (* MAIN PROGRAM *)
    Initialize_for_memory_test;
    Data_input;
    While NOT(Test_Done) do
        Begin
            Initialize_for_one_pass;
            While NOT(Pass_done) do
                Begin
                    Mem[Segment_address:Offset_address]:=Test_pattern[pointer];
                    Test_for_pass_done;
                End;
            Initialize_for_one_pass;
            While NOT(Pass_done) do
                Begin
                    Data_read:=Mem[Segment_address:Offset_address];
                    If Data_read <> Test_pattern[pointer] then Do_error_message;
                    Test_for_pass_done;
                End;
            Test_for_test_done;
        End;
        Print_end_of_test_message;
End.
```

Figure 7.47 (continued)

SELF-REVIEW 7.7 (answers on page 346)

7.7.1. A permanent type of memory error is referred to as a _____ error.

7.7.2. Explain the purpose of the instruction DEC DI following STOSB in Fig. 7.45.

7.7.3. What types of errors (if any) would be missed by a test program that wrote and verified a test pattern of 00 to all bytes and then FFH to all bytes?

7.7.4. How many different bytes are written to each memory location using the walking-bit memory test pattern?

CHAPTER 7 SELF-TEST

1. Of the following, which memory part could be considered a nonvolatile RAM? (a) 2764; (b) 2817A; (c) TMM2016; (d) 2164A.

2. State the memory *organization* for each of the memory parts in question 1.

3. Give the word interpretation for the 8086 timing specification TRLDV.

4. In the minimum mode, the _____ signal indicates if the current bus cycle is an I/O or memory operation.

5. In the minimum or maximum mode, data is guaranteed to be valid on the leading edge of the RD or MRDC control signals. (True/False)

6. The following conditions are observed on the buses of the 8086 when operated in the minimum mode:

$$address\ bus\ =\ 30000H$$
$$data\ bus\ =\ 1234H$$
$$\overline{BHE}\ =\ 0,\ M/\overline{IO}\ =\ 1,\ \overline{RD}\ =\ 0,\ \overline{DEN}\ =\ 0,\ DT/\overline{R}\ =\ 0$$

Explain the type of bus cycle being performed.

7. When interfacing ROM to the 8086, it is not necessary to use AB0 and $\overline{BHE}$ to control byte or word access of the memory. (True/False)

8. Refer to the 8088 memory interface in Fig. 7.20. An I/O read instruction from port 0 will cause AB11–AB19 to store 00H and the SRAM will be enabled. Will this cause contention problems on the data bus between the memory and the I/O device?

9. An address decoder which requires that AB19–AB15 = 11000B will be enabled for addresses in the range _____ to _____.

10. In question 9 the total amount of memory decoded is _____ bytes.

11. In Fig. 7.20, if IC1a is removed and AB11–AB15 are not tested, the 2K-byte memory will actually occupy _____ bytes of memory space from address _____ to _____.

12. It is desired to use a bipolar PROM as an address decoder for an 8086-based microcomputer. The system has 8K bytes of SRAM using TMM2016s and 16K bytes of ROM using 2764A EPROMs. Describe the organization of the minimum-size PROM that can be used as the address decoder.

13. Although an n-input ROM can generate all 2^n product terms, its AND array is less flexible than that of a PLA or PAL. Explain why.

14. The _____ signal is normally used to request WAIT states by a memory unit unable to exchange data within the timing windows imposed by the CPU.

15. Calculate the maximum allowable address access time for a maximum mode double-buffered 8086-1 microcomputer. Assume 8287 and 8283 buffers and an address decode time of 25 ns.

16. The access time of a DRAM normally refers to the time from _____ to _____.

17. When operated in the page mode, the access time for a DRAM becomes _____.

18. Each memory chip in a DRAM memory must be refreshed separately by sequencing through all row addresses once every 2 ms. (True/False)

19. The 8203 _____ signal goes low to indicate that data is available on the DO pins of each DRAM chip.

20. The ''checkerboard'' memory test is effective for locating which types of memory errors?

ANALYSIS AND DESIGN QUESTIONS

7.1. It might seem that an EPROM such as the 2716 would be a good choice for an easily reprogrammable address decoder. Why would this part *not* be a good choice?

7.2. At the end of every bus cycle DT/$\overline{R}$ is driven high by the 8086. Is this done to prepare for the next bus cycle (which may be a write operation), or is there another reason?

7.3. List all the "design errors" you can find in the 4K-byte minimum mode 8086 memory interface shown in Fig. 7.48.

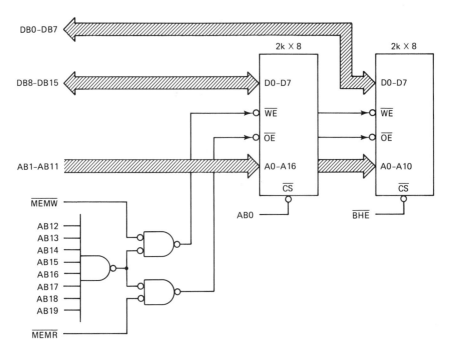

Figure 7.48 Circuit to be analyzed for design errors in Analysis and Design Question 7.3.

7.4. Refer to the 2167 SRAM data sheet in App. F. Look up the t_{WZ} specification for a memory write cycle. Now determine if the DI and DO pins can be shorted together and buffered by octal transceivers versus the separate configuration shown in Fig. 7.34. Support your answer.

7.5. Make a photocopy of the PAL10L8 in Fig. 7.30. Now using X's to indicate AND connections, select pin numbers for the input and output signals and "program" the PAL to duplicate the function of the 87S181A PROM address decoder shown in Fig. 7.28.

7.6. Repeat question 7.5, but program the PAL to replace all the combinational logic (except the data bus buffers) in the memory interface shown in Fig. 7.34.

7.7. Use the 87S181A PROM to replace all the combinational logic (except the data bus buffers) in the memory interface shown in Fig. 7.3.4. Supply the data table required to program the PROM.

Main Memory System Design   Chap. 7

7.8. Design a 4K-byte SRAM interface that begins at address 01000H. Use a 74ALS677 address comparator for the address decoding.

7.9. Figure 7.49 shows a single-step circuit connected to the 8284A RDY2 input. When the SS-RUN switch is moved to the SS position, the CPU enters a WAIT state. Depressing the STEP switch will allow one bus cycle to occur before reentering the WAIT state. Analyze and explain the operation of this circuit.

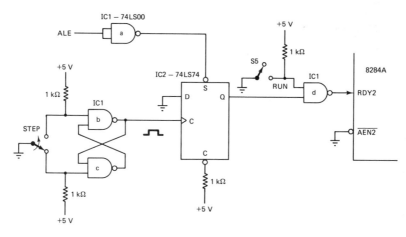

Figure 7.49 Single-step circuit for the 8086/88.

7.10. Using LEDs as indicators and the single-step circuit in question 7.8, design a circuit that will indicate the processor *state* as each bus cycle is single-stepped. (*Hint:* See Tables 6.7 and 6.9.)

7.11. Design a 128K-byte DRAM interface for the 8088 microprocessor operated in the maximum mode. Use 2164A DRAM chips and the 8203 dynamic RAM controller. Design your circuit such that its location in memory is programmable via a three-position DIP switch. When this switch is set to 000, the interface should occupy memory from 00000 to 1FFFFH, 001 should correspond to 20000–3FFFFH, and so on.

7.12. Write the 8086 assembly language version of the complement memory test. Assume that the starting segment address is passed in register DS with the number of bytes to be tested in register CX. Retrun with CF set if there is an error.

7.13. Write the Pascal code for the function BIN in Fig. 7.47. Your routine should accept a decimal number between 0 and 255 and return a binary result between 00000000 and 11111111. (*Hint:* Your result can be of type string.)

SELF REVIEW ANSWERS

7.1.1 main

7.1.2 time from application of address to data out

7.1.3 nonvolatile

7.1.4 16, 5

7.1.5 UV EPROM

7.1.6 reprogrammable and eraseable, no byte erasure and must be removed from PCB to erase

7.1.7 dynamic

7.1.8 False (128)

7.1.9 8 16k × 1 chips are required to build a practical (byte wide) memory

7.2.1 address access

7.2.2 False

7.2.3 rising

7.2.4 $\overline{\text{normal}}$ write $\overline{\text{control}}$ signals $\overline{\text{MWTC}}$ and $\overline{\text{IOWC}}$ (maximum mode only)

7.2.5 transmit

7.2.6 175 ns

7.3.1 even, odd

7.3.2 (1) 003H, (2) 0, (3) 0, (4) 1

7.3.3 DB0-DB7

7.3.4 A0, ROM

7.3.5 write

7.3.6 80000-80FFFH

7.3.7 no need to provide even and odd banks

7.4.1 AB14-AB19

7.4.2 00000, 0FFFFH

7.4.3 70000H, 7FFFFH

7.4.4 different

7.4.5 AND, OR

7.4.6 True

7.4.7 PLA

7.4.8 HAL

7.5.1 until chip selected the memory cannot release its data

7.5.2 double buffered minimum or maximum mode

7.5.3 open circuit (disabled)

7.5.4 RDY

7.5.5 True

7.6.1 falling edge of $\overline{\text{RAS}}$, valid data

7.6.2 $\overline{\text{RAS}}$

7.6.3 there is little dead time on the buses due to the BIU prefetching instructions while others are executing

7.6.4 512 (9 bit row address)

7.6.5 RAM 16

7.6.6 during a refresh

7.6.7 DRAM: approximately the width of the $\overline{\text{CAS}}$ low pulse SRAM: as long as the CPU holds the address and $\overline{\text{RD}}$ inputs active

7.6.8 $\overline{\text{MRDC}}$ or $\overline{\text{AMWC}}$

7.7.1 hard

7.7.2 repositions DI to the byte under test so it can be read back

7.7.3 shorted data and address lines

7.7.4 17

8

BASIC INPUT/OUTPUT

Now that the CPU module has been designed, the system buses defined, and main memory interfaced properly, it is time to turn our attention to the I/O. But rather than talk about specific I/O devices, we first consider the design of an *I/O port*. This port will then become the *pathway* for data as it is transferred between the microprocessor and its *peripherals*.

At the most basic level there are two types of I/O ports: *parallel* and *serial*. Because the microprocessor naturally works with data in 8- or 16-bit "chunks," the parallel port is the easiest to implement. All bits comprising the data word are input or output together in *parallel*.

A serial I/O port is quite different. The data bits are lined up and transmitted in single-file fashion one bit at a time. It should be apparent that this technique will be slower than the parallel port design, but it does have certain advantages. For one, full-duplex communications (simultaneous transmission and reception) can occur with only a three-conductor cable: one wire for transmitted data, another for received data, and a third to establish a common ground between the computer and peripheral.

The serial data bits can also be converted to audio tones (using a circuit called a *modem*) and transmitted over the telephone network. A receiving modem converts the tones back into digital 1's and 0's. In this way one computer can communicate with another thousands of miles away.

Regardless of the I/O port design—parallel or serial—the microprocessor must be *synchronized* to the speed of the peripheral. Some peripherals, like printers and plotters, cannot accept data as fast as the microprocessor would like to output it. On the other hand, floppy-disk drives and Winchester disks may require data faster than the processor can supply it. Both cases must be handled carefully to prevent a loss of data.

This chapter is the first of three dealing with microprocessor I/O. Its intention is to present the basic *concepts* of serial and parallel I/O ports and the techniques used to control the flow of data through these ports. We will begin with a discussion of the hardware requirements for parallel and serial I/O ports. This is followed by an introduction to the three common methods for controlling or synchronizing the data flow through these ports: polling, interrupts, and DMA (direct memory access).

Chapter 9 is devoted to *peripheral controller* chips that make the design of a particular type of I/O port much simpler. For example, the 8259A PIC (programmable interrupt controller) is designed specifically for the 8086 and 8088 family of microprocessors. It provides all the circuitry required to interface as many as eight separate (interrupt-controlled) peripherals to the processor.

Chapter 10 is the third chapter in this sequence and discusses the industry standards that have been developed for transferring data between a computer and a peripheral. This includes error detection and correction schemes, electrical specifications for the logic 1's and 0's, maximum cable lengths for a given data rate, and even connector pinouts for the data cables.

For now, however, let us delve into the basic I/O port and the techniques used to control it. The major topics in this chapter are:

8.1 Parallel I/O

8.2 Serial I/O

8.3 Programmed I/O

8.4 Interrupt-Driven I/O

8.5 Direct Memory Access

8.6 Summary

8.1 PARALLEL I/O

The hardware requirements for a parallel I/O port are similar to those of a RAM or ROM interface. When the CPU performs an output instruction (I/O write cycle) the data on the bus must be stored by the port. Similarly, when an input instruction is executed (I/O read cycle), the I/O port must gate its data onto the data bus lines. Just as each memory location has its own (memory) address, each I/O port has its own (port) address.

In this section we discuss the hardware required for parallel input and output ports and verify that these circuits meet the timing constraints imposed by the 8086. We also consider the special case of I/O mapped into the memory space of the processor, called *memory-mapped* I/O.

I/O Bus Cycle Timing

The 8086 and 8088 have only two I/O instructions: IN AL (or AX),port and OUT port,AL (or AX). As Table 8.1 indicates, there are two forms of each instruction. In the *direct*

TABLE 8.1 8086 I/O INSTRUCTIONS

Type	Instruction	Address bus	Data bus	Control bus[a]	
				Min. mode	Max. mode
Direct	IN AL (or AX),port	A0–A7 = port address[b] A8–A19 = 0	D0–D7 = even byte D8–D15 = odd byte D0–D15 = even word	$M/\overline{IO}$ = 0 $\overline{RD}$ = 0	$\overline{IORC}$ = 0
	OUT port,AL (or AX)	A0–A7 = port address[b] A8–A19 = 0	D0–D7 = even byte D8–D15 = odd byte D0–D15 = even word	$M/\overline{IO}$ = 0 $\overline{WR}$ = 0	$\overline{IOWC}$ = 0 $\overline{AIOWC}$ = 0
Indirect	IN AL (or AX),DX	A0–A15 = port address[c] A16–A19 = 0	As above	As above	As above
	OUT DX,AL (or AX)	A0–A15 = port address[c] A16–A19 = 0	As above	As above	As above

[a]$\overline{BHE}$ and A0 are encoded as follows:

$\overline{BHE}$	A0	
0	0	Word access
0	1	Even-byte access
1	0	Odd-byte access
1	1	No action

[b]The port address is supplied within the instruction.
[c]The port address is supplied in register DX.

form the I/O port address is supplied within the instruction and restricts the access to ports with addresses between 0 and 255. The *indirect* form uses register DX to hold the port address. This allows access to the full range of I/O ports from 0 to 65,535.

The advantage of the indirect form is that an I/O procedure can be set up and *shared* between several peripherals by passing the port address (in register DX) to the procedure.

In Table 8.1, note that the "footprint" left on the buses during an I/O cycle is similar to that which occurs during a memory cycle. The address bus carries the port address on A0–A7 for direct I/O cycles, and A0–A15 for indirect I/O cycles. The D0–D7 data bus lines are used to transfer data from even-addressed ports, and D8–D15 are used for odd-addressed ports. As the note in Table 8.1 indicates, $\overline{BHE}$ and A0 are used to identify the type of transfer.

In the minimum mode, the condition $M/\overline{IO} = 0$ is used to identify the current bus cycle as an I/O operation. $\overline{RD}$ and $\overline{WR}$ then indicate the direction of data flow. This means that the timing specifications for minimum-mode I/O cycles are identical to those for minimum-mode memory cycles.

In the maximum mode the 8288 bus controller provides separate I/O read and write commands. However, studying the detailed timing diagrams in App. C, the timing for these commands is identical to that for the memory read and write commands. Once again the timing specifications for memory and I/O cycles are the same. As a result, the definitions and formulas given in Tables 7.3 and 7.4 can also be used to verify I/O port timing. If we consider an I/O read cycle, the timing shown in Fig. 7.11 or 7.13 can be used. The following sequence occurs:

1. $M/\overline{IO} = 0$ (minimum mode only) and $DT/\overline{R} = 0$.
2. The 8- or 16-bit I/O port address is output.
3. DEN = active (data bus transceivers are enabled to input data).
4. $\overline{RD}$ or $\overline{IORC} = 0$.
5. TRLDV nanoseconds after the falling edge of $\overline{RD}$ or $\overline{IORC}$, data is expected by the 8086.
6. $\overline{RD}$ or $\overline{IORC} = 1$, $DT/\overline{R} = 1$, and DEN = inactive (the data bus transceivers are pointed in the transmit direction and disabled).

Based on this sequence of events, the input port must be designed to detect an I/O read bus cycle—$M/\overline{IO}$ and $\overline{RD}$ or $\overline{MRDC} = 0$—decode the port address and gate the input data onto the appropriate data bus lines through tri-state gates. The data bus connection would look like that shown in Fig. 6.16, where one bit of input device 2 is shown driving the bus.

An I/O write cycle would have the timing shown in Fig. 7.12 or 7.14. The sequence of events is as follows:

1. $M/\overline{IO} = 0$ (minimum mode only) and $DT/\overline{R} = 1$ (from previous cycle).
2. The 8- or 16-bit port address is output.
3. DEN = active (data bus transceivers are enabled to output data).

4. $\overline{WR}$ or $\overline{AIOWC} = 0$ 100 ns *before* the data is output.

5. Data is output by the 8086.

6. $\overline{IOWC} = 0$ 100 ns *after* the data is output.

7. All write commands $= 1$; data is held on the bus for TWHDX nanoseconds.

8. DEN $=$ inactive (the data bus transceivers are disabled).

The job of the output port hardware will again be to detect an I/O bus cycle and decode the port address, but this time the data on the bus must be *latched*. This is because the data will only be on the bus for approximately two clock periods. The data bus connection would look like Fig. 6.16, where one bit of the output port is shown as a *D* flip-flop.

Note that both types of I/O ports require a signal that identifies the current bus cycle as a read or write I/O cycle from a selected port address. In the next section we call this signal the *device select pulse* (DSP) and show how it is used to construct a parallel input port.

Designing a Parallel Input Port

Figure 8.1 shows a 16-bit input port that meets the requirements specified in the preceding section. Sixteen switches are used to simulate the input data. IC1 and IC2 decode the (direct) port address on AB1–AB7. The output of IC2 is the *port select signal* $\overline{SEL\ 30\text{-}31H}$. IC3a combines this signal with $\overline{IORB}$[1] to generate the device select pulse signal (DSP) $\overline{IN\ 30\text{-}31H}$. This signal is so called because it will be active only for input instructions that select the devices wired to ports 30H or 31H.

Just as the 8086's memory must be divided into even- and odd-addressed memory banks, its I/O must be divided into even- and odd-addressed ports. Data from the even ports is transferred via D0–D7, and D8–D15 are used to transfer data from the odd-addressed ports. As shown in Fig. 8.1, $\overline{BHEB}$ and AB0 are combined with $\overline{IN\ 30\text{-}31H}$ to generate separate even- and odd-device select pulses. These signals are then used to enable the tri-state buffers and allow the data set up on the switches to be placed onto the data bus lines.

Example 8.1

Write a procedure (subroutine) to check if switches 13, 11, 3, or 2 are open. If the condition is met, return with CF $= 1$; if the condition is not met, return with CF $= 0$.

Solution An open switch will present a logic 1 level on its input line. Thus the problem becomes one of determining if any of bits 13, 11, 3, or 2 are logic 1's. This can be done with the instruction TEST AX,280CH. A nonzero result means that at least one of the bits is set. Figure 8.2 provides a listing for the program. The statement **PUBLIC FIG8_2** will allow this routine to be linked by another calling program. This will be done in Ex. 8.4.

---

[1]$\overline{IORB}$ is generated as shown in Fig. 6.21 (minimum mode) or Fig. 6.23 (maximum mode). In the latter case, the 8288 signal $\overline{IORCB}$ is the equivalent.

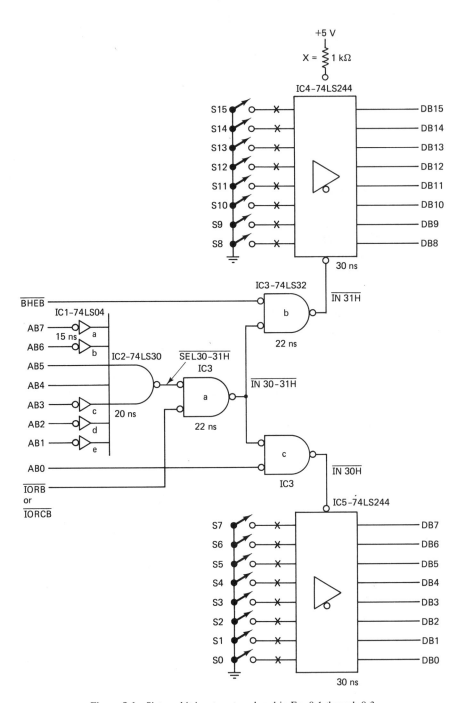

Figure 8.1 Sixteen-bit input port analyzed in Ex. 8.1 through 8.3.

```
                    ;Function:  Test if bits 13, 11, 3 or 2 of
                    ;           the 16-bit data port are high.
                    ;Inputs:    Status information from IPORT.
                    ;Outputs:   CF=1 if condition TRUE, else CF=0.
                    ;Destroys:  AX, flags.

                             PUBLIC FIG8_2
     = 0030               IPORT   EQU       30H              ;Data input port

     0000             CODE     SEGMENT BYTE PUBLIC
                               ASSUME CS:CODE

     0000             FIG8_2   PROC      NEAR
     0000   F8                 CLC                           ;Be sure CF=0
     0001   E5 30              IN        AX,IPORT            ;Sample data
     0003   A9 280C            TEST      AX,0010100000001100B ;Test input data
     0006   74 01              JZ        DONE                ;No bits high
     0008   F9                 STC                           ;At least 1 bit high
     0009   C3        DONE:    RET
     000A             FIG8_2   ENDP
     000A             CODE     ENDS
                               END
```

Figure 8.2 Control program for Ex. 8.1.

The input port in Fig. 8.1 will work with any of the following instructions:

IN AL,30H	;SW0–SW7 → AL via DB0–DB7
IN AL,31H	;SW8–SW15 → AL via DB8–DB15
IN AX,30H	;SW0–SW15 → AX via DB0–DB15
IN AL,DX	;If DX = XX30H, then SW0–SW7 → AL
	;If DX = XX31H, then SW8–SW15 → AL
IN AX,DX	;If DX = XX30H, then SW0–SW15 → AX

Note that for byte input the destination is always register AL. This is true even though the data may be transferred via the DB0–DB7 (for even ports) or DB8–DB15 (for odd ports) data bus lines. The BIU automatically selects the proper set of data lines.

For indirect I/O instructions using register DX, the I/O address is 16 bits long. This means that the circuit in Fig. 8.1 will be *partially* decoded for these instructions. In particular, any input instruction from a port whose address ends in 30H or 31H will enable the circuit. The "XX" in the example port address thus translates into "don't care."

One final point. The instruction IN AX, 31H (or IN AX,DX with DX = XX31H) performs a word input from an odd port address. This is similar to reading a word from an odd memory address. The penalty is one extra bus cycle (four additional T states). For this reason 16-bit ports should normally be mapped to even addresses.[2]

---

[2]As always, the 8088 pays the extra bus cycle penalty with all word accesses (memory or I/O). Thus there is no need to assign 16-bit I/O ports to even addresses for this processor.

Sec. 8.1   Parallel I/O

Example 8.2

Verify that the input port in Fig. 8.1 meets the 5-MHz minimum-mode 8086 TAVDV and TRLDV specifications. Assume a (noninverting) fully buffered configuration.

Solution TAVDV is the delay from output of a valid address by the CPU until data is received by the CPU from the input port. In this case it is the sum of the buffer delays plus the address decoding logic delays. The buffer delays can be found from Fig. 7.33. Note that $IC4-5$'s delay is included in this total (i.e., $IC4-5$ drives the data bus directly).

$$T = t_{buf} + t_{IC1} + t_{IC2} + t_{IC3a} + t_{IC3b-c}$$
$$= 120 \text{ ns} + 15 \text{ ns} + 20 \text{ ns} + 22 \text{ ns} + 22 \text{ ns} = 199 \text{ ns}$$

The specification is 460 ns maximum.

TRLDV is the delay from $\overline{RD}$ low to data valid at the CPU. Because the address is output well before $\overline{RD}$, only the delays through IC3a and IC3b-c (plus the buffer delays) need be considered.

$$T = t_{buf} + t_{IC3a} + t_{IC3b-c}$$
$$= 130 \text{ ns} + 22 \text{ ns} + 22 \text{ ns} = 174 \text{ ns}^3$$

The specification is 205 ns maximum.

Example 8.3

Explain how to troubleshoot the circuit shown in Fig. 8.1 using (a) a single-step circuit and logic probe; (b) a logic analyzer.

Solution (a) Set up a simple test program that will "exercise" the port.

```
AGAIN:  IN   AX,30H      ;Make all select signals active
        JMP  AGAIN       ;Push the single-step key to stop
                         ;in the middle of this loop
```

After the single-step switch has stopped the processor, the logic probe can be used to locate the input read bus cycle. This can be identified by the $\overline{IN\ 30H}$ and $\overline{IN\ 31H}$ DSP signals both being low. $\overline{IORB}$ should also be low, as well as $\overline{BHEB}$, ABO, and $\overline{SEL\ 30-31H}$. IC4 and IC5 should be enabled and as each data switch is changed, the corresponding data bus line should also change.

(b) Set the logic analyzer to the state mode using $\overline{RD}$ as the clock signal. Monitor the 16 data bus lines, DB0–DB15, and the $\overline{IN\ 30H}$ and $\overline{IN\ 31H}$ DSP signals. Using the same test program as in part (a), the analyzer will sample the data bus with each memory or I/O read cycle. You should see the hex codes (or mnemonics) for each instruction, and when the DSP signals are low, DB0–DB15 will hold the data setup on the 16 input switches.

Designing a Parallel Output Port

The hardware required for an output port is similar to that of an input port except that the DSP signal is used to strobe a latch instead of the tri-state buffers. The latch is required due to the short time that data is placed on the bus by the processor.

Figure 8.3 shows a circuit that provides 16 separate select signals. $\overline{BHEB}$ and ABO

---

[3]The $\overline{IORB}$ gating in Fig. 6.21 delays $\overline{IORB}$ by 40 ns. In the maximum mode this gating is not required and T = 164 ns (assuming 8286 buffers as shown in Fig. 7.33).

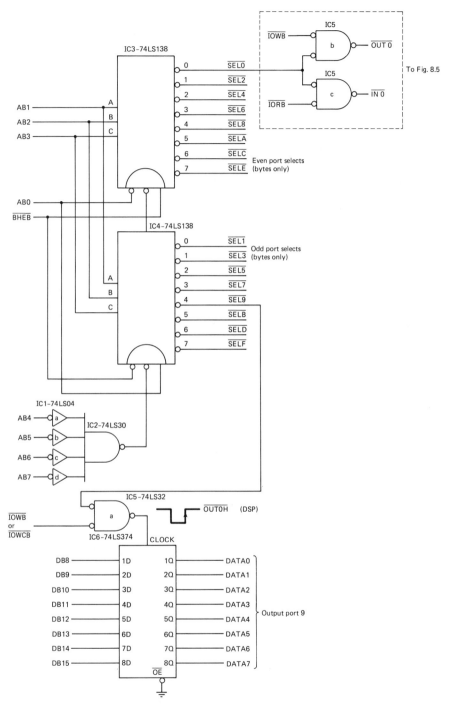

Figure 8.3 I/O port address decoder and 8-bit output port. Eight even-addressed and eight odd-addressed port select signals are generated.

```
                              ;This program calls the routine in Fig. 8.2.
                              ;If switches 13, 11, 3 or 2 are open, FFH is
                              ;output to OPORT, else 00 is output.

                              EXTRN     FIG8_2:NEAR
= 0009                        OPORT     EQU     9        ;Output port

0000               CODE       SEGMENT
                              ASSUME    CS:CODE

0000   B3 FF       START:     MOV       BL,0FFH          ;Open switches code
0002   E8 0000 E              CALL      FIG8_2           ;Test switches
0005   72 02                  JC        SET              ;Condition met
0007   B3 00                  MOV       BL,0             ;Condition not met
0009   8A C3       SET:       MOV       AL,BL            ;Output code
000B   E6 09                  OUT       OPORT,AL         ;to OPORT.
000D   EB F1                  JMP       START            ;Monitor continuously
000F               CODE       ENDS
                              END       START
```

Figure 8.4 Control program for Ex. 8.4.

are wired such that IC3 provides select signals for the even addresses, while IC4 provides selects for the odd addresses. Note that for a word select ($\overline{BHEB}$ and ABO both low), both decoders are disabled. This might be desirable for byte-oriented peripherals that you do not want selected ''accidentally'' by an inadvertent 16-bit I/O cycle.

In this particular case $\overline{SEL\ 9}$ is combined with $\overline{IOWB}$ in IC5a to generate the $\overline{OUT\ 9}$ DSP signal. The rising edge of this signal (and therefore $\overline{IOWB}$) causes the 74LS374 latch to store the data on DB8–DB15. As shown in Fig. 7.12 or 7.14, data is guaranteed valid on this rising edge.

Which instructions will work with this output port circuit? There are only two: OUT 9,AL or OUT DX,AL, where DX = XX09. In particular, the decoding scheme used in Fig. 8.3 protects the circuit against the instruction OUT 8,AX, which would otherwise write data to ports 8 and 9.

Example 8.4

Write a program that tests if any of the switches 13, 11, 3, or 2 in the input port of Fig. 8.1 are open. If the condition is met, output FFH to port 9 in Fig. 8.3. If the condition is not met, output 00 to this port. The program should cycle indefinitely.

Solution We can take advantage of the procedure written in Ex. 8.1 to test the input port. Depending on the condition of CF, FFH or 00 can then be output to port 9. Figure 8.4 is a listing of the program. FIG8_2 is declared as an external symbol, so that this routine can be linked to the program in Fig. 8.4 without having to rewrite that procedure's code.

Example 8.5

The 74LS374 used for the output port latch in Fig. 8.3 has a data setup time of 20 ns and a hold time of 0 ns. Verify that these specifications are met assuming a 5-MHz maximum mode fully buffered 8086 CPU module.

Solution Data is output by the 8086 TDVWH nanoseconds before the rising edge of $\overline{IOWC}$. In Fig. 7.14 this is shown to be 300 ns. The data will be delayed through the system data bus buffers a maximum of 60 ns. However, the trailing edge of $\overline{IOWC}$ will also be delayed a similar amount, plus the delay of IC5a. The worst-case analysis would require that

$$t_{su} \geq \text{TDVWHmin} - (t_{\text{DBbuf}}\text{max} - t_{\text{CBbuf}}\text{min} - t_{\text{IC5}}\text{min})$$

where t_{DBbuf} represents the data bus buffer delay and t_{CBbuf} represents the control bus delay for $\overline{\text{IOWC}}$. Even assuming 0 ns for the minimum delays, the setup time is 300 ns − 60 ns, or 240 ns and the specification is easily met.

Again referring to Fig. 7.14, data is held on the bus lines TWHDX nanoseconds after $\overline{\text{IOWC}}$ returns high. In this case the worst-case analysis requires that

$$
\begin{aligned}
t_h &\geq \text{TWHDXmin} - (t_{\text{CBbuf}}\text{max} + t_{\text{IC5}}\text{max} - t_{\text{DBbuf}}\text{min}) \\
&\geq 93 \text{ ns} - (30 \text{ ns} + 22 \text{ ns} - 0 \text{ ns}) \\
&\geq 41 \text{ ns}
\end{aligned}
$$

Again the specification is easily met, even assuming 0 ns for the minimum data bus buffer delay.

Applications for the Device Select Pulse

Normally the DSP signal is used to enable a latch or set of tri-state gates. However, in some cases the pulse alone is sufficient. Figure 8.5 provides an example. Using the $\overline{\text{IN 0}}$ and $\overline{\text{OUT 0}}$ DSP signals from the decoder in Fig. 8.3, this circuit controls a mechanical relay. An *IN AL,0* instruction resets the flip-flop and turns on the transistor. This, in turn, allows current to flow through the relay coil. The normally open (NO) contact closes and some external (non-TTL-compatible) device can be turned on. An *OUT 0,AL* instruction turns the relay off.

The 74LS05 is an open-collector buffer. This allows its output to be pulled to +5 V and the transistor base drive to be supplied through the pull-up resistor. Transistor Q1 is required because the relay's ON current exceeds the sink capability of the 74LS05.

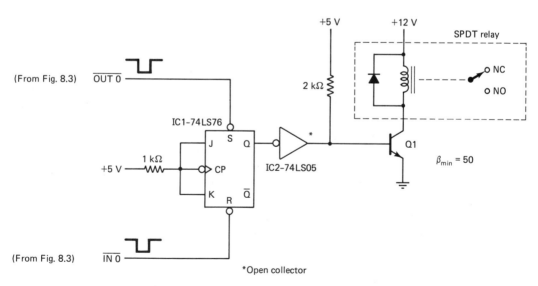

Figure 8.5 Using device select pulses to control a relay. An IN AL,0 instruction will turn the relay ON, an OUT 0,AL instruction will turn it OFF.

Sec. 8.1 Parallel I/O

A similar application for the DSP is to trigger a one-shot to generate pulse widths of a particular length. Be sure to note that it is only the DSP that is used. No data is transferred. For this reason the contents of register AL is a ''don't care'' when an output instruction is executed, and indeterminate when an input instruction is executed.

Memory-Mapped I/O

The address space of the 8086 is divided into 1,048,576 bytes of memory space and 65,536 bytes of I/O space. These two regions do not overlap because memory addresses are selected with the memory commands ($\overline{\text{MEMR}}$, $\overline{\text{MRDC}}$, $\overline{\text{MEMW}}$, $\overline{\text{MWTC}}$), while the I/O addresses are selected with the I/O commands ($\overline{\text{IOR}}$, $\overline{\text{IORC}}$, $\overline{\text{IOW}}$, $\overline{\text{IOWC}}$).

But consider designing a one-byte (or word) read/write memory. We would use latches to store the data written during a memory write cycle, and tri-state gates to drive the bus during a memory read cycle—exactly the same hardware that we would use for an output or input port.

This is the essence of memory-mapped I/O. In hardware it appears to be a conventional I/O port. But because it is mapped to a *memory* address, it is accessible in software using any of the memory read or write instructions. For example, the instruction *MOV BH,MEMBDS* becomes an input instruction (input the data at ''port'' MEMBDS to register BH). Indirect I/O is also possible. The instruction sequence

```
LEA   SI,  MEMWDS      ;Point SI at the port
MOV   [SI],CX          ;Output CX to the port
```

allows CX to be output to the 16-bit port at address DS:MEMWDS.

As you can see, the advantage of memory-mapped I/O is the large number of instructions and addressing modes available for referencing memory. This is compared to the single input and output commands available with an I/O-mapped port.

Figure 8.6 shows an 8-bit input port memory-mapped to address FFFFFH. Two 74ALS677 address comparators are required to decode all 20 address lines and two control signals. Note that the decoding is such that only this odd-addressed byte can be accessed ($\overline{\text{BHE}}$ = 0, AB0 = 1). You can also see one of the disadvantages to memory-mapped I/O. Full decoding requires that 20 address lines be tested. Partial decoding can be used, simplifying the decoder, but this will ''steal'' memory space away from the processor.

Memory-mapped I/O is most appropriate when the peripheral to be interfaced requires a large block of *consecutive* addresses. One example would be a digital clock chip with separate registers for the seconds, minutes, hours, days, months, and year.

Figure 8.7 shows an interface to such a chip. The registers within this circuit are all assumed to be 8 bits wide (as is usually the case). The eight data bus lines on the chip are bidirectional, allowing the device to be read or written with the same set of I/O lines. In this example there are 16 read/write registers.

However, the 8-bit data path also causes a problem. The 8086 wants even-addressed data bytes to be transported on DB0–DB7, while odd-addressed bytes must use DB8–DB15. We can either decode the peripheral so that each register resides at an even (or odd) address (A0000H, A0002H, A0004H, etc.) or use a data bus *multiplexer* to convert

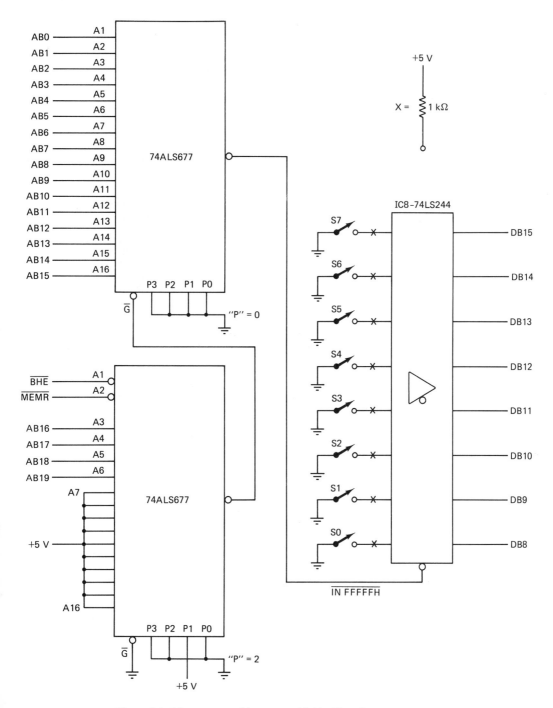

Figure 8.6 Memory-mapped input port. All 20 address lines must be decoded.

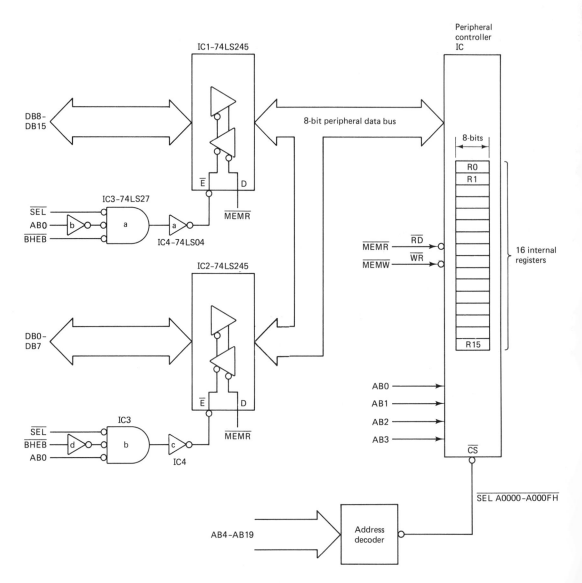

Figure 8.7 Interfacing an 8-bit peripheral to the 8086. This circuit is memory-mapped and appears as 16 consecutive memory locations from A0000H through A000FH.

the 8086's 16-bit bus into an 8-bit bus compatible with the peripheral. In Fig. 8.7 the latter approach has been chosen.

IC1 and IC2 form the multiplexer. IC1 is enabled for odd addresses (AB0 = 1 and $\overline{\text{BHEB}}$ = 0), while IC2 is enabled for even addresses (AB0 = 0 and $\overline{\text{BHEB}}$ = 1). Note that both buffers are disabled if a word access is attempted. $\overline{\text{MEMR}}$ is used to control the direction of the buffers.

The address decoder has been arbitrarily selected to decode the address range A0000–A000FH. This signal drives the peripheral controller's chip select ($\overline{\text{CS}}$) input.

When selected, $\overline{\text{MEMR}}$ and $\overline{\text{MEMW}}$, connected to the chips $\overline{\text{RD}}$ and $\overline{\text{WR}}$ inputs, determine if data is to be written to or read from the chip. AB0–AB3 select one of the 16 internal registers.

Example 8.6

Write a procedure to initialize all 16 registers of the peripheral controller shown in Fig. 8.7.

Solution Figure 8.8 is the program listing. The PERIPH segment contains the offset and address of the (memory mapped) peripheral controller chip using the name IO_BLOCK_ADDR. The 16 data bytes to be programmed follow these four bytes. After fetching the segment address and offset of this table, the REP MOVSB instruction automatically programs all 16 registers. This is an example of the software flexibility afforded by a memory-mapped I/O port.

The data bus multiplexer shown in Fig. 8.7 is not required with the 8-bit 8088 microprocessor. In this case, the peripheral's data bus lines can be connected directly to the system data bus lines. Because most peripheral controller chips utilize 8-bit internal registers and data buses, you will find that it is usually easier to interface these chips to the 8088 than to the 8086.

```
                        TITLE  Fig. 8.8

                        ;This program initializes the 16 registers of
                        ;the memory-mapped peripheral controller chip
                        ;shown in Fig. 8.7.

0000                    PERIPH SEGMENT BYTE
0000  00 00 00 A0       IO_BLOCK_ADDR   DD          0A0000000H
                        ;
                        ;Fill in the following table with the 16 bytes
                        ;to be programmed.
                        ;
0004     10 [           TABLE           DB          16 DUP (?)
              ??
                 ]

0014                    PERIPH          ENDS

0000                    CODE    SEGMENT
                                ASSUME CS:CODE, DS:PERIPH

0000                    FIG8_8  PROC    NEAR
0000  B8  ---- R                MOV     AX,PERIPH        ;Point DS:SI at the
0003  8E D8                     MOV     DS,AX            ;programming codes.
0005  8D 36 0004 R              LEA     SI,TABLE         ;ES:DI at A000:0000.
0009  C4 3E 0000 R              LES     DI,IO_BLOCK_ADDR

000D  B9 0010                   MOV     CX,16            ;16 bytes to program
0010  FC                        CLD                      ;Auto increment

0011  F3/ A4                    REP     MOVSB            ;Program the chip
0013  C3                        RET
0014                    FIG8_8 ENDP
0014                    CODE    ENDS
                                END
```

Figure 8.8 Control program to initialize the peripheral interface chip shown in Fig. 8.7.

8.1.1. When the instruction IN AL,27H is executed, the 8086 inputs the data byte over the _____ data bus lines.

8.1.2. For direct I/O, the 8086 is restricted to _____ I/O ports with addresses in the range _____ to _____.

8.1.3. In the minimum mode, I/O bus cycle timing is exactly the same as memory timing except for the state of the _____ signal.

8.1.4. When an I/O port select signal is combined with the $\overline{\text{IOR}}$ or $\overline{\text{IOW}}$ control signals, the resulting signal is referred to as a _____ _____ _____.

8.1.5. Input or output ports can be interfaced to the 8086 only in 8-bit pairs. (True/False)

8.1.6. Memory-mapped I/O is most useful when the I/O devices require a block of _____ I/O ports.

8.1.7. Which of the following instructions could *not* be used for memory-mapped input? (a) INC AX; (b) CMP DX,MEMWDS; (c) MOV BX,MEMWDS; (d) MOV BP,[BX].

8.2 SERIAL I/O

One way of visualizing a serial I/O port is as a 1-bit parallel port. Figure 8.9 shows an example. Partial decoding is used such that all even (byte) ports between XXF0H and XXFEH are selected. The $\overline{\text{IN F0H}}$ and $\overline{\text{OUT F0H}}$ DSP signals strobe DB0 into the latch or gate the serial input data onto the DB0 data bus line. The serial data is thus transmitted and received as bit 0 of port F0H (or port F2H, F4H, etc.).

But there are several questions to be answered about this serial I/O port. How can we tell when the data starts or stops? How long should each data bit persist? How are the microprocessor and peripheral *synchronized*?

In this section we answer these questions by considering the two basic methods used for serial data transmission and reception: *asynchronous* and *synchronous* serial communications.

Asynchronous Serial Communications

One of the most common applications for a serial I/O port is to interface the keyboard on a video display terminal (VDT). In this circuit, each keystroke generates a 7-bit ASCII code which is converted to bit-by-bit serial and then transmitted to a computer over a two- or three-conductor cable. Because even the fastest typist cannot exceed data rates of 60 to 100 words per minute, it is a good match for the (relatively) slow transmission rate of the serial port.

Note an important characteristic of this interface. At some times the serial port will be required to transfer data at 10 to 20 characters/s, but at other times the data rate may be only 1 or 2 characters/s. Indeed, most of the time the keyboard is not in use and the data rate is zero. Because of this erratic data rate, an asynchronous communications *protocol* (set of universally accepted rules) must be established.

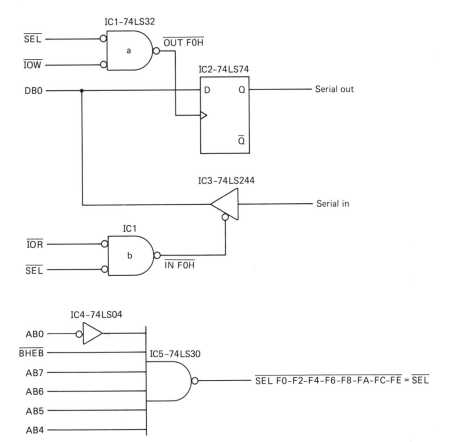

Figure 8.9 One-bit input and output port. With appropriate software this circuit can function as a serial I/O channel.

Start bits, stop bits, and the baud rate. The accepted technique for asynchronous serial communications is to hold the serial output line at a logic 1 level (a *"mark"*) until data is to be transmitted. Each character is required to begin with a logic 0 (a *"space"*) for one bit time. This first bit is called the *start bit* and is used to synchronize the transmitter and receiver. Figure 8.10 illustrates how the data byte 7BH would look when transmitted in the asynchronous serial format. The data is sent least significant bit first and framed between a start bit (always a 0) and one or two stop bits (always a 1).

The start and stop bits carry no information but are required because of the asynchronous nature of the data. The data rate can be expressed as bits/s or characters/s. The term bits/s is also called the *baud rate*.[4]

[4]In Chap. 10 you will learn that the baud rate is more accurately defined as the number of *signal events* per second.

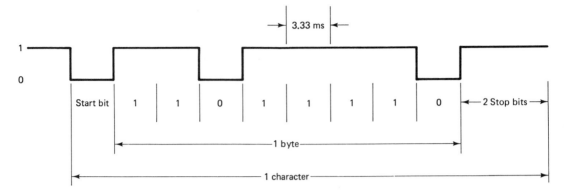

Figure 8.10 Standard asynchronous serial data format. The data byte is framed between the start bit and two stop bits. In this example the data byte is 7BH. (From J. Uffenbeck, *Microcomputers and Microprocessors: The 8080, 8085, and Z-80*. Prentice-Hall, Englewood Cliffs, N.J., 1985.)

Example 8.7

Calculate the baud rate and character rate for the serial data shown in Fig. 8.10.

Solution   Because one bit persists for 3.33 ms, the bits/s rate is 1/3.33 ms = 300 bits/s, or 300 baud. Because there are 11 bits per character, it will require 11 × 3.33 ms = 36.63 ms to transmit the entire byte. The character rate is therefore 1/36.63 ms = 27.3 characters/s.

Example 8.8

Most VDTs have 80 characters per line and 24 lines per screen. At 300 baud, how long will it take to fill the screen of such a terminal?

Solution   The total number of characters required is 80 × 24 = 1920. The total time is thus

$$1920 \text{ characters}/27.3 \text{ characters/s} = 70.3 \text{ s}$$

Generating and recovering asynchronous serial data.   All microprocessors are capable of generating serial data without special hardware. For example, consider the 8086 program in Fig. 8.11. Assume that bit 0 of the DPORT is used as the serial output pin (see Fig. 8.9). Each bit to be transmitted is rotated to the bit 0 position of the accumulator and output. The DELAY procedure determines the baud rate.

Recovering the serial data requires a more complex program, but again no special hardware is required. Assuming that a 1-bit input port is used (see Fig. 8.9), Fig. 8.12 flowcharts the process. The program begins by waiting for the one-to-zero transition of the start bit. Once found, the middle of the bit is located by waiting for DELAY/2 seconds. If the input bit is still 0, a valid start bit is assumed and the program then waits for one additional bit time (thus sampling in the middle of all following bits).

As each bit is read it is rotated right—through the carry—and after eight reads the entire byte has been recovered. The ninth read should return the first stop bit, but if this bit is low a *framing* error is indicated, that is, the program is out of "sync" with the

```
;Function:   Serial data transmitter.  DELAY
;            procedure determines baud rate.
;Inputs:     Character to be transmitted assumed
;            passed in AL.
;Ouputs:     Serial data on bit 0 of DPORT.

;Destroys:   AL,CX,flags.
```

		EXTRN	DELAY:NEAR	
= 00F0		DPORT	EQU 0F0H	
0000		CODE	SEGMENT	
		ASSUME	CS:CODE	
0000		FIG8_11 PROC	NEAR	
0000	B9 000B	MOV	CX,11	;11 bits/char
0003	F8	CLC		;Start bit
0004	D0 D0	RCL	AL,1	;Move to position 0
0006	E6 F0	TRANS: OUT	DPORT,AL	;Transmit bit
0008	E8 0000 E	CALL	DELAY	;Wait
000B	D0 D8	RCR	AL,1	;Next bit
000D	F9	STC		;Stop bit
000E	E2 F6	LOOP	TRANS	;Do 11 times
0010	C3	RET		
0011		FIG8_11 ENDP		
0011		CODE	ENDS	
			END	

Figure 8.11 8086 serial transmitter program. Bit 0 of the DPORT is used for the serial output line.

data. If high, the data byte can be saved and the program begins searching for the next start bit.

It has been implied in our discussion thus far that the receiver and transmitter data rates are exactly matched. But is this necessary? Can we tolerate slight differences? For example, using software timing loops it is unlikely that the DELAY procedure in two different computers will be *exactly* the same.

Figure 8.13 illustrates the results of trying to recover data that is too fast or too slow for the receiver. In either case, note how the error *accumulates*. If sampling is done in the middle of the bit time, the maximum allowable error will cause the ninth bit to be shifted ½ bit time to the right or left. If all bits are shifted equally (because of a data rate mismatch), the amount of error in one bit will be ½ bit time ÷ 9 = $1/18$ bit time. This means that the received and transmitted data rates must match within 5.6%.

This is an interesting result. You might have guessed that the data rates had to match exactly. This would be true if there were no start or stop bits. But because of these bits, synchronization need only be held from the beginning of one start bit to the beginning of the first stop bit. The technique *self-synchronizes* itself after each character. Of course, the price we pay for this is that each data byte must be increased in length by 3 bits, or 37.5% (25% with only 1 stop bit). If these bits were not required, the character rate calculated in Ex. 8.8 would rise to 37.5 characters/s and the VDT screen could be filled in 52 s instead of 70 s.

In some cases a logic 1 might be delayed more than a logic 0 (or vice versa) when passing through the transmission medium. This can lead to individual bit errors rather

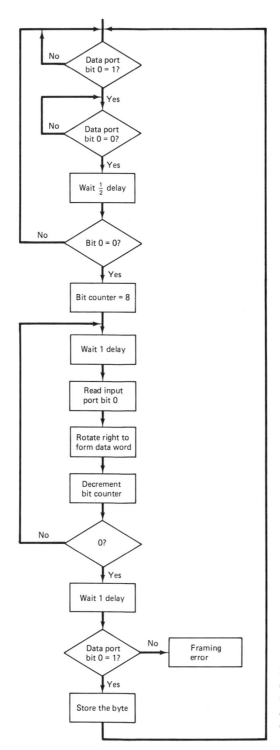

Figure 8.12 Flowchart of the process required to recover asynchronous serial data. (From J. Uffenbeck, *Microcomputers and Microprocessors: The 8080, 8085, and Z-80*. Prentice-Hall, Englewood Cliffs, N.J., 1985.)

Basic Input/Output   Chap. 8

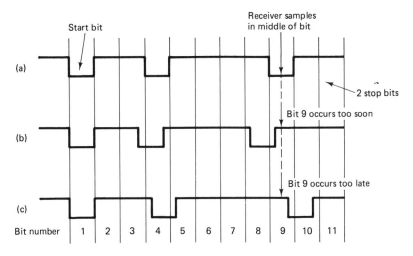

Figure 8.13 (a) Data transmitted at the proper rate. (b) The data rate is too fast. (c) The data rate is too slow. (From J. Uffenbeck, *Microcomputers and Microprocessors: The 8080, 8085, and Z-80*. Prentice-Hall, Englewood Cliffs, N.J., 1985.)

than framing errors. Because of this, the rule of thumb is to try to match receiving and transmitting data rates to 1% or less.

Standard asynchronous serial communications protocols. As mentioned previously, protocols define certain rules that should be followed to help standardize the communications technique. An example is the adoption of a logic 0 for a start bit and a logic 1 for a stop bit. Certain baud rates have also become standard and are listed in Table 8.2.

TABLE 8.2 COMMON BAUD RATES FOR SERIAL DATA COMMUNICATIONS

75
110
150
300
600
1,200
2,400
4,800
9,600
19,200

Source: J. Uffenbeck, *Microcomputers and Microprocessors: The 8080, 8085, and Z-80*. Prentice-Hall, Englewood Cliffs, N.J., 1985.

When setting up a serial port several parameters must be specified. The most common are:

1. Data bits/character, usually 5 to 8
2. Stop bits, one or two
3. Parity bit, used to detect single bit errors, may be specified as odd or even or no parity[5]
4. Baud rate (see Table 8.2 for standard frequencies)

One of the considerations to be made when designing or using a serial port is to select a *compatible* set of communications parameters for the computer and peripheral. In fact, this is one of the most common problems with serial ports. The receiver may be set for one baud rate but the transmitter to another.

The UART.   Writing a program compatible with all the different asynchronous communications protocols can be quite a task. It is also an *inefficient* use of the microprocessor, as much of its time will be spent in timing loops waiting to transmit or receive another character.

Because of this, the semiconductor companies have developed the *universal asynchronous receiver/transmitter* (UART). Figure 8.14 is a block diagram of the General Instruments AY-5-1013, which features a separate serial transmitter and serial receiver in the same IC package. Several control pins allow the selection of 5 to 8 data bits/word; even, odd, or no parity bit; and 1 or 2 stop bits.

Status pins indicate when a new character has been received ("Receiver data ready") or when the transmitter is ready for another character ("Transmitter buffer empty"). Other status indicators show when a framing error, parity error, or overrun condition (character received before the previous character has been read) has occurred.

The UART requires an accurate clock signal, which then determines the baud rate. Most UARTs use a signal *16 times* the intended data rate. This has the effect of breaking each bit time into 16 "slices" and allows the center of the bit to be located more accurately. As an example, to operate the AY-5-1013 in Fig. 8.14 with a 1200-baud peripheral, a 19.2-kHz clock signal should be connected to the transmitter and receiver clock inputs (*16 × 1200*).

It is interesting to note that to the microprocessor a serial port (the UART) appears as a conventional *parallel* port. When the transmitter buffer is empty, all the bits in the word to be transmitted are output to the port at once (in parallel). Similarly, all bits of the received word are input at once when the received data is ready.

The job of converting the data from serial to parallel, or parallel to serial, has been transferred to the UART. This is interesting because we usually think of using the microprocessor to replace hardware with software. However, the UART is an example of a case in which it is more efficient to replace software with hardware.

In Chap. 9 we discuss the Intel 8251A USART (*universal synchronous/asynchronous receiver/transmitter*). This peripheral controller chip has all the features of the AY-

---

[5]Parity and other error-detection techniques are discussed in Chap. 10.

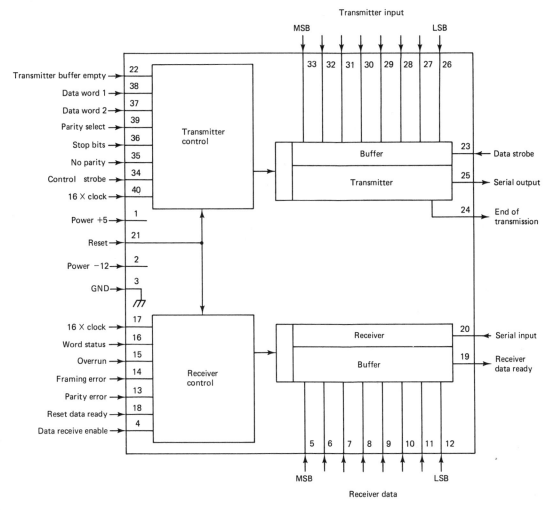

Figure 8.14 AY-5-1013 UART. A separate transmitter and receiver are provided. Control functions are hardwired. (From J. Uffenbeck, *Microcomputers and Microprocessors: The 8080, 8085, and Z-80.* Prentice-Hall, Englewood Cliffs, N.J., 1985.)

5-1013 but is programmable via an 8-bit bidirectional data bus (similar to the clock circuit discussed previously).

Synchronous Serial Communications

The start and stop bits of asynchronous serial data represent wasted overhead bytes that reduce the overall character rate no matter what the baud rate. Even adding a parity bit can reduce the transfer rate by 10%.

But giving up the start and stop bits will require some means of *synchronizing* the data. How will we know when the data starts and when to sample it? In this section we examine two common synchronous serial protocols that answer these questions.

Bisync protocol. Because there is no start bit, a special *sync character* is required in all synchronous serial formats. This character tells the receiver that data is about to follow. The USART, accordingly, must have a special "hunt" or "search" mode so that the sync character can be found.

Because there is no stop bit, a clock signal usually accompanies the synchronous data to maintain synchronization. When synchronous serial data is to be transmitted over the telephone network, it is not possible to provide a separate clock channel. In this case a special *synchronous modem* is used that encodes the data and clock into a single signal. The receiving modem separates the data and clock signals.

Another difference when compared to asynchronous serial is that the clock rate is the same as the baud rate (i.e., a $1 \times$ clock is used).

In the *bisync* protocol several special (ASCII) characters are used to control the data transfer as shown in Table 8.3. Figure 8.15 illustrates one "frame" of a synchronous message. Just as asynchronous data is framed between start and stop bits, synchronous data is framed between special control codes. In Fig. 8.15 two sync characters are output followed by *STX*—start of text. The data bytes follow. This block may consist of 100 or more data bytes or simply be other control codes. *ETX* signifies end of text. *BCC* is a block check character used for error detection (discussed in Chap. 10). *PAD* is the

TABLE 8.3 SPECIAL CHARACTERS USED IN THE BISYNC SYNCHONOUS SERIAL PROTOCOL

Character	ASCII code	Description
SYNC	16	Sync character
PAD	FF	End of frame pad
DLE	10	Data link escape
ENQ	05	Enquiry
SOH	01	Start of header
STX	02	Start of text
ITB	0F	End of intermediate transmission block
ETB	17	End of transmission block
ETX	03	End of text

Source: J. Uffenbeck, *Microcomputers and Microprocessors: The 8080, 8085, and Z-80.* Prentice-Hall, Englewood Cliffs, N.J., 1985.

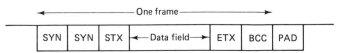

Figure 8.15 One frame of a synchronous message using the bisync protocol. (From J. Uffenbeck, *Microcomputers and Microprocessors: The 8080, 8085, and Z-80.* Prentice-Hall, Englewood Cliffs, N.J., 1985.)

character output when no data is being transmitted and corresponds to the "mark" output in asynchronous serial.

Be sure to note that the bisync protocol is simply a set of rules that everyone has agreed to follow. It is not necessarily any better or worse than some other set of rules.

Example 8.9

Calculate the percentage of "wasted" bits using the bisync protocol compared to 8-data-bit, 2-stop-bit, 1-parity-bit asynchronous serial. Assume that the data block size is 100 bytes.

Solution The overhead required for the asynchronous character is 50% (4 extra bits for each byte). The bisync protocol requires six extra bytes (see Fig. 8.15 and assuming a 16-bit BCC) for the 100-byte block. The overhead is 6%.

The consequences of the reduced overhead should be clear. For a given baud rate, synchronous data will have a considerably higher character rate.

Serial data link control (SDLC). This format was developed by IBM for use with their *Systems Network Architecture* (SNA) communications package. Figure 8.16 illustrates one frame of data using this protocol. It is similar to bisync but is not byte oriented.

The SDLC receiver searches for the beginning flag (01111110) as its sync character. An 8-bit address field follows, allowing each frame to be addressed to a particular station among a network of stations. Control characters are identified by a sequence of six or more logic 1's.

The information field can be of any format (i.e., it does not have to consist of an integral number of bytes). The transmitter will automatically insert 0's in this field if five or more logic 1's should appear in sequence. This will avoid inadvertent control characters appearing in the information field. The receiver automatically deletes these 0's.

The 16-bit frame check is used for error detection, similar to the BCC character in bisync. The frame ends with the ending flag.

SDLC is actually a subset of HDLC (high-level data link control), which is an international synchronous communications protocol. As with bisync, SDLC is simply a set of rules that have been agreed upon for the transfer of serial data.

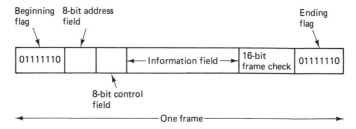

Figure 8.16 One frame of a synchronous message using the SDLC protocol. (From J. Uffenbeck, *Microcomputers and Microprocessors: The 8080, 8085, and Z-80*. Prentice-Hall, Englewood Cliffs, N.J., 1985.)

8.2.1. How long will it take to transmit the ASCII letter "B" assuming 1200 baud, 7 data bits, 1 start bit, no parity, and 2 stop bits?

8.2.2. Sketch the transmitted waveform for the conditions described in question 8.2.1.

8.2.3. A _____ error occurs when the receiver detects a missing stop bit.

8.2.4. The _____ is a microprocessor-compatible peripheral interface chip used to convert parallel data into serial and serial data into parallel.

8.2.5. What clock rate is required by a UART transmitting the data described in question 8.2.1?

8.2.6. The character rate for the conditions in question 8.2.1 is _____ characters/s.

8.2.7. Which serial communications technique normally achieves the highest character rate? Why?

8.2.8. _____ is a byte-oriented synchronous serial data technique, while _____ is a bit-oriented synchronous technique.

8.3 PROGRAMMED I/O

Regardless of the type of I/O port, serial or parallel, a strategy must be developed to control or synchronize the flow of data through that port. For example, assume that a 100-character/s (cps) printer is interfaced to a parallel output port. This printer is capable of printing a new character every 10 ms (1/100 cps). But consider the following 8086 output routine, which might be used to supply data to the printer.

```
AGAIN:  LODSB                    ;Fetch byte to AL      [12]
        OUT     DPORT, AL        ;Send to printer       [10]
        LOOP    AGAIN            ;Do CX times           [17]
```

The numbers in brackets represent the number of T states required for each instruction (assuming that the instruction is already in the queue). Using this routine, the 8086 can output a new byte to the printer every 39 T states. At 5 MHz this is a new character every 7.8 μs and corresponds to 128,205 characters/s! There is an obvious mismatch in the data rates of the printer and microprocessor.

There are different ways of solving this problem. In this section we develop a set of "handshaking" signals that can be polled via software to ensure a smooth transfer of data between the peripheral and the microprocessor.

Polling

Let us continue to consider the problem of interfacing a parallel printer to a microprocessor. Table 8.4 gives the pin assignments and signal descriptions for a popular parallel printer.[6] A 36-conductor cable is required between computer and printer. However, pins 19 through

---

[6]The Epson MX-80. The signals described are common to most parallel printers. Indeed, the interface has become known as the "Centronic's standard parallel printer interface."

TABLE 8.4 PARALLEL PRINTER SIGNAL DESCRIPTIONS

Signal pin	Return pin	Signal	Direction	Description
1	19	$\overline{\text{STROBE}}$	In	STROBE pulse to read data in. Pulse width must be more than 0.5 μs at receiving terminal. The signal level is normally "HIGH"; read-in of data is performed at the "LOW" level of this signal.
2	20	DATA 1	In	
3	21	DATA 2	In	
4	22	DATA 3	In	These signals represent information of the first to eighth bits of parallel data, respectively. Each signal is at "HIGH" level when data is logical "1" and "LOW" when logical "0".
5	23	DATA 4	In	
6	24	DATA 5	In	
7	25	DATA 6	In	
8	26	DATA 7	In	
9	27	DATA 8	In	
10	28	$\overline{\text{ACKNLG}}$	Out	Approx. 5-μs pulse. "LOW" indicates that data has been received and that the printer is ready to accept other data.
11	29	BUSY	Out	A "HIGH" signal indicates that the printer cannot receive data. The signal becomes "High" in the following cases: 1. During data entry 2. During printing operation 3. In OFF-LINE state 4. During printer error status.
12	30	PE	Out	A "HIGH" signal indicates that the printer is out of paper.
13	—	SLCT	Out	This signal indicates that the printer is in the selected state.
14	—	$\overline{\text{AUTO}}$ $\overline{\text{FEED XT}}$	In	With this signal being at "LOW" level, the paper is automatically fed one line after printing. (The signal level can be fixed to "LOW" with DIP SW pin 2-3 provided on the control circuit board.)
15	—	NC		Not used.
16	—	OV		Logic GND level.

TABLE 8.4 CONTINUED

Signal pin	Return pin	Signal	Direction	Description
17	—	CHASSIS-GND	—	Printer chassis GND. In the printer, the chassis GND and the logic GND are isolated from each other.
18	—	NC	—	Not used.
19 to 30	—	GND	—	TWISTED-PAIR RETURN signal GND level.
31	—	$\overline{\text{INIT}}$	In	When the level of this signal becomes "LOW", the printer controller is reset to its initial state and the print buffer is cleared. This signal is normally at "HIGH" level, and its pulse width must be more than 50 μs at the receiving terminal.
32		$\overline{\text{ERROR}}$	Out	The level of this signal becomes "LOW" when the printer is in: 1. PAPER END state 2. OFF-LINE state 3. Error state
33	—	GND	—	Same as with pins 19 to 30.
34	—	NC	—	Not used.
35				Pulled up to +5 V through 4.7-kΩ resistance.
36	—	$\overline{\text{SLCT IN}}$	In	Data entry to the printer is possible only when the level of this signal is "LOW" (Internal fixing can be carried out with DIP SW 1-8. The condition at the time of shipment is set "LOW" for this signal.)

Notes:

1. "Direction" refers to the direction of signal flow as viewed from the printer.

2. "Return" denotes "TWISTED PAIR RETURN" and is to be connected at signal ground level. As to the wiring for the interface, be sure to use a twisted-pair cable for each signal and never fail to complete connection on the Return side. To prevent noise effectively, these cables should be shielded and connected to the chassis of the host computer and the printer, respectively.

3. All interface conditions are based on TTL level. Both the rise and fall times of each signal must be less than 0.2 μs.

4. Data transfer must not be carried out by ignoring the $\overline{\text{ACKNLG}}$ or BUSY signal. (Data transfer to this printer can be carried out only after confirming the $\overline{\text{ACKNLG}}$ signal or when the level of the BUSY signal is "LOW".)

Source: Seiko Epson Corporation, Nagano, Japan.

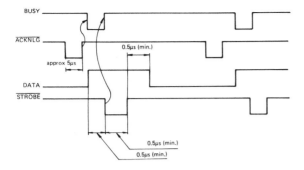

Figure 8.17 Parallel printer timing showing the relationship between the handshaking signals. (Courtesy of Seiko Epson Corporation, Nagano, Japan)

30 are connected to the printer chassis ground and are used to shield each signal wire in the cable (a flat ribbon cable is normally used with every other conductor a ground wire).

There are eight data wires, labeled DATA1 through DATA8. The printer will latch the data on these pins when its $\overline{\text{STROBE}}$ input is pulsed low for 0.5 μs or longer. Figure 8.17 illustrates the timing. The data requires a 0.5-μs setup time before the leading edge of $\overline{\text{STROBE}}$ occurs. A 0.5-μs hold time is also required after $\overline{\text{STROBE}}$ returns high.

Two other control signals are provided by the printer, labeled BUSY and $\overline{\text{ACKNLG}}$. In Table 8.4, BUSY is an active-high signal that indicates that the printer is "busy" printing a character, has some error condition, or is in an OFF-LINE state. Taken literally, it means "I am busy now and can't accept data from you."

The $\overline{\text{ACKNLG}}$ signal is an active-low pulse provided by the printer after a character has been accepted and printed. Be sure to note the difference between these two signals. BUSY is best suited for a level-triggered input; $\overline{\text{ACKNLG}}$ is most appropriate with an edge-triggered input.

The $\overline{\text{STROBE}}$, BUSY, and $\overline{\text{ACKNLG}}$ signals form a set of "handshaking" signals exchanged between the CPU and the printer. The CPU extends its "hand" with the $\overline{\text{STROBE}}$ pulse, saying "Here is the data." The printer acknowledges via the $\overline{\text{ACKNLG}}$ pulse, saying "I've got it. You can send me some more." BUSY is the same as $\overline{\text{ACKNLG}}$ but provides a *level* to be monitored instead of a pulse.

Figure 8.18 is a flowchart of the process required to transfer data to the printer. In this example we assume that the data to be printed is stored in consecutive memory locations thought of as a print buffer. A pointer is used to identify the head of this buffer, and a counter is used to store the total number of bytes to be printed.

The decision block, "BUSY = 1?", forms a *polling loop* in which the CPU continually tests the printer's BUSY flag. When this line goes low the CPU fetches a byte from the buffer, outputs it to the printer, pulses the $\overline{\text{STROBE}}$ input, advances the table pointer, and decrements the byte counter. If more data remains to be printed, control returns to the polling loop.

Before we actually write this program, let's design the hardware required to interface the printer. Figure 8.19 shows the circuit. An 8-bit latch is required to hold the data on the input pins of the printer. This latch is clocked by the $\overline{\text{OUT 2}}$ DSP signal from IC2a. The $\overline{\text{SEL 2}}$ and $\overline{\text{SEL 3}}$ signals are derived from the address decoder in Fig. 8.3.

A 1-bit input port is constructed with IC4 and enabled by the $\overline{\text{IN 3}}$ DSP. Finally, the $\overline{\text{STROBE}}$ signal is manufactured using a flip-flop set and reset by the $\overline{\text{IN 3}}$ and $\overline{\text{OUT 3}}$ DSP signals. Ideally, the $\overline{\text{OUT 2}}$ DSP signal alone could be used for this purpose.

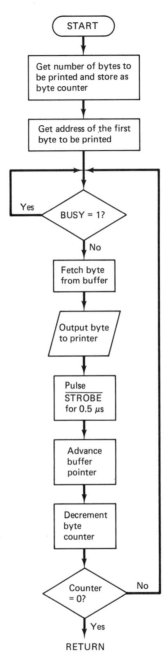

Figure 8.18 Flowchart for the printer control program.

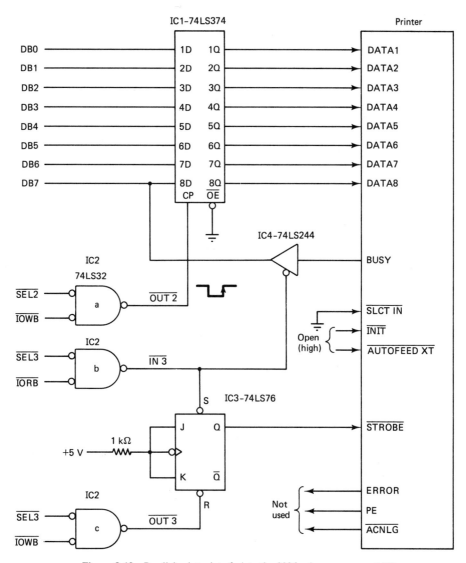

Figure 8.19 Parallel printer interface to the 8086 using programmed I/O.

However, the pulse width of this signal is too short—375 ns at best (using the $\overline{\text{AIOWC}}$ signal). It would also not meet the 500-ns setup time shown in Fig. 8.17. The $\overline{\text{ACKNLG}}$ signal is not used in this example.

The following instruction sequence can be used to generate the $\overline{\text{STROBE}}$ pulse (assuming that the flip-flop is initially set).

```
OUT 3,AL      ;STROBE = 0
IN AL,3       ;STROBE = 1
```

Because the IN instruction requires 10 T states to execute, $\overline{\text{STROBE}}$ will be low for 10 × 200 ns = 2 μs (assuming a 5-MHz clock). This is four times longer than required. Note that the *IN AL,3* instruction will also read the BUSY signal status as bit 7 of input port 3. Finally, the hold-time requirement of the printer is met because the data will be held in the latch until a new output instruction occurs.

Figure 8.20 is a listing of the program and it follows the flowchart step for step. Equates are used to define the printer output port and BUSY input port addresses. Note that the IN AL,BUSY instruction resets the $\overline{\text{STROBE}}$ pulse. Because the instruction *LOOP POLL* occurs between the reset and set $\overline{\text{STROBE}}$ instructions, the $\overline{\text{STROBE}}$ pulse width increases to 27 T states or 5.4 μs.

The most important point to note about this interface is the use of the $\overline{\text{STROBE}}$ and BUSY signals to synchronize the microprocessor and peripheral. Because the transfer

```
                          TITLE    Fig8.20

                     ;Function:   Fig. 8.19 polled printer driver.
                     ;Inputs:     Number of bytes and address of first
                     ;            byte assumed stored in PRINT_DATA segment.
                     ;Outputs:    Character to be printed at port PRINTER.
                     ;Calls:      None
                     ;Destroys:   AX, CX, SI, DS, flags


0000                 PRINT_DATA   SEGMENT  WORD
0000    ????              NUMB        DW    ?          ;Number of bytes
0002    ????????          ADDR        DD    ?          ;Address of first byte
0006                 PRINT_DATA   ENDS

= 0002                    PRINTER     EQU   2          ;Printer port
= 0003                    STATUS      EQU   3          ;BUSY status port

0000                 CODE      SEGMENT
                          ASSUME   CS:CODE, DS:PRINT_DATA

                     FIG8_20  PROC     FAR
0000    B8  ---- R   START:   MOV      AX,PRINT_DATA    ;Load DS with
0003    8E D8                 MOV      DS,AX            ;address of PRINT_DATA.
0005    8B 0E 0000 R          MOV      CX,NUMB          ;Get number of bytes
0009    C5 36 0002 R          LDS      SI,ADDR          ;Get address of data
                                                        ;to DS:SI.
000D    FC                    CLD                       ;Auto increment

000E    E4 03        POLL:    IN       AL,STATUS        ;Set STROBE = 1    +[10]
                                                        ;Input BUSY flag
0010    A8 80                 TEST     AL,10000000B     ;Test BUSY         + [4]
0012    75 FA                 JNZ      POLL             ;Wait until READY +[16]

0014    AC                    LODSB                     ;Get byte          [12]
                                                        ;and advance pointer.
0015    E6 02                 OUT      PRINTER,AL       ;Output to printer [10]
0017    E6 03                 OUT      3,AL             ;STROBE = 0        [10]
0019    E2 F3                 LOOP     POLL             ;Do CX times       [17]

001B    E4 03                 IN       AL,STATUS        ;Quit with STROBE = 1
001D    CB                    RET                       ;Then return
001E                 FIG8_20  ENDP
001E                 CODE     ENDS
                              END      START
```

Figure 8.20 Control program for the parallel printer interface shown in Fig. 8.19.

of data to the printer is done under program control, the technique is referred to as *programmed I/O*.

Note the three instructions in the program marked with the symbol " + ". These three instructions form the polling loop. Using the T-state information enclosed in brackets, the 8086 requires 30 T states or 6 μs (at 5 MHz) to poll the printer. However, the printer requires 10 ms, or 10,000 μs, to print each character. Therefore, the instructions in the polling loop will be executed 10,000/6 = 1666 times between each printed character.

Stated another way, the CPU will ask the printer "Are you ready?" and receive the reply "No!" 1666 times before the next character can finally be output. This suggests that polling may be a rather inefficient way of controlling the printer. Most of the time the CPU is simply waiting for the printer to be READY. And even when it is, only about 10 μs is required to feed the printer another character (49 T states). Then the CPU must wait another 10,000 μs for that character to be printed.

But maybe you are thinking, what does it matter? What else does the CPU have to do anyway? Depending on the system, perhaps nothing. But if the printer is being used to print a 40-page report, you may have a 30-minute wait (or longer) before the system can be used for some other job. It also seems intuitively "wrong" to have a microprocessor as powerful as the 8086 simply "spinning its wheels" waiting for the slow printer to be done.

So now you ought to be thinking about a way to make the CPU (appear to) do two jobs simultaneously. Then you could work on some other task while the long text file was being printed. In Sec. 8.4 we see exactly how to do this.

Data Transfer Rate

Clearly, the 8086 is capable of interfacing faster peripherals than the printer in the last example. But how fast? We can calculate the maximum rate at which the program can transfer data by assuming the peripheral will be ready after only one loop through the polling instructions. In this example 30 T states are required to test the BUSY flag, and 49 T states to fetch the data byte, advance the pointer, generate the strobe pulse, and test for done. In all, 79 T states are required or 15.8 μs at 5 MHz. This corresponds to a *data transfer rate* of 63,291 characters/s.

To put this number into perspective, an 8-inch double-density disk drive reads and writes data to a floppy disk at 62,500 bytes/s. Thus the 8086 might be (marginally) fast enough to interface this peripheral.[7] Usually, when a fast peripheral such as a disk drive must be controlled, a *direct memory access* (DMA) approach is used. This is discussed in Sec. 8.5.

Response Time

A typical microcomputer system may have several different peripherals. These might include floppy-disk drives, dot-matrix printers, daisy-wheel printers, modems, video

---

[7]The T states shown in Fig. 8.20 are "best case." They assume that all instructions are in the queue, and no memory WAIT states.

Video terminal	Modem	DAC	ADC	Plotter	Daisy-wheel printer	Line printer	Floppy disk
7	6	5	4	3	2	1	0

Figure 8.21 One 8-bit input port can be used to monitor the BUSY/READY status of eight separate peripherals. (From J. Uffenbeck, *Microcomputers and Microprocessors: The 8080, 8085, and Z-80*. Prentice-Hall, Englewood Cliffs, N.J., 1985.)

display terminals, and so on. If polling is to be used to control these devices, each must supply a BUSY/READY flag. Figure 8.21 shows an example in which the BUSY status of eight different peripherals can be monitored through one input (status) port.

A routine to test each of these flags and branch to the appropriate program is shown in Fig. 8.22. When several peripherals are interfaced in this manner, the response time, that is, the time from BUSY/READY = READY to service by the microprocessor, becomes important. For example, in the previous printer example, the polling loop required 6 µs to execute. Thus in the worst case, this loop would require 6 µs to detect BUSY/READY = READY and transfer control to a printer output routine.

But what happens as additional peripherals are added? Referring to Fig. 8.22, if

```
POLL     IN      AL,2            ;Read status port         [10]
         ;
         TEST    AL,00000001B    ;Test bit 0               [4]
         JZ      SKIP0           ;Not ready so skip        [4/16]
         JMP     FD              ;Floppy-disk              [15]
         ;
SKIP0:   TEST    AL,00000010B    ;Test bit 1               [4]
         JZ      SKIP1           ;Not ready so skip        [4/16]
         JMP     LP              ;Line printer             [15]
         ;
SKIP1:   TEST    AL,00000100B    ;Test bit 2               [4]
         JZ      SKIP2           ;Not ready so skip        [4/16]
         JMP     FD              ;Daisy-wheel printer      [15]
         ;
SKIP2:   TEST    AL,00001000B    ;Test bit 3               [4]
         JZ      SKIP3           ;Not ready so skip        [4/16]
         JMP     LP              ;Plotter                  [15]
         ;
SKIP3:   TEST    AL,00010000B    ;Test bit 4               [4]
         JZ      SKIP4           ;Not ready so skip        [4/16]
         JMP     FD              ;Analog-digital conv.     [15]
         ;
SKIP4:   TEST    AL,00100000B    ;Test bit 5               [4]
         JZ      SKIP5           ;Not ready so skip        [4/16]
         JMP     LP              ;Digital-analog conv.     [15]
         ;
SKIP5:   TEST    AL,01000000B    ;Test bit 6               [4]
         JZ      SKIP6           ;Not ready so skip        [4/16]
         JMP     FD              ;Modem                    [15]
         ;
SKIP6:   TEST    AL,10000000B    ;Test bit 7               [4]
         JZ      POLL            ;Not ready so redo        [4/16]
         JMP     LP              ;Terminal                 [15]
```

Figure 8.22 Polling can be extended to several peripherals. This routine tests the BUSY/READY status of all eight peripherals in Fig. 8.21. T states are listed along the right margin. (From J. Uffenbeck, *Microcomputers and Microprocessors: The 8080, 8085, and Z-80*. Prentice-Hall, Englewood Cliffs, N.J., 1985.)

the video terminal becomes READY just as the JZ POLL instruction is being executed, all the other peripherals will have to be polled before this device can be serviced. The response time will be

$$T = [16 + 10 + (4 + 16) \times 7 + 4 + 4 + 15] \times 200 \text{ ns}$$
$$= 189 \text{ T states} \times 200 \text{ ns} = 37.8 \text{ } \mu\text{s}$$

Now if the terminal is running at 19,200 baud, a new character will be received only once every

$$\frac{1 \text{ s}}{19,200 \text{ bits}} \times \frac{9 \text{ bits}}{\text{character}} = 469 \text{ } \mu\text{s}$$

assuming 7 data bits, 1 start bit, and 1 stop bit. This still leaves 469 μs − 38 μs = 431 μs to process this character.

But now consider a floppy-disk interface. Using an 8-inch double-density controller, data is transferred at the rate of 500,000 bits per second. This is 62,500 bytes per second or one new character every 16 μs. Assuming the same worst case as for the video terminal, 37.8 μs could elapse before the floppy-disk routine is started. The response time is obviously too long and several characters will be lost.

The situation could actually be much worse. If each of the peripherals happens to be READY, the floppy disk would have to wait for each of these devices to be serviced. At 100 μs per routine, this could add another 700 μs to the response time.

One solution to this problem is to have the CPU supply its own BUSY/READY flag. This flag tells the peripheral not to send any new data until the CPU announces READY. This technique is used in many RS-232C serial interfaces and will be discussed in Chap. 10. However, some peripherals, like the floppy-disk drive, cannot be stopped once they have begun sending their data. These devices must be given a high *priority* so that they are serviced before all others. With polling this is easily done by polling the highest-priority device first.

Establishing a polling priority may still not be a satisfactory solution, however. If each service routine returns control to the head of the polling loop—as it should to maintain the priority structure—the higher-priority devices may "hog" all of the CPU's time. The result will be that the lower-priority devices become "starved" for service.

The real problem is the polling concept itself. Although very simple to implement in hardware and software, it is inefficient in its use of the resources of the computer system. When multiple peripherals are involved, polling may become totally unsatisfactory.

In Sections 8.4 and 8.5 we introduce the topics of *interrupts* and *DMA*. Both of these techniques are alternatives to polling but at the expense of more complex hardware.

SELF-REVIEW 8.3 (answers on pages 410-411)

8.3.1. Polling a peripheral's BUSY/READY flag is one way of _____ the microprocessor to a slow-speed peripheral.

8.3.2. List the handshaking signals supplied by the printer in Fig. 8.19.

8.3.3. Why is polling an inefficient way of controlling a slow peripheral?

8.3.4. In Fig. 8.19 the _____ signal initiates the $\overline{\text{STROBE}}$ pulse and the _____ signal terminates this pulse.

8.3.5. Using the polling routine shown in Fig. 8.22, the plotter has _____ priority than the line printer.

8.4 INTERRUPT-DRIVEN I/O

When interfacing a peripheral to a microprocessor the real problem for the microprocessor is not knowing when the peripheral is READY. That is, the peripheral operates *asynchronously* with respect to the microprocessor.

As we have just seen, one solution is to program the CPU to repeatedly poll the peripheral's BUSY/READY flag. However, this has a built-in disadvantage in that all the resources of the processor are devoted to waiting for this flag. No other tasks can be performed. If the peripheral is READY only once every 10,000 μs (as was true with the parallel printer), the CPU will spend most of its time waiting.

A more logical approach would be to have the peripheral "tell the CPU" when it is READY. This is the purpose of the microprocessor's *interrupt* input. At the end of each instruction the processor samples this line. If it is active, control is transferred to a special *interrupt service routine* (ISR).

Figure 8.23 diagrams the CPU's response to an interrupt. During time 1 the processor is assumed to be executing its main task. At time 2 the peripheral's READY flag causes an interrupt to occur. After finishing the current instruction at time 3, the CS, IP, and flag registers are pushed onto the stack at time 4. Control then transfers to the ISR at time 5. During time 6 the ISR is executed, terminating with the instruction IRET (interrupt return). The CS, IP, and flag registers are recovered from the stack during time 7 and the original task is resumed at time 8.

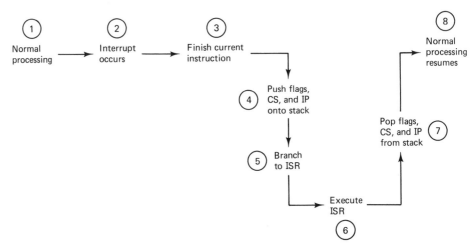

Figure 8.23 When an interrupt occurs, normal processing is suspended while a special interrupt service routine (ISR) is executed. Normal processing resumes when this routine is completed.

If we assume that 100 µs is required to respond to the interrupt and supply the peripheral with data, then in the case of the 10,000-µs/character printer, 9,900 µs will be available to the processor for its main task. In effect, the processor can perform two jobs at the same time.

The 8086 has two interrupt pins, labeled *INTR* and *NMI*. In this section we see how to use these pins to generate an interrupt request and study the CPU's response to each. The parallel printer interface will again be used as an example with appropriate modifications to accommodate the 8086's INTR input.

Types of Interrupts

The 8086 has seven different interrupt types, as listed in Table 8.5. NMI and INTR are external interrupts requested via hardware. INT n, INTO, and the special single-byte INT 3 breakpoint instruction are software interrupts placed as desired within a program. The divide-by-0 and single-step interrupts are initiated by the CPU: the former if the quotient produced by a divide instruction exceeds the capacity of the destination register, and the latter at the completion of each instruction, if TF is set.

Figure 8.24 flowcharts the 8086's response to each of these types of interrupts. In all cases the current instruction is allowed to finish before the interrupt is processed. Internal interrupts (except single-step) have precedence or *priority* over simultaneous (within the same instruction) external interrupt requests. For example, if an interrupt request occurs on INTR, but the current instruction causes a divide-by-zero interrupt, the later will be serviced first. Similarly if simultaneous interrupts occur on INTR and NMI, NMI will be serviced first.

When the interrupt is serviced, the flags, CS, and IP registers are pushed onto the stack, saving the CPU's "place" in memory. This means that six bytes will be pushed onto the stack. The TF status is saved so that the interrupted instruction will still be single-stepped (if TF is set). However, before executing the ISR, TF and IF are cleared, disabling INTR and the single-step mechanism within this routine. If desired, these flags can be set, enabling these interrupts. That is, interrupts can be allowed to interrupt themselves.

Be sure that you understand the difference between simultaneous interrupts and interrupts occurring within an ISR. In the first case the priority structure shown in Fig. 8.24 applies—the highest-priority input will be serviced first.

However, if an internal interrupt is being serviced and an NMI (or INTR if IF is set) occurs, the ISR for the internal interrupt will be suspended and the external interrupt honored, even though it is of lower priority. The priority structure applies only to *simultaneous* interrupt requests.

NMI is a *nonmaskable interrupt*, which means that it cannot be blocked. INTR, on the other hand, is maskable via the IF flag. Only when this flag is set will interrupts on this input be accepted. Also note that although internal interrupts have priority over external interrupts, the NMI request will be honored as soon as the internal interrupt's ISR begins (note the NMI decision block located after the CALL ISR block in Fig. 8.24). The same is *not* true for the INTR input, however. This is because IF is cleared automatically when the internal interrupt is serviced.

Because the NMI input is nonmaskable, care must be taken when using this interrupt.

TABLE 8.5 8086 INTERRUPT TYPES[a]

Name	Initated by:	Maskable?	Trigger	Priority	Acknowledge signal?	Vector table address	Interrupt latency
NMI	External hardware	No	↑ Edge, hold 2 T states min.	2	None	00008H–0000BH	Current instruction + 51 T states
INTR	External hardware	Yes via IF	High level until acknowledged	3	$\overline{\text{INTA}}$	n * 4[b]	Current instruction + 61 T states
INT n	Internal via software	No	None	1	None	n * 4	51 T states
INT 3 (breakpoint)	Internal via software	No	None	1	None	0000CH–0000FH	52 T states
INTO	Internal via software	No	None	1	None	00010H–00013H	53 T states
Divide-by-0	Internal via CPU	Yes via OF	None	1	None	00000H–00003H	51 T states
Single-step	Internal via CPU	Yes via TF	None	4	None	00004H–00007H	51 T states

[a]All interrupt types cause the flags, CS, and IP registers to be pushed onto the stack. In addition, the IF and TF flags are cleared.
[b]n is an 8-bit type number read during the second INTA pulse.

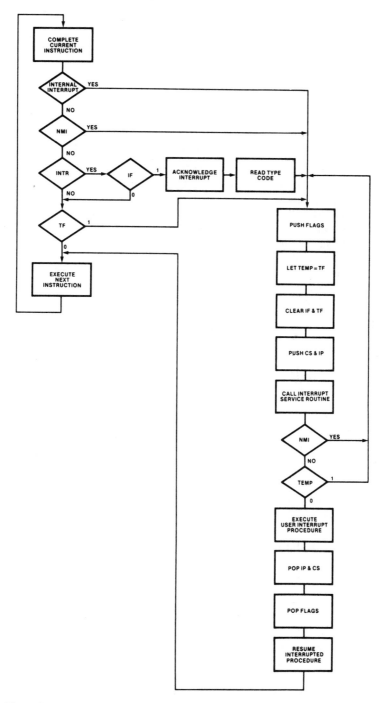

Figure 8.24 8086 interrupt processing sequence. INT n, INTO, INT 3, and INT 0 are considered internal interrupts. (Courtesy of Intel Corporation.)

This is because there may be some programs that you do not want interrupted—reading or writing data to a disk drive, for example. For this reason, the NMI input is normally reserved for *catastrophic* events such as memory error or an impending power failure.

The following example will illustrate how the priority is resolved when multiple interrupts occur within the same instruction.

Example 8.10

Assume that TF and IF = 1. If NMI and INTR interrupts occur simultaneously, which interrupt will be accepted? Will the ISR be single-stepped?

Solution Figure 8.25 diagrams the instruction flow. When the current instruction completes, three interrupts will be pending: NMI, INTR, and single-step. As shown in Fig. 8.24, NMI has highest priority, so it will be recognized first. However, after pushing the flags, clearing IF and TF, and pushing CS, single-step will be recognized (because TEMP = 1). This means the current instruction's single-step procedure will be executed *before* the NMI ISR. In effect, the single-step interrupt has highest priority.

When this routine completes, the flags will be restored to their pre-single-step values (IF and TF = 0) and the NMI procedure executed. Because both flags are cleared, neither single-step nor INTR will be recognized within this routine. When the IRET instruction is executed (interrupt return), the flags will be restored to their original values (TF and IF = 1) *but not until the next main line instruction is executed*.

INTR will now be recognized, the flags pushed and then cleared, and CS and IP pushed. Because TEMP is again set, the single-step routine (for the second mainline instruction) will first be allowed to execute. Upon completion, the INTR procedure will execute. Again, because TF is cleared, this routine will not be single-stepped.

Note: As with IRET, the STI instruction will not enable interrupts on INTR until after the *next* instruction has executed.

The address of the interrupt service routine is stored in four consecutive memory locations (a double word) in an *interrupt vector table* beginning at address 00000H. All the interrupts listed in Table 8.5 except INTR either supply an 8-bit *type number* as part of the instruction or have a *predefined* type number that points to one of the 256 ISR addresses in this vector table.

The 8086 determines the particular vector to be used by multiplying the type number by 4. The 10-bit result points to one of the 256 four-byte vectors.

Example 8.11

A particular interrupt has a type number n = 41H. If the ISR begins at address 09E3:0010H, determine the locations in the vector table to store this address.

Solution The vector address is calculated by multiplying 41H by 4. This is done most easily by rotating 41H left twice. 41H = 01000001; rotate left twice → 100000100 = 104H or 00104H. IP is stored in the low word location and CS in the high word location.

00107H:	09H
00106H:	E3H
00105H:	00H
00104H:	10H

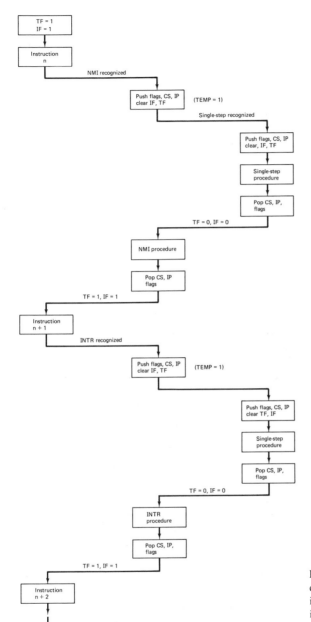

Figure 8.25 When an NMI or INTR request occurs, TF is cleared, causing the service routine to run at normal speed. The IRET instruction restores TF, causing the mainline program to be single-stepped.

As shown in Table 8.5, the NMI interrupt is predefined as type 2 and thus extracts its vector from locations 00008–0000BH. INTR, however, must gate its type number onto data bus lines AD0–AD7 during a special *interrupt acknowledge bus cycle*. The timing for this cycle and the hardware required to read the type number are explained in the next section.

External Interrupt Timing

The 8086 samples the INTR and NMI inputs during the last T state of the last bus cycle of each instruction. The NMI input is rising-edge triggered and internally synchronized. It must be held high for at least two clock states to guarantee recognition by the CPU.

The INTR input is level triggered and must be held high until acknowledged by the CPU. INTA is the acknowledge signal output by the CPU for this purpose. When INTA = 0 it indicates that the 8086 has detected and accepted the interrupt request. This can occur only if IF = 1, enabling this interrupt. Note that the INTA output applies only to INTR. The NMI input (and all internal interrupts) are not acknowledged.

Figure 8.26 shows the timing for an interrupt acknowledge bus cycle. INTR must meet a two-T-state setup time prior to state T4 of the interrupted instruction. If this condition is not met, the interrupt will not be accepted until the end of the *next* instruction. Note that this wait might involve more than 100 T states in the case of the multiplication and division instructions.

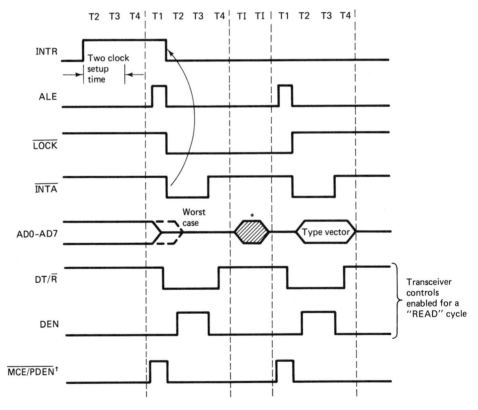

*Redriven by CPU if queue is not full
†Used to enable master 8259A PIC cascade address onto local bus

Figure 8.26 Maximum-mode timing for the INTR input. Two interrupt acknowledge bus cycles are executed.

Basic Input/Output   Chap. 8

When the interrupt is accepted, two interrupt acknowledge cycles are executed, separated by two bus idle cycles, as shown in Fig. 8.26. The first $\overline{\text{INTA}}$ pulse acknowledges the interrupt request and alerts the external hardware to prepare to gate the type number onto the data bus lines. During the second $\overline{\text{INTA}}$ pulse the CPU will input the contents of AD0–AD7 and interpret this data as one of 256 possible type numbers.

Notice that the data bus transceiver control signals DT/$\overline{\text{R}}$ and DEN are enabled the same as they would be for an I/O or memory read bus cycle. The $\overline{\text{LOCK}}$ signal (maximum mode only) is output during the first $\overline{\text{INTA}}$ cycle and can be used to prevent another processor from requesting use of the buses while the type number is being read.

Figure 8.27(a) shows a circuit that can be used to drive the INTR input of the 8086. In this case the peripheral is assumed to supply a falling edge to indicate that it is ready for more data. This signal clocks the flip-flop, driving INTR high. The first $\overline{\text{INTA}}$ pulse resets Q, removing INTR before it can be interpreted as a second interrupt request. The RESET input ensures that INTR will be low after the system is reset.

Figure 8.27(b) illustrates a technique for gating the type number onto the low data bus lines. The $\overline{\text{LOCK}}$ signal is combined with $\overline{\text{INTA}}$ to enable the tri-state gates during the *second* $\overline{\text{INTA}}$ pulse when the CPU expects the type number. In this case the gates are wired to input n = 41H.

The circuits in Fig. 8.27 limit the 8086 to one (maskable) hardware interrupt. This may be sufficient in some small systems but will be inadequate for most CPU configurations. For this reason Intel has developed the 8259A *programmable interrupt controller* (PIC).

The PIC is a very flexible peripheral controller chip programmed via software commands from the 8086. It accepts eight interrupt inputs (expandable to 64), each of which can be masked. Various priority schemes can also be programmed. When an interrupt occurs, the PIC determines the highest-priority request, activates the 8086 via its INTR input, and gates the type number onto the data bus during the $\overline{\text{INTA}}$ bus cycle. The PIC is discussed in detail in Chap. 9.

Response Time

As we learned in Sec. 8.3, the basic polling loop of IN, TEST, and JNZ requires 30 T states and can be executed in 6 μs with a 5-MHz 8086 microprocessor. This means that the 8086 can respond to a peripheral's BUSY/READY flag within 6 μs. Of course, the wait can be much longer when several peripherals are to be polled and serviced.

The interrupt response time or *interrupt latency* consists of the time to perform the following:

1. Finish executing the current instruction.
2. Perform two interrupt-acknowledge bus cycles.
3. Push the flags, IP, and CS onto the stack.
4. Calculate the vector table address and transfer control to the ISR.

Figure 8.28 illustrates an example in which the interrupt occurs just before the instruction OUT 27H,AL is about to be executed. Assuming that the setup time has not

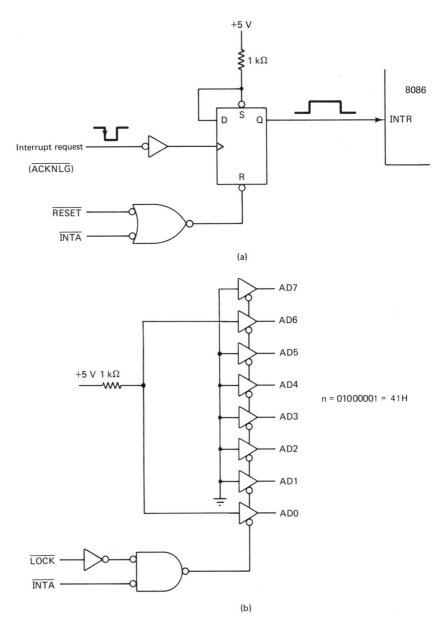

Figure 8.27 (a) Terminating INTR when the interrupt request has been acknowledged; (b) gating the type number onto the data bus with the second $\overline{\text{INTA}}$ pulse.

been met, the CPU will have to wait 10 T states for the OUT instruction to complete, 10 more T states for the interrupt acknowledge cycle, and 51 T states to store the flags, IP, and CS registers, and to branch to the ISR. At 5MHz the response time is 14.2 μs.

In a worst case, the result could be much longer. For example, what if the current instruction was ROR [BX+DI+7],CL with CL = FFH? The execution time of this

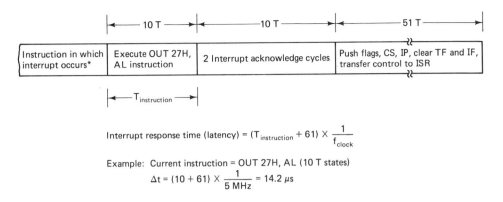

$$\longleftarrow 10\ T \longrightarrow \longleftarrow 10\ T \longrightarrow \longleftarrow 51\ T \longrightarrow$$

| Instruction in which interrupt occurs* | Execute OUT 27H, AL instruction | 2 Interrupt acknowledge cycles | Push flags, CS, IP, clear TF and IF, transfer control to ISR |

$$\longleftarrow T_{instruction} \longrightarrow$$

Interrupt response time (latency) = $(T_{instruction} + 61) \times \dfrac{1}{f_{clock}}$

Example: Current instruction = OUT 27H, AL (10 T states)

$$\Delta t = (10 + 61) \times \frac{1}{5\ \text{MHz}} = 14.2\ \mu s$$

*Just missed setup time.

Figure 8.28 The interrupt response time is made up of the time to finish the current instruction, the two interrupt acknowledge bus cycles, and 51 T states to save CS, IP, and the flags and transfer control to the ISR address.

instruction is

$$T = (20 + EA + 4 \times CL) \times \frac{1}{f}$$

The based and indexed addressing mode requires 12 T states for the effective address calculation, and with CL = 255, 1052 total T states are required. The response time becomes 210.4 μs.

Because the NMI input does not perform interrupt acknowledge cycles, its latency is the current instruction plus 51 T states. Although this saves 10 T states, this would only shorten the preceding result to 208.4 μs.

Are you surprised by this result? Until now interrupts appeared to be the ideal solution to combat the inefficiency associated with polling. Unfortunately, there is a considerable amount of "software overhead" associated with interrupt-driven I/O. The 8086's powerful instruction set is its own demise in this case.

But we should also keep things in perspective. The 210-μs response time represents less than 3% of the time required by the 100-cps printer to print one character. Allowing another 1% to supply the printer with data still leaves 96% of the CPU's time free for some other task.

It is also interesting to note that the 80186 microprocessor executes most of the 8086's instructions with one-third to one-fourth the number of T states. For example, the ROR instruction requires only 1 T state per rotate instead of the 8086's 4 T states. This can have a significant effect on the interrupt latency.

Finally, you should note that some instructions cannot be interrupted: namely, the POP *segment register* and MOV *segment register* instructions. An interrupt occurring during these instructions will not be accepted until the instruction following the POP or MOV. This is done to protect the program from ending up with a new stack segment but the "old" stack pointer.

The LOCK and segment override prefixes are considered part of the instruction they preface and thus also cannot be interrupted. The REP prefix is an exception, however.

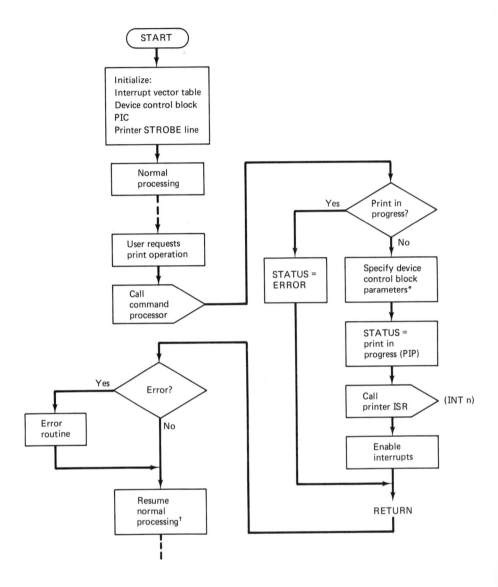

*This block could transfer control to a disk read routine, transferring one sector of data to the print buffer
†Printer periodically interrupts as necessary for additional data

Figure 8.29 The printer command processor is called from within the mainline program whenever the user requires a print operation.

Used with the string group of instructions, interrupts will be honored between repeated string operations. Interrupts are also honored while the WAIT instruction is "waiting" for the TEST input to go low.

Setting Up the Interrupt Vector and Service Routine

Having seen the hardware details of the 8086's interrupt inputs, we need to turn our attention to the software. There are two problems to be solved:

1. Store the ISR address at the appropriate location in the interrupt vector table.
2. Write the ISR as a procedure terminated with IRET.

Let us continue to use the parallel printer interface shown in Fig. 8.19 as an example. However, rather than poll the BUSY line, the printer's $\overline{\text{ACKNLG}}$ signal will be connected to the interrupt request circuit shown in Fig. 8.27(a). Let's assume a type number n = 20H as shown in Fig. 8.27(b).

When the printer finishes printing a character its $\overline{\text{ACKNLG}}$ pulse will request an interrupt. The 8086 will suspend its current task and transfer control to the printer service routine. This program will output a new byte to the printer and then return control to the suspended program by executing an IRET instruction.

The software required to control an interrupt-driven peripheral such as this parallel printer is called a *device driver*. This program is actually made up of two parts: a *command processor* and the *interrupt service routine*. Figure 8.29 shows how the command processor is activated from within the mainline program.

The main program begins by performing a system initialization. This is a sequence of instructions that program the I/O devices to a known state (STROBE = high, for example), specify the interrupt vectors, and load initial data into any memory tables. The program then begins normal processing, depending on its function.

At some point in the main program the user requests that a print operation occur. The program responds by transferring control to the printer *command processor*. This procedure checks to make sure that a previous print is not in progress, and then specifies the parameters of the printer *device control block* (DCB). This is a section of memory used to transfer data between the main program and the interrupt service routine. Table 8.6 defines the DCB parameters used for this example.

Note that the command processor may transfer control to another routine, which retrieves the data to be printed and fills in the DCB parameters. Alternatively, these

TABLE 8.6 PRINTER DEVICE CONTROL BLOCK DEFINITIONS

Name	Description
STATUS	A one-byte field used to identify if the previous print has completed (GOOD), is in progress (PIP), or if an error has occurred (ERROR)
BUF_ADDR	A four-byte field storing the base address of the data table containing the characters to be printed
CHAR_COUNT	A two-byte field storing the number of bytes to be printed
CHAR_XFER	A two-byte field storing the current number of bytes transferred

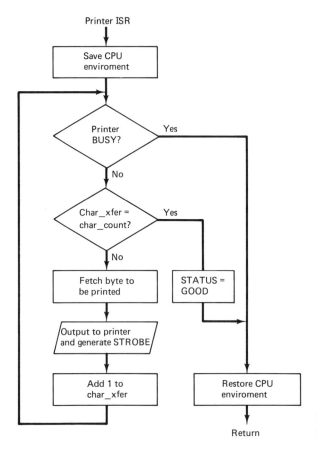

Printer ISR

Save CPU
enviroment

Printer BUSY? — Yes

No

Char_xfer = char_count? — Yes

No

Fetch byte to be printed

STATUS = GOOD

Output to printer and generate STROBE

Add 1 to char_xfer

Restore CPU enviroment

Return

Figure 8.30 Flowchart for the printer interrupt service routine.

parameters might be passed from the main program when the print is first requested. In either case, the STATUS byte is loaded with PIP (print in progress) and a software interrupt is used to transfer control to the printer's interrupt service routine. This is done to start up the print process for the first time.

Upon returning from the ISR, the command processor enables interrupts. This allows the printer's $\overline{\text{ACKNLG}}$ signal to initiate all further print requests. The command processor is not executed again until the user requests another print operation.

Figure 8.30 flowcharts the printer ISR. Because some printers have an internal buffer, polling is used to write bytes to this buffer until the BUSY flag is set. In this way several hundred bytes may be output to the printer with each ACKNLG pulse. When the number of characters transferred equals the character count, the print job is finished and the ISR sets the STATUS to GOOD.

The assembly language listing for the entire program is given in Figs. 8.31(a) through 8.31(e). There are several important points to note about this program.

1. The statements in Fig. 8.31(a) set up an interrupt vector table segment and DCB. Note the use of the **SEGMENT AT** statement. Although this cannot be used to

```
                        ;*******
                        ; Parallel Printer Device Driver -
                        ;    Interrupt vector table, device control
                        ;    block, program equates
                        ;*******

                        ; Set up segment at absolute address 0000
                        ; Printer generates type 65 interrupt

0000                    INT_VEC_TABLE   SEGMENT AT 0
0104                            ORG             65*4
0104                            PRINT_INT       LABEL   DWORD
0104                    INT_VEC_TABLE   ENDS

                        ;Set up and initialize the device control block

0000                    DEV_CTRL_BLK    SEGMENT BYTE

                        ;The following equates define the status byte

= 0000                          GOOD            EQU     00H     ;Good transfer
= 0001                          ERROR           EQU     01H     ;Previous print in progress
= 0002                          PIP             EQU     02H     ;Print in progress flag

0000  00                        STATUS          DB      GOOD        ;Current print status
0001  00 00 00 20               BUF_ADDR        DD      20000000H   ;Print buffer starting address
0005  ????                      CHAR_COUNT      DW      ?           ;Number of bytes to be printed
0007  ????                      CHAR_XFER       DW      ?           ;Current number of bytes transferred
0009                    DEV_CTRL_BLK    ENDS

                        ;Printer equates

= 0002                          PR_PORT         EQU     02H     ;Printer output port address
= 0003                          PR_STATUS       EQU     03H     ;BUSY/READY status port address
= 0003                          STROBE          EQU     03H     ;STROBE signal port address
= 0080                          BUSY            EQU     80H     ;Mask for BUSY/READY - bit D7

                        ;8259A PIC equates

= 0013                          ICW1    EQU     00010011B       ;Edge triggerred,single,ICW4 to follow
= 0040                          ICW2    EQU     01000000B       ;PIC base vector = 40H
= 0001                          ICW4    EQU     00000001B       ;NSFNM,non buffered,normal EOI,8086
= 00FD                          PMASK   EQU     11111101B       ;Mask all but IR1, the printer interrupt
= 00F2                          PIC_A   EQU     0F2H            ;PIC base port address
= 00F3                          PIC_B   EQU     0F3H            ;Second port
= 0020                          EOI     EQU     20H             ;OCW2 - nonspecific EOI
```

Figure 8.31   (a) Program to set up the interrupt vector segment and device control block. Equates are used to identify the printer and PIC program codes.

```
                              ;********
                              ;  Parallel Printer Device Driver -
                              ;      Initialization routines
                              ;********

0000                          CODE    SEGMENT PUBLIC
                                      ASSUME  CS:CODE, DS:INT_VEC_TABLE

                              ;Load printer interrupt vector

0000 FA                       START:  CLI                              ;No interrupts until initialized
0001 B8 0000                          MOV     AX,0                     ;Base of INT_VEC_TABLE
0004 8E D8                             MOV     DS,AX                    ;Point DS at INT_VEC_TABLE
0006 C7 06 0104 R 0069 R               MOV     PRINT_INT,OFFSET PR_ISR  ;Store offset of printer ISR
000C C7 06 0106 R  ---- R              MOV     PRINT_INT+2,SEG PR_ISR   ;Store segment of printer ISR

                              ;Ouptut PIC program codes

0012 B0 13                             MOV     AL,ICW1                  ;Program PIC
0014 E6 F2                             OUT     PIC_A,AL
0016 B0 40                             MOV     AL,ICW2
0018 E6 F3                             OUT     PIC_B,AL
001A B0 01                             MOV     AL,ICW4
001C E6 F3                             OUT     PIC_B,AL
001E B0 FD                             MOV     AL,PMASK
0020 E6 F3                             OUT     PIC_B,AL

                              ;Make sure STROBE line is high

0022 E4 03                             IN      AL,STROBE                ;DSP sets flip-flop
```

Figure 8.31 (b) Interrupt vector and PIC initialization routines.

force code to be loaded at a particular address, it does allow a *label* to be defined at specific locations in memory.

In this example the **ORG 65*4** statement causes the location counter to associate the label PRINT_INT with address 0000:0104. This corresponds to the vector location for a type 41H interrupt assumed generated by the printer interrupt interface.

2. The DCB is defined as a segment, with the DB, DW, and DD operators used to reserve space for the appropriate parameters (to be specified later by the command processor). The print buffer is arbitrarily selected to begin at 2000:0000H.

3. Equates are used liberally throughout the program to make it more "readable."

4. Instead of using the interrupt interface shown in Fig. 8.27, an 8259A PIC is assumed. This is transparant to the printer except to note that the PIC is programmed for a rising-edge trigger (instead of the 8086's high-level trigger). The programming codes shown in Fig. 8.31(a) initialize the PIC and programs it such that a type number of 65 will be gated onto the data bus when the printer's $\overline{\text{ACKNLG}}$ pulse occurs. These codes are explained in detail in Chap. 9.

5. Figure 8.31(b) shows how the offset and segment addresses of the printer ISR (PR_ISR) are loaded into the interrupt vector. This was the point of defining the label PRINT_INT in Fig. 8.31(a).

```
                        ;#######
                        ;  Parallel Printer Device Driver -
                        ;     Main program
                        ;#######


                        ;Normal processing occurs

                        ;User requests a file to be printed

                                ASSUME  CS:CODE, DS:DEV_CTRL_BLK      ;Following labels are in DEV_CTRL_BLK
0024  1E                        PUSH    DS                           ;Save main program's DS
0025  B8 ---- R                 MOV     AX,DEV_CTRL_BLK              ;Point DS at DEV_CTRL_BLK
0028  8E D8                     MOV     DS,AX
002A  E8 0046 R                 CALL    COM_PROC                     ;Transfer control to command processor

                        ;Command processor returns control to main
                        ;program after starting the I/O.  STATUS
                        ;holds error condition (if any).

002D  80 3E 0000 R 01          CMP     STATUS,ERROR                 ;Was a print already in progress?
0032  1F                        POP     DS                           ;Recover main program's DS
0033  74 0F                     JE      ERROR_ROUTINE                ;Notify user of error

                        ;Normal processing now resumes (simulated by
                        ;the closed loop that follows)

0035  90              SIMU:     NOP
0036  EB FD                     JMP     SIMU

0038                    ERROR_ROUTINE:
                        ;This routine might notify the user that a
                        ;previous print job is already in progress.
                        ;Control then returns to the main program.

0038  EB FB                     JMP     SIMU                         ;Just a dummy in this case
```

Figure 8.31   (c) Mainline program showing how control is transferred to the command processor.

6. Figure 8.31(c) shows how the main program transfers control to the command processor. The error routine is executed if the command processor returns with STATUS = ERROR.

7. Figure 8.31(d) is the command processor procedure. Note the JMP SHORT QUIT instruction. The SHORT pointer prevents the assembler from generating an unnecessary three-byte near jump instruction.

8. Figure 8.31(e) is the printer interrupt service routine. Because the segment registers will have unknown values when this routine is called, it is necessary to load DS with the DEV_CTRL_BLK address. The CHAR_XFER is used as an index into the buffer so that the instruction ADD SI,AX forms a pointer into this buffer.

9. The EOI byte output to the PIC in Fig. 8.31(e) is required to reset the interrupt request (latched by the PIC). If this is not done, further interrupts will not be honored (by the PIC).

```
                        ;*******
                        ;  Parallel Printer Device Driver -
                        ;      Command processor procedure
                        ;*******

                        ;Function:   Process print command and specify
                        ;            DEV_CTRL_BLK parameters.
                        ;
                        ;Inputs:     DS assumed to point at DEV_CTRL_BLK
                        ;Outputs:    STATUS=ERROR if previous print in
                        ;            progress, else STATUS=PIP.
                        ;Calls:      Printer ISR to start I/O.
                        ;Destroys:   flags

003A                    COM_PROC     PROC   NEAR
003A  80 3E 0000 R 00                CMP    STATUS,GOOD      ;Make sure previous print complete
003F  74 07                          JE     SKIP             ;Else
0041  C6 06 0000 R 01                MOV    STATUS,ERROR     ;Let STATUS = ERROR
0046  EB 14                          JMP    SHORT QUIT       ;And quit
0048  C7 06 0007 R 0000  SKIP:       MOV    CHAR_XFER,0      ;Reset characters transferred to 0
004E  C7 06 0005 R 0200              MOV    CHAR_COUNT,512   ;This example prints 512 byte buffers
0054  C6 06 0000 R 02                MOV    STATUS,PIP       ;Update STATUS to print-in-progress
0059  CD 41                          INT    65               ;Start the first byte "manually"
005B  FB                             STI                     ;Remaining bytes will print automatically
005C  C3                 QUIT:       RET                     ;So return to main program
005D                    COM_PROC     ENDP
```

Figure 8.31   (d) Command processor routine.

As you can see, the software required to interface an interrupt-driven peripheral is more complex than that associated with a status-driven or polled peripheral. This is because the interrupt procedure must be written such that other tasks (the mainline program) can be executed while the I/O is in progress.

Of course, this is precisely the advantage of interrupt-driven I/O. The CPU need service the peripheral only when the peripheral is READY, thus allowing time for other tasks (or peripherals) to be serviced.

The primary disadvantage is the software overhead required. Each time the ISR is entered the buffer address must be retrieved, the character fetched and printed, and the number of characters transferred incremented. In addition, any registers used within the ISR must be pushed onto the stack. The polled routine must fetch the same variables, but only once when the program is first started.

The net effect is to increase the interrupt latency (to the print instruction) and decrease the transfer rate. As a result, some fast peripherals that can be controlled with polling or DMA cannot be controlled with interrupts.

```
;########
;  Parallel Printer Device Driver -
;    Printer interrupt service routine
;########

;Function:    Output bytes from buffer to
;             printer port until printer is
;             BUSY.
;Inputs:      Data to be printed stored
;             beginning at BUF_ADDR
;Outputs:     Data to be printed at PR_PORT.
;             Returns with STATUS=GOOD when
;             all bytes printed.
;Calls:       Nothing
;Destroys     Nothing


005D                  PR_ISR  PROC    NEAR
005D  56                      PUSH    SI                ;Save any registers about to be changed
005E  1E                      PUSH    DS
005F  50                      PUSH    AX

0060  E4 03         POLL:     IN      AL,PR_STATUS      ;If printer BUSY (or off-line)
0062  A8 B0                   TEST    AL,BUSY
0064  75 29                   JNZ     EXIT              ;Then exit this procedure
0066  B8  ---- R               MOV     AX,DEV_CTRL_BLK   ;Make sure DS points to DEV_CTRL_BLK
0069  8E D8                   MOV     DS,AX
006B  A1 0007 R               MOV     AX,CHAR_XFER      ;Check to see if all bytes
006E  3B 06 0005 R            CMP     AX,CHAR_COUNT     ;have been printed.
0072  74 16                   JE      JOB_DONE          ;Then the job is done
0074  1E                      PUSH    DS                ;Save DEV_CTRL_BLK segment
0075  C5 36 0001 R            LDS     SI,BUF_ADDR       ;Point DS at base of the print buffer
0079  03 F0                   ADD     SI,AX             ;Point SI at character to be printed
007B  8A 04                   MOV     AL,[SI]           ;Fetch the byte
007D  E6 02                   OUT     PR_PORT,AL        ;Output to printer
007F  E6 03                   OUT     STROBE,AL         ;STROBE low
0081  E4 03                   IN      AL,STROBE         ;STROBE high
0083  1F                      POP     DS                ;Recover DEV_CTRL_BLK segment
0084  FF 06 0007 R            INC     CHAR_XFER         ;Update characters transferred
0088  EB D6                   JMP     POLL              ;See if printer will accept another

008A          JOB_DONE:
008A  C6 06 0000 R 00         MOV     STATUS,GOOD       ;When all bytes printed STATUS=GOOD

008F  B0 20         EXIT:     MOV     AL,EOI            ;Reset interrupt within PIC
0091  E6 F2                   OUT     PIC_A,AL
0093  58                      POP     AX                ;Restore used registers
0094  1F                      POP     DS
0095  5E                      POP     SI
0096  CF                      IRET                      ;Return to main program
0097                  PR_ISR  ENDP
0097                  CODE    ENDS
                              END     START
```

Figure 8.31   (e) Printer interrupt service routine.

8.4.1. The 8086 has two external interrupt inputs, labeled _____ and _____.

8.4.2. Which registers are saved by the 8086 when an interrupt occurs?

8.4.3. What is the purpose of the interrupt acknowledge bus cycle? Which interrupt types will cause this cycle to occur?

8.4.4. For a single peripheral, the worst-case response time from READY to execution of the first instruction in the service routine is fastest if polling is used.   (True/False)

8.4.5. Assume that IF = 1 and an NMI occurs. While servicing the NMI, an INTR occurs. When will INTR be serviced?

8.4.6. The _____ _____ statement allows a label to be associated with a *specific* memory location.

8.4.7. The _____ _____ _____ allows a mainline program to pass parameters to the command processor and interrupt service routine.

8.4.8. How will the program in Fig. 8.31 respond if the printer is in an *off-line* (BUSY) state when the user selects a print operation?

8.4.9. Why should RET *not* be used to terminate an ISR?

8.5 DIRECT MEMORY ACCESS

We have now seen two different methods for controlling the flow of data through a microcomputer I/O port. In this section we consider a third technique, called *direct memory access* (DMA). Using DMA, the peripheral is synchronized to *main memory*, not the microprocessor.

To appreciate the DMA concept, you must understand that the real bottleneck in the data transfer process is the microprocessor itself. When a text file is output to a disk drive, we are concerned with transferring data from memory to that drive. Yet with the programmed or interrupt-driven I/O approaches, that data must first be read from memory into the CPU and then transferred to the disk drive. The microprocessor is an unnecessary "middleman" in this process, with the result that the transfer rate is decreased.

The DMA approach is to "turn off" the processor and let the disk drive access the data file in memory itself: a sort of *direct memory access*. If the memory can supply a new byte of data every 200 ns, data can potentially be transferred at a rate of 5 million bytes per second!

In this section we consider the protocols used by the 8086 for transferring control of its buses to another bus master, in this case the DMA controller (DMAC). Once the DMAC takes over the buses, there are several different types of DMA operations that can be performed, and these are also covered. Finally, we compare DMA with polling and interrupts and consider the advantages and disadvantages of each technique.

DMA Protocols

Minimum mode.   The term *protocol* is used here to represent the handshaking mechanism used by the processor to release control of its buses to another processor. In the minimum mode two control signals are available: HOLD and HLDA. Figure 8.32 shows how these signals are used by the DMAC.

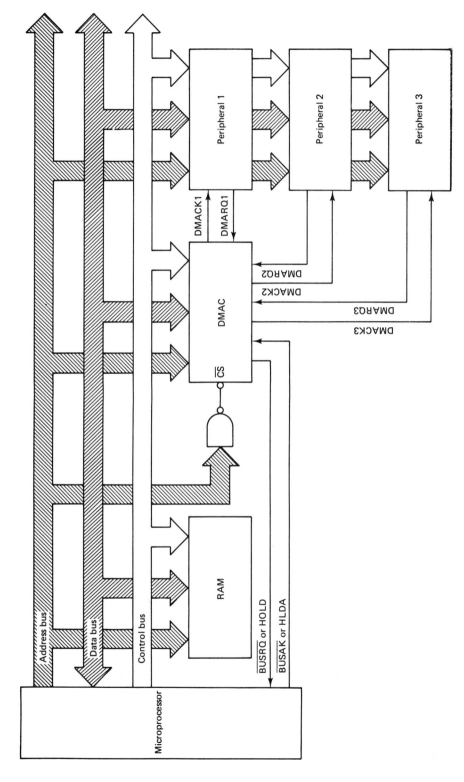

Figure 8.32 A DMA controller allows the peripheral to interface directly with memory without CPU intervention. This allows the data transfer rate to approach the access time of the memory. (From J. Uffenbeck, *Microcomputers and Microprocessors: The 8080, 8085, and Z-80.* Prentice-Hall, Englewood, N.J., 1985.)

The cycle begins with the peripheral requesting service via the DMARQn (DMA request) input of the DMAC. The DMAC, in turn, drives the 8086's HOLD input high, requesting that the CPU enter a HOLD state. The processor responds by finishing the current bus cycle (if any) and then open circuits (tri-states) its address, data, and (most) control signals as shown in Table 8.7. HLDA is then output high by the 8086, acknowledging the hold request. In a system with address, data, and control bus buffers, HLDA is used to disable these buffers so that the CPU is completely disconnected from the memory and I/O. This can be seen in Fig. 6.21.

TABLE 8.7 8086 BUS CONDITION DURING HOLD (MINIMUM MODE)

Signal	Condition
AD0–AD15	
A16/S3–A19/S6	
RD	
IO/$\overline{\text{M}}$	Open circuit
$\overline{\text{WR}}$	
$\overline{\text{INTA}}$	
DT/$\overline{\text{R}}$	
$\overline{\text{DEN}}$	
ALE	Low
HLDA	High

Upon receiving HLDA, the DMAC applies DMACK (DMA acknowledge) to the peripheral requesting service—normally via the *chip select* input of the peripheral. The DMAC is now in control of the system, outputting all the control and address bus signals just as if it were the system processor (which, in fact, it is).

The DMAC is normally programmed by the 8086 prior to the DMA operation for a particular type of transfer. For example, it might be programmed to transfer 100 bytes from memory beginning at address 1000:0000H to I/O port A3H. When the DMAC takes over the buses, it chip selects the output port at A3H, drives the $\overline{\text{IOW}}$ and $\overline{\text{MEMR}}$ control signals low, and then sequentially outputs the address for each of the 100 bytes to be transferred. Note that the data moves directly from memory to the I/O port, not through the DMAC. This allows a very high transfer rate.

Figure 8.33 shows the timing for HOLD and HLDA. The HOLD request must be received THVCH nanoseconds before the rising edge of the last system clock pulse in the current bus cycle. If this setup time is met, HLDA will be output TCLHAV nanoseconds after the second falling edge of the clock. This means that the minimum latency from HOLD to HLDA will be 314 ns, as shown in Fig. 8.33 (assuming a 5-MHz system clock).

In the worst case, the BIU will have just initiated a bus cycle when the HOLD request is received. The latency is calculated as follows:

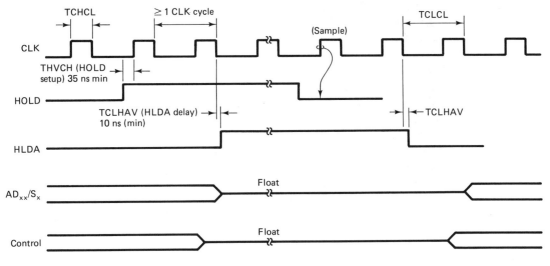

Notes:
1. 5-MHz 8086 minimum-mode CPU assumed
2. DMA processor drives buses during float
3. HOLD-HLDA latency (min) = THVCHmin + TCHCLmin + TCLCL + TCLHAVmin
   = 35 ns + 69 ns + 200 ns + 10 ns
   = 314 ns
4. See the text for worst-case latency

Figure 8.33 HOLD/HLDA timing (minimum mode only).

	THVCH	34 ns	(just missed setup time)
+	TCHCLmax	82 ns	
+		1400 ns	(7–T state instruction)
+	TCLHAVmax	160 ns	
		1.676 μs	

In a "real" worst case, the current bus cycle will require a word access from an odd address. This will require four additional T states (latency = 2.476 μs), as HLDA will not be output during the middle of the two bus cycles.[8]

The HOLD input has a higher priority than INTR or NMI. Thus simultaneous HOLD and interrupt requests will result in the HOLD acknowledge cycle being performed first. However, if the HOLD request occurs at the beginning of an interrupt-acknowledge cycle, that cycle will be allowed to complete before HLDA is output. This increases the HOLD-HLDA latency to 2.876 μs [34 ns + 82 ns + 2600 ns (13 clock cycles for INTA) + 160 ns] assuming a 5-MHz clock.

---

[8]For the 8088, this worst case applies for all word-access bus cycles.

Finally, the LOCK prefix can be used to delay generation of the HLDA signal until the LOCKED instruction has been executed. Note, however, that the $\overline{\text{LOCK}}$ signal itself is not available in the minimum mode.

Maximum mode. When operated in the maximum mode, the 8086 supports a request-grant-release protocol using the bidirectional control lines $\overline{\text{RQ0/GT0}}$ and $\overline{\text{RQ1/}}$ $\overline{\text{GT1}}$. This is a more sophisticated technique that the HOLD-HLDA scheme used in the minimum mode and can be used to allow three processors (including the 8086) to access the local (multiplexed) buses.

Upon receipt of a request pulse, the 8086 open circuits its address/data lines, the $\overline{\text{S0}}$, $\overline{\text{S1}}$, and $\overline{\text{S2}}$ status signals, and the $\overline{\text{RD}}$ and $\overline{\text{LOCK}}$ control signals. The address/data latches and buffers and the 8288 system controller are not disabled, however. This is due to internal pull-up resistors within the 8288 on $\overline{\text{S0}}$, $\overline{\text{S1}}$, and $\overline{\text{S2}}$ forcing the 8288 to assume an idle bus cycle. This allows the coprocessor to access the system memory and I/O utilizing the address/data buffers and 8288 system controller. $\overline{\text{RQ0/GT0}}$ has priority over $\overline{\text{RQ1/GT1}}$ for impending requests that have not yet been granted.

Figure 8.34 illustrates timing for the $\overline{\text{RQ/GT}}$ pins. The request is initiated by pulsing the 8086's $\overline{\text{RQ/GT}}$ input low for no more than one clock cycle. The pulse must be synchronized to the system clock to meet the setup and hold times shown.

The CPU may respond with a grant pulse on the next low-to-high system clock pulse subject to the restrictions mentioned when operating in the minimum mode. To prevent bus contention, the coprocessor must wait TCLAZ nanoseconds after the high-to-low clock transition following the grant pulse before attempting to drive the local bus.

Control of the buses is returned to the 8086 by applying a third pulse on $\overline{\text{RQ/GT}}$. The 8086 may then drive the buses three clock cycles after detecting this release pulse.

Minimum latency from request to grant occurs during an idle bus cycle and is one T state or 200 ns with a 5-MHz clock. All other cases are the same as the minimum-mode calculations, but minus 476 ns (THVCH, TCHCL, and TCLHAV do not apply).

As you can see, the $\overline{\text{RQ/GT}}$ mechanism of the maximum-mode 8086 is intended for more than DMA operations. It allows two other processors full use of the resources of the system, including the bus buffers and system controller. The multiprocessing capabilities of the 8086 were discussed in Sec. 6.6.

In either mode, minimum or maximum, a special DMA controller is required to implement the data transfer. The Intel 8237A can be used for minimum mode configurations. This peripheral controller chip is interfaced as a normal I/O port, allowing it to be programmed by the CPU. It includes three separate, prioritized DMA channels (similar to that shown in Fig. 8.32).

The 8237A outputs a 16-bit memory address. This necessitates the use of a separate ''page'' latch to store address lines A16–A19. In the maximum mode, the 8237A is *not* compatible with the 8086's $\overline{\text{RQ/GT}}$ protocol. For these reasons, Intel has developed the 8089 I/O processor.

The 8089 interfaces to the 8086's local *multiplexed* buses and shares the bus buffers and system controller of the host system. Compatible with the 8086's $\overline{\text{RQ/GT}}$ protocol, it outputs the full 20-bit memory address without the need for an external latch. It is designed to handle all the I/O processing needs of the 8086, and includes two high-speed DMA channels. This chip is discussed in detail in Chap. 11.

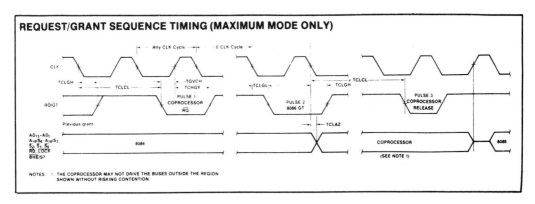

REQUEST/GRANT SEQUENCE TIMING (MAXIMUM MODE ONLY)

Figure 8.34 Request/grant/release sequence timing (maximum mode only). (Courtesy of Intel Corporation.)

Types of DMA

Two types of DMA cycles are possible. In *sequential DMA* the DMAC first performs a read operation, fetching the data byte into the DMAC. Next, a write operation is performed, transferring the data byte to the I/O port. The opposite sequence is also possible—read a byte from the I/O port, write the byte to memory. Generally, two to four clock periods are required for each read or write operation (four to eight for the total transfer). The 8089 performs sequential DMA.

Simultaneous DMA provides the fastest transfers. With this technique the read and write operations are performed at the same time (as discussed at the beginning of this section). This requires $\overline{\text{MEMR}}$ and $\overline{\text{IOW}}$ (or $\overline{\text{IOR}}$ and $\overline{\text{MEMW}}$) to be active simultaneously. In this way data does not flow through the DMAC at all, but directly from memory to the I/O port (or vice versa). The result is a factor-of-2 speed improvement over the sequential approach.

In either case the data tansfer is done completely in hardware involving only the DMAC, the peripheral, and main memory. Because the CPU is not involved, there is no software overhead.

DMA requests take precedence over all other bus activities, including interrupts. In fact, no interrupts—maskable or nonmaskable—will be recognized during a DMA cycle.

Several DMA transfer combinations are possible:

1. Memory to peripheral
2. Peripheral to memory
3. Memory to memory
4. Peripheral to peripheral

Before the data transfer can occur, the CPU must program the DMAC for the type of transfer that is to take place, the destination and source addresses, and the number of bytes to be transferred.

Sec. 8.5   Direct Memory Access

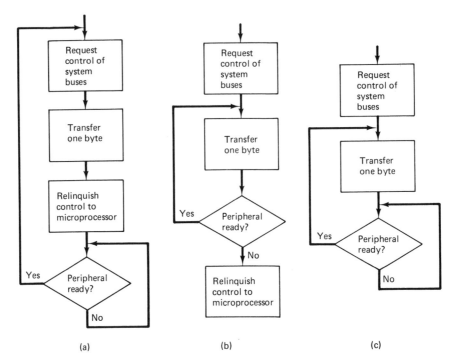

Figure 8.35 The three modes of DMA operation: (a) byte; (b) burst; (c) block. (From J. Uffenbeck, *Microcomputers and Microprocessors: The 8080, 8085, and Z-80.* Prentice-Hall, Inc., Englewood Cliffs, N.J., 1985.)

For a given DMA type, there are three ways of mixing the DMA cycles among normal processor bus cycles. These are shown in Fig. 8.35. In *byte* or *single* mode, the DMAC, after gaining control of the system buses, transfers a single data byte. Control of the buses is then relinquished until the peripheral's READY flag is again active.

The *burst* or *demand* mode is intended for peripherals that have high-speed data buffers. After gaining control of the buses, data is transferred until the peripheral's READY flag is no longer active. Control of the buses is then relinquished to the CPU. When READY again becomes active, another burst of DMA occurs. The advantage of this technique is that the buffers can be filled very rapidly by the DMAC and then emptied at the peripheral's leisure.

A third type of DMA is called *continuous* or *block* mode DMA. This is similar to burst mode except that control of the buses is not relinquished until the entire data block has been transferred. This technique is very effective, with a high-speed peripheral that can keep up with the DMAC. Slow peripherals will cause long periods of inactivity on the buses as the DMAC waits for the READY flag.

8.6 SUMMARY

In this chapter we have discussed the two basic I/O paths used for transferring data between a microprocessor and peripheral: the serial port and the parallel port. We have also covered three techniques for *synchronizing* the microprocessor to the data rate of the peripheral.

The simplest is *polling*, which provides a fast response time and relatively high transfer rate, provided that only one peripheral is to be controlled at a time. Its main disadvantage is that all of the resources of the processor are dedicated to this one peripheral.

The *interrupt* approach is more efficient, as the CPU only services the peripheral when data is required. This allows the processor to perform some other task, occasionally stopping to service the peripheral when data is required. The main disadvantage is the software overhead required to save the CPU and processing environments. This means that the response time may be quite lengthy and the transfer rate less than that for polling.

The ultimate in transfer rate and response time is achieved with DMA. DMA latency is less than 3 μs, and data transfer rates approaching the access time of the memory are possible. The disadvantage is that a special DMA controller is required, increasing the overall complexity (and cost) of the system.

All three techniques are supported by special *peripheral controller chips*. These devices can be programmed by the processor so that their configurations can be changed to meet the particular needs of the peripheral interfaced. Several of these devices are discussed in Chap. 9, and the 8089 is discussed in Chap. 11.

SELF-REVIEW 8.5 (answers on page 411)

8.5.1. Using simultaneous DMA to transfer a date byte from an input port to memory, the _____ and _____ control bus signals will both be active.

8.5.2. When operated in the minimum mode, the 8086 uses the _____ and the _____ handshaking signals to allow the DMAC to gain control of the system buses.

8.5.3. If the BIU is idle when a DMA request occurs, the 8086 will enter the HOLD state in approximately _____ T state(s).

8.5.4. The $\overline{RQ}/\overline{GT}$ protocol used by the 8086 in the maximum mode follows a _____ - _____ - _____ sequence.

8.5.5. _____ DMA provides the fastest data transfer rate.

8.5.6. The _____ mode of DMA is appropriate for peripherals with a data buffer.

8.5.7. Why do the flags, CS, and IP registers not have to be saved during a DMA cycle?

CHAPTER 8 SELF-TEST

1. Indicate the logic levels to be found on the following minimum mode 8086 CPU module lines when the instruction OUT 47H,AL is executed. Assume that AL = 10H.

(1) A15–A0:	_____
(2) D7–D0:	_____
(3) D15–D8:	_____
(4) $\overline{\text{BHE}}$:	_____
(5) M/$\overline{\text{IO}}$:	_____
(6) $\overline{\text{RD}}$:	_____
(7) $\overline{\text{WR}}$:	_____
(8) DT/$\overline{\text{R}}$:	_____
(9) $\overline{\text{DEN}}$:	_____

2. Using *indirect* I/O, the 8086 can access up to _____ different I/O ports.

3. What two signal types are combined to form the *device select pulse* (DSP)?

4. Give two input instructions that can be used to input the byte (only) at input port 30H in Fig. 8.1.

5. With regard to Fig. 8.3, if the instruction OUT 0,AX is executed, which $\overline{\text{SEL}}$ signal will be active?

6. The instruction MOV BX,MEMWDS when used for memory-mapped I/O will _____ a word from "port" _____.

7. Sketch the output wave shape you would expect to see on the output of a serial port transmitting the ASCII letter "A" at 9600 baud with 1 start bit, 1 stop bit, and no parity bit.

8. Calculate the character rate for the serial transmitter in question 7.

9. A *synchronous* serial data port will achieve a higher character rate than an *asynchronous* serial data port even though both ports operate at the same baud rate. (True/False).

10. The _____ protocol is used when serial data is to be transmitted synchronously in bit format.

11. Explain what is meant by "synchronizing the microprocessor to the peripheral."

12. The printer interfaced in Fig. 8.19 must not be strobed unless its BUSY output is _____.

13. Refer to Fig. 8.20. What is the purpose of the segment labeled PRINT_DATA?

14. Explain how priorities can be established in a polling routine.

15. Assume that a peripheral has an interrupt service routine stored at 0783:0000H. Determine the contents and location of the interrupt vector if type number C8H is used.

16. Explain why the 8086's interrupt latency can vary from less than 15 μs to more than 200 μs.

17. Under what conditions (if any) can an interrupt on INTR interrupt an NMI service routine?

18. Normally, if an interrupt occurs while TF is set, the ISR will not execute in single-step mode. Explain why.

19. Explain why the latency from a DMA request is so much shorter than from an interrupt request.

20. Assume that a 2400-baud serial printer is interfaced using a UART and the 8237A DMAC. Which of the following DMA modes would be appropriate for this interface? (a) burst; (b) byte; (c) block.

ANALYSIS AND DESIGN QUESTIONS

8.1. Design an 8-bit input and output port both mapped to direct port address 56H. Write a program to read data from the input port (set up on a DIP switch, for example) and output this data to the output port (monitored via two seven-segment displays, for example).

8.2. Modify the circuit designed in question 8.1 so that it is memory mapped to the (partially decoded) address range EXX56H. Rewrite the test program as necessary.

8.3. Design the hardware such that a pushbutton switch can be used to generate a type 40H interrupt request. Write a test program that increments the count displayed in a seven-segment display wired to output port 56H (see question 8.1) each time the switch is pushed.

8.4. What, if anything, is "wrong" with the output port design shown in Fig. 8.36?

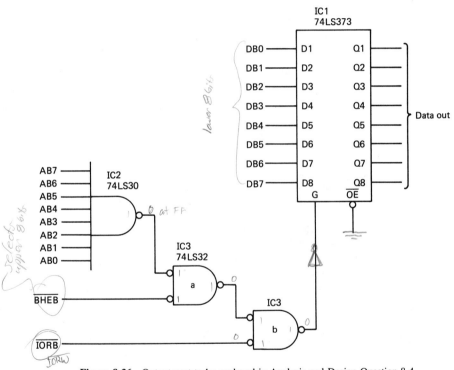

Figure 8.36 Output port to be analyzed in Analysis and Design Question 8.4.

8.5. Redesign the peripheral controller interface shown in Fig. 8.7 so that registers 0–15 are memory mapped to addresses A0000H–A001EH (i.e., the even addresses in this range only).

8.6. Using the 74ALS677 address comparator, redesign the address decoder shown in Fig. 8.1.

8.7. Write a procedure following the flowchart in Fig. 8.12 to read incoming serial data on bit 0 and return with the character in register AL.

8.8. What (if anything) is wrong with the ISR shown in Fig. 8.37?

```
ISR        PROC    NEAR
           PUSH    SI                           ;Save CPU environment
           PUSH    AX
           PUSH    DS
           PUSH    CX

           POP     SI                           ;Recover old data pointer
           POP     DS
           POP     CX

           MOV     AL,[SI]                      ;Fetch byte to be printed
           OUT     PRINTER_PORT,AL              ;Output byte to printer
           OUT     STROBE,AL                    ;Strobe printer

     ·     INC     SI                           ;Advance pointer
           DEC     CX                           ;Decrement byte counter

           PUSH    CX                           ;Save counter and pointer
           PUSH    DS
           PUSH    SI

           POP     CX                           ;Restore CPU registers
           POP     DS
           POP     AX
           POP     SI

           IRET                                 ;Return to interrupted routine
ISR        ENDP
```

Figure 8.37   ISR for Analysis and Design Question 8.8.

8.9. Using the 8086's $\overline{\text{TEST}}$ input and the WAIT instruction, redesign the printer interface shown in Fig. 8.19. Describe the changes needed in the printer control program in Fig. 8.20. Can this technique be used to decrease the response time and increase the transfer rate for polling? Explain. *Note:* The WAIT instruction requires $3 + 5n$ T states to execute, where n is the number of WAIT states inserted.

8.10. Refer to Fig. 8.7. Could the data bus multiplexer concept used in this interface be used in a RAM or ROM interface? In this way single byte-wide memory parts could be interfaced to the 8086.

SELF REVIEW ANSWERS

8.1.1 DB8-DB15

8.1.2 256, 0, FF

8.1.3 $M/\overline{IO}$

8.1.4 device select pulse

8.1.5 False

8.1.6 consecutive

8.1.7 (a)

8.2.1 $10/1200 = 8.3$ ms

8.2.2   start 0 1 0 0 0 0 1 2 stop
           start   bits

8.2.3 framing

8.2.4 UART (or USART)

8.2.5 19.2 KHz (assuming a 16X clock)

8.2.6 120

8.2.7 synchronous - less overhead

8.2.8 bisync, SDLC

8.3.1 synchronizing

8.3.2 $\overline{\text{STROBE}}$, BUSY, $\overline{\text{ACKNLG}}$

8.3.3 the CPU spends most of its

time waiting for the peripheral to be ready

8.3.4 $\overline{\text{OUT 3}}$, $\overline{\text{IN 3}}$

8.3.5 lower

8.4.1 NMI, INTR

8.4.2 flags, CS, IP

8.4.3 input the interrupt type number, INTR only

8.4.4 True

8.4.5 after completion of the current instruction

8.4.6 SEGMENT AT

8.4.7 device control block

8.4.8 the ERROR_ROUTINE will be executed

8.4.9 it only pops IP (and CS for a far call) but not the flags

8.5.1 IO read, memory write

8.5.2 HLD, HLDA

8.5.3 1.5

8.5.4 request-grant-release

8.5.6 burst

8.5.7 the microprocessor is inactive during DMA cycles so none of these registers are changed

9

PERIPHERAL CONTROLLERS FOR THE 8086/88 FAMILY

Peripheral interfacing refers to the hardware and software techniques utilized to control the flow of data between a microcomputer and its peripherals. As we saw in Chap. 8, the actual data path may be *serial* or *parallel*. The synchronization technique may use *polling*, *interrupts*, or *DMA*.

A typical interface will require address decoding circuitry, latches and buffers to exchange the data, and control logic to generate the device select pulses. Once again we are faced with a situation in which the LSI microprocessor is "surrounded" by numerous SSI packages.

For this reason the LSI *peripheral controller* IC has been developed. In fact, we are not talking about a single IC, but an entire "family" of devices designed to simplify the task of peripheral interfacing. Table 9.1 lists several representative chips available from Intel.

The one common theme in all the devices listed in this table is *programmability*. Because each chip interfaces directly to the CPU's bidirectional data bus lines, it is possible for the microprocessor to change the function of the device by outputting a new program code. For example, the 8255 has three 8-bit I/O ports. The instruction sequence

```
MOV   AL,80H
OUT   CONTROL_PORT,AL
```

programs all three ports as outputs. If the control byte 80H is changed to 9BH, all ports are reprogrammed to become inputs.

TABLE 9.1 I/O SUPPORT DEVICES FOR THE 8086 AND 8088 MICROPROCESSORS

Part number	Description
8155/56[a]	RAM with I/O and timer
8185[a]	1K × 8 RAM
8755/8355[a]	EPROM/ROM with I/O
8231	Arthmetic processing unit
8237	Programmable DMA controller
8251	Programmable communications interface
8254	Programmable interval timer
8255	Programmable peripheral interface
8256	Multifunction universal asynchronous receiver/transmitter
8259A	Programmable interrupt controller
8272	Single/double-density floppy-disk controller
8275	Programmable CRT controller
8279	Programmable keyboard display interface
8295	Dot-matrix printer controller
82720	Graphics display controller

[a]Compatible with the 8085 multiplexed address and data bus.

Source: J. Uffenbeck, *Microcomputers and Microprocessors: The 8080, 8085, and Z-80.* Prentice-Hall, Englewood Cliffs, N.J.: 1985.

All the chips listed in Table 9.1 are *byte* oriented by design. They interface to the microprocessor via an 8-bit data bus and internally are organized as a number of 8-bit registers (see Fig. 8.7 for an example). As you will see, connecting these devices to the 8-bit 8088 microprocessor is quite straightforward.

Interfacing to the 8086 can be more involved. Unless a data bus multiplexer is used, a given chip will reside only on the high-order or low-order side of the 8086's data bus. This means that the internal registers will occupy even or odd addresses only.

The important point to keep in mind is that all the I/O techniques discussed in Chap. 8—serial or parallel, polling, interrupts, or DMA—can be implemented more easily using these devices. This chapter covers the following devices:

9.1 The 8255 Programmable Peripheral Interface (PPI)

9.2 The 8251A Universal Synchronous/Asynchronous Receiver/Transmitter (USART)

9.3 The 8259A Programmable Interrupt Controller (PIC)

9.1 THE 8255 PROGRAMMABLE PERIPHERAL INTERFACE (PPI)

The 8255 is a general-purpose parallel I/O interfacing device. It provides 24 I/O lines organized as three 8-bit I/O ports labeled A, B, and C. Pin definitions and a block diagram are provided in Fig. 9.1.

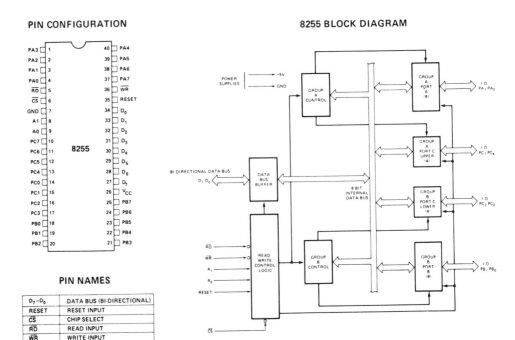

PIN CONFIGURATION

PA3	1	40	PA4
PA2	2	39	PA5
PA1	3	38	PA6
PA0	4	37	PA7
$\overline{RD}$	5	36	$\overline{WR}$
$\overline{CS}$	6	35	RESET
GND	7	34	D_0
A1	8	33	D_1
A0	9	32	D_2
PC7	10	31	D_3
PC6	11	30	D_4
PC5	12	29	D_5
PC4	13	28	D_6
PC0	14	27	D_7
PC1	15	26	V_{CC}
PC2	16	25	PB7
PC3	17	24	PB6
PB0	18	23	PB5
PB1	19	22	PB4
PB2	20	21	PB3

8255

8255 BLOCK DIAGRAM

PIN NAMES

$D_7 - D_0$	DATA BUS (BI-DIRECTIONAL)
RESET	RESET INPUT
$\overline{CS}$	CHIP SELECT
$\overline{RD}$	READ INPUT
$\overline{WR}$	WRITE INPUT
A0, A1	PORT ADDRESS
PA7-PA0	PORT A (BIT)
PB7-PB0	PORT B (BIT)
PC7-PC0	PORT C (BIT)
V_{CC}	+5 VOLTS
GND	0 VOLTS

Figure 9.1 8255A programmable peripheral interface (PPI). Twenty-four I/O pins are provided, grouped as three 8-bit I/O ports. There is one 8-bit control port. (Courtesy of Intel Corporation.)

Programming of the ports is restricted to bytes or nibbles (4 bits). Each of the ports A or B can be programmed as an 8-bit input or output port. Port C can be divided in half with the topmost or bottom-most 4 bits programmed as inputs or outputs. Individual bits of a particular port cannot be programmed.

The 8255 is a very versatile device. It can be programmed to look like three simple I/O ports (called *mode 0*), two handshaking I/O ports (called *mode 1*), or a bidirectional I/O port with five handshaking signals (called *mode 2*). The modes can also be intermixed. For example, port A can be programmed to operate in mode 2 while port B operates in mode 0. There is also a bit set/reset mode that allows individual bits of port C to be set or reset for control purposes.

Table 9.2 shows how the four internal registers (or ports) are accessed for read and write operations by the CPU. Two address input lines, labeled A0 and A1, determine which register is to be selected. For example, the control port is accessed when A1 A0 = 11.

The $\overline{RD}$ and $\overline{WR}$ input pins determine the direction of data flow over the chip's 8-bit bidirectional data bus. Note that each of the *data* ports can be read from or written to. The *control* port, however, can only be written to. As you will see, the byte written to this port determines the mode of operation of the three data ports.

Similar to the memory devices discussed in Chap. 7, the 8255 can be accessed

TABLE 9.2 TRUTH TABLE FOR THE 8255A PPI

A_1	A_0	$\overline{RD}$	$\overline{WR}$	$\overline{CS}$	
					Input operation (READ)
0	0	0	1	0	Port A → data bus
0	1	0	1	0	Port B → data bus
1	0	0	1	0	Port C → data bus
					Output operation (WRITE)
0	0	1	0	0	Data bus → port A
0	1	1	0	0	Data bus → port B
1	0	1	0	0	Data bus → port C
1	1	1	0	0	Data bus → control
					Disable function
X	X	X	X	1	Data bus → tri-state
1	1	0	1	0	Illegal condition
X	X	1	1	0	Data bus → tri-state

Source: Courtesy of Intel Corporation.

only when its $\overline{CS}$ (chip select) input is low. Thus this input is normally driven by an address decoder to assign the device to a specific range of I/O addresses.

If you are wondering about compatibility with the 16-bit 8086, remember the processor's ability to access its I/O (or memory) in bytes as well as words.

Interfacing the 8255

As a starting point, let's consider an interface between the 8255 and the 8088 microprocessor. The circuit diagram is shown in Fig. 9.2. Because the 8088 data bus uses only DB0–DB7, there is no need to worry about providing for an even or odd byte access. AB0 and AB1 then select one of the four internal ports.

Example 9.1

Determine the addresses of ports A, B, C and the control port in the interface in Fig. 9.2.

Solution The $\overline{CS}$ input will be driven low whenever the low-order address lines A2–A7 = 111100. This can occur during memory or I/O bus cycles. However, the $\overline{RD}$ (connected to $\overline{IORB}$) and $\overline{WR}$ (connected to $\overline{IOWB}$) inputs are active only for I/O bus cycles. Thus port A is accessed as input or output port F0 (111100 00). For all four ports:

Port	I/O address
A	F0
B	F1
C	F2
Control	F3

Note: The 8255 can be *memory-mapped* by connecting $\overline{MEMR}$ (or $\overline{MRDC}$) and $\overline{MEMW}$ (or $\overline{MWTC}$) to the $\overline{RD}$ and $\overline{WR}$ inputs of the chip.

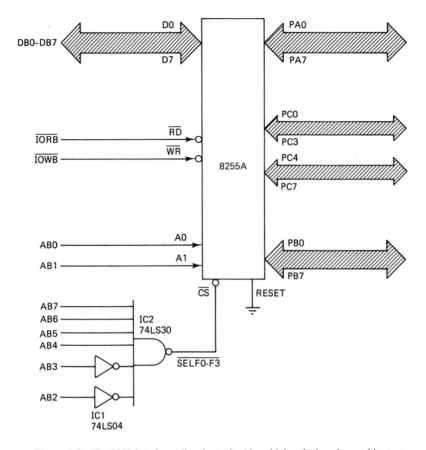

Figure 9.2 The 8255 interfaces directly to the (demultiplexed) three-bus architecture of the 8088 microprocessor. Four consecutive I/O ports are required. (From J. Uffenbeck, *Microcomputers and Microprocessors: The 8080, 8085, and Z-80.* Prentice-Hall, Englewood Cliffs, N.J., 1985.)

The port addresses calculated in this example assume that the 8088's *direct* I/O instructions are used. For *indirect* I/O, the interface is partially decoded. This is because AB8–AB15 are not examined by the address decoder. The circuit will then respond to addresses in the range XXXX XXXX 1111 00--. In addition to ports F0–F3, ports 01F0–01F3, 02F0–02F3, ... , FEF0–FEF3, and FFF0–FFF3 will all enable the 8255. If this is undesirable, the eight high-order address lines must be decoded.

With this circuit as background, consider the 8255–8086 interface shown in Figure 9.3. The address decoder is similar to that used when interfacing memory and provides even and odd port-select signals. These are, in turn, used to chip select an even 8255 (interfaced to the low-order data bus lines) and an odd 8255 (interfaced to the high order data bus lines).

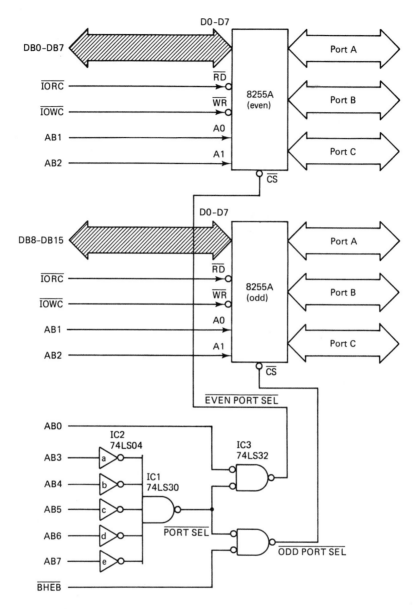

Figure 9.3 Interfacing the 8255 to the 8086 maximum-mode CPU module. Two 8255s provide three consecutively addressed 16-bit I/O ports. (From J. Uffenbeck, *Microcomputers and Microprocessors: The 8080, 8085, and Z-80.* Prentice-Hall, Englewood Cliffs, N.J., 1985.)

Example 9.2

Determine the 8255 port addresses in Fig. 9.3 for direct I/O instructions and indirect I/O instructions.

Solution The direct I/O instructions supply an 8-bit fixed address as part of the instruction on AB0–AB7. The decoding in Fig. 9.3 will cause $\overline{\text{PORT SEL}}$ to be active over the range

$$\text{AB7–AB0} = 00000\text{XXX} = 00\text{H} - 07\text{H}$$

IC3 combines the $\overline{\text{PORT SEL}}$ signal with AB0 and $\overline{\text{BHE}}$ to produce $\overline{\text{EVEN PORT SEL}}$ and $\overline{\text{ODD PORT SEL}}$. There will be four combinations of each of these signals because they do not include AB1 and AB2. For example, $\overline{\text{EVEN PORT SEL}}$ will be active if the direct port address is 0, 2, 4, or 6. Similarly, $\overline{\text{ODD PORT SEL}}$ will be active if the direct port address is 1, 3, 5, or 7.

Because AB1 and AB2 are used to select one of the four ports within the 8255, the four combinations of the $\overline{\text{EVEN PORT SEL}}$ and $\overline{\text{ODD PORT SEL}}$ signals correspond to ports A, B, C, and the control port of the 8255. This is shown more clearly in Table 9.3.

When indirect I/O instructions are given, register DX is used to hold a 16-bit port address. Because AB8–AB15 are not decoded, the circuit is *partially* decoded for these instructions. The port address range is 0000H–0007H, 0100H–0107H, 0200H–0207H, . . . , FF00H–FF07H.

Be careful to not be misled by the interface in Fig. 9.3. It is *not* necessary to interface pairs of 8255s to the 8086. If an 8-bit I/O port is sufficient, the even- or odd-addressed PPI chip (and corresponding OR gate—IC3) can be deleted. The resulting interface will still span eight consecutive port locations, but every other address will be empty. Analysis and Design Question 9.3 explores the possibility of using a data bus multiplexer to map a single 8255 to four *consecutive* port addresses.

Finally, it is constructive to compare the interface in Fig. 9.3 with the similar 16-

TABLE 9.3 8255 PORT ADDRESSES FOR THE INTERFACE IN FIG. 9.3

AB7–AB3	AB2	AB1	AB0	BHE	Port	Description	Comment
00000	0	0	0	1	0	Port A	Even port on
00000	0	1	0	1	2	Port B	DB0–DB7
00000	1	0	0	1	4	Port C	
00000	1	1	0	1	6	Control port	
00000	0	0	1	0	1	Port A	Odd port on
00000	0	1	1	0	3	Port B	DB8–DB15
00000	1	0	1	0	5	Port C	
00000	1	1	1	0	7	Control port	
00000	0	0	0	0	0 and 1	Port A	Even port on
00000	0	1	0	0	2 and 3	Port B	DB0–DB7 and
00000	1	0	0	0	4 and 5	Port C	odd port on
00000	1	1	0	0	6 and 7	Control port	DB8–DB15

Source: J. Uffenbeck, *Microcomputers and Microprocessors: The 8080, 8085, and Z-80.* Prentice-Hall, Englewood Cliffs, N.J., 1985.

bit interfaces shown in Figs. 8.1 and 8.3. The 8255 circuit provides three 16-bit I/O ports and requires only five chips. In addition, each of the six 8-bit ports can be individually programmed as an input or an output port. In the next section you will learn how to specify the control word to program the ports and see an application for mode 0 operation.

Specifying the Control Word

Applying an active-high pulse to the 8255's RESET input will leave the three data ports programmed as inputs. Thus the first few instructions of the applications software will normally program the PPI for the desired operating mode and I/O configuration. This will require one to three bytes to be output to the control port.

Figure 9.4 shows how the control word is formed. Bit 7 determines if a *bit*

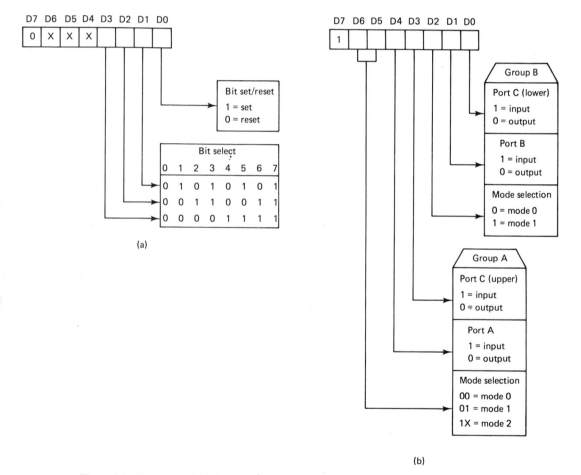

Figure 9.4 Two types of 8255 control words: (a) when bit 7 = 0, a bit set/reset operation is indicated; (b) when bit 7 = 1, any of the modes 0, 1, or 2 can be programmed. (From J. Uffenbeck, *Microcomputers and Microprocessors: The 8080, 8085, and Z-80.* Prentice-Hall, Englewood Cliffs, N.J., 1985.)

Sec. 9.1   The 8255 Programmable Peripheral Interface (PPI)   **419**

set/reset or *mode* definition byte is to be written. The bit set/reset function is not really a control word (it does not alter the previously specified operating mode). Instead, it allows individual bits of port C to be set or reset. This is discussed further in the next section.

When bit 7 of the control byte is a 0, one of three operating modes can be specified. As Fig. 9.4 illustrates, the three data ports are separated into two groups, labeled group A and group B. The ports in group A can be programmed for any of modes 0, 1, or 2. The ports in group B can be programmed for mode 0 or 1 only.

Example 9.3

Write the 8086 initialization routine required to program both 8255s in Fig. 9.3 for mode 0 with, port A an output and port B and C inputs.

Solution In Fig. 9.4 the control word is formed as

$$1\ 00\ 0\ 1\ 0\ 1\ 1 = 8\text{BH}$$

The direct or indirect I/O instructions can be used. By duplicating the code in both halves of register AX, both PPI chips can be programmed simultaneously. The program is as follows:

```
MOV   DX,0006H      ;DX points at ports 6 and 7
MOV   AX,8B8BH      ;Control word duplicated in AL and AH
OUT   DX,AX         ;Write AL to even PPI and AH to odd PPI
```

One of the most powerful features of the 8255 is that only one control byte is required to program the mode selection—this is true no matter how complex the configuration may be. The following example illustrates the ease of programming and versatility of the 8255.

Example 9.4

Write an 8086 program to input a byte from port B of the even PPI chip in Fig. 9.4 and output this byte to port A of the odd PPI. Assume that both chips have been programmed as in Ex. 9.3.

Solution The program is very simple.

```
IN    AL,02H      ;Read port B of the even PPI
OUT   01H,AL      ;Write the byte to port A of the odd PPI
```

Using MODE 0 to Interface a Matrix Keyboard

When programmed for mode 0 operation, as in Ex. 9.4, the PPI offers three simple (nonhandshaking) I/O ports. This mode is appropriate for I/O devices that do not need special synchronizing signals to exchange data with the CPU. A common example is a keyboard used for data entry. This could range from a full-sized ASCII keyboard to a calculator-like keypad used to control some industrial process.

Figure 9.5 shows an example of the latter case, in which a 16-key switch matrix is interfaced to a microcomputer using the 8255. In this example port A is programmed as a mode 0 input port and the high-order nibble of port C is programmed as an output

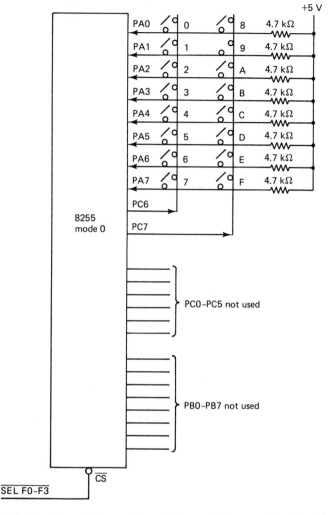

Figure 9.5 Interfacing a 16-key switch matrix to the 8255 (assumed interfaced to the 8088 microprocessor as shown in Fig. 9.2). Port A is programmed as a mode 0 input port and port C (upper) as a mode 0 output port.

port. Before discussing the details of this interface, three problems associated with interfacing a keyboard to a microcomputer should be mentioned:

1. Determine that at least one key in the matrix is closed.
2. Debounce the switch closure and release.
3. Encode the key with a particular value.

There are many approaches that can be taken to solve these problems. They range from an all-hardware solution in which the keyboard is simply "plugged into" an available input port, to an all-software solution in which only the bare keyswitches themselves are connected to the microcomputer. As you can see in Fig. 9.5, this example will follow the latter approach.

Our first problem is to be able to detect that one of the switches in the matrix is closed. This can be done by inputting the byte from PPI port A. With all switches open, the result will be FFH. Now consider outputting a 0 to PC6 and PC7, the two column lines. If one of the switches is closed, say switch 6, the code 10111111 or DFH will be read. The following instruction sequence can be used to detect this non-FFH code.

```
MOV   AL,00XXXXXX      ;Make PC6 and PC7 low
OUT   Port_C,AL        ;Both column lines now low
IN    AL,PORT_A        ;Scan the keyboard for a closed switch
CMP   AL,0FFH          ;Compare with all-keys-up code
JNE   KEY_DOWN         ;A nonzero result means that a key is
                       down
```

Once it is known that a key has been pressed, it must be *debounced*. This is because the contacts of all mechanical switches will bounce open and closed for several milliseconds after first being depressed or released. If you are not careful, the microcomputer may be able to process the first contact closure and return in time to pick up several of the bounces. In most cases this will result in erroneous operation of the control function.

Debouncing can be handled in software by inserting time delays of sufficient length to ensure that the switch contacts are stable. This will have to be done when the switch is first detected closed, and also when the switch returns open.

The final problem of encoding the key with a particular value is solved by setting up a data table of desired keyboard values. The "raw" code read from the keyboard is then used as an *index* into this table to extract that key's value. This is a particularly elegant solution because it allows the key values (or functions) to be changed to suit the application.

Figure 9.6 flowcharts the entire process of detecting, debouncing, and encoding. Notice that we begin by ensuring that the keyboard is clear (all switches up). This is done to prevent the computer from processing the same key over and over due to the operator holding the key down longer than it takes the CPU to process that key. Some keyboards have a "typamatic" feature which causes the key value to be repeated at a 10 to 20-Hz rate if the key is held down for longer than $\frac{1}{2}$ s.

To encode the key with a value, its particular column must be found. This is done by first testing column 1 (PC6 = 0, PC7 = 1). An input of FFH means that the key must be in column 2.

After setting the pointer into the data table, the contents of AL can be rotated right, the table pointer incremented, and CF tested. When CF = 0, the pointer will have located the key's value in the table. This code can then be fetched to register AL.

Figure 9.7 is the 8086 assembly language listing for the keyboard problem. It is written as a procedure so that some other program need only call this routine when it is desired to read the keyboard. This main program can then process the key value as desired.

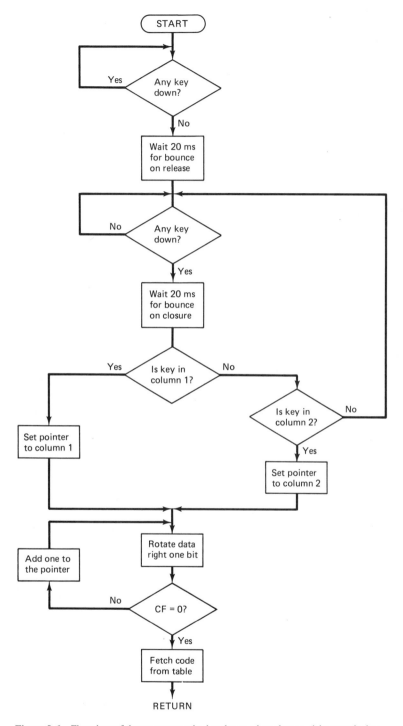

Figure 9.6 Flowchart of the process required to detect a key closure, debounce the key, and encode with a value between 0 and F.

```
;Function:      Scan the keyboard shown in Fig. 9.5
;               and return with the encoded key
;               value in register AL.
;Inputs:        none
;Outputs:       hex key value in AL.
;Calls:         20 ms delay procedure for debouncing
;Destroys:      AX and flags


;*******
;  Set up segment to store key values
;*******
```

```
0000                            KEY_CODE      SEGMENT BYTE
0000  00 01 02 03 04 05         TOP           DB       0,1,2,3,4,5,6,7
000B  08 09 0A 0B 0C            MIDDLE        DB       8,9,0AH,0BH,0CH
000D  0D 0E 0F                                DB       0DH,0EH,0FH
0010                            KEY_CODE      ENDS

0000                            CODE          SEGMENT BYTE
                                              ASSUME   CS:CODE,DS:KEY_CODE
```

```
;*******
;Program equates
;*******
```

```
= 00F0                          PORT_A        EQU      0F0H            ;PPI port A address (see Fig. 9.2)
= 00F2                          PORT_C        EQU      0F2H            ;PPI port C address
= 00BF                          COL_1_LOW     EQU      10111111B       ;PC6 low
= 007F                          COL_2_LOW     EQU      01111111B       ;PC7 low
= 003F                          BOTH_COL_LOW  EQU      00111111B       ;PC6 and PC7 low
= 00FF                          KEY_UP        EQU      0FFH            ;Input 0FFH when no keys are down
= 143D                          T1            EQU      5181            ;~ 20 ms time delay assuming 5 MHz 8088
```

```
;*******
;   20 ms time delay for debouncing
;*******
```

```
0000                            DELAY         PROC     NEAR
0000  B9 143D                                 MOV      CX,T1
0003  E2 FE                     COUNT:        LOOP     COUNT
0005  C3                                      RET
0006                            DELAY         ENDP
```

Figure 9.7 Program listing for the keyboard interface in Fig. 9.5 and flowchart in Fig. 9.6.

```
                        ;*******
                        ;  Main program begins here
                        ;*******

0006                    KEYBOARD    PROC    NEAR
0006  1E                            PUSH    DS              ;Save registers about to be used
0007  51                            PUSH    CX
0008  56                            PUSH    SI
0009  B8 ---- R                     MOV     AX,KEY_CODE     ;Point DS to the key codes
000C  8E D8                         MOV     DS,AX

                        ;Wait for previous key to be released

000E  B0 3F                         MOV     AL,BOTH_COL_LOW ;Scan both columns
0010  E6 F2                         OUT     PORT_C,AL       ;Column lines on PC6 and PC7
0012  E4 F0             POLL1:      IN      AL,PORT_A       ;Read keyboard
0014  3C FF                         CMP     AL,KEY_UP       ;All keys up?
0016  75 FA                         JNE     POLL1           ;No - so wait
0018  E8 0000 R                     CALL    DELAY           ;Yes - wait for bounce on release

                        ;Wait for a new key to be pressed

001B  E4 F0             POLL2:      IN      AL,PORT_A       ;Read keyboard
001D  3C FF                         CMP     AL,KEY_UP       ;Any keys down?
001F  74 FA                         JE      POLL2           ;No - so wait
0021  E8 0000 R                     CALL    DELAY           ;Yes - wait for bounce

                        ;See if the key is in column 1

0024  B0 BF                         MOV     AL,COL_1_LOW    ;Test for column 1
0026  E6 F2                         OUT     PORT_C,AL       ;PC6 low
0028  E4 F0                         IN      AL,PORT_A       ;Read column 1 keys
002A  3C FF                         CMP     AL,KEY_UP       ;Any key down?
002C  74 07                         JE      CHECK_COL_2     ;No - check for column 2
002E  8D 36 0000 R                  LEA     SI,TOP          ;Yes - point SI at the key values 0-7
0032  EB 0F 90                      JMP     LOOKUP          ;Now lookup code

                        ;If not column 1 then column 2

0035  B0 7F             CHECK_COL_2: MOV    AL,COL_2_LOW    ;Test for column 2
0037  E6 F2                         OUT     PORT_C,AL       ;PC7 low
0039  E4 F0                         IN      AL,PORT_A       ;Read column 2 keys
003B  3C FF                         CMP     AL,KEY_UP       ;Any key down?
003D  74 DC                         JE      POLL2           ;No - false input so repeat
003F  8D 36 0008 R                  LEA     SI,MIDDLE       ;Yes - point SI at key values 8-F

                        ;Now lookup the key's value and store in AL

0043  D0 DB             LOOKUP:     RCR     AL,1            ;Rotate keyboard input code right
0045  73 03                         JNC     MATCH           ;If 0 key is found - so retrieve it
0047  46                            INC     SI              ;No - advance pointer to next value
0048  EB F9                         JMP     LOOKUP          ;Repeat the loop

004A  8A 04             MATCH:      MOV     AL,[SI]         ;Get the key code
004C  5E                            POP     SI              ;Restore all registers
004D  59                            POP     CX              ;(except AX and flags)
004E  1F                            POP     DS
004F  C3                            RET
0050                    KEYBOARD    ENDP
0050                    CODE        ENDS
                                    END
```

Figure 9.7 continued

Bit Set/Reset

When bit 7 of the 8255 control word is a 0, a bit set/reset operation will be performed. In this mode any one bit of port C can be set to a logic 1 or reset to a logic 0. Note that only one bit can be set or reset at a time.

One of the advantages of this mode is that individual bits of port C can be changed without changing any of the others. This is important when port C is used to control the ON/OFF status of several external devices. The device connected to PC4 can be turned ON without affecting the status of any devices connected to the other seven outputs.

The bit set/reset mode also lends itself to the easy generation of strobe pulses. Consider the following instruction sequence:

```
MOV   AL,00001001
OUT   CTRL_PORT,AL      ;Set PC4 high
DEC   AL
OUT   CTRL_PORT,AL      ;Reset PC4
```

The bit set/reset function is used in modes 1 and 2 to enable interrupt outputs available in these modes. This will be covered later in this section.

Electrical Characteristics of the Ports

All three 8255 ports have an I_{OL} specification of 1.7 mA and an I_{OH} specification of 200 µA. This means they can drive one standard TTL load or four LSTTL loads. A special feature of ports B and C is that any set of eight lines can source 1-mA at 1.5 V. This is useful for driving solid-state relays and transistor drivers. Note that the outputs *cannot* sink the typical 10- to 20-mA current required to light an LED; a TTL buffer should be used, as shown in Fig. 9.8.

There are two speed versions of the 8255, labeled the 8255A and the 8255A-5. Table 9.4 compares the 8255 specifications for t_{RD} (RD low to data valid) and t_{WW} (the minimum write pulse width) with the similar specifications for the 5-MHz 8086. Table 9.5 indicates that the 8255A will require one wait state for all 8086 CPU configurations. The 8255A-5 will require one wait state only when interfaced to the buffered minimum mode CPU module. Also note that when operated in the maximum mode the advanced write command should be used in order to meet the minimum write pulse-width specification of the 8255.

Mode 1: Strobed I/O

Mode 1 is intended for handshaking and interrupt-driven I/O interfaces. In this mode ports A and B are programmed as data ports and port C is programmed to carry status

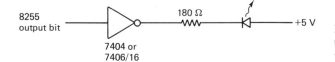

Figure 9.8 A TTL buffer should be used to sink the 15 to 20 mA of current required when driving an LED with the 8255.

TABLE 9.4 8255 READ/WRITE TIMING SPECIFICATIONS

	8255A (ns)	8255A-5 (ns)	8086 Minimum mode[a] (ns)	8086 Maximum mode[a] (ns)
t_{RD} (t_{RLDV})	250	200	205	335
t_{WW} (t_{WLWH})	400	300	340	175 (375)[b]

[a]Unbuffered 8086 CPU.

[b]Advanced write command (t_{WLWHA}).

TABLE 9.5 8255A WAIT STATES WITH THE 8086 CPU

	Minimum mode		Maximum mode	
	Unbuffered	Buffered	Unbuffered	Buffered
8255A	1	1	1	1
8255A-5	0	1	0	0

signals. One of the unique features of this mode is that data transfers can take place without direct CPU intervention.

There are four possible configurations for the 8255 when operated in this mode as shown in Fig. 9.9. These correspond to the four combinations of ports A and B as inputs and outputs. The two separate control words shown in Fig. 9.9(a) and (b) illustrate the fact that port A, port B, or both ports can be programmed for mode 1 operation. This means that it is possible to program port A for mode 1 while using port B in mode 0, for example.

Input port timing. When port A or B is programmed as an input port, three control signals are dedicated to supporting data transfers with this port. These are IBF, $\overline{STB}$, and INTR. Table 9.6 gives a word explanation for each of these signals and Fig. 9.10 illustrates the timing.

When the peripheral device has data for the microprocessor, it places that data on the port A or B input lines and then pulses the 8255 $\overline{STB}$ input. The PPI replies by latching this data and raising its IBF (input buffer full) line. This is a signal to the peripheral that data has been latched but not yet read by the microprocessor.

If the INTE (interrupts enabled) bit of the input port has been set, IBF will also cause the INTR output of that port to go high. The processor now has the choice of polling the IBF line—by reading the mode 1 status word at port C (see Fig. 9.11)—or letting INTR generate an interrupt, thereby alerting the processor that the input buffer is full.

In either case the processor should branch to a routine that reads the data port. The falling edge of $\overline{RD}$ causes the 8255 INTR output to be reset and the rising edge of $\overline{RD}$ resets IBF. The data transfer is now complete and the peripheral (detecting IBF low) can strobe in the next byte of data.

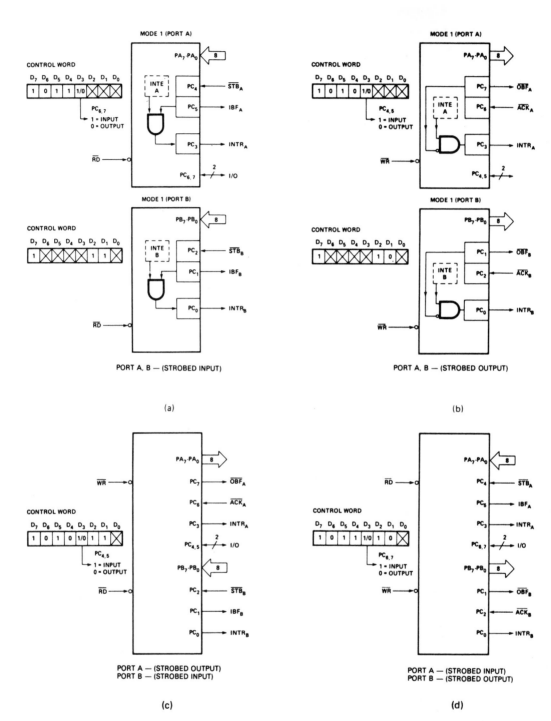

Figure 9.9 Four possible I/O configurations for ports A and B when the 8255 is programmed for mode 1 operation. Port C becomes a status port in this mode. (Courtesy of Intel Corporation.)

TABLE 9.6 PORT C OF THE 8255A SUPPLIES SEVERAL HANDSHAKING SIGNALS WHEN PROGRAMMED FOR MODE 1 OPERATION

Signal	Direction	Description
		Input Port
IBF	OUT	A 1 on this output indicates that the data has been loaded into the input latch; in essence an acknowledgment; IBF is set by the falling edge of the $\overline{\text{STB}}$ input and is reset by the rising edge of the $\overline{\text{RD}}$ input
$\overline{\text{STB}}$	IN	A 0 on this input loads data into the input latch
INTR	OUT	A 1 on this output can be used to interrupt the CPU when an input device is requesting service; INTR is set by the rising edge of $\overline{\text{STB}}$ if IBF is a 1 and INTE is a 1; it is reset by the falling ege of $\overline{\text{RD}}$. This procedure allows an input device to request service from the CPU simply by strobing its data into the port; INTE A is controlled by bit set/reset of PC4 and INTE B by bit set/reset of PC2
		Output Port
$\overline{\text{OBF}}$	OUT	The $\overline{\text{OBF}}$ output will go low to indicate that the CPU has written data out to the specified port; the $\overline{\text{OBF}}$ flip-flop will be set by the rising edge of the $\overline{\text{WR}}$ input and reset by the falling edge of the $\overline{\text{ACK}}$ input signal
$\overline{\text{ACK}}$	IN	A 0 on this input informs the 8255 that the data from port A or port B has been accepted; in essence, a response from the peripheral device indicating that it has received the data output by the CPU
INTR	OUT	A 1 on this output can be used to interrupt the CPU when an output device has accepted data transmitted by the CPU; INTR is set by the rising edge of $\overline{\text{ACK}}$ if $\overline{\text{OBF}}$ is a 0 and INTE is a 1; it is reset by the falling edge of $\overline{\text{WR}}$; INTE A is controlled by the bit set/reset of PC6 and INTE B by bit set/reset of PC2

Source: J. Uffenbeck, *Hardware Interfacing with the Apple II Plus.* Prentice-Hall, Englewood Cliffs, NJ, 1983.

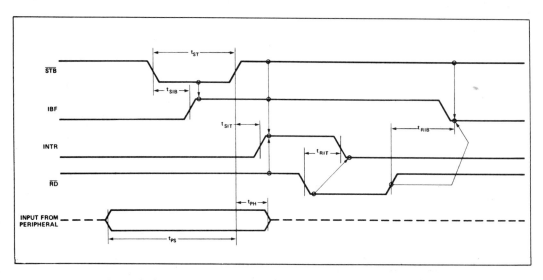

Figure 9.10 8255 mode 1 input port timing. (Courtesy of Intel Corporation.)

Sec. 9.1   The 8255 Programmable Peripheral Interface (PPI)   **429**

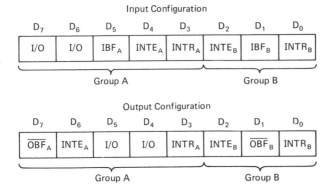

Input Configuration

D₇	D₆	D₅	D₄	D₃	D₂	D₁	D₀
I/O	I/O	IBF_A	INTE_A	INTR_A	INTE_B	IBF_B	INTR_B

Group A — Group B

Output Configuration

D₇	D₆	D₅	D₄	D₃	D₂	D₁	D₀
$\overline{OBF}_A$	INTE_A	I/O	I/O	INTR_A	INTE_B	$\overline{OBF}_B$	INTR_B

Group A — Group B

Figure 9.11 8255 mode 1 status word format. This byte is read via an input read from port C. (From J. Uffenbeck, *Microcomputers and Microprocessors: The 8080, 8085, and Z-80.* Prentice-Hall, Englewood Cliffs, N.J., 1985.)

Output port timing. When ports A or B are programmed as mode 1 output ports, three lines of port C are dedicated to supporting this function: $\overline{OBF}$, $\overline{ACK}$, and INTR. Their word descriptions are also provided in Table 9.6. Figure 9.12 illustrates output port timing.

Assuming that data has been previously written to one of the data ports, the peripheral monitors $\overline{OBF}$ (output buffer full). When this line is low, data is available to be read by the peripheral. Using $\overline{OBF}$ as a $\overline{STROBE}$ input, the peripheral latches the data byte and responds with an $\overline{ACK}$ (acknowledge) pulse. The falling edge of this pulse sets $\overline{OBF}$ high, and if INTE is high, the rising edge causes INTR to also go high.

Again the CPU has the choice of polling or interrupts. $\overline{OBF}$ can be polled by reading the mode 1 status word at port C (see Fig. 9.11). INTR can be used to request an interrupt alerting the CPU that $\overline{OBF}$ is high; that is, the peripheral is ready for more data. In either case, the processor should write a new byte of data to the output port. The falling edge

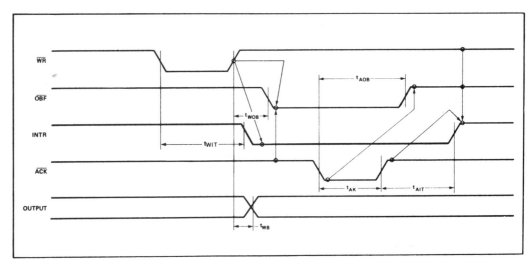

Figure 9.12 8255 mode 1 output port timing. (Courtesy of Intel Corporation.)

of $\overline{WR}$ will reset INTR, and the rising edge of $\overline{WR}$ will force $\overline{OBF}$ low. The peripheral, monitoring $\overline{OBF}$, can latch the new data byte and the cycle repeats.

Polling versus interrupts. The advantages of polling and interrupts have been previously discussed. Let's make sure that we appreciate what is involved for each technique when using the 8255 in mode 1.

When polling is used, an input read from port C (IN AL,OF2H for the hardware shown in Fig. 9.2) will load the accumulator with the mode 1 status word shown in Fig. 9.11. Note that if port A is programmed as an input port and port B as an output port, the status word will be made up of the group A bits as an input and the group B bits as an output. Standard bit-testing techniques may be used to monitor $\overline{OBF}$ or $\overline{IBF}$.

Note also that PC6 and 7 (when port A is programmed as an input) or PC4 and 5 (when port A is programmed as an output) are not involved in the handshaking logic and can be programmed as general-purpose input and output lines. This is shown in Fig. 9.9. They can also be read as part of the mode 1 status word.

When interrupts are used, the INTR output will be set as $\overline{OBF}$ goes high (the buffer is available for more data) or as $\overline{STB}$ goes high (the input buffer contains data to be read). However, INTR can be set only if the corresponding INTE bit has been previously set by the processor. This is where the bit set/reset mode comes in.

INTE is controlled as follows (refer to Fig. 9.11):

Port	Type	Name	Controlled by bit set/reset of:
A	Input	INTEA	PC4
A	Output	INTEA	PC6
B	Input	INTEB	PC2
B	Output	INTEB	PC2

A few examples should help illustrate how the control word is formed and interrupts enabled.

Example 9.5

Determine the 8255 control word to be used when programming port A as a mode 1 input port and port B as a mode 1 output port. INTEA and INTEB should both be enabled and the two unused port C lines should be defined as outputs. Assuming the 8088 interface shown in Fig. 9.2, write the 8086 initialization routine required.

Solution The desired port configuration is shown in Fig. 9.9(d). Programming PC6 and 7 as outputs, the control word is 1011010X. Setting INTEA will require a bit set for PC4 and INTEB will require a bit set for PC2. The initialization routine is as follows:

```
MOV   AL,0B4H      ;Control word
OUT   0F3H,AL      ;Control port
MOV   AL,09H       ;Bit set PC4
OUT   0F3H,AL      ;Control port
MOV   AL,05H       ;Bit set PC2
OUT   0F3H,AL      ;Control port
```

Example 9.6

Repeat Ex. 9.5 with port B programmed as a mode 0 output port. Program all free pins of port C as inputs.

Solution Refer to Fig. 9.9(a) to determine the port A portion of the control word. This is 10111XXX. Now refer to Fig. 9.4 for the group B (or port B) portion of the control word. The last 3 bits should be 001. The resulting control word is 10111001. Only INTEA will need to be set, requiring a bit-set operation on PC4. The program is given below. PC0–PC2 and PC6 and PC7 are all available as general-purpose inputs.

```
MOV   AL,0B9H      ;Control word
OUT   0F3H,AL      ;Control port
MOV   AL,09H       ;Bit set PC4
OUT   0F3H,AL      ;Control port
```

As a final example, let's use the 8255 again to interface a parallel printer. We will program the PPI for mode 1 operation and use *interrupts* to control the flow of data. Refer to the timing diagram in Fig. 9.12 for the following discussion.

The circuit diagram is shown in Fig. 9.13. We assume that the even PPI chip in

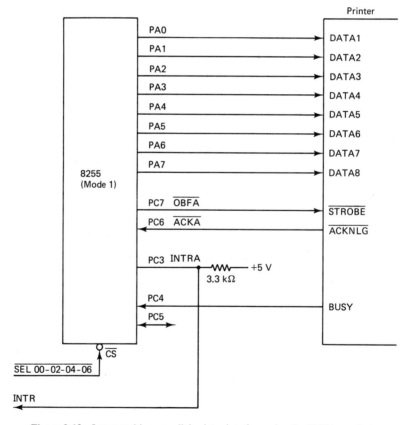

Figure 9.13 Interrupt-driven parallel printer interface using the 8255 in mode 1.

the interface in Fig. 9.3 is to be used. Port A has been chosen as the data output port requiring the $\overline{\text{ACKNLG}}$ signal from the printer to be connected to PC6. The $\overline{\text{OBFA}}$ output from the 8255 will serve as the $\overline{\text{STROBE}}$ input to the printer. The printer's BUSY signal can be polled via PC4, one of two *extra* pins available when group A of the 8255 is programmed for mode 1.

The software to control this interface is nearly identical to the routines flowcharted in Figs. 8.29 and 8.30. After the 8255 has been initialized, its port A output buffer will be empty, causing $\overline{\text{OBFA}}$ to be high. Thus the printer's $\overline{\text{STROBE}}$ input will also be high. When the user requests a print operation, the command processor procedure will be called. This routine will specify the device control block parameters and call the printer ISR. Polling PC4, the first character will be written to the 8255 and then control will return to the main program. The rising edge of the I/O write command will reset $\overline{\text{OBFA}}$ and initiate the $\overline{\text{STROBE}}$ pulse. INTRA is low at this time.

Eventually, the printer will acknowledge the character, causing $\overline{\text{OBFA}}$ to return high, ending the $\overline{\text{STROBE}}$ pulse. In effect, the 8255 generates the $\overline{\text{STROBE}}$ signal "automatically." There is no need for a STROBE flip-flop (IC3 in Fig. 8.19). The printer's $\overline{\text{ACKNLG}}$ pulse also sets INTRA. Assuming that interrupts are enabled (both for the processor and the 8255), the printer interrupt service routine will be called, a new byte output to the printer, and $\overline{\text{OBFA}}$ and INTRA both driven low. The cycle then repeats until all bytes have been output.

A comparison of the hardware in Fig. 9.13 with that shown in Fig. 8.19 is striking. The 8255 requires no additional circuits even though it is used to poll the printer's BUSY flag, generate the $\overline{\text{STROBE}}$ pulse, and request the interrupt—certainly a good example of the flexibility of the 8255 PPI.

The software driver developed in Chap. 8 can also be used with this interface. The following changes are required.

1. Add or change the following equates in Fig. 8.31(a):

```
PR_PORT      EQU F0H           ;8255 port A
PR_STATUS    EQU F4H           ;8255 port C
CTRL_P       EQU F6H           ;8255 control port
MODE         EQU 10101011B     ;Mode 1 control byte
EI_PPI       EQU 00001101B     ;INTEA enable
DI_PPI       EQU 00001100B     ;INTEA disable
BUSY         EQU 00010000B     ;Mask for BUSY on PC4
```

Delete the STROBE EQU; it is no longer needed.

2. Modify the initialization routine in Fig. 8.31(b) by deleting the IN AL,STROBE instruction and add the following:

```
MOV   AL,MODE
OUT   CTRL_P,AL
```

3. In the command processor routine [Fig. 8.31(d)], add the following after the STI instruction:

MOV   AL,EI_PPI
OUT   CTRL_P,AL

This enables interrupts from INTRA of the 8255.

4. In the interrupt service routine [Fig. 8.31(e)] delete the OUT STROBE,AL and IN STROBE,AL instructions. Add the following after the MOV STATUS,GOOD instruction:

MOV   AL,DI_PPI
OUT   CTRL_P,AL

This disables 8255 interrupts once the print job has completed.

You should be able to see the advantage of using a liberal number of equates in your programs. By changing the equate values, the same program can be used with entirely different hardware.

Mode 2: Strobed Bidirectional I/O

When operated in mode 2, port A of the 8255 becomes a *bidirectional* data port supported by five handshaking signals. This is shown in Fig. 9.14. The handshaking signals are identical to those provided in mode 1 except that they now refer only to port A. This particular mode of operation is useful when transferring data between two computers.

When port A is programmed to operate in mode 2, port B can operate in mode 0 or mode 1. If programmed for mode 0, PC0–PC2 can be programmed as mode 0 inputs or outputs. If port B is programmed for mode 1, PC0–PC2 become handshake signals for this port.

Considering all the possible combinations, there are four configurations of the 8255 in mode 2. These are shown in Fig. 9.15. As an example, if we choose to program port A for mode 2, port B as a mode 0 input port, and PC0–PC2 as mode 0 output pins, the control word is 11XXX010.

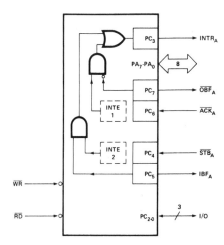

Figure 9.14 8255 pin definitions for mode 2. Port A is a bidirectional port supported by five handshaking signals from port C. (Courtesy of Intel Corporation.)

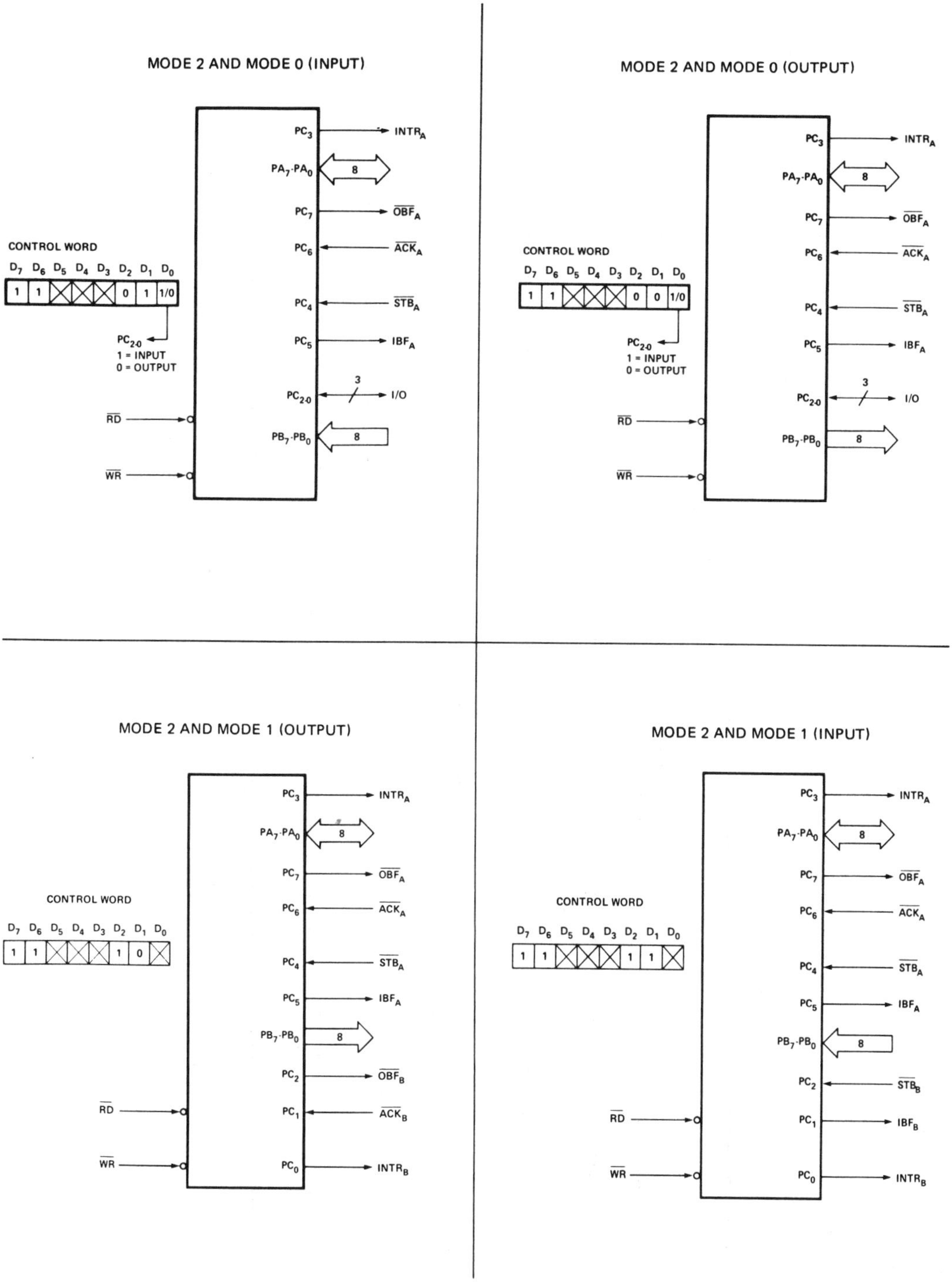

Figure 9.15 Four possible configurations of the 8255 when programmed for mode 2. (Courtesy of Intel Corporation.)

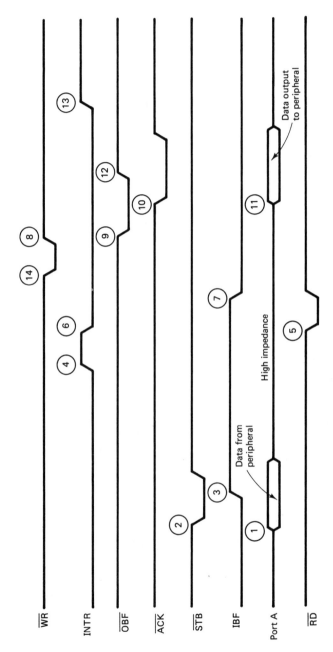

Figure 9.16 Input and output port timing relationships for mode 2. The numbers are keyed to the text. (From J. Uffenbeck, *Microcomputers and Microprocessors: The 8080, 8085, and Z-80.* Prentice-Hall, Englewood Cliffs, N.J., 1985.)

Input port timing.　Figure 9.16 is a timing diagram for mode 2 illustrating the sequence of events as a data byte is first transferred to the 8255 by the peripheral and then back to the peripheral by the 8255. The numbers in the diagram are keyed to the explanation. We begin with the peripheral outputting a byte to the 8255.

1. Data is output by the peripheral.
2. The peripheral applies a $\overline{STB}$ pulse to the 8255.
3. When the data is latched, IBF goes high.
4. After $\overline{STB}$ returns high with IBF still set, INTR goes high, requesting an interrupt if this feature is used.
5. Polling or interrupts can now be used to service the peripheral. The 8255 buffer is read when $\overline{RD}$ goes low.
6. The falling edge of $\overline{RD}$ resets INTR.
7. The rising edge of $\overline{RD}$ resets IBF.

Output port timing.　The following sequence occurs as the processor outputs a byte of data to the peripheral through the 8255.

8. Data is output by the processor and latched by the 8255 (note that the peripheral bus is in a high-impedance state at this time).
9. The rising edge of $\overline{WR}$ causes $\overline{OBF}$ to switch low ("the output buffer is full").
10. The peripheral acknowledges $\overline{OBF}$ by causing $\overline{ACK}$ to go low.
11. On the falling edge of $\overline{ACK}$ the 8255 releases its data onto the bus.
12. $\overline{OBF}$ returns high ("the output buffer is empty").
13. The rising edge of $\overline{ACK}$ sets INTR, requesting an interrupt if this feature is used.
14. Polling or interrupts can now be used to write the next data byte to the 8255.

A subtle point concerning mode 2 operation is that only a single INTR output is available. This raises the question of how the processor can determine if the interrupt requires data to be read or written—that is, who requested the interrupt? Two solutions are possible.

One is to use software to *poll* the mode 2 status word shown in Fig. 9.17. In this way IBFA and $\overline{OBFA}$ can be tested to determine which one requested the interrupt. Control is then transferred to the proper routine.

A hardware solution is also possible. The interrupt request can be combined with $\overline{OBF}$ or IBF to generate two separate interrupts. These could be connected to the interrupt

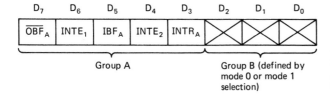

Figure 9.17　8255 mode 2 status word. (From J. Uffenbeck, *Microcomputers and Microprocessors: The 8080, 8085, and Z-80.* Prentice-Hall, Englewood Cliffs, N.J., 1985.)

inputs of the 8259A PIC (programmable interrupt controller). The PIC would then vector each to its own service routine. The 8259A is discussed later in this chapter.

Note that it is possible to *mask* interrupts generated by IBF or $\overline{OBF}$. This is done by resetting INTE1 or INTE2 with a *bit reset* operation. PC6 corresponds to INTE1 and PC4 to INTE2. The same bits must be set if interrupts are to be enabled. This can be seen by studying Fig. 9.14.

Using mode 2 to interface two microcomputers. Most microcomputer peripherals are not bidirectional and thus are interfaced to the 8255 using modes 0 or 1. However, mode 2 can be useful when it is desired to interface two microcomputers over a common (bidirectional) data bus. Figure 9.18 illustrates such a circuit.

The 8255 is connected to the *master* CPU via the $\overline{CS}$ and $\overline{RD}$ and $\overline{WR}$ inputs. It is then programmed for mode 2 operation. The bidirectional port A bus is connected directly to the *slave* CPU's 8-bit data bus. In this example the IBF and $\overline{OBF}$ status bits are connected to the slave as bits D0 and D1 of input port Y. Thus the instruction IN AL,PORT Y can be used by the slave to poll the master CPU and determine if data should be input or output.

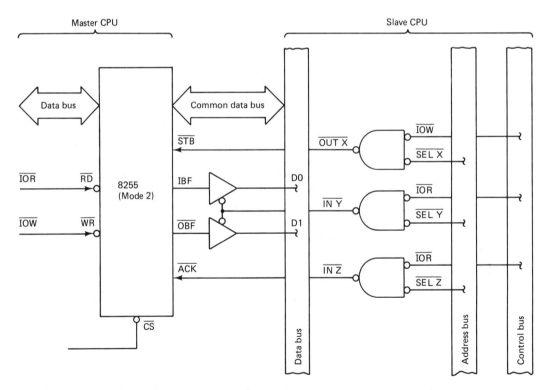

Figure 9.18 When operated in mode 2 the 8255 can be used to interface two separate microcomputer systems. To the slave CPU, the master CPU appears to be an 8-bit input and output port.

When the master has data to be output to the slave, it first checks $\overline{OBF}$ (via the mode 2 status word at port C), and if high, outputs the byte to port A. The slave, polling $\overline{OBF}$ via input port Y, detects $\overline{OBF}$ = 0 and performs an input instruction from port Z (IN AL,PORT_Z). Note that the *IN Z* DSP causes the 8255 to place its data onto the port A data lines (via $\overline{ACK}$) and also causes $\overline{OBF}$ to return high. In this way full handshaking is achieved between the master and slave CPUs.

When the slave has data to be sent to the master, it first polls input port Y. If IBF is low, the 8255's input buffer is empty and ready to receive data. The slave then executes an output instruction to port X (OUT PORT_X,AL). The *OUT X* DSP strobes the 8255, causing it to accept the data and force IBF high. The master CPU can then poll its mode 2 status port and input the data from port A when IBF is high. This read cycle will then reset IBF and another byte can be transferred.

What are some applications for this interface? The slave CPU can be thought of as an *I/O processor*. For example, it might be programmed to take temperature samples once every 5 minutes for 24 hours. At the end of this time it will have stored 288 temperature samples in its memory. The master, busy with other tasks, can now read all 288 samples from the slave and process this information. In this way the master need not be tied up with the "nitty gritty" details of the temperature interface. In fact, the slave could be programmed to *preprocess* the data and supply only the mean, or the extremes, if desired.

In another application the slave CPU could be thought of as a *print buffer*. Each time the master is called on for a print job it can transfer the data to be printed to its slave CPU (at high speed via the port A parallel interface between the two CPUs). The slave can then print the data at the rate required by the printer, while the master busies itself with some other task.

SELF-REVIEW 9.1 (answers on page 473)

9.1.1. The 8255 provides a total of _____ pins that can be programmed as inputs or outputs.

9.1.2. Unless a data bus multiplexer is used, the 8255 must be interfaced to the 8086 in pairs, providing four sets of even and odd ports. (True/False)

9.1.3. What action is taken by the 8255 if the control byte OEH is written to the control port?

9.1.4. To construct an output port supported by handshaking control signals, the 8255 should be programmed for mode _____.

9.1.5. Determine the control byte necessary to program port A of the even PPI chip in Fig. 9.3 for mode 1 output, port B for mode 0 output, and all available pins of port C as outputs.

9.1.6. Write the sequence of 8086 instructions required to initialize the 8255 as described in question 9.1.5 with INTEA enabled.

9.1.7. State the conditions for which an interrupt will occur for the initialization routine in question 9.1.6.

9.1.8. In mode 2, port _____ becomes a bidirectional I/O port, while port _____ can be programmed for mode _____ or _____.

Peripheral interfacing may involve a parallel or serial data path. As we have seen, the 8255 PPI simplifies the task of designing a parallel interface and is directly compatible with a polled or interrupt-driven control scheme.

The 8251A USART provides a similar function when a serial interface is required. It provides two basic functions. In the transmit mode it serializes the parallel data output by the processor, automatically inserting start, stop, and parity bits (asynchronous mode), or sync characters (synchronous mode). In the receive mode it converts the incoming serial data to parallel and checks for parity, framing, and overrun errors.

The 8251A has an 8-bit bidirectional data bus, allowing the microprocessor to *program* its function via one to three control bytes. This can be contrasted with the less flexible AY-5-1013 UART presented in Fig. 8.14. This circuit required all control functions to be *hardwired*.

In this section you learn how to interface the 8215A to the 8086 and 8088 microprocessors and how to initialize the device for the asynchronous or synchronous modes of operation. A polled transmitter procedure will also be presented.

Interfacing the 8251A

Figure 9.19 provides a block diagram and pin description for the 8251A. Note that a separate receiver and transmitter are provided, each with their own clock inputs (RxC and TxC). RxD is the serial data input and TxD is the serial data output. The RxRDY and TxRDY status signals indicate that the receiver and transmitter data buffers are ready to be read or written, respectively. These lines can be polled to synchronize the processor

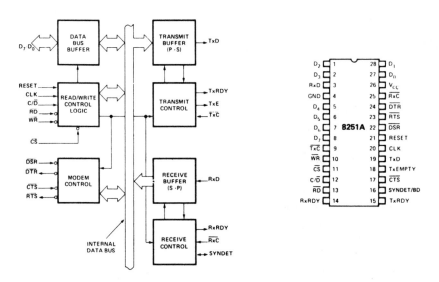

Figure 9.19 Block diagram and pin descriptions for the Intel 8251A USART. (Courtesy of Intel Corporation).

to the data rate of the USART. For this purpose, the pins are duplicated in an internal status port.

SYNDET/BD is a signal that goes high when the sync character has been detected while operating in the synchronous mode. The processor can poll this signal, and when high, begin inputting characters (polling RxRDY). In the asynchronous mode SYNDET/BD indicates a "break" condition. This is a continuous logic 0 level on the received line (RxD). It is sent by a receiver to the transmitter to request a break in transmission—perhaps because of an error condition. SYNDET/BD is also available via the internal status port.

All parallel data exchanged between the CPU and USART travels over the eight bidirectional data bus lines D0–D7. The $\overline{RD}$ and $\overline{WR}$ inputs control the direction of data flow. As with the 8255, the $\overline{CS}$ input must be low for the chip to be selected. The receiver and transmitter, however, continue to function independent of the $\overline{CS}$ input.

Figure 9.20 shows an interface between the 8251A and the 16-bit 8086 microprocessor. In this circuit a data bus multiplexer is used, routing odd port accesses through IC1, and even port accesses through IC2. Note the USART C/$\overline{D}$ input. When this input is low, the internal data port is selected. When high, the control port is chosen. Because of the multiplexer, AB0 can be used to select these ports.

Full decoding is provided for all 16 I/O address lines such that the USART is mapped to consecutive ports 0070H and 0071H (selected by AB0). Table 9.7 summarizes the read and write functions of each of these ports.

Without the multiplexer, D0–D7 of the 8251A would have to be connected to one side of the 8086's data bus or the other. The resulting circuit would then be mapped to two consecutive even addresses (70H and 72H, say) or two consecutive odd addresses (71H and 73H, say).[a]

Figure 9.20 also shows the four modem control signals: $\overline{DSR}$, $\overline{DTR}$, $\overline{RTS}$, and $\overline{CTS}$. Except for $\overline{CTS}$, these signals are general-purpose inputs or outputs and do not affect the operation of the 8251A in any way. They can be controlled via the internal status port (discussed later in this section). $\overline{CTS}$, however, must be low if the 8251A internal transmitter is to be enabled. There is no similar receiver enable. In Chap. 10 we discuss the use of these modem control signals to implement an RS-232C interface.

The CLK input shown in Fig. 9.20 is required by the 8251A for internal timing, but no external inputs or outputs are related to this signal. It must have a frequency of at least 30 times that of the synchronous receiver or transmitter clock and at least 4.5 times the asynchronous receiver or transmitter clock frequency. The maximum clock frequency is 3.125 MHz. In this example the 8284A's PCLK (peripheral clock) is used. This signal has a frequency of one-half the system clock frequency and is 2.5 MHz for an 8086 processor.

The 8251A has t_{RD} of 200 ns maximum and a minimum write pulse width of 250 ns. This means that one wait state will be required with the buffered 8086 minimum mode CPU configuration. No wait states are required in the other modes or configurations. As with the 8255, the advanced write command must be used for maximum mode interfaces.

[a]Most peripheral controller chips are interfaced without the data bus multiplexer. The circuit in Fig. 9.20 is intended as an example when bus multiplexing is desired.

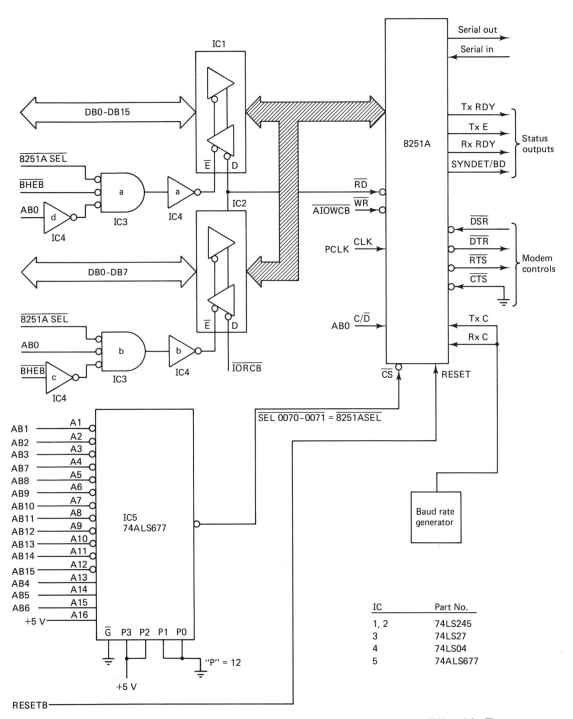

Figure 9.20 Interfacing the 8251A to the 8086 microprocessor maximum-mode CPU module. The data bus multiplexer allows the chip to occupy two consecutive I/O port locations.

TABLE 9.7 8251A CONTROL LOGIC TRUTH TABLE

C/$\overline{\text{D}}$	$\overline{\text{RD}}$	$\overline{\text{WR}}$	Figure 9.20 port address	Function
0	0	1	70H	Read data byte
0	1	0	70H	Write data byte
1	0	1	71H	Read status byte
1	1	0	71H	Write control byte

Generating the asynchronous baud rate clock. As mentioned in Chap. 8, the baud rate clocks of the receiver and transmitter do not have to be exactly matched when the USART is operated asynchronously. However, it is important that the clock frequency be stable. This precludes the use of *RC* oscillators and similar circuits whose frequency will change with temperature and component aging.

Figure 9.21 shows three different approaches for generating the baud rate clock signal. Each circuit uses a crystal time base for accuracy and stability. The circuit in part (a) is simplest but may require a nonstandard crystal to achieve a particular baud rate. For example, at 1200 baud and assuming a 16× clock rate (recall that the baud rate clock is normally 16 times the bit rate), the crystal frequency must be 16 × 1200 = 19,200 Hz. Another disadvantage of this circuit is that it is good only for one baud rate.

The circuit in Fig. 9.21(b) uses the crystal oscillator in the 8284A clock generator to establish a stable base frequency. A frequency divider is then required to step this frequency down to the desired frequency. In this example, PCLK operates at 2.5 MHz, which when divided by 130, yields 19,230 Hz. This in turn yields a baud rate of 1201 assuming a 16× clock. The problem with this circuit is that depending on the base frequency, some baud rates may not be achievable. For example, 9600 baud requires a 153,600-Hz clock (assuming 16×). This in turn requires a divide-by-16.276 counter.

Figure 9.21(c) shows the best solution. This single chip combines the features from the previous two circuits. Using a crystal time base for stability, its 1.8432-MHz base frequency can be divided by integers to achieve 10 different baud rates all within 0.1%.

The 8251A can be programmed to accept a 16× or 64× baud rate clock. This feature can be taken advantage of to switch between two different baud rates with the same clock frequency.

Example 9.7

What frequency is required for a baud rate of 1200, assuming that the 8251A is programmed for a 16× clock? What does the baud rate become if the 8251A is reprogrammed for a 64× clock?

Solution For 1200 baud the clock frequency must be 1200 × 16 = 19,200 Hz. Now if the USART interprets this as a 64× clock, the baud rate becomes 19,200/64 = 300 baud.

In the asynchronous mode the baud rate is limited to 19,200 using a 16× clock. Using a 64× clock, the maximum baud rate is 9600. The latter restriction is imposed due to the CLK input's maximum frequency specification. In the synchronous mode the 8251A baud rate clock is limited to 64 kHz (a 1× clock must be used).

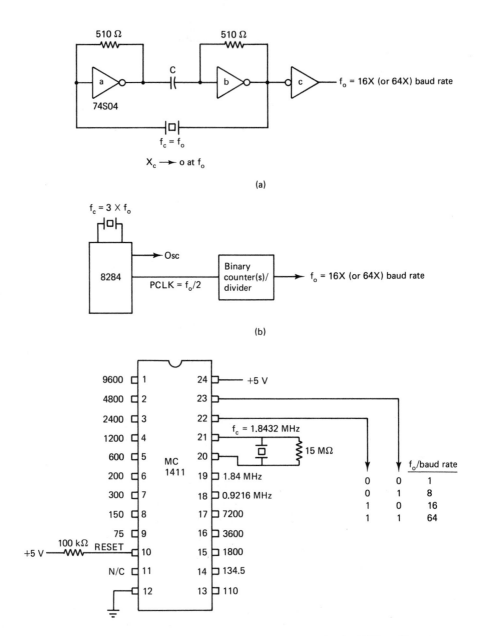

Figure 9.21 Three methods of generating the baud rate clock signal: (a) TTL oscillator; (b) 8284A peripheral clock and frequency divider; (c) single-chip baud rate generator.

Application. The advantages of serial data transmission versus parallel have already been mentioned in Chap. 8. In most cases, however, the TTL levels on the serial in and out lines must be translated to EIA (Electronics Industries Associates) RS-232C specifications. This is (typically) -12 V for a logic 1 and $+12$ V for a logic 0. Special drivers and receivers are available for this purpose. In Chap. 10 we provide more detail on RS-232C.

Many computer peripherals use the asynchronous serial RS-232C format, including printers, plotters, and modems. By following this standard, equipment from several different manufacturers can readily be interfaced.

Another application for asynchronous serial that should not be overlooked is *remote control*. After translating the USART's TTL levels to RS-232C levels, the serial data can be transmitted for several hundred, even thousands of feet, to a remote location. Using an 8-bit data byte, 256 devices could potentially be controlled using only a two-conductor (signal and ground) cable.

Programming the 8251A for the Asynchronous Mode

When programming the 8251A, the following sequence must be followed:

1. Reset the chip (via external input or internal control byte).
2. Write the mode instruction to the control port.
3. Write the command instruction to the control port.

Figure 9.22 describes the form of the mode and command instructions. A reset command must be used to start the initialization sequence. The following command (only) will be interpreted as a *mode* instruction. After this byte has been written, all further writes to the control register will be interpreted as *command* instructions. *The only way to return to the mode instruction is to apply a reset pulse or write a command byte with bit 6 high.*

Example 9.8

Write the initialization routine required to program the 8251A USART in Fig. 9.20 for asynchronous transmission with 7 data bits, 2 stop bits, and odd parity. Select a 16× clock and program $\overline{DTR}$ and $\overline{RTS}$ to be low.

Solution   The program is as follows:

```
        MOV   AL,01000000B      ;Reset command
        OUT   71H,AL            ;Control port
        MOV   AL,11011010B      ;Mode instruction:
                                ;7 data, 2 stop, odd parity, 16×
        OUT   71H,AL            ;Control port
        MOV   AL,00110111B      ;Command instruction:
                                ;RTS and DTR low, error reset, enable
        OUT   71H,AL            ;Command Port
        IN    AL,70H            ;Dummy read to clear receiver
```

The receiver enable (bit 2 of the command instruction) only inhibits the RxRDY flag—not the receiver itself. Thus it is possible for the receiver to have captured a character before or during the initialization routine. The dummy read ensures that the receiver holding register is clear.

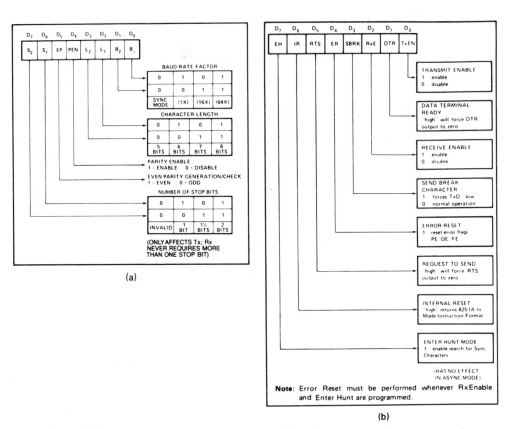

(a)

(b)

Figure 9.22 (a) Asynchronous mode instruction format; (b) synchronous or asynchronous command instruction format. (Courtesy of Intel Corporation.)

Once initialized the USART will automatically begin looking for the start bit of any incoming serial data. Similarly, the transmitter will serialize any data written to the transmitter buffer (output port 70H in Fig. 9.20). However, you must not forget the need to *synchronize* the processor to the data rate of the USART. For example, even at 19,200 baud, more than 0.5 ms is required to transmit or receive one character (assuming 8 data bits, 1 start bit, and 1 stop bit). This is a very long time to the processor.

Figure 9.23 shows the 8251A status bit definitions obtained when the control port is read. Pay particular attention to TxRDY and RxRDY. Data should not be output unless TxRDY is high, nor should received data be input until RxRDY is high. By polling these pins the processor can be synchronized to the data rate of the peripheral.

Figure 9.24 gives an example of such a routine. It is written as a printer procedure, outputting the contents of a print buffer to the 8251A interface in Fig. 9.20. In this example we assume that the USART has previously been initialized (see Ex. 9.8). As you can see, the program is straightforward, simply testing bit 0 of port 71H (TxRDY of the control port) and outputting a new byte from the table when the transmitter is ready.

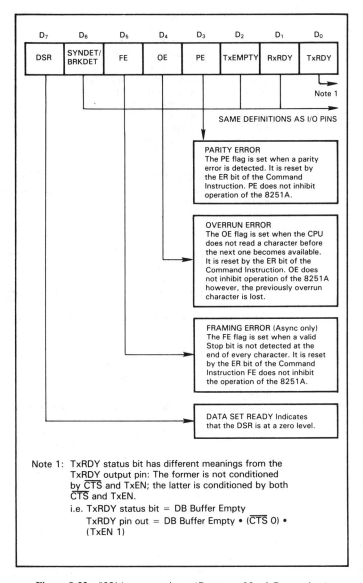

Figure 9.23 8251A status register. (Courtesy of Intel Corporation.)

Processing rate versus data rate. There is one problem with this simple synchronization scheme. We have synchronized the processor to the *data rate* of the peripheral but not to the *processing speed* of the peripheral. The control program outputs one character after the other as fast as the baud rate will allow. The assumption is that the receiver (the printer) can process these characters as fast as they are being sent.

But can it? For example, what happens if the printer receives a *carriage return* character? The print head will have to return all the way to the left margin of the paper.

TITLE FIG. 9.24

```
                ;Function:      Empty the print buffer specified in
                ;               the device control block and terminated
                ;               with a '$' symbol.
                ;Inputs:        Data buffer beginning at address PRINT_BUF.
                ;Outputs:       Each character to be printed is
                ;               output to the 8251A USART data port
                ;               shown in Fig. 9.20.
                ;Calls:         nothing
                ;Destroys       AX,DS,SI,flags


0000            DEV_CTRL_BL     SEGMENT BYTE
0000 ????????   PRINT_BUF       DD      ?              ;Put address of buffer here
0004            DEV_CTRL_BL     ENDS


                ;Program equates


= 0024          LAST_BYTE       EQU     '$'            ;Data terminated with a '$'
= 0070          DATA_PORT       EQU     70H            ;See Fig. 9.20
= 0071          CTRL_P          EQU     71H            ;
= 0001          TXRDY           EQU     00000001B      ;Mask for TXRDY


                ;Procedure assumes the USART has been programmed.
                ;See Ex. 9.8.


0000            CODE            SEGMENT BYTE
                                ASSUME  CS:CODE, DS:DEV_CTRL_BL


0000            SERIAL_XMTR     PROC    NEAR
0000 B8 ---- R                  MOV     AX,DEV_CTRL_BL ;Point DS at DEV_CTRL_BL
0003 8E D8                      MOV     DS,AX
0005 C5 36 0000 R               LDS     SI,PRINT_BUF   ;Fetch buffer address to DS:SI
0009 FC                         CLD                    ;Auto increment


000A E4 71      POLL:           IN      AL,CTRL_P      ;Get TXRDY status
000C A8 01                      TEST    AL,TXRDY       ;Ready for a new byte?
000E 74 FA                      JZ      POLL           ;No - so wait


0010 AC                         LODSB                  ;Yes - fetch byte and increment pointer
0011 3C 24                      CMP     AL,LAST_BYTE   ;Is this the last byte?
0013 74 04                      JE      QUIT           ;Yes - so return to caller
0015 E6 70                      OUT     DATA_PORT,AL   ;No - output the byte
0017 EB F1                      JMP     POLL           ;Repeat the cycle
0019 C3         QUIT:           RET
001A            SERIAL_XMTR     ENDP
001A            CODE            ENDS
                                END
```

Figure 9.24   Polled procedure to output a block of data to the 8251A operated in the asynchronous mode.

Depending on the printer, this may require several milliseconds. The CPU, having no way of knowing this, continues to send characters. The result will be several lost characters as the printer processes this special (carriage return) character.

Several handshaking protocols have been established to solve this problem, including the ASCII exchange characters ETX/ACK, X-ON/X-OFF, and the modem control signals $\overline{RTS}$ and $\overline{DTR}$. These protocols are discussed in Chap. 10. The important point to note for now is that polling RxRDY and TxRDY will not necessarily guarantee synchronization between the microprocessor and peripheral.

Control schemes. The long time interval between characters at 9600 baud (even longer with lower baud rates) should suggest that polling will be an inefficient control scheme. Interrupts or DMA may be good alternatives. The 8251A supports both techniques because the status bits are also available as external outputs. For example, the TxRDY pin will go high to indicate that the USART is ready to accept a new character. Connecting this output to the 8086's INTR input (or that of a PIC) would allow the processor to perform some other task, stopping only when necessary to service the USART.

DMA is usually associated with transferring large blocks of data to a high-speed peripheral. However, this technique can also be put to good use when controlling slow serial transmitters and receivers such as the 8251A. The "trick" is to program the DMAC for *byte transfers*. The starting address of the memory buffer and number of bytes to be transferred are also programmed into the DMAC. When TxRDY becomes active, a byte DMA transfer occurs. The CPU then resumes normal processing. The advantage is that the DMAC maintains all the data normally stored in the device control block. The software overhead is reduced considerably.

Programming the 8251A for the Synchronous Mode

The 8251A is a character-oriented serial device and is compatible with the bisync synchronous communications protocol discussed in Chap. 8. This is a technique in which the serial data is transmitted framed between sync *characters* instead of sync *bits*. As noted in Chap. 8, the advantage is a much higher character rate because fewer bytes are devoted to maintaining synchronization.

When operated in the synchronous mode the 8251A clock must be set for $1 \times$ operation (bits D0 and D1 of the mode instruction must be 0). The clock signal must also accompany the data, either as an additional conductor in a hard-wired system, or encoded with the data when used with a synchronous modem. This is because the receiving and transmitting clock rates must match exactly (0.1%).

When programming the 8251A for synchronous mode operation, the following sequence must be followed:

1. Reset the chip (via external input or internal control byte).
2. Write the mode instruction to the control port.
3. Write one or two sync characters to the control port.
4. Write the command instruction to the control port.

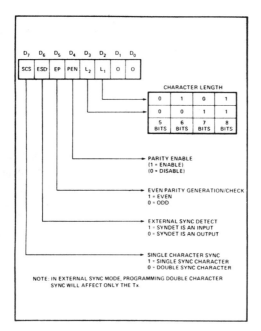

Figure 9.25 Synchronous mode instruction format. The command instruction format is the same as in Fig. 9.22(b). (Courtesy of Intel Corporation).

As with the asynchronous mode, the mode instruction can only be written immediately after a reset. Following this instruction, the USART expects one or two sync characters to be specified. The next (and all following) writes will be interpreted as command instructions.

Figure 9.25 indicates the format for the mode instruction when the USART is operated in the synchronous mode. The command instruction format does not change from that shown in Fig. 9.22(b).

After programming the $\overline{\text{USART}}$ for the synchronous mode, the serial output line will be high (marking) until $\overline{\text{CTS}}$ goes low. At this time the contents of the transmitter buffer will be serialized and transmitted. Normally, this will be one or two sync characters.

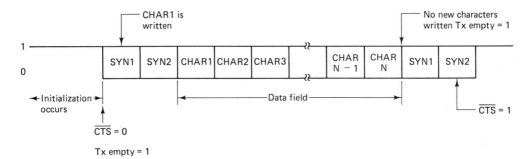

Figure 9.26 Synchronous data format when the 8251A is programmed for two sync characters. (From J. Uffenbeck, *Microcomputers and Microprocessors: The 8080, 8085, and Z-80.* Prentice-Hall, Englewood Cliffs, N.J., 1985.)

Polling TxRDY, the processor begins outputting the data to be transmitted. If at any time the transmitter's buffer becomes empty, the SYNC characters will automatically be inserted by the 8251A. This is done to maintain synchronization, as illustrated in Fig. 9.26. Because of the $1 \times$ clock, one data bit is transmitted with each clock pulse.

In the receive mode the final command instruction should set bit 7, requesting the 8251A to enter the "hunt" mode. As each new bit is shifted into the receiver buffer, the resulting character is compared against the sync character(s). If no match is found, a new bit is input. SYNDET/BD goes high to indicate synchronization when the characters match (two contiguous characters if two sync bytes have been specified). Data can now be input by the CPU polling RxRDY, as in the asynchronous mode.

SELF-REVIEW 9.2 (answers on page 473)

9.2.1. To the microprocessor the 8251A appears as _____ read/write I/O ports or memory locations.

9.2.2. Refer to the interface in Fig. 9.20. The control port can be read when $\overline{\text{8251A SEL}}$ = _____, $C/\overline{D}$ = _____, $\overline{\text{BHEB}}$ = _____, AB0 = _____, $\overline{\text{RD}}$ = _____, and $\overline{\text{WR}}$ = _____.

9.2.3. Calculate the modulus of the frequency divider required to use a 5MHz 8086's PCLK as the baud rate clock for 300 baud. Assume that the 8251A is programmed for a $16 \times$ clock.

9.2.4. Upon reset, the next write cycle to the 8251A control register will be interpreted as a _____ instruction.

9.2.5. Write the 8086 instruction sequence to program the 8251A in Fig. 9.20 for asynchronous transmission with a $64 \times$ clock, 7 data bits, 1 stop bit, and no parity. Program all modem control signals (except $\overline{\text{CTS}}$) to be inactive.

9.2.6. If polling is used to input characters from the 8251A, the _____ status bit should be tested before each character is input.

9.2.7. Explain how the 8251A synchronizes itself to the incoming data when operated in the synchronous mode.

9.3 THE 8259A PROGRAMMABLE INTERRUPT CONTROLLER (PIC)

When Intel designed the 8-bit 8085 microprocessor they included five separate interrupt inputs. This was deemed adequate for a processor of the 8085's capabilities. However, when the 8086 family was designed, the philosophy changed. The 8086 is a general-purpose microprocessor designed to be compatible with a number of optional *coprocessors* and *peripheral controllers*. It has only a single (maskable) interrupt input. However, by using the 8259A programmable interrupt controller (PIC), up to 64 prioritized interrupt inputs can be interfaced.

The basic functions of the PIC can be summarized as follows.

1. Accept up to eight interrupt requests (expandable to 64 in the cascade mode).
2. Prioritize these inputs such that the highest-priority device receives service when simultaneous interrupts occur.

3. Issue a single interrupt request compatible with the 8086's INTR input.

4. Output a unique type number for each interrupt input in response to the CPU's $\overline{\text{INTA}}$ bus cycle.

Figure 9.27 provides a block diagram of the 8259A and includes the pin number description. Like the 8255 and 8251A, the PIC is programmed via an 8-bit bidirectional data bus. In this section you will see how to interface this chip to the 8086 or 8088, study the various modes of operation, and learn how to specify the initialization and operation control instructions.

Interfacing the 8259A

To the microprocessor the PIC appears to be two memory or I/O-mapped 8-bit ports selected by the (PIC's) A0 input. The direction of data flow, to or from the PIC, is controlled by the $\overline{\text{RD}}$ and $\overline{\text{WR}}$ inputs. Because of its 8-bit bus, the PIC is normally connected to either the even or odd side of the 8086's data bus.

Figure 9.28 shows an I/O-mapped interface in which the PIC is mapped to the addresses 007CH and 007EH. Notice that the $\overline{\text{SEL}}$ signal will be active only for *byte* accesses within this address range (because $\overline{\text{BHE}}$ must be high).

Basic Operation of the PIC

Before the PIC can be used the interrupt *type* numbers must be programmed. In addition, the operating mode and priority scheme must be selected. These software codes are written via the 8-bit bidirectional data bus lines (DB0–DB7 in Fig. 9.28).

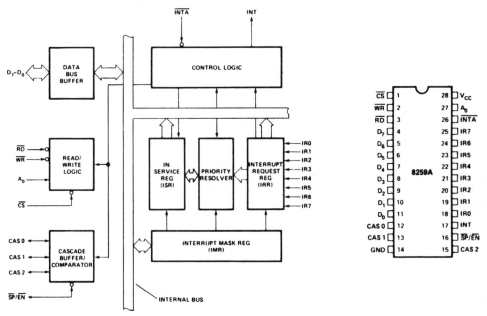

Figure 9.27 Block diagram and pin definitions for the 8259A programmable interrupt controller (PIC). (Courtesy of Intel Corporation.)

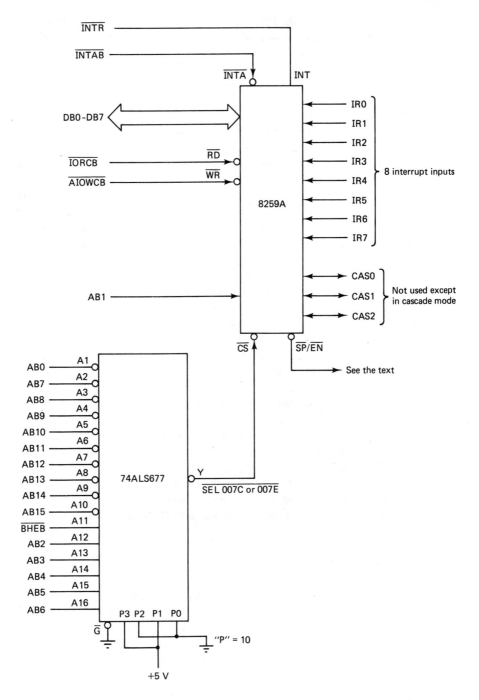

Figure 9.28 Interfacing the 8259A PIC to the 8086 microprocessor. Because of its 8-bit data bus, the PIC must reside on the even or odd side of the 8086's data bus.

Once initialized, the PIC responds to interrupt requests on IR0–IR7. For example, if an interrupt request occurs that is of a higher priority than that currently being serviced (if any), the PIC drives its INT output high. Assuming that IF (the CPU's interrupts enabled flag) is set, the processor finishes the current instruction and responds by outputting the first of two $\overline{\text{INTA}}$ pulses. This pulse freezes (stores) all interrupt requests within the PIC in a special *interrupt request register* (IRR). The interrupt signal can now be removed.

When the second $\overline{\text{INTA}}$ pulse is received by the PIC, one bit of the *in-service* (IS) register is set. For example, if a request on IR3 is acknowledged by the CPU, the PIC will set IS3 to indicate that this input is now active. Furthermore, inputs of equal or lower priority will be inhibited.

Next, the PIC outputs a *type number* corresponding to the active IR input. This number is multiplied by 4 within the CPU and then used as a pointer into the interrupt vector table located at address 00000 through 003FFH. Thus if the PIC outputs a type number of A0H (1010 0000), the CPU will retrieve the vector stored in 00280H–00283H (10 1000 00XX).

Before transferring to the vector address, the CPU pushes CS, IP, and the flag register onto the stack. The interrupt service routine (ISR) then executes. Upon completion, the ISR must issue a special *end-of-interrupt* (EOI) command to the PIC. This resets the IS register bit corresponding to the active IR input. If this bit is not reset, all interrupts of equal or lower priority will remain inhibited by the PIC.

The interrupt cycle ends when the IRET instruction is executed. This retrieves CS, IP, and the flags and transfers control back to the interrupted program.

Using the PIC in a buffered environment. Figure 9.29 illustrates a typical interface when the PIC is used with a buffered CPU. The $\overline{\text{SP/EN}}$ signal is output low during the $\overline{\text{INTA}}$ cycle and should be used to disable the system data bus transceivers. To see why this is necessary, turn to Fig. 8.26. During an $\overline{\text{INTA}}$ bus cycle the CPU control signals DT/$\overline{\text{R}}$ and DEN are enabled to allow the type number to be read by the CPU. However, when the PIC is interfaced to the CPU's local address/data bus, the enabled buffers will contend with the data bus of the PIC as it attempts to output the interrupt type number. Using $\overline{\text{SP/EN}}$ as a qualifier with DEN, as shown in Fig. 9.29, avoids this problem.

Cascading the PIC

Figure 9.30 illustrates the technique used to expand the capabilities of the PIC beyond the eight inputs of a single chip. One PIC is designated the *master* ($\overline{\text{SP/EN}}$ = +5 V) and the others become slaves. Each slave's INT output drives an IR input of the master. This allows the priority structure of the master to be extended to the slave PICs. This is because only the master PIC can request an interrupt of the processor.

When an interrupt request occurs on one of the slave's IR inputs, its priority is resolved among the other inputs within that slave. If this input is enabled, the request is passed on to the master. Again the priority is resolved, this time among all the slaves. Presuming the interrupt level to be enabled, the master requests an interrupt by forcing its INT output high.

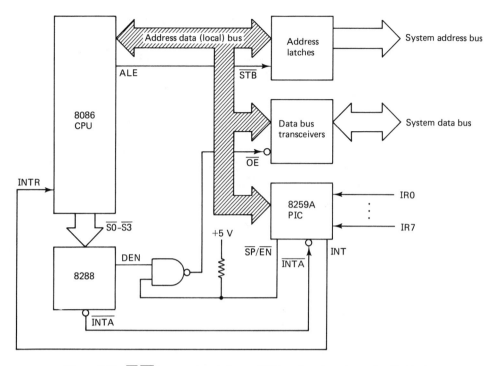

Figure 9.29 $\overline{\text{SP/EN}}$ is output low during an INTA cycle and can be used to disable the data bus buffers when the PIC is connected to the 8086's local bus in a buffered mode.

Now assuming processor interrupts to be enabled, the CPU outputs the first $\overline{\text{INTA}}$ pulse. Upon receipt of this pulse the master PIC outputs a *cascade address* on CAS0–CAS2. This enables the selected PIC, causing it to output its type number during the second $\overline{\text{INTA}}$ pulse.

Be sure to notice that this interconnection scheme allows each slave to be programmed separately from the master. Indeed, each PIC can be programmed to operate in a different mode.

When the service routine completes, it issues an EOI command to the slave PIC, resetting the appropriate IS bit. Next, the IS register of the slave should be read to ensure that another interrupt from that slave is not in progress. If this read returns zero, an EOI command can also be sent to the master. If the slave's IS register is not zero, the master IS bit should be left high until the lower-priority routine completes.

The Interrupt Control Registers

All interrupt requests must pass through three registers within the PIC, as shown in Fig. 9.31. The first register is IRR, the interrupt request register mentioned previously. This is a transparent latch clocked by the FREEZE signal. Bits in this register are not latched until the first $\overline{\text{INTA}}$ pulse occurs.

Because IRR is transparent, all requests are passed on to the *interrupt mask register* (IMR). If the corresponding mask bit is a zero, the request is routed to the *priority*

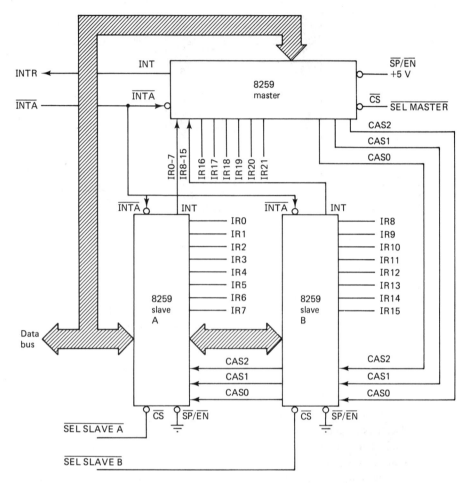

Figure 9.30 Cascading the 8259A. Up to 64 interrupts can be accommodated using one master and eight slaves. (From J. Uffenbeck, *Microcomputers and Microprocessors: The 8080, 8085, and Z-80.* Prentice-Hall, Englewood Cliffs, N.J., 1985.)

resolver. This is a circuit designed to select the highest-priority input when simultaneous requests occur or when the request has higher priority than the routine currently executing.

If the request meets either of these two criteria, the INT output is driven high. When the CPU acknowledges this request, the FREEZE signal is generated, latching the IR inputs. When the INTA cycle completes, the IS bit is set, indicating that the interrupt is now in service. Simultaneously, all bits of IRR are cleared.

Notice that the PIC does not "remember" interrupt requests that are not acknowledged. It is up to you to hold the request until the FREEZE signal latches it. If an interrupt is requested but no IR bit is found high during INTA—that is, IR is removed before being acknowledged—the PIC will default to an IR7. For this reason, this input can be reserved for "spurious" interrupts and an IRET instruction used for the IR7 service

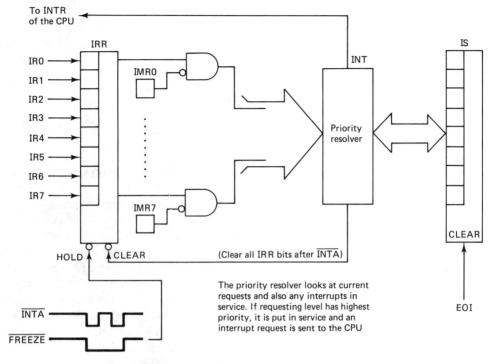

To INTR
of the CPU

IRR

IR0 →
IR1 →   IMR0
IR2 →
IR3 →
IR4 →   Priority
IR5 →   resolver
IR6 →
IR7 →
           IMR7

INT

IS

CLEAR

HOLD   CLEAR   (Clear all IRR bits after $\overline{INTA}$)

The priority resolver looks at current
requests and also any interrupts in
service. If requesting level has highest
priority, it is put in service and an
interrupt request is sent to the CPU

EOI

$\overline{INTA}$

$\overline{FREEZE}$

Figure 9.31 All interrupt requests must pass through the PIC's interrupt request register (IRR) and interrupt mask register (IMR). If put in service, the appropriate bit of the in-service (IS) register is set.

routine. If the IR7 input is used for a legitimate device, the service routine should read the IS register and test that bit 7 is high. A routine to do this is given later in this section.

It is important to remember that the CPU has ultimate control over its interrupt input via the STI and CLI instructions. In fact, when servicing an interrupt the CPU automatically clears IF (see the flowchart in Fig. 8.24). Thus it is quite possible that the PIC could receive an interrupt request of higher priority than that currently executing but not receive an acknowledge from the CPU. For this reason, an STI instruction must be explicitly placed in the ISR if the priority capabilities of the PIC are to be extended to interrupts in progress. For example (assuming IR0 to have highest priority and IR7 lowest priority):

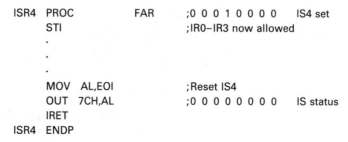

```
ISR4  PROC        FAR       ;0 0 0 1 0 0 0 0   IS4 set
      STI                   ;IR0–IR3 now allowed
      .
      .
      .
      MOV  AL,EOI           ;Reset IS4
      OUT  7CH,AL           ;0 0 0 0 0 0 0 0   IS status
      IRET
ISR4  ENDP
```

If interrupts are not to be allowed during the execution of the service routine, the STI instruction should be omitted.

There are several ways of setting the priority within the PIC and these are explained in the next section.

Operating Modes

The PIC can be programmed to operate in one of six modes. Following is a brief description of each.

1. Fully nested. This is the default mode of the PIC and prioritizes the IR inputs such that IR0 has highest priority and IR7 lowest priority. This priority structure extends to interrupts currently in service, as well as simultaneous interrupt requests.

For example, if an interrupt on IR3 is being serviced (IS3 = 1) and a request occurs on IR2, the PIC will issue an interrupt request because the IR2 input has higher priority. But if an IR4 is received, the PIC will not issue the request. Note, however, that the IR2 request will not be acknowledged unless the CPU has set IF within the IR3 service routine.

In all operating modes, the IS bit corresponding to the active routine must be reset to allow other lower-priority interrupts to be acknowledged. This can be done by outputting a special *nonspecific EOI* instruction to the PIC. Normally, this is done just before the IRET instruction within the service routine. Alternatively, the PIC can be programmed to perform this nonspecific EOI automatically when the second INTA pulse occurs. Note however, that in this later case, lower-priority interrupts will be enabled throughout the higher-priority service routine.

2. Special fully nested. This mode is selected for the master PIC in a cascaded system. It is identical to the fully nested mode but extends the priority structure to the cascaded PICs. For example, if the service routine for IR13 in Fig. 9.30 is in progress, a request from IR8 will be honored because it has higher priority (even though both requests use the same master IR input). In effect, the special fully nested mode allows the master PIC to accept requests on a (master) IR input that is already in service.

3. Nonspecific rotating mode. This mode is intended for systems with several interrupt sources, all of equal priority. When the EOI command is issued, the corresponding IS bit is reset and then assigned lowest priority. The priority of the other inputs rotates accordingly. Figure 9.32 illustrates the technique. Simultaneous interrupts are shown to arrive on IR4 and IR6. The IR4 routine is put in service (IS4 = 1), as it has highest priority [Fig. 9.32(a)].

When the rotate-on-nonspecific-EOI command is given by the IR4 service routine, IS4 is reset and becomes the lowest priority [Fig. 9.32(b)]. Notice that this moves IR6 up to second-highest priority. A second rotate-on-nonspecific-EOI command, given upon completion of the IR6 service routine, resets IS6, leaving the IR7 input with highest priority [Fig. 9.32(c)].

The rotate-on-nonspecific-EOI mode ensures that no input will ever have to wait for more than seven devices to be serviced before being serviced itself. The rotate-on-

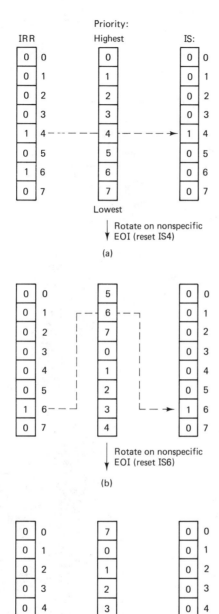

Figure 9.32 (a) Simultaneous interrupt requests arrive at IR4 and IR6. IR4 has highest priority and its IS bit is set as the IR4 service routine is put in service. (b) The IR4 service routine issues a rotate-on-nonspecific-EOI command, resetting IS4 and assigning it lowest priority. IR6 is now placed in service. (c) The IR6 service routine issues a rotate-on-nonspecific-EOI command, resetting IS6 and assigning it lowest priority.

nonspecific-EOI command can be output within the service routine or programmed to occur automatically after the second $\overline{\text{INTA}}$ pulse occurs.

There is one caution to be observed with this mode. The EOI command always resets the *lowest-numbered* IS bit. In the fully nested mode this will always correspond to the routine in service. However, in the rotating priority mode this may not always be the current in-service bit. Figure 9.33 shows an example in which an IR4 is in progress but interrupted by an IR6 (the IR6 is assumed to have higher priority). Issuing a nonspecific EOI command within the IR6 service routine will cause IS4 to be reset—the wrong bit.

There are two solutions to this problem. One is to select the automatic nonspecific rotating mode. This will automatically clear the IS bit as soon as the CPU acknowledges

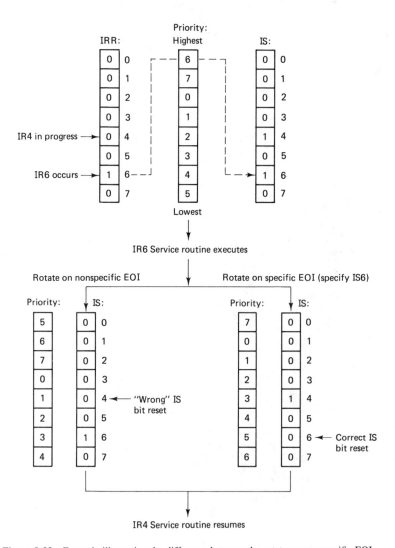

Figure 9.33 Example illustrating the difference between the rotate-on-nonspecific-EOI command and the rotate-on-specific-EOI command.

the request. Two IS bits will never be set simultaneously, and thus the "wrong" bit can never be cleared. However, this also means that all other IR inputs will be enabled throughout the service routine, which may be undesirable.

The second solution is to select the *specific rotating* mode.

4. Specific rotating. This mode again allows the priorities to be rotated, but the EOI command can indicate the specific IS bit to reset and assign lowest priority. Figure 9.33 illustrates how this command can be used to solve the "wrong bit" problem mentioned above.

A variation of this command allows the priorities to be specified without resetting the IS bit. This allows the programmer to control the priority structure within the service routine. For example, while executing the IR4 service routine it may be important to assign the IR7 input highest priority. The specific rotating command allows you to do this.

5. Special mask. As we have seen, the PIC normally inhibits interrupt requests of equal or lower priority than that currently in service. In the special mask mode, this is altered to allow interrupts on all inputs except the input currently in service.

6. Poll. In this mode the INT output of the PIC is inhibited and the device is used as a prioritized poller. Performing an I/O read instruction from the PIC (either port address) returns the status word shown in Fig. 9.34. Typically, a polling routine is written to test bit 7 of the PIC status word. If this bit is high, bits 0 through 2 encode the highest-priority device requesting service.

Programming the Initialization Control Registers

As you can imagine, the key to using the PIC is to perform the proper initialization sequence required for the desired operating mode. Figure 9.35 defines the format for the four initialization control words (ICWs).

ICW1. This byte is required in all modes and is written to port 7CH in Fig. 9.28 (A0 = 0). Bits D7–D5 and D2 are required only when used with the 8085 microprocessor. Bit D4 must be a 1. Bit D3 specifies the IR trigger, either level or rising edge. Remember,

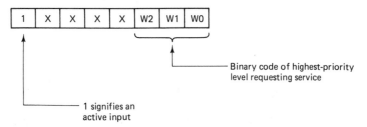

Figure 9.34 In the polled mode the 8259A acts as a prioritized status port. (From J. Uffenbeck, *Microcomputers and Microprocessors: The 8080, 8085, and Z-80.* Prentice-Hall, Englewood Cliffs, N.J., 1985.)

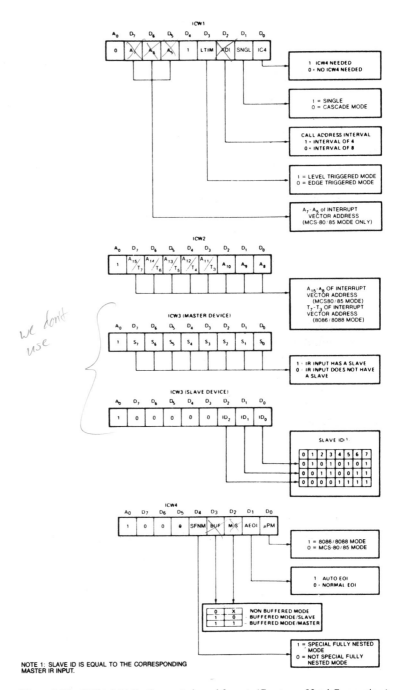

we don't use

NOTE 1: SLAVE ID IS EQUAL TO THE CORRESPONDING MASTER IR INPUT.

Figure 9.35 8259A initialization control word format. (Courtesy of Intel Corporation.)

however, that the input must be held until acknowledged by the CPU. In addition, if you program for the level trigger mode, you must be sure to remove the input after the acknowledge pulses occur to avoid multiple interrupt requests.

Bit D1 is used to specify that the PIC is to be used in the cascade mode (requiring a subsequent ICW3). Bit D0 must be a 1 for an 8086 or 8088 microprocessor.

As an example, the following instructions program the PIC in Fig. 9.28 for the 8086 mode, rising edge trigger, and a single PIC.

```
MOV    AL,00010011B
OUT    7CH,AL
```

ICW2.   ICW2, written to port 7EH in Fig. 9.28 (A0 = 1), specifies the five high-order bits of the interrupt type number to be output by the PIC during the INTA bus cycle. The PIC assigns the three low-order bits 000–111 to correspond to the active IR input, IR0–IR7. Thus the base type number of the PIC must end with 000B.

Example 9.9

Determine the value for ICW2 if the PIC is to be programmed for a base address of C8H. What type numbers will be output by the PIC for each IR input, and from which memory locations will the CPU fetch the interrupt vectors?

Solution   ICW2 is equal to the base address and thus should be programmed for 11001000B. Table 9.8 summarizes the type numbers output for each IR input and the corresponding interrupt vector locations in memory.

ICW3.   This byte is also output to port 7EH in Fig. 9.28 (A0 = 1) but is required only if the PIC is to be used in a cascaded system. For a master it specifies the IR input to which a slave is connected. Thus, setting ICW3 to 00000011 indicates that slave PICs are connected to the master's IR1 and IR0 inputs.

For a slave PIC, ICW3 indicates the *cascade address* (master IR input) to which that slave is connected. For example, if the slave is connected to IR6 of the master, ICW3 = 00000110. During the INTA bus cycle the master will output this address on CAS0–CAS2. If the address matches, the slave will output the type number corresponding to its highest-priority active IR input.

TABLE 9.8   PIC INTERRUPT VECTORS FOR EX. 9.9

Input	Type number output by PIC	Interrupt vector location
IR0	C8H	0000:0320–0323H
IR1	C9H	0000:0324–0327H
IR2	CAH	0000:0328–032BH
IR3	CBH	0000:032C–032FH
IR4	CCH	0000:0330–0333H
IR5	CDH	0000:0334–0337H
IR6	CEH	0000:0338–033BH
IR7	CFH	0000:033C–033FH

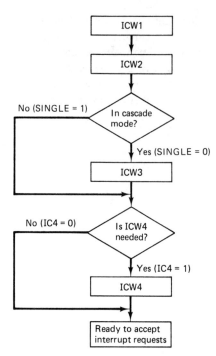

Figure 9.36 8259A initialization sequence. (Courtesy of Intel Corporation.)

ICW4. This byte is also output to port 7EH in Fig. 9.28 (A0 = 1) and is required to specify the 8086 mode (bit D0 = 1). Bit D1 activates the automatic EOI instruction used in the fully nested and automatic rotating priority modes. Bits D2 and D3 specify if the PIC is the master or slave in a buffered CPU environment, and thus control the $\overline{SP/EN}$ output discussed previously. Bit D4 selects the fully nested or special fully nested operating mode.

You have probably noticed that ICW2–ICW4 are all written to the same port address. This works because the 8259A expects these bytes to be written in sequence, as shown in the flowchart in Fig. 9.36. ICW3 and ICW4 are optional depending on the presence of slave PICs in the system and if the 8086 is to be used.

Example 9.10

Write the initialization instructions required to program the PIC for the nonbuffered 8086 mode with rising-edge IR trigger, noncascade mode, and a fully nested priority structure. Assume that IR1 is to produce a type number of 65 and that the normal EOI command will be used to reset the IS bit.

Solution These requirements meet those of the 8086 printer driver routine in Fig. 8.31. The type number of 65 corresponds to 40H for IR0. This is the base type number for the PIC. Figure 8.31(a) shows the three equates required for ICW1, ICW2, and ICW4. The PIC port addresses are assumed to be PIC_A and PIC_B. Figure 8.31(b) shows how these ICWs are output to the PIC. Note that all except ICW1 are sent to address PIC_B. PMASK is explained in the next section.

Programming the Operation Control Registers

After the three (or four) initialization control words have been written, the PIC is ready to receive interrupts on IR0–IR7 and will operate in the fully nested or special fully nested mode. To specify the rotating priority modes, the special mask mode, the polled mode, the interrupt mask, or the EOI commands requires that the *operation control registers* (OCWs) be programmed.

Figure 9.37 explains the bit definitions for the three operation control registers, OCW1, OCW2, and OCW3.

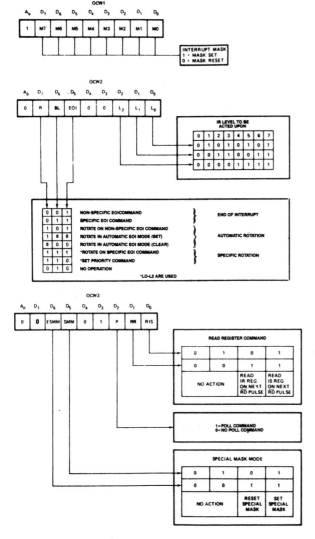

Figure 9.37 8259A operation control word format. (Courtesy of Intel Corporation.)

OCW1. This register can be written to or read from using port address 7EH (A0 = 1) for the hardware in Fig. 9.28. Bits set to a 1 mask the corresponding IR input, inhibiting it from requesting an interrupt. In Figs. 8.31(a) and 8.31(b), PMASK is used to mask all inputs except IR1, which is driven by the printer's $\overline{ACKNLG}$ signal.

OCW2. OCW2 is written to port 7CH (A0 = 0) in Fig. 9.28 and is used to specify the EOI command to the PIC. Note that bit D4 is a 0, so the PIC will not confuse this byte with ICW1 (in which bit D4 = 1). Table 9.9 summarizes the commands that can be written to this register.

Example 9.11

Describe the form of the interrupt service routine when the PIC has been programmed for the fully nested mode.

Solution   Assuming the port addresses in Fig. 9.28:

```
ISR  PROC  FAR
          .                    ;ISR begins
          .
          .                    ;ISR ends
     MOV   AL,00100000B        ;Nonspecific EOI
     OUT   7CH,AL              ;OCW2
     IRET
ISR  ENDP
```

Note: The printer ISR [Fig. 8.31(e)] provides an additional example of the non-specific EOI command.

There is no need to worry about resetting the wrong IS bit when operating in the fully nested mode. This is because the nonspecific EOI instruction always resets the lowest-numbered IS bit. In the fully nested mode, this will correspond to the currently executing routine.

OCW3. This is a write register accessible as port 7CH in Fig. 9.28. It is distinguished from ICW1 and OCW2 by bits D3 and D4, which must be 1 and 0, respectively. Bits D5 and D6 allow the special mask mode to be programmed, allowing lower-priority interrupts to be accepted. For example, consider the following instructions given within an IR4 service routine.

```
MOV   AL,00010000        ;Mask IR4
OUT   7EH,AL             ;OCW1 (IMR)
MOV   AL,01101000        ;Special mask mode
OUT   7CH,AL             ;OCW3
```

By masking itself and selecting the special mask mode, interrupts on IR5–IR7 will now be accepted by the PIC (as well as those of higher priority on IR0–IR3).

Bit D2 of OCW3 is used to select the poll mode, and D0 and D1 allow IRR or IS to be read.

TABLE 9.9 OCW2 COMMAND SUMMARY

R	SL	EOI	Command	Description
0	0	1	Nonspecific EOI	Use in fully nested mode to reset IS bit; if ICW4 bit 1 is set, this command is performed automatically during INTA bus cycles
0	1	1	Specific EOI	Use to reset a specific IS bit; bits D0–D2 specify IS bit to reset
1	0	1	Rotate on non-specific EOI	Use to operate in nonspecific rotating mode; resets lowest-numbered IS bit and assigns that input lowest priority
1	0	0	Set rotate in auto EOI mode	If ICW4 bit 1 is set, this command will automatically cause the PIC to perform a rotate on nonspecific EOI command during INTA bus cycles
0	0	0	Clear rotate in auto EOI mode	Use to disable the auto rotate mode
1	1	1	Rotate on specific EOI command	Use to operate in specific rotating mode; bits D0–D2 specify the IS bit to reset and assign lowest priority
1	1	0	Set priority command	Use to assign a specific IR input lowest priority, thus fixing all other priorities

Example 9.12

Write a service routine to verify that the interrupt on IR7 is "legitimate."

Solution Recall that the PIC defaults to an IR7 if the interrupt request is not held until acknowledged by the CPU. In this case IS7 will *not* be set. The program is as follows.

```
ISR7    PROC    FAR
        MOV     AL,00001011    ;Read IS on next IOR
        OUT     7CH,AL         ;OCW3
        IN      AL,7CH         ;Get IS status
        TEST    AL,80H         ;IS7 set?
        JZ      FALSE          ;No—spurious input
         .                     ;Yes—process good interrupt
         .
         .
FALSE:  IRET
ISR7    ENDP
```

9.3.1. Using the 8259A, the INTR input of the 8086 can be expanded to accommodate up to _____ prioritized interrupt inputs.

9.3.2. Interrupt requests received by the PIC must be held until the first _____ _____ occurs.

9.3.3. A certain PIC has ICW2 programmed for 80H. What is the type number output by an interrupt request on IR4?

9.3.4. When operated in the slave mode, the PIC outputs its type number only if the cascade address received on CAS0–CAS2 matches the address programmed in _____ bits D0–D2.

9.3.5. How does the PIC's fully nested mode differ from the priority scheme imposed by the 8086 microprocessor?

9.3.6. When several equal-priority peripherals are to be interfaced, the _____ _____ mode of the PIC should be selected.

9.3.7. To allow interrupts of lower priority than that currently executing, the _____ _____ mode of the PIC should be selected.

9.3.8. Assume that an interrupt on IR5 is currently being processed. Write the program sequence required to reset IS5 and assign this input lowest priority, rotating all others accordingly.

9.3.9. Sketch the resulting priority structure after the instructions in question 9.3.8 have been executed.

9.3.10. To operate a single PIC in the fully nested mode with an 8086 microprocessor, _____, _____, and _____ must first be programmed.

CHAPTER 9 SELF-TEST

1. Because of the 8255's 8-bit data bus, two chips are required when interfacing to the data bus of the 8086 microprocessor.   (True/False)

2. Assume that it is required to set bit PC2 of the 8255 PPI chip. Describe two ways of doing this. What are the advantages of each method?

3. Assume that the hardware in Fig. 9.3 applies and show the initialization instructions required to program both PPI chips for mode 0 with ports A and B programmed as outputs and port C programmed as an input.

4. When programmed for mode 1 the _____ signal is supplied by the peripheral and causes input data to be latched by the 8255.

5. When programmed for mode 1 a CPU write operation to the 8255 will force _____ low. When the peripheral accepts this data, the rising edge of $\overline{ACK}$ drives _____ high.

6. Refer to Figs. 9.5 and 9.7. What is the data byte input in the POLL1 loop if key ''D'' only is held down?

7. Write the initialization routine required to program the odd 8255 in Fig. 9.3 such that ports A and B both operate in mode 1 as interrupt-driven output ports. Program any unused bits as outputs.

8. The _____ instruction is used to specify the number of stop bits, data bits, parity bit, and baud rate clock factor for the 8251A USART.

9. Following the mode instruction, the 8251A will interpret the next and all following CPU write instructions to the USART as command instructions. (True/False)

10. Assuming a data rate of 9600 baud and a $16 \times$ baud rate clock factor, determine the frequency of the baud rate generator required.

11. If the 8251A is to be operated in an interrupt-driven environment, the _____ output should be used to request an interrupt and cause the CPU to input the data character from the USART.

12. Assume that the USART in Fig. 9.20 is operating in the asynchronous mode with 7 data bits and 2 stop bits. Write the instruction sequence required to *reprogram* the USART for 8 data bits, 1 stop bit, even parity, and a $16 \times$ clock. Assume that all modem control signals are to be disabled.

13. When the 8251A is operated in the synchronous mode, one bit is output or input for every 16 pulses of the baud rate clock. (True/False)

14. The IR inputs of the 8259A can be programmed for a _____-edge trigger or a _____ levl trigger.

15. As an input, the $\overline{SP}/\overline{EN}$ signal identifies the 8259A as a _____ or a _____. As an output, it is used to _____ the data bus transceivers during the $\overline{INTA}$ bus cycle.

16. In the fully nested mode the _____ input has highest priority.

17. Under what conditions will a lower-priority service routine be allowed to interrupt a higher-priority routine using the 8259A PIC?

18. Write the 8259A initialization instructions required for the following: (1) single PIC; (2) level triggered; (3) IR0 type number E0H; (4) automatic EOI; (5) buffered CPU module; (6) fully nested. Assume the PIC port addresses shown in Fig. 9.28.

19. Assume that the PIC in Fig. 9.28 is operating in the fully nested mode with ICW4 bit 1 low. A request on IR3 occurs and the service routine begins. A second request occurs on IR2 which is serviced and terminated with a nonspecific EOI command. Will this command reset the correct IS bit?

20. Sketch the resulting priority structure if the IR2 service routine in question 19 terminates with the instructions

```
MOV   AL,11100010B
OUT   7CH,AL
```

ANALYSIS AND DESIGN QUESTIONS

9.1. Modify the matrix keyboard interface shown in Fig. 9.5 to become interrupt driven. When any key is closed a rising-edge interrupt signal should be generated compatible with the 8259A PIC.

9.2. Rewrite the keyboard scanner program (Fig. 9.7) to be compatible with your interrupt-driven interface in question 9.1. Be sure to include the PIC initialization instructions. Assume that the procedure is to return with the *ASCII* value of the key in register AL.

9.3. Design an 8255 interface using a data bus multiplexer such that your circuit is *memory mapped* to cover the address range EXXX0–EXXX3H, where "X" indicates "don't care." Write the mode 0 initialization routine required to program ports A and B as inputs and port C as an output.

9.4. Design a mode 0 8255 parallel printer interface similar to Fig. 9.13 but without interrupts. Use the bit set/reset mode to generate the $\overline{\text{STROBE}}$ signal. Write the driver routine using polling to synchronize the flow of data to the printer.

9.5. Write the polled serial receiver routine corresponding to the transmitter program given in Fig. 9.24. Have your program test for errors and output a "break" condition if present. If no errors are present, store the data in a print buffer. Assume that the end of data is indicated by the "$" character.

9.6. The two-CPU 8255 interface shown in Fig. 9.18 would be more realistic if the data bus connections between the two computers were buffered. Design a circuit to accomplish this buffering.

9.7. Figure 9.38 is a function table for the MSM5832 microprocessor real-time clock chip. The timing relationships for read and write cycles are given in Fig. 9.39. Design a circuit to interface this chip to the 8255 PPI. Write a control program in BASIC to set the clock and display the time of day on the CRT screen.

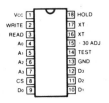

A0 to A3: Address Inputs

WRITE: Write Enable

READ: Read Enable

HOLD: Count Hold Enable

CS: Chip Select

D0 to D3: Data Input/Output

TEST: Test Input

±30 ADJ: ±30 Second
    Correction Input

XT & $\overline{\text{XT}}$: xtal oscillator
    connections

Vcc: +5 V Supply

GND: Ground

Figure 9.38 (a) Pin description, and (b) function table for the MSM5832 real-time clock chip. Sixteen registers can be accessed via the A0–A3 inputs and provide indication of the seconds, minutes, hours, weeks, days, months, and years. (Courtesy of OKI Semiconductor, Inc.)

FUNCTION TABLE

ADDRESS INPUTS				INTERNAL COUNTER	DATA I/O				DATA LIMITS	NOTES
A_0	A_1	A_2	A_3		D_0	D_1	D_2	D_3		
0	0	0	0	S 1	*	*	*	*	$0 \sim 9$	S_1 or S_{10} are reset to zero irrespective of input data $D_0 \sim D_3$ when write instruction is executed with address selection
1	0	0	0	S 10	*	*	*		$0 \sim 5$	
0	1	0	0	MI 1	*	*	*	*	$0 \sim 9$	
1	1	0	0	MI 10	*	*	*		$0 \sim 5$	
0	0	1	0	H 1	*	*	*	*	$0 \sim 9$	
1	0	1	0	H 10	*	*	†	†	$0 \sim 1 / 0 \sim 2$	$D_2 =$ "1" for PM $D_3 =$ "1" for 24 hour format $D_2 =$ "0" for AM $D_3 =$ "0" for 12 hour format
0	1	1	0	W	*	*	*		$0 \sim 6$	
1	1	1	0	D 1	*	*	*	*	$0 \sim 9$	
0	0	0	1	D 10	*	*	†		$0 \sim 3$	$D_2 =$ "1" for 29 days in month 2 (2) $D_2 =$ "0" for 28 days in month 2
1	0	0	1	MO 1	*	*	*	*	$0 \sim 9$	
0	1	0	1	MO 10	*				$0 \sim 1$	
1	1	0	1	Y 1	*	*	*	*	$0 \sim 9$	
0	0	1	1	Y 10	*	*	*	*	$0 \sim 9$	

(1) * data valid as "0" or "1"
   blank does not exist (unrecognized during a write and held at "0" during a read)
   † data bits used for AM/PM, 12/24 HOUR and leap year
(2) If D_2 previously set to "1", upon completion of month 2 day 29, D_2 will be internally reset to "0"

Figure 9.38   continued

READ CYCLE

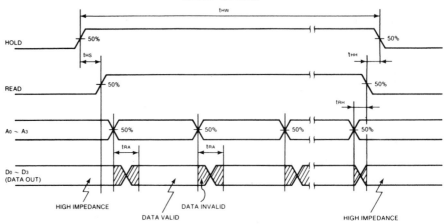

Notes: 1. A Read occurs during the overlap of a high CS and a high READ
2. Output Load: 1 TTL Gate, CL = 50 pf and RL = 4.7 KΩ
3. CS may be a permanent "1", or may be coincident with HOLD pulse

WRITE CYCLE

(Vcc = 5V ± 5%; Ta = 25°C)

Parameter	Symbol	Min.	Typ.	Max.	Unit
HOLD Set-up Time	tHS	150			μS
HOLD Hold Time	tHH	0			μS
HOLD Pulse Width	tHW			1	SEC
ADDRESS Pulse Width	tAW	1.7			μS
DATA Pulse Width	tDW	1.7			μS
DATA Set-up Time	tDS	0.5			μS
DATA Hold Time	tDH	0.2			μS
WRITE Pulse Width	tWW	1.0			μS

WRITE CYCLE   **FIGURE 5**

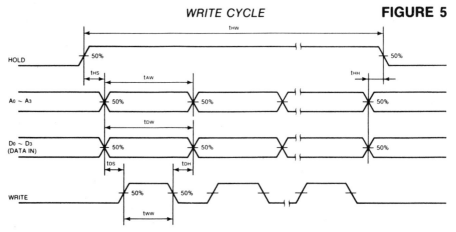

Notes: 1. A WRITE occurs during the overlap of a high CS, a high HOLD and a high WRITE
2. CS may be a permanent "1", or may be coincident with HOLD pulse

Figure 9.39 (a) Read cycle timing. The HOLD and READ inputs must both be high. (b) Write cycle timing. The HOLD input must be high, the register address selected, and the WRITE input strobed. (Courtesy of OKI Semiconductor.)

SELF REVIEW ANSWERS

9.1.1 24

9.1.2 False

9.1.3 bit 7 (only) of port C is reset

9.1.4 1

9.1.5 A0H

9.1.6
```
MOV AL,0A0H      ;Control byte
OUT 06H,AL       ;Control port
MOV AL,0DH       ;Bit set PC6
OUT 06H,AL       ;Control port
```

9.1.7 after the CPU writes a byte to the PPI and it is acknowledged (rising edge of $\overline{ACK}$) by the peripheral

9.1.8 A, B, 0, 1

9.2.1 2

9.2.2 0, 1, 0, 1, 0, 1

9.2.3 521

9.2.4 mode

9.2.5
```
MOV AL,01000000B      ;Reset command
OUT 71H,AL            ;Control port
MOV AL,01001011B      ;Mode instruction
OUT 71H,AL            ;Control port
MOV AL,00010101B      ;Command instruction
```

9.2.6 RxRDY

9.2.7 it hunts for the sync character(s)

9.3.1 64

9.3.2 $\overline{INTA}$ pulse

9.3.3 84H

9.3.4 ICW3

9.3.5 The PIC will allow higher priority interrupts to interrupt the ISR in progress - the CPU will not, unless IF is specifically set in which case all interrupts will be enabled.

9.3.6 non-specific rotating

9.3.7 special mask

9.3.8
```
MOV AL, 11100101B      ;reset IS5 and rotate others
OUT 7CH,AL             ;OCW2
```

9.3.9 lowest →5 4 3 2 1 0 7 6 ↘ highest

9.3.10 ICW1, ICW2, ICW4

10

DATA COMMUNICATIONS STANDARDS

Data communications refers to the ability of one computer to exchange data with another computer or peripheral. Physically, the data communications path may be a short 5- to 10-ft ribbon cable connecting a microcomputer and parallel printer. It might also take the form of a two- or three-conductor serial interface cable to a *modem*. This is a special device that interfaces with the telephone lines and allows communications with other computers thousands of miles away.

The ability to communicate with other computers and computer peripherals is essential to nearly every computer system, from the mainframe to the micro. Because of this need, it is to everyone's advantage to establish a *standard* data communications port. Equipped with this port, interfacing a computer and peripheral becomes a simple matter of plugging a cable into each device's standard data port.

In practice, there are several different standards. For example, the Centronic's parallel printer interface described in Chap. 8 has become a ''de facto'' parallel interface standard simply because everyone uses it. Other standards are more formal.

An organization of U.S. manufacturers known as the Electronic Industries Association (EIA) has proposed a series of standards prefixed with the letters RS. The best known is RS-232C, describing a serial communications standard.

The Institute of Electrical and Electronic Engineers (IEEE) publishes several standards and recommended practices based on the work of several member committees. Their recommendations cover both hardware and software. In this chapter we consider the IEEE 488-1978 parallel interface standard.

There is also an agency of the United Nations called the Consultive Committee in International Telegraphy and Telephony (CCITT) which concerns itself with worldwide aspects of telecommunications. Their work is published in a V and an X series of documents. For example, V.28 is similar to the EIA RS-232C standard.

What exactly constitutes a standard? First there is the *physical layer*, which describes the mechanical design of the connectors, the pin assignments and signal definitions, and the electrical characteristics of the signals. For example, RS-232C uses a negative logic scheme in which a logic 0 is a voltage more positive than $+3$ V and a logic 1 a voltage more negative than -3 V.

The second part of the standard is the *data link layer*. This establishes the protocol that is to be used for exchanging data within the standard. This is basically a set of rules and conventions that have been agreed upon. An example is the use of the BUSY signal in the Centronic's interface. Only when BUSY is low should data be sent to the printer.

Although not usually part of the standard, most communications channels use some sort of *data protection* scheme to ensure that data is transferred reliably. This can take the form of a *parity* bit added to each character transmitted, or a *block check character* transmitted at the end of a block of data. Still more elaborate schemes can detect and correct the bit in error (assuming single-bit errors).

Most data communications channels today are implemented using a serial pathway, and in this chapter we discuss the two most common such standards: current loop and RS-232C. Parallel interfaces are limited to shorter distances and are usually used to connect printers and plotters. Because the Centronic's parallel interface has been discussed previously, in this chapter we focus on the other popular parallel standard: IEEE 488-1978. This is quite different from the simpler Centronic's technique because it allows bidirectional communications on a bus-oriented data path.

The main topics of this chapter are:

10.1 The Current Loop Interface
10.2 The EIA RS-232C Serial Interface Standard
10.3 The IEEE 488-1978 General-Purpose Interface Bus Standard
10.4 Error Detection and Correction

10.1 THE CURRENT LOOP INTERFACE

The current loop represents one of the earliest schemes for transmitting serial data. Originally designed for teletypewriter (TTY) machines, a logic 1 is indicated by the presence of current—20 mA and 60 mA were the standard—and a logic 0 by the absence of current. Typing on the keys of the electromechanical TTY produces a series of current pulses at a particular data rate. The ASR-33 TTY operates at 110 baud and uses ASCII-encoded characters.

Although the TTY is used infrequently today, its current loop-transmission technique still has application. The main reason is that baud rates up to 9600 can be achieved with cables up to 1500 ft long. In fact, this exceeds the specified capabilities of the newer RS-232C standard.

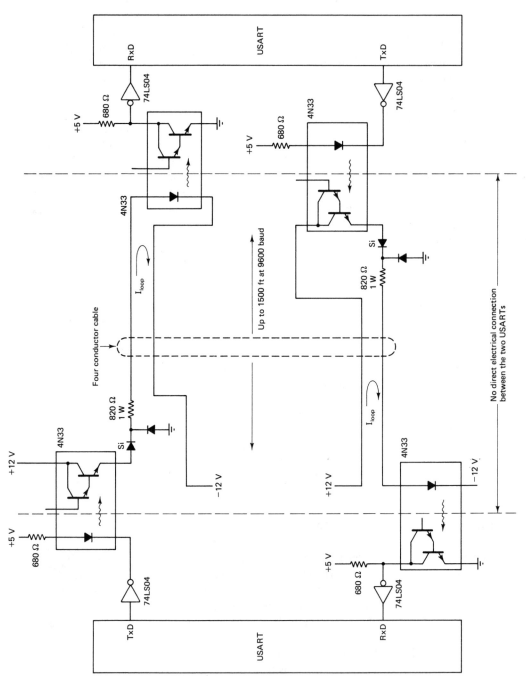

Figure 10.1 Serial data can be transmitted for distances up to 1500 feet at data rates as high as 9600 baud using a current loop interface.

Figure 10.1 shows a current loop interface between two TTL serial data ports. Note that two wires are required for each USART's transmit and receive signal. In this example a four-conductor cable allows full-duplex (simultaneous transmission and reception) operation.

The optoisolators are used to protect the USARTs from transients along the lines. In this example, the exact magnitude of the current in the loop is not as important as it is when interfacing a TTY. In the latter case too little current would not "pull in" the relay contacts, and too much current might damage the relay coils.

The loop current for the interface in Fig. 10.1 is approximately 26 mA. This is adequate to ensure that the infrared LEDs (IREDs) within the optoisolators are biased ON. The light path is then used to couple this signal into the bases of the photo Darlington transistors. This means that the USARTs (and associated computer equipment) are *isolated* from any transients on the transmission cable. When the photo Darlington is ON, the transmitter allows current to flow through the loop and the receiver outputs a logic 1 (via the 74LS04).

Note that the current loop power sources (± 12 V) can be located at one end of the cable only. This is an advantage over some other schemes (such as RS-232C), which require special power sources at the receiving and transmitting ends of the cable. Because the current transients can couple noise into adjacent conductors, sensitive lines such as telephone cables should be routed away from current loop cabling.

Notice that the interface in Fig. 10.1 is not supported by any *handshaking* signals. In addition, there is no standard connector. In fact, it has become common to use "spare" pins in an RS-232C connector to implement this interface. For these reasons the current loop is more of an interface technique than a serial communications standard.

SELF-REVIEW 10.1 (answers on page 525)

10.1.1. The current loop interface is a _____ transmission technique in which a logic 1 is indicated by the _____ of current and a logic 0 by the _____ of current.

10.1.2. Assuming a 1.5 V drop across the IRED, 0.6 V across the series silicon diode, and a V_{CEsat} for the Darlington transistors of 0.1 V, calculate the IRED current in the transmitting optoisolator in Fig. 10.1.

10.2 THE EIA RS-232C SERIAL INTERFACE STANDARD

RS-232C is by far the most popular serial interface standard. First introduced in 1962, it was intended to describe the interface between a computer terminal and a modem. In RS-232C jargon, the terminal is referred to as a DTE (data terminal equipment) and the modem as a DCE (data communications equipment).

The specification limits the baud rate to 19,200 with a 50-ft cable. In practice, much longer cables can be accommodated but at lower data rates. As mentioned previously, RS-232C is a voltage standard with typical logic levels of -12 V for a logic 1 and $+12$ V for a logic 0.

In addition to the electrical characteristics, the standard also defines a 25-pin connector with signals defined for all but three of these pins. In this section we consider the electrical characteristics of RS-232C and see how it is interfaced with standard TTL logic levels. The signals that make up the standard are explained together with the data exchange protocol. Finally, an example of an interface between an RS-232C data port and a 300-baud single-chip modem is presented.

Electrical Characteristics of RS-232C

Figure 10.2 compares the logic-level specifications of RS-232C with those of standard TTL. As you know, TTL uses positive logic and provides 0.4 V of noise immunity. RS-232C is quite different. The higher voltage levels—a typical driver outputs ± 12 V—are necessary to ensure reliable operation with long cables. The 2-V noise immunity specification allows the cables to be routed through noisy environments that would be a problem for TTL.

To interface RS-232C with TTL, special line drivers and receivers are required. These are shown in Fig. 10.3(a). The MC1488 accepts TTL-level inputs and provides RS-232C output levels. The MC1489 does the opposite, converting the RS-232C levels on the transmission line to TTL levels for the receiving USART. Because of these drivers and receivers, the negative logic aspect of RS-232C is "transparent" to the user.

One of the requirements of the RS-232C standard is that the transition time from one logic level to the other must not exceed 4% of one bit time. Thus at 19,200 baud the transition time must be less than $0.04 \times 1/19,200 = 2.1$ μs. This in turn imposes a limit on the length of cable that can be driven. The longer the cable, the greater the capacitive load on the driver and the slower the transition time. At 19,200 baud, the maximum cable length is restricted to 50 ft.

One of the main problems with RS-232C is that the drivers and receivers are *unbalanced* or *single-ended*. This means that the input and output signals are referenced to a common ground [see Fig. 10.3(a)]. Because it is likely that the ground potentials at the receiving and transmitting nodes will be at different potentials, a current will flow in the common ground wire connection. The resulting *IR* drop in this conductor then reduces the 2.0 V of noise immunity. The unbalanced nature of the driver and receiver thus becomes another limiting factor in the length of cable that can be used.

Figure 10.3(b) and (c) illustrates two new electrical interface standards: RS-423A and RS-422A. RS-422A uses a *differential* transmitter and receiver. This eliminates the common ground wire. The receiver detects the difference between its two inputs as positive or negative. RS-423A is similar but uses a single-ended driver with a differential receiver. Again no common ground path exists. Figure 10.4 compares the logic-level specifications for these two standards.

Because of its differential design, RS-422A can tolerate a much smaller transition region than can RS-232C. This in turn allows a much higher baud rate. For example, 100,000 baud is possible with a 4000-ft cable.

The EIA would like to see the electronics industry move to the newer RS-422A standard. However, as you can see by comparing RS-232C in Fig. 10.2(b) with RS-422A in Fig. 10-4(a), the two are not compatible. This is one of the reasons that RS-423A was developed. An RS-423A driver produces voltages within the RS-232C specifications. In

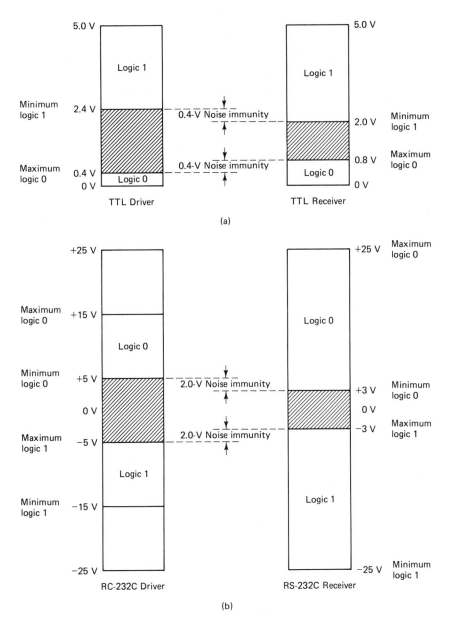

Figure 10.2 Comparing the logic-level specifications of (a) TTL and (b) RS-232C. The RS-232C standard uses negative logic (true = low).

addition, its receiver will correctly convert RS-232C levels to TTL. Thus RS-423A establishes a sort of interim standard between RS-422A and RS-232C.

Table 10.1 compares several important electrical characteristics of the three standards discussed. You should be aware that RS-422A and RS-423A actually represent just the *electrical standards* for yet another EIA standard called RS-449. This is a new serial

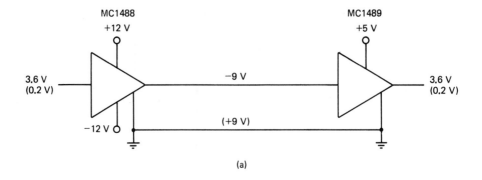

(a)

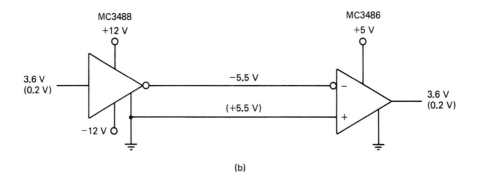

(b)

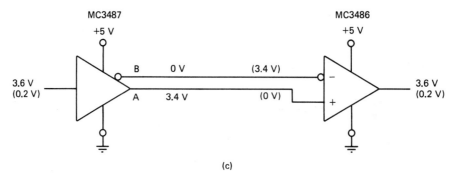

(c)

Figure 10.3 Line drivers are available to convert TTL levels to any of the three standards: (a) RS-232C; (b) RS-423A; (c) RS-422A. (From J. Uffenbeck, *Microcomputers and Microprocessors: The 8080, 8085, and Z-80*. Prentice-Hall, Englewood Cliffs, N.J., 1985.)

interface standard comparable with RS-232C. However, unlike RS-232C, it specifies two data connectors, a 37-pin connector for the main interface signals, and a 9-pin connector for an (optional) secondary channel. For data rates below 20,000 baud, either RS-422A or RS-423A can be used. For data rates above 20,000 baud, RS-422A must be used.

Will RS-449 replace RS-232C? At present, the industry is solidly entrenched with

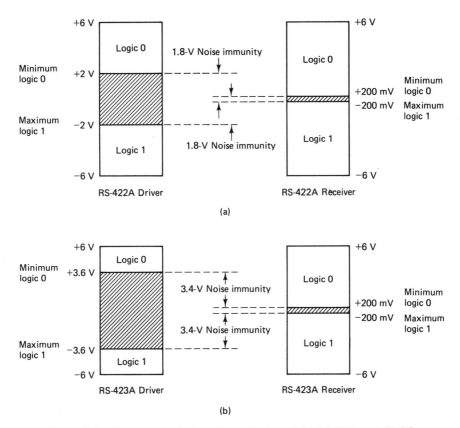

Figure 10.4 Comparing the logic-level specifications of (a) RS-422A, and (b) RS-423A.

RS-232C. However, the performance benefits of RS-449 are slowly attracting converts. The best bet is to expect this conversion process to continue for many years.

RS-232C Signal Descriptions and Mechanical Interface

Table 10.2 lists the signal names and source and destination for the 25 pins of the RS-232C interface standard. The data pins are grouped into a *primary channel* and a *secondary channel*. The latter is seldom used but does allow a path for confirmation or interruption of the data flow.

The control pins $\overline{\text{DTR}}$, $\overline{\text{DSR}}$, $\overline{\text{CTS}}$, $\overline{\text{RTS}}$, and $\overline{\text{DCD}}$ establish a protocol between the modem (DCE) and terminal (DTE). They are explained in detail in the next section. The remaining signals are used less frequently and support a secondary data channel, synchronous modems (requiring separate transmit and receive clock signals), a ring indicator for auto-dialing modems, and a baud rate select pin for dual-rate modems.

Note that the signal names are defined from the DTE's point of view. *This is very important.* Why? If we simply consider pin 2 to be transmitted data, we could easily end

TABLE 10.1 ELECTRICAL CHARACTERISTICS FOR RS-232C, RS-422A, AND RS-423A

Parameter	RS-232C	RS-422A	RS-423A
Line length (max.)	50 ft	4000 ft	4000 ft
Frequency (max.)	20 kbaud/50 ft	10 Mbaud/40 ft 1 Mbaud/400 ft 100 kbaud/4000 ft	100 kbaud/30 ft 10 kbaud/300 ft 1 kbaud/4000 ft
Mode of operation	Single-ended input and output	Differential input and output	Single-ended output, differential input
Driver logic levels "0" "1"	 $> +5$ to $+15$ V < -5 to -15 V	 $> +2$ to $+5$ V < -2 to -5 V	 $> +3.6$ to $+6$ V < -3.6 to -6 V
Noise immunity	2.0 V	1.8 V	3.4 V
Number of receivers allowed on one line	1	10	10
Input impedance	$3-7$ kΩ and 2500 pF	> 4 kΩ	> 4 kΩ
Output impedance	—	< 100 Ω balanced	< 50 Ω
Short circuit current	500 mA	150 mA	150 mA
Output slew rate	30 V/μs maximum	—	Controls provided
Receiver input voltage range	± 15 V	± 7 V	± 12 V
Maximum voltage applied to driver output	± 25 V	-0.25 to $+6$ V	± 6 V

up with two transmitters connected to the same pin. Fortunately, the standard allows any two pins to be shorted without damage, but the interface will certainly not work.

Example 10.1

Show the minimum connections required to interface a microcomputer serial port wired as a DCE to a video terminal serial port wired as a DTE.

Solution Figure 10.5 shows the connections. Only three signals are required: transmitted data, received data, and signal ground. Technically, protective ground, pin 1, should also be used to help eliminate the ground-loop problem mentioned earlier. However, the connections shown in Fig. 10.5 are very common.

Although not part of the standard, the 25-pin DB-25S and DB-25P connectors shown in Fig. 10.6 are universally used when interfacing two RS-232C data ports. You must exercise caution when interfacing to such a connector, however. First, many of the pins may not be used (the circuit in Fig. 10.4 used only three of the 25 pins). Remember, just because the pin exists on the connector does not mean there is a wire soldered to the other side!

Second, it has become popular to use DB-25 connectors to implement Centronic's parallel printer interfaces. Thus simply "spying" a DB-25 connector does not guarantee an RS-232C interface. Always check the documentation of the equipment to be interfaced, and pay particular attention to the signals brought out to the serial connectors. In the next

TABLE 10.2 SIGNAL DESIGNATIONS FOR THE RS-232C SERIAL INTERFACE STANDARD

Pin	Signal name	Data		Control	
		From DTE to DCE	To DTE from DCE	From DTE to DCE	To DTE from DCE
1	Protective ground				
2	Transmitted data	×			
3	Received data		×		
4	Request to send ($\overline{\text{RTS}}$)			×	
5	Clear to send ($\overline{\text{CTS}}$)				×
6	Data set ready ($\overline{\text{DSR}}$)				×
7	Signal ground				
8	Data carrier detect ($\overline{\text{DCD}}$)				×
9/10	Reserved for data set testing				
11	Unassigned				
12	Secondary data carrier detect				×
13	Secondary clear to send				×
14	Secondary transmitted data	×			
15	Transmit signal element timing				×
16	Secondary received data		×		
17	Receive signal element timing				×
18	Unassigned				
19	Secondary request to send			×	
20	Data terminal ready ($\overline{\text{DTR}}$)			×	
21	Signal-quality detector (indicates probability of error)				×
22	Ring indicator				×
23	Data signal rate select (allows selection of two different baud rates)				×
24	Transmit signal element timing			×	
25	Unassigned				

Source: J. Uffenbeck, *Microcomputers and Microprocessors: The 8080, 8085, and Z-80.* Prentice-Hall, Englewood Cliffs, N.J., 1985.

section an example is provided showing how to interface two devices both wired as DTEs—a common situation with RS-232C.

RS-232C Data Exchange Protocol

The need for handshaking signals with a serial data port may not be immediately obvious. Normally, the microcomputer is synchronized to the character rate of the USART by testing the latter's TxRDY flag. The flaw in this technique is that the readiness of the data receiver is not being tested.

For example, when interfacing a particular VDT, the ASCII sequence 1BH 7AH

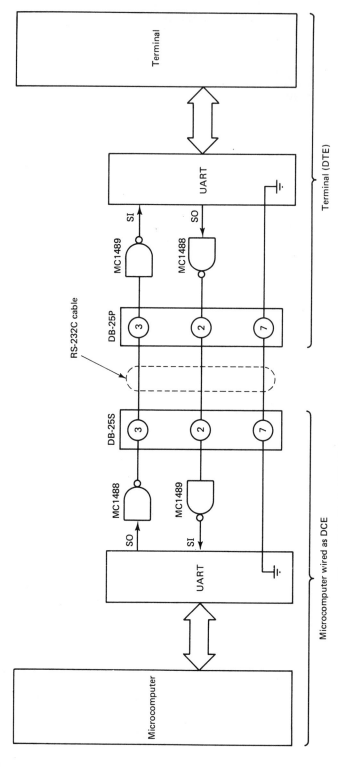

Figure 10.5 Typical RS-232C interface between a microcomputer wired as a DCE and a VDT wired as a DTE. (From J. Uffenbeck, *Microcomputers and Microprocessors: The 8080, 8085, and Z-80*. Prentice-Hall, Englewood Cliffs, N.J., 1985.)

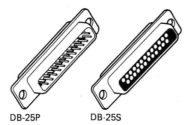

Figure 10.6 DB-25S socket connector and DB-25P plug connector universally used with all RS-232C communications ports. (From J. Uffenbeck, *Microcomputers and Microprocessors: The 8080, 8085, and Z-80.* Prentice-Hall, Englewood Cliffs, N.J., 1985.)

DB-25P   DB-25S

(ESC "z") will clear the screen. Usually, this requires several milliseconds. However, at 9600 baud, new characters are being transmitted to the VDT approximately once each millisecond. Because the transmitter has no way of knowing that the receiver is "busy," several characters will be lost.

The five modem control signals mentioned in the preceding section are included in the RS-232C standard to allow a handshaking protocol to be established. The word interpretation for each of these signals is as follows:

1. *Data carrier detect (DCD).* This signal is output by the DCE and indicates that the modem has detected a valid carrier (i.e., a logic 1 level).
2. *Data terminal ready (DTR).* This signal is output by the DTE to indicate that it is ready for communications. It can be used to switch on a modem.
3. *Data set ready (DSR).* This signal is output by the DCE in response to DTR and indicates that the DCE is on and connected to the communications channel.
4. *Request to send (RTS).* This signal is output by the DTE to indicate that it is ready to transmit data.
5. *Clear to send (CTS).* This signal is output by the DCE and acknowledges RTS. It indicates that the DCE is ready for transmission.

Figure 10.7 flowcharts the handshaking process when an RS-232C data port is used to exchange data with a modem. In practice, a subset of these signals is usually used. For example, a full-duplex modem may only use $\overline{\text{DSR}}$ and $\overline{\text{DCD}}$. The microcomputer polls $\overline{\text{DSR}}$ to verify that the modem is ready and not in a test mode. After manually placing the call to the distant station, $\overline{\text{DCD}}$ is polled to verify that a carrier is present. Data transmission then begins.

For half-duplex operation $\overline{\text{DSR}}$, $\overline{\text{RTS}}$, $\overline{\text{CTS}}$, and $\overline{\text{DCD}}$ are commonly used. $\overline{\text{DSR}}$ and $\overline{\text{DCD}}$ serve the same purpose as in the preceding paragraph. $\overline{\text{RTS}}$ is used to request that the line be "turned around" so that the microcomputer can transmit. $\overline{\text{CTS}}$ acknowledges this request. Removing $\overline{\text{RTS}}$ returns the line to the receive mode.

Interfacing Nonmodem Peripherals

How, you may be wondering, do these modem control signals help us solve the VDT's clear-screen problem? When RS-232C is used to interface a microcomputer and a nonmodem peripheral, any of these control lines can be selected for handshake control. After

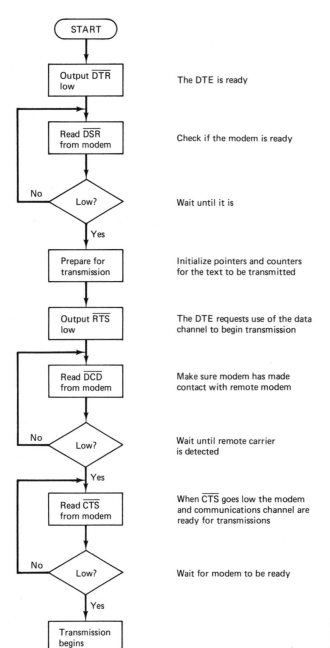

START	
Output $\overline{DTR}$ low	The DTE is ready
Read $\overline{DSR}$ from modem	Check if the modem is ready
Low? — No / Yes	Wait until it is
Prepare for transmission	Initialize pointers and counters for the text to be transmitted
Output $\overline{RTS}$ low	The DTE requests use of the data channel to begin transmission
Read $\overline{DCD}$ from modem	Make sure modem has made contact with remote modem
Low? — No / Yes	Wait until remote carrier is detected
Read $\overline{CTS}$ from modem	When $\overline{CTS}$ goes low the modem and communications channel are ready for transmissions
Low? — No / Yes	Wait for modem to be ready
Transmission begins	

Figure 10.7 RS-232C data exchange protocol between a terminal (DTE) and a modem (DCE).

all, they are only pins on a connector. However, this unfortunately means that the "standard" may not be so standard. The printer manufacturer may have chosen to wire the printer's BUSY flag to DSR, but your computer may be wired to monitor DTR. Another common problem occurs when computer and peripheral are both wired as DTEs.

Example 10.2

Show how to wire a serial printer to a microcomputer assuming that both ports are configured as DTEs with the printer's BUSY flag connected to DTR.

Solution The interface and cable are shown in Fig. 10.8. Because both devices are wired as DTEs, it is necessary to exchange or "cross" the wires connecting pins 2 and 3. This requirement occurs so frequently when interfacing with RS-232C that the cable is given the special name *null modem* (there is no DCE). The DTR output from the printer is connected to DSR, which should be an input pin on a DTE connector (CTS could also have been used for this purpose). The 8251A can now poll DSR as bit 7 of its status word (see Fig. 9.23).

One other problem remains. The serial port connectors are integral to the microcomputer and printer. One may use a DB-25P and the other a DB-25S, or they may both use DB-25S socket connectors. Thus you must also pay special attention to the connectors you put on the ends of the transmission cable.

It has been said that the main problem with the RS-232C standard is that it is not a standard! Of course, it was never designed to interface a microcomputer and a printer. It is a modem to terminal standard.

Example 10.3

Write a procedure to output a character passed on the stack to the printer shown in Fig. 10.8.

Solution The program is shown in Fig. 10.9. It begins by polling DSR to see if the printer is ready. If so, TxRDY of the USART is tested, and if high, the character is fetched from the stack and output to the USART. The RET 2 instruction discards the character from the stack and returns control to the calling program.

You may have wondered why the transmitted data line was required in the interface in Fig. 10.8. The control program in Fig. 10.9 did not use it. However, there are two alternate protocols, called X-ON/X-OFF and ETX/ACK, that require this connection.

Using the X-ON/X-OFF protocol the printer can request that data transmission be halted by sending the character 13H (X-OFF or control-S) to the transmitter. Transmission resumes when the character 11H (X-ON or control-Q) is received. The advantage of this technique is that it eliminates the need for the handshaking wire. The disadvantage is that the USART may have one or two characters stored in its buffer when X-OFF is received. These characters will still be transmitted and thus may be lost.

The ETX/ACK protocol is similar to X-ON/X-OFF but is *block* oriented. After a block of text has been sent, it is terminated with 03H (ETX or end of transmission). Further transmissions are inhibited until 06H (ACK or acknowledge) is received from the printer. This technique is suitable for peripherals with data buffers that can be filled as fast as the USART can output data.

Notice that both of these protocols are simply rules or conventions that have been agreed upon. No special hardware support is required.

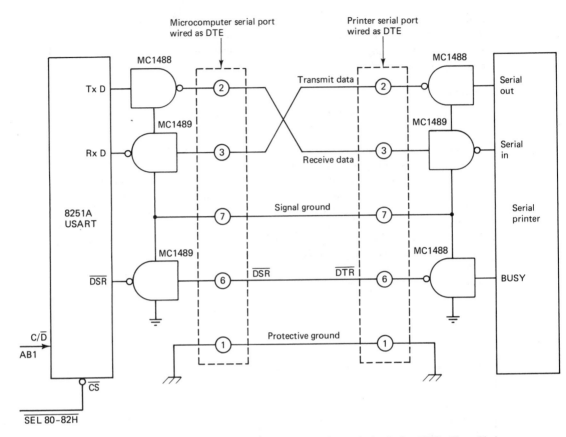

Figure 10.8 Connections required to interface two serial ports both wired as DTEs. The cable is referred to as a *null modem*.

Interfacing a 300-Baud FSK Modem

As you have learned, RS-232C was initially designed to interface a terminal and a modem. For that reason most modems come equipped with an RS-232C data port. However, any attempt to transmit the RS-232C serial data directly over the telephone network is doomed to failure. This is because the phone system is optimized for *voice transmissions* and has a 300- to 3300-Hz bandwidth. A digital signal with submicrosecond rise and fall times exhibits frequency components well into the tens of megahertz. The result of attempting to pass such signals through this low-pass filter (the telephone network) would be a signal unrecognizable as a logic 1 or 0.

For this reason the modem—short for modulator/demodulator—was invented. It is designed to convert input serial data (usually in RS-232C levels) to audio frequencies within the bandpass of the telephone network. Figure 10.10 illustrates the basic concept. A technique called *frequency-shift keying* (FSK) is used by the modem to convert the binary 1's and 0's to two different sine-wave frequencies that can be passed by the telephone network.

TITLE FIG. 10.9

```
;Function:     Output one byte to to the serial
;              printer interface shown in Fig. 10.8.
;Inputs:       Character to be printed passed on stack.
;Ouputs:       Print-character to USART data port.
;Calls:        nothing
;Destroys:     flags,BP,AL

              ;Program equates

= 0082        STATUS_PORT       EQU    82H    ;USART status port
= 0080        DATA_PORT         EQU    80H    ;USART data port
= 0080        DSR               EQU    80H    ;BUSY = DSR on bit 7
= 0001        TXRDY             EQU    01H    ;TXRDY on bit 0

              ;Procedure assumes USART has been programmed.

0000          CODE          SEGMENT BYTE
              ASSUME        CS:CODE

0000          BYTE_OUT      PROC    NEAR
0000  E4 82   WDSR:         IN      AL,STATUS_PORT   ;Get DSR and TXRDY
0002  A8 80                 TEST    AL,DSR           ;Printer busy?
0004  74 FA                 JZ      WDSR             ;Yes - so wait

0006  A8 01                 TEST    AL,TXRDY         ;USART ready?
0008  74 F6                 JZ      WDSR             ;No - so wait

000A  8B EC                 MOV     BP,SP            ;Stack holds character
000C  8A 46 02      .        MOV    AL,[BP+2]        ;Fetch it
000F  E6 80                 OUT     DATA_PORT,AL     ;Output to USART
0011  C2 0002               RET     2                ;Discard and return
0014          BYTE_OUT      ENDP
0014          CODE          ENDS
              END
```

Figure 10.9 Serial transmission program for the hardware shown in Fig. 10.8.

Once converted to sine waves, the binary information can be transmitted over the telephone lines just as a voice signal. The distant modem demodulates the signal, outputting the serial data in standard 0V-5V form.

A voltage-controlled oscillator (VCO) is used for the modulation process and a phase-locked loop (PLL) for the demodulation process. Thus a modem is made from a combination of linear and digital circuitry.

There are two basic types of modems, called *originate* modems and *answer* modems. The originate modem is used to originate the call and an answer modem is used at the distant computer site to answer the call. For these two modems to communicate with each other simultaneously (i.e., in *full duplex*), two sets of frequencies are required. Specifications for the Bell 103 full-duplex 300-baud modem are given in Fig. 10.11. In this standard the originate modem transmits using the low set of frequencies and receives on the high set. The answer modem operates just the opposite.

The data rate for a 103-type modem is 300 bits per second (bps). The maximum standard data rate using FSK techniques and the frequency assignments shown in Fig. 10.11 is 600 bps. This can be verified by noting that one period of the 1070-Hz sine wave is 0.93 ms (1/1070). However, at 1200 bps, the next highest standard baud rate,

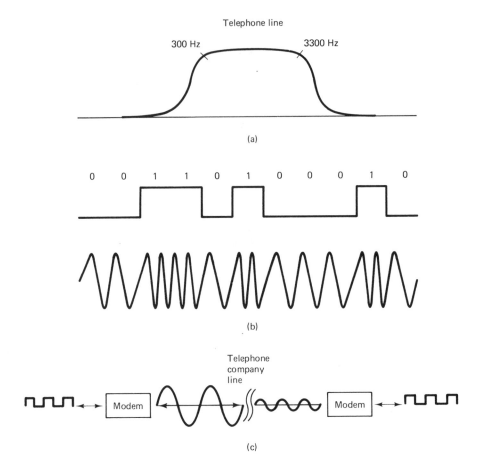

Figure 10.10 Telecommunications concept: (a) the switched telephone network has a 300-Hz bandwidth; (b) using frequency-shift keying (FSK), the modem converts the binary 1's and 0's into two different-frequency sine waves; (c) these sine waves are transmitted over the telephone company lines. (From J. Uffenbeck, *Microcomputers and Micrprocessors: The 8080, 8085, and Z-80*. Prentice-Hall, Englewood Cliffs, N.J., 1985.)

only 0.83 ms (1/1200) is available for one bit time. This is insufficient for even one period of the 1070-Hz tone.

When interfacing to the telephone network, two techniques are possible:

1. Acoustic coupling (cradle, speaker, microphone)
2. Direct connect

Acoustic coupling is the simplest to accomplish, requiring no special interface between the modem and the telephone. The audio tones output by the modem are used to drive a loudspeaker acoustically coupled to the microphone of the telephone handset. The tones received are coupled from the handset earpiece to a microphone and hence to the modem receiver.

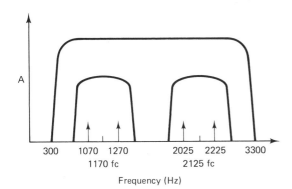

Specifications

Data:

Serial, binary, asynchronous, full duplex

Data transfer rate:

0 to 300 bps

Modulation:

Frequency shift-keyed (FSK) FM

Frequency assignment:

	Originating end	Answering end
Transmit	1070 Hz space 1270 Hz mark	2025 Hz space 2225 Hz mark
Receive	2025 Hz space 2225 Hz mark	1070 Hz space 1270 Hz mark

Transmit level:

0 to −12 dBm

Receive level:

0 to −50 dBm simultaneous with adjacent channel transmitter at as much as 0 dBm

Specifications and channel assignments for the full-duplex 300-bps asynchronous Bell 103/113 modem are shown in this illustration. The Bell 103 modem can transmit and receive the low or high band. The ability to switch modes has been termed "originate and answer." The Bell 113A/D operates only in the originate mode; the Bell 113B/C operates only in the answer mode.

Figure 10.11 Specifications for the 103 300-bps full-duplex modem standard. (Courtesy of Racal Vadic.)

Acoustic coupling restricts operation to a manual mode. The operator must dial the call, wait for the distant carrier, and then place the handset in the acoustic coupler of the modem. The connection is also subject to external room noise, packing of the carbon microphone granules, and mechanical vibrations.

Prior to 1976 a *direct-access arrangement* (DAA) had to be leased from the telephone company when it was desired to use a direct-connect modem. However, using a *registered protective circuit*, it is now possible to buy or build equipment that connects directly to the telephone company lines, provided that it is registered with the FCC (Federal Communications Commission).

The 103-style modem offers full-duplex asynchronous operation at 300 bps. It is probably the most common type of modem in use today, primarily because of its low cost. A one-chip 103-style modem called the TMS99532 is available from Texas Instruments. An interface to this circuit is shown in Fig. 10.12. This circuit can be driven in two ways:

1. Directly, by Serial out and Serial in of a USART
2. From an RS-232C serial port using the MC1488 and MC1489 line receiver and line driver

The TMS99532 can be programmed to operate in the answer or originate mode via the four control pins SQT, ALB, A/O, and $\overline{ATE}$. Table 10.3 summarizes the operating modes of the modem selected by these four lines. These pins can be hard-wired or controlled by the output port of a PPI chip.

The TMS99532 features an on-board oscillator requiring only a 4.032-MHz external crystal. Figure 10.13(a) illustrates an acoustically coupled interface and Fig. 10.13(b)

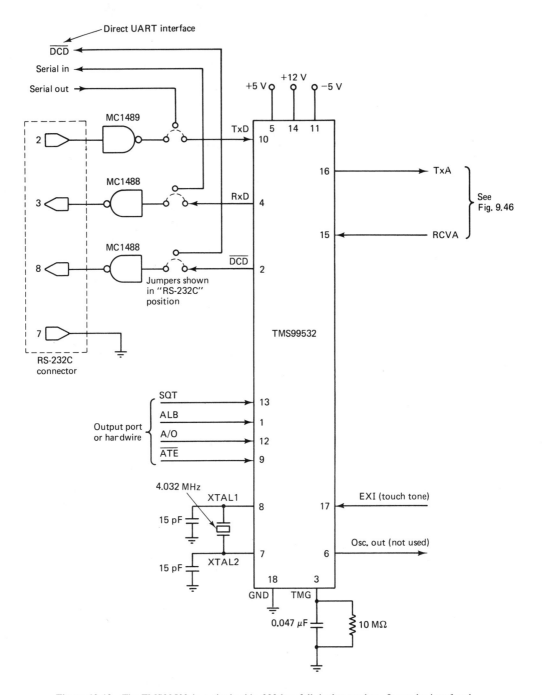

Figure 10.12 The TMS99532 is a single-chip 300-bps full-duplex modem. It can be interfaced directly to a UART chip or to the serial data lines of an RS-232C port. (From J. Uffenbeck, *Microcomputers and Microprocessors: The 8080, 8085, and Z-80.* Prentice-Hall, Englewood Cliffs, N.J., 1985.)

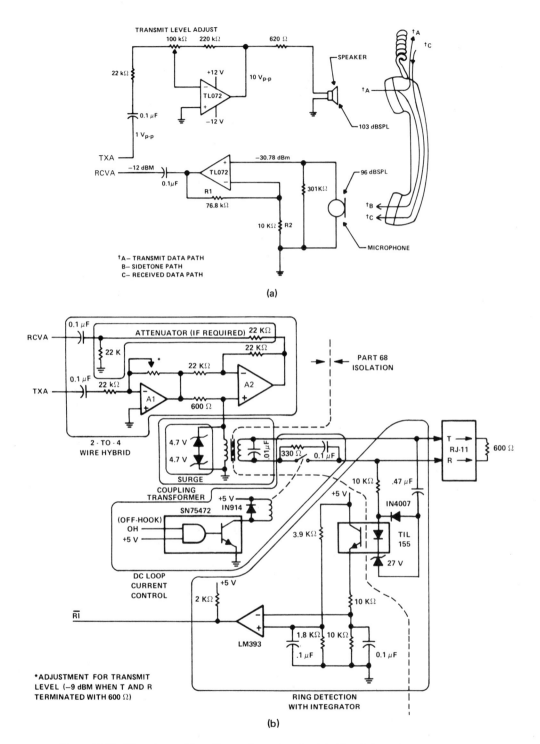

Figure 10.13 The output and input lines to the modem circuit in Fig. 10.12 can be (a) acoustically coupled to the phone line, or (b) direct-connected. (Courtesy of Texas Instruments.)

TABLE 10.3 OPERATING MODES FOR THE TMS99532 300-BPS MODEM[a,b]

Mode	Mode controls SQT ALB A/O ATE (Digital)	Transmitted data		Received data		Touch tones EXI (Analog)
		XMTD (Digital)	TXA (Analog) (Hz)	RVCA (Analog) (Hz)	RCVD (Digital)	
Answer	0 0 0 1	Mark = 1 — Space = 0 —	2225 2025	Mark = 1270 — Space = 1070 —	1 0	×
Originate	0 0 1 1	Mark = 1 — Space = 0 —	1270 1070	Mark = 2225 — Space = 2025 —	1 0	×
Answer, squelch	1 0 0 1	×	Disabled	Mark = 1270 — Space = 1070 —	1 0	×
Originate, squelch	1 0 1 1 —	×	Disabled	Mark = 2225 — Space = 2025 —	1 0	×
Analog loop back, answer	0 1 0 1	Mark = 1 Space = 0	Disabled	Disabled	1 0	×
Analog loop back, originate	0 1 1 1	Mark = 1 Space = 0	Disabled	Disabled	1 0	×

494

State										
ALB test, answer	1 1 0 1	×	×	Disabled	Disabled	1	×
ALB test, originate	1 1 1 1	×	×	Disabled	Disabled	1	×
EXI as input	1 0 1 0	×	×	Same as EXI, inverted[c]	×	Tri-state HBPF active	External tone source
EXI as input[d]	1 0 0 0	×	×	Same as EXI, inverted[c]	×	Tri-state LBPF active	External tone source
2100 Hz[d] CCITT V.25 answer tone	0 0 0 0	×	×	2100	×	Tri-state	×

[a]These states are undefined and should not be used:

```
0 0 1 0
0 1 0 0
0 1 1 0
1 1 0 0
1 1 1 0
```

[b]×, don't care; HBPF, high-bandpass filter; LBPF, low-bandpass filter.

[c]Assumes ac coupling at EXI.

[d]Typically not used in U.S. applications.

Source: Courtesy of Texas Instuments, Inc.

shows a direct connection. In either case external operational amplifiers are required to provide signal levels within telephone company specifications.

Note that the direct-coupled circuit is completely *isolated* from the phone line, as required by FCC regulations. There are four components to this circuit:

1. Ring detector
2. DC loop current control
3. Coupling transformer and surge protection
4. Two- to-four-wire hybrid

Normally, the phone line rests at 48 V when the phone is "on hook" (not used). To ring the phone a 40- to 130-V rms ring signal at 17 to 33 Hz is superimposed on this level. In the modem's ring detector circuit, this signal causes the 27-V zener diode and infrared LED in the TIL 155 optoisolator to conduct. The inverting input of the LM393 comparator becomes more positive than the noninverting input and the $\overline{RI}$ signal goes low. This can be used to alert the control circuit to apply the OH (off-hook) signal, thus implementing an auto-answer modem.

The 75472 relay driver allows OH to "answer the phone" by closing the dc loop current switch. Note that the OH input can also be used to implement an *auto-dial* feature (see Analysis and Design Question 10.9).

A 600-Ω transformer is used to couple the data signal on and off the 600-Ω phone line. Back-to-back zener diodes prevent excessive voltages (due to lightning, for example) from damaging the modem.

The transmit and receive signals are mixed onto a two-wire line by the phone company. These must be converted to separate receive (and ground) and transmit (and ground) signals for the modem. The two op-amps accomplish this function. The transmitted signal is amplified by A1 but rejected by A2, a *differential amplifier* with 0 gain. However, to the received signal A2 appears to be a noninverting amplifier with 6-dB gain. The result is a circuit that separates the receive and transmit signals for the modem but mixes them for transmission over the phone lines.

SELF-REVIEW 10.2 (answers on pages 525-526)

10.2.1. The RS-232C standard was originally written to specify the connections between a _____ and a _____.

10.2.2. Using the MC1488 RS-232C line driver, a logic 1 is transmitted as a voltage level of typically _____.

10.2.3. Which of the following electrical standards uses a balanced line driver and receiver? (a) RS-232C; (b) RS-422A; (c) RS-423A; (d) V.28.

10.2.4. An RS-423A receiver can be used with an RS-232C driver. (True/False)

10.2.5. An RS-232C cable with pins 2 and 3 reversed is called a _____ _____.

10.2.6. The _____ and _____ have become the standard connectors to be used with RS-232C.

10.2.7. A serial printer is to be interfaced using the RS-232C standard. Will handshaking signals be required? Explain.

10.2.8. Instead of using $\overline{\text{DTR}}/\overline{\text{DSR}}$, some peripherals support an _____ or _____ data exchange protocol. These peripherals require both the transmit and receive data lines of the RS-232C interface to be used.

10.2.9. An FSK modem converts the ± 12-V pulses of RS-232C into two separate _____ _____.

10.2.10. What are the advantages of a direct-connect modem versus an acoustically coupled modem?

10.3 THE IEEE 488-1978 GENERAL-PURPOSE INTERFACE BUS STANDARD

One of the areas in which the microcomputer is finding increasing application is that of electronic instrumentation. A common problem is to collect analog data samples—the temperature or pressure of two different gases, for example—at a periodic rate, say once every minute. The collected data is recorded and later analyzed. Although this can be a tedious process when performed manually, it is a "natural" for the microcomputer.

Because of Hewlett-Packard's instrumentation background, the company began to recognize the need for a *standard* interface between an instrumentation device and a microcomputer. Their goal was to develop an interface that would allow several instruments to communicate with each other over a common set of bus lines.

The RS-232C standard was rejected for this application because it requires a separate port for each peripheral to be interfaced. In addition, the serial data format results in a data rate that was judged to be too slow.

In the early 1970s the IEEE became interested in the HPIB (Hewlett-Packard Interface Bus, as it had become known) and in 1975 adopted it as an IEEE standard. In 1978 it was revised to its present form and is now known as IEEE 488-1978 *Standard Digital Interface for Programmable Instrumentation*. It is often referred to as the *General Purpose Interface Bus* (GPIB).

Figure 10.14 illustrates the bus structure of the standard. Unlike RS-232C, an 8-bit bidirectional data bus is defined, supported by three handshake control signals and five general-purpose interface management lines. The bus is said to be *byte serial and bit parallel*. This means that the data bus is made up of (eight) parallel data bits, which are transmitted one byte after another in sequence, or serially.

The standard allows up to 15 devices to be connected to the parallel bus at one time. Each has its own address, usually set by DIP switches on the instrument's back panel. Because there is no address bus defined in the standard, addresses are passed over the data lines when the ATN (attention) management line is asserted. When ATN is inactive, information on the bus is to be interpreted as data.

The bus is rated to handle data rates as high as 1MB/s (1 million bytes per second). In practice, this rate is seldom achieved. Most applications operate at 250,000 bytes/s or less. The maximum cable length is restricted to 60 m. However, no more than 2 m should separate individual devices on the bus. Thus the GPIB is not intended to interface a terminal or other peripheral located at a remote site such as an adjacent building.

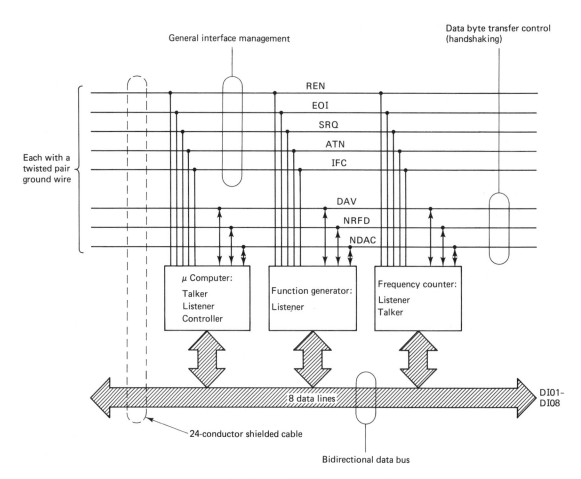

Figure 10.14 General-purpose interface bus (GPIB). Sixteen signal lines are defined with up to 15 devices allowed in a "daisy-chain" or "star" configuration.

The standard defines three types of devices that may be connected to the bus. These are called *talkers*, *listeners*, and *controllers*.

1. Talkers are devices capable of putting data onto the bus for transmission to listeners or the controller in charge.
2. Listeners are devices capable of reading data on the bus output by talkers or the controller.
3. The controller programs devices on the bus. For example, it might cause a digital multimeter (DMM) to switch to the dc volts function. It also decides which device will be allowed to talk and which devices allowed to listen. It can also relinquish control to another controller (only one controller may be in charge at a given time, however).

In Fig. 10.14 the microcomputer is wired as the controller. A GPIB-compatible function generator is shown as a listener, and a GPIB-compatible frequency counter as both a listener and a talker.

IEEE 488 is an important parallel interface standard, particularly in the electronic instrumentation industry. Accordingly, in this section we present the electrical characteristics, mechanical considerations, control signal functions, and data exchange protocol for IEEE 488. In addition, a design using four LSI chips to implement the hardware is shown. We begin with a brief example illustrating a typical application.

Example: Using BASIC to Control a GPIB Instrument

One of the advantages of the GPIB is that users can program the interface using a high-level language without having to specify each step required in the control sequence. To understand why this is important, consider an example in which it is desired to program the function generator in Fig. 10.14 to output a 2-V peak-to-peak (p-p) 37-kHz sine wave. The frequency counter is to be used to measure this frequency, "talking" the result back to the microcomputer (controller). The following sequence of events is required.

1. The controller asserts the IFC (interface clear) signal, putting the system controller in charge and causing all talkers to cease talking.
2. The controller asserts the ATN (attention) signal and places the message DCL (device clear) on the bus. This causes all devices to revert to their factory default setup mode.
3. The controller asserts ATN and outputs the listen address of the function generator. Now in the listen mode, the function generator receives the device-dependent data to program the 2-V p-p 37-kHz sine wave. ATN is removed during the transmission of this data.
4. The controller asserts ATN and "unlistens" the function generator.
5. Steps 3 and 4 are repeated as the frequency counter is programmed to measure the waveform.
6. The controller asserts ATN and assigns the frequency counter as a talker and itself as a listener.
7. The controller polls the SRQ line waiting for the measurement to be complete. This poll can either be done serially, reading one status byte from each device on the bus, or in parallel, reading the status of eight devices at once.
8. When ready, the frequency counter "talks" its data to the controller. If only one data byte is to be transferred, the EOI (end or identify) line is asserted simultaneously with the data byte, indicating the end of data.
9. The microcomputer may use polling, interrupts, or DMA to read the data byte(s). The data transfer being complete, the controller returns to an idle state.

Notice that two forms of messages are passed over the bus. The first are called *interface messages*. These do not interact directly with the measurement process but rather, carry out commands required for setting up the proper protocol for transmitting and receiving the device data. Examples are the device clear (DCL) and unlisten commands.

The bus is also used to transfer *device-dependent messages*. These include setup information such as the amplitude and frequency of a sine-wave output by a function generator, or the full-scale voltage range of a DMM. The actual measurement data is also considered a device-dependent message.

GPIB interfaces are available as plug-in boards for many microcomputer systems. Software driver routines are normally included that allow users to control the interface through a high-level language such as BASIC or Pascal. Figure 10.15 illustrates a program written in *Tek BASIC*, a special version of BASIC developed by Tektronix for controlling their GPIB-compatible instruments. A 4041 System Controller is required to translate the BASIC commands into IEEE 488 interface and device-dependent messages.

The program in Fig. 10.15 begins by assigning the instruments at addresses 16 and 12 to logical units 5 and 7. Variable names suggesting the type of instrument involved are then assigned to these unit numbers—in this case a programmable power supply and digital multimeter.

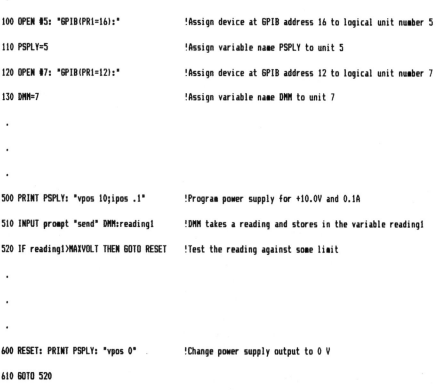

```
100 OPEN #5: "GPIB(PRI=16):"        !Assign device at GPIB address 16 to logical unit number 5

110 PSPLY=5                         !Assign variable name PSPLY to unit 5

120 OPEN #7: "GPIB(PRI=12):"        !Assign device at GPIB address 12 to logical unit number 7

130 DMM=7                           !Assign variable name DMM to unit 7




500 PRINT PSPLY: "vpos 10;ipos .1"  !Program power supply for +10.0V and 0.1A

510 INPUT prompt "send" DMM:reading1 !DMM takes a reading and stores in the variable reading1

520 IF reading1>MAXVOLT THEN GOTO RESET  !Test the reading against some limit




600 RESET: PRINT PSPLY: "vpos 0"    !Change power supply output to 0 V

610 GOTO 520
```

Figure 10.15 A pseudo-high-level language can be used to control the instruments on the GPIB.

Line 500 sets the power supply output for 10.0 V with a 0.1-A current limit. Line 510 instructs the DMM to take a voltage reading. The result is stored in the program variable *reading1*. This value is tested against a predefined limit in line 520. If greater than this value, control transfers to the RESET instructions in lines 600–610. Note that program lines can be assigned labels—line 600 is RESET—enhancing the readability of the program.

The advantage of using BASIC to control instruments on the GPIB bus should be obvious. The electrical protocol of the bus becomes transparent to the user. Since BASIC is easily learned, users can quickly develop control programs for their instrumentation problems.

As mentioned, the actual form of the data received from the talker or expected by the listener is device dependent. In addition, some manufacturers encode these messages in ASCII, terminating the byte string with the carriage return and line feed characters. Others use binary. ASCII has the advantage that the data can also be routed to a printer for display and analysis.

This inconsistency is the major problem of the IEEE 488 standard today. Although the electrical and mechanical specifications are very precise, the nature and format of the codes used in the message have been left to individual manufacturers. To encode $+6.52$ V, some use 6.52, others 25.6, and still others E1F7G6.

The IEEE is aware of this problem and has produced a new standard—IEEE 728-1982, "IEEE Recommended Practice for Code and Format Conventions for Use with ANSI/IEEE Std 488-1978." In addition, committees have been formed to extend and refine the current standards. In time it is hoped that all manufacturers will adhere to a well-defined hardware and software standard.

Electrical Characteristics

IEEE 488 specifies a low true (negative) logic system. The voltage levels are TTL compatible. The requirements for a driver are

$$V_{OL} \leq 0.5 \text{ V at 48 mA sink current}$$

and

$$V_{OH} \geq 2.4 \text{ V at 5.2 mA source current}$$

The requirements for a receiver are

$$V_{IH} \geq 2.0 \text{ V}$$

and

$$V_{IL} \leq 0.8 \text{ V}$$

The noise immunity is thus 0.3 V in the low state and 0.4 V in the high state. The Intel 8293 is a GPIB transceiver that meets the full requirements of the standard and includes Schmitt triggers with 0.4 V of hysteresis within each receiver. A GPIB interface using this chip is presented later in this section.

As mentioned previously, the maximum data rate is 1MB/s. However, this is restricted to cables less than 15 m in length. Normally, devices are connected in a "daisy chain" or star configuration with less than 4 m (2 m preferable) between connections. Used in this way, up to 15 devices can be accommodated with the 60-m-maximum-length cable.

Mechanical Interface

Figure 10.16 shows the 24-pin GPIB connector and pin assignments. Each of the eight control signals has a separate ground pin (EOI and REN share pin 24) and a shield or frame ground is also provided. Figure 10.17 shows one way in which these conductors can be arranged in a cable. The large number of grounds and cable shielding are responsible for the standard's excellent noise immunity. Be advised, however, that GPIB cables can be very expensive, typically more than $75 for a short 2-m cable with connectors.

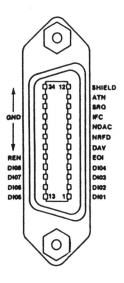

Contact	Signal Line	Contact	Signal Line
1	DIO 1	13	DIO 5
2	DIO 2	14	DIO 6
3	DIO 3	15	DIO 7
4	DIO 4	16	DIO 8
5	EOI (24)	17	REN (24)
6	DAV	18	Gnd, (6)
7	NRFD	19	Gnd, (7)
8	NDAC	20	Gnd, (8)
9	IFC	21	Gnd, (9)
10	SRQ	22	Gnd, (10)
11	ATN	23	Gnd, (11)
12	SHIELD	24	Gnd, LOGIC

Figure 10.16 A GPIB interface requires a 24-pin connector with pin assignments as shown. (Courtesy of IEEE.)

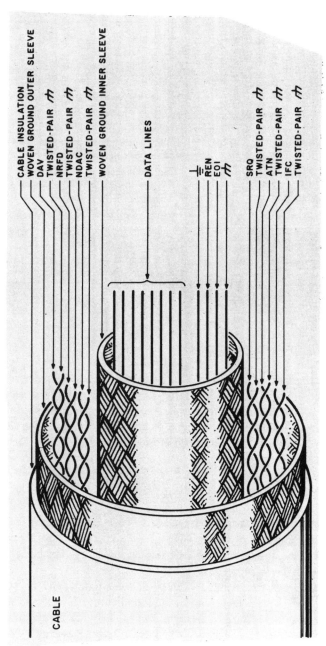

Figure 10.17 Cutaway view of a GPIB cable assembly. (Redrawn from "Interfacing for Data Acquisition" by Thomas R. Clune, appearing in the February 1985 issue of *BYTE* magazine. Copyright © 1985 by McGraw Hill, Inc. Used with permission.)

TABLE 10.4 GPIB INTERFACE FUNCTIONS

Mnemonic	Function name	Description
SH	Source handshake	Ability to transfer data from a talker to one or more listeners using the three handshake lines
AH	Acceptor handshake	Ability to receive data from a talker using the three handshake lines
T	Talker	Ability to send status and data bytes when addressed to talk
L	Listener	Ability to receive data when addressed to listen
SR	Service request	Ability to request service (interrupt) from the controller
RL	Remote local	Ability to operate in remote mode via GPIB or local mode via front-panel controls
PP	Parallel poll	Ability to present one bit of status to the controller without being addressed to talk and without handshake
DC	Device clear	Ability to be cleared (initialized) by the controller
DT	Device trigger	Ability to have its basic operation started either individually or as part of a group
C	Controller	Ability to send addresses as well as universal and addressed commands to other devices

Signal Descriptions

The GPIB standard specifies 10 different capabilities or *functions* for devices conr
to the bus. These are listed in Table 10.4. Note that it is not necessary for each c
to have all 10 functions. For example, the function generator shown in Fig. 10.14 re
the L and AH functions in order to receive data from the controller. However, be
it functions only as a listener, it need not support the T or C functions. This allo
designer flexibility in designing GPIB-compatible instruments. The standard recom
that the *capability code* be marked just above the connector on a GPIB instru
indicating which functions the device supports.

Commands and addresses.   When interface management line ATN
serted, the contents of the data bus is to be interpreted as an interface command
address (as opposed to a device-dependent message). The binary format for these
mands is given in Table 10.5.

Note that the commands can be either *uniline* (Type = ''U'') or *multiline*
= ''M''). As their name implies, uniline commands activate one (sometimes tw
the five interface management control lines. They do not require that the bus be
command mode. For example, when the controller asserts IFC, the active talke
immediately relinquish control of the data bus to the controller. The five interface
agement control signals are described in Table 10.6.

TABLE 10.5 REMOTE MESSAGE CODING[a]

Mnemonic	Message name	Notes	Type	Class	DIO8	DIO7	DIO6	DIO5	DIO4	DIO3	DIO2	DIO1	DAV	NRFD	NDAC	ATN	EOI	SRQ	IFC	REN
ACG	Addressed command group		M	AC	Y	0	0	0	X	X	X	X	X	X	X	1	X	X	X	X
ATN	Attention		U	UC	X	X	X	X	X	X	X	X	X	X	X	1	X	X	X	X
DAB	Data byte	(Notes 1,9)	M	DD	D_8	D_7	D_6	D_5	D_4	D_3	D_2	D_1	X	X	X	0	X	X	X	X
DAC	Data accepted		U	HS	X	X	X	X	X	X	X	X	X	X	0	X	X	X	X	X
DAV	Data valid		U	HS	X	X	X	X	X	X	X	X	1	X	X	X	X	X	X	X
DCL	Device clear		M	UC	Y	0	0	1	0	1	0	0	X	X	X	1	X	X	X	X
END	End	(Note 9)	U	ST	X	X	X	X	X	X	X	X	X	X	X	0	1	X	X	X
EOS	End of string	(Notes 2, 9)	M	DD	E_8	E_7	E_6	E_5	E_4	E_3	E_2	E_1	X	X	X	0	X	X	X	X
GET	Group execute trigger		M	AC	Y	0	0	0	1	0	0	0	X	X	X	1	X	X	X	X
GTL	Go to local		M	AC	Y	0	0	0	0	0	0	1	X	X	X	1	X	X	X	X
IDY	Identify		U	UC	X	X	X	X	X	X	X	X	X	X	X	1	1	X	X	X
IFC	Interface clear		U	UC	X	X	X	X	X	X	X	X	X	X	X	X	X	X	1	X
LAG	Listen address group		M	AD	Y	0	1	X	X	X	X	X	X	X	X	1	X	X	X	X
LLO	Local lock out		M	UC	Y	0	0	1	0	0	0	1	X	X	X	1	X	X	X	X
MLA	My listen address	(Note 3)	M	AD	Y	0	1	L_5	L_4	L_3	L_2	L_1	X	X	X	1	X	X	X	X
MTA	My talk address	(Note 4)	M	AD	Y	1	0	T_5	T_4	T_3	T_2	T_1	X	X	X	1	X	X	X	X
MSA	My secondary address	(Note 5)	M	SE	Y	1	1	S_5	S_4	S_3	S_2	S_1	X	X	X	1	X	X	X	X
NUL	Null byte		M	DD	0	0	0	0	0	0	0	0	X	X	X	0	X	X	X	X
OSA	Other secondary address		M	SE	$OSA = SCG \wedge \overline{MSA}$															
OTA	Other talk address		M	AD	$OTA = TAG \wedge \overline{MTA}$															
PCG	Primary command group		M	—	$PCG = ACG \vee UCG \vee LAG \vee TAG$															
PPC	Parallel poll configure		M	AC	Y	0	0	0	0	1	0	1	X	X	X	1	X	X	X	X

TABLE 10.5 CONTINUED

Bus signal line(s) and coding that asserts the true value of the message

Mnemonic	Message name	Type	Class	DIO8	DIO7	DIO6	DIO5	DIO4	DIO3	DIO2	DIO1	DAV	NRFD	NDAC	ATN	EOI	SRQ	IFC	REN
PPE	Parallel poll enable (Note 6)	M	SE	Y	1	1	0	S	P_3	P_2	P_1	X	X	X	1	X	X	X	X
PPD	Parallel poll disable (Note 7)	M	SE	Y	1	1	1	X	X	X	X	X	X	X	1	X	X	X	X
PPR1	Parallel poll response 1	U	ST	X	X	X	X	X	X	X	1	X	X	X	1	1	X	X	X
PPR2	Parallel poll response 2	U	ST	X	X	X	X	X	X	1	X	X	X	X	1	1	X	X	X
PPR3	Parallel poll response 3	U	ST	X	X	X	X	X	1	X	X	X	X	X	1	1	X	X	X
PPR4	Parallel poll response 4 (Note 10)	U	ST	X	X	X	X	1	X	X	X	X	X	X	1	1	X	X	X
PPR5	Parallel poll response 5	U	ST	X	X	X	1	X	X	X	X	X	X	X	1	1	X	X	X
PPR6	Parallel poll response 6	U	ST	X	X	1	X	X	X	X	X	X	X	X	1	1	X	X	X
PPR7	Parallel poll response 7	U	ST	X	1	X	X	X	X	X	X	X	X	X	1	1	X	X	X
PPR8	Parallel poll response 8	U	ST	1	X	X	X	X	X	X	X	X	X	X	1	1	X	X	X
PPU	Parallel poll unconfigure	M	UC	Y	0	0	1	0	1	0	1	X	X	X	1	X	X	X	X
REN	Remote enable	U	UC	X	X	X	X	X	X	X	X	X	X	X	X	X	X	X	1
RFD	Ready for data	U	HS	X	X	X	X	X	X	X	X	X	X	X	X	X	X	X	X
RQS	Request service (Note 9)	U	ST	X	1	X	X	X	X	X	X	X	X	X	0	X	X	X	X
SCG	Secondary command group	M	SE	Y	1	1	X	X	X	X	X	X	X	X	1	X	X	X	X
SDC	Selected device clear	M	AC	Y	0	0	0	0	1	0	0	X	X	X	1	X	X	X	X
SPD	Serial poll disable	M	UC	Y	0	0	1	1	0	0	1	X	X	X	1	X	X	X	X
SPE	Serial poll enable	M	UC	Y	0	0	1	1	0	0	0	X	X	X	1	X	X	X	X
SRQ	Service request	U	ST	X	X	X	X	X	X	X	X	X	X	X	X	X	1	X	X
STB	Status byte (Notes 8, 9)	M	ST	S_8	X	S_6	S_5	S_4	S_3	S_2	S_1	X	X	X	0	X	X	X	X

(PPR1 through PPR8 are grouped together by a brace.)

		M															
TCT	Take control	M	AC	Y	0	0	0	1	0	0	1	XXX	1	X	X	X	X
TAG	Talk address group	M	AD	Y	1	0	X	X	X	X	X	XXX	1	X	X	X	X
UCG	Universal command group	M	UC	Y	0	0	1	X	X	X	1	XXX	1	X	X	X	X
UNL	Unlisten	M	AD	Y	0	1	1	1	1	1	1	XXX	1	X	X	X	X
UNT	Untalk (Note 11)	M	AD	Y	1	0	1	1	1	1	1	XXX	1	X	X	X	X

a The 1/0 coding on ATN when sent concurrent with multiline messages has been added to this revision for interpretive convenience. 0 = logical 0. 1 = logical 1. X = don't care (received message) or do not drive unless directed by another message (transmitted message). Y = don't care (transmitted message).

Notes:

1. D1-D8 specify the device-dependent data bits.
2. E1-E8 specify the device-dependent code used to indicate the EOS message.
3. L1-L5 specify the device-dependent bits of the device's listen address.
4. T1-T5 specify the device-dependent bits of the device's talk address.
5. S1-S5 specify the device-dependent bits of the device's secondary address.
6. S specifies the sense of the PPR.

S	Response
0	0
1	1

P1-P3 specify the PPR message to be sent when a parallel poll is executed.

P3	P2	P1	PPR Message
0	0	0	PPR1
.	.	.	
.	.	.	
1	1	1	PPR8

7. D1-D4 specify don't care bits that shall not be decoded by the receiving device. It is recommended that all zeros be sent.
8. S1-S6, S8 specify the device-dependent status. (DIO7 is used for RQS message.)
9. The source of the message on the ATN line is always the C function, whereas the messages on the DIO and EOI lines are enabled by the T function.
10. The source of the messages on the ATN and EOI lines is always the C function, whereas the source of the messages on the DIO lines is always the PP function.
11. This code is provided for system use.

TABLE 10.6 GPIB MANAGEMENT BUS CONTROL SIGNALS

Mnemonic	Signal name	Source	Description
ATN	Attention	Controller	Indicates address or control byte is on the bus
EOI	End or identify	Talker or controller	Talker asserts simultaneous with last byte to indicate end of data; controller asserts with ATN to initiate a parallel poll
SRQ	Service request	Talker or listener	Request controller to take some action; controller must perform serial poll to determine device requiring service
IFC	Interface clear	Controller	Initialize all devices to a known state with the system controller the active controller in the system
REN	Remote enable	Controller	Enables a device to go remote when addressed to listen

Multiline commands pass their messages over the eight data bus lines. Because ATN is asserted for these commands, they are not confused with the data output by a talker.

Example 10.4

Describe the commands that must be given to program a DMM at device address 19 for normal front-panel control.

Solution The commands are as follows:

[1] MLA; ATN = 1, data = 00110011
[2] GTL; ATN = 1, data = 00000001
[3] UNL; ATN = 1, data = 00111111

The first command asserts "My Listen Address" to device 19, enabling it to receive the following command, Go To Local. The device is now under front-panel control. The last command, Unlisten, prevents device 19 from accepting further interface messages (until the next MLA).

Some messages are sent to all devices on the bus and thus do not need to be preceded by an MLA command. These are the *universal* (Class = "UC") commands. DCL, for example, clears all devices to their factory presets. LLO (Local Lock Out) disables the front-panel controls of all devices on the bus.

Data Exchange Protocol

The actual exchange of data on the bus between a talker and a listener is coordinated via a three-wire (interlocked) handshaking process. Figure 10.18 shows the timing. The handshake is also flowcharted in Fig. 10.19.

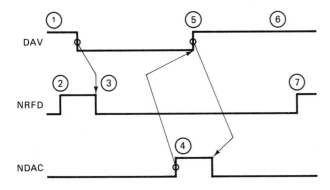

① Data is output

② All listeners are ready for data

③ Listeners begin to accept data

④ Last listener latches data

⑤ Talker removes data and prepares for next transfer

⑥ Next data byte is output

⑦ Last listener acknowledges processing of previous data byte

Figure 10.18 The GPIB standard specifies a three-wire handshake mechanism.

DAV (data available) is initially high, indicating that data is not available on the bus (recall that all signals are asserted active low). When all listeners are ready for data, NRFD (not ready for data) will be high. The talker than asserts DAV low, alerting the listeners that valid data is on the bus. Each listener now reads the data byte from the bus, asserting NRFD and deasserting NDAC (not data accepted). That is, NRFD = 0 and NDAC = 1. This is interpreted to mean that the data byte has been latched and accepted (NDAC = 1) but not yet processed (NRFD = 0).

Because NRFD and NDAC are implemented with open-collector gates, NDAC does not go high until *all* listeners have accepted the data byte. It is this feature of the handshake that allows devices with different speeds to be interfaced to the bus.

When all listeners do acknowledge receipt of the data, the talker sets DAV high, indicating that valid data is no longer on the bus. The listeners then assert NDAC in preparation for the next transfer. Note, however, that NRFD is still asserted (low) as each listener processes the data. Only when this line returns high, indicating that *all* listeners have processed the data, can the next data transfer take place.

The purpose of NRFD is to allow the talker to remove the data from the bus (and begin to fetch the next data byte) even though the listeners have not yet "digested" the previous byte. This increases the data transfer rate of the bus, as the talker can have the next byte ready as soon as the previous one has been processed (NDAC = 0).

The standard requires the talker to indicate the end of the data stream. Two methods are used. One is to assert EOI (end or identify) simultaneously with the last data byte. When the data format is ASCII, another technique is to send the carriage return character (ODH) as the delimiter.

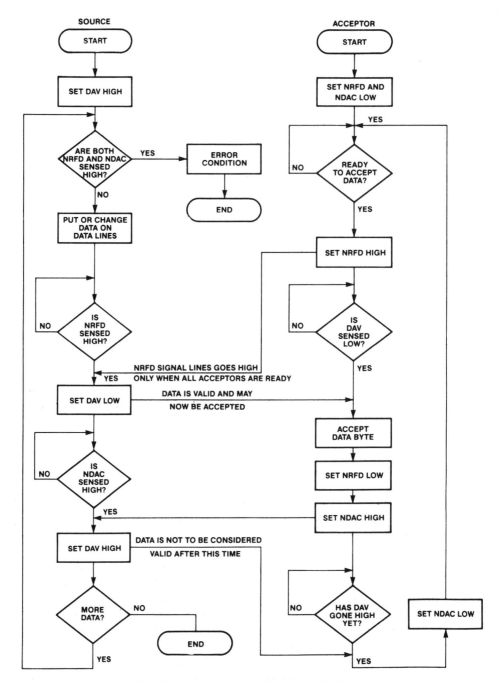

Figure 10.19 Flowchart showing the relationship between the handshaking signals DAV, NRFD, and NDAC. (Courtesy of Intel Corporation.)

Implementing the GPIB with the 8291A, 8292, and 8293

The complexity of designing a GPIB interface—40 to 50 SSI and MSI chips are required to implement the controller function—has prevented the standard from gaining the widespread acceptance of RS-232C. However, it is now possible to implement talker/listener functions with only three ICs, and a fully functional controller can be built from only four chips.

Figure 10.20 shows a design based on the Intel 8291A talker/listener and the 8292 controller (actually a preprogrammed 8041 UPI microcomputer). Because these chips cannot meet the standard's bus driver specifications—48-mA sink current and 5.2-mA source current—two 8293 GPIB bus transceivers are required to complete the interface.

The 8291A and 8292 interface to the host processor via a set of eight bidirectional data bus lines similar to the other peripheral controller chips discussed in Chap. 9. When the 8291A's $\overline{CS}$ input is low, RS0–RS2 selects one of eight internal read/write registers. Thus the chip occupies eight I/O ports (or memory locations) within the host processor's I/O (or memory) address space.

The 8292 is interfaced in a similar manner and appears as two input and output ports selected by the AO address input line when its $\overline{CS}$ input is low. The internal RAM of the 8292/8041 is used as a special-purpose register bank organized as six read registers and five write registers. Most of these registers are accessed by writing special command bytes to the chips command register (written whenever AO is high).

The actual transfer of data using these chips can be done using polling, DMA (via the 8291A's DREQ and DACK pins), or interrupts. The 8292 controller provides interrupts on task complete (TCI), output buffer full (OBFI), input buffer full (IBFI), and a special (non-CPU-initiated) interrupt (SPI).

A detailed description of the registers within these chips and their operation is beyond the scope of this book but is available in the data sheets available from Intel Corporation.[1]

SELF-REVIEW 10.3 (answers on page 526)

10.3.1. Using RS-232C, one peripheral can be interfaced to a microcomputer for each RS-232C port. However, as many as _____ devices can be interfaced in a "daisy chain" configuration using one GPIB "port."

10.3.2. In the IEEE 488 GPIB standard, devices that transmit on the bus are called _____, while devices that accept information from the bus are called _____.

10.3.3. The minimum GPIB configuration requires at least one talker or listener and a controller. (True/False)

10.3.4. Although the GPIB standard allows up to 60-m cable lengths, devices on the bus should not be separated by more than _____ m.

10.3.5. When the GPIB interface management line ATN is asserted, the contents of the data bus carries a(n) _____ message.

---

[1]See also Ronald M. Williams, "LSI Chips Ease Standard 488 Bus Interfacing," *Computer Design*, October 1979.

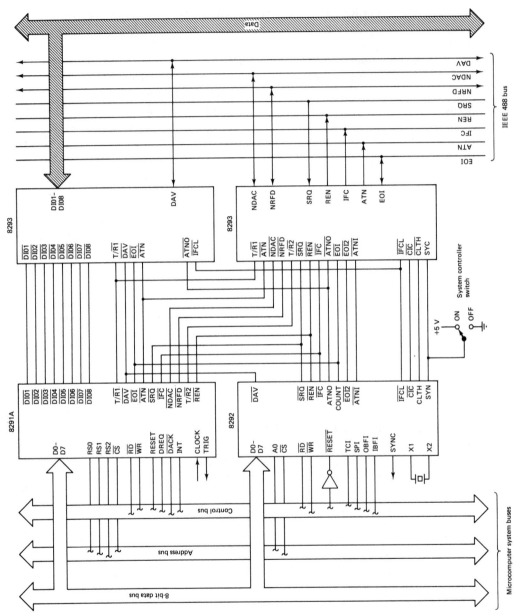

Figure 10.20 Fully functional talker/listener GPIB interface.

10.3.6. GPIB command messages may be either _____ or _____.

10.3.7. The binary code for the command that assigns GPIB device 7 as a talker is _____.

10.3.8. When GPIB handshake signal NDAC switches from high to low, this indicates that all receivers have accepted and processed the previously output data byte. (True/False)

10.4 ERROR DETECTION AND CORRECTION

In this context, data errors refer to those errors electrically induced by crosstalk between adjacent conductors, signal distortion, or impulse noise due to lightning or high current or voltage switching. The long lines of the switched telephone network are particularly susceptible to these noise sources, but data errors can occur on any medium used for data transmissions. This includes the traces on a printed-circuit board used to transport data between a microprocessor and its memory chips.

Data errors cause the receiving node to misinterpret the incoming data—often with disastrous results. For example, the ASCII line feed character has the hex code OAH. If a noise pulse should occur changing this to 4AH—only one bit need change—the letter "J" is received. Sent to a printer or VDT, this may cause the next line of text to overwrite the previous one.

Sometimes the data being sent is a control code telling a device to operate in a particular mode or take a particular action. A one-bit data error could have serious—even life threatening—consequences if the data is meant for a robotic arm or other industrial process controller.

All methods of error control involve *redundancy*, that is, sending extra information that is not a part of the data message. The redundant information is sent in the form of *check bits* which are used by the receiver to detect errors in the incoming data.

Two error control methods are used. *Automatic request for repeat* (ARQ) is most common and has the receiver request that the last character or block of data be retransmitted if an error has been detected. This has the built-in disadvantage of reducing the data rate of the communications channel in direct proportion to the error rate.

The second technique is called *forward error correction* (FEC). This method requires the receiver to have more intricate logic circuitry such that it not only detects data errors, but also identifies and corrects those bits in error. FEC is based on a data-encoding technique called the *Hamming code* and requires several check bits for each character transmitted. The obvious advantage is the elimination of the need for data retransmission.

In this section we discuss the most common redundant check bit strategies and also show how the Hamming code can be used to identify and correct data errors.

Parity

A parity bit is a redundant checking bit added to a data word or stream of bits in such a way that the total number of logic 1's in the data stream, including the parity bit, is even or odd (the receiving and transmitting stations must decide beforehand on even or odd parity). As shown in Fig. 10.21, parity can be applied vertically (VRC) or longitudinally (LRC).

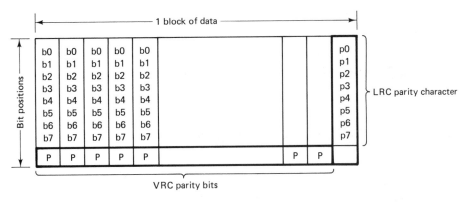

Figure 10.21 Vertical redundancy check (VRC) and longitudinal redundancy check (LRC). One VRC bit is appended to each data character. One LRC character is appended to each block of data.

Vertical redundancy check (VRC). VRC is a very common form of error control used with asynchronous serial data. One reason for this is that the transmitting and receiving USARTs (or UARTs) can easily append and check the extra parity bit with minimal additional hardware. Used with ASCII-encoded data, the parity bit becomes an eighth data bit chosen to make the number of logic 1's in the resulting byte even or odd.

Example 10.5

The following data bytes are ASCII characters encoded with an even-parity bit in the MSB position: D1H, 36H, E5H. Which of these bytes, if any, are in error?

Solution Convert each byte to binary:

$$D1H = 11010001$$
$$36H = 00110110$$
$$E5H = 11100101$$

On inspecting each byte, only E5 has an odd number of 1's and must therefore be in error. The actual bit in error, however, is unknown.

Figures 9.22 and 9.23 show the mode instruction and status registers of the 8251A USART. During initialization the mode register can be programmed for even or odd parity via bits D4 and D5 (PEN and EP). Thereafter, the 8251A will automatically insert the proper parity bit. On data reception, the parity of the incoming characters is determined. Bit 3 of the status register (PE) is then set if the parity does not agree with that programmed in the mode register.

RAM parity check. The use of a vertical check bit is not limited to asynchronous serial data. Figure 10.22 illustrates the pin descriptions and truth table for the 74LS280 9-bit parity generator/checker. This chip can be used effectively to add a ninth (redundant) data bit to a byte array of RAM chips. This is shown in Fig. 10.23.

During a memory write cycle the data byte output by the microprocessor is examined by the 74LS280. The Σ E output is used to write an *odd* parity bit into the ninth bit of the memory array. Note that 74LS280 input A is low during this (memory write) cycle.

DECEMBER 1972–REVISED DECEMBER 1983

- **Generates Either Odd or Even Parity for Nine Data Lines**

- **Cascadable for n-Bits**

- **Can Be Used to Upgrade Existing Systems using MSI Parity Circuits**

- **Typical Data-to-Output Delay of Only 14 ns for 'S280 and 33 ns for 'LS280**

- **Typical Power Dissipation:**
  'LS280 . . . 80 mW
  'S280 . . . 335 mW

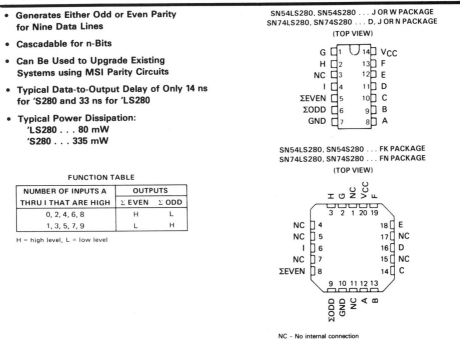

FUNCTION TABLE

NUMBER OF INPUTS A	OUTPUTS	
THRU I THAT ARE HIGH	Σ EVEN	Σ ODD
0, 2, 4, 6, 8	H	L
1, 3, 5, 7, 9	L	H

H = high level, L = low level

Figure 10.22 The 74LS280 will generate/check the parity of 9 input data bits. (Courtesy of Texas Instruments.)

During a memory read cycle the AND gate is enabled, allowing the 74LS280 to check the parity of the 9-bit word stored in memory. A logic 0 on the Σ0 output indicates even parity and thus a parity error. This level is clocked into a flip-flop whose Q output is used to drive one input of an 8259A PIC. Depending on the priority of this input, the interrupt service routine will be called and appropriate action taken.

The 74LS280 has a 50-ns worst-case propagation delay time, and this must be considered when verifying memory read and write timing. If necessary, the 74AS280 can be used. This chip has a typical input-to-output delay of only 7.5 ns.

Longitudinal redundancy check (LRC). Adding a VRC bit to a data character can detect odd numbers or error bits only. For example, if the data byte D1H is received as D2H, its parity does not change—even though 2 bits are now in error. VRC is best suited for environments where multiple bit errors are unlikely. A typical situation would be data transmissions between two computers connected via twisted-pair conductors or shielded cable.

Analysis of data errors transmitted over long distances, particularly via a modem and the switched telephone network, reveals that data errors occur in "bursts." A lightning strike may induce noise into the transmission path that may persist for several milliseconds. At 9600 baud, 20 to 25 bits will be transmitted in 2 ms. Thus several characters may be affected by the burst noise source.

Sec. 10.4   Error Detection and Correction   **515**

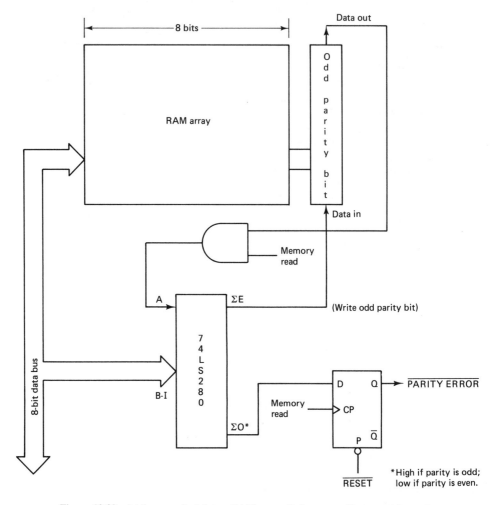

Figure 10.23 Adding a parity bit to a RAM array. Parity errors, if any, are detected during a memory read cycle.

For this reason, a redundant *block checking character* or checksum is often used to detect multiple bit errors. The block check character (BCC) may be computed as a LRC parity bit, as shown in Fig. 10.21, or calculated in software as the 2's complement sum of all the preceding bytes in the data block. Figure 10.24 shows an 8086 program that calculates and appends a BCC to a block of 255 data bytes. The (256-byte) data block can then be transmitted using serial or parallel techniques as desired.

Example 10.6

Calculate the checksum byte for the four hex data bytes 10, 23, 45, and 04.

Solution The sum is calculated first.

$$10$$
$$23$$
$$45$$
$$04$$
$$\overline{}$$
$$7C$$

Then invert 7C and add 1 (forming the 2's complement):

$$\overline{01111100} + 1 = 10000011 + 1 = 10000100 = 84H$$

Example 10.7

Assume that the following data bytes are received and that the last byte is the checksum character: 10, 23, 45, 04, 84. Has the data been received correctly?

Solution   The receiver need only add the five data bytes.

$$10$$
$$23$$
$$45$$
$$04$$
$$84$$
$$\overline{}$$

$$00$$

Discarding the carry, the result is 00. No error has been detected. The reason for forming the 2's complement should now be clear. Correctly received data will always sum to 0.

Besides its ability to detect multiple-bit errors, there is another advantage to using the BCC. For a 255-byte data block, one extra byte or 0.4% of redundancy is required. Using a VRC technique, one extra bit is required per byte. This amounts to an overhead of 12.5%. Thus the BCC is an effective way to detect multiple-bit errors without significantly decreasing the data rate of the channel.

BCC is not perfect, however. When an error is detected, the entire data block must be retransmitted—unlike VRC, in which only the errant character need be repeated. In addition, some error combinations will go undetected by the BCC. In Exs. 10.6 and 10.7, if the data byte 45H changes to become 44H and the data byte 04H becomes 05H, the BCC remains the same. In general, to go undetected, even numbers of bits must change in the same bit position.

Cyclic Redundancy Check (CRC)

The CRC character is another form of longitudinal redundancy calculated on a block of data. It is commonly used when reading and writing data to a floppy or rigid disk and to ensure data integrity in programmable ROMs. It is universally used for detecting errors in synchronous data communications.

```
                            ;Function:      Append BCC byte to a data block
                            ;Inputs:        Block address passed in DS:SI
                            ;Outputs:       BCC added to the block as last byte
                            ;Calls:         nothing
                            ;Destroys:      flags,CX,SI,AL,BL

                            ;Program Equates

= 00FF                      BLOCK_SIZE      EQU   255

                            ;Procedure Begins

0000                        CODE      SEGMENT   BYTE
                            ASSUME    CS:CODE

0000                        BCC       PROC      NEAR
0000   FC                             CLD                   ;Auto increment
0001   B9 00FF                        MOV     CX,BLOCK_SIZE ;CX is counter
0004   B3 00                          MOV     BL,0          ;Sum to BL
0006   AC               SUM:          LODSB                 ;Get one byte
0007   02 D8                          ADD     BL,AL         ;Accumulate sum
0009   E2 FB                          LOOP    SUM           ;Do until CX=0
000B   F6 DB                          NEG     BL            ;Form 2s compl
000D   88 1C                          MOV     [SI],BL       ;Append BCC
000F   C3                             RET                   ;Done
0010                        BCC       ENDP
0010                        CODE      ENDS
                                      END
```

Figure 10.24 Program to generate the BCC for a 255-byte block of data.

Unlike the checksum, the CRC method is not byte oriented. Instead, the data block is thought of as a "stream" of serial data bits. The bits in this n-bit block are considered the coefficients of a *characteristic polynomial* [usually referred to as $M(X)$—"M of X"]. $M(X)$ has the form

$$M(X) = b_n + b_{n-1} X + b_{n-2}X^2 + \cdots + b_1X^{n-1} + b_0 X^n$$

where b_0 is the least significant bit (LSB) and b_n is the most significant bit (MSB).

Example 10.8

Calculate the data polynomial $M(X)$ for the 16-bit data stream 26F0H.

Solution   First visualize this data in binary form:

$$0\ 0\ 1\ 0 \quad 0\ 1\ 1\ 0 \quad 1\ 1\ 1\ 1 \quad 0\ 0\ 0\ 0$$

Now write this as $M(X)$:

$$M(X) = 0 + 0X^1 + 1X^2 + 0X^3 + 0X^4 + 1X^5 + 1X^6 + 0X^7 + 1X^8$$
$$+ 1X^9 + 1X^{10} + 1X^{11} + 0X^{12} + 0X^{13} + 0X^{14} + 0X^{15}$$

and eliminate the 0 terms:

$$M(X) = X^2 + X^5 + X^6 + X^8 + X^9 + X^{10} + X^{11} \tag{10.1}$$

Equation 10.1 is a unique polynomial representing the data in the 16-bit block. If one or more of the data bits was to change, the polynomial would also change. The CRC is found by applying the following equation:

$$\frac{M(X) \times X^n}{G(X)} = Q(X) + R(X) \tag{10.2}$$

In this equation $G(X)$ is called the *generator polynomial*. For the bisync protocol $G(X)$ is

$$G(X) = X^{16} + X^{15} + X^2 + 1 \tag{10.3}$$

The SDLC protocol uses:

$$G(X) = X^{16} + X^{13} + X^5 + 1 \tag{10.4}$$

When the division is performed, the result will be a *quotient $Q(X)$* and a *remainder $R(X)$*. The CRC technique consists of calculating $R(X)$ for the data stream and *appending* the result to the data block. Now when $R(X)$ is again calculated by the receiver, the result should be $R(X) = 0$. Also note that because $G(X)$ is of power 16, the remainder, $R(X)$, cannot be of order higher than 15, and is thus represented by two bytes (no matter what the block length itself).

Example 10.9

Calculate the CRC bytes for the data block 26F0H using the bisync generator polynomial.

Solution   Figure 10.25 shows the arithmetic. The remainder is

$$R(X) = X^{15} + X^{13} + X^9 + X^8 + X^6 + X^4 + X^3 + X + 1$$

When expressed in binary this becomes (recalling that the coefficient of the highest power becomes the LSB)

$$1101 \quad 1010 \quad 1100 \quad 0101 = \text{DAC5H}$$

If the two bytes DAC5 are appended to the 26F0 data stream, the received CRC calculation should result in R(X) = 0, indicating that no errors have been detected. If an error is indicated, a request for retransmission must be made, as with BCC. The effectiveness of CRC for detecting errors can be summarized as follows assuming a CRC length of n bits.

1. All data blocks with an even (or odd) number of errors are detected if n is even (or odd).
2. All data blocks with burst errors less than n bits long are detected.
3. All data blocks with a total number of error bits less than approximately $n/4$ are detected.
4. Of all remaining error patterns, 1 in 2^n is undetected.

As an example, if a 25-bit CRC is appended to a 1000-bit data stream, only 3 error bits in 100 million will go undetected!

In practice the CRC character can be computed in hardware or software. However, it has become common for the data communications peripheral controller chip to implement the function on-board. Intel's 8273 programmable HDLC/SDLC protocol controller automatically checks for CRC errors during reception, and automatically appends R(X)

$$\frac{M(X)\,X^{16}}{G(X)} =$$

$$X^{16} + X^{15} + X^2 + 1$$

Quotient: $X^{11} + X^9 + X^6 + X^2 + X + 1$

$$X^{16} + X^{15} + X^2 + 1 \; \big)\; X^{27} + X^{26} + X^{25} + X^{24} + X^{22} + X^{21} + X^{18}$$

$$X^{27} + X^{26}$$

$$X^{25} + X^{24} + X^{22} + X^{21} + X^{18} \qquad\qquad\qquad\qquad\quad + X^{13} + X^{11}$$

$$X^{25} + X^{24} \qquad\qquad\qquad\qquad\qquad\qquad\qquad\quad + X^{13} + X^{11}$$

$$\qquad\qquad\qquad\qquad\qquad\qquad\qquad\qquad\qquad\qquad + X^{11} + X^9$$

$$X^{22} + X^{21} + X^{18} \qquad\qquad\qquad\qquad\quad + X^{13} \qquad + X^9$$

$$X^{22} + X^{21}$$

$$X^{18} \qquad\qquad\qquad\qquad\quad + X^{13} \qquad + X^9 + X^8 + X^6$$

$$X^{18} + X^{17} \qquad\qquad\qquad + X^{13} \qquad + X^9 + X^8 + X^6$$

$$X^{17} \qquad\qquad\qquad\qquad\quad + X^{13} \qquad + X^9 + X^8 + X^6 \qquad + X^4$$

$$X^{17} + X^{16} \qquad\qquad\qquad + X^{13} \qquad + X^9 + X^8 + X^6 + X^4 \qquad + X^2$$

$$X^{16} \qquad\qquad\qquad\qquad\quad + X^{13} \qquad + X^9 + X^8 + X^6 + X^4 + X^3 \qquad + X^2 \quad + X$$

$$X^{16} + X^{15} \qquad\qquad\qquad\qquad\qquad\qquad\qquad\qquad\qquad\qquad\qquad + X^2 \qquad\quad + 1$$

$$R(X) = X^{15} + X^{13} \qquad\qquad\quad + X^9 + X^8 + X^6 + X^4 + X^3 \qquad\qquad\quad + X + 1$$

Figure 10.25 Generating the CRC bytes from the bisync data stream 26F0H. (From J. Uffenbeck, *Microcomputers and Microprocessors: The 8080, 8085, and Z-80.* Prentice-Hall, Englewood Cliffs, N.J., 1985.)

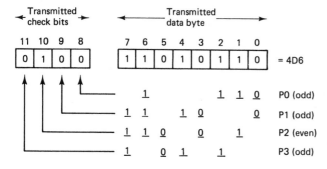

Figure 10.26 Four parity bits are required to encode one byte in the Hamming code. (From J. Uffenbeck, *Microcomputers and Microprocessors: The 8080, 8085, and Z-80*. Prentice-Hall, Englewood Cliffs, N.J., 1985.)

to the end of the data stream during transmission. Thus the CRC becomes "transparent" to the user.

Error Correction

The preceding error detection techniques—VRC, LRC, CRC, BCC—all rely on the receiver to request retransmission of the data blocks or characters in which an error was detected. This is called the ARQ (automatic request for repeat) method of data error control.

As mentioned, the alternative to ARQ is forward error correction (FEC). This is a technique based on work done by mathematician Richard Hamming at Bell Laboratories in the early 1950s. It can be used to detect and correct single-bit data errors. Figure 10.26 illustrates the Hamming code applied to an 8-bit data byte. Four check bits are required, each calculated on a different subset of bits in the data byte. In Fig. 10.26 the data byte D6H is transmitted as the 12-bit data stream 4D6H.

When the data is received, a 4-bit *error code* is generated by again calculating the parity on the four subsets of bits (including the four checkbits). This is shown in Fig. 10.27. The resulting error code can then be used to identify the particular bit (if any) in error. This is shown in Table 10.7.

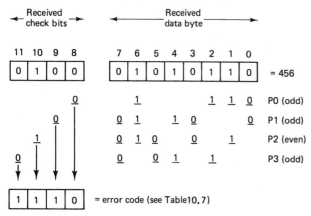

Figure 10.27 The receiver computes an error code based on the four check bits and the data byte. An error code of 0000 indicates that no error has been detected. (From J. Uffenbeck, *Microcomputers and Microprocessors: The 8080, 8085, and Z-80*. Prentice-Hall, Englewood Cliffs, N.J., 1985.)

TABLE 10.7 ERROR CODES FOR THE 8-BIT
MODIFIED HAMMING CODE TECHNIQUE IN
FIG. 10.27

Error code	Bit in error
0000	No error detected
0001	Check bit 0
0010	Check bit 1
0011	Data bit 0
0100	Check bit 2[a]
0101	Data bit 1
0110	Data bit 3
0111	Data bit 6
1000	Check bit 3
1001	Data bit 2
1010	Data bit 4
1011	All data and parity set to 0
1100	Data bit 5
1101	Multibit error
1110	Data bit 7
1111	Multibit error

[a]All data and parity bits are set to a 1.

Source: J. Uffenbeck, *Microcomputers and Micropro-cessors: The 8080, 8085, and Z-80*. Prentice-Hall, Englewood Cliffs, N.J., 1985.

Figure 10.27 illustrates the case where the data byte D6H (Hamming encoded as 4D6H) is received as 456H. The error code generated is 1110, which (correctly) indicates that data bit 7 is in error.

The overhead of 4 extra parity bits for each data byte makes this technique undesirable for many applications. The data rate of the communications channel is also adversely affected by these 4 extra bits. However, as the word length increases, the overhead decreases. A 16-bit word requires only 5 check bits, resulting in a 31% overhead. Such a system has been developed by Data General Corporation. It will correct all single-bit errors and reportedly detect an average of 97% of all multiple-bit errors.[2]

The final choice of error control method depends on the application at hand. As the price of memory chips continues to drop, FEC may find increasing application in microcomputer systems. On the other hand, CRC with ARQ will probably remain the choice for secure transmissions over bursty data channels.

[2]George J. Walker, "Error Checking and Correcting for Your Computer," *BYTE*, Vol. 5, No. 5 (1980), p. 260.

10.4.1. Two general methods for controlling errors in data transmissions are _____ and _____ .

10.4.2. List three error-detection schemes used with ARQ error control.

10.4.3. When the ASCII character "T" is sent using even parity, the hex code transmitted is _____ .

10.4.4. Using the CRC code, the receiving terminal computes a remainder polynomial which should be _____ if no errors are detected.

10.4.5. What is the advantage of using a block-checking error-detection scheme such as LRC or CRC, versus a character-oriented scheme such as VRC?

10.4.6. Using the Hamming error-detection and error-correction code, the data byte 3CH would be transmitted as _____ .

CHAPTER 10 SELF-TEST

1. The current loop interface in Fig. 10.1 (will/will not) operate in dull duplex.

2. When not transmitting data, the typical voltage level on an RS-232C transmission line is _____ .

3. To avoid ground loops, RS-422 uses _____ line drivers and receivers.

4. If an RS-232C connector is wired such that data is output on pin 3 of that connector and input on pin 2, the port is wired as a _____ .

5. When not transmitting data, a 300 baud originate modem will be outputting a _____ tone.

6. What handshaking protocol can be implemented between two computers communicating over the telephone network using 300-baud full-duplex modems?

7. Devices on the GPIB use a _____ -bit primary address.

8. For a GPIB-compatible instrument to output its data onto the bus, it must first be enabled as a talker via the _____ command.

9. A GPIB driver must be able to sink _____ in the low state and source _____ in the high state.

10. When NRFD is _____ and NDAC is _____ , all GPIB receivers are ready for new data.

11. What feature of the GPIB standard allows talkers to communicate with listeners with different data rate capabilities?

12. All GPIB uniline commands are output by the controller only. (True/False)

13. Which of the following error-detection schemes are *not* associated with the ARQ method of error control? (a) VRC; (b) Hamming codes; (c) BCC; (d) CRC.

14. List three disadvantages of using the VRC method of error control.

15. Using a generator polynomial $X^8 + X^6 + X^5 + X^4 + X^3 + 1$ will result in a _____ -bit CRC character.

16. The data byte A5H is transmitted as _____ using the 12-bit Hamming code.

17. The Hamming encoded data stream C37H is received and decoded. The (corrected) data byte
is _____.

ANALYSIS AND DESIGN QUESTIONS

10.1. Figure 10.28 shows an RS-232C interface between a VDT and a microcomputer using an
8251A USART. Unfortunately, the circuit does not work. What do you think is wrong?

10.2. Using the 8215A USART and TMS99532, design an acoustically coupled modem interface
to an 8086 microprocessor. Write the following software routines as *procedures*.

1. *8251A initialization:* 7 data bits, even parity, 2 stop bits, and 64× clock.
2. *Data carrier detect:* poll the modem waiting for a valid carrier.
3. *Character out:* output the character passed on the stack to the modem for transmission.
4. *Character in:* input one character from the modem and return with that character in
register AL.

10.3. Design an RS-233C interface between an 8251A and a serial printer wired as a DTE. Assume
that the printer's BUSY signal is wired to $\overline{\text{RTS}}$ on the DTE connector. Describe the required
RS-232C cable and connectors, including pin assignments.

10.4. The printer described in question 10.3 has a 128-byte buffer used to hold characters until
they have been printed. Depending on the data rate, it is possible for the computer to fill
this buffer faster than the printer can empty it. For this reason, the printer will send X-OFF
when the buffer stores 112 characters. X-ON will be sent when the buffer has been reduced
to 96 characters. The BUSY signal is set if the buffer is completely filled. Write an 8086
procedure that will output characters to the printer to accommodate this protocol. Assume
that the number of bytes to be output is passed in register CX and the address of the first
byte in register DS:SI.

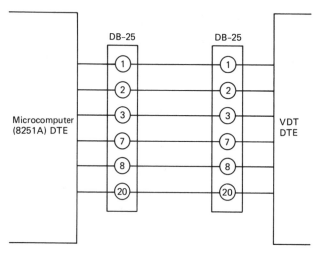

Figure 10.28 RS-232C interface for Analysis and Design Question 10.1.

10.5. Assume that the following instruments have been interfaced via the GPIB.

> DC power supply at address 4
> DMM1 at address 5
> DMM2 at address 9

Using Fig. 10.15 as a guide, write a program in Tek BASIC to set the power supply to 18.0 V with a 50 mA current limit. Now monitor the voltage difference between DMM1 and DMM2. If greater than +4.5 V, decrease the power supply output to 9.0 V. If the difference is less than +4.5 V, maintain the power supply voltage at 18.0 V. The program should run continuously.

10.6. Write an 8086 procedure to check a 256-byte block of BCC-encoded characters (see Fig. 10.24) for data errors. Return with the carry flag set if an error is detected; reset if there is no error. Assume that the segment address of the block is passed in register BX and the offset address in register CX.

10.7. Calculate M(X), Q(X) and R(X) for the 16-bit data stream 8030H. Assume the bisync generator polynomial.

10.8. Write an 8086 procedure that adds an even-parity bit (in bit position 7) to a 7-bit word passed in register CL. Return with the encoded character in register CL.

10.9. The OH input to the dc loop current control circuit in Fig. 10.13(b) can be used to implement a computer-controlled automatic dialing circuit. Fig. 10.29 illustrates the timing required to dial the two-digit sequence ''4'' ''3''. Write a procedure that pulses the OH line in Fig. 10.29 the appropriate number of times and with proper interdigit timing to facilitate a computer-controlled auto dialer. Assume the digit to be dialed is passed on the stack and that the OH input is connected to $\overline{\text{DTR}}$ of the 8251A interface in Fig. 9.20.

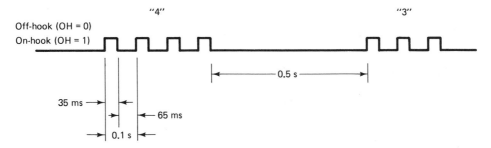

Figure 10.29 Telephone pulse timing required to dial the two-digit sequence ''4'' ''3''.

SELF REVIEW ANSWERS

10.1.1 serial, presence, absence

10.1.2 (24V − 1.5V − 0.6V − 0.1V)/820 = 26.6 mA

10.2.1 modem, terminal

10.2.2 − 12V

10.2.3 (c)

10.2.4 True

10.2.5 null modem

10.2.6 DB-25S, DB-25P

10.2.7 Yes - the microcomputer must be synchronized to the processing rate of the printer

10.2.8 ETX/ACK, X-ON/X-OFF

10.2.9 audio tones

10.2.10 allows automatic dialing by the modem and is not susceptible to external room noise

10.3.1 15

10.3.2 talkers, listeners

10.3.3 True

10.3.4 2

10.3.5 interface

10.3.6 uniline, multiline

10.3.7 01000111 (MTA)

10.3.8 False (the data has been accepted but not processed until NRFD returns high)

10.4.1 automatic request for repeat, forward error checking

10.4.2 parity (VRC), BCC and CRC (LRC)

10.4.3 D4H

10.4.4 0

10.4.5 less overhead and therefore higher character rate

10.4.6 23CH

11

USING THE 80186 HIGH-INTEGRATION MICROPROCESSOR AND THE COPROCESSORS

In Chap. 1 the point was made that the 8086 was one chip in a family of (compatible) microprocessors available from Intel. In this chapter we take a closer look at three of these family members, each designed specifically to improve the performance of the 8086 (or 8088).

We begin with the 80186, an enhanced version of the 8086. It was designed to eliminate much of the SSI and MSI support circuitry required in 8086 designs. This includes the clock generator, bus controller, and chip select logic. Like the 8086, the 80186 is a general-purpose microprocessor executing all the instructions in the 8086's instruction set.

In Sections 11.2 and 11.3 we cover the coprocessors: the 8087 numeric data processor (NDP) and the 8089 I/O processor (IOP). The 8087 extends the instruction set of the 8086 (and 80186) to include extensive high-speed arithmetic and comparison operations. Benchmark tests have shown that an 8086 equipped with an 8087 approaches (within a factor of 10) the speed of a DEC VAX 11/780 minicomputer.

The 8089 is an I/O system on a chip. It is designed to handle all of the system's I/O operations, thus freeing the applications software of these details. When operated in the remote mode, the 8086 can work on other tasks while the 8089 manages the transfer of data between itself and the system peripherals.

In this chapter we present applications examples for each of these chips. Included are typical hardware interfaces and the software control programs required. Emphasis is

527

placed on the performance improvement compared to the single CPU 8086 designs presented previously.

The main topics in this chapter include:

11.1 The 80186 High-Integration 16-Bit Microprocessor
11.2 The 8087 Numeric Data Processor
11.3 The 8089 I/O Processor

11.1 THE 80186 HIGH-INTEGRATION 16-BIT MICROPROCESSOR

Since its inception in the early 1960s, the integrated-circuit industry has continually searched for ways to pack more transistors on a single chip of silicon. This has led, in turn, to increasingly more sophisticated (and more complex) microprocessor designs. The 80186 microprocessor is a good example of this trend. Designed to be object-code compatible with the 8086, it incorporates, in one 68-pin package, a clock generator, chip select unit, programmable wait-state generator, two 20-bit DMA channels, three 16-bit timers, and an 8259A-compatible interrupt controller. Figure 11.1 is a block diagram of this chip.

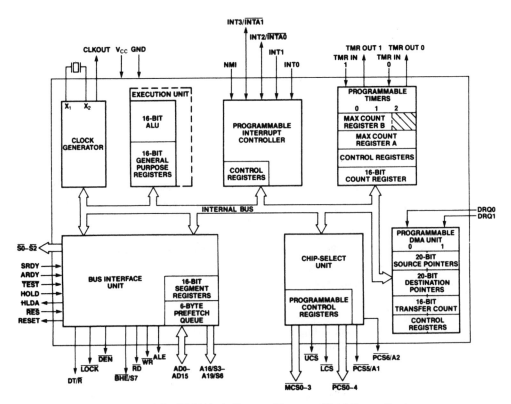

Figure 11.1 80186 block diagram. (Courtesy of Intel Corporation.)

TABLE 11.1 iAPX 186, 188 RELATIVE PERFORMANCE[a]
(8-MHz STANDARD CLOCK RATE)

Instruction	8086 (5MHz)	8086-2 (8MHz)
MOV REG TO MEM	2.0–2.9X	1.2–1.8X
ADD MEM TO REG	2.0–2.9X	1.2–1.8X
MUL REG 16	>5.4X	>3.4X
DIV REG 16	>6.1X	>3.8X
MULTIPLE (4 bits) SHIFT/ROTATE MEMORY	3.1–3.7X	1.95–2.3X
CONDITIONAL JUMP	1.9X	1.2X
BLOCK MOVE (100 bytes)	3.4X	2.1X

[a]Overall: 2x performance of 5-MHz iAPX 86

        1.3x performance of 8-MHz iAPX 86.

Note: Same comparisons apply to iAPX 188 and iAPX 88

Source: Intel Corporation.

Included in the new chip's design are a number of hardware enhancements in the 8086's BIU and EU (bus interface and execution units). For example, integer multiply-and-divide hardware is now provided such that the corresponding instructions operate more than three times as fast as those of the 8086. Overall, the standard 8-MHz 80186 achieves a factor-of-2 increase in performance over the standard 5-MHz 8086. Table 11.1 lists the particulars.

An 8-bit version of the part is also available, called the 80188. Like the 8088, it pays a performance penalty of four extra clock cycles for all 16-bit memory and I/O operations. However, when accessing the on-board peripherals, the full 16-bit (internal) data bus is used.

In this section we cover the bus structure, internal peripheral interface, and the new (non-8086) instructions provided by the 80186 microprocessor. With the exception of external memory and I/O access timing, these comments apply to the 80188 as well.

Bus Structure

Figure 11.2 shows the package outline and pin definitions for the 80186. The large number of pins required a change from the standard dual-in-line package used in the past. In this case a leadless JEDEC type A hermetic *chip carrier* is used, providing 17 pins per side.

Note that there are two V_{cc} pins and two grounds (V_{ss}). Current consumption for the 8-MHz 80186 is rated at 550 mA maximum compared to 350 mA for the similar 8086 part. A 6-MHz version of the chip is also available with part number 80186-6. The following discussion concentrates on the pins required for the system bus interface.

Timing control: X1, X2, CLKOUT, $\overline{\text{RES}}$, RESET, ARDY, SRDY. The clock frequency is determined by a crystal connected to pins X1 and X2 as shown in Fig. 11.1. The CPU will operate at half this frequency. A system clock signal with a 50% duty

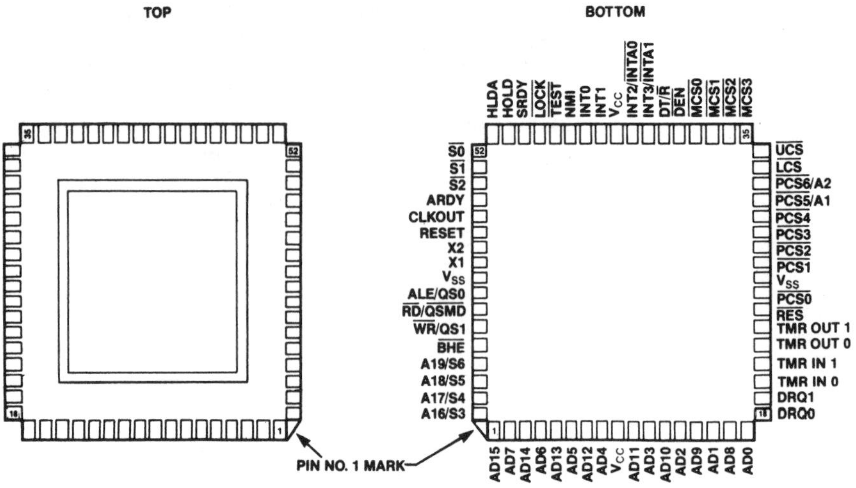

Figure 11.2 80186 pinout diagram. The package is a 68-pin leadless JEDEC type A hermetic chip carrier. (Courtesy of Intel Corporation.)

cycle is available via the CLKOUT pin. Note that there is no PCLK or OSC output as on the 8284A clock generator used with the 8086.

The processor can be reset by grounding the $\overline{\text{RES}}$ input. A power-on reset circuit such as that shown in Fig. 6.21 or 6.23 is typically used. RESET is an active-high system reset output signal. Like the 8086, following reset, the first instruction will be fetched from memory beginning at address FFFF0H.

Slow memory or I/O can request wait states via the (asynchronous) ARDY or (synchronous) SRDY inputs. A "not ready" state is indicated only when both inputs are low. Unlike the 8284A, there are no enables ($\overline{\text{AEN1}}$ and $\overline{\text{AEN2}}$) to qualify ARDY or SRDY.

Address/data: AD0–AD15, A16/S3–A19/S6. The 80186 uses a multiplexed 20-bit address and 16-bit data bus identical to that of the 8086. ALE is provided as a demultiplexing signal for transparent latches (e.g., 8282s or 8283s).

Local bus control: ALE/QS0, $\overline{\text{RD}}$/QSMD, $\overline{\text{WR}}$/QS1, $\overline{\text{BHE}}$/S7, DT/$\overline{\text{R}}$, $\overline{\text{DEN}}$.
All the signals in this group have exactly the same function as their counterparts in the 8086. ALE, $\overline{\text{RD}}$, and $\overline{\text{WR}}$ are multiplexed with queue status signals explained later in this section.

Notice that the 80186 does not provide a minimum/maximum-mode selection as does the 8086. This is because (most of) the signals associated with these two modes are provided in the standard design. One difference, however, is the absence of the 8086's M/$\overline{\text{IO}}$ signal. This signal is incorporated as part of the on-board memory and peripheral chip select logic. If necessary, it can be synthesized by latching the S2 status bit. The status bit definitions will be explained in a moment.

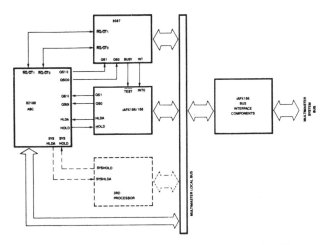

Figure 11.3 The 82188 advanced bus controller (ABC) translates the $\overline{\text{RQ}}/\overline{\text{GT}}$ protocol of the 8087 coprocessor to a HOLD/HLDA protocol compatible with the 80186. (Courtesy of Intel Corporation.)

Another difference compared to the 8086 (maximum mode) is that $\overline{\text{WR}}$ is an "early write" signal compatible with the 8288's $\overline{\text{AMWTC}}$ and $\overline{\text{AIOWC}}$ signals. There is no "late write" signal. The implication is that data should not be latched on the leading (falling) edge of $\overline{\text{WR}}$.

Local bus arbitration: HOLD, HLDA. The 80186 uses a HOLD/HLDA protocol when releasing its local bus to another bus master. This is the same as the 8086 minimum mode. It does not support the $\overline{\text{RQ}}/\overline{\text{GT}}$ protocol of the 8086 maximum mode— the protocol used by the 8087 and 8089 coprocessors. When interfacing these coprocessors the 82188 *advanced bus controller* (ABC) must be used. This is explained in the next section.

Coprocessor control: $\overline{\text{TEST}}$, ALE/QS0, $\overline{\text{WR}}$/QS1, $\overline{\text{RD}}$/QSMD, $\overline{\text{LOCK}}$. Both the 8087 and 8089 coprocessors require knowledge of the processor's queue status. To support these devices, the 80186 includes a *queue status mode*. This is entered by grounding the $\overline{\text{RD}}$/QSMD pin and performing a system reset. In this mode, ALE and $\overline{\text{WR}}$ become queue status signals QS0 and QS1. Their definitions are the same as those given for the 8086 in Table 6.6.

In addition to supplying the queue status for the coprocessors, the HOLD/HLDA protocol of the 80186 must be converted to a compatible $\overline{\text{RQ}}/\overline{\text{GT}}$ protocol. This is done with the 82188 ABC as shown in Fig. 11.3.

The $\overline{\text{TEST}}$ input is used with the WAIT instruction to suspend CPU instruction execution until the coprocessor drives this input low, indicating ready. The $\overline{\text{LOCK}}$ output is driven low by the 80186 to prevent another bus master from gaining control of the bus during this one (locked) instruction. This signal is intended for the 8289 bus arbiter.

Status: S0–S2, A16/S3–A19/S6, S7/$\overline{\text{BHE}}$. When operated in the queue status mode the control bus signals $\overline{\text{RD}}$, $\overline{\text{WR}}$, and ALE are "lost" to provide queue status for the coprocessors. In this case the status outputs S0–S2 can be decoded to provide a system control bus. The 8288 and 82188 bus controllers are provided for this purpose. Figure 11.4 provides an example.

Unlike the 8086, the S0–S2 status outputs are always available. This means separate local and system control buses can be provided (assuming that $\overline{\text{RD}}$, $\overline{\text{WR}}$, and ALE are not required by a coprocessor).

Of the remaining status signals, S6 is low when the data bus is being driven by the CPU, and high when driven by another processor (during a DMA cycle, for example). S3–S5 are always low and S7 is identical to $\overline{\text{BHE}}$.

Peripheral Interface

Like the other peripheral controllers we have studied, all of the on-board 80186 peripherals are controlled via software. A special set of 16-bit control registers are provided in a 256-byte block of I/O or memory space called the *peripheral control block* (PCB). Figure 11.5 shows the offsets within this block for the various peripherals.

When the 80186 is reset, the PCB is located in I/O space at ports FF00–FFFFH. This means, for example, that timer 0 can be accessed via the four 16-bit I/O ports at FF50H, FF52H, FF54H, and FF56H. If desired, the location of the PCB can be moved to a new location by writing to the *relocation register* at offset FEH. This register also allows the interrupt mode to be programmed and enables an interrupt trap to occur when

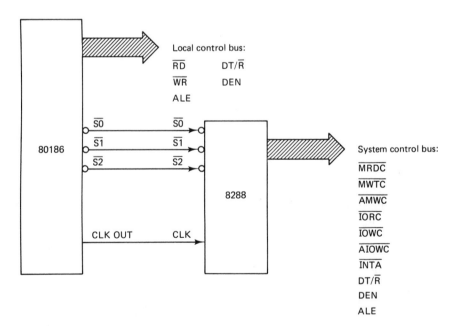

Figure 11.4 Using the 8288 bus controller to generate a system control bus. The 80186 control signals provide a *local* control bus.

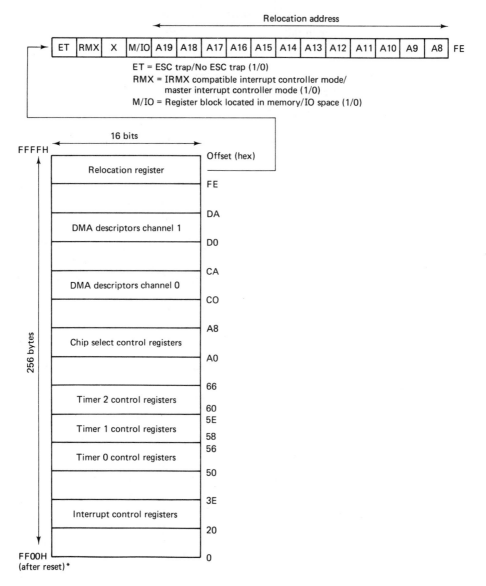

Figure 11.5 Peripheral control block (PCB). The 16-bit registers contained within this block are used to control all of the 80186's on-board peripherals. The relocation register defines the base address of the block to be in memory or I/O space.

any of the escape op-codes (D8H–DFH) are executed. These options will be discussed in more detail later in this section.

Example 11.1

Write the instructions necessary to relocate the PCB to memory space beginning at address EFF00H. Select master interrupt mode and no ESC trap.

Solution   The program is as follows:

```
        MOV   DX,OFFFEH                  ;Offset of relocation register
        MOV   AX,0001111011111111B       ;ET = 0
                                         ;RMX = 0
                                         ;M/IO = 1
                                         ;A19–A8 = EFF
        OUT   DX,AX                      ;Output control word
```

For the most part, the peripherals operate independent of the CPU. For example, if a timer is programmed to produce a particular square wave, it does so without further CPU intervention. Using the integrated peripherals is thus a matter of learning the register addresses and functions.

The following paragraphs provide an overview of the register sets for each of the peripherals and a brief example illustrating a typical application.

Memory and peripheral chip select logic.   Often a microprocessor must be supported by several SSI and MSI chips used for address decoding and device selection. Although PALs and PLAs can be used to minimize the number of devices required, once programmed, they cannot be changed. The 80186 provides 13 pins for memory and peripheral selection—all programmable via five registers within the PCB.

Referring to Fig. 11.1, the memory chip selects are $\overline{\text{LCS}}$, $\overline{\text{UCS}}$, and $\overline{\text{MCS0-3}}$. $\overline{\text{LCS}}$ (low-memory chip select) is active from a programmable base address to address 00000. $\overline{\text{UCS}}$ (upper-memory chip select) is active from a programmable base address to address FFFFF. $\overline{\text{MCS0-3}}$ (mid-memory chip selects) are active for four *consecutive* blocks of memory. The base address and block size are both programmable.

Peripherals may be selected with $\overline{\text{PCS0-3}}$, $\overline{\text{PCS5}}$/A1, and $\overline{\text{PCS6}}$/A2. Depending on the mode, $\overline{\text{PCS0-6}}$ select seven consecutive I/O or memory-mapped 128-byte blocks. $\overline{\text{PCS5}}$ and $\overline{\text{PCS6}}$ can also be programmed to provide latched A1 and A2 outputs, useful when interfacing peripheral controllers with internal registers such as the 8255.

Figure 11.6 provides the details for the five chip select registers within the PCB. UMCS programs the base address for $\overline{\text{UCS}}$, LMCS the base address for $\overline{\text{LCS}}$, PACS the base address for $\overline{\text{PCS0-6}}$, and MMCS the base address for $\overline{\text{MCS0-3}}$. MPCS is used to define the mid-memory block size. It is also used to determine if the peripheral chip selects are mapped to I/O or memory space, and if $\overline{\text{PCS5}}$ and $\overline{\text{PCS6}}$ are chip selects or latched address bits. Be sure to note the restrictions on the various block sizes and base addresses (notes 1, 3, 4, and 5). Note that A19 and A18 must be low for LMCS and high for UMCS.

Bits 0–2 of each register allow the number of wait states associated with that chip select signal to be programmed. For example, if R2–R0 of UMCS equals 110, two wait

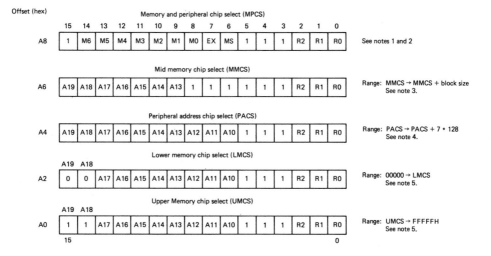

Figure 11.6 Chip-select generation and programmable wait-state registers of the 80186.

states will automatically be inserted for all memory accesses within this block of memory. If the external ready inputs are used, they *overlap* the programmed ready states. That is, one external wait state request, combined with two programmed wait states, results in two actual wait states—not three.

When the 80186 is reset, UMCS automatically stores FFF8H, defining the 1K byte

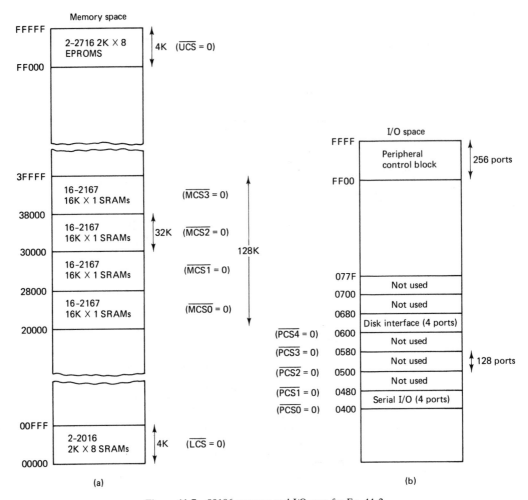

Figure 11.7 80186 memory and I/O map for Ex. 11.2.

address range FFC00H–FFFFFH (A19–A10 all high). This allows a *boot ROM* to be located in this memory space. The first few instructions in this ROM should program the chip select registers. This is particularly important, as the memory and I/O configuration is undefined until these registers are programmed.

Example 11.2

Program the 80186 chip select registers to accommodate the memory and I/O configuration mapped in Fig. 11.7.

Solution The program is given in Fig. 11.8. Note that the five program codes are included in the code segment and the LODS instruction (with segment override) is used to retrieve them. Indirect I/O is used with register DX holding the control register address.

Figure 11.9 shows the circuit diagram. $\overline{UCS}$ selects the boot ROM which starts the system up upon reset. $\overline{LCS}$ selects the low RAM, which can be used to store the interrupt vector table and other system variables. The program RAM is made up of four 32K-byte blocks selected by $\overline{\text{MCS0-3}}$.

There are only two I/O devices and these are selected by $\overline{\text{PCS0}}$ and $\overline{\text{PCS4}}$. Note that both of these devices are *partially decoded*, as only four of the 128 available ports are required. PCS5/A1 and PCS6/A2 are used as latched address bits to select one of four registers within the I/O devices.

DMA controller. During DMA cycles the CPU must suspend normal instruction fetching and relinquish its buses to another processor. In a typical DMA interface, data is transferred directly from memory to an I/O port, or from an I/O port directly into

```
                TITLE   FIG. 11.8

                ;Function:    Program the five chip-select
                ;             registers of the 80186 PCB.
                ;Inputs:      none
                ;Ouputs:      Program codes for UMCS, LMCS
                ;             PACS, MMCS, and MPCS beginning
                ;             at offset A0H of the PCB.
                ;Calls:       nothing
                ;Destroys:    AX,CX,DX,SI,flags

                ;Program equates

= 0005          BYTES_TO_PROG EQU    5
= FFA0          BASE_PORT     EQU    0FFA0H

0000            CODE          SEGMENT  BYTE
                              ASSUME CS:CODE

0000            CHIP_SELECT   PROC     FAR
0000  FF38      PROG_CODES    DW       1111 1111 0011 1000B    ;UMCS: FF000-FFFFF
0002  00FB                    DW       0000 0000 1111 1000B    ;LMCS: 00000-00FFF
0004  0078                    DW       0000 0100 0011 1000B    ;PCS0-6: 0400-077F
0006  21FF                    DW       0010 0001 1111 1000B    ;MCS0-3 base: 20000H
0008  9038                    DW       1001 0000 0011 1000B    ;Block size: 128K total,
                                                               ;Latched address bits

000A  FC        START:        CLD                              ;Auto increment
000B  B9 0005                 MOV      CX,BYTES_TO_PROG        ;Byte counter
000E  2E: 8D 36 0000 R        LEA      SI,PROG_CODES           ;Point SI at program codes
0013  BA FFA0                 MOV      DX,BASE_PORT            ;UMCS is chip select register base

0016  2E: AD    NEXT:         LODS     CS:PROG_CODES           ;Fetch code and advance pointer
0018  EF                      OUT      DX,AX                   ;Output code
0019  42                      INC      DX                      ;Point to next register port
001A  42                      INC      DX
001B  E2 F9                   LOOP     NEXT                    ;Repeat for all 5 registers
001D  CB                      RET
001E            CHIP_SELECT   ENDP

001E            CODE          ENDS
                              END      START
```

Figure 11.8 Program to illustrate the chip generation logic of the 80186.

Sec. 11.1   The 80186 High-Integration 16-Bit Microprocessor   **537**

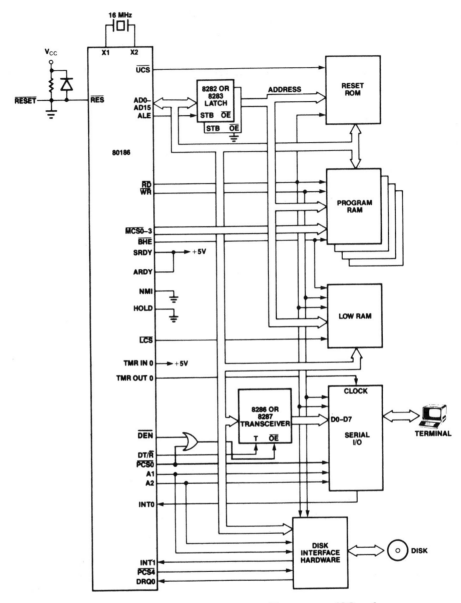

Figure 11.9 Typical 80186-based microcomputer system. The memory and I/O conform to the mapping shown in Fig. 11.7. (Courtesy of Intel Corporation.)

memory. Because the CPU "middleman" is disconnected, the data transfer rate can be quite high. Indeed, for fast peripherals such as Winchester disk drives, DMA is the only feasible I/O control scheme.

As discussed in Chap. 8, using an external DMA controller like the 8237 with the 8086 is difficult. This is related to the 8237's 16-bit address bus limitation. In addition,

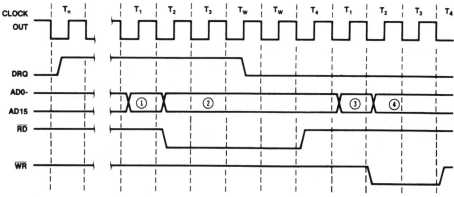

1. Source address
2. Source data
3. Destination address
4. Destination data

NOTE: Wait states are inserted by the bus condition during the bus cycle, not by the DMA controller

Figure 11.10 DMA transfer cycle on the 80186. Two bus cycles are required. (Courtesy of Intel Corporation.)

the 8237's HOLD/HLDA protocol requires that the 8086 be operated in the minimum mode.

The 80186 solves these problems by incorporating a 20-bit DMA controller on-board. When a DMA cycle is to be performed, the CPU portion of the 80186 enters an (internal) hold state while the DMA controller proceeds to take control of the local buses (including the on-board chip select logic).

Figure 11.10 illustrates a typical 8-T-state DMA cycle. It consists of back-to-back I/O or memory read and write cycles. For example, the source address might be a 20-bit memory location, and the destination address a 16-bit I/O port. Because the timing is exactly the same as for a conventional CPU read or write bus cycle,[1] the memory and I/O cannot tell the difference. Using an 8-MHz system clock, one data word can be transferred in 1 μs. This corresponds to a 2MB/s data transfer rate. For byte I/O ports the data rate is 1MB/s.

DMA requests can occur from any of three sources:

1. Externally via the DRQ input
2. Internally when timer 2 reaches its maximum count
3. Internally by the DMA unit itself

The first two cases are referred to as *synchronized* DMA transfers, as one DMA cycle is run for each request pulse. In the third case the DMA unit generates its own requests, and transfers will be run continuously at the maximum bus bandwidth until the

---

[1]Except that S6 = 1 during all DMA-initiated cycles.

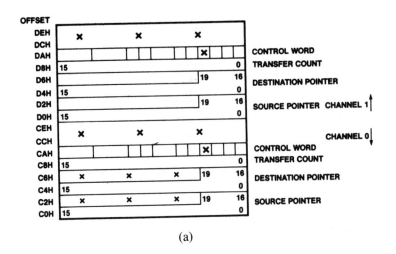

(a)

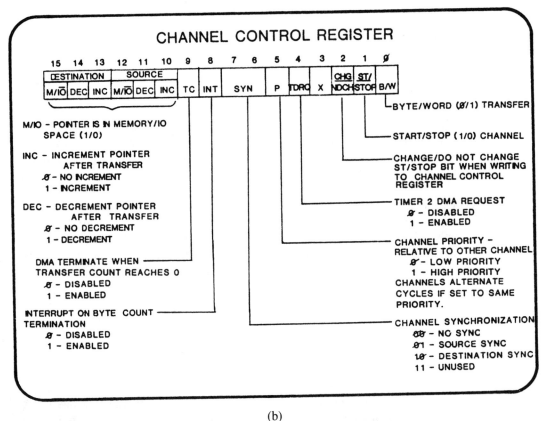

(b)

Figure 11.11 (a) 80186 DMA register layout. Two channels are provided. (b) The control register determines the mode of operation for each channel. (Courtesy of Intel Corporation.)

programmed number of DMA transfers have occurred. This mode is referred to as *unsynchronized* DMA.

There are two separate DMA channels, each with its own set of control registers located at offset C0H-DBH in the PCB. This is shown in Fig. 11.11(a). The control register defines the location (memory or I/O space) of the source and destination of data, and also the source of the request: timer 2 (TDRQ = 1 and SYN = 11), DRQ (SYN = 01 or 10), or continuous (SYN = 00). Each unit can also be programmed to generate an interrupt when all bytes have been transferred.

Upon a system reset, bit 1 (ST/STOP) of the control register will be reset, preventing any DMA cycles from being run. The source and destination registers can then be loaded with the appropriate addresses. Note that a (16-bit) register *pair* is required for each (20-bit) address. The number of bytes to transfer is loaded into the transfer count register. Finally, the control register is written, defining the mode of DMA to occur and setting the ST/STOP bit.

Example 11.3

Assume that 512 bytes are to be transferred via DMA from a WD2797 floppy-disk controller (FDC) to a memory buffer. The WD2797 DRQ (data request) output will be used to synchronize the transfer. The FDC's data register is assumed mapped to port 0200H in I/O space. Write the DMA control program required and use an interrupt to signify the end of the transfer.

Solution The program is shown in Fig. 11.12. A DISK__BUFFER segment is set up to store the data. Register DX is then initialized to point to the base of the channel 0 DMA registers. The WD2797 16-bit port address is written to the source pointer.

Writing the destination address is more complex, as the 20-bit address must first be computed, the low 16 bits written at offset C4H, and the high 4 bits written at offset C6H. This is accomplished by computing the 20-bit segment address in DX:AX and adding the offset of the memory buffer. AX is then written to offset C4H and DX to offset C6H.

The transfer count register is loaded next, using the LENGTH operator to specify the capacity of the buffer. Finally, the control register is programmed for source synchronized DMA (i.e., DRQ of the WD2797), and interrupt upon termination. The program then halts the processor.

One DMA cycle will be run for each DRQ pulse received from the WD2797. When all bytes have been transferred the interrupt "sparks" the CPU back to life and normal processing resumes.

Programmable timers. The three 16-bit timers of the 80186 are shown in block diagram form in Fig. 11.13. Via software these timers can be programmed to:

> Produce programmable one-shot pulses
> Produce variable-duty-cycle square waves
> Function as a baud rate generator clock
> Count events
> Function as a real-time clock

Timers 0 and 1 have external input and output pins—TMR IN and TMR OUT. Timer 2 is special. It can act as a *prescaler* for the other timers or as a DMA request

```
= FF00                      BASE_PCB     EQU        0FF00H

0000                        DISK_BUFFER  SEGMENT
0000   0200 [               BUFFER       DB         512 DUP(?)
            ??
       ]

0200                        DISK_BUFFER  ENDS

0000                        CODE         SEGMENT BYTE
                                         ASSUME CS:CODE, DS:DISK_BUFFER

0000   B8 ---- R            START:       MOV        AX,DISK_BUFFER          ;Point DS to DISK_BUFFER
0003   8E D8                             MOV        DS,AX

0005   BA FFC0                           MOV        DX,BASE_PCB+0C0H        ;DMA source pointer bits 0-15
0008   B8 0200                           MOV        AX,200H                 ;FDC data port address
000B   EF                                OUT        DX,AX                   ;Write to source pointer

000C   83 C2 02                          ADD        DX,2                    ;DMA source pointer bits 16-19
000F   B8 0000                           MOV        AX,0                    ;Bits 16-19 are 0 for I/O address
0012   EF                                OUT        DX,AX                   ;Write to source pointer

0013   83 C2 02                          ADD        DX,2                    ;DMA destination pointer bits 0-15
0016   8C D8                             MOV        AX,DS                   ;Prepare to multiply DS by 16
0018   8B CA                             MOV        CX,DX                   ;Save port address
001A   BB 0010                           MOV        BX,16                   ;Multiplier
001D   F7 E3                             MUL        BX                      ;DX:AX holds 20 bit segment address
001F   8D 1E 0000 R                      LEA        BX,BUFFER               ;Get offset of BUFFER
0023   03 C3                             ADD        AX,BX                   ;Add to segment address
0025   83 D2 00                          ADC        DX,0                    ;Add any carry to upper four bits
0028   87 D1                             XCHG       DX,CX                   ;Recover port address
002A   EF                                OUT        DX,AX                   ;Low 16 bits to destination pointer
002B   83 C2 02                          ADD        DX,2                    ;DMA destination pointer bits 16-19
002E   8B C1                             MOV        AX,CX                   ;Fetch upper 4 bits
0030   EF                                OUT        DX,AX                   ;Write to destination pointer

0031   83 C2 02                          ADD        DX,2                    ;DMA transfer count register
0034   B8 0200                           MOV        AX,LENGTH BUFFER        ;Number of bytes to transfer
0037   EF                                OUT        DX,AX                   ;Write to transfer count register

0038   83 C2 02                          ADD        DX,2                    ;DMA control register offset
003B   B8 A366                           MOV        AX,1010001101100110B    ;Destination: memory and increment
                                                                           ;Source: I/O and stationary
                                                                           ;Terminate when transfer count = 0
                                                                           ;Interrupt when transfer count = 0
                                                                           ;Source synchronization
                                                                           ;High priority
                                                                           ;Timer 2 disabled
                                                                           ;Change START/STOP to START
                                                                           ;Byte transfers

003E   EF                                OUT        DX,AX                   ;Write to control register
003F   F4                                HLT                               ;Wait for interrupt

0040                        CODE         ENDS
                                         END
```

Figure 11.12   Program to illustrate the DMA capabilities of the 80186.

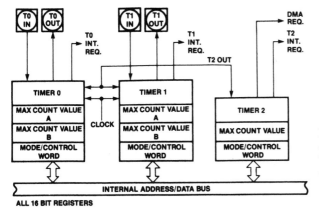

Figure 11.13 80186 time/counter block diagram. Timers 0 and 1 are general purpose. Timer 2 can be used as a prescaler for timers 0 and 1, or to generate a timed DMA or interrupt request. (Courtesy of Intel Corporation.)

signal. In the first case its output becomes the clock source to timers 0 or 1. This cascading can allow very long time delays to be generated using the system clock as the base frequency.

When used as a DMA request signal, the timer 2 output can facilitate the refresh of dynamic RAMs. By pulsing the DMA unit once every 10-20µs, a "dummy" read cycle can be performed (via DMA), effectively refreshing the DRAM array.

The three timers are controlled by a set of 12 registers within the PCB. This is shown in Fig. 11.14. When enabled, the count register is incremented once for every input clock pulse. When this count equals the value in the maximum count register (A or B), the count register is reset to 0, maximum count (bit 5 of the control register) is set, and if interrupts are enabled (bit 13 of the control register set), an interrupt is generated.

Timers 0 and 1 contain two maximum count registers, labeled A and B. When ALT (bit 1 of the control register) is set, the count register will first count up to the value in maximum count register A, reset to 0, and then count up to the value in maximum count register B, both times setting the maximum count bit and generating interrupts (if enabled). In this mode the TMR OUT pin and status bit RIU (bit 12 of the control register) indicate which register is in use at a particular time. This allows variable-duty-cycle waveforms to be generated. For example, if maximum count register A = 4 and maximum count register B = 6, a 40% duty cycle square wave will be generated.

Figure 11.15 illustrates the operating modes for timers 0 and 1. The input clock signal to the timer can either be external via TMR IN (control register EXT bit = 1) or internal (EXT = 0). In the latter case the control register prescaler mode bit (P) determines if every fourth CPU clock (P = 0) or the timer 2 output (P = 1) will act as the clock source.

When the control register retrigger bit (RTG) is set, the TMR IN pin acts as a trigger resetting the counter to 0 and beginning the count cycle. When RTG = 0, TMR IN acts as a gated input. These two cases are shown in Fig. 11.15(a) and (b).

The TMR OUT signal can either be a single pulse as shown in Fig. 11.15(c) or a variable-duty-cycle square wave as shown in Fig. 11.15(d). This is controlled by the ALT bit in the control register. The waveform will repeat continuously when the CONT bit is set; if not, only the single period is obtained before the counter halts.

Offset

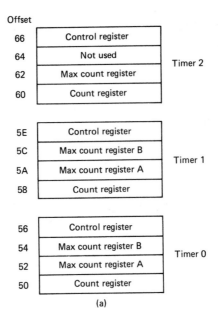

(a)

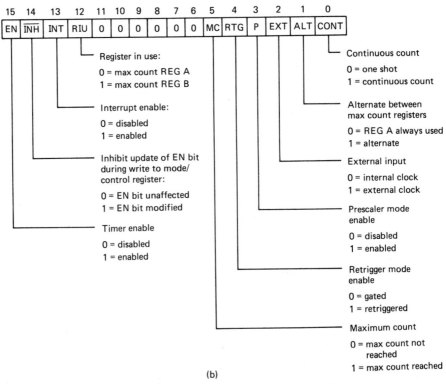

(b)

Figure 11.14 Bit definitions: (a) 80186 timer registers; (b) mode/control register.

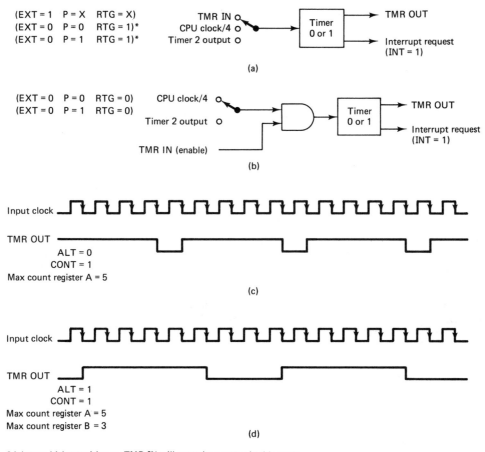

Figure 11.15 Timer 0 and 1 options: (a) counting internal or external pulses; (b) gated timer; (c) single pulse; (d) variable-duty-cycle waveform.

Figure 11.16 is a procedure that programs timer 1 as a baud rate generator clock. Using the system clock as the clock input, timer 1 receives a pulse every 500 ns (four system clock periods at 8 MHz). After receiving 13 such pulses 6.5 µs will have elapsed and the timer will output a pulse. Assuming a $16 \times$ baud rate clock, this corresponds to a data rate of 9600 baud. By programming the control register for the continuous mode, the timer will run on its own without further CPU intervention. A typical application (using timer 0) is shown in Fig. 11.9.

Interrupt controller. Figure 11.17 is a block diagram of the 80186 programmable interrupt controller. It accepts five external interrupt requests via the INT0–INT3 and NMI input pins. NMI is a nonmaskable interrupt exactly like that of the 8086. INT0–INT3 are general-purpose (maskable) interrupts. There are also three internal in-

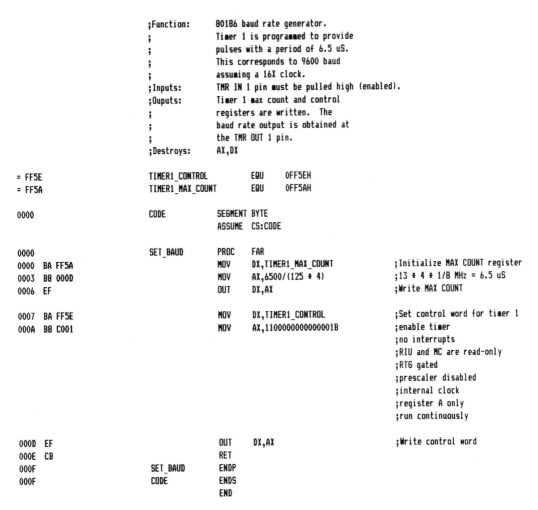

```
                        ;Function:      80186 baud rate generator.
                        ;               Timer 1 is programmed to provide
                        ;               pulses with a period of 6.5 uS.
                        ;               This corresponds to 9600 baud
                        ;               assuming a 16X clock.
                        ;Inputs:        TMR IN 1 pin must be pulled high (enabled).
                        ;Ouputs:        Timer 1 max count and control
                        ;               registers are written.  The
                        ;               baud rate output is obtained at
                        ;               the TMR OUT 1 pin.
                        ;Destroys:      AX,DX


= FF5E                  TIMER1_CONTROL        EQU     0FF5EH
= FF5A                  TIMER1_MAX_COUNT      EQU     0FF5AH


0000                    CODE          SEGMENT BYTE
                                      ASSUME  CS:CODE


0000                    SET_BAUD      PROC    FAR
0000  BA FF5A                         MOV     DX,TIMER1_MAX_COUNT       ;Initialize MAX COUNT register
0003  BB 000D                         MOV     AX,6500/(125 * 4)         ;13 * 4 * 1/8 MHz = 6.5 uS
0006  EF                              OUT     DX,AX                     ;Write MAX COUNT

0007  BA FF5E                         MOV     DX,TIMER1_CONTROL         ;Set control word for timer 1
000A  BB C001                         MOV     AX,1100000000000001B      ;enable timer
                                                                       ;no interrupts
                                                                       ;RIU and MC are read-only
                                                                       ;RTG gated
                                                                       ;prescaler disabled
                                                                       ;internal clock
                                                                       ;register A only
                                                                       ;run continuously

000D  EF                              OUT     DX,AX                     ;Write control word
000E  CB                              RET
000F                    SET_BAUD      ENDP
000F                    CODE          ENDS
                                      END
```

Figure 11.16   Program to use 80186 timer 1 as a baud rate generator.

terrupt sources: one each for the two DMA channels and one shared by the three timers. In addition, there are several CPU-initiated interrupts, as with the 8086.

Table 11.2 lists the preassigned interrupt type numbers associated with the interrupt sources just mentioned. Vectors 0–4 are the same as those found in the 8086. Vectors 5–7 are new CPU-initiated interrupts unique to the 80186.

The array bounds trap is used with the new instruction BOUND and occurs whenever an array element is accessed outside its specified limits. The unused op-code trap occurs whenever the CPU attempts to execute an instruction with one of the following (unused) op-codes: 63H–67H, F1H, FEH XX111XXXB, and FFH XX111XXXB. The escape op-code trap occurs whenever the CPU executes an instruction with an escape prefix. As such instructions are intended for a coprocessor, it provides a mechanism for emulating the coprocessor function in software.

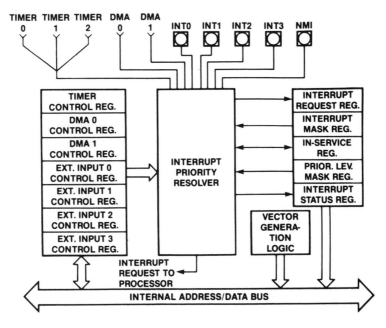

Figure 11.17 80186 priority interrupt controller block diagram. (Courtesy of Intel Corporation.)

TABLE 11.2 iAPX 186,188 PREASSIGNED INTERRUPT TYPES

Interrupt name	Vector type	Comment
Type 0	0	Divide error trap
Type 1	1	Single step trap
NMI	2	Nonmaskable interrupt
Type 3	3	Breakpoint trap
INTO	4	Trap on overflow
Array bounds trap	5	BOUND instruction trap
Unused op trap	6	Invalid op-code trap
ESCAPE op trap	7	Supports 8087 emulation
Timer 0	8	Internal h/w interrupt
Timer 1	18	Internal h/w interrupt
Timer 2	19	Internal h/w interrupt
DMA 0	10	Internal h/w interrupt
DMA 1	11	Internal h/w interrupt
Reserved	9	*Reserved*
INT0	12	External interrupt 0
INT1	13	External interrupt 1
INT2/INTA0	14	External interrupt 2
INT3/INTA1	15	External interrupt 3

Source: Intel Corporation.

Sec. 11.1   The 80186 High-Integration 16-Bit Microprocessor

The 80186 interrupt controller has two basic modes of operation, called *master* (acts like a master 8259A PIC) and iRMX 86 (acts as a slave to an external master). Bit 14 of the relocation register in the PCB (see Fig. 11.5) determines this selection. The following discussion applies to the (more common) master mode.

Fifteen 16-bit registers within the PCB control the operation of the interrupt controller. These are shown in Fig. 11.18.[2] Control registers are provided at offset 32H–3EH for each general-purpose interrupt input, the two DMA channels, and the timers. To allow arbitration of multiple interrupt requests, bits PR0–PR2 allow each input to be assigned a priority between 0 and 7 (0 is highest). Each input can also be masked from consideration by setting its mask bit. LTM allows the trigger mode to be specified.

INT0 and INT1 can also be used in a *cascade* mode. In this case INT2 and INT3 become acknowledge signals to external 8259A PICs. These PICs can in turn be programmed as masters, supporting eight additional PICs connected to IR0–IR7. In this way up to 128 prioritized interrupt inputs can be accommodated. In the cascade mode the SFNM bit should be set to allow multiple interrupt requests on a single input pin (INT0 or INT1).

The *interrupt request register* is read-only and indicates which inputs are active (regardless of their priority or mask status). The *interrupt status register* is required to determine which specific timer is active—all three share the TMR bit in the interrupt request and service registers.

DMA cycles have priority over interrupt requests; that is, an interrupt request received during a DMA cycle will not be honored. This is consistent with the 8086. However, unlike the 8086, if a nonmaskable interrupt occurs, all internal DMA activity will be halted and the DHLT bit of the interrupt status register will be set automatically. This allows the CPU to respond quickly to the NMI request. The IRET instruction will reset DHLT, allowing the DMA to resume. If desired, DHLT can be set via software, preventing DMA cycles while a critical section of code is executed.

The *in-service register* indicates which interrupt has actually been acknowledged and is currently in service. Writing the end-of-interrupt command to the EOI register resets the in-service bit.

Instead of reading or writing the MSK bit in each of the seven control registers the *mask register* can be accessed. All of the bits in this register are functionally the same as the MSK bits in the corresponding control registers. Changing a bit in this register will change the MSK bit in the control register, and vice versa.

The *priority mask register* is written to specify the lowest priority level that can be serviced. For example, writing 101 to bits 2–0 masks interrupts at levels 6 and 7 from being serviced (recall that bits 0–2 of the control register specifies that input's priority). In the read mode this register indicates the current priority level being serviced. When the service routine issues an EOI instruction, these bits are automatically set to the next-lowest priority level.

The interrupt controller can also be used in a polled mode. In this case bit 15 of the *poll status register* will be set whenever a device of sufficient priority requires service.

---

[2]In iRMX 86 mode an interrupt vector register resides at offset 20H.

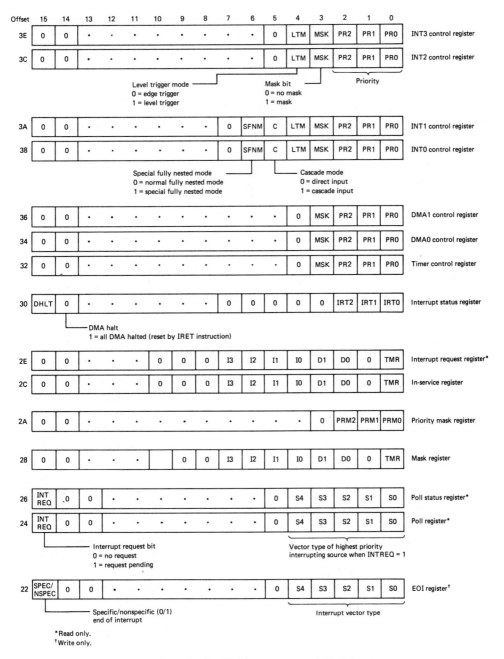

Figure 11.18 80186 interrupt control block format.

Bits 0–4 will indicate the type (vector) number of the device requiring service (see Table 11.2). The *poll register* is identical to the poll status register except that reading this register will set the corresponding in-service bit just as if an interrupt acknowledge cycle had been run.

The *EOI register* is written at the end of the interrupt service routine. If bit 15 is set, a nonspecific end of interrupt will occur, resetting the highest-priority in-service bit currently set. If bit 15 is reset, a specific EOI is indicated. In this case bits 0–4 indicate the type number of the interrupt to be reset. For example, to reset the in-service bit for an interrupt on INT2:

```
MOV   DX,0FF22H    ;EOI register
MOV   AX,0EH       ;Specific EOI, INT2
OUT   DX,AX
```

Figure 11.19 is an example of a typical 80186 interrupt controller initialization routine. One by one the seven control registers are written specifying their priority level, trigger mode, and mask status. In this case only INT2 and INT3 are masked. Like the 8259A, each service routine will be expected to supply an EOI instruction before executing IRET.

New Instructions

The 80186 includes 10 new instructions or instruction types not available with the 8086. These are summarized in Table 11.3. Two new "push" instructions allow immediate data to be temporarily saved on the stack or all the general-purpose CPU registers saved and recovered with one instruction. The PUSHA instruction executes in 36 T states versus 88 T states for the equivalent 8086 instructions. This can have a significant effect on interrupt latency.

The integer multiply instruction now allows immediate data as one of the operands. In addition, the result need not be confined to register AX. For example, IMUL CX,BX,1234H is interpreted as CX = BX x 1234H. Note, however, that the answer is limited to the low 16 bits of the result operand.

The shift and rotate instructions have also been expanded to accommodate immediate data (instead of using register CL). Thus the instruction SAR AL,5 will shift the contents of register AL right 5 bits.

The input and output instructions have been expanded to include two new *block* I/O commands. They allow an entire block of memory to be input or output without having to pass that data through the accumulator. Using the REP prefix the entire memory block can be input or output with one instruction. This amounts to a one instruction DMA command. See Analysis and Design Question 11.3.

Three instructions have been included to support high-level-language development: BOUND for checking that array indices are within limits, and ENTER and LEAVE for setting up stack frames within high-level-language procedures. Figure 11.20 shows how an entire stack frame can be saved using the ENTER instruction.

```
                    ;Function      80186 interrupt controller initialization.
                    ;              The following priorities are assigned:
                    ;              Timers: 0
                    ;                DMA0: 1
                    ;                DMA1: 2
                    ;                INT0: 3    level triggered, normal mode
                    ;                INT1: 4    edge triggereed, normal
                    ;                INT2: masked
                    ;                INT3: masked
                    ;Inputs:        none
                    ;Ouputs:        Initialization codes to interrrupt control
                    ;              block registers assumed located at
                    ;              the default I/O addresses.
                    ;Calls:         nothing
                    ;Destroys:      AX,DX

= FF00              BASE_PCB    EQU     0FF00H

0000                CODE        SEGMENT BYTE
                                ASSUME CS:CODE

0000                INT_INIT    PROC    FAR
0000  BA FF32                   MOV     DX,BASE_PCB+32H          ;Timer control register
0003  B8 0000                   MOV     AX,0                     ;Priority 0 nonmasked
0006  EF                        OUT     DX,AX

0007  83 C2 02                  ADD     DX,2                     ;DMA0 control register
000A  40                        INC     AX                       ;Priority 1 nonmasked
000B  EF                        OUT     DX,AX

000C  83 C2 02                  ADD     DX,2                     ;DMA1 control register
000F  40                        INC     AX                       ;Priority 2 nonmasked
0010  EF                        OUT     DX,AX

0011  83 C2 02                  ADD     DX,2                     ;INT0 control register
0014  B8 0013                   MOV     AX,13H                   ;Priority 3, normal, level
0017  EF                        OUT     DX,AX                    ;triggered, nonmasked

0018  83 C2 02                  ADD     DX,2                     ;INT1 control register
001B  B8 0004                   MOV     AX,4                     ;Priority 4, normal, edge
001E  EF                        OUT     DX,AX                    ;triggered, nonmasked

001F  83 C2 02                  ADD     DX,2                     ;INT3 control register
0022  B8 8000                   MOV     AX,8000H                 ;masked
0025  EF                        OUT     DX,AX

0026  83 C2 02                  ADD     DX,2                     ;INT4 control register
0029  EF                        OUT     DX,AX                    ;masked
002A  CB                        RET
002B                INT_INIT    ENDP

002B                CODE        ENDS
                                END
```

Figure 11.19   Program to illustrate initialization of the 80186 interrupt controller.

TABLE 11.3 80186 NEW INSTRUCTIONS

	Mnemonic	Example	Object code	Description
PUSH	*immediate data*	PUSH 1234H PUSH 12H	68 34 12 6A 00 12	Decrement SP by 2 and transfer the immediate data byte or word to the top of the stack now pointed to by SP; for byte operations, the data byte is sign extended
PUSHA		PUSHA	60	The data, pointer, and index registers are pushed onto the stack in the following order: AX, CX, DX, BX, SP, BP, SI, DI; the SP value pushed is the value before the first register (AX) is pushed
POPA		POPA	61	All data, pointer, and index registers are popped from the stack; the SP value popped is discarded
IMUL	*result, source, immediate data*	IMUL CX,BX,1234H IMUL CX,[SI], −5	69 XX 34 12 6B XX FF FB	Signed multiplication of the byte or word source operand and the immediate byte or word; the lower 16 bits of the result are saved in a general-purpose or pointer register specified by the result operand
SAR, SHR, SAL,	*dest, immediate count*	SAR AL,5	C0 F8 05	Rotate/shift the destination operand in the indicated direction a number of times specified in the immediate operand.

552

Mnemonic	Example	Opcode	Description
RCR, ROR, RCL, ROL			
INS *dest,port*	INS WORD_BUF, WORD_PORT	6D	Input a byte or word from the I/O port addressed by DX and store the result in the memory location addressed by DI; if DF = 0, increment DI, else decrement DI
	INS BYTE_BUF, BYTE_PORT	6C	
OUTS *port,dest*	OUTS WORD_PORT, WORD_BUF	6F	Output a byte or word from the memory location addressed by SI and store the result at the port addressed by DX; if DF = 0, increment SI, else decrement SI
BOUND *dest,source*	BOUND AX,1000H	62 06 00 10	Compare the array index in the destination operand with the upper and lower boundaries stored in memory and addressed by the source operand; execute an INT 5 if the index is out of limits
ENTER *disp,level*	ENTER 28,3	C8 28 00 03	Save the current frame pointed (BP) and any old frame pointers in lower levels and allocate space on the stack (disp) for any local variables
LEAVE	LEAVE	C9	Deallocate all local variables and restore SP and BP to their values immediately after the procedure's call

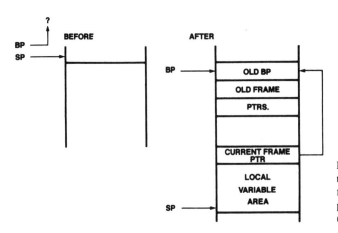

Figure 11.20 The ENTER instruction is used to construct a high-level-language "stack frame" made up of the old and new frame pointers, and the set of local variables. (Courtesy of Intel Corporation.)

SELF-REVIEW 11.1 (answers on page 595)

11.1.1. An assembly language program written for the 8086 microprocessor will run without changes on the 80186 microprocessor. (True/False)

11.1.2. The control bus of the 80186 is nearly the same as that of the 8086 except that _____ is not provided.

11.1.3. When interfacing the 8089 or 8087 coprocessors to the 80186, the _____ advanced bus controller is required to convert the coprocessor's $\overline{RQ}/\overline{GT}$ protocol to a _____ protocol.

11.1.4. After reset, the 80186 chip select registers are located at ports _____ to _____.

11.1.5. To install an 8K-byte EPROM at the top of the 80186's memory space, the _____ chip select signal should be used and register UMCS programmed for _____ H (assuming no wait states).

11.1.6. Referring to the program in Fig. 11.8, $\overline{PCS3}$ decodes all CPU I/O accesses to ports in the range _____ to _____.

11.1.7. Assume that the channel 0 control register of the 80186 DMA stores 17A7H. What type of DMA cycle is programmed? Describe the channel synchronization.

11.1.8. To produce a pulse once every 2 ms, the 80186 timer 2 maximum count register should be programmed for _____ H. Assume an 8-MHz system clock.

11.1.9. If INT2 is to be programmed as an edge-triggered interrupt with priority level 3, the control word _____ H should be written at offset _____ in the 80186 PCB.

11.1.10. When the 80186 poll status register contains 8013H an interrupt request from _____ is indicated.

11.1.11. What is the word interpretation for the 80186 instruction IMUL CX,[SI],-5?

11.2 THE 8087 NUMERIC DATA PROCESSOR

The 8086 and 80186 are general-purpose microprocessors suitable for most data processing tasks. However, many "real world" problems cannot be solved with integer arithmetic and the four basic math functions provided by the 8086. For example, calculating the sine of an angle or the area of a circle requires a fractional number system and transcendental math functions.

Traditionally, software routines have been written to implement these functions. For example, $\sin x$ can be approximated as

$$\sin x = x - \frac{x^3}{3!} + \frac{x^5}{5!} - \frac{x^7}{7!} + \cdots$$

As you can imagine, in some applications the time to execute these functions can become excessive. For this reason, math coprocessors have become popular accessories in microcomputers intended for scientific or other calculation-intensive applications.

In fact, Intel offers two coprocessors for the 8086 family. These are the 8087 numeric data processor (NDP) discussed in this section and the 8089 I/O processor (IOP) covered in Sec. 11.3. Each of these chips is quite complex—truly "microprocessors" themselves—capable of executing special coprocessor instructions in parallel with the host CPU. Indeed, Intel would have us consider the coprocessor as an *extension* of the main CPU. In their numbering scheme an 8086/8087 system is an iAPX 86/20 two-chip CPU. An 8086/8087/8089 is an iAPX 86/21 three-chip CPU.

In this section we consider the iAPX 86/20 CPU configuration. In particular, we concentrate on the electrical interface between CPU and coprocessor. The programming model, which is quite different from that of the 8086, is also presented. It includes registers capable of processing numbers in eight different data formats. The section concludes with a survey of the instruction set and a simple program example. This is an 8087 procedure written to calculate the area of a circle.

Host Interface[3]

Figure 11.21 illustrates that the 8087 is organized as a separate *control unit* (CU) and *numeric execution unit* (NEU). The CU receives and decodes all NDP instructions. Those involving the data registers (requiring arithmetic processing) are passed on to the NEU. Other control instructions are executed by the CU itself.

Like the BIU and EU of the 8086, these two units can operate independently. In fact, the NEU can be busy executing a numeric instruction—calculating a square root, for example—while the CU is executing a special control instruction.

Figure 11.22 shows how the 8087 is interfaced to the 8086 or 8088 microprocessors. Basically the two chips are wired in "parallel" with common connections for the address, data, and most control signals. Note that the host must be operated in the maximum

---

[3]In the following discussion the term *host* will refer to any of the 8086 family of processors—the 8086, 8088, 80186, and 80188.

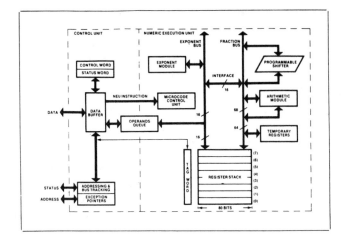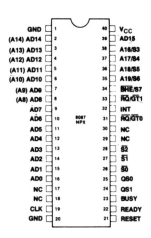

Figure 11.21 Block diagram and pin configuration for the 8087 numeric data processor (NDP). The chip is divided into a control unit (CU) and a numeric execution unit (NEU). (Courtesy of Intel Corporation.)

mode. This is to accommodate the $\overline{RQ}/\overline{GT}$ DMA protocol of the coprocessor and also allows the coprocessor to monitor the host's status via $\overline{S0}$–$\overline{S2}$ and $\overline{QS0}$–$\overline{QS1}$.

Typical operation.　As the host fetches instructions from memory the 8087 does likewise—"looking" for an instruction with a special ESC prefix. Because of the host's prefetch queue, instructions being fetched are not the same as those being executed. $\overline{QS0}$ and $\overline{QS1}$ allow the coprocessor to track instructions as they proceed through the queue. $\overline{S0}$–$\overline{S2}$ provide information on the bus status (see Tables 6.6 and 6.7 for a review of these status bits).

In some special cases, instructions on the bus are not intended for the host processor. This can occur when an 8089 IOP is executing a channel program in main memory. During this time S6 will be high to indicate that the local bus is being used by a coprocessor. Monitoring S6, the 8087 will ignore these coprocessor fetches.

When the host encounters an ESC instruction it calculates the effective address (EA) and performs a "dummy" read cycle from this location. That is, the data read is not stored. The 8087, however, captures this address. Now, depending on the coprocessor instruction, a memory read or write cycle will be performed by the NDP from this address. Thus the 8087 works in tandem with the host CPU, using it to generate the EA of coprocessor memory operands. The 8087 itself has no EA generation capability.

As you will see, several of the data formats used by the 8087 require multiple-word memory operands. To read or write these numbers, the 8087 requests control of the local bus via $\overline{RQ}/\overline{GT}$. All the required bytes are then read or written in consecutive DMA cycles.

Note the 8087 BUSY output. This signal alerts the CPU (via its $\overline{TEST}$ input) that an 8087 calculation is in progress. Only when $\overline{TEST}$ is high should the CPU attempt to access an 8087 memory result. The 8086 memory WAIT instruction is provided for this purpose.

Interfacing 8- and 16-bit hosts. The 8087 is compatible with the 16-bit 8086 and 80186 as well as the 8-bit 8088 and 80188 microprocessors. If the host has a 16-bit data bus width, the NDP will access memory following the same rules defined for that host: namely, two-byte operations for word operands starting at an odd address, and single-word accesses for operands starting at an even address.

When the host has an 8-bit data bus width, all memory accesses are performed as byte operations. The 8087 determines the appropriate bus width by monitoring pin 34 during a system reset. For a 16-bit host, a word access from FFFF0H will be performed and pin 34 ($\overline{\text{BHE}}$) will be low. However, with an 8-bit host, a byte access from FFFF0H will be performed and pin 34 ($\overline{\text{SS0}}$) will be high. Be sure to note that the width of the host data bus has no effect on 8087 instructions except for the execution time penalty associated with the byte versus word memory accesses.

Handling numeric errors. As the 8087 is executing instructions, it automatically checks for the following error or *exception* conditions.

1. *Invalid operation.* Examples are attempting to calculate the square root of a negative number, or popping an operand from an empty register.
2. *Zero divide.*
3. *Denormalized.* An attempt has been made to operate on an operand that has not been normalized.
4. *Overflow.* Exponent of the result is too large for the destination real format.
5. *Underflow.* Exponent of the result is too small to be represented.
6. *Precision.* Operand is not exactly representable in destination format, causing the 8087 to round the result.

The 8087's response to each of these exception conditions is to set the appropriate flag bit in the status word. It then checks the exception mask in the control register. If the mask bit is set (masked), a built in fix-up procedure is followed. For example, a zero-divide exception, when masked, causes the NDP to return an infinite result signed with the exclusive OR of the operand signs.

If the exception is unmasked (mask bit = 0), an interrupt is requested via pin 32, INT (assuming that the interrupt enable mask bit in the 8087 has been set). INT is normally connected to one of the interrupt inputs of an 8259A PIC. In this way unmasked exceptions trap to user-written exception handlers.

Multiple coprocessors. When multiple coprocessors are used the 8087 extends the CPU's $\overline{\text{RQ}}/\overline{\text{GT1}}$ pin to accommodate an additional coprocessor. This is shown in Fig. 11.23. If IOPB should request use of the system buses while the 8087 is performing a DMA cycle, the current transfer will be finished. The 8087 will then relinquish control to IOPB. That is, the NDP assigns a higher priority to external bus requests than to an

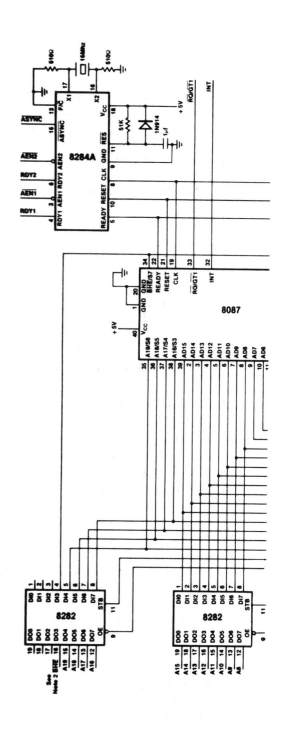

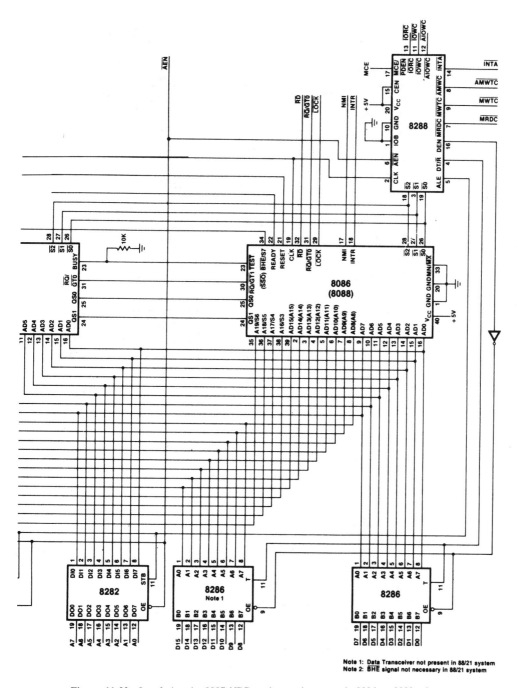

Figure 11.22 Interfacing the 8087 NDP to the maximum-mode 8086 or 8088 microprocessors. (Courtesy of Intel Corporation.)

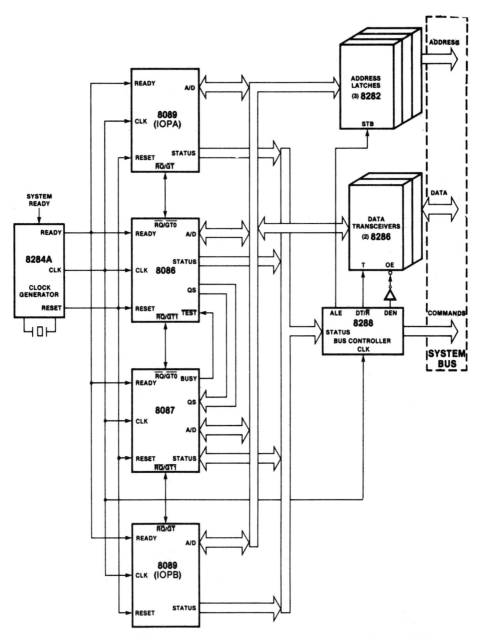

Figure 11.23 Using the 8087 with multiple coprocessors. Bus requests from IOPB are passed on to the host by the 8087. (Courtesy of Intel Corporation.)

internal request. If IOPB's bus request occurs while the 8087 does not own the bus, the request will be passed on to the CPU.

In Fig. 11.23 IOPB will have a shorter worst-case bus request latency than IOPA, even though IOPA is connected to a higher-priority CPU $\overline{\text{RQ}}/\overline{\text{GT}}$ input. This is because bus requests by IOPA that occur during NDP DMA cycles will be ignored (the CPU is disabled, and the NDP cannot know that IOPA is making a request). Thus in systems with one 8089 and one 8087—an iAPX 86/21—the 8089 $\overline{\text{RQ}}/\overline{\text{GT}}$ pin should interface through the 8087, not directly to the CPU.

Programming Model

Figure 11.24 is the programmer's view of the iAPX 86/20. Shown on the left are the registers contained within the host CPU. Those on the right comprise the register set of the 8087. These are divided into eight data registers and a tag field, R1–R8, and five control/status registers. Note that the tag word is the tag field represented as one 16-bit word.

Data registers. The eight data registers are organized as a "push down" stack within the NEU. Each of these registers is 80 bits wide and designed to accommodate several different data formats. The numeric instructions operate on data in this stack using a *relative* addressing scheme. This is shown in Fig. 11.25.

At a given time, any register can be "on top of" the stack. The stack top is indicated symbolically as ST(0). When data is loaded into the stack from memory, a "push" operation occurs. The data loaded now sits atop the stack, with each of the other registers pushed down one position.

Data is stored in memory by popping the stack, causing the contents of ST(0) to be transferred to memory and all data registers moved up one position. That is, ST(1) becomes ST(0), ST(2) becomes ST(1), and so on.

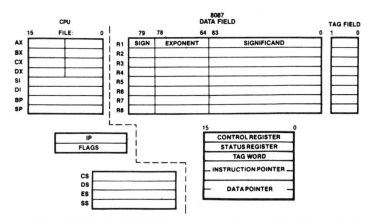

Figure 11.24 The iAPX86/20 register set. (Courtesy of Intel Corporation.)

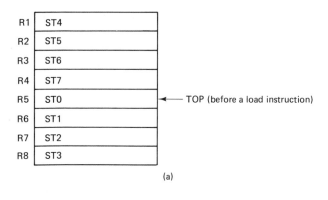

(a)

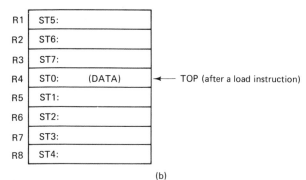

(b)

Figure 11.25 (a) The eight data registers of the NDP are organized as a pushdown stack. (b) The 8087 load instructions retrieve data from memory and store the result by pushing the data onto the top of the stack.

Table 11.4 defines the eight numeric data formats supported by the 8087. These are 2's-complement signed integers, signed 18-digit BCD numbers, and signed real— also called "floating point"—numbers. The signed real numbers are expressed in "binary scientific notation." This is explained in notes e–g of the table. Note that the sign bit for these numbers is a 0 for positive numbers and a 1 for negative numbers.

Example 11.4

Express the decimal number 0.080078125 as a long real floating-point number.

Solution This number can be converted to binary by extracting the appropriate powers of 2 or via the repeated multiplication-by-2 method. The result is 0.000101001. Expressing this in binary scientific notation yields

$$0.000101001 = 1.01001 \times 2^{-4}$$

The 52-bit mantissa is thus as shown in note f of Table 11.4. Note that the binary point and leading 1 are implied. The exponent bits are found by adding -4 (the power of 2) to 1023 (the long real bias). The result is 1019, or 01111111011 (written for 11 bits). Because the original number is positive, S = 0. The final result is shown in note f of Table 11.4.

The 8087 data registers use the 80-bit temporary real format. Data read from memory is automatically converted to this form by the 8087. Data written back to memory is written in a form dependent on the instruction used. This will be shown later when the instruction set is surveyed.

Control registers. The two main registers in the CU are the control and status registers shown in Fig. 11.26. The TOP bits in the status register reflect the register currently atop the register stack. The condition code bits, C2–C0, are set by various 8087 operations similar to the flags within the CPU. Bits 0–5 indicate the exception status, as described earlier.

The control register defines the type of infinity, rounding, and precision to be used as the NDP performs its calculations. Bit 7 must be reset to allow interrupts. Bits 0–5 allow any of the exception cases to be masked. The 8087 will then default to the built-in fix-up procedure for these masked exceptions.

The instruction and data pointer registers (see Fig. 11.24) are each 20 bits long. Whenever the NEU executes an instruction, the CU saves the op-code and memory address of that instruction, and its operand, in these registers. A control instruction can be given to store their contents to memory. This is useful for program debugging. For example, if an unmasked error occurs, the interrupt handler can be written to display the op-code and operand that caused the problem.

Unlike the general-purpose CPU registers, the 8087 data registers are initially considered *empty*. As data is written to these registers they can become *valid* (the register holds a valid number in temporary real format), *zero*, or *special* (indefinite due to an error condition). Each data register has a tag field identifying its contents as being in one of these four states. The tagword groups these eight fields into one 16-bit word. Its primary purpose is to optimize the NDP's performance under certain circumstances. It is not normally needed by the programmer.

Instruction Set

The instruction set of the 8087 should be viewed as an extension to that of the 8086. Each instruction begins with the letter "F" for floating point. When the instruction

```
FILD  MEMORY_WORD
```

is encountered in the 8086's instruction stream, it is "seen" by the 8086 as ESC 38H, MEMORY_WORD.[4] The ESC prefix tells the 8086 to perform a "dummy" read cycle from address MEMORY_WORD. The 8087 "sees" this instruction as an integer load operation. When memory places the word onto the data bus lines, it is captured by the NDP and pushed onto the top of the data stack (automatically converting it to temporary real format).

Normally, the 8087 would be programmed using a compatible assembler such that all of the NDP mnemonics are recognized and the proper hex codes generated. An 8086 assembler can be used if macros are created for each of the 8087 instructions. This idea was mentioned briefly in Sec. 4.7. In either case, the memory operands can be accessed

---

[4]38H represents bits 5–10 of the FILD op-code.

TABLE 11.4 NUMERIC DATA FORMATS SUPPORTED BY THE 8087

Data format	Range	Precision	Most significant byte										
			7 07	07	07	07	07	07	07	07	07	07	0
Byte integer	10^2	8 bits	$I_7\ I_0$ 2's complement										
Word integer[a]	10^4	16 bits	I_{15} I_0 2's complement										
Short integer[b]	10^9	32 bits	I_{31} I_0 2's complement										
Long integer[c]	10^{18}	64 bits	I_{63} I_0 2's complement										
Packed BCD[d]	10^{18}	18 digits	S|— $D_{17}D_{16}$										D_1D_0
Short real[e]	$10^{\pm38}$	24 bits	S|$E_7\ E_0$|F_1 $F_{23}F_0$ Implicit										
Long real[f]	$10^{\pm308}$	53 bits	S|$E_{10}\ E_0$|F_1 $F_{52}F_0$ Implicit										
Temporary real[g]	$10^{\pm4932}$	64 bits	S|E_{14}|E_0F_0 F_{63}										

564

^aSigned integers in the range −32,768 to 32,767. Only data format directly compatible with 8086. Specified in a program with the DW operator.

WORD	DW	1234H	;2 bytes

^bSigned integers in the range −2^{32} to 2^{32} − 1. Specified in a program with the DD operator.

SHORT INTEGER	DD	12345678H	;4 bytes

^cSigned integers in the range 2^{64} to 2^{64} − 1. Specified in a program with the DQ operator.

LONG INTEGER	DQ	123456789ABCDEFOH	;8 bytes

^dS = 0 for positive, 1 for a negative number. Specified in a program with the DT operator

PACKED_BCD	DT	00123456789012345678	;10 bytes
	DT	80000000000000005678	;−5678

^eThe exponent bits (E7–E0) are calculated as 127D (7FH) + the signed exponent. F0 is implied to be 1. F1–F23 specify the 23-bit mantissa. For example, 13.625D = 1101.101B = 1.101101 × 2^3 is written

$$0 \quad 10000010 \quad 10110100000000000000000$$
$$S \qquad exp \qquad \text{mantissa (23 bits)}$$

^fThe exponent bits (E10–E0) are calculated as 1023D (3FFH) + the signed exponent. F0 is implied to be 1. F1–F52 specify the 52-bit mantissa. For example, 0.080078125D = 0.000101001B = 1.01001 × 2^{-4} is written

$$0 \quad 01111111011 \quad 0100100000000000000000000000000000000000000000000000$$
$$S \qquad exp \qquad \text{mantissa (52 bits)}$$

^gThe exponent bits (E14–E0) are calculated as 16383D (3FFFH) + the signed exponent. F0–F63 specify the 64-bit mantissa. For example, −4096D = −0001000000000000 = −1.0 × 2^{12} is written

$$1 \quad 100000000000110 \quad 1000000000000000000000 \cdots 00000000000000000000000$$
$$S \qquad exp \qquad \text{mantissa (64 bits)}$$

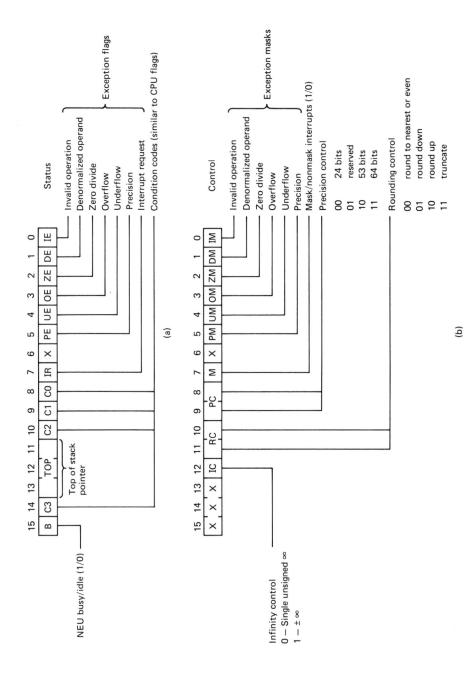

Figure 11.26 (a) The 8087 status word can be read to check the state of the NDP. (b) The control word can be written to select various processing options.

TABLE 11.5 8087 INSTRUCTIONS FOR MOVING DATA

Real Transfers	
FLD	Load real
FST	Store real
FSTP	Store real and pop
FXCH	Exchange registers
Integer Transfers	
FILD	Integer load
FIST	Integer store
FISTP	Integer store and pop
Packed Decimal Transfers	
FBLD	Packed decimal (BCD) load
FBSTP	Packed decimal (BCD) store and pop

Source: Intel Corporation

using any of the addressing modes available to the host processor. Indeed, it is the host that generates the EA!

Data transfer instructions. Table 11.5 lists all those instructions that can be used to move data among the registers on the data stack, and between the stack top and a memory location. There are two basic instruction types. *Load* instructions, with the suffix "LD," push the register or memory operand onto the stack top. For example, FLD ST(5) replaces the stack top with the contents of ST(5). The value that was in ST(5) moves to ST(6), as does ST(0) to ST(1), and so on.

Unlike the 8086, the 8087 uses different mnemonics for different data types. Thus the instruction

FBLD   TBYTE PTR [BX]

has the word interpretation "Load the 18-digit (10-byte) BCD number pointed to by register BX in the data segment to register ST(0)."

Data transfer instructions may also specify a *store* operation (suffix "ST"). This causes the stack top to be transferred to another data register or a memory location. For example,

FST   LONG_REAL

converts ST(0) to long real format (the format of the memory destination) and stores the result in eight consecutive bytes beginning at memory location LONG_REAL. Store instructions ending with a "P" store the register via a "pop" operation. Thus the instruction

FBSTP   BCD_INTEGER

TABLE 11.6 8087 CONSTANTS FOR
SCIENTIFIC CALCULATIONS

FLDZ	Load $+0.0$
FLD1	Load $+1.0$
FLDPI	Load π
FLDL2T	Load $\log_2 10$
FLDL2E	Load $\log_2 e$
FLDLG2	Load $\log_{10} 2$
FLDLN2	Load $\log_e 2$

Source: Intel Corporation

converts ST(0) to an 18-digit BCD number and pops the result from the stack top to memory location BCD_INTEGER. ST(1) now becomes the new stack top.

The 8087 also has a number of constants useful for scientific calculations that can be loaded to ST(0). These are shown in Table 11.6.

Control instructions.   The 8087 control instructions are listed in Table 11.7. These instructions are executed by the CU and are not used for any arithmetic processing. Most of these can be given without waiting for a previous 8087 result to be generated. Several of the instructions have alternate mnemonics beginning with "FN" for *not synchronized*. This instructs the assembler not to prefix the instruction with a CPU WAIT instruction. Forms without the "N" will have the WAIT prefix automatically inserted by the assembler.

FLDCW MEMORY_WORD is used to write the control word by transferring the memory operand to the 8087 control register. FSTCW MEMORY_WORD and FSTSW

TABLE 11.7 8087 CONTROL INSTRUCTIONS

FINIT/FNINIT	Initialize processor
FDISI/FNDISI	Disable interrupts
FENI/FNENI	Enable interrupts
FLDCW	Load control word
FSTCW/FNSTCW	Store control word
FSTSW/FNSTSW	Store status word
FCLEX/FNCLEX	Clear exceptions
FSTENV/FNSTENV	Store environment
FLDENV	Load environment
FSAVE/FNSAVE	Save state
FRSTOR	Restore state
FINCSTP	Increment stack pointer
FDECSTP	Decrement stack pointer
FFREE	Free register
FNOP	No operation
FWAIT	CPU wait

Source: Intel Corporation.

MEMORY_WORD allow the status and control registers to be read by transferring each to the specified memory operand. Without these instructions the status and control registers cannot be accessed by the CPU.

The FLDENV and FSTENV instructions allow the 8087 *environment*—that is, the control registers—to be saved and recovered. With reference to Fig. 11.24, 14 memory bytes are required.

The FSAVE and FRSTOR instructions save and restore the 8087 *state*. This is the environment plus all data registers. Ninety-four consecutive memory bytes are required. The point of these two groups of instructions is to allow the 8087 to be used within an interrupt handler. They can also be used for debugging purposes.

The FFREE instruction is used to define a stack register as *empty:* for example, to empty ST(3): FFREE ST(3). Recall that the tag word keeps track of this status.

Finally, the FWAIT instruction is not an 8087 instruction at all. It is included as an alternate CPU WAIT mnemonic so that it can be flagged and removed for 8087 emulation. If this is not done, the host processor will enter an endless ''wait'' when this instruction is encountered and no 8087 is actually present.

FWAIT should be inserted before CPU instructions that access memory before the 8087 is ready. Following is a typical example:

```
FNSAVE  BUFFER       ;Save state in 94-byte buffer
FWAIT                ;Wait for all 94 bytes to be written
MOV     AX,BUFFER    ;Fetch first word
```

Numeric instructions.   At the heart of the 8087 are the numeric instructions. The basic functions are shown in Table 11.8. The reversed forms reverse the roles of source and destination in the calculation (only). Each of the instructions in this group can be written in five different forms. This is shown in Table 11.9 using the FMUL instruction as an example. Thus the operand may be an 8087 data register (forms 1–3) or a memory location (forms 4 and 5). Instructions with a ''P'' suffix store the result of the operation in a data register and then pop the stack.

Other instructions in this group include FSCALE, which uses ST(1) as a scale factor for ST(0).

$$ST(0) \leftarrow ST(0) \times 2^{ST(1)}$$

FPREM returns the partial remainder of ST(0) mod ST(1). This instruction is intended for repeated operation in a loop. One of the condition code flag bits is set when the instruction has completed. FRNDINT rounds ST(0) to an integer using the rules currently in effect (set via the RC [rounding and control] bits in the control register). FXTRACT breaks ST(0) into a fractional part [ST(0)] and an exponent [ST(1)].

Table 11.10 lists the comparison instructions. These instructions compare ST(0) with a register or memory operand. The condition code bits are set accordingly. For example,

FICOM SHORT_INTEGER

TABLE 11.8 ARITHMETIC INSTRUCTIONS

	Addition
FADD	Add real
FADDP	Add real and pop
FIADD	Integer add

	Subtraction
FSUB	Subtract real
FSUBP	Subtract real and pop
FISUB	Integer subtract
FSUBR	Subtract real reversed and pop
FSUBRP	Subtract real reversed and pop
FISUBR	Integer subtract reversed

	Multiplication
FMUL	Multiply real
FMULP	Multiply real and pop
FIMUL	Integer multiply

	Division
FDIV	Divide real
FDIVP	Divide real and pop
FIDIV	Integer divide
FDIVR	Divide real reversed
FDIVRP	Divide real reversed and pop
FIDIVR	Integer divide reversed

	Other Operations
FSQRT	Square root
FSCALE	Scale
FPREM	Partial remainder
FRNDINT	Round to integer
FXTRACT	Extract expoonent and significand
FABS	Absolute value
FCHS	Change sign

Source: Intel Corporation

compares ST(0) with the short integer in memory location SHORT_INTEGER. Note that you must use FSTSW to store the status word to memory to allow the host to test the condition codes. The 8087 cannot test these bits itself.

FTST tests ST(0) for 0. FXAM sets the status bits to reflect the kind of number on the stack top—positive or negative normal, empty, ± infinity, invalid.

Table 11.11 shows the transcendental instructions necessary for most trigonometric functions. Note that these are lower-level functions from which the more typical sin and

TABLE 11.9 8087 ARITHMETIC INSTRUCTION FORMS

	Form	Mnemonic	Operand	Description
1.	ST0 and ST1 only	FMUL		ST0 ← ST0 × ST1
2.	ST0 and STi	FMUL	ST3	ST0 ← ST0 × ST3
3.	STi and ST0	FMULP	ST2,ST	ST2 ← ST0 × ST2 (pop stack)
4.	Real memory	FMUL	LONG_REAL	ST0 ← ST0 × LONG_REAL[a]
5.	Integer memory	FMUL	WORD_INTEGER	ST0 ← ST0 × WORD_INTEGER[b]

[a]Memory operand may be short or long real only.

[b]Memory operand may be byte, word, or short integer only.

TABLE 11.10 8087 COMPARISON INSTRUCTIONS

FCOM	Compare real
FCOMP	Compare real and pop
FCOMPP	Compare real and pop twice
FICOM	Integer compare
FICOMP	Integer compare and pop
FTST	Test
FXAM	Examine

Source: Intel Corporation

TABLE 11.11 8087 TRANSCENDENTAL INSTRUCTIONS

FPTAN	Partial tangent
FPATAN	Partial arctangent
F2XM1	$2^x - 1$
FYL2X	$Y \cdot \log_2 X$
FYL2XP1	$Y \cdot \log_2(X + 1)$

Source: Intel Corporation

cos can be derived. For example, assuming a right triangle with height Y and base X such that $Y/X = \tan \Theta$, two functions are provided.

1. FPTAN assumes that ST(0) is the angle in radians and returns X in ST(0) and Y in ST(1). Note that this allows $\sin \Theta$ to be calculated as $Y/(SQR(X^2 + Y^2))$.
2. FPATAN assumes that X is in ST(0) and Y is in ST(1). It pops the stack and puts the angle in ST(0) (formerly Y).

There are also three base 2 logarithm functions.

1. F2XM1 stores $2^{ST(0)} - 1$ in ST(0). ST(0) is limited to the range 0–0.5.
2. FYL2X stores $ST(1) \times Log_2 ST(0)$ in ST(0).
3. FYL2XP1 stores $ST(1) \times Log_2(ST(0) + 1)$ in ST(0).

```
;Function        8087 procedure to calculate
;                the area of a circle.
; Inputs:        Radius in AH (byte integer).
;Outputs:        Area in BX:AX (short integer).
;Calls:          nothing
;Destroys        nothing


CODE          SEGMENT BYTE
              ASSUME CS:CODE

RADIUS   DB        ?                        ;Memory variables required to
AREA     DD        ?                        ;exchange data with 8087.

AREA_OF_CIRCLE        PROC     NEAR
                     MOV      RADIUS,AH        ;Put radius in memory
                     FILD     RADIUS           ;ST0 = r
                     FMUL     ST(0),ST(0)      ;ST0 = r * r
                     FLDPI                     ;ST0 = pi and ST1 = r * r
                     FMUL     ST(0),ST(1)      ;ST0 = pi * r * r = area
                     FIST     AREA             ;Store rounded result
                     FWAIT                     ;Be sure data is stored
                     MOV      AX,AREA          ;Then fetch low 16-bits
                     MOV      BX,AREA + 2      ;Then high 16-bits
                     RET                       ;Done
AREA_OF_CIRCLE        ENDP
CODE                 ENDS
                     END
```

Figure 11.27   8087 procedure to calculate the area of a circle.

Example 11.5

Write an 8086/8087 procedure to calculate the area of a circle. Assume that the integer radius is passed in register AH and return the area (rounded to the nearest integer) in BX:AX.

Solution   The program is shown in Fig. 11.27. Note that the data must be passed through memory variables, in this case RADIUS and AREA. The DD operator will cause the 8087 FIST store instruction to convert the result to a short integer. Note the use of the FWAIT instruction to synchronize the 8086 to the NDP.

SELF-REVIEW 11.2 (answers on pages 595-596)

11.2.1. The 8087 NDP is made up of a separate _____ unit and _____ _____ unit.

11.2.2. The 8087 fetches instructions in parallel with the host processor "looking" for an _____ instruction.

11.2.3. The 8087 is compatible with 8- or 16-bit host processors. How can it tell which type of processor it is interfaced to?

11.2.4. Although the 8087 can access memory using any of the 8086 addressing modes, it has no effective address-calculating capability of its own.   (True/False) ____

11.2.5. Specify an 8087 instruction that would require DMA cycles via the $\overline{RQ/GT}$ control line.

11.2.6. The CPU should preface instructions that access 8087 memory variables with the _____ instruction.

11.2.7. It is not possible to move data directly from the 8086 CPU to the 8087 NDP. (True/False)

11.2.8. When a memory variable is pushed onto the 8087 data stack, it is automatically converted to _____ _____ format.

11.2.9. The 8087 will fix up errors or exceptions that occur during processing if the _____ _____ in the _____ _____ are set.

11.2.10. What is the word interpretation for the 8087 instruction FADD ST2,ST3?

11.3 THE 8089 I/O PROCESSOR

All computer systems—from mainframes to micros—are designed to input information, process that information, and output the result. The speed with which these operations can be carried out is a measure of the system's capability. For example, a mainframe computer such as the Control Data Corporation Cyber can perform a floating-point multiplication in about 1 μs. A similar calculation on the 8086 will require about 1600μs.

One way of improving a microcomputer system's performance—the approach adopted by Intel—is through the use of optional *coprocessors*. For example, the 8087 NDP can perform the floating calculation above in about 19 μs (still slower than the Cyber but nearly 100 times faster than the 8086 alone).

Another area affecting system performance is management of the I/O devices. If the CPU is involved in each and every input/output operation, as is true in a typical microcomputer system, the overall processing speed of that system will be degraded. Even if interrupts are employed, the CPU must still have its "hand" in each data transfer.

Mainframe designers have solved this problem by employing special "front end" processors. These are minicomputers to which all the system's I/O devices are connected. The main CPU communicates with its front end at high speed and only when all data has been input or a new block of data is to be output.

The 8089 is designed to be a front-end processor for the 8086/88 and 80186/188. As such, it is actually a microprocessor designed specifically for I/O operations. Executing a task program from its own private memory, it is capable of concurrent operation with the host CPU. Data transfers can be under program control or DMA, the latter initiated by the special 8089 instruction XFER.

Do not confuse the 8089 with peripheral controller chips such as the 8255 PPI or 8251A USART. These chips are designed to simplify I/O hardware design by incorporating all the logic for parallel (8255) or serial (8251A) ports in one package. However, as we have seen, each controller chip requires its own unique initialization sequence before it can be used. Of course, the actual data transfers must be controlled by the CPU.

The 8089 is not designed to replace these chips. In fact, it has no built-in I/O ports of its own. Instead, it is designed to *control* these devices by executing all the I/O software formerly run by the host CPU. It does this by fetching and executing instructions from private or shared memory. The former is called the *remote mode* and allows concurrent operation with the host CPU. In the latter case the 8089 must share the system buses with the host CPU. Concurrency is not possible. This is referred to as the *local mode*.

In this section you are introduced to these two modes of 8089 operation. The internal registers or programming model will also be explained and the instruction set surveyed. A design example in which the 8089 is used to control a printer will illustrate a typical application.

Bus Configuration

Figure 11.28 provides a block diagram and pin definitions for the 8089 I/O processor (IOP). It is designed to be compatible with the (maximum mode) 8086 family of host processors. The bus interface unit (BIU) is in control of all bus cycles. Notice that the IOP itself does not output any of the control bus signals ($\overline{\text{IOW}}$, $\overline{\text{IOR}}$, $\overline{\text{MEMR}}$, $\overline{\text{MEMW}}$, DT/$\overline{\text{R}}$, ALE, or DEN). This information is encoded via the status outputs $\overline{\text{S0}}$–$\overline{\text{S2}}$, which must be connected to an 8288 bus controller. The 8288 then generates the appropriate control bus signals.

The multiplexed address/data bus is identical to that of the 8086 and 80186. This can be changed during initialization to an 8-bit bus, making it compatible with the 8088 and 80188. $\overline{\text{BHE}}$ is active for the 16-bit configuration and controls the gating of data on AD8–AD15 as in the 8086/186.

The $\overline{\text{LOCK}}$ signal is intended for the 8289 bus arbiter. When active it prevents another processor from accessing the system buses. This is typically used to ensure that the contents of system memory are not changed until the locked instruction has executed. The $\overline{\text{RQ/GT}}$ pin supports the standard bus access protocol used by the 8086 family in the maximum mode. This will be covered more fully when the local and remote modes are discussed.

One 8089 can control two separate I/O devices. That is, the 8089 has two control channels. DRQ (an input) and EXT (an output) are provided to synchronize the exchange of data on these channels. DRQ is used to initiate each DMA transfer. EXT can be used to terminate DMA cycles.

Like the 8087, the 8089 and host CPU cannot communicate with each other directly. As you will see, the normal technique is through a series of commonly accessible message blocks in system memory. SINTR provides another method. Connecting this output to one of the inputs of an 8259A PIC, the CPU can be alerted (via an interrupt) that the task program has completed or an error condition has occurred.

The common control unit (CCU) oversees the two data channels. In particular, it determines which channel will execute the next cycle. In cases where both channels have equal priority, an interleave scheme is used in which a cycle is run alternately for each channel.

The CA input—channel attention—functions similar to a CPU interrupt. The falling edge of this signal causes the CCU to read a special channel control word (CCW) stored in system memory. If the channel select (SEL) input is low, the CCW for channel 0 is accessed. If high, channel 1's CCW is read. Based on this word, the selected channel's task program may be started, suspended, resumed, or halted.

The assembly/disassembly registers allow the 8089 to accommodate an 8- or 16-bit data bus width. It is also possible to mix the two types. For example, during a DMA transfer from an 8-bit I/O device to a 16-bit memory interface, the IOP will read two bytes from the I/O port before writing them as one word to memory.

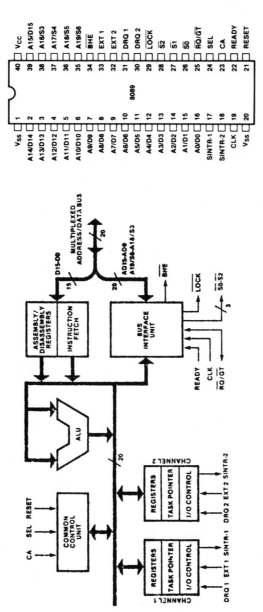

Figure 11.28 Pin configuration and block diagram of the 8089 I/O processor (IOP). (Courtesy of Intel Corporation.)

Local mode.   Figure 11.29 illustrates the local mode of operation for the 8089. It is very similar to an 8087 interface. The CPU and IOP *share* all system resources, including the bus buffers, latches, and bus controller. In this mode the 8089's data bus width must match that of the CPU.

The IOP gains control of the buses by pulsing the bidirectional $\overline{RQ}/\overline{GT}$ line. The CPU acknowledges by pulsing $\overline{RQ}/\overline{GT}$ a second time and open circuiting its address/data and $\overline{S0}$–$\overline{S2}$ status lines. The 8089 now drives these lines using the 8288 to generate its control bus signals as mentioned before. To the memory and I/O, the bus timing appears identical to that of the CPU.

The CPU begins channel activity by asserting CA. In Fig. 11.29 this is done via the *device select pulse* (DSP) obtained by decoding A1–A15 and $\overline{IOWC}$. The SEL input is driven by A0. An OUT PORT,AX instruction to an even port selects channel 0, an odd port selects channel 1. The data in register AX is of no concern, as it is only the CA pulse that is required.

In a typical application, the peripheral will supply a synchronizing signal (DMQ) to one of the IOP's DRQ inputs. Data will then be transferred from memory to the I/O device (or vice versa) until all bytes have been transferred or EXT is received. In either case, the task program will halt, $\overline{RQ}/\overline{GT}$ will be pulsed a third time, and the CPU will resume its control program.

Be sure to notice that concurrent operation is not possible in this mode. The CPU must enter a hold state while the IOP executes its task program and performs the DMA cycles. Thus when configured in the local mode, the IOP operates more like an intelligent DMA controller (a 20-bit 8237A?) than a concurrent processor.

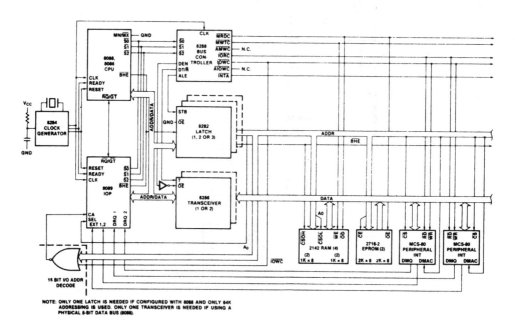

Figure 11.29   Operating the 8089 in the *local* mode. The CPU and IOP share all system resources. (Courtesy of Intel Corporation.)

Remote mode. Figure 11.30 illustrates a typical remote configuration for the 8089 IOP. In this case the IOP buses (the local bus) are physically separated from the CPU system buses by buffers. The key to this circuit is the 8288. It is operated in the *IO bus* mode such that $\overline{PDEN}$ is active only when the 8089 is executing an I/O instruction. This allows the IOP to have a separate and private *I/O bus* accessible only to itself and its I/O devices.

The 8289 is required to arbitrate requests for the system bus among other bus masters. When the IOP requires access to system memory, the 8289 checks that the system buses are available. It then examines $\overline{S0}$–$\overline{S2}$ and enables the 8288 memory read and write commands as required by the IOP. In effect, the 8289 and 8288 take the place of the $\overline{RQ}/\overline{GT}$ mechanism used by the IOP in the local mode to gain control of the buses.

Because the IOP's private bus is enabled only for I/O reference instructions, its address bus is limited to 16 bits (A0–A15). The private data bus width can be 8 or 16 bits, as required (except that 16-bit I/O devices will require a 16-bit data bus). The system bus interface must have the same width as the CPU system bus.

Instructions in the IOP's instruction set do not distinguish between I/O devices and memory locations. That is, there are no specific I/O instructions. Instructions may reference an I/O address (via the private bus) or a system address. If an I/O device resides at the specified I/O address, this instruction is effectively an "I/O" instruction. In Chap. 8 we called this *memory-mapped* I/O.

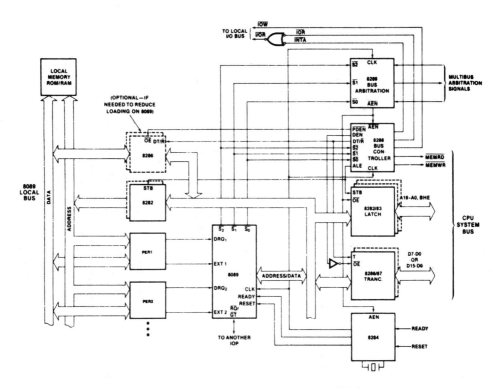

Figure 11.30 Operating the 8089 in the *remote* mode. The IOP has its own *private* memory and I/O, not accessible by the system CPU. (Courtesy of Intel Corporation.)

If the IOP's task program is located in private memory, the task program can be executed independent of the system CPU. That is, the IOP can operate *concurrently* with the CPU. This is the preferred mode of operation for the 8089. The price, however, is the extensive support circuitry required, as shown in Fig. 11.30. In contrast, the local mode of operation allows the IOP to share all system resources. No additional components are required, but concurrency is not possible.

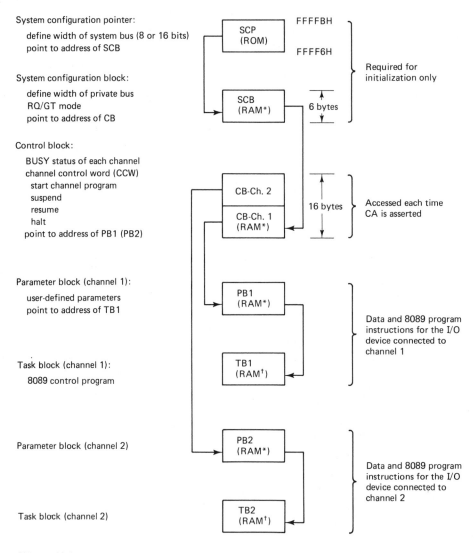

*Must reside in system memory
†May reside in system or local memory

Figure 11.31   The 8089 uses a series of five linked memory message blocks. All except the task block must be located in memory accessible to the 8089 and the host processor.

Communicating with the Host CPU

There is no way for the host CPU to directly access any of the internal registers of the IOP. Instead, a series of five linked memory blocks are used. The layout and definition of each of these is shown in Fig. 11.31. After the 8089 is reset, the very first CA pulse it receives will cause it to begin an initialization sequence. The following events occur.

1. On the falling edge of CA, the SEL input is sensed. If low, the IOP assumes a remote configuration. If high, the local mode is assumed.
2. The byte at FFFF6H in system memory is read to determine the width of the system bus. The system configuration pointer (SCP) is then read to determine the location of the system configuration block (SCB).
3. The byte at the base of the SCB is read to determine the width of the 8089's private bus. The base address of the control block (CB) is then read.
4. The BUSY byte for channel 1 is cleared. This ends the initialization process.

It is up to the host processor to initialize these three memory blocks after each system reset and before the first CA pulse is applied to the IOP. Note that because the SCB is located in RAM, it can be rewritten to allow additional IOPs to be initialized.

Following the initialization sequence, subsequent CA pulses cause the IOP to access the control block bytes for channel 1 or 2, depending on the state of SEL. The channel control word (CCW) is read first. Next, the base address of the parameter block is read. This block is user defined (except for the first two words) and is typically used to pass parameters to the IOP task program.

Figure 11.32 shows an example in which the IOP is used to control a floppy-disk controller (FDC). The parameter block holds the base address of the FDC controller, the address of a memory buffer where the data read is to be stored, and specific information about the drive, track, and sector to be accessed. The RESULT byte is returned to the CPU and indicates the success or failure of the operation.

By passing parameters in this way, the host CPU can implement many of its I/O functions via *high-level* commands: for example, **READ 1,32,4** (read drive 1, track 32,

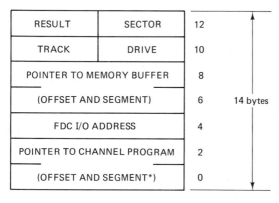

RESULT	SECTOR	12
TRACK	DRIVE	10
POINTER TO MEMORY BUFFER		8
(OFFSET AND SEGMENT)		6
FDC I/O ADDRESS		4
POINTER TO CHANNEL PROGRAM		2
(OFFSET AND SEGMENT*)		0

14 bytes

*Segment required only if task program located in system memory

Figure 11.32 Example of an 8089 parameter block designed for a floppy-disk controller.

sector 4). The IOP can then execute the command without further CPU intervention. The task program can be written so that the command repeats if soft errors occur. Again the CPU need not be concerned.

The first two words in the PB point to the task program, which may be located in system memory or the IOP's private memory. Depending on the CCW, the task program may then be started. This causes the BUSY byte to be loaded with FFH. For the floppy-disk example, the task program would program the FDC to access the proper track and sector and then transfer the data to the memory buffer whose address was passed in the PB. Upon completion of the program, the BUSY byte is cleared and (optionally) a CPU interrupt is generated.

Programming Model

As mentioned, the 8089 has two separate I/O channels. Each has its own CB, PB, and TB, as shown in Fig. 11.31. Internally, each channel also has its own identical set of programming registers. One set is shown in Fig. 11.33. Note that most of these registers have *dedicated* functions when DMA transfers are occurring. For example, GA and GB are general-purpose registers that function as the source and destination pointers during DMA. If desired, the data input during DMA can be used as an index into a 256-byte translation table. GC points to the base of this table. The indexed byte is then written to the destination address.

Register TP is the 8089's equivalent of the 8086 instruction pointer. It points to the next task program instruction to be fetched. The system CPU indicates the task to be performed by passing the task program address as the bottom two words in the PB. This is shown in Fig. 11.32.

Registers GA, GB, GC, TP, and PP are called *pointer* registers, as each is capable of storing all 20 bits of a system memory address. Each of these registers (except PP) can also be made to point into the 8089's private I/O space. This is done by setting the associated *tag* bit for that register. If high, bits 16–19 are ignored and the pointer defines one of 64K addresses in the 8089's I/O space. If the tag bit is low, all 20 bits are considered, and the pointer defines one of 1M addresses in system memory space.

When the CPU writes the CCW (in the control block) and TP address for a particular channel, it also defines register TP's tag bit. This allows the CPU to specify that the task program is located in system or 8089 I/O space. If the 8089 MOV instruction is used to load any of registers GA, GB, GC, or TP, the tag bit will automatically be set. Thus the data moved should be interpreted as an I/O address. Loading these registers via the LDP instruction—load pointer register—will clear the tag bit, thus specifying a system memory address. The IOP's instruction set is covered in more detail in the next section.

When the task program is first started, register PP is loaded with the base address of the PB. Although this register cannot be altered by a channel program, it can be used with any of the indexed, based, or offset addressing modes to access parameters passed in the PB. For example, assuming that register IX = 10H and the PB shown in Fig. 11.32, the 8089 instruction MOV BC,[PP + IX] would load register BC with the floppy-disk track and drive number to be accessed.

The remaining four registers in Fig. 11.33 are all 16 bits wide. As mentioned, IX can be used as an index with any of the pointer registers. It is not used for DMA. Register

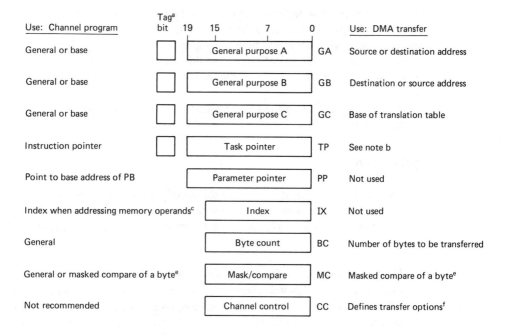

Use: Channel program	Tag[a] bit	19 15 7 0		Use: DMA transfer
General or base	☐	General purpose A	GA	Source or destination address
General or base	☐	General purpose B	GB	Destination or source address
General or base	☐	General purpose C	GC	Base of translation table
Instruction pointer	☐	Task pointer	TP	See note b
Point to base address of PB		Parameter pointer	PP	Not used
Index when addressing memory operands[c]		Index	IX	Not used
General		Byte count	BC	Number of bytes to be transferred
General or masked compare of a byte[e]		Mask/compare	MC	Masked compare of a byte[e]
Not recommended		Channel control	CC	Defines transfer options[f]

Notes:

a. GA, GB, GC, and TP may address either memory space (20-bits, tag bit = 0) or I/O space (16 bits, tag bit = 1)

b. Upon completion of the DMA transfer TP is adjusted to point to a particular address, depending on the cause of the DMA termination

c. May be optionally auto-incremented as the last step in the instruction. This allows arrays and strings to be stepped through

d. BC is decremented for each byte transferred

e. Compare a byte with the masked compare value computed as shown:

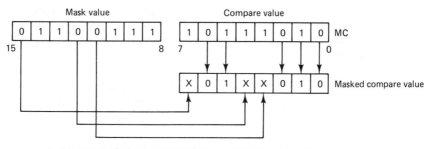

In this example the byte compares if it equals X01XX010 (X = "don't care").

f. See Fig. 11.34

Figure 11.33 Channel register set for the 8089. One set is provided for each channel. Some of the registers have a dedicated function when DMA transfers are occurring, versus a channel program.

BC is a general-purpose register that holds the number of bytes to be transferred during DMA cycles. Register MC allows the source data byte to be compared against a masked compare value. Two 8089 instructions—jump if mask compare equal (JMCE), and jump if mask compare not equal (JMCNE)—use this register. DMA cycles can also be made to terminate based on the results of this compare. This will be illustrated later in this chapter.

Finally, register CC allows several DMA options to be programmed. These will be covered in the next section.

Input/Output

The 8089 has been designed to manage the transfer of data from a source address to a destination address. The source and destination can be located in system memory space, or private 8089 I/O space. The data can be transferred under program control or via DMA.

Programmed I/O. The 8089 does not have specific I/O instructions. Setting the tag bit of a pointer register will allow that register to access locations in the 8089's I/O space. If an I/O device is located at that address, an I/O read or write effectively occurs. For example, the instruction MOVBI [GB],0A3H has the word interpretation "Move (or write) the immediate data byte 0A3H to the I/O device whose address is in register GB." Programmed I/O instructions such as this are typically used to initialize peripheral controllers prior to performing DMA cycles.

Example 11.6

Specify the 8089 instructions required to intialize an 8255 PPI for mode 0 with all ports programmed as outputs. Assume that the PPI is interfaced at ports FF00–FF03H in the 8089's I/O space.

Solution The instructions are as follows:

```
MOVI    GB,0FF03H    ;GB points to 8255 control port
MOVBI   [GB],80H     ;Program all ports as outputs
```

Note that the MOVI instruction also sets register GB's tag bit, ensuring that this register points to I/O space.

DMA. The 8089 XFER instruction puts the IOP into the DMA mode. In this mode no channel instructions can be executed. Each DMA transfer requires two separate IOP cycles:

1. Fetch the source data and store in the IOP.
2. Write the data to the destination address.

Using a 5-MHz clock with 4 T states per bus cycle, 8 T states are required for one DMA transfer. This yields a maximum transfer rate of 1.25MB/s (assuming a 16-bit data bus). Of course, most DMA transfers must be *synchronized* to the source or destination device and will not be able to operate at this rate. An exception is memory-to-memory transfers, which can be allowed to operate unsynchronized.

As discussed in Chap. 8, simultaneous DMA provides the fastest data transfer rate. Two-cycle or sequential DMA requires an extra bus cycle to store the source data in the DMA controller. However, this technique simplifies the timing as each bus cycle appears identical to a CPU read or write operation. It also allows different bus widths for the source and destination of data. Transferring data from an 8-bit I/O device to a 16-bit memory will require two I/O read cycles but only one memory write cycle. One bus cycle is saved.

Another advantage to two-cycle DMA is that the input data can be processed before it is written to the destination address. For example, the 8089 allows a *data translation* or *mask compare* operation to be done on the source data. This requires one extra bus cycle (4 T states).

Before the XFER instruction is given, the channel control (CC) register must be programmed. The bit definitions for this register are shown in Fig. 11.34. Note that any combination of source and destination can be specified via the ''F'' bits. The ''TR'' bit activates the translation function, as discussed previously.

The ''SYN'' bits allow the type of synchronization to be specified. For example, when writing data to a peripheral the I/O device will normally supply a flag indicating that it is ready for the next DMA transfer (data write). This is referred to as *destination synchronized*. On the other hand, reading data from a peripheral normally requires *source synchronization*. In this case the peripheral's flag indicates that new data can be read. Because memory access times are much faster than DMA cycle times, memory-to-memory transfers are normally unsynchronized.

Register GA or GB can be programmed as the source or destination pointer for the DMA cycles. Bit ''S'' controls this selection. If desired, the bus can be locked during the DMA transfer by setting the ''L'' bit. The ''C'' bit is not used for DMA but when set raises the channel program to highest priority. If this is not done, the CCU will give highest priority to DMA cycles on the other channel. This will cause the channel program to be suspended if DMA is required from the other channel.

There are several ways to terminate DMA cycles.

1. Terminate after one byte or word has been transferred.
2. Terminate when the EXT input is sensed high.
3. Terminate when the specified number of bytes (in register BC) have been transferred.
4. Terminate when the source data does (or does not) compare with the masked compare value.

Note that in all cases an offset of 0, 4, or 8 bytes can be added to register TP when the terminate condition occurs. In this way the task program can branch to different locations depending on the outcome of the DMA cycles. For example, if the TX bits = 11, the DMA mode will end when an EXT pulse is received, and the task program will resume at TP + 8.

Figure 11.35 flowcharts the activities that occur during one DMA transfer cycle. If source synchronization is programmed, the IOP waits for a DRQ input before reading

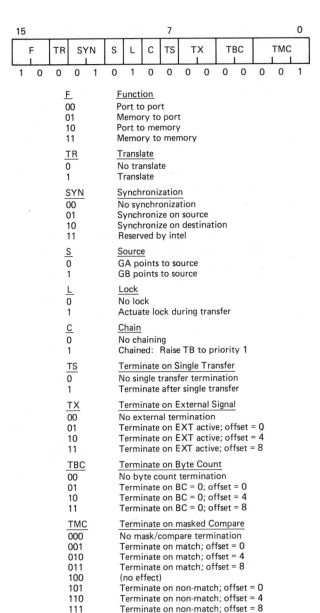

15				7					0
F	TR	SYN	S	L	C	TS	TX	TBC	TMC
1 0	0	0 1	0	1	0	0	0 0	0 0	0 0 1

F	**Function**
00	Port to port
01	Memory to port
10	Port to memory
11	Memory to memory

TR	**Translate**
0	No translate
1	Translate

SYN	**Synchronization**
00	No synchronization
01	Synchronize on source
10	Synchronize on destination
11	Reserved by intel

S	**Source**
0	GA points to source
1	GB points to source

L	**Lock**
0	No lock
1	Actuate lock during transfer

C	**Chain**
0	No chaining
1	Chained: Raise TB to priority 1

TS	**Terminate on Single Transfer**
0	No single transfer termination
1	Terminate after single transfer

TX	**Terminate on External Signal**
00	No external termination
01	Terminate on EXT active; offset = 0
10	Terminate on EXT active; offset = 4
11	Terminate on EXT active; offset = 8

TBC	**Terminate on Byte Count**
00	No byte count termination
01	Terminate on BC = 0; offset = 0
10	Terminate on BC = 0; offset = 4
11	Terminate on BC = 0; offset = 8

TMC	**Terminate on masked Compare**
000	No mask/compare termination
001	Terminate on match; offset = 0
010	Terminate on match; offset = 4
011	Terminate on match; offset = 8
100	(no effect)
101	Terminate on non-match; offset = 0
110	Terminate on non-match; offset = 4
111	Terminate on non-match; offset = 8

Figure 11.34 The 16-bit channel control (CC) register specifies how the DMA transfer is to occur. (Courtesy of Intel Corporation.)

the source byte or word. Note that, depending on the width of the bus and size of the data to be read, an additional byte may have to be fetched (and assembled as one word with the preceding byte).

Next, a data translation can occur if this option has been programmed (TR = 1). If the IOP is destination synchronized, a DRQ pulse must occur before the data is written.

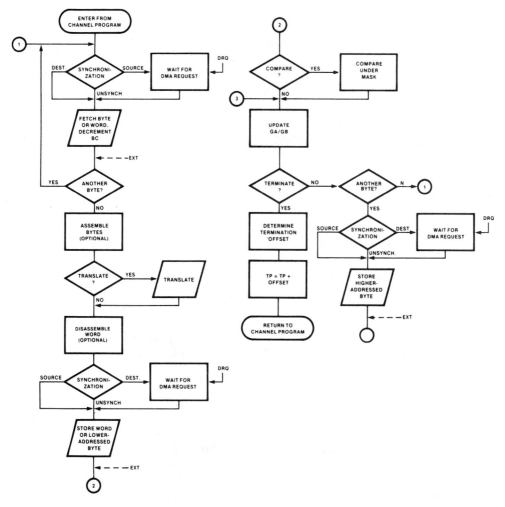

Figure 11.35 8089 DMA transfer flowchart. (Courtesy of Intel Corporation.)

Note that only the low-order byte of a 16-bit word will be written if the destination bus width is 8 bits. If the masked compare option has been selected, the low-order byte is compared with the compare value before the source and destination registers (GA and GB) are adjusted. Note that the register(s) pointing to memory will be incremented, but the register pointing to I/O space will be held constant.

The IOP then determines if the terminate condition has been met. If not, the cycle repeats and the next data element is fetched. Note that for 8-bit destination bus widths, the high-order byte of the source word (if present) will be written before the new cycle begins. When the terminate condition is finally met, the offset (if any) is added to TP and the channel program resumes.

Instruction Set

Although designed as a coprocessor for the 8086 family, the 8089 executes an entirely different set of instructions from the 8086. Each consists of at least two bytes. Some instructions may require as many as five bytes to describe memory addresses and offsets. Intel provides an 8089 IOP software support package that includes ASM-89, a macro assembler, and RBF-89, a symbolic software debugger.

Data transfer instructions. Table 11.12 lists the three data transfer instructions. There are actually four forms of the MOV instruction:

MOV: move word

MOVB: move byte

MOVI: move immediate word

MOVBI: move immediate byte

All forms set the tag bit when the destination is a pointer register. This means that the pointer will be accessing 8089 I/O space.

The 8089 has no stack, so the MOVP instruction is used to save and restore the pointer registers (and their tag bits) in memory (e.g., MOVP TP,[GC + IX]). This instruction allows a pointer to be saved prior to DMA cycles and then recovered when the DMA has ended. This is necessary because GA, GB, and GC may be used during the DMA transfer.

The LPD instruction is used to load one of the four pointer registers with a 20-bit memory address. The associated tag bit will be reset causing the pointer to access system memory space.

Arithmetic, logical, and bit manipulation instructions. These instructions are shown in Table 11.13 and include the typical instructions also available with the 8086. The AND, ADD, and OR instructions have the four forms mentioned previously for the MOV instruction. The INC, DEC, and NOT instructions operate on byte or word operands only—not immediate data.

The NOT instruction is unique in that the inverted register or memory data source

---

TABLE 11.12 8089 DATA TRANSFER INSTRUCTIONS

MOV *dest,source*	Transfer a byte or word from: Memory to memory Memory to a register Register to memory Tag bit = 1
MOVP *dest,source*	Transfer physical address between pointer register and memory
LPD *dest,source*	Load pointer register with double word. Tag bit = 0

TABLE 11.13 8089 ARITHMETIC, LOGICAL, AND BIT MANIPULATION INSTRUCTIONS

ADD *dest,source*	Add register to memory, memory to register, or memory to memory
INC *dest*	Add 1 to the contents of a register or memory
DEC *dest*	Subtract 1 from the contents of a register or memory
AND *dest,source*	AND register with memory, memory with a register, or memory with memory
OR *dest,source*	OR register with memory, memory with a register, with memory to memory
NOT *dest*	Invert all bits of a register or memory
NOT *dest,source*	Invert all bits of the memory or register source; store the result in the destination register or memory
SETB *dest,bit-select*	Set selected bit of the destination memory byte; for example, if bit-select = 0, the low-order bit will be set; if bit-select = 7, the high-order bit will be set
CLR *dest,bit-select*	Clear selected bit of the destination memory byte

can be written to a destination register or memory location. The SETB and CLR instructions are handy for setting one bit in an 8-bit device register without changing any of the others.

Example 11.7

Write the 8089 instructions to set bit 3 of the output port at I/O address 0040H.

Solution Only two instructions are required:

```
MOVI   GA,0040H      ;GA points to the port
SETB   [GA],3        ;Set bit 3
```

Addressing modes. Table 11.14 provides several examples of the six 8089 addressing modes. These are:

1. *Register*. The data is obtained in an IOP register.
2. *Immediate*. The data is obtained as part of the instruction.
3. *Based*. The data is obtained from the memory location whose address is stored in the pointer register.
4. *Offset*. The data is obtained from the memory location whose address is stored in the pointer register plus an 8-bit unsigned offset.
5. *Indexed*. The data is obtained from the memory location whose address is the sum of a pointer register plus the 16-bit unsigned contents of the IX register.
6. *Indexed with autoincrement*. Same as indexed except that IX is incremented automatically after the data has been accessed.

As shown in Table 11.14, any instruction may use a combination of these addressing modes.

TABLE 11.14 8089 ADDRESSING MODES

Instruction		Addressing mode	Comment
ANDI	GA,8000H	Register, immediate	Clear bits 0–14 of GA
AND	GA,[GB]	Register, memory (based)	GA ← GA AND [GB]
ANDBI	[GA],80H	Memory(based), immediate	Clear bits 0–6 of [GA]
ANDB	GA,[GB].5	Register, memory (offset)	GA ← GA AND [GB + 5]
AND	[GA + IX],BC	Memory (indexed), register	[GA + IX] ← [GA + IX] AND BC
ANDI	[GA + IX +], 8000H	Memory (indexed autoincrement), immediate	Clear bits 0–14 of [GA + IX] IX ← IX + 2[a]
ANDB	[GA].5,[GB]	Memory (offset), memory (based)	[GA + 5] ← [GA + 5] AND [GB]

[a]Increment by 1 for byte operands.

Program transfer instructions. Table 11.15 lists the instructions in this group. The CALL instruction is unique because there is no stack on which to save the return address. Instead, a *TPsave* address must be specified. A return is implemented by MOVing the contents of TPsave back to register TP.

The remaining instructions are the unconditional and conditional jumps. Because the 8089 has no flags, the jumps test the *contents* of the source operand and transfer control to the target address if the test is true. Individual bits can be tested with the JMCE/JMCNE and JBT/JNBT instructions. The former use the MC register to mask particular bits of the compare value. This is shown in note e of Fig. 11.33. The latter instructions allow a particular bit to be tested. Note that both groups combine the bit test and jump in one instruction (unlike the 8086).

TABLE 11.15 8089 PROGRAM TRANSFER INSTRUCTIONS[a]

CALL *TPsave,target*	Transfer control to the subroutine at the target address; save TP and its tag bit in the TPsave operand—a physical address variable at an even address
JMP *target*	Unconditional transfer to target location
JZ *source,target*	Jump to target if the source operand is 0; the JZB form is used to test byte values
JNZ *source,target*	Jump to target if the source operand is not 0; the JNZB form is used to test byte values
JMCE *source,target*	Jump to target if the masked compare of the source and register MC are equal (see Fig. 11.33, note e)
JMCNE *source,target*	Jump to target if the masked compare of the source and register MC are not equal
JBT *source,bit-select,target*	Jump to target if the specified source bit is a 1; for example, if the bit-select is 7, the jump is taken if bit 7 of the source is a 1
JNBT *source,bit-select, target*	Jump to target if the specified source bit is a 0

[a]The mnemonic shown for all instructions in this group is the "short" form. The *target* address is computed using a 2's-complement 8-bit displacement, allowing a transfer to a location in the range −128 through +127 bytes from the end of the transfer instruction. If the instruction is prefaced with the letter "L," the long form is indicated, which uses a 2's-complement 16-bit displacement. The target address can be located within the range −32,768 to +32,767 bytes from the end of the transfer instruction.

TABLE 11.16 8089 PROCESSOR CONTROL INSTRUCTIONS

TSL *dest,set-value,target*	Test and set $\overline{\text{LOCK}}$; activate $\overline{\text{LOCK}}$ and test destination for 0; if not 0, jump to target, else store the set-value in the destination, deactivate $\overline{\text{LOCK}}$, and execute the next instruction in sequence
WID *source-width, dest-width*	Set logical bus widths; note that the logical bus width cannot exceed its physical width
XFER	Enter DMA transfer mode following the next instruction
SINTR	Activate channel's SINTR line if enabled
NOP	No operation
HLT	Halt; the BUSY byte is cleared

Example 11.8

Write an 8089 program to poll bit 7 of input port 0040H, waiting for this bit to be low.

Solution Again only two instructions are required.

```
        MOVI  GA,0040H       ;GA points to the input port
POLL:   JBT   [GA],7,POLL    ;Jump to self if bit 7 is high
```

Processor control instructions. These instructions are shown in Table 11.16. They control hardware functions of the IOP. The TSL instruction activates the $\overline{\text{LOCK}}$ output. Specifying the target address as itself, this instruction will wait until the system resource is ready (destination byte = 0) before proceeding with the task program.

The WID instruction allows the logical bus width to be specified as different from the physical bus width. This would allow an 8-bit peripheral to be interfaced to a 16-bit I/O bus.

IOP Design Example

In a multiple-CPU system it is common to share one printer among the several CPUs. A design for implementing such a scheme is shown in Fig. 11.36. The IOP is configured in the remote mode with its own private data and address buses. It uses an 8288 bus controller to generate the $\overline{\text{IOR}}$ and $\overline{\text{IOW}}$ control signals and an 8284A to generate the clock signal.

The parallel printer is driven by an 8255 PPI programmed for mode 1—strobed I/O. As a byte is written to port A of the PPI, its $\overline{\text{OBFA}}$ output will go low. This strobes the printer until $\overline{\text{ACKA}}$ is received, acknowledging the data byte. The PPI then drives its INTRA output high. This signal is used to request that another byte be written to the PPI by the IOP (destination synchronized DMA). Refer to Fig. 9.12 for a review of 8255 mode 1 output port timing.

When one of the system CPUs requires use of the printer, it checks the BUSY byte in channel 1's control block located in system memory. If this byte is low, the starting address of the task program, location of the print buffer, and the desired I/O space address for the print buffer are written to channel 1's parameter block. CA is then asserted with the SEL input high.

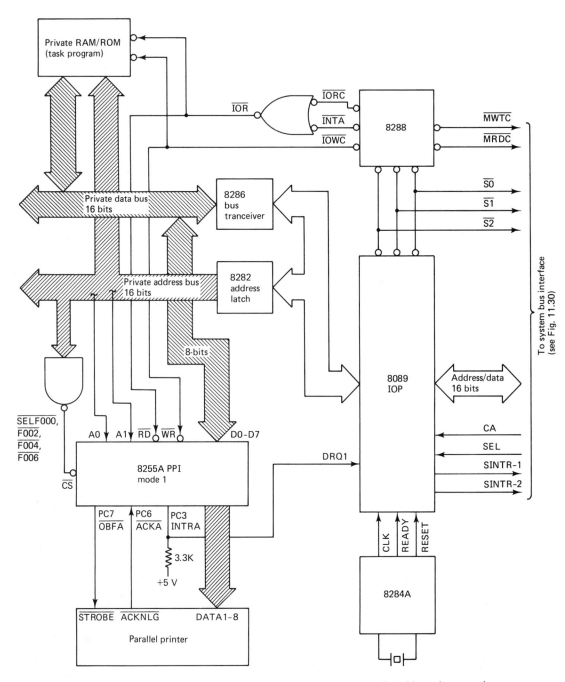

Figure 11.36 In this design the 8089 is configured for the remote mode and is used to control a parallel printer driven by an 8255.

The task program has two parts. To allow concurrency, it begins by transferring the print buffer to private IOP RAM. This can be done using a memory-to-memory unsynchronized DMA transfer run at the full bandwidth of the system (1.25MB/s). Analysis and Design Question 11.9 investigates this program. The second part of the program initializes the PPI, and then transfers data, byte by byte, to the 8255 using destination-synchronized DMA.

Figure 11.37 is a listing for this part of the program. It begins at address START by calling PPI_MODE1, a subroutine to initialize the PPI for mode 1 operation. Note that TP is saved in the double word TPSAVE. The subroutine writes the mode 1 control word and then uses the bit set/reset mode of the PPI to enable the INTRA output. The subroutine "returns" by recovering TP from the TPSAVE variable.

The program then continues by initializing GA as the source pointer and GB as the destination pointer. In this example we are assuming that the data to be printed is a text file terminated with the character *control Z* (ASCII 1AH). Register MC is thus loaded to look for the pattern X0011010. The channel control word is written such that the DMA cycles will terminate when a match occurs. The XFER instruction is given next, enabling the DMA to begin following the next instruction. This is WID 16,8, which matches the logical bus widths to the physical source and destination bus widths.

The IOP now enters the DMA mode transferring data to the PPI until a control Z character is received. Because the terminate condition specifies 0 offset, the HLT instruction will then be executed clearing the BUSY byte and idling the channel.

SELF-REVIEW 11.3 *(answers on page 596)*

11.3.1. For concurrent operation with the host CPU the 8089 must be configured in the _____ mode.

11.3.2. Explain how the 8089 generates the control bus signals $\overline{\text{IOR}}$, $\overline{\text{IOW}}$, $\overline{\text{MEMR}}$, and $\overline{\text{MEMW}}$ when operated in the local and remote modes.

11.3.3. Why is the IOP's private address bus limited to 16 bits?

11.3.4. For concurrent operation with the host CPU the 8089 must locate its SCP, SCB, CB, PB, and TB in private I/O space. (True/False)

11.3.5. To reset the IOP the CPU must apply a pulse to the CA input. (True/False)

11.3.6. Explain how the IOP determines the address of its task program. Which internal register stores this address?

11.3.7. List all possible bytes that will "compare" if IOP register MC = 773AH.

11.3.8. _____ synchronized DMA transfers should be used when transferring a block of memory to a floppy-disk controller.

11.3.9. For what condition will the 8089 instruction below transfer control to BEGIN?

JNBT [GC].5,4,BEGIN

11.3.10. Which addressing modes are used by the instruction in question 11.3.9?

11.3.11. After the IOP instruction MOVI GB,8000H register GB points to _____ space.

```
;Function:     8089 program to drive the parallel
;              printer shown in Fig. 12.36.

;Inputs:       Data is fetched from a print buffer
;              in 8089 I/O space.

;Ouputs:       Using destination synchronized DMA, each
;              byte is written to port A of the PPI.

;Calls:        PPI_MODE1 - procedure to initialize
;              the PPI for mode 1 operation.


;Program equates

CTRL_PORT      EQU    0F006H             ;8255A control port
DATA_PORT      EQU    0F000H             ;8255A port A
MODE1          EQU    0A0H               ;1010XXXX mode 1 for port A
INTEA          EQU    0DH                ;Bit set for PC6
END_OF_TXT     EQU    7F1AH              ;Mask value = 7FH
                                         ;Compare value = Ctrl Z
BUFFER         EQU    NNNN               ;Base of print buffer retrieved
                                         ;from parameter block


IOP_PRINT      SEGMENT

TPSAVE         DD     ?                  ;Storage for TP


PPI_MODE1      PROC
               MOVI   GA,CTRL_PORT       ;GA points to control port
               MOVI   [GA],MODE1         ;Mode 1 control word
               MOVI   [GA],INTEA         ;Enable 8255A INTR output
               MOVP   TP,[GB]            ;Recover TP, that is, return
PPI_MODE1      ENDP



START:         CALL   TPSAVE,PPI_MODE1   ;Init PPI for mode 1
               MOVI   GA,BUFFER          ;Init source pointer
               MOVI   GB,DATA_PORT       ;Init dest pointer
               MOVBI  MC,END_OF_TXT      ;Init mask/compare
               MOVI   CC,1001H           ;Memory to port F=00
                                         ;No translate TR=0
                                         ;Sync on dest SYN=10
                                         ;GA source S=0
                                         ;No lock L=0
                                         ;No chaining C=0
                                         ;No single xfer terminate TS=0
                                         ;No EXT terminate TX=00
                                         ;No byte count terminate TBC=00
                                         ;Terminate on match no offset
                                         ;    TMC=001
               XFER                      ;Enable xfer on next instruction
               WID    16,8               ;16-bit source bus
                                         ;8-bit dest bus
               HLT                       ;Reset BUSY byte and quit
IOP_PRINT      ENDS
               END    START
```

Figure 11.37 8089 program to print the contents of a (private) memory buffer. This routine assumes
that the data to be printed has been transferred to private memory beginning at location BUFFER.

CHAPTER 11 SELF-TEST

1. Write the instructions required to relocate the 80186 PCB to begin at I/O port 8000H. Select master interrupt mode and no escape trap.

2. When should the 80186 be operated in the queue status mode? How is this done?

3. Interpret the contents of register UMCS in the 80186 PCB if it stores the word E039H.

4. 80186 DMA requests may be external via the _____ inputs or internal via the _____ output or the _____ itself.

5. To program an 8 MHz 80186 timer 0 for a free-running 50% duty cycle 5 kHz square wave, control bit P = _____, ALT = _____, CONT = _____, maximum count register A = _____, and maximum count register B = _____.

6. 80186 internal DMA cycles will be halted if a _____ interrupt occurs.

7. Write the instructions necessary to mask all 80186 interrupts with a priority level less than 2. Assume the default PCB addresses.

8. Under what conditions will the 8087 request control of the buses to perform DMA cycles?

9. How can the host processor tell that the 8087 NEU is currently executing an instruction?

10. Express 47.3125 as an 8087 short real number.

11. The 8087 instruction _____ will divide ST(0) by ST(6) storing the result in ST(0).

12. To save all of the registers within the 8087, the _____ instruction should be given.

13. The 8087 has the capability of calculating the sine of an angle in one instruction. (True/False)

14. List the advantages and disadvantages of operating the 8089 IOP in the local and remote modes.

15. The host CPU can check the busy status of one IOP channel by testing the _____ byte located in that channel's _____ _____.

16. Of the five linked IOP message blocks, which can be located in system memory or private I/O space?

17. When their _____ bits are set, the IOP pointer registers will access _____ space.

18. Assume that the 8089 IOP is used to transfer one sector of data from system memory to a floppy-disk controller. The DMA transfer should terminate when register BC = 0 with no offset. Assume register GA holds the starting memory address. Specify the channel control word required assuming no lock, chaining, or translation.

19. Write the 8089 instruction sequence required to load register GB with the FDC port address passed in the parameter block shown in Fig. 11.32.

20. Calculate the maximum data transfer rate for the 8089 when performing memory-to-port transfers assuming an 8-bit memory and I/O bus, and a 5 MHz clock. Repeat assuming a 16-bit memory bus but an 8-bit I/O bus.

ANALYSIS AND DESIGN QUESTIONS

11.1. Refer to Fig. 11.12 and verify that the destination register is properly loaded if the DISK_BUFFER begins at physical address 09D3:0100H.

11.2. Write an 8086/80186 program to generate a 1-kHz 50% duty cycle square wave at the T1 output pin of the 80186.

11.3. The 80186 block move instructions require 8 T states per byte or word transferred plus an initial 8 T states to execute. Calculate the maximum data transfer rate assuming an 8-MHz system clock signal. Is this rate fast enough to keep up with a 5MB/s Winchester disk drive? Can you think of any problems with this design? *Hint:* Consider synchronization between the CPU and disk controller.

11.4. Write the 80186 initialization code necessary to set up the address maps shown in Fig. 11.38. Assume that the PCB is left in its default location.

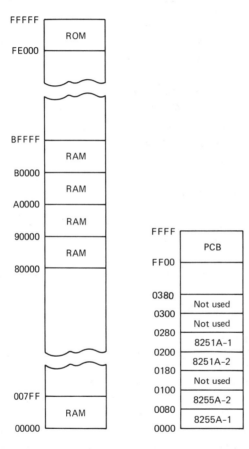

Figure 11.38 Memory map for Analysis and Design Question 11.4.

11.5. What is the purpose of the following sequence of 8086/8087 instructions?

```
FNSTCW    C_WORD
AND       C_WORD,0080H
FLDCW
```

11.6. What is the function of the following 8087 procedure? Answer this by providing a comment for each program line. *Hint:* Analyze the contents of the data stack after each instruction.

```
FLD     ANGLE
FPTAN
FLD     ST(0)
FMUL    ST(0)
FLD     ST(2)
FMUL    ST(0)
FADD
FSQRT
FLD     ST(2)
FLD     ST(1)
FDIV
FSTP    COSINE
```

11.7. Write an 8089 program that monitors bit 5 of port A002H. With each falling edge of this bit, have your program increment a count in register BC and output the result to port A002H.

11.8. Under what conditions will the 8089 program below transfer control to address FIX_UP?

```
START:   MOVI    MC,0FE3CH
         MOVI    GB,8000H
POLL:    JMCNE   [GB],POLL
FIX_UP:                         ;Program continues
```

11.9. Write an 8089 program to transfer a print buffer from system memory to private I/O space. Assume that the CPU sets up a parameter block for the program as follows.

NUMB_BYTES	10
DEST_ADDR	8
	6
SOURCE_ADDR	4
Pointer to	2
Channel Program	0

SELF REVIEW ANSWERS

11.1.1 True

11.2.1 M/$\overline{\text{IO}}$

11.1.3 82188, HOLD/HLDA

11.1.4 FFA0H, FFA8H

11.1.5 $\overline{\text{UCS}}$, FE38H

11.1.6 0580-05FFH

11.1.7 memory to I/O (word transfers), destination synchronized

11.1.8 0FA0H (4000 × 500 ns)

11.1.9 0003H, 3CH

11.1.10 timer 2

11.1.11 CX = [SI] × −5

11.2.1 control, numeric execution

11.2.2 escape

11.2.3 monitor pin 34 ($\overline{\text{BHE}}$ − 16 bit CPU; $\overline{\text{SS0}}$ − 8 bit CPU)

11.2.4 True

11.2.5 FSAVE (94 bytes are written)

11.2.6 FWAIT

11.2.7 True (all data must pass through memory)

11.2.8 temporary real

11.2.9 exception masks, control register

11.2.10 ST2 ← ST2 + ST3

11.3.1 remote

11.3.2 it outputs $\overline{\text{S0-S2}}$ which are decoded by the 8288 bus controller to generate the control bus signals

11.3.3 the 8288 uses $\overline{\text{PDEN}}$ (which is only active for I/O bus cycles) to enable the local bus

11.3.4 False (only the TB need be in private I/O space)

11.3.5. False (the 8089 is reset by pulsing its RESET pin)

11.3.6. base word of the PB points to the TB base address and register TP serves as the IOP instruction pointer

11.3.7. X011X010

11.3.8. destination

11.3.9. if bit 4 of [GC + 5] is a 0

11.3.10. memory (offset), immediate

11.3.11. I/O

ANSWERS TO SELECTED ANALYSIS AND DESIGN QUESTIONS

Chapter 1

1.1 671308

1.3 00000000 − 10110110 = 01001010
= 4AH = > −74

1.5 Two bus cycles are required: (1) memory read (op-code and operand), (2) I/O read

1.7 The logic of a program is difficult to decipher from the object code but much easier from the source code.

Chapter 2

2.1 If the EU executes instructions faster than the BIU can fetch them the queue will be emptied. This will force the EU to wait for the next instruction(s) to be fetched increasing the effective execution time.

2.3 OF = 0; SF = 1; ZF = 0; AF = undefined; PF = 0; CF = 0

2.5 BP = > stack segment: 5D270H + 1080H + 007FH + 30H = 5E39F

2.7 The data bytes from the string are repeatedly stored in AL overwriting each other before they can be processed.

2.9 Port 0 receives a two-digit BCD count sequence—00 through 99—repeating indefinitely.

2.11 SCASB should be CMPSB; REPNE should be REPE

Chapter 3

3.2 MOV AL,12H   ;segments a,c,d,f, and g on
OUT PORT,AL   ;5 appears in display

3.4

```
START:  MOV   DX,OFFFAH   ;OUTPUT PORT ADDRESS
        MOV   AL,0        ;ALARM BIT RESET
        OUT   DX,AL       ;ALARM OFF
READ:   MOV   DX,OFFF8H   ;INPUT PORT ADDRESS
        IN    AL,DX       ;READ SENSORS
        AND   AL,03H      ;MASK BITS 2-7
        JZ    ALARM       ;TEMP AND PRESSURE TOO LOW FOR PROCESS A?
        CMP   AL,3        ;NO—TEST FOR TOO HIGH
        JZ    ALARM       ;
        IN    AL,DX       ;READ SENSORS AGAIN
        AND   AL,0C0H     ;MASK BITS 0-5
        JZ    ALARM       ;TEMP AND PRESSURE TOO LOW FOR PROCESS B?
        CMP   AL,0C0H     ;NO—TEST FOR TOO HIGH
        JZ    ALARM       ;
        JMP   START       ;NO PROBLEMS—TURN ALARM OFF
ALARM:  MOV   DX,OFFFAH   ;OUTPUT PORT ADDRESS
        MOV   AL,04H      ;ALARM BIT SET
        OUT   DX,AL       ;ALARM ON
        JMP   READ        ;SAMPLE INPUTS AGAIN
```

Chapter 4

4.2 $[4 + ([2 + 4 + (1114095 - 12) + 2 + 17] \times 65535) - 12] \times 200$ ns
$= 73{,}013{,}067{,}000$ (T states) $\times 200$ ns $= 14{,}602.6$ sec $= 4$ hrs 3 min 23 sec

4.6

START	STOP	LENGTH	NAME
00000	0002A	002B	CODE
0002C	000AB	0080	STACK

4.7 09E30 + 003E (first byte of seven segment code table) = 09E6E = >
DS = 09E6. The code for digit 0 is thus
stored at DS:000E.

Chapter 5

5.2

Control Panel ---------> Switches	Read control panel settings, activate appropriate washer control signals based on sensor inputs. Display current state of machine in LED displays.	---> Control Signals: COLD_IN, HOT_IN DRAIN, SPEED_BYTE
Sensors --------->		---> LED Display (front panel)

5.4 (1) Form separate hardware and software design teams

(2) Begin building hardware modules and test

(3) Begin writing software modules and test

(4) Integrate software and hardware using in-circuit emulation where necessary

(5) Repeat steps 2–4 until all hardware and software completed and debugged

(6) Move software to ROM in prototype

(7) Provide documentation to allow production of product

Chapter 6

6.1 Ensures that the data bus buffers will be disabled avoiding contention with the active address lines.

6.3
$$R < \frac{5V - 2.7V}{3 \times 20uA + 20uA} = 28.8K\Omega$$

$$R > \frac{5V - 0.4V}{12mA} = 383\Omega$$

6.5 The resident 8288 drives the resident buses for nonsystem addresses (decoder output = 0V). For system addresses the 8289 enables the system 8288 (via AEN) depending on its priority.

6.7 Make the following changes to Fig. 6.23: (1) $\overline{BHE}$/S7 becomes $\overline{SS0}$ (and need not be latched); (2) IC2 becomes a 74LS244 buffer (no latching required).

Chapter 7

7.2 This ensures that the data bus transceivers will not be driving the address/data lines during the T1 state (when these lines are driven by the CPU).

7.4 Because the Dout pin does not go into a high impedance state until twz nanoseconds after WE goes low, bus contention may occur between the buffer driving the Din pin (now shorted to the Dout pin) and Dout.

7.5 10 inputs and 4 outputs are required:
$\overline{RAMO} = \overline{A19}\ \overline{A18}\ \overline{A17}\ \overline{A16}$; RAM1 $= \overline{A19}\ \overline{A18}\ \overline{A17}$ A16; $\overline{RAMSEL} =$ A19 $\overline{A18}$ A17 $\overline{A16}\ \overline{A15}\ \overline{A14}$;

$\overline{BRAMSEL} =$ A19 A18 A17 A16 A15 A14 A13 A12 A11 A10

7.9 Each time the STEP switch is pushed RDY2 is driven high and one bus cycle is executed. The rising edge of ALE sets the flip-flop forcing the CPU into a wait until the next STEP pulse.

7.13 (* ############################ *)

type
   String1 = string[8];

Function Bin(n: real): String1;

(* ############################ *)

(* This function returns an 8-bit binary number—in string form—*)

(* equal to the binary value of the decimal number n.   *)

```
var
    power: integer;
    result: string1;
    temp: real;

Begin
    power: = 7;
    result: = '';
    Repeat
      temp: = Round(Exp(power*Ln(2)));
      If n - temp >= 0 then
        Begin
          result: = result + '1';
          n: = n - temp;
          power: = power - 1;
        End
      Else
        Begin
          result: = result + '0';
          power: = power - 1
        End;
      Until power = -1;
      bin: = result;
End;
```

Chapter 8

8.2
```
            MOV   AX,0E000H
            MOV   DS,AX
AGAIN:  MOV   AL,[0056H]
            JMP   AGAIN
```

8.4 (1) $\overline{IORB}$ should be $\overline{IOWB}$; (2) DB0-DB7 should be DB8-DB15; (3) $\overline{OE}$ should be grounded.

8.7 Note: procedure assumes ES:D1 initialized to first location in a storage buffer.

```
BIT_0           PROC    NEAR
                IN      AL,D_PORT        ;Input data
                TEST    AL,01H           ;Check bit 0
BIT_0           ENDP

;Main program begins here

SERIAL_RCVR     PROC    NEAR
WAIT_HIGH:      CALL    BIT_0            ;Check bit 0
                JZ      WAIT_HIGH        ;Wait until high
WAIT_LOW:       CALL    BIT_0            ;Check bit 0
                JNZ     WAIT_LOW         ;Wait for start bit
                MOV     BX,HALF_DELAY    ;Delay parameter
                PUSH    BX               ;Expected on stack
                CALL    DELAY            ;Sample in middle of start bit
```

```
                    CALL     BIT_0              ;Make sure bit 0 is still low
                    JNZ      WAIT_HIGH          ;Else false start bit
                    MOV      CX,8               ;8 data bits per character
    FORM_BYTE:      MOV      BX,FULL_DELAY      ;Sample in middle of each data bit
                    PUSH     BX                 ;
                    CALL     DELAY              ;
                    IN       AL,D_PORT          ;Get next data bit
                    RDR      AL,1               ;Prepare for next bit
                    LOOP     FORM_BYTE          ;Do for all 8 bits
                    MOV      BX,FULL_DELAY      ;Wait one more bit time
                    PUSH     BX                 ;
                    CALL     DELAY              ;
                    CALL     BIT_0              ;Then check for stop bit
                    JZ       FRAMING_ERROR      ;Framing error?
                    STOSB                       ;No—so save byte
    SERIAL_RCVR     ENDP
```

8.10 No—word read and write bus cycles require the full 16-bit data bus.

Chapter 9

9.3
```
    MOV   AX,E000H       ;PPI is located in E000 data segment
    MOV   DS,AX          ;Load DS
    MOV   AL,92H         ;Ports A and B inputs, C is an output
    MOV   [0003H],AL     ;Write to control register at E000:0003H
```

9.5
```
                        TITLE SERIAL RECEIVER
```

;Function:	Store incoming serial data in a print buffer specified in the device control block below.
;Inputs:	Serial data from the USART data port shown in Fig. 9.20.
;Outputs:	Characters stored in PRINT_BUF
;Calls:	Nothing
;Destroys:	AX, DS, DI, flags

```
    DEV_CTRL_BL  SEGMENT  BYTE
    PRINT_BUF    DD       ?              ;Put address of buffer here
    DEV_CTRL_BL  ENDS

    LAST_BYTE    EQU      "$"
    DATA_PORT    EQU      70H
    CTRL_PORT    EQU      71H
    RXRDY        EQU      00000010B
    ERROR        EQU      00111000B
    BREAK_COND   EQU      00011101B

    CODE         SEGMENT  BYTE
                 ASSUME   CS:CODE,DS:DEV_CTRL_BL
```

SERIAL_RCVR	PROC	NEAR	
	MOV	AX,DEV_CTRL_BL	;Point DS at DEV_CTRL_BL
	MOV	DS,AX	
	LES	DI,PRINT_BUF	;Fetch buffer address to ES:DI
	MOV	DS,AX	
	LES	DI,PRINT_BUF	;Fetch buffer address to ES:DI
	CLD		;Auto increment
POLL:	IN	AL,CTRL_PORT	;Get status
	TEST	AL,ERROR	;FE, PE, or OE?
	JE	BREAK	;Send break code
	TEST	AL,RXRDY	;Character received?
	JZ	POLL	;No—then wait
	CMP	AL,LAST_BYTE	;End of data?
	JE	QUIT	;Then quit
	STOSB		;Store the byte in the print buffer
	JMP	POLL	;Next character
BREAK:	MOV	AL,BREAK_COND	;Break character and reset error flags
	OUT	CTRL_PORT,AL	;Command instruction
	JMP	POLL	;Resume polling

9.7 Connect the 8255 as follows: PA0-PA3 to D0-D3 of the MSM5832; PC4-PC7 to A0-A3 of the MSM5832; PC4 to HOLD; PC5 TO READ; PC6 to WRITE; PC7 and port B are not used.

```
10  CLS: DIM TIME(13)
20  A=940: B=941: C=942: CP=943          '8255 port addresses
30  OUT CP,128                            'Program all ports as outputs
40  INPUT "Enter the time as: (0832) ";T  'Get the current time as 4 digits
50  FOR J=1 TO 4                          'Set up to store 4 digits
60  T1=INT(T/10)                          'Get 1 digit from T
65  TIME(J+1)=T-10*T1: T=T1               'Write to TIME array TIME(2) - TIME(5)
70  NEXT J                                'Do for all 4 digits
80  FOR J=2 TO 5                          'Set up to write 4 digits to MSM5832
90  OUT C,16: OUT C,16+J                  'Make HOLD high then apply register address
100 OUT A,TIME(J): OUT C,16+J+64:         'Output 1 time digit then take HOLD and
    OUT C,0                                      WRITE high
110 NEXT J                                'Repeat for all 4 time digits
120 PRINT: PRINT "Done"                   'Job done
```

Chapter 10

10.1 The microcomputer and VDT are both wired as DTEs. A null modem cable is required with pins 2 and 3 crossed and pins 8 and 20 crossed.

10.4   TITLE SERIAL TRANSMITTER WITH X-ON/X-OFF PROTOCOL

```
;Function:  Output characters to a serial printer with 128 byte buffer
;Inputs:    BUSY signal on RTS, X-ON/X-OFF at serial input (see 10.3 solution)
;           CX holds number of bytes to transmit
;           DS:SI points to first byte to transmit
;Outputs:   Characters to be printed at serial output pin
;Calls:     Nothing
;Destroys:  AL, SI, CX, flags

PROB10.4 PROC    NEAR
         CLD                         ;Auto increment
POLL:    IN      AL,CTRL_PORT        ;Get RXRDY, TXRDY, and DSR status
         TEST    AL,02H              ;Has printer sent a character?
         JNZ     X_OFF               ;Yes—so check for X-OFF
         TEST    AL,80H              ;Is printer BUSY?
         JZ      POLL                ;Yes—so wait
         TEST    AL, 01H             ;Ready to xmit next byte?
         JZ      POLL                ;No—so wait
         LODSB                       ;Fetch byte
         OUT     DATA_PORT,AL        ;Output to USART
         LOOP    POLL                ;Repeat until CX=0
         JMP     EXIT                ;Then return
X_OFF:   IN      AL,DATA_PORT        ;Read the character
         CMP     AL,13H              ;Is it X-OFF?
         JNE     POLL                ;No—so return to main polling loop
POLL1:   IN      AL,CTRL_PORT        ;Get RXRDY status
         TEST    AL,02H              ;Received character?
         JZ      POLL1               ;Wait for next charcter
         IN      AL,DATA_PORT        ;Read character
         CMP     AL,11H              ;Is it X-ON?
         JNE     POLL1               ;No—so continue waiting
         JMP     POLL                ;Yes—back to main polling loop
EXIT:    RET
PROB10.4 ENDP
```

10.5   100 OPEN #4: ''GPIB(PR1=4):''
    110 PSPLY=4
    120 OPEN #5: ''GPIB(PR1=5):''
    130 DMM1=5
    140 OPEN #9: ''GPIB(PR1=9):''
    150 DMM2=9
    160 PRINT PSPLY: ''vpos 18;ipos .05''

    200 SAMPLE: INPUT prompt ''send'' DMM1:v1
    210 INPUT prompt ''send'' DMM2:v2
    220 IF v1-v2>4.5 THEN GOTO 240
    230 GOTO SAMPLE
    240 PRINT PSPLY: ''vpos 9''
    250 GOTO SAMPLE

10.7 $M(X) = X^{11} + X^{10} + 1; Q(X) = X^{11} + 1; R(X) = X^{15} + X^{13} + X^{11} + X^2 + 1 => A015H$

Chapter 11

11.3 Transfer time $= 8T + n * 8T$ where n is the number of bytes or words to be transferred. The maximum transfer rate becomes 8 T states per word or 4 T states per byte $= 2$ MB/s. This is much faster than the 5M-bps (625,000 bytes/s) rate of the Winchester disk drive. Because of this, the Winchester will have to supply a BUSY signal to synchronize the DMA transfers.

11.5 Bit 7 of the NDP control register is set masking all NDP interrupts.

11.7

```
             MOV1  GA,0A002H          ;GA points to I/O port address
             MOV1  BC,0000            ;Init count to 0
WAIT_HIGH:   JNBT  [GA],5,WAIT_HIGH   ;Wait for bit 5 to go high
WAIT_LOW:    JBT   [GA],5,WAIT_LOW    ;Wait for bit 5 to go low
             INC   BC                 ;Found a falling edge—add 1 to counter
             MOV   [GA],BC            ;Output the count to the I/O port
             JMP   WAIT_HIGH          ;Repeat indefinitely
```

11.8 If [GB] $= 3$CH or 3DH

Appendix A

USING THE BINARY AND HEXADECIMAL NUMBER SYSTEMS

Digital computers are designed with logic circuits that operate in an ''on'' state or an ''off'' state only. Using TTL (transistor-transistor-logic) gates, a logic 1 is an output voltage more positive than $+2.4V$ and a logic 0 a voltage less than $+0.4V$. This type of logic assignment in which the most positive output voltage is considered a logic 1 is referred to as positive logic.

When several digital outputs are grouped together a binary ''word'' is formed. Each digit in a word is referred to as a bit. Depending on the number of bits grouped together we can define:

$$4\text{-bits} = \text{nibble}$$
$$8\text{-bits} = \text{byte}$$
$$16\text{-bits} = \text{word}$$
$$32\text{-bits} = \text{double word}$$

The grouping of bits to form words is an essential concept of the modern digital computer. Consider that a single bit can only represent two pieces of information. However, expanding to a four bit word allows 2^4 or 16 unique 1–0 combinations. This is shown in Table A.1.

The general result is that given n bits, 2^n unique combinations will exist. This means that even the largest decimal numbers can be represented in binary provided enough bits are allocated.

TABLE A.1 BINARY AND HEXADECIMAL EQUIVALENTS OF THE DECIMAL NUMBERS 0 THROUGH 15

Decimal	Binary	Hexadecimal
0	0000	0
1	0001	1
2	0010	2
3	0011	3
4	0100	4
5	0101	5
6	0110	6
7	0111	7
8	1000	8
9	1001	9
10	1010	A
11	1011	B
12	1100	C
13	1101	D
14	1110	E
15	1111	F

BINARY AND DECIMAL NUMBER BASE CONVERSIONS

The binary number system is built into the basic hardware of all digital computers such that the computer "thinks" and calculates in binary much as we think and calculate in decimal. And like the decimal number system, each digit in a binary number is given a weight based on its position relative to the radix or binary point.

For example, the binary word 1101 can be expressed in decimal as:

$$1 \times 2^3 + 1 \times 2^2 + 0 \times 2^1 + 1 \times 2^0$$
$$\text{or} \quad 8 + \quad 4 + \quad 0 + \quad 1 = 13$$

Note that the rightmost digit has the weight 2^0 and each succeeding digit is a factor of two higher than this. The bit in the rightmost position is called the least significant bit (LSB) while the leftmost bit is referred to as the most significant bit (MSB).

As the example illustrates, a binary word can be converted to decimal by adding up the factors of two in which the corresponding bit is set. This is most easily accomplished by beginning with the LSB and counting using the sequence 1, 2, 4, 8, 16, 32, 64, etc. Thus the decimal value of the binary word:

$$1011011010010101$$

is: $32768 + 8192 + 4096 + 1024 + 512 + 128 + 16 + 4 + 1 = 46{,}281$.

When it is desired to convert a decimal number into binary, two methods can be used. In the first, the highest powers of two in the decimal number are removed recording a 1 in the appropriate bit positions. For example, converting 39 to binary:

1. Start with the highest power of 2 less than 39:
$$39 - 32 \ (2^5) = 7$$

2. The highest power of 2 in 7 is 4:
$$7 - 4 \ (2^2) = 3$$

3. The highest power of 2 in 3 is 2:
$$3 - 2 \ (2^1) = 1$$

4. Finally we subtract 2^0 as the last bit. The result is:
$$2^5 + 2^2 + 2^1 + 2^0 => 100111$$

A second method called repeated division by 2 is often less tedious when large numbers must be converted. For example, 39 is converted to binary as follows:

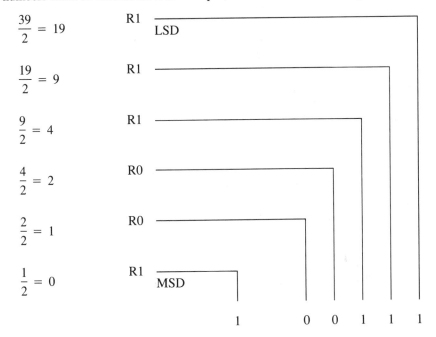

THE HEXADECIMAL NUMBER SYSTEM

It does not take long to realize that the binary number system is very inefficient. For example, assume the 8086 microprocessor is accessing a memory byte at memory location 762489. The binary address output by the 8086 will be:

$$10111010001001111001$$

Twenty bits are required to express this six digit decimal number!

Because of the awkwardness associated with handling large binary numbers, the hexadecimal number system is often used. This is a base 16 number system requiring 16

Appendix A

unique symbols for its digits. The first ten are no problem—hexadecimal uses 0–9 just as decimal. The last six digits borrow the first six letters of the alphabet A–F. Table A.1 shows the decimal and binary equivalents of the 16 hexadecimal (or simply hex) digits.

You might wonder why a base 16 number system is chosen instead of a base 12 or base 5, say. The reason is shown in Table A.1. The 16 hex digits exactly map into all combinations of four binary bits from 0000 through 1111. This would not be true with a base 12 number system—the binary combinations 1100, 1101, 1110 and 1111 would require two base 12 digits.

If you want to convert the binary number 10111010001001111001 into hex, simply break the number into groups of four bits each beginning with the LSB, and apply the definitions in Table A.1. Thus:

$$1011 \quad 1010 \quad 0010 \quad 0111 \quad 1001 \quad => \text{BA279H}$$

where the suffix H indicates that the number is to be interpreted in hexadecimal.

The advantages of hex are (1) easy conversion to binary or back into hex from binary and (2) efficiency. In the example a 20 digit binary number can be expressed with only 5 hex digits (one less than the decimal representation).

The main disadvantage to hex is that the decimal magnitude is not apparent. However, by adding the powers of 16 a hex number can be quickly converted to decimal. For example:

$$\begin{aligned}
\text{BA279H} &= 11 \times 16^4 + 10 \times 16^3 + 2 \times 16^2 + 7 \times 16^1 + 9 \times 16^0 \\
&= 720896 \quad + 40960 \quad + 512 \quad + 112 \quad + 9 \\
&= 762489
\end{aligned}$$

In fact, in some cases it may be quicker to convert a binary number to hex and then to decimal, rather than to decimal directly.

If it is required to convert a decimal number to hex this can be done by removing the highest powers of 16 in the source number or via a repeated division by 16 method. The first method can be done easily with a pocket calculator.

Consider the number 762489. The powers of 16 are 1, 16, 256, 4096, 65536, etc. To convert to hex:

1. $\dfrac{762489}{65536} = 11.634659$ Write down B (for 11).

2. $.634659 \times 65536 = 41593.$

3. $\dfrac{41593}{4096} = 10.154541$ Write down A (for 10).

4. $.154541 \times 4096 = 633.$

5. $\dfrac{633}{256} = 2.4726563$ Write down 2.

6. $.4726563 \times 256 = 121$

7. $\dfrac{121}{16} = 7.5625$ Write down 7.

8. $.5625 \times 16 = 9$ Write down 9.

The result is 762489 = BA279H.

BINARY AND HEXADECIMAL ARITHMETIC

The power of a digital computer is based on its ability to perform mathematical and logical functions at very high speed. Yet these operations must all be done in binary. If we consider basic binary addition, only four possibilities exist:

$$
\begin{array}{cccc}
 & & & 1 \text{ (carry)} \\
0 & 0 & 1 & 1 \\
+0 & +1 & +1 & +1 \\
\hline
0 & 1 & 1\ 0 & 1\ 1
\end{array}
$$

Remembering these four rules binary addition problems for any sized word can be solved.

$$
\begin{array}{ccc}
1111 & 1 & \\
10101101\ = & \text{ADH}\ = & 173 \\
+\,11001011\ = & +\,\text{CBH}\ = & +\,203 \\
\hline
1\ 01111000 & 1\ \ 78 & 376
\end{array}
$$

Note how the carry propagates to the left as in decimal arithmetic. The hex result is found by noting that $D + B = 13 + 11 = 24$ or $16 + 8$ (8 carry 1). Similarly $A + C + 1 = 10 + 12 + 1 = 23$ or $16 + 7$ (7 carry 1).

Binary subtraction is performed in a similar manner remembering that a borrow causes two 1's to be added to the bit immediately to the right of the borrowed bit.

$$
\begin{array}{ccc}
1\ \ 11\ 1 & & \\
1\ \ 11\ 1\ = & \text{A1} & \\
10110010\ = & \text{B2H}\ = & 178 \\
-\,01100101\ = & -\,65\text{H}\ = & -\,101 \\
\hline
01001101 & 4\text{DH} & 77
\end{array}
$$

The multiplication and division functions are obtained by repeated applications of addition and subtraction. Many microprocessor circuits now include special multiplication and division instructions relieving the programmer of the task of writing these routines.

TWO'S COMPLEMENT ARITHMETIC

In addition to representing a number's magnitude, a computer must also be able to represent the sign of that number. Unfortunately, while this is easy to do on paper, it is not so easily done by a computer.

Numbers to be processed by a computer can be stored as unsigned binary numbers or signed binary numbers. In the later case a special 2's complement code is required. The rules for converting a binary number to its 2's complement form are as follows:

1. If the number is positive make no changes.
2. If the number is negative, complement all bits and add 1.*

For example, to convert -27 to 2's complement binary we first express the number in binary (assuming 8-bit words):

$$27 = 00011011$$

Now inverting all bits and adding 1:

$$
\begin{array}{r}
11100100 \\
+1 \\
\hline
11100101
\end{array}
$$

If we assume an 8-bit word size (which is typical for many microprocessor chips) then the range of positive numbers is from 0 to $+127$ and the range of negative numbers is from -1 to -128. Table A.2 illustrates these extremes. Studying this table you can see that a negative number is always indicated when the MSB is set. A positive number when the bit is reset.

Microprocessors have special instructions for testing this bit (sometimes called the sign bit) causing program control to be transferred to a new location if the bit is set or reset.

When it is desired to determine the magnitude of a 2's complement number, the following rules are applied.

1. If the MSB is 0 no conversion is necessary.
2. If the MSB is 1 a negative number is indicated. Convert the number by inverting all bits and adding 1 (as described above). On paper prefix the number with a negative sign.

For example, given the 2's complement binary number 10110110 we note that the MSB is set. Forming the 2's complement:

$$
\begin{array}{r}
01001001 \\
+1 \\
\hline
01001010
\end{array} => -4AH \text{ or } -74
$$

From the microprocessor's standpoint the advantage of expressing numbers in 2's complement form is that addition and subtraction can be performed with the same (adder) circuit. As an example, suppose we wish to find the result of $13 - 9$. This can be done by expressing both numbers in 2's complement form and adding.

---

*An alternate method is to subtract the number from 0.

TABLE A.2
SIGNED BINARY NUMBERS[a]

Decimal	Binary	Hexadecimal
−128	10000000	80
−127	10000001	81
−126	10000010	82
−125	10000011	83
−124	10000100	84
⋮	⋮	⋮
−3	11111101	FD
−2	11111110	FE
−1	11111111	FF
0	00000000	0
+1	00000001	1
+2	00000010	2
⋮	⋮	⋮
+125	01111101	7D
+126	01111110	7E
+127	01111111	7F

[a] Positive numbers are formed without change. Negative numbers are formed by complementing all bits and adding 1. Thus −6 becomes $00000110 \rightarrow 11111001 + 1 = 11111010$.

$$
\begin{array}{lll}
+13 => & = & 00001101 \\
-9 \ => 11110110 + 1 = & + & 11110111 \\
\hline
& 1 \ 00000100 & = \ +4 \text{ (ignoring the carry)}
\end{array}
$$

Note that this signed subtraction also corresponded to the unsigned addition of 13 and 247 (11110111). The result, 1 00000100 (260), corresponds to the sum of these two numbers. The significance of this result is that it is up to the programmer to know when his or her data must be in unsigned binary form or in 2's complement form as a signed binary number. The computer will add both types of data correctly.

Finally, care must be taken when performing 2's complement arithmetic that an overflow condition does not occur. For example, consider the addition of the two positive numbers 64 + 96.

$$
\begin{array}{lll}
+64 & = & 01000000 \\
+96 & = & +01100000 \\
\hline
160 & = & 10100000
\end{array}
$$

└────→ indicates a negative number

This condition is called an overflow as the correct sum exceeds the capacity (+127) of an 8-bit signed binary number. Most microprocessors have an overflow flag that can be tested for this error condition.

Appendix B

 IAPX 86/10

ABSOLUTE MAXIMUM RATINGS*

Ambient Temperature Under Bias........0°C to 70°C
Storage Temperature............ – 65°C to + 150°C
Voltage on Any Pin with
  Respect to Ground.................. – 1.0 to + 7V
Power Dissipation .... 2.5 Watt

*NOTICE: Stresses above those listed under "Absolute Maximum Ratings" may cause permanent damage to the device. This is a stress rating only and functional operation of the device at these or any other conditions above those indicated in the operational sections of this specification is not implied. Exposure to absolute maximum rating conditions for extended periods may affect device reliability.

D.C. CHARACTERISTICS
(8086: T_A = 0°C to 70°C, V_{CC} = 5V ± 10%)
(8086-1: T_A = 0°C to 70°C, V_{CC} = 5V ± 5%)
(8086-2: T_A = 0°C to 70°C, V_{CC} = 5V ± 5%)

Symbol	Parameter	Min.	Max.	Units	Test Conditions
V_{IL}	Input Low Voltage	– 0.5	+ 0.8	V	
V_{IH}	Input High Voltage	2.0	V_{CC} + 0.5	V	
V_{OL}	Output Low Voltage		0.45	V	I_{OL} = 2.5 mA
V_{OH}	Output High Voltage	2.4		V	I_{OH} = – 400 µA
I_{CC}	Power Supply Current: 8086 8086-1 8086-2		340 360 350	mA	T_A = 25°C
I_{LI}	Input Leakage Current		± 10	µA	0V ≤ V_{IN} ≤ V_{CC}
I_{LO}	Output Leakage Current		± 10	µA	0.45V ≤ V_{OUT} ≤ V_{CC}
V_{CL}	Clock Input Low Voltage	– 0.5	+ 0.6	V	
V_{CH}	Clock Input High Voltage	3.9	V_{CC} + 1.0	V	
C_{IN}	Capacitance of Input Buffer (All input except $AD_0 – AD_{15}$, $\overline{RQ/GT}$)		15	pF	fc = 1 MHz
C_{IO}	Capacitance of I/O Buffer ($AD_0 – AD_{15}$, $\overline{RQ/GT}$)		15	pF	fc = 1 MHz

Appendix C

ințel 	IAPX 86/10

A.C. CHARACTERISTICS (8086: $T_A = 0°C$ to $70°C$, $V_{CC} = 5V \pm 10\%$)
(8086-1: $T_A = 0°C$ to $70°C$, $V_{CC} = 5V \pm 5\%$)
(8086-2: $T_A = 0°C$ to $70°C$, $V_{CC} = 5V \pm 5\%$)

MINIMUM COMPLEXITY SYSTEM
TIMING REQUIREMENTS

Symbol	Parameter	8086		8086-1 (Preliminary)		8086-2		Units	Test Conditions
		Min.	Max.	Min.	Max.	Min.	Max.		
TCLCL	CLK Cycle Period	200	500	100	500	125	500	ns	
TCLCH	CLK Low Time	118		53		68		ns	
TCHCL	CLK High Time	69		39		44		ns	
TCH1CH2	CLK Rise Time		10		10		10	ns	From 1.0V to 3.5V
TCL2CL1	CLK Fall Time		10		10		10	ns	From 3.5V to 1.0V
TDVCL	Data in Setup Time	30		5		20		ns	
TCLDX	Data in Hold Time	10		10		10		ns	
TR1VCL	RDY Setup Time into 8284A (See Notes 1, 2)	35		35		35		ns	
TCLR1X	RDY Hold Time into 8284A (See Notes 1, 2)	0		0		0		ns	
TRYHCH	READY Setup Time into 8086	118		53		68		ns	
TCHRYX	READY Hold Time into 8086	30		20		20		ns	
TRYLCL	READY Inactive to CLK (See Note 3)	−8		−10		−8		ns	
THVCH	HOLD Setup Time	35		20		20		ns	
TINVCH	INTR, NMI, TEST Setup Time (See Note 2)	30		15		15		ns	
TILIH	Input Rise Time (Except CLK)		20		20		20	ns	From 0.8V to 2.0V
TIHIL	Input Fall Time (Except CLK)		12		12		12	ns	From 2.0V to 0.8V

A.C. CHARACTERISTICS (Continued)

TIMING RESPONSES

Symbol	Parameter	8086 Min.	8086 Max.	8086-1 (Preliminary) Min.	8086-1 (Preliminary) Max.	8086-2 Min.	8086-2 Max.	Units	Test Conditions
TCLAV	Address Valid Delay	10	110	10	50	10	60	ns	
TCLAX	Address Hold Time	10		10		10		ns	
TCLAZ	Address Float Delay	TCLAX	80	10	40	TCLAX	50	ns	
TLHLL	ALE Width	TCLCH−20		TCLCH−10		TCLCH-10		ns	
TCLLH	ALE Active Delay		80		40		50	ns	
TCHLL	ALE Inactive Delay		85		45		55	ns	
TLLAX	Address Hold Time to ALE Inactive	TCHCL−10		TCHCL−10		TCHCL−10		ns	
TCLDV	Data Valid Delay	10	110	10	50	10	60	ns	*C$_L$ = 20-100 pF for all 8086 Outputs (In addition to 8086 self-load)
TCHDX	Data Hold Time	10		10		10		ns	
TWHDX	Data Hold Time After WR	TCLCH−30		TCLCH−25		TCLCH−30		ns	
TCVCTV	Control Active Delay 1	10	110	10	50	10	70	ns	
TCHCTV	Control Active Delay 2	10	110	10	45	10	60	ns	
TCVCTX	Control Inactive Delay	10	110	10	50	10	70	ns	
TAZRL	Address Float to READ Active	0		0		0		ns	
TCLRL	RD Active Delay	10	165	10	70	10	100	ns	
TCLRH	RD Inactive Delay	10	150	10	60	10	80	ns	
TRHAV	RD Inactive to Next Address Active	TCLCL−45		TCLCL−35		TCLCL−40		ns	
TCLHAV	HLDA Valid Delay	10	160	10	60	10	100	ns	
TRLRH	RD Width	2TCLCL−75		2TCLCL−40		2TCLCL−50		ns	
TWLWH	WR Width	2TCLCL−60		2TCLCL−35		2TCLCL−40		ns	
TAVAL	Address Valid to ALE Low	TCLCH−60		TCLCH−35		TCLCH−40		ns	
TOLOH	Output Rise Time		20		20		20	ns	From 0.8V to 2.0V
TOHOL	Output Fall Time		12		12		12	ns	From 2.0V to 0.8V

NOTES:
1. Signal at 8284A shown for reference only.
2. Setup requirement for asynchronous signal only to guarantee recognition at next CLK.
3. Applies only to T2 state. (8 ns into T3).

WAVEFORMS

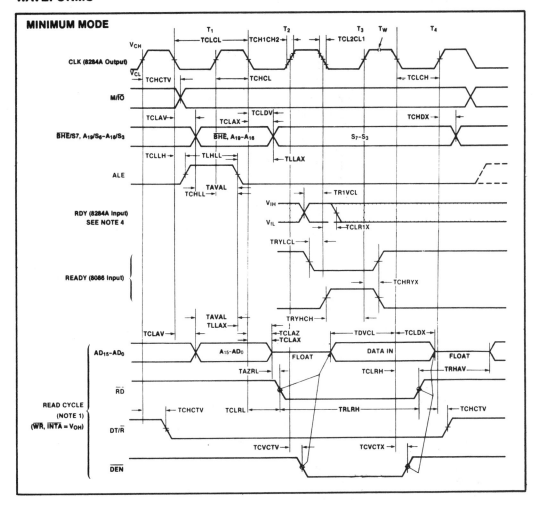

WAVEFORMS (Continued)

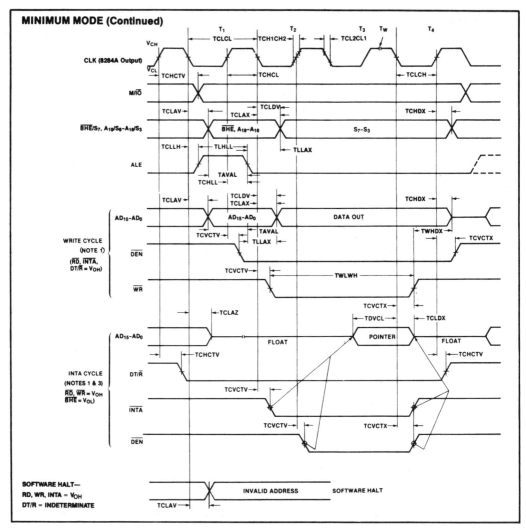

NOTES:

1. All signals switch between V_{OH} and V_{OL} unless otherwise specified.
2. RDY is sampled near the end of T_2, T_3, T_W to determine if T_W machines states are to be inserted.
3. Two INTA cycles run back-to-back. The 8086 LOCAL ADDR/DATA BUS is floating during both INTA cycles. Control signals shown for second INTA cycle.
4. Signals at 8284A are shown for reference only.
5. All timing measurements are made at 1.5V unless otherwise noted.

A.C. CHARACTERISTICS

MAX MODE SYSTEM (USING 8288 BUS CONTROLLER)
TIMING REQUIREMENTS

Symbol	Parameter	8086		8086-1 (Preliminary)		8086-2 (Preliminary)		Units	Test Conditions
		Min.	Max.	Min.	Max.	Min.	Max.		
TCLCL	CLK Cycle Period	200	500	100	500	125	500	ns	
TCLCH	CLK Low Time	118		53		68		ns	
TCHCL	CLK High Time	69		39		44		ns	
TCH1CH2	CLK Rise Time		10		10		10	ns	From 1.0V to 3.5V
TCL2CL1	CLK Fall Time		10		10		10	ns	From 3.5V to 1.0V
TDVCL	Data in Setup Time	30		5		20		ns	
TCLDX	Data In Hold Time	10		10		10		ns	
TR1VCL	RDY Setup Time into 8284A (See Notes 1, 2)	35		35		35		ns	
TCLR1X	RDY Hold Time into 8284A (See Notes 1, 2)	0		0		0		ns	
TRYHCH	READY Setup Time into 8086	118		53		68		ns	
TCHRYX	READY Hold Time into 8086	30		20		20		ns	
TRYLCL	READY Inactive to CLK (See Note 4)	−8		−10		−8		ns	
TINVCH	Setup Time for Recognition (INTR, NMI, TEST) (See Note 2)	30		15		15		ns	
TGVCH	RQ/GT Setup Time	30		12		15		ns	
TCHGX	RQ Hold Time into 8086	40		20		30		ns	
TILIH	Input Rise Time (Except CLK)		20		20		20	ns	From 0.8V to 2.0V
TIHIL	Input Fall Time (Except CLK)		12		12		12	ns	From 2.0V to 0.8V

NOTES:
1. Signal at 8284A or 8288 shown for reference only.
2. Setup requirement for asynchronous signal only to guarantee recognition at next CLK.
3. Applies only to T3 and wait states.
4. Applies only to T2 state (8 ns into T3).

A.C. CHARACTERISTICS (Continued)

TIMING RESPONSES

Symbol	Parameter	8086		8086-1 (Preliminary)		8086-2 (Preliminary)		Units	Test Conditions
		Min.	Max.	Min.	Max.	Min.	Max.		
TCLML	Command Active Delay (See Note 1)	10	35	10	35	10	35	ns	
TCLMH	Command Inactive Delay (See Note 1)	10	35	10	35	10	35	ns	
TRYHSH	READY Active to Status Passive (See Note 3)		110		45		65	ns	
TCHSV	Status Active Delay	10	110	10	45	10	60	ns	
TCLSH	Status Inactive Delay	10	130	10	55	10	70	ns	
TCLAV	Address Valid Delay	10	110	10	50	10	60	ns	
TCLAX	Address Hold Time	10		10		10		ns	
TCLAZ	Address Float Delay	TCLAX	80	10	40	TCLAX	50	ns	
TSVLH	Status Valid to ALE High (See Note 1)		15		15		15	ns	
TSVMCH	Status Valid to MCE High (See Note 1)		15		15		15	ns	
TCLLH	CLK Low to ALE Valid (See Note 1)		15		15		15	ns	
TCLMCH	CLK Low to MCE High (See Note 1)		15		15		15	ns	
TCHLL	ALE Inactive Delay (See Note 1)		15		15		15	ns	C_L = 20-100 pF for all 8086 Outputs (In addition to 8086 self-load)
TCLMCL	MCE Inactive Delay (See Note 1)		15		15		15	ns	
TCLDV	Data Valid Delay	10	110	10	50	10	60	ns	
TCHDX	Data Hold Time	10		10		10		ns	
TCVNV	Control Active Delay (See Note 1)	5	45	5	45	5	45	ns	
TCVNX	Control Inactive Delay (See Note 1)	10	45	10	45	10	45	ns	
TAZRL	Address Float to Read Active	0		0		0		ns	
TCLRL	RD Active Delay	10	165	10	70	10	100	ns	
TCLRH	RD Inactive Delay	10	150	10	60	10	80	ns	
TRHAV	RD Inactive to Next Address Active	TCLCL−45		TCLCL−35		TCLCL−40		ns	
TCHDTL	Direction Control Active Delay (See Note 1)		50		50		50	ns	
TCHDTH	Direction Control Inactive Delay (See Note 1)		30		30		30	ns	
TCLGL	GT Active Delay	0	85	0	45	0	50	ns	
TCLGH	GT Inactive Delay	0	85	0	45	0	50	ns	
TRLRH	RD Width	2TCLCL−75		2TCLCL−40		2TCLCL−50		ns	
TOLOH	Output Rise Time		20		20		20	ns	From 0.8V to 2.0V
TOHOL	Output Fall Time		12		12		12	ns	From 2.0V to 0.8V

WAVEFORMS

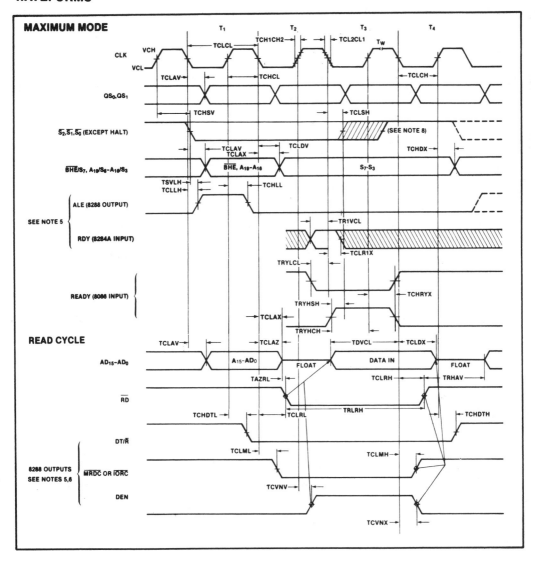

WAVEFORMS (Continued)

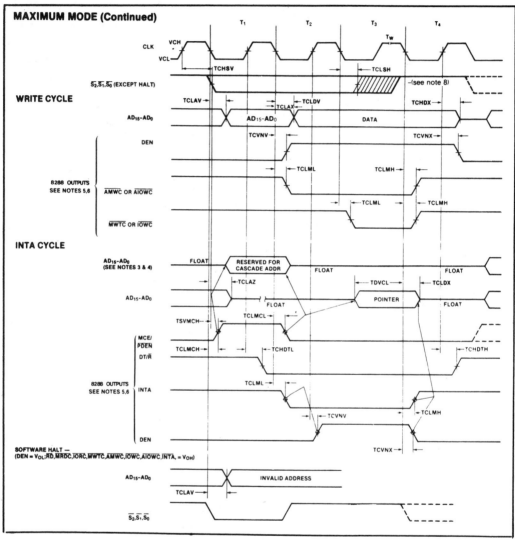

NOTES:

1. All signals switch between V_{OH} and V_{OL} unless otherwise specified.
2. RDY is sampled near the end of T_2, T_3, T_W to determine if T_W machines states are to be inserted.
3. Cascade address is valid between first and second INTA cycle.
4. Two INTA cycles run back-to-back. The 8086 LOCAL ADDR/DATA BUS is floating during both INTA cycles. Control for pointer address is shown for second INTA cycle.
5. Signals at 8284A or 8288 are shown for reference only.
6. The issuance of the 8288 command and control signals ($\overline{MRDC}$, $\overline{MWTC}$, $\overline{AMWC}$, $\overline{IORC}$, $\overline{IOWC}$, $\overline{AIOWC}$, $\overline{INTA}$ and DEN) lags the active high 8288 CEN.
7. All timing measurements are made at 1.5V unless otherwise noted.
8. Status inactive in state just prior to T_4.

620   Appendix C

Appendix D

intel

Table 2. Instruction Set Summary

DATA TRANSFER

MOV = Move:

	76543210	76543210	76543210	76543210
Register/memory to/from register	1 0 0 0 1 0 d w	mod reg r/m		
Immediate to register/memory	1 1 0 0 0 1 1 w	mod 0 0 0 r/m	data	data if w 1
Immediate to register	1 0 1 1 w reg	data	data if w 1	
Memory to accumulator	1 0 1 0 0 0 0 w	addr-low	addr-high	
Accumulator to memory	1 0 1 0 0 0 1 w	addr-low	addr-high	
Register/memory to segment register	1 0 0 0 1 1 1 0	mod 0 reg r/m		
Segment register to register/memory	1 0 0 0 1 1 0 0	mod 0 reg r/m		

PUSH = Push:

Register/memory	1 1 1 1 1 1 1 1	mod 1 1 0 r/m
Register	0 1 0 1 0 reg	
Segment register	0 0 0 reg 1 1 0	

POP = Pop:

Register/memory	1 0 0 0 1 1 1 1	mod 0 0 0 r/m
Register	0 1 0 1 1 reg	
Segment register	0 0 0 reg 1 1 1	

XCHG = Exchange:

Register/memory with register	1 0 0 0 0 1 1 w	mod reg r/m
Register with accumulator	1 0 0 1 0 reg	

IN=Input from:

Fixed port	1 1 1 0 0 1 0 w	port
Variable port	1 1 1 0 1 1 0 w	

OUT = Output to:

Fixed port	1 1 1 0 0 1 1 w	port
Variable port	1 1 1 0 1 1 1 w	
XLAT=Translate byte to AL	1 1 0 1 0 1 1 1	
LEA=Load EA to register	1 0 0 0 1 1 0 1	mod reg r/m
LDS=Load pointer to DS	1 1 0 0 0 1 0 1	mod reg r/m
LES=Load pointer to ES	1 1 0 0 0 1 0 0	mod reg r/m
LAHF=Load AH with flags	1 0 0 1 1 1 1 1	
SAHF=Store AH into flags	1 0 0 1 1 1 1 0	
PUSHF=Push flags	1 0 0 1 1 1 0 0	
POPF=Pop flags	1 0 0 1 1 1 0 1	

ARITHMETIC

ADD = Add:

Reg./memory with register to either	0 0 0 0 0 0 d w	mod reg r/m		
Immediate to register/memory	1 0 0 0 0 0 s w	mod 0 0 0 r/m	data	data if s w 01
Immediate to accumulator	0 0 0 0 0 1 0 w	data	data if w 1	

ADC = Add with carry:

Reg./memory with register to either	0 0 0 1 0 0 d w	mod reg r/m		
Immediate to register/memory	1 0 0 0 0 0 s w	mod 0 1 0 r/m	data	data if s w 01
Immediate to accumulator	0 0 0 1 0 1 0 w	data	data if w 1	

INC = Increment:

Register/memory	1 1 1 1 1 1 1 w	mod 0 0 0 r/m
Register	0 1 0 0 0 reg	
AAA=ASCII adjust for add	0 0 1 1 0 1 1 1	
DAA=Decimal adjust for add	0 0 1 0 0 1 1 1	

SUB = Subtract:

Reg./memory and register to either	0 0 1 0 1 0 d w	mod reg r/m		
Immediate from register/memory	1 0 0 0 0 0 s w	mod 1 0 1 r/m	data	data if s w 01
Immediate from accumulator	0 0 1 0 1 1 0 w	data	data if w 1	

SBB = Subtract with borrow:

Reg./memory and register to either	0 0 0 1 1 0 d w	mod reg r/m		
Immediate from register/memory	1 0 0 0 0 0 s w	mod 0 1 1 r/m	data	data if s w 01
Immediate from accumulator	0 0 0 1 1 1 0 w	data	data if w 1	

DEC Decrement:

	76543210	76543210	76543210	76543210
Register/memory	1 1 1 1 1 1 1 w	mod 0 0 1 r/m		
Register	0 1 0 0 1 reg			
NEG Change sign	1 1 1 1 0 1 1 w	mod 0 1 1 r/m		

CMP Compare:

Register/memory and register	0 0 1 1 1 0 d w	mod reg r/m		
Immediate with register/memory	1 0 0 0 0 0 s w	mod 1 1 1 r/m	data	data if s w 01
Immediate with accumulator	0 0 1 1 1 1 0 w	data	data if w 1	
AAS ASCII adjust for subtract	0 0 1 1 1 1 1 1			
DAS Decimal adjust for subtract	0 0 1 0 1 1 1 1			
MUL Multiply (unsigned)	1 1 1 1 0 1 1 w	mod 1 0 0 r/m		
IMUL Integer multiply (signed)	1 1 1 1 0 1 1 w	mod 1 0 1 r/m		
AAM ASCII adjust for multiply	1 1 0 1 0 1 0 0	0 0 0 0 1 0 1 0		
DIV Divide (unsigned)	1 1 1 1 0 1 1 w	mod 1 1 0 r/m		
IDIV Integer divide (signed)	1 1 1 1 0 1 1 w	mod 1 1 1 r/m		
AAD ASCII adjust for divide	1 1 0 1 0 1 0 1	0 0 0 0 1 0 1 0		
CBW Convert byte to word	1 0 0 1 1 0 0 0			
CWD Convert word to double word	1 0 0 1 1 0 0 1			

LOGIC

NOT Invert	1 1 1 1 0 1 1 w	mod 0 1 0 r/m
SHL/SAL Shift logical/arithmetic left	1 1 0 1 0 0 v w	mod 1 0 0 r/m
SHR Shift logical right	1 1 0 1 0 0 v w	mod 1 0 1 r/m
SAR Shift arithmetic right	1 1 0 1 0 0 v w	mod 1 1 1 r/m
ROL Rotate left	1 1 0 1 0 0 v w	mod 0 0 0 r/m
ROR Rotate right	1 1 0 1 0 0 v w	mod 0 0 1 r/m
RCL Rotate through carry flag left	1 1 0 1 0 0 v w	mod 0 1 0 r/m
RCR Rotate through carry right	1 1 0 1 0 0 v w	mod 0 1 1 r/m

AND And:

Reg/memory and register to either	0 0 1 0 0 0 d w	mod reg r/m		
Immediate to register/memory	1 0 0 0 0 0 0 w	mod 1 0 0 r/m	data	data if w 1
Immediate to accumulator	0 0 1 0 0 1 0 w	data	data if w 1	

TEST And function to flags, no result:

Register/memory and register	1 0 0 0 0 1 0 w	mod reg r/m		
Immediate data and register/memory	1 1 1 1 0 1 1 w	mod 0 0 0 r/m	data	data if w 1
Immediate data and accumulator	1 0 1 0 1 0 0 w	data	data if w 1	

OR Or:

Reg/memory and register to either	0 0 0 0 1 0 d w	mod reg r/m		
Immediate to register/memory	1 0 0 0 0 0 0 w	mod 0 0 1 r/m	data	data if w 1
Immediate to accumulator	0 0 0 0 1 1 0 w	data	data if w 1	

XOR Exclusive or:

Reg/memory and register to either	0 0 1 1 0 0 d w	mod reg r/m		
Immediate to register/memory	1 0 0 0 0 0 0 w	mod 1 1 0 r/m	data	data if w 1
Immediate to accumulator	0 0 1 1 0 1 0 w	data	data if w 1	

STRING MANIPULATION

REP=Repeat	1 1 1 1 0 0 1 z
MOVS=Move byte/word	1 0 1 0 0 1 0 w
CMPS=Compare byte/word	1 0 1 0 0 1 1 w
SCAS=Scan byte/word	1 0 1 0 1 1 1 w
LODS=Load byte/wd to AL/AX	1 0 1 0 1 1 0 w
STOS=Stor byte/wd from AL/A	1 0 1 0 1 0 1 w

Mnemonics ©Intel, 1978

Table 2. Instruction Set Summary (Continued)

CONTROL TRANSFER

CALL = Call:

	7 6 5 4 3 2 1 0	7 6 5 4 3 2 1 0	7 6 5 4 3 2 1 0
Direct within segment	1 1 1 0 1 0 0 0	disp-low	disp-high
Indirect within segment	1 1 1 1 1 1 1 1	mod 0 1 0 r/m	
Direct intersegment	1 0 0 1 1 0 1 0	offset-low	offset-high
		seg-low	seg-high
Indirect intersegment	1 1 1 1 1 1 1 1	mod 0 1 1 r/m	

JMP = Unconditional Jump:

	7 6 5 4 3 2 1 0	7 6 5 4 3 2 1 0	7 6 5 4 3 2 1 0
Direct within segment	1 1 1 0 1 0 0 1	disp-low	disp-high
Direct within segment-short	1 1 1 0 1 0 1 1	disp	
Indirect within segment	1 1 1 1 1 1 1 1	mod 1 0 0 r/m	
Direct intersegment	1 1 1 0 1 0 1 0	offset-low	offset-high
		seg-low	seg-high
Indirect intersegment	1 1 1 1 1 1 1 1	mod 1 0 1 r/m	

RET = Return from CALL:

	7 6 5 4 3 2 1 0	7 6 5 4 3 2 1 0	7 6 5 4 3 2 1 0
Within segment	1 1 0 0 0 0 1 1		
Within seg, adding immed to SP	1 1 0 0 0 0 1 0	data-low	data-high
Intersegment	1 1 0 0 1 0 1 1		
Intersegment, adding immediate to SP	1 1 0 0 1 0 1 0	data-low	data-high
JE/JZ=Jump on equal/zero	0 1 1 1 0 1 0 0	disp	
JL/JNGE=Jump on less/not greater or equal	0 1 1 1 1 1 0 0	disp	
JLE/JNG=Jump on less or equal/not greater	0 1 1 1 1 1 1 0	disp	
JB/JNAE=Jump on below/not above or equal	0 1 1 1 0 0 1 0	disp	
JBE/JNA=Jump on below or equal/not above	0 1 1 1 0 1 1 0	disp	
JP/JPE=Jump on parity/parity even	0 1 1 1 1 0 1 0	disp	
JO=Jump on overflow	0 1 1 1 0 0 0 0	disp	
JS=Jump on sign	0 1 1 1 1 0 0 0	disp	
JNE/JNZ=Jump on not equal/not zero	0 1 1 1 0 1 0 1	disp	
JNL/JGE=Jump on not less/greater or equal	0 1 1 1 1 1 0 1	disp	
JNLE/JG=Jump on not less or equal/greater	0 1 1 1 1 1 1 1	disp	

	7 6 5 4 3 2 1 0	7 6 5 4 3 2 1 0
JNB/JAE Jump on not below/above or equal	0 1 1 1 0 0 1 1	disp
JNBE/JA Jump on not below or equal/above	0 1 1 1 0 1 1 1	disp
JNP/JPO Jump on not par/par odd	0 1 1 1 1 0 1 1	disp
JNO=Jump on not overflow	0 1 1 1 0 0 0 1	disp
JNS Jump on not sign	0 1 1 1 1 0 0 1	disp
LOOP Loop CX times	1 1 1 0 0 0 1 0	disp
LOOPZ/LOOPE Loop while zero/equal	1 1 1 0 0 0 0 1	disp
LOOPNZ/LOOPNE Loop while not zero/equal	1 1 1 0 0 0 0 0	disp
JCXZ Jump on CX zero	1 1 1 0 0 0 1 1	disp

INT Interrupt

	7 6 5 4 3 2 1 0	7 6 5 4 3 2 1 0
Type specified	1 1 0 0 1 1 0 1	type
Type 3	1 1 0 0 1 1 0 0	
INTO Interrupt on overflow	1 1 0 0 1 1 1 0	
IRET Interrupt return	1 1 0 0 1 1 1 1	

PROCESSOR CONTROL

	7 6 5 4 3 2 1 0	7 6 5 4 3 2 1 0
CLC Clear carry	1 1 1 1 1 0 0 0	
CMC Complement carry	1 1 1 1 0 1 0 1	
STC Set carry	1 1 1 1 1 0 0 1	
CLD Clear direction	1 1 1 1 1 1 0 0	
STD Set direction	1 1 1 1 1 1 0 1	
CLI Clear interrupt	1 1 1 1 1 0 1 0	
STI Set interrupt	1 1 1 1 1 0 1 1	
HLT Halt	1 1 1 1 0 1 0 0	
WAIT Wait	1 0 0 1 1 0 1 1	
ESC Escape (to external device)	1 1 0 1 1 x x x	mod x x x r/m
LOCK Bus lock prefix	1 1 1 1 0 0 0 0	

Footnotes:

AL = 8-bit accumulator
AX = 16-bit accumulator
CX = Count register
DS = Data segment
ES = Extra segment
Above/below refers to unsigned value.
Greater = more positive;
Less = less positive (more negative) signed values
if d = 1 then "to" reg; if d = 0 then "from" reg
if w = 1 then word instruction; if w = 0 then byte instruction

if mod = 11 then r/m is treated as a REG field
if mod = 00 then DISP = 0*, disp-low and disp-high are absent
if mod = 01 then DISP = disp-low sign-extended to 16-bits, disp-high is absent
if mod = 10 then DISP = disp-high: disp-low

if r/m = 000 then EA = (BX) + (SI) + DISP
if r/m = 001 then EA = (BX) + (DI) + DISP
if r/m = 010 then EA = (BP) + (SI) + DISP
if r/m = 011 then EA = (BP) + (DI) + DISP
if r/m = 100 then EA = (SI) + DISP
if r/m = 101 then EA = (DI) + DISP
if r/m = 110 then EA = (BP) + DISP*
if r/m = 111 then EA = (BX) + DISP
DISP follows 2nd byte of instruction (before data if required)

*except if mod = 00 and r/m = 110 then EA = disp-high: disp-low.

if s:w = 01 then 16 bits of immediate data form the operand.
if s:w = 11 then an immediate data byte is sign extended to
   form the 16-bit operand.
if v = 0 then "count" = 1; if v = 1 then "count" in (CL)
x = don't care
z is used for string primitives for comparison with ZF FLAG.

SEGMENT OVERRIDE PREFIX

0 0 1 reg 1 1 0

REG is assigned according to the following table:

16-Bit (w = 1)	8-Bit (w = 0)	Segment
000 AX	000 AL	00 ES
001 CX	001 CL	01 CS
010 DX	010 DL	10 SS
011 BX	011 BL	11 DS
100 SP	100 AH	
101 BP	101 CH	
110 SI	110 DH	
111 DI	111 BH	

Instructions which reference the flag register file as a 16-bit object use
the symbol FLAGS to represent the file:

FLAGS = X:X:X:X:(OF):(DF):(IF):(TF):(SF):(ZF):X:(AF):X:(PF):X:(CF)

Appendix D

Appendix E

intel®

8288
BUS CONTROLLER
FOR iAPX 86, 88 PROCESSORS

- **Bipolar Drive Capability**
- **Provides Advanced Commands**
- **Provides Wide Flexibility In System Configurations**
- **3-State Command Output Drivers**

- **Configurable for Use with an I/O Bus**
- **Facilitates Interface to One or Two Multi-Master Busses**
- **Available In EXPRESS**
  - **Standard Temperature Range**
  - **Extended Temperature Range**

The Intel® 8288 Bus Controller is a 20-pin bipolar component for use with medium-to-large iAPX 86, 88 processing systems. The bus controller provides command and control timing generation as well as bipolar bus drive capability while optimizing system performance.

A strapping option on the bus controller configures it for use with a multi-master system bus and separate I/O bus.

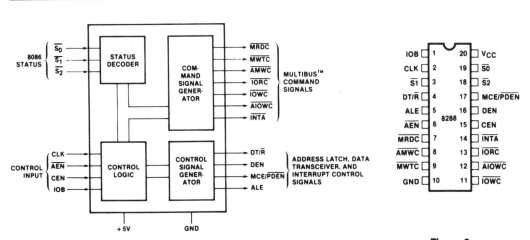

Figure 1. Block Diagram

**Figure 2.
Pin Configuration**

A.C. CHARACTERISTICS (V_{CC} = 5V ± 10%, T_A = 0°C to 70°C)*

TIMING REQUIREMENTS

Symbol	Parameter	Min.	Max.	Unit	Test Conditions
TCLCL	CLK Cycle Period	100		ns	
TCLCH	CLK Low Time	50		ns	
TCHCL	CLK High Time	30		ns	
TSVCH	Status Active Setup Time	35		ns	
TCHSV	Status Inactive Hold Time	10		ns	
TSHCL	Status Inactive Setup Time	35		ns	
TCLSH	Status Active Hold Time	10		ns	

*Note: For Extended Temperature EXPRESS the Preliminary Values are TCLCL = 125; TCLCH = 50; TCHCL = 30; TCVNX = 50; TCLLH, TCLMCH = 25; TSVLH, TSVMCH = 25.

intel   8288

A.C. CHARACTERISTICS (Continued)
TIMING RESPONSES

Symbol	Parameter	Min.	Max.	Unit	Test Conditions	
TCVNV	Control Active Delay	5	45	ns		
TCVNX	Control Inactive Delay	10	45	ns		
TCLLH, TCLMCH	ALE MCE Active Delay (from CLK)		20	ns		
TSVLH, TSVMCH	ALE MCE Active Delay (from Status)		20	ns		
TCHLL	ALE Inactive Delay	4	15	ns	MRDC	
TCLML	Command Active Delay	10	35	ns	IORC	
TCLMH	Command Inactive Delay	10	35	ns	MWTC	I_{OL} = 32 mA
TCHDTL	Direction Control Active Delay		50	ns	IOWC	I_{OH} = −5 mA
TCHDTH	Direction Control Inactive Delay		30	ns	INTA	C_L = 300 pF
TAELCH	Command Enable Time		40	ns	AMWC	
TAEHCZ	Command Disable Time		40	ns	AIOWC	
TAELCV	Enable Delay Time	115	200	ns		I_{OL} = 16 mA
TAEVNV	AEN to DEN		20	ns	Other	I_{OH} = −1 mA
TCEVNV	CEN to DEN, PDEN		25	ns		C_L = 80 pF
TCELRH	CEN to Command		TCLML	ns		
TOLOH	Output, Rise Time		20	ns	From 0.8V to 2.0V	
TOHOL	Output, Fall Time		12	ns	From 2.0V to 0.8V	

WAVEFORMS

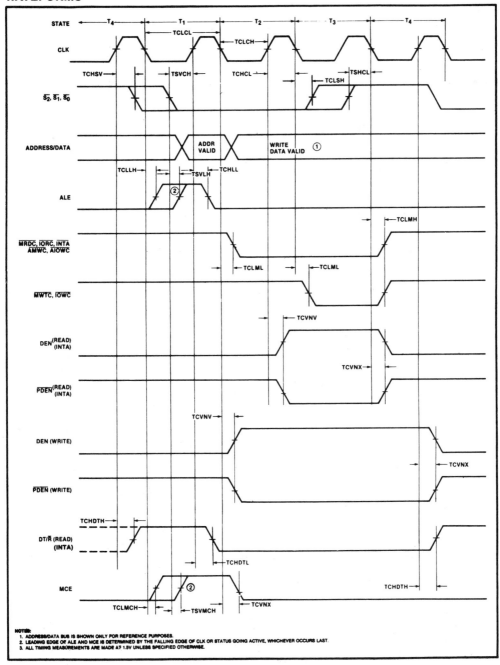

NOTES:
1. ADDRESS/DATA BUS IS SHOWN ONLY FOR REFERENCE PURPOSES.
2. LEADING EDGE OF ALE AND MCE IS DETERMINED BY THE FALLING EDGE OF CLK OR STATUS GOING ACTIVE, WHICHEVER OCCURS LAST.
3. ALL TIMING MEASUREMENTS ARE MADE AT 1.5V UNLESS SPECIFIED OTHERWISE.

Appendix E

625

Appendix F

BUS STRUCTURE OF THE IBM PC (AND COMPATIBLES)

PIN NUMBER SIGNAL DEFINITIONS

Figure F.1 provides the pin number definitions for the expansion card slots in the IBM PC. Each slot receives the same set of signals. Prototyping cards with compatible 62-pin card-edge signal tabs are available from:

Vector Electronics Co., Inc.
12460 Gladstone Ave.
Sylmar, Ca. 91342

SIGNAL DESCRIPTIONS

A0-A19. These 20 output lines are the 8088 microprocessor's address bus.

D0-D7. These eight lines are the 8088 microprocessor's bidirectional data bus.

MEMR (memory read). This is an active low output signal driven by the 8288 bus controller. It indicates that the address bus (A0-A19) contains a valid memory read address.

MEMW (memory write). This is an active low output signal driven by the 8288 bus controller. It indicates that the address bus (A0-A19) contains a valid memory write address.

IOR (I/O read). This is an active low output signal driven by the 8288 bus controller. It indicates that the address bus (A0-A15) contains a valid I/O port read address.

IOW (I/O write). This is an active low output signal driven by the 8288 bus controller. It indicates that the address bus (A0-A15) contains a valid I/O port write address.

ALE (address latch enable). This is an active high output signal driven by the 8288 bus controller. It indicates that a valid (memory or I/O) address is available on A0-A19. *Note that D0-D7 do not contain address information, and ALE cannot be used to demultiplex addresses from the data bus..*

OSC (oscillator). This is the crystal oscillator output of the 8284A clock generator. It has a frequency of 14.31818 MHz.

CLK (clock). This is the CLK output of the 8284A clock generator and serves as the clock signal for the 8088 microprocessor. It has a frequency of 4.77 MHz (14.31818 MHz/3) and a 33% duty cycle.

RESET DRV (reset driver). This is an active high output signal driven by the 8284A clock generator. It is active during the system power-on sequence only.

IRQ2–IRQ7 (interrupt request). These six input lines are connected directly to the 8259A peripheral interrupt controller (PIC). The PC-DOS operating system initializes the PIC such that IRQ2 has highest priority and IRQ7 lowest priority. Each input is rising edge triggered and must be held until an interrupt acknowledge (INTA) signal occurs. Note: INTA is not available on the PC bus. It will be up to the interrupt service routine (ISR) to remove the interrupt request once acknowledged.

DRQ1–DRQ3 (DMA request). These three active high input lines are used to request a DMA cycle from the 8237-5 DMA controller (DMAC). The PC-DOS operating system initializes the DMAC such that DRQ1 has highest priority and DRQ4 lowest priority. DRQ0—unavailable on the system bus—has the highest overall priority and is used to refresh the dynamic memory array.

DACKO–DACK3 (DMA acknowledge). These four active low output signals are output by the 8237-5 DMAC to acknowledge that the corresponding DMA request has been honored. The signal is active throughout the DMA cycle.

I/O CH CK (I/O channel check). This active low input signal will cause a non-maskable interrupt (NMI). As such, it allows a peripheral to report an error condition. *Note: Although the 8088's NMI input is nonmaskable, I/O CH CK is masked via one bit of I/O port 00A0H which must be enabled before an NMI can be received by the 8088.*

I/O CH RDY (I/O channel ready). This active high input signal can be used to request an integer number of wait states during memory and I/O bus cycles. It must be low 60 ns prior to the rising edge of the T2 CLK signal to request a wait state, and high 75 ns before the rising edge of the T3 clock signal to avoid an additional wait state.

AEN (address enable). This is an active high output signal. It indicates that a DMA cycle is in progress and should be used to disable all I/O port decoders. This is necessary because the 8237-5 performs simultaneous DMA transfers in which IOR or IOW may be active with memory addresses on A0-A19.

TC (terminal count). This is an active high output signal issued by the 8237-5 DMAC. It indicates that one of the DMA channels has reached its terminal count of preprogrammed transfers.

Power and ground (+5V, +12V, −12V, −5V, GND). The current levels available from each power pin depends on the particular power supply used and the number of auxiliary cards installed in the computer.

A DESIGN EXAMPLE: INTERFACING THE 8255A-5

Figure F.2 illustrates a PC interfacing example using the 8255A-5 PPI chip. IC1 is an octal comparator used as an address decoder. Note that address lines A0-A9 only are examined. The reason for this is that the I/O ports on the system board are partially decoded, with high order address lines A10-A15 unused. This reduces the I/O port address space from 65,536 ports to 1,024 ports.

Another address restriction also applies. Address bit A9 serves as an input port enable bit. When low, input data will only be accepted from ports on the system board. That is, input data from the card slots is disabled. When A9 is high, input data is accepted from the card slots. There is no similar restriction for output ports.

The circuit in Fig. F.2 allows the 8255 to be mapped to any four consecutive addresses in the range 0000-03FFH. Care must be taken when setting switches S1 through S8 to not select an address range that overlaps the address space used by one of the standard adapter cards. For example, picking the unused address range 03C0-03C3H, S8 through S1 should be set to:

$$11110000 \quad S8 \ldots S1$$

where a ''1'' indicates an open switch and a ''0'' a closed switch. The resulting circuit will then provide three programmable I/O ports controlled by the command byte written to the control port at 03C3H.

signal	pin		pin	signal
GND	B1	+	A1	I/O CH CK
RESETDRV	B2	+	A2	D7
+5V	B3	+	A3	D6
IRQ2	B4	+	A4	D5
-5V	B5	+	A5	D4
DRQ2	B6	+	A6	D3
-12V	B7	+	A7	D2
not used	B8	+	A8	D1
+12V	B9	+	A9	D0
GND	B10	+	A10	I/O CH RDY
MEMW	B11	+	A11	AEN
MEMR	B12	+	A12	A19
IOW	B13	+	A13	A18
IOR	B14	+	A14	A17
DACK3	B15	+	A15	A16
DRQ3	B16	+	A16	A15
DACK1	B17	+	A17	A14
DRQ1	B18	+	A18	A13
DACK0	B19	+	A19	A12
CLK	B20	+	A20	A11
IRQ7	B21	+	A21	A10
IRQ6	B22	+	A22	A9
IRQ5	B23	+	A23	A8
IRQ4	B24	+	A24	A7
IRQ3	B25	+	A25	A6
DACK2	B26	+	A26	A5
TC	B27	+	A27	A4
ALE	B28	+	A28	A3
+5V	B29	+	A29	A2
OSC	B30	+	A30	A1
GND	B31	+	A31	A0

Figure F-1

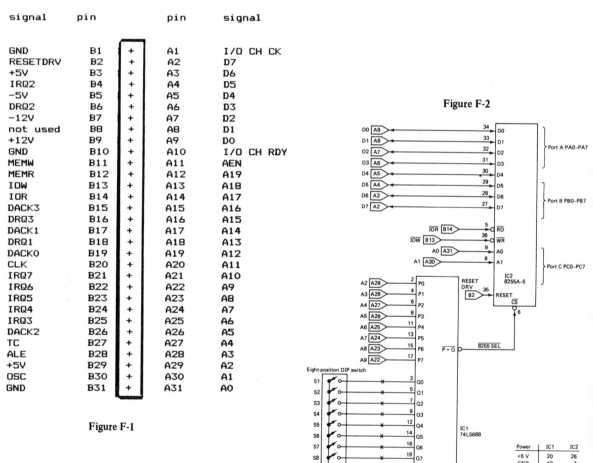

Figure F-2

628

INDEX